International Trade and the New Global Economy

The International Library of Critical Writings in Economics

Founding Editor: Mark Blaug

Late Professor Emeritus, University of London, UK
Late Professor Emeritus, University of Buckingham, UK

This series is an essential reference source for students, researchers and lecturers in economics. It presents by theme a selection of the most important articles across the entire spectrum of economics. Each volume has been prepared by a leading specialist who has written an authoritative introduction to the literature included.

Wherever possible, the articles in these volumes have been reproduced as originally published using facsimile reproduction, inclusive of footnotes and pagination to facilitate ease of reference.

For a list of all Edward Elgar published titles visit our website at
www.e-elgar.com

International Trade and the New Global Economy

Edited by

Edward D. Mansfield

Hum Rosen Professor of Political Science
and Director of the Christopher H. Browne Center for International Politics
University of Pennsylvania, USA

THE INTERNATIONAL LIBRARY OF CRITICAL WRITINGS IN ECONOMICS

An Elgar Research Collection
Cheltenham, UK • Northampton, MA, USA

Published by
Edward Elgar Publishing Limited
The Lypiatts
15 Lansdown Road
Cheltenham
Glos GL50 2JA
UK

Edward Elgar Publishing, Inc.
William Pratt House
9 Dewey Court
Northampton
Massachusetts 01060
USA

A catalogue record for this book is available from the British Library

Library of Congress Control Number: 2015938869

FSC www.fsc.org MIX Paper from responsible sources FSC® C013056

ISBN 978 1 78471 259 4

Printed and bound in Great Britain by T.J. International Ltd, Padstow

Contents

Acknowledgements

The editor and publishers wish to thank the authors and the following publishers who have kindly given permission for the use of copyright material.

Blackwell Publishing Ltd for article: Yotam Margalit (2012), 'Lost in Globalization: International Economic Integration and the Sources of Popular Discontent', *International Studies Quarterly*, **56** (3), September, 484–500.

Brookings Institution for article: Kevin H. O'Rourke and Richard Sinnott (2001), 'The Determinants of Individual Trade Policy Preferences: International Survey Evidence' and J. David Richardson and Dani Rodrik (2001), 'Comments and Discussion', *Brookings Trade Forum*, 157–206.

Cambridge University Press for articles: Andy Baker (2003), 'Why Is Trade Reform So Popular in Latin America? A Consumption-Based Theory of Trade Policy Preferences', *World Politics*, **55** (3), April, 423–55; Kerry A. Chase (2003), 'Economic Interests and Regional Trading Arrangements: The Case of NAFTA', *International Organization*, **57** (1), Winter, 137–74; Edward D. Mansfield and Eric Reinhardt (2003), 'Multilateral Determinants of Regionalism: The Effects of GATT/WTO on the Formation of Preferential Trading Arrangements', *International Organization*, **57** (4), Fall, 829–62; Jens Hainmueller and Michael J. Hiscox (2006), 'Learning to Love Globalization: Education and Individual Attitudes Toward International Trade', *International Organization*, **60** (2), Spring, 469–98; Jude C. Hays, Sean D. Ehrlich, and Clint Peinhardt (2005), 'Government Spending and Public Support for Trade in the OECD: An Empirical Test of the Embedded Liberalism Thesis', *International Organization*, **59** (2), Spring, 473–94; Edward D. Mansfield and Diana C. Mutz (2009), 'Support for Free Trade: Self-Interest, Sociotropic Politics, and Out-Group Anxiety', *International Organization*, **63** (3), Summer, 425–57; Mark S. Manger (2012), 'Vertical Trade Specialization and the Formation of North–South PTAs', *World Politics*, **64** (4), October, 622–58; Daniel W. Drezner (2014), 'The System Worked: Global Economic Governance during the Great Recession', *World Politics*, **66** (1), January, 123–64.

Elsevier Ltd for articles: Kenneth F. Scheve and Matthew J. Slaughter (2001), 'What Determines Individual Trade-Policy Preferences?', *Journal of International Economics*, **54** (2), 267–92; Scott L. Baier and Jeffrey H. Bergstrand (2004), 'Economic Determinants of Free Trade Agreements', *Journal of International Economics*, **64** (1), 29–63; Anna Maria Mayda and Dani Rodrik (2005), 'Why Are Some People (and Countries) More Protectionist than Others?', *European Economic Review*, **49** (6), 1393–430; Richard Baldwin and Dany Jaimovich (2012), 'Are Free Trade Agreements Contagious?', *Journal of International Economics*, **88** (1), 1–16; Chad P. Bown and Meredith A. Crowley (2013), 'Import Protection, Business Cycles, and Exchange Rates: Evidence from the Great Recession', *Journal of International Economics*, **90** (1), 50–64.

Oxford University Press via the Copyright Clearance Center's RightsLink Service for article: Kishore Gawande, Bernard Hoekman, and Yue Cui (2014), 'Global Supply Chains and Trade Policy Responses to the 2008 Crisis', *World Bank Economic Review*, **29** (1), 102–28.

President and Fellows of the Harvard College and the Massachusetts Institute of Technology for articles: Edward D. Mansfield, Helen V. Milner, and B. Peter Rosendorff (2002), 'Why Democracies Cooperate More: Electoral Control and International Trade Agreements', *International Organization*, **56** (3), Summer, 477–513; Hiau Looi Kee, Cristina Neagu, and Alessandro Nicita (2013), 'Is Protectionism on the Rise? Assessing National Trade Policies during the Crisis of 2008', *Review of Economics and Statistics*, **95** (1), March, 342–6.

Every effort has been made to trace all the copyright holders but if any have been inadvertently overlooked the publishers will be pleased to make the necessary arrangement at the first opportunity.

In addition the publishers wish to thank the Library of Indiana University at Bloomington, USA, for their assistance in obtaining these articles.

Introduction

Edward D. Mansfield

The past few decades have witnessed a set of important developments in the international trading system. Preferential trade agreements (PTAs) have spread rapidly, the World Trade Organization (WTO) has struggled to address a variety of new challenges, and the 'Great Recession' of 2007–2009 created concerns that protectionism would rise and the trading system might collapse. At the same time, economic globalization and international trade have continued to grow. Many observers celebrate this growth, but globalization and trade have also provoked protest and fierce opposition. This volume includes a selection of well-known articles that address a number of these developments.

The first section takes up the political and economic factors that give rise to PTAs, institutions that include free trade areas, customs unions, common markets, and economic unions. Since the conclusion of World War II, these agreements have proliferated. Currently, hundreds of them are in force; virtually every country participates in at least one, and roughly half of all merchandise trade is conducted between PTA members. Until recently, however, relatively little empirical research had addressed the formation of PTAs, an issue analyzed in the first six chapters of this book.

The second section of this volume examines mass attitudes toward international trade. The sharp rise in trade and economic globalization over the past half-century has been heralded by economists and others who point to the attendant welfare and efficiency gains. However, it is widely recognized that trade has distributional consequences: some groups in society realize benefits from trade whereas others are harmed. Until recently, few studies analyzed whether these distributional consequences shape the attitudes of individuals toward trade or whether trade attitudes stem from other sources. Over the past 15 years, various studies have addressed the factors that drive opinions about overseas commerce. Eight of them are included herein.

The third section of this book addresses the effect of the Great Recession and the 2008 financial crisis on international trade. This episode precipitated the worst economic downturn in the US since the Great Depression and severely damaged other countries as well. Many observers expressed concern that the recession would stimulate protectionist pressure, damage the multilateral trading system, and prompt the outbreak of mercantilist policies. Yet this is not what transpired. Although international trade volumes collapsed during this episode, they have rebounded in the recession's aftermath. Moreover, most countries did not experience a rise in protectionism, an outcome at odds with political economy models that expect recessions to stimulate heightened trade barriers. The final four chapters in this book analyze how the recession and the financial crisis influenced international trade and why most countries did not respond to these events by increasing trade barriers.

Part I: The Sources and Features of Preferential Trade Agreements

PTAs have generated considerable interest among social scientists and policymakers alike. A substantial amount of research has focused on explaining the effects of PTAs. It is widely argued, for example, that PTAs shape trade relations and trade flows (Frankel 1997). There is also evidence that they guide foreign investment (Büthe and Milner 2008). For over half a century, economists have debated whether PTAs promote or undermine the welfare of countries (Viner 1950). Similarly, scholars sharply disagree about whether the formation of these agreements will erode the multilateral trading system or promote multilateral openness and stability (Bhagwati 2008; Lawrence 1996). From a political standpoint, some have argued that PTAs can promote peace, enhance international environmental coordination, and improve human rights enforcement (Mansfield and Pevehouse 2000; Limão 2005; Hafner-Burton 2009).

Until recently, however, relatively little attention had been focused on the factors that give rise to PTAs (Mansfield and Milner 2012). In light of the vast amount of research that has been conducted on the consequences of PTAs, the relative dearth of work on their origins is surprising. In this book, I include six studies that aimed to help fill that gap.

In Chapter 1, Scott L. Baier and Jeffrey H. Bergstrand analyze the economic sources of PTAs. From an economic perspective, Baier and Bergstrand argue that states should form PTAs when doing so will be welfare improving. In their framework, three sets of factors affect the welfare implications of PTAs: geography, intra-industry trade determinants, and inter-industry trade determinants. States creating a PTA will experience welfare gains if they are located in close proximity to one another, if the country pair is located farther from other countries in the world, if their economies are large and similarly sized, and if their economies are marked by wide differences in relative factor endowments. Baier and Bergstrand test these arguments using a cross-section of 54 countries in 1996. Their findings confirm each hypothesis and lead them to conclude that countries tend to establish PTAs when doing so generates economic gains.

The next four chapters address the political economy of PTA formation. In Chapter 2, Edward D. Mansfield, Helen V. Milner, and B. Peter Rosendorff analyze whether a country's regime type influences its propensity to enter preferential agreements. They argue that chief executives in democratic countries have particular reason to enter trade agreements because voters have difficulty distinguishing between adverse economic outcomes that are beyond the leader's control and poor economic performance stemming from the leader's actions. As a result, voters may remove a democratic head of state from office because they erroneously believe he or she is responsible for an economic downturn that is actually beyond his or her control. Entering into a trade agreement can help chief executives to guard against this possibility. Such institutions often furnish reliable information about the behavior of member-states. Countries that violate their commitments will trip an alarm sounded by other participants in the agreement or the institution itself. Entering a trade agreement therefore reduces the prospect that a democratic leader will be turned out of office because voters mistakenly believe he or she has performed poorly. In non-democracies, by contrast, electoral dynamics are far less important, giving leaders much less incentive to join trade agreements. The results of a series of statistical tests support the argument that democracies are more likely to enter PTAs than other countries.

In Chapter 3, Kerry A. Chase shifts attention from domestic institutions to domestic interest groups. His central focus is on the conditions that lead firms to lobby governments for membership in a PTA. More specifically, Chase maintains that industries characterized by economies of scale will press for entry into PTAs because the arrangements offer access to a larger market, thereby allowing them to realize significant reductions in per unit production costs. Furthermore, firms support PTAs when these arrangements seem likely to allow them to increase profits by shifting stages of production across borders. Chase tests this argument by analyzing lobbying by US firms on the North American Free Trade Agreement (NAFTA). Consistent with his claims, he finds that the firms supporting NAFTA were in a position to exploit economies of scale and to benefit from expanding procurement networks throughout North America.

In Chapter 4, Mark S. Manger addresses the formation of those PTAs that include both developed countries and either developing countries or formerly communist countries. Manger argues that trade between such countries tends to be intra-industry and driven by differences in factor prices—what is referred to as vertical intra-industry trade (VIIT). PTAs created to take advantage of VIIT face fewer political obstacles than those formed to take advantage of inter-industry trade based on comparative advantage. To produce goods at the lowest cost, multinational corporations (MNCs) should produce lower unit-value (that is, less capital intensive) goods in developing or post-communist countries and higher unit-value (that is, more capital intensive) goods in developed countries. MNCs typically have contractual ties to local suppliers in both the developed and the developing or post-communist country. These 'rent chains' create a common interest in open trade across all of these firms that lead them to lobby both governments for a PTA. The government of the developing or post-communist country has reason to expect an inflow of foreign direct investment as a result of this agreement, and the government of the developed country has a bargaining advantage that it can use to avoid liberalizing politically sensitive sectors. As such, there is reason to expect that 'North–South' PTAs are particularly likely to form between countries in which VIIT is an important part of the bilateral trade relationship. A case study of the Japan–Thailand Economic Partnership Agreement and the results of a quantitative analysis spanning 1995–2007 support this argument.

It is noteworthy that the proliferation of PTAs over the past half-century has been accompanied by the unprecedented growth of multilateral trade openness, spurred by the General Agreement on Tariffs and Trade (GATT) and the WTO. It is not clear why states form preferential agreements when they belong to a successful multilateral trade regime. In Chapter 5, Edward D. Mansfield and Eric Reinhardt examine this issue. They argue that conditions within the multilateral regime can create incentives for states to expand their bargaining power, and forming a PTA is one way to enhance such power. First, the growth of GATT/WTO membership reduces each participant's leverage and fosters collective action problems within the regime. Entering a PTA composed of countries with similar economic interests can provide states with insurance against the emergence of these problems. Second, the multilateral trade negotiations sponsored by the GATT/WTO can prompt members to enter PTAs to insure against the possibility of the negotiations faltering and to bolster their bargaining position in the talks. Third, during GATT/WTO disputes, states may form PTAs with third parties to improve their leverage in the conflict; and losing a GATT/WTO dispute may convince states to form PTAs with third parties to gain countervailing market access and added bargaining leverage. The results of Mansfield and Reinhardt's statistical analysis support each of these hypotheses.

It widely argued that PTAs often form in reaction to one another. More specifically, various observers have pointed out that the establishment of a preferential grouping by a set of countries often prompts third parties to follow suit in order to avoid being placed at a competitive disadvantage. In Chapter 6, Richard Baldwin and Dany Jaimovich analyze the contagion of free trade agreements (FTAs). They advance a model in which an FTA between two countries leads a third party that trades with these states to respond by forming an FTA with one of the two original signatories. Doing so eliminates the discrimination on the third party's exports created by the initial agreement and the accompanying downward pressure on the profits of its exporting firms. Baldwin and Jaimovich test this model using an innovative spatial measure of contagion. Based on an analysis of the period 1976–2005, they find that FTAs are contagious, and the extent of contagion grows as the importance of the partners' markets increases.

Part II: What Does the Public Think about Trade?

During the post-World War II era, there has been a tremendous increase in international trade. Economists have argued that this development has contributed to greater efficiency, growth, and welfare gains. Among the mass public, however, there is less consensus on the virtues of trade.

Over the past two decades, a variety of studies have analyzed why some individuals support open trade while others oppose it. In general, the literature on trade preferences has been guided by two models. First, the factor endowments or Heckscher–Ohlin (HO) model assumes that all factors of production within a country are mobile across sectors, markets are perfectly competitive, and there are constant returns to scale in production. Based on these assumptions, Wolfgang Stolper and Paul Samuelson (1941) showed that, in a given country, open trade benefits owners of factors of production that are abundant, relative to the remainder of the world, and harms owners of scarce factors. Consequently, in a country endowed with an abundance (scarcity) of highly skilled labor relative to the rest of the world, free trade benefits (harms) highly skilled workers and harms (benefits) less skilled individuals (Leamer 1984). In such a country, open trade increases (decreases) the demand for skilled workers, since this nation has a comparative advantage in the production of goods that use this input intensively. As the demand for such workers rises (falls), so do their wages. Conversely, heightened trade decreases (increases) the demand for low skilled labor and depresses its wage rate, since goods produced using such labor intensively can be produced more efficiently abroad. The factor endowments approach therefore predicts that highly skilled workers in capital-abundant countries should be pro-trade, whereas less skilled workers should hold more protectionist views.

Second, the specific factors or Ricardo–Viner (RV) model is an alternative framework that assumes that, at least in the short run, certain factors of production cannot be shifted across sectors. If workers cannot easily move from sector to sector, then they will base their trade preferences on how changes in trade policy are expected to affect the industry in which they are currently employed. This model suggests that individuals who work in export-oriented sectors of the economy will support open trade because they personally benefit from it, while those in import-competing sectors will naturally be more protectionist. Equally, an individual employed in a non-traded sector of the economy should be more pro-trade than someone employed in an industry that faces substantial competition from foreign imports.

A variety of studies included in this volume have probed whether these models help to explain trade attitudes. In Chapter 7, Kenneth F. Scheve and Matthew J. Slaughter analyze mass opinion about trade in the US. Using individual-level survey data drawn from a representative sample of Americans, Scheve and Slaughter find that people's attitudes toward trade correspond closely to the HO framework, but not the RV framework. Interestingly, they also find that such attitudes depend on home ownership and the mix of industries in a respondent's area. Home owners are more protectionist if they reside in regions marked by a concentration of comparative disadvantage industries. They are less protectionist if they reside in areas with a concentration of comparative advantage sectors.

The next two chapters address mass attitudes about trade from a cross-national perspective. In Chapter 8, Kevin H. O'Rourke and Richard Sinnott analyze such attitudes in 24 countries during the mid-1990s. The data used in this study do not permit them to analyze the RV framework, but their results are broadly consistent with the HO framework. Low skilled individuals tend to support trade in poorer countries and oppose trade in richer ones. High skilled workers tend to support trade, but this effect is stronger in richer than poorer countries. Furthermore, non-economic factors also influence trade attitudes. Particularly interesting is that nationalist attitudes are associated with hostility toward trade.

In Chapter 9, Anna Maria Mayda and Dani Rodrik further address cross-national patterns in trade attitudes during the mid-1990s. Like Scheve and Slaughter and O'Rourke and Sinnott, they find ample support for the HO framework. Unlike most other studies, however, they also find some support for the RV approach. Using sector-specific trade data, they report that whether individuals are employed in a sector with a comparative advantage has no significant effect on trade preferences. But they also find that individuals employed in non-traded sectors are most supportive of free trade and that those in sectors with a revealed competitive disadvantage are most protectionist. They interpret these results as being broadly consistent with the specific factors model. Furthermore, Mayda and Rodrik find that non-economic factors—especially social status, values, and nationalism—shape trade attitudes.

In Chapter 10, Jude C. Hays, Sean D. Ehrlich, and Clint Peinhardt analyze trade attitudes in a group of countries that belong to the Organisation for Economic Co-operation and Development (OECD). Their central purpose is to test a set of hypotheses stemming from research on 'embedded liberalism' conducted by John Ruggie (1982) and others. Ruggie argues that after World War II, leaders of the advanced industrial democracies undertook two tasks: to liberalize the international trading system and to manage the adjustment costs of such liberalization by establishing social policies at home to offset the adverse distributional consequences of open trade. This combination of foreign and domestic policies was intended to reduce any domestic opposition to trade liberalization that might otherwise undermine the multilateral trade regime. To test this argument, Hays, Ehlrich, and Peinhardt start by analyzing surveys of OECD country residents. Consistent with the embedded liberalism argument and with the RV approach, they find that individuals employed in import-competing industries are more protectionist than individuals who work in non-tradable or export-oriented sectors. They also find that government policies that help to cushion the adverse effects of trade increase the support for open overseas commerce. Finally, turning from survey results to macroeconomic evidence, Hays, Ehrlich, and Peinhardt find that governments do in fact increase spending as imports increase and that this effect grows larger if a substantial portion of the work force is employed in tradable industries.

Much of the literature on trade attitudes focuses on tests of the HO and RV approaches. The next four chapters, however, take different tacks. In Chapter 11, Andy Baker analyzes trade attitudes in Latin America. He argues that neither of these approaches explains the popularity of trade liberalization in this region. Instead, it is the fact that open trade has various beneficial effects on consumption. More specifically, trade reduces the price and improves the quality and variety of many goods, enhancing the welfare of consumers. Baker finds that his consumption-based theory does a better job of explaining trade policy preferences across Latin American than either the HO or the RV approach.

As I discussed earlier, the HO approach stresses that individuals' trade attitudes derive from their skills. Most studies of such attitudes have used formal educational attainment as a proxy for skill level. In Chapter 12, however, Jens Hainmueller and Michael J. Hiscox argue that education represents something more than skill. They find that education predicts trade preferences just as well among those who are not currently employed as among those who are employed, even those who are retired and are not likely to re-enter the work force. Since education cannot be serving as a proxy for skill level among the latter individuals, they argue that it represents the effects of exposure to economic ideas among the college-educated, where most of the impact of education comes into play. Because economists believe that open trade is beneficial, college-educated individuals will have more exposure to arguments about the economic benefits of foreign commerce than those with less formal education.

Economic ideas, however, are not the only sources of information that might influence trade attitudes. In Chapter 13, Edward D. Mansfield and Diana C. Mutz analyze mass attitudes about trade in the US. They argue that 'sociotropic' perceptions about whether trade is good or bad for the national economy are more important than the material factors emphasized by both the HO and the RV approach for the purposes of explaining mass attitudes about trade. These sociotropic perceptions tend to grow out of information that individuals are exposed to (for example, mass media coverage of economic issues). Consistent with their argument, Mansfield and Mutz find that people who believe that trade is good for the US, more generally, tend to support open trade, whereas those who feel that trade is bad for the US as a whole oppose it. They also find that trade attitudes are shaped in important ways by domestic ethnocentrism and foreign policy attitudes. There is little support for free trade among people who believe the US should take an isolationist stance on international affairs or those who feel that members of other ethnic and racial groups are less praiseworthy than their own racial or ethnic group.

In Chapter 14, Yotam Margalit addresses some similar themes. In addition to the material consequences of trade, he argues that opposition to trade often stems from its perceived social and cultural consequences, especially among the less educated. Margalit's results, based on surveys conducted across a wide range of countries, support this argument. Perceived cultural threats from trade dampen support for open trade, and this effect is especially pronounced among individuals with less schooling.

Part III: The Great Recession and International Trade

The single biggest shock to the international trading system over the past few decades grew out of the 2008 financial crisis and the Great Recession of 2007–2009. During this period, global trade collapsed. Moreover, there was widespread concern that this episode would precipitate a bout of protectionism, since the received wisdom is that protectionism is countercyclical, rising during downturns in the business cycle (Irwin 2002; Bagwell and Staiger

2003). Interestingly, however, protectionism did not spike during this period, an issue that is examined in the final four chapters of this volume.

In Chapter 15, Hiau Looi Kee, Cristina Neagu, and Alessandro Nicita analyze whether the financial crisis stimulated heightened protectionism. Based on an analysis of roughly 100 countries, they find that the crisis led only a handful of countries to raise their tariffs. A number of others—including the US and the EU—raised antidumping duties to protect domestic industries; but even after accounting for such duties, rising protectionism accounts for only about 2 percent of the fall in global trade during the recession.

In Chapter 16, Chad P. Bown and Meredith A. Crowley analyze why there was not more protection during the Great Recession, given the received wisdom that protectionism tends to be countercyclical. They focus on estimating the effects of macroeconomic fluctuations on temporary trade barriers (TTBs)—including antidumping, countervailing duty, and various other safeguards—imposed by the US, the EU, Australia, Canada, and South Korea from 1988–2010. During the period prior to the Great Recession, Bown and Crowley find evidence that trade policy is countercyclical. Rising unemployment in a home country, falling growth in a trade partner of this country, and an appreciated bilateral real exchange rate between the two countries each lead to a significant rise in TTBs imposed by the home country. The effects of growth, however, changed during the Great Recession. Policymakers in these five countries were far less likely to impose TTBs on their many trade partners in the midst of downturns. Equally, the US and the EU both experienced significant real currency depreciations during this period. Both of these developments contributed to far fewer TTBs than would otherwise have been expected.

In Chapter 17, Kishore Gawande, Bernard Hoekman, and Yue Cui offer a different explanation for the lack of protectionism after the 2008 crisis, and one that resembles Manger's explanation for the formation of North–South PTAs. A great deal of global trade is intra-industry, involving global supply chains and two way trade in intermediate goods. This type of trade, argues Gawande, Hoekman, and Cui, discourages protection since it would harm downstream domestic firms within the chain that rely on imports. Furthermore, declining transportation costs and other technological developments have led firms to locate the links in such supply chains throughout the world, increasing the amount of intra-industry and reducing protectionist pressures. Gawande, Hoekman, and Cui also maintain that the WTO system helped to limit the willingness of governments to respond to the Great Recession by increasing protectionist barriers.

This latter issue is addressed in greater detail by Daniel W. Drezner in Chapter 18. Drezner points out that many observers have lamented the erosion of international economic governance over the last decade or so. These concerns escalated in the aftermath of the 2008 financial crisis. However, he argues that such concerns are misplaced. Despite a set of shocks that were even more severe than the 1929 crisis that precipitated the Great Depression, the global economy functioned relatively well. The economy rebounded relatively quickly, the trading system did not succumb to protectionism, the major economic actors (especially the US) continued to provide leadership and promote coordination in the system, and the international institutions that undergird the system—including the WTO—were robust enough to help manage the crisis and its aftermath.

Conclusion

Recent years have been marked by various important developments in the international trading system. This volume contains a set of studies on a number of these developments. The following articles have improved our understanding of the contemporary global economy and have shed light on a set of key theoretical and empirical issues in the fields of international trade and international political economy.

References

Bagwell, Kyle, and Robert W. Staiger. 2003. Protection and the Business Cycle. *Advances in Economic Analysis & Policy* 3 (1): 1–43.

Bhagwati, Jagdish. 2008. *Termites in the Trading System: How Preferential Agreements Undermine Free Trade*. New York: Oxford University Press.

Büthe, Tim, and Helen V. Milner. 2008. The Politics of Foreign Direct Investment into Developing Countries: Increasing FDI through International Trade Agreements? *American Journal of Political Science* 52 (4): 741–762.

Frankel, Jeffrey A. 1997. *Regional Trading Blocs in the World Economic System*. Washington, DC: Institute for International Economics.

Hafner-Burton, Emilie. 2009. *Forced to be Good: Why Trade Agreements Boost Human Rights.* Ithaca, NY: Cornell University Press.

Irwin, Douglas A. 2002. *Free Trade under Fire*. Princeton, NJ: Princeton University Press.

Lawrence, Robert Z. 1996. *Regionalism, Multilateralism, and Deeper Integration*. Washington, DC: Brookings Institution.

Leamer, Edward E. 1984. *Sources of International Comparative Advantage*. Cambridge, MA: MIT Press.

Limão, Nuno. 2005. Trade Policy, Cross-Border Externalities and Lobbies: Do Linked Agreements Enforce More Cooperative Outcomes? *Journal of International Economics* 67 (1): 175–199.

Mansfield, Edward D., and Helen V. Milner. 2012. *Votes, Vetoes, and the Political Economy of International Trade Agreements*. Princeton, NJ: Princeton University Press.

Mansfield, Edward D., and Jon C. Pevehouse. 2000. Trade Blocs, Trade Flows, and International Conflict. *International Organization* 54 (4): 775–808.

Ruggie, John Gerard. 1982. International Regimes, Transactions, and Change: Embedded Liberalism in the Postwar Economic Order. *International Organization* 36 (2): 195–231.

Stolper, Wolfgang Friedrich, and Paul A. Samuelson. 1941. Protection and Real Wages. *Review of Economic Studies* 9: 58–73.

Viner, Jacob. 1950. *The Customs Union Issue*. New York: Carnegie Endowment for International Peace.

Part I
The Sources and Features of Preferential Trade Agreements

[1]

ELSEVIER

Journal of International Economics 64 (2004) 29–63

Journal of INTERNATIONAL ECONOMICS

www.elsevier.com/locate/econbase

Economic determinants of free trade agreements

Scott L. Baier[a,b], Jeffrey H. Bergstrand[c,*]

[a] *John E. Walker Department of Economics, Clemson University, Clemson, SC 29634, USA*

[b] *Research Department, Federal Reserve Bank of Atlanta, Atlanta, GA 30309, USA*

[c] *Department of Finance and Business Economics, Mendoza College of Business, Kellogg Institute for International Studies, University of Notre Dame, Notre Dame, IN 46556, USA*

Received 29 June 2001; received in revised form 27 June 2002; accepted 4 December 2002

Abstract

The purpose of this study is to provide the first systematic empirical analysis of the economic determinants of the formation of free trade agreements (FTAs) and of the likelihood of FTAs between pairs of countries using a qualitative choice model. We develop this econometric model based upon a general equilibrium model of world trade with two factors of production, two monopolistically-competitive product markets, and explicit intercontinental and intracontinental transportation costs among multiple countries on multiple continents. The empirical model correctly predicts, based solely upon economic characteristics, 85% of the 286 FTAs existing in 1996 among 1431 pairs of countries and 97% of the remaining 1145 pairs with no FTAs.

Keywords: Free trade agreements; International trade; Qualitative choice models

JEL classification: F11; F12; F15

1. Introduction

> Free trade areas may well be an endogenous variable—that is, a response to, rather than a source of, large trade flows.... Presumably, (governments) are more likely to form free trade areas, (if) the benefits outweigh the costs. (Lawrence, 1998, p. 59)

Ever since Viner (1950), international economists have debated whether or not free trade agreements (FTAs)—on net—enhance or reduce economic agents' welfare. While

* Corresponding author. Tel.: +1-574-631-6761; fax: +1-574-631-5255.
E-mail address: bergstrand.1@nd.edu (J.H. Bergstrand).

0022-1996/$ - see front matter
doi:10.1016/S0022-1996(03)00079-5

most of the literature has focused on theoretical welfare gains or losses from FTAs for member (and nonmember) countries, there is no study in the literature that has tried to explain—or predict—FTAs between pairs of countries. As the quote above notes, FTAs may well be an endogenous variable. Lawrence's remark should come as no surprise to trade economists as there is a large literature in international economics on endogenous trade policy. While a large literature exists explaining empirically tariff and nontariff barriers cross-sectionally, no study has analyzed econometrically cross-sectional determinants of FTAs—much less one based upon a formal economic model.

The goal of this paper is to determine key economic factors influencing the likelihood of pairs of countries forming an FTA in a given year, based upon a qualitative choice methodology. We hope to provide an empirical benchmark for the determinants of FTAs, upon which strategic and political factors can be embedded subsequently. Qualitative choice models were designed to provide economists with the ability to evaluate decision behavior when choices are discrete (e.g. voting 'yes' or 'no') and characteristics of the population are unobservable (e.g. utility gain or loss from a policy decision). The decision to form an FTA is essentially a binary choice by a pair of countries' governments since, according to the GATT's Article XXIV, only complete (no partial) FTAs can be formed between a pair of countries. Qualitative choice models provide a framework to estimate the probability that a pair of governments are making a decision as if maximizing their respective agents' utilities.

What economic factors should influence the likelihood of an FTA? In his seminal survey of the theory of customs unions, Lipsey (1960) stated: "If one wishes to predict the welfare effects of a customs union it is necessary to predict the relative strengths of the forces causing trade creation and trade diversion (p. 498)". For the impatient reader, we find that trade-creating and trade-diverting economic characteristics matter considerably in explaining the probability of an FTA. Pairs of countries with FTAs tend to have the particular economic characteristics that the theory suggests should enhance the two countries' net trade creation and welfare (though possibly reducing nonmembers' net welfare). We find strong evidence that pairs of countries' governments tend to form FTAs: (i) the closer are two countries in distance; (ii) the more remote a pair of continental trading partners is from the rest of the world (ROW); (iii) the larger and more similar in economic size are two trading partners; (iv) the greater the difference of capital–labor ratios between two partners; and (v) the smaller the difference of the members' capital–labor ratios with respect to the ROW's capital–labor ratio. In the case of our framework, these 'pure economic' characteristics can predict accurately 85% of the 286 FTAs existing among 1431 country pairs in 1996 for which data were available and 97% of the remaining 1145 country pairs with no FTAs.

The remainder of the paper is as follows. Section 2 motivates the analysis. Section 3 presents the theoretical model. Section 4 discusses the econometric methodology and data requirements. Section 5 discusses simulations demonstrating theoretical relationships between the utility changes from an FTA and intercontinental and intracontinental transport costs, countries' real GDPs, and relative factor endowments, and presents empirical results on 'testable' hypotheses. Section 6 presents an evaluation of the robustness of the empirical results. Section 7 presents estimates of quantitative effects of typical changes in various economic characteristics on probabilities of FTAs. Section 8 interprets the results. Section 9 concludes.

2. Motivation and related literature

> The pure economic theory of trading blocs is essentially part of the broader theory of preferential trading arrangements. This theory... is a subject of inherent complexity and ambiguity; theory per se identifies the main forces at work, but offers few presumptions about what is likely to happen in practice. To make any headway, one must either get into detailed empirical work, or make strategic simplifications and stylizations that one hopes do not lead one too far astray. Obviously *detailed empirical work is the right direction*... (Krugman, 1993, p. 60; italics added)

Krugman (1991b) delineated sharply for the 1990s the debate on the relative merits of regional FTAs. In that paper, he appropriately separated discussions of the (pure) 'economics of trading blocs' and the 'political economy of FTAs'. In the 1990s, the debate about regional FTAs has subsequently followed these tracks. The 'economics' of trading blocs literature addresses FTAs in a competitive framework, either perfect or monopolistic competition. Baldwin and Venables (1995) discuss the economics of FTAs in terms of competitive frameworks[1]. Rodrik's (1995) survey addresses political economy frameworks. We discuss each approach in turn, with our focus on the former.

In addressing the economics of FTAs, Krugman (1991a,b) addressed the relative merits of FTAs in a static monopolistically-competitive framework, but emphasized economic geography. With zero intercontinental transport costs, continental FTAs decrease welfare unambiguously. With prohibitive intercontinental transport costs, such agreements increase welfare unambiguously. Krugman (1991b) concluded that, because most FTAs are among 'natural' trading partners, the likelihood of much trade diversion was small and "prospective moves toward regional free trade would almost surely do more good than harm to the members of the free trade areas" (p. 21). However, in a subsequent commentary, Bergsten (1991) noted: "This is an empirical question on which Krugman offers little supportive evidence" (p. 48). Our paper is concerned with providing supportive evidence.

The Krugman work led Frankel (1997), Frankel et al. (1995, 1996, 1998) to investigate the continuum between zero and prohibitive intercontinental transport costs. First, for high intercontinental transport costs, FTAs between countries geographically close—that is, continental or natural FTAs—are welfare enhancing on net and should lead social planners in these countries to adopt FTAs, because large intracontinental trade creation would

[1] The static effects are the net gains to a country's representative household from an FTA due to changes in trade volumes, trade distortion costs, or terms of trade that would arise in a perfectly competitive framework (with constant returns). These potential gains would be supplemented in the monopolistically competitive framework with scale and variety effects. The potential dynamic gains arise once factor accumulation is allowed, leading to potential investment creation and diversion.

dominate small intercontinental trade diversion. However, as intercontinental transport costs fall, continental FTAs may become welfare decreasing. Second, for any level of intercontinental transport costs, FTAs between countries geographically distant or on separate continents—that is, unnatural FTAs—are welfare decreasing and should lead countries' social planners to avoid FTAs, as the welfare loss from intracontinental trade diversion exceeds the welfare gain from intercontinental trade creation.

In the context of a qualitative choice framework with social planners, the FSW analysis suggests two hypotheses. First, all else constant, the more remote from the ROW are continental trading partners, the more likely an FTA will be formed due to less potential trade diversion. Second, the more natural (i.e. closer in distance) are two trading partners, the more likely an FTA will be formed by the countries' governments due to more potential trade creation. Consequently, the FSW model suggests two economic factors that could predict FTAs.

However, the Krugman and FSW theoretical results were generated in a model with identical economies, one industry and zero intracontinental transport costs. In reality, the world is not so generous as to make countries identical in terms of economic size or relative factor endowments, nor are intracontinental transport costs zero. As even noted in comments on Frankel et al. (1998) by Krugman (1998), the restriction of identical economic sizes may not be innocuous:

> My second, more analytical, concern is with the way Frankel, Stein, and Wei map the theoretical model onto the real world... there is a crucial assumption in the model that is not nearly true of the real world: that countries themselves are of equal economic size. In reality, of course, the size distribution of GDPs is highly unequal, and this surely makes a major difference when we try to model the effects of integration. (p. 115)

See Srinivasan (1998) and Panagariya (2000) for more on the problems raised by the symmetry assumption.

Second, the models in Krugman and FSW assume a world with one factor and one industry. As noted in Deardorff and Stern (1994) and Haveman (1996), such a model precludes trade in traditional comparative advantages, such as Heckscher–Ohlin trade. By eliminating traditional comparative advantages, the model may be relying too heavily on imperfect substitution among products that 'stacks the cards' against bilateralism.

Third, the Krugman and FSW models assume intra-continental transport costs are zero. Just as FSW noted Krugman's conclusions are sensitive to intercontinental transport costs, Nitsch (1996) challenged the FSW work by noting that the results are sensitive to intracontinental transport costs. Nitsch argued that introducing an intra-continental transport cost may cause the FSW phenomenon of 'supernatural' FTAs to disappear[2]. In FSW, the assumption of zero intracontinental transport costs is not innocuous; the trade diversion effect on welfare of a continental FTA is enhanced with zero intracontinental transport costs.

[2] In Frankel et al. (1995), the term 'supernatural FTA' refers to a continental FTA that is welfare-reducing on net due to low intercontinental transport costs.

Our paper generalizes the Krugman–FSW model to allow for economies with different absolute and relative factor endowments, and intra- as well as inter-continental transport costs. In our framework, governments are assumed to maximize their citizens' economic welfare. The net welfare gain or loss of two countries from forming an FTA depends on the trade creation versus trade diversion of the members. Economic determinants of trade creation and diversion can be categorized into three groups. The first is economic geography factors. Trade creation is greater the closer are two countries, and trade diversion is less the more remote two (continental) trading partners are from the ROW. The second category is intra-industry trade determinants. Trade creation is greater the larger and more similar are two countries' economic sizes, and trade diversion is less the smaller is the economic size of the ROW. The third category is inter-industry trade determinants. Trade creation is greater the wider are relative factor endowments between two countries, and trade diversion is less the smaller the difference between the relative factor endowments of the pair and that of the ROW. We find empirical support for all three groups of characteristics in predicting FTAs.

We now discuss briefly issues that we do not address to make our analysis tractable and to limit the paper's scope and length. First, as noted, the alternative track to the 'pure economics' of FTAs is the literature on the 'political economy' of FTAs. The latter literature is concerned largely with explaining theoretically the level of trade liberalization in general, or an FTA in particular, based on the relevant economic actors in an imperfect market structure with little competition. In the absence of special interest lobbies or distributional preferences, a government would act as a social planner, maximizing welfare of the country's agent.

As this paper is the first attempt to explain empirically the determinants of FTAs, we choose here to assume a social planner for each country that maximizes consumer welfare. While political lobbies and government distributional preferences may well influence FTA decisions, we intentionally ignore these factors initially to limit the scope and enhance the tractability of our analysis[3]. We find empirical support for our approach in Goldberg and Maggi (1999) which found "the weight of (consumer economic) welfare in the government's objective function is many times larger than the weight of (political) contributions" (p. 1135; italics added). Specifically, they estimated the weight of consumer welfare (political contributions) in government trade policy decisions to be 98% (2%)[4]. Our empirical investigation of select economic determinants of FTAs, based upon a model with monopolistically competitive firms and a social planner maximizing consumer welfare, consequently complements the political economy literature on empirical determinants of trade protection. Our paper intends to develop an empirical 'benchmark' for economic factors, hoping future research will address empirically political economy factors.

Second, we assume that the decision for a pair of countries' governments to form an FTA is based upon the welfare of only representative agents of the country pair, and ignore the possible net welfare loss to nonmember countries. We assume a social planner for each

[3] Moreover, we do not create any explicit coalition-formation structure in the model, as in Bond and Syropoulos (1996).

[4] Using a similar framework, Gawande and Bandyopadhyay (2000) estimated an even higher relative weight for consumer welfare versus contributions; their estimate ($a = 3175$) implies a welfare weight of 99%.

country, not for the world. In the (more restrictive) symmetric models of Krugman and FSW, inferences could be made about world welfare, and whether FTAs were good or bad for the world. We cannot attempt to address world welfare empirically; we restrict our analysis to the net welfare gain or loss of trade creation versus trade diversion for member countries. As in Baldwin and Venables (1995), tension between trade creation versus trade diversion makes the net welfare gain ambiguous for nonmember and member countries[5].

Third, we treat the decision to enter an FTA as a bilateral, rather than multilateral, one. While the decision of a country to form an FTA with the European Union (EU), for instance, may appear to be a multilateral one, every country in the EU has the ability to veto an FTA with a nonmember. In effect, every country in the EU decides bilaterally whether the net national welfare gain from an FTA with another country warrants formation[6].

Fourth, as we are interested in explaining empirically the cross-sectional variation in FTAs for a given year (1996), we assume that each country pair makes a decision in 1996 to form or not form an FTA, or to enforce or not enforce an FTA formed prior to 1996. This 'static' approach is in conformity with most cross-sectional 'gravity' analyses of bilateral trade flows where the presence or absence of an FTA is determined exogenously annually based upon government documentation. In theory, the presence or absence of an FTA in a given year depends only upon the economic characteristics in that year, similar to empirical cross-sectional endogenous trade-policy studies. Dynamic issues are important, but are outside the scope of the present paper and are left for future research.

3. The Model

In this section, we generalize the model in Frankel et al., (1995, 1996, 1998), Frankel (1997) to allow for asymmetries between countries and sectors, and intra- versus inter-continental transport costs. We use this theoretical model in Section 5 as the basis for a computable general equilibrium (CGE) model to illustrate the relationships between net utility gains (losses) from an FTA and relative transport costs, national outputs, and factor-endowment ratios. These relationships are employed to motivate the likely key empirical economic determinants of the probabilities of FTAs between pairs of countries.

International trade within each of two monopolistically-competitive sectors is generated by the interaction of consumers having tastes for diversity and production being characterized by economies of scale. Assume two factors of production, capital and labor, each perfectly mobile between sectors and each immobile internationally. We label the two sectors goods and services. Initially, these labels are arbitrary. Only much later will we differentiate the two sectors along conventional Balassa–Samuelson lines: goods (services) will be capital (labor) intensive in production and more (less) tradable. Within each

[5] As Baldwin and Venables (1995) note, "Perhaps the most important conclusion to be drawn is that—despite theoretical ambiguities—RIAs (regional integration agreements) seem to have generated welfare gains for the participants, with small, but possibly negative spillovers onto the rest of the world" (p. 1638).

[6] However, a bilateral decision does not imply a pair of countries ignores economic factors external to the pair. We address these considerations later.

sector, taste for diversity is captured formally by Dixit–Stiglitz preferences. Increasing returns to scale internal to the firm are captured with fixed costs and linear cost functions.

To capture the effects of asymmetries on regionalism, we assume three continents (indexed by 1, 2, 3) with two countries on each continent (countries indexed by A and B). Each country is allowed potentially to have different absolute and relative factor endowments of capital and labor. The two sectors are allowed potentially to differ in terms of relative factor intensities, tastes for variety, and trade barriers (transportation costs and/or tariffs). While earlier CGE models address the relative welfare benefits of regionalism, they do not explore these effects with explicit intercontinental and intracontinental transport costs, emphasizing—in the spirit of the Krugman and FSW frameworks—world geography.

3.1. Consumers

Each country i has a representative consumer who derives utility from consuming goods and services (g and s, respectively), based upon Cobb–Douglas preferences. Within each sector, the consumer has a taste for diversity captured formally by Dixit–Stiglitz (CES) preferences. The representative consumer for each of the six countries (i=1A, 1B, 2A, 2B, 3A, 3B) has a nested utility function:

$$U_i = [(\Sigma_{k=1}^{n_i^g} g_{iik}^{\theta^g} + \Sigma_{k=1}^{n_{i'}^g} g_{ii'k}^{\theta^g} + \Sigma_{j\neq i,i'} \Sigma_{k=1}^{n_{j\neq i,i'}^g} g_{ijk}^{\theta^g})^{1/\theta^g}]^{\gamma}[(\Sigma_{k=1}^{n_i^s} s_{iik}^{\theta^s} + \Sigma_{k=1}^{n_{i'}^s} s_{ii'k}^{\theta^s} + \Sigma_{j\neq i,i'} \Sigma_{k=1}^{n_{j\neq i,i'}^s} s_{ijk}^{\theta^s})^{1/\theta^s}]^{1-\gamma} \quad (1)$$

where U_i denotes the utility of the representative household in i. Let g_{iik} (s_{iik}) be consumption in country i of differentiated good (service) k produced in the home country (i), $g_{ii'k}$($s_{ii'k}$) is consumption in country i of good (service) k produced in the foreign country on the same continent (i'), and g_{ijk} (s_{ijk}) is consumption in country i of good (service) k produced in each of the four foreign countries on other continents (j). Let θ^g (θ^s) denote the parameter determining the elasticity of substitution in consumption in goods (services) with $0<\theta^g$, $\theta^s<1$. Let γ $(1-\gamma)$ be the Cobb–Douglas preference parameter for goods (services). Finally, let n_i^g (n_i^s) be the number of varieties of goods (services) produced in the home country, $n_{i'}^g$ ($n_{i'}^s$) the number of varieties of goods (services) produced in the foreign country on the same continent, and n_j^g (n_j^s) the number of varieties of goods (services) produced by a foreign country on another continent.

Within any country, households and firms are assumed symmetric; with symmetry, subscript k can be eliminated. Consequently, the budget constraint for the representative consumer in country i is:

$$w_i + r_i\left(\frac{K_i}{L_i}\right) + T_i = n_i^g p_i^g g_{ii} + n_{i'}^g p_{ii'}^g g_{ii'} + \sum_{j\neq i,i'} n_j^g p_{ij}^g g_{ij} + n_i^s p_i^s s_{ii} + n_{i'}^s p_{ii'}^s s_{ii'} + \sum_{j\neq i,i'} n_j^s p_{ij}^s s_{ij} \quad (2)$$

where w_i is the wage rate of the representative consumer–worker (or household) in country i, r_i is the rental rate on capital per household, K_i/L_i is the amount of capital exogenously supplied (or endowed) per household, T_i is tariff revenue redistributed back to households in a lump sum, p_i^g (p_i^s) is the price of the good (service) produced in the home country, $p_{ii'}^g$ ($p_{ii'}^s$) is country i's c.i.f. price of the good (service) produced in the foreign country on the same continent, and p_{ij}^g (p_{ij}^s) is country i's c.i.f. price of the good (service) produced in a foreign country on another continent.

Following FSW, c.i.f. prices differ from home prices due to Samuelson-type 'iceberg' transportation costs and ad valorem tariffs. Let a (b) represent the fraction of output exported by a country that is 'consumed' (or lost) due to intra- (inter-) continental transport[7]. Let $t_{ii'}$ and t_{ij} denote the ad valorem tariff rates in country i (that can potentially differ by trading partner). In the presence of positive tariffs and transport costs, country i's price of the good (service) produced by the foreign country on the same continent, $p_{ii'}^g$ ($p_{ii'}^s$), is

$$p_{ii'}^g = p_{i'}^g \left[\frac{1}{(1-a^g)}\right] + p_{i'}^g t_{ii'}^g \tag{3}$$

$$p_{ii'}^s = p_{i'}^s \left[\frac{1}{(1-a^s)}\right] + p_{i'}^s t_{ii'}^s \tag{4}$$

Country i's price of the good (service) produced by a foreign country on a different continent, p_{ij}^g (p_{ij}^s), is:

$$p_{ij}^g = p_j^g \left\{\frac{1}{[(1-a^g)(1-b^g)]}\right\} + p_j^g t_{ij}^g \tag{5}$$

$$p_{ij}^s = p_j^s \left\{\frac{1}{[(1-a^s)(1-b^s)]}\right\} + p_j^s t_{ij}^s \tag{6}$$

Tariff rates and transport costs can differ across sectors[8]. For each country's consumer, maximizing Eq. (1) subject to Eqs. (2)–(6) yields a set of demand equations which, for brevity, are omitted here.

3.2. Firms

Each firm in the goods industry is assumed to produce output subject to the technology

$$g_i = z_i^g (k_i^g)^{\alpha g} (l_i^g)^{1-\alpha g} - \varphi^g \tag{7}$$

where g_i denotes output of the representative firm in this industry in country i, z_i^g is an exogenous productivity term for goods producers, k_i^g is the amount of capital used by this

[7] Note these transport costs are of the hub-and-spoke variety discussed in Frankel et al. (1995) where each continent represents a hub. For intercontinental shipments, costs are broken down into two components. The cost of transporting a good (service) from one hub to another is given by b^g (b^s) and the cost to distribute the good (service) to each spoke is a^g (a^s).

[8] Asymmetries in transport costs across pairs of countries is beyond the scope of the present model; thus, a change in a or b changes transport costs for all country pairs. Note that a and b both contribute to total "inter-continental" transport costs.

firm, l_i^g is the amount of labor used by this firm, and φ^g represents a fixed cost facing each firm (e.g. marketing costs absorbing both capital and labor), the latter assumed identical across countries for simplicity. Each firm in the services industry is assumed to have a similar technology:

$$s_i = z_i^s (k_i^s)^{\alpha s} (l_i^s)^{1-\alpha s} - \varphi^s \tag{8}$$

where s_i denotes output of the representative firm, z_i^s, k_i^s, l_i^s, and φ^s are defined analogously for services, and factor intensities α^g and α^s can differ.

Firms in each industry in each country maximize profits subject to the technology defined in Eqs. (7) and (8), given the demand schedules implied by Section 3.1 above. Equilibrium in these types of models is characterized by two conditions. First, profit maximization ensures that prices are a markup over marginal production costs:

$$p_i^g = (\theta^g)^{-1} \left[\left(\frac{C}{z_i^g} \right) r_i^{\alpha g} w_i^{1-\alpha g} \right] \tag{9}$$

$$p_i^s = (\theta^s)^{-1} \left[\left(\frac{D}{z_i^s} \right) r_i^{\alpha s} w_i^{1-\alpha s} \right] \tag{10}$$

where $C=(\alpha^g)^{-\alpha g}(1-\alpha^g)^{-(1-\alpha g)}$ and $D=(\alpha^s)^{-\alpha s}(1-\alpha_s)^{-(1-\alpha s)}$. Second, firms earn zero economic profits which implies:

$$g_i = \frac{\theta^g \varphi^g}{(1-\theta^g)} \tag{11}$$

$$s_i = \frac{\theta^s \varphi^s}{(1-\theta^s)} \tag{12}$$

Common to such models, output of the representative firm in each industry is determined parametrically.

3.3. Factor endowment constraints

As standard, we assume that endowments of capital (K_i) and labor (L_i) are exogenous, with both factors internationally immobile. Assuming full employment

$$K_i = K_i^g + K_i^s = n_i^g k_i^g + n_i^s k_i^s \tag{13}$$

$$L_i = L_i^g + L_i^s = n_i^g l_i^g + n_i^s l_i^s \tag{14}$$

3.4. Equilibrium

The number of firms and product varieties in each industry and country, factor employments and prices in each industry and country, consumptions of each good, and product prices can be determined uniquely given parameters of the model (γ, θ^g, θ^s, α^g, α^s,

φ^g, φ^s) and initial transport costs, tariffs, and factor endowments. All together, the model includes 204 equations in 204 endogenous variables; the remaining equations are described in a technical appendix available from the corresponding author on request.

3.5. The social planner

To enable comparison with FSW, we assume that the social planner in each country sets tariffs initially at 30%. The formation of an FTA eliminates tariffs between members, leaving the members' tariffs on nonmember countries' products at 30%[9]. If the changes in utility for two countries' agents from an FTA are positive, we assume each social planner would choose to enter an FTA with the other country's planner. Thus, for a bilateral FTA to be formed, it must be the case that the change in utility is positive for both countries' agents. If the change in utility is negative for either country, we assume an FTA is not formed.

4. Econometric issues and data

4.1. Econometric issues

The econometric framework we employ is the qualitative choice model of McFadden (1975, 1976). A qualitative choice model can be derived from an underlying latent variable model. For instance, let y^* denote an unobserved (or latent) variable, where for simplicity we ignore the observation subscript. As in Wooldridge (2000), let y^* in the present context represent the difference in utility levels from an action (the formation of an FTA), where

$$y* = \beta_0 + x\beta + e \tag{15}$$

where x is a vector of explanatory variables (i.e. economic characteristics), β is a vector of parameters, and error term e is assumed to be independent of x and to have a

[9] The calibration exercise later requires initial (or pre-integration) and post-integration tariffs. We use 0.30 as our initial tariffs and as our post-integration tariff rates on nonmember imports, similar to FSW. Frankel (1997, pp. 167–168) discusses the empirical rationale for using 0.30. The ideal approach would be to consider the Nash equilibrium tariffs; the Nash equilibrium tariffs in a post-integration situation are likely to differ from those in the pre-integration situation. Addressing this limitation, however, is beyond the scope of the present paper, especially due to the emphasis here on asymmetric economies with intra- and inter-continental transport costs; many papers solving for Nash equilibrium tariffs benefit from a symmetry assumption, such as Krugman (1991a). Bond and Syropoulos (1996) address how the Nash equilibrium tariffs change between pre- and post-integration situations; the authors show conditions under which the Nash equilibrium tariffs of FTA members with nonmembers may even fall. Bond and Syropoulos also show when the Krugman (1991a) approach is a limiting case; in the symmetric trading-blocs model in Krugman, the optimal tariff is $1/(\varepsilon - 1)$ where ε is the elasticity of demand for the country's exports, and this (in his model) is a function of the representative bloc's absolute economic size or number of blocs and the elasticity of substitution, $1/(1 - \theta)$. Yi (2000) shows in a model with "taste-for-variety" preferences that an FTA could alter the Nash equilibrium tariffs of members with nonmembers downward to "balance" the varieties of imported goods. Ornelas (2001) shows that the Nash equilibrium tariffs of members with nonmembers may fall due to rent dissipation. See Bagwell and Staiger (1999) also for a detailed discussion of Nash equilibrium tariff structures in the presence of preferential and multilateral trade policies.

standard normal distribution. In the context of our model formally, $y^* = \min(\Delta U_i, \Delta U_j)$. Hence, both countries' consumers need to benefit from an FTA for their governments to form one.

Since y^* is unobservable, we define an indicator variable, FTA, which takes the value 1 if two countries have a FTA (indicating $y^*>0$), and 0 otherwise (indicating $y^* \leq 0$). The response probability, P, for FTA is

$$P(\text{FTA} = 1) = P(y* > 0) = G(\beta_0 + x\beta) \tag{16}$$

where $G(\cdot)$ is the standard normal cumulative distribution function, which ensures that $P(\text{FTA}=1)$ lies between 0 and 1. The standard errors of the estimates of β are asymptotically normally distributed and z-statistics reported in Section 5 will indicate whether estimates of β are statistically significant (see Wooldridge, 2000). While the statistical significance of the probit estimates can be determined, the coefficient estimates can only reveal the signs of the partial effects of changes in x on the probability of an FTA, due to the nonlinear nature of $G(\cdot)$. Letting $E(\cdot)$ denote the expectation of a variable, the direction of the effect of variable x_j on $E(y^*|x) = \beta_0 + x\beta$ is only qualitatively (not quantitatively) identical to the effect of x_j on $E(\text{FTA}|x) = G(\beta_0 + x\beta)$. We estimate directly the partial effects on the response probabilities in Section 7. In Section 8, we compare predicted FTAs to actual FTAs.

4.2. Data issues

Since Linnemann (1966), a plethora of trade studies have measured the presence or absence of an FTA between a pair of countries using a binary variable; see Frankel (1997, Ch. 4) for a survey. Following those studies, variable FTA_{ij} will have the value 1 for a pair of countries (i, j) with an FTA in 1996, and 0 otherwise. This variable was constructed for the pairings of 54 countries (hence, $(54 \times 53)/2$ or 1431 pairings) using appendices in Lawrence (1996) and Frankel (1997) and FTAs notified to the GATT/WTO under GATT Article XXIV or the Enabling Clause for developing economies as of May 2002 (WTO, 2002). We included only full (no partial) FTAs or customs unions.

In the Krugman and FSW models, the dichotomy between inter- and intra-continental transport costs was simply an abstraction to emphasize that two countries that are closer geographically will tend to have lower transport costs. The lower are transport costs between two countries (ignoring their distance from the ROW), the more each country can consume the other's varieties, enhancing trade creation regionally. As the primary factor influencing such costs is bilateral distance, this task amounted to calculating 1431 bilateral distances among 54 countries' economic centers. Similar to Bergstrand (1985, 1989), distances were calculated in nautical miles using US Department of the Navy Oceanographic Office (1965) for sea distances and Road Atlas of Europe (1988) for land distances (the latter multiplied by a standard factor of 2 for the transport-cost differential between land and sea transport). We used Linnemann (1966) for identifying countries' economic centers. NATURAL_{ij} (denoting natural trading partners) is the natural logarithm of the inverse of the distance between the economic centers of i and j.

While measuring closeness is straightforward, measuring the 'remoteness' of a pair of continental trading partners from the ROW is not. We constructed REMOTE as

$$\mathrm{REMOTE}_{ij} = \mathrm{DCONT}_{ij} \times \left\{ \frac{\left[\log\left(\sum_{k=1,k\neq j}^{N} \mathrm{Distance}_{ik}/N-1\right) + \log\left(\sum_{k=1,k\neq i}^{N} \mathrm{Distance}_{jk}/N-1\right)\right]}{2} \right\}$$

The interpretation of REMOTE is as follows. First, DCONT is a binary variable assuming the value 1 if both countries are on the same continent, and 0 otherwise. If two countries (i, j) are on the same continent, REMOTE measures the simple average of (the natural logarithms of) the mean distance of country i from all of its trading partners except j and the mean distance of country j from all of its trading partners except i. If two countries (i, j) are on different continents, REMOTE has the value 0. This measure captures the spirit of b for natural FTAs because it measures how far two countries on the same continent are from other countries, but it has no value for unnatural trading partners. As will be discussed in Section 5 below, for any given value of intracontinental transport costs, only the welfare gains from a continental FTA increase monotonically with increases in intercontinental transport costs (b) in our model.

Other economic variables were readily measurable. Data on real GDPs and per worker physical capital stocks (all in international dollars) are from Baier et al. (2000), assembled from primary data in Mitchell (1992, 1993, 1995); availability of capital stock data determined the sample of countries[10]. Data on tariff rates for countries are from World Bank (2000). Despite the cross-sectional nature of the decision, an issue of potential endogeneity arises. In the context of our theoretical model, the decision between two countries to have an FTA or not in 1996 depends upon economic characteristics in 1996. However, income and factor endowments vary over time and have likely been influenced by trade liberalization. For many pairs, an FTA between two countries in 1996 was formed well before 1996, the earliest (the original six-member EEC) phased in over 10 years beginning in 1958. Since an FTA formed several years prior to 1996 likely influenced subsequent trade—which then influenced economic growth—incomes and capital stocks in 1996 may well be endogenous. To account for this, we used the earliest data on incomes and capital and labor stocks in Baier et al. (2000) for a wide sample, namely, 1960 data.

5. Numerical analysis and empirical results

This section offers seven theoretical hypotheses about the relationships between the net gains from an FTA and various economic characteristics of country pairs, using a calibrated CGE model based upon the theoretical model in Section 3. Following each hypothesis (except

[10] The 54 countries include Algeria, Egypt, Nigeria, South Africa, Hong Kong, Iran, Iraq, Japan, Singapore, Austria, Belgium, Denmark, France, Germany (W. Germany in 1960), Greece, Ireland, Italy, Netherlands, Norway, Portugal, Spain, Sweden, Switzerland, Turkey, United Kingdom, Canada, Costa Rica, El Salvador, Guatemala, Honduras, Mexico, Nicaragua, Panama, United States, Argentina, Bolivia, Brazil, Chile, Colombia, Ecuador, Paraguay, Peru, Uruguay, Venezuela, Bulgaria, Czech Republic (Czechoslovakia in 1960), Hungary, Poland, Romania, South Korea, Philippines, Thailand, Indonesia, and Australia.

one), we evaluate empirically the relationship between the likelihood of an FTA and the various economic characteristics using the qualitative choice framework outlined in Section 4.

Hypothesis 1. The net gain from an FTA between two countries increases as the distance between them decreases.

One of the key implications from Krugman (1991b), Frankel et al. (1995, 1996, 1998) is that natural FTAs are unambiguously welfare superior to unnatural FTAs; hence, the two countries' social planners will form an FTA the smaller the distance between them. For a given distance between country pair and the ROW (other things equal), the closer are two countries, the lower their transport costs of international trade and consequently the higher is their trade volume. Elimination of the ad valorem tariff between close members alleviates the price distortion on a large amount of trade, improving utility of consumers more in continental FTAs[11].

As a benchmark, consider initially a special case of our model where countries and continents are identical in factor endowments ($K_i = L_i = 100$ for $i = 1A, \ldots, 3B$) and industries are identical, analogous to FSW's single-industry case[12]. Fig. 1 illustrates the relationship between intercontinental transport costs, intracontinental transport costs, and net benefits from either a natural FTA or an unnatural FTA. The top (bottom) surface is the net welfare gain from a natural (unnatural) FTA. Consistent with FSW, the welfare effects of a natural FTA exceed (or equal) those of an unnatural FTA for any levels of inter- and intra-continental transport costs. Frankel et al. (1995) Fig. 2 is a special case of our Fig. 1 evaluated at $a = 0$; this special case is shown in Fig. 1 by the plane relating 'Percent Change in Welfare' to 'Intercontinental T.C. Factor'. Thus, the FSW relationship is robust to varying intracontinental transport costs (a).

In the context of our qualitative choice framework and theoretical model, two countries will have a higher probability of an FTA if the welfare benefits outweigh the welfare costs. The first testable hypothesis is that the probability of an FTA is higher as the distance between the countries' economic centers falls. Specification (column) 1 in Table 1 shows that the first hypothesis is supported; the likelihood of an FTA is larger the more natural are two countries as trading partners.

Hypothesis 2. The net welfare gain from an FTA for two continental trading partners increases as their remoteness from the ROW increases.

A second important implication from the FSW model is that the net welfare gains from a continental FTA increase the greater are intercontinental transport costs (b) relative to intracontinental transport costs (a). As relative intercontinental transport costs increase, the volume of trade with remote countries (on other continents) decreases and that with near countries (on the same continent) increases. With less trade with remote countries, the

[11] We use "continental" and "natural" interchangeably, "intercontinental" and "unnatural" interchangeably.

[12] With perfect symmetry, tariff rates between sectors and countries ($t_{ij}^g, t_{ij}^g, t_{ij}^s, t_{ij}^s$) are identical, transport costs between continents (b^g, b^s) and countries on the same continent (a^g, a^s) are identical between sectors, factor intensities (α^g, α^s) are identical, CES preference parameters θ^g and θ^s are identical and equal to 0.75 as in FSW (implying elasticities of substitution in consumption in both sectors of four), and preferences for goods versus services are identical ($\gamma = 1 - \gamma = 1/2$). For simplicity, fixed costs in each sector (φ^g, φ^s) are unity, tariff rates are 0.30 initially in both sectors as in FSW (see [9]), and total factor productivity is normalized to unity ($z_i^g = z_i^s = 1$).

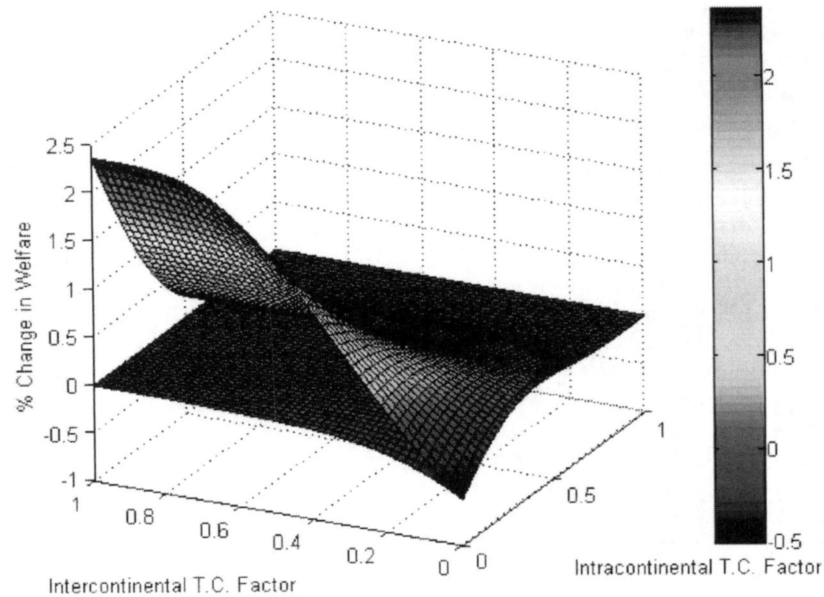

Fig. 1. Net welfare gains from natural and unnatural FTAs.

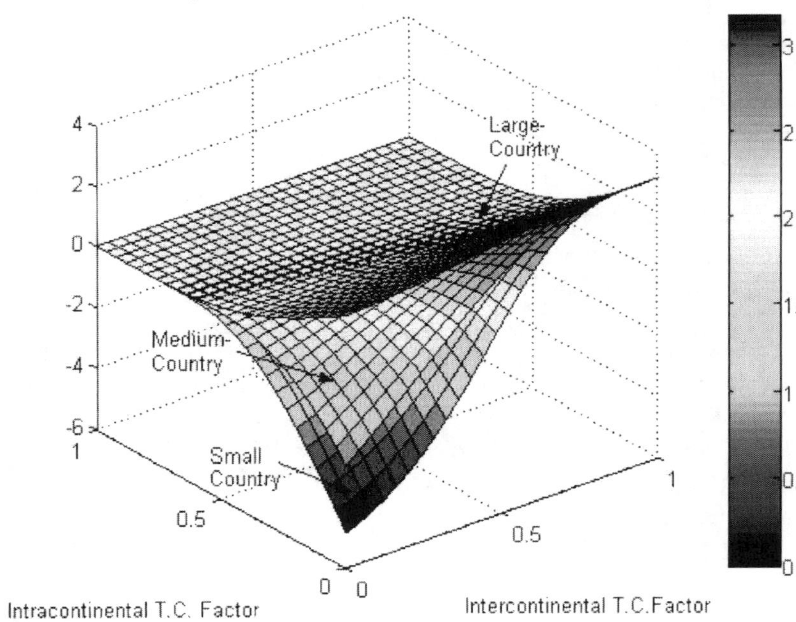

Fig. 2. Net welfare gains from natural FTAs and economic size.

Table 1
Probit results for the probability of an FTA

Variable:	Specification						
	1	2	3	4	5	6	7
Constant	13.42[a] (20.29)	9.76[a] (12.46)	4.31[a] (3.48)	3.49[a] (2.72)	4.22[a] (3.05)	4.22[a] (3.05)	7.90[a] (4.92)
NATURAL	1.74[a] (21.21)	1.36[a] (14.29)	1.49[a] (13.97)	1.52[a] (13.74)	1.64[a] (13.59)	1.65[a] (13.59)	1.76[a] (13.43)
REMOTE		0.15[a] (10.37)	0.15[a] (9.86)	0.16[a] (9.98)	0.17[a] (10.28)	0.17[a] (10.24)	0.18[a] (10.03)
RGDP			0.19[a] (5.33)	0.23[a] (5.94)	0.22[a] (5.28)	0.22[a] (5.27)	0.17[a] (3.67)
DRGDP				− 0.25[a] (-4.29)	− 0.27[a] (− 4.68)	− 0.28[a] (− 4.69)	− 0.34[a] (− 5.45)
DKL					0.43[a] (5.42)	0.49[b] (2.10)	0.85[a] (7.37)
SQDKL						− 0.02 (− 0.27)	
DROWKL							− 1.29[a] (− 5.53)
Pseudo R^2	0.571	0.647	0.668	0.683	0.704	0.704	0.728
Log likelihood	− 306.9	− 252.5	− 237.4	− 227.1	− 211.7	− 211.7	− 194.4
Number of observations	1431	1431	1431	1431	1431	1431	1431

[a] Denotes statistically significant z-statistic at 1% level in two-tailed test.
[b] Denotes statistically significant z-statistic at 5% level in two-tailed test.

relative tariff distortion with remote countries has less impact on utility; in Vinerian terms, there is less 'trade diversion'. With more trade with near countries, the elimination of the tariff distortion has greater utility gains.

The top surface in Fig. 1 reveals clearly for any level of a the monotonic relationship between greater intercontinental transport costs (b) and the larger net welfare benefits from a natural FTA. At $a=0$, the welfare effect of a regional FTA increases monotonically with b, and replicates (in the left-hand-side plane at $a=0$) FSW's Fig. 2 natural FTA line[13].

At higher values of a, the shape of this relationship remains monotonic, but 'flattens' considerably. The intuition is the following. First, suppose b is low. If a is zero, the utility loss of consumption of varieties intercontinentally (trade diversion) from a continental FTA exceeds the utility gain from more intracontinental trade (trade creation); with a equal to zero, there is no cost to transporting goods intracontinentally. However, at high levels of a, there is relatively little international trade, so there is relatively little welfare loss from increased relative discrimination against remote trading partners as well as little welfare gain from the continental FTA.

Next, suppose b is high. Even if a is zero, there is little intercontinental and much intracontinental trade, and hence little potential loss of trade volume intercontinentally (trade diversion) from a continental FTA. If a increases, intracontinental trade is dampened, decreasing the welfare gains from a continental FTA. Thus, the relationship between b and welfare from a continental FTA flattens as a increases[14].

The second testable hypothesis from the theory is that—for a given distance of two countries from one another—two continental trading partners will have a higher probability of forming an FTA the more remote the countries are from the ROW, measured by REMOTE_{ij}. Column 2 in Table 1 demonstrates that REMOTE is positively related to the probability of an FTA as expected and the coefficient estimate is statistically significant at the 1% level.

Hypothesis 3. The net welfare gain from an FTA between a pair of countries increases the larger are their economic sizes (i.e. average real GDPs).

We now introduce asymmetric sizes in terms of absolute factor endowments to determine scale-economies effects and address concerns raised earlier in Krugman (1998). We examine this in two exercises, first for natural trading partners and second for unnatural partners. In the first exercise, we allow countries on continent 1 (1A, 1B) to have larger absolute endowments of capital and labor than countries on continent 2 (2A, 2B), and 2A and 2B to have larger absolute endowments than countries on continent 3 (3A,

[13] FSW also showed that the net welfare loss from an unnatural FTA decreases unambiguously as intercontinental transport costs increase, possibly suggesting another testable hypothesis. However, in a world with asymmetric economies, this theoretical conclusion is not robust. We show, in the discussion below of Hypothesis 3, the ambiguous relationship between the net gains (losses) from an unnatural FTA and b.

[14] This result is in contrast to Nitsch (1996). Like Nitsch, we find that—for a given b—the welfare cost of a continental FTA decreases as a rises; however, FSW's "supernatural" region of welfare loss does not disappear. Only for higher values of a (such as 0.2–0.4) does the supernatural effect disappear. Moreover, Nitsch found that the entire two-dimensional line shifted up. We found this result counterintuitive. At high intercontinental transport costs, there is little intercontinental trade, and so a continental FTA generates large trade creation intracontinentally relative to little trade diversion intercontinentally. Thus, higher intracontinental transport costs should, on net, reduce the trade and welfare gains from a continental FTA as our figure confirms, counter to Nitsch's findings.

3B). Countries on the same continent have identical factor endowments. Moreover, for now relative factor endowments (capital–labor ratios) in every country are identical. Intuitively, the welfare gains from natural FTAs should be higher for countries with larger absolute factor endowments (and thus larger real GDPs). An FTA between two large partners (1A, 1B) increases the volume of trade in more varieties than an FTA between two small partners (3A, 3B), and reduces trade in fewer varieties from nonmembers than two small natural partners would, improving utility more in large countries relative to small countries. Second, the consequent larger increase in trade among two large economies causes a larger net expansion of demand and hence a larger rise in real income. Small countries 3A and 3B face considerable trade diversion when 1A and 1B form an FTA; the excess relative supply of factors in the small countries causes an erosion of terms of trade[15]. Fig. 2 illustrates that—for any values of a or b—the welfare gains from natural FTAs on all three continents are monotonically higher the larger the endowments of the countries.

Analogous reasoning applies to an unnatural FTA, the second exercise. Fig. 3 confirms the monotonic relationship—for any given values of a and b—between economic size and the welfare benefits of an unnatural FTA; net welfare gains (losses) increase (decrease) monotonically with economic size.

The third testable hypothesis is that the probability of an FTA is higher the larger economically are the trading partners, after accounting for distance and remoteness. $RGDP_{ij}$ measures the sum of the logs of real GDPs of countries i and j in 1960. Column 3 in Table 1 reveals that pairs of countries with larger average real GDPs have a higher probability of an FTA, in accordance with Hypothesis 3.

Figs. 2 and 3 also lend insight into the previous hypothesis about remoteness and FTA welfare gains. Fig. 2 illustrates also that—for a natural FTA—for a given economic size, net welfare gains (losses) increase (decrease) as remoteness (b) increases. However, Fig. 3 illustrates that such a monotonic relationship does not exist for unnatural FTAs. For $a=b=0$, larger economies on net gain from an unnatural FTA due to trade in a larger number of varieties and favorable terms-of-trade effects. However, as b increases (relative to a) these relative benefits for the largest economies erode. By contrast, for smaller economies, the loss of consumption of varieties from discriminating against natural and other unnatural trading partners by introducing an FTA offsets the gain in trade with an unnatural partner, but the welfare losses of this distortion decrease as b rises[16]. In some

[15] This is a theoretical argument for the potential endogeneity of incomes in the subsequent empirical work. Simulations of real income confirm this.

[16] Note that the formation of an FTA is symmetric; each pair of countries on each continent is assumed to form an FTA, as in Krugman and FSW. However, in the empirical work that will follow, we are more interested in the likely effect of an increase in the economic size of a pair of countries on the formation of an FTA between that pair of countries (i.e. probit analysis). We find that the effect on net welfare of a single natural or unnatural FTA still increases monotonically with the countries' absolute factor endowment sizes; figures are not shown but are available on request. Welfare effects are qualitatively similar but quantitatively larger; with one pair of countries forming an FTA, there is less trade diversion. As this discussion suggests, the net welfare gains (losses) from an FTA are sensitive to what other bilateral decisions are being made. That is, the net welfare gain from an FTA between country 1A and 1B is sensitive to whether country 1A is considering one with (in a broader context) another country on the continent. While this issue important, it is beyond the scope of the present theoretical analysis which focuses on "bilateral" decisions, not multilateral ones; we leave this issue for future theoretical research. However, we do address this issue of bilateral decisions empirically in a limited fashion in the econometric analysis.

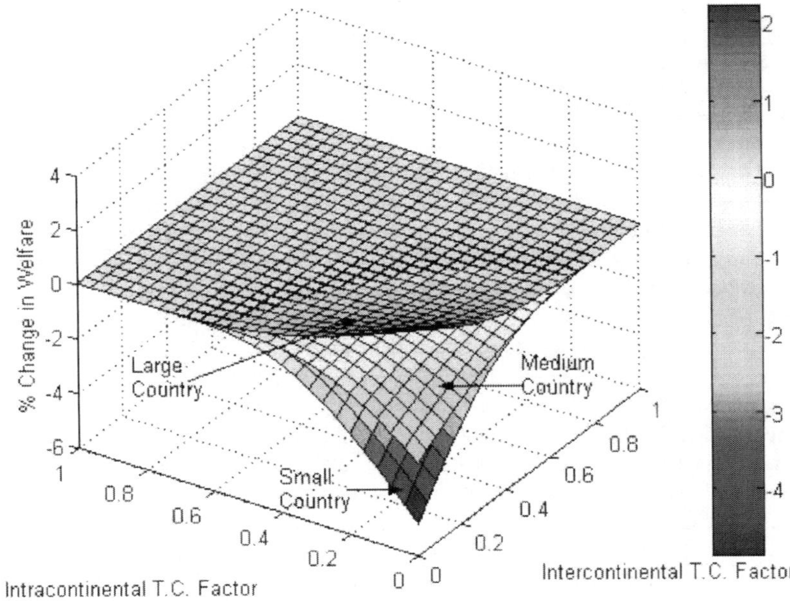

Fig. 3. Net welfare gains from unnatural FTAs and economic size.

cases, we can show the relationship between net welfare gains (losses) from an unnatural FTA and b is even quadratic.

Hypothesis 4. The net welfare gain from an FTA between a pair of countries increases the more similar are their economic sizes (i.e. real GDPs).

In this class of models, the more similar are the two countries' market sizes the larger the gains from an FTA. In the context of the first exercise, suppose 1A and 1B have identical shares of the two countries' factor endowments. The formation of a natural FTA provides gains from an increase in the volume of trade as the tariff distortion is eliminated on much continental trade. By contrast, if 1A has virtually all of the capital and labor on continent 1, formation of an FTA provides little welfare increase since there is virtually no trade between 1A and 1B. Similar reasoning applies to unnatural FTAs.

Fig. 4 illustrates the relationship between disparity in country sizes and the welfare benefits from a natural FTA for any given values of a and b (here, assuming $a=0$). As disparity increases, the loss of trade vis-a-vis the ROW for the larger country rises relative to its diminishing trade being created with a smaller and smaller FTA partner. Since one of the countries' net welfare declines with size disparity, the likelihood of an FTA decreases with disparity.

The fourth testable hypothesis is that the probability of an FTA is higher the more similar economically are the trading partners. $DRGDP_{ij}$ measures the absolute value of the difference between the logs of real GDPs of countries i and j in 1960. Column 4 in Table 1

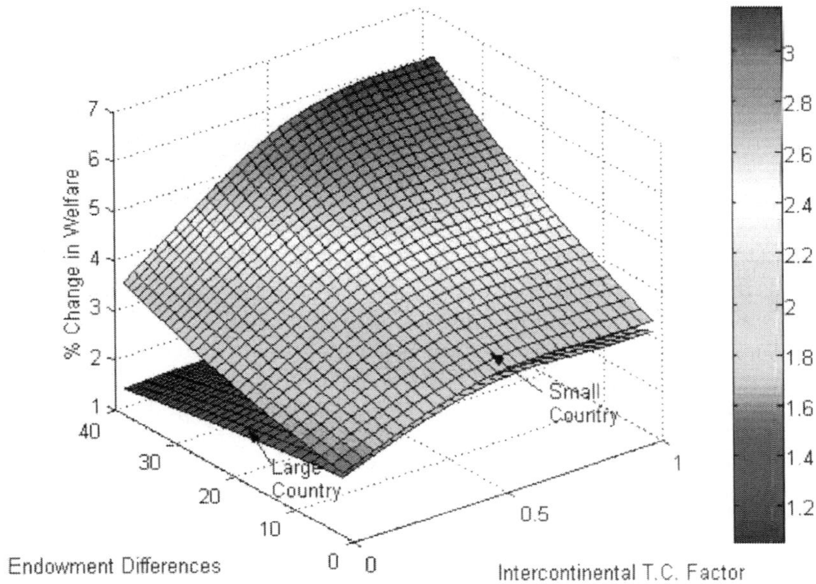

Fig. 4. Net welfare gains from a natural FTA for disparate economic sizes.

reveals that pairs of countries with smaller differences in real GDPs have a higher probability of an FTA.

Hypothesis 5. The net welfare gain from an FTA between a pair of countries decreases the larger is the economic size of countries outside the FTA (i.e. ROW real GDP).

The previous two hypotheses address the economic sizes of only those two countries. Surely the economic size of the ROW matters also. We can demonstrate (figure not shown) that the trade diversion from an FTA between a country pair is less the smaller the absolute factor endowment size of the ROW. As the ROW shrinks, the loss of consumption of varieties from the ROW due to an FTA is diminished. Moreover, the terms of trade effect is enhanced.

Unfortunately, the fifth hypothesis is difficult to evaluate empirically. In a cross-section of country pairs, the ROW's GDP does not vary much across the 1431 observations. Not surprisingly, the variance of this variable is trivial (coefficient of variation of 0.002) and consequently it was excluded.

Hypothesis 6. The net welfare gain from an FTA between a pair of countries increases with wider relative factor endowments, but might eventually decline due to increased specialization (if intercontinental transport costs are low).

At this point, asymmetries have been introduced between economies, but not between industries; a limitation of the Krugman–FSW model raised by Deardorff and Stern (1994) is the assumption of only one factor and one industry. As suggested in

Haveman (1998), the only paper in the literature that attempts to synthesize the complementary approaches of traditional Hecksher–Ohlin comparative advantage under perfect competition with the Krugman–FSW approach featuring imperfect competition to analyze the welfare benefits of regional FTAs in the presence of transport costs is Spilimbergo and Stein (1998). The limitation of Spilimbergo and Stein's two-factor two-industry extension is that each industry uses only one factor of production (capital in manufactures, labor in agriculture); in their framework, countries' factor endowments "differ only in their capital endowment" (p. 128). Consequently, differing capital–labor ratios only create differences in per capita income through scale-economies effects, not traditional comparative advantages. Changes in relative factor endowments cannot influence production shares and relative employment of capital and labor in sectors, since factors are immobile between sectors (an uncommon assumption to capture traditional Heckscher–Ohlin effects). Haveman (1998) notes that the Spilimbergo–Stein model "is really a world full of endowment economies" (p. 147). By contrast, our model allows endogenous adjustment of capital and labor between sectors (perfect factor mobility between sectors but not between countries) and endogenous determination of numbers of varieties of products in each industry. Our model can potentially separate differences between countries in per capita incomes due to scale-economies effects as well as specialization due to traditional comparative advantages; we allow also for differences in per capita incomes due to productivity differences.

Following most work, we assume 'goods' are capital-intensive and 'services' are labor-intensive in production in the spirit of the Balassa–Samuelson model, cf. Bergstrand (1991). As in Roland-Holst et al. (1994), we set $\alpha_g = 0.36$ and $\alpha_s = 0.27$ (capital shares in production). All other parameters for the two sectors are assumed identical. Starting with countries initially having identical capital and labor endowments, we increase the capital stock of country 1A to initiate a difference between the capital–labor ratios of 1A and 1B, but reduce 1A's productivity proportionately in both sectors (z^g, z^s) to hold 1A's real GDP fixed (to suppress scale-economies effects).

In traditional trade models (ignoring transport costs), the benefits of an FTA between a pair of countries should be enhanced the wider their relative factor endowments because traditional comparative advantages would be exploited more fully. Fig. 5 illustrates the relationship between differences in capital–labor endowment ratios and the net welfare benefits from a natural FTA for the capital-abundant country (1A). At high intercontinental transport costs, the relationship is positive and monotonic. At high values of b, there is little intercontinental trade. Consequently, most variety is exchanged intra-continentally. As relative factor endowments widen, both countries specialize more in the industries where they have comparative advantages and enjoy more net welfare gains from an FTA. There is little loss of variety (trade diversion) for 1A due to high intercontinental transport costs.

However, at low intercontinental transport costs, the net gains from an FTA increase at first with wider relative factor endowments, but eventually decline. At low values of b, there is considerable intercontinental trade in goods and services. As relative factor endowments widen, country 1A gains initially from specialization in goods. Yet, at high levels of specialization, 1A relies more on intra- and inter-continental trade to

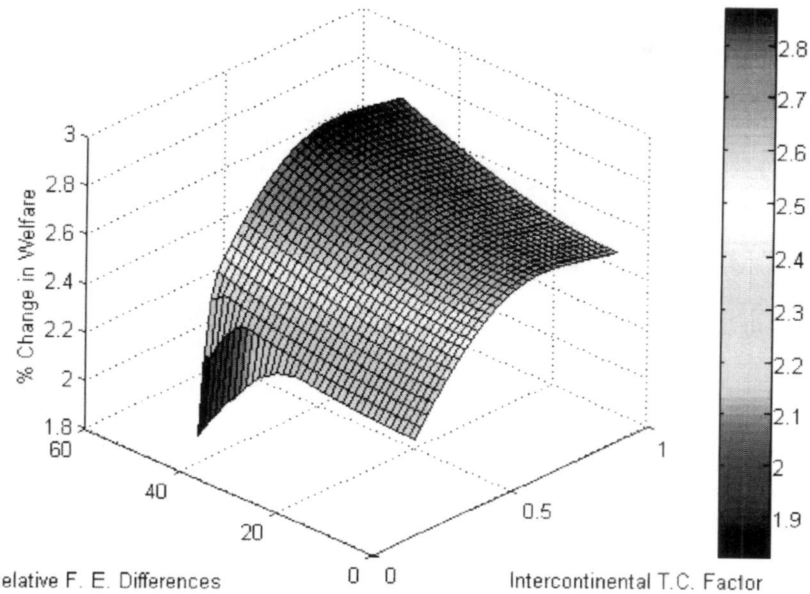

Fig. 5. A natural FTA and relative factor-endowment differences.

meet its demand for varieties of services. A natural FTA causes considerable trade diversion of services intercontinentally. With increasing specialization, the net welfare gains from inter-industry trade are eventually offset by the net trade diversion due to intra-industry trade. A qualitatively similar relationship holds for an unnatural FTA (figure not shown).

The sixth hypothesis is that the probability of an FTA is higher the larger the difference between two countries relative factor endowments, but possibly only up to a point. If intercontinental transport costs are not very low or relative factor endowment differences not high, the quadratic term may be unimportant. DKL_{ij} measures the absolute value of the difference between the logs of the capital–labor ratios of countries i and j in 1960; $SQDKL_{ij}$ measures the square of DKL. DKL should be positively related to $P(FTA=1)$ while SQDKL should be negatively related to it. Column 5 in Table 1 reveals that DKL has the expected positive effect. Larger relative factor endowment differences between country pairs have a positive and statistically significant relationship with the probability of an FTA.

Column 6 reveals that the variables have the expected quadratic relationship with $P(FTA=1)$, but the statistical significance of the coefficient estimate of DKL erodes and the coefficient estimate for the quadratic term—while having the expected negative sign—is statistically insignificant. The overall explanatory power from adding the quadratic term is negligible; the pseudo-R^2 of specification 6 is virtually identical to that of specification 5. Hence, for parsimony, we omitted the quadratic term in subsequent regressions.

Hypothesis 7. The net welfare gain from an FTA between a pair of countries decreases the larger is the difference between the relative factor endowment of the pair and that of the ROW.

The previous hypothesis concerns only trade between the country pair and the pair's capital–labor ratios. The loss in welfare from an FTA for the country pair will be higher the more Heckscher–Ohlin trade is foregone with the ROW (up to a point). We can demonstrate readily (figure not shown) that the loss of gains from specialization from an FTA between a country pair is less the smaller the difference between the pair's relative factor endowment size and that of the ROW.

The last testable hypothesis is that the probability of an FTA declines the wider is the (absolute) difference between the capital–labor ratios of the member countries and the ROW's capital–labor ratio, due to potential trade diversion. This variable—DROWKL_{ij}—is measured as

$$\text{DROWKL}_{ij} = \frac{\left\{\left|\log\left[\left(\sum_{k=1,k\neq j}^{N} K_k\right)/\left(\sum_{k=1,k\neq i}^{N} L_k\right)\right] - \log[K_i/L_i]\right| + \left|\log\left[\left(\sum_{k=1,k\neq j}^{N} K_k\right)/\left(\sum_{k=1,k\neq i}^{N} L_k\right)\right] - \log[K_j/L_j]\right|\right\}}{2}$$

Column 7 in Table 1 reveals that DROWKL has a negative relationship with the probability of an FTA and its coefficient estimate is statistically significant, likely due to the potential inter-industry trade diversion.

On net, the probit model works well. All six RHS variables in specification 7 have the expected sign and their coefficient estimates are statistically significant. Using the pseudo-R^2 term as a summary measure of explanatory power, specification 7 'explains' 73% of the variation of FTAs among 1431 country pairings in 1996. The pseudo-R^2 measure is the one discussed in Wooldridge (2000), one minus the ratio of the log-likelihood value for the estimated model to that for the model with only an intercept.

An alternative measure of goodness-of-fit for probit models is the 'percent correctly predicted,' also discussed in Wooldridge (2000). If the estimated probability of the pair exceeds 0.5, we define a variable *PredFTA* to be one; if the probability is less than 0.5, *PredFTA* takes on the value zero. The percentage of times that *PredFTA* matches FTA (which equals 1 if an FTA exists, and 0 otherwise) is an alternative measure of goodness-of-fit. However, Wooldridge notes that it is even more useful to report the percentage correctly predicted for each of the two possible outcomes, for the following reason. With 1431 country pairs and 286 FTAs, a probit specification of FTA on a constant only would result in predicted values of FTA of 0.2 for every observation (i.e. 286/1431). In this naive specification, however, *PredFTA* would still match FTA for 1145 of the 1431 cases, or 80% of the time. Even if the model failed to predict even one FTA correctly, this goodness-of-fit measure would suggest a predictive power of 80%.

Consequently, we report the percentage correctly predicted for each of the two possible outcomes. In our sample of 1431 pairs, 286 pairs have an FTA and 1145 pairs do not have an FTA. Using the rule described, 243 of the 286 FTAs are predicted correctly, or 84.97%. Also, 1114 of the 1145 pairs without an FTA are predicted correctly, or 97.29%. Thus, using alternative criteria the model appears to have a reasonably good fit.

6. Robustness of the empirical results

In this section, we evaluate the sensitivity of the results to several potential econometric issues.

6.1. Clustering and heteroskedasticity

First and foremost, the specifications assume that FTA_{ij} is independent across observations. In reality, a FTA between the United States and Mexico is not independent of such an agreement between the United States and Canada. Certain pairings of countries belong to a group or 'cluster'. The lack of independence of observations can influence the econometric results in several ways. First, it might influence the variance-covariance matrix of the econometric model. Akin to adjusting for heteroskedasticity, we re-estimated the specification in column 7 to adjust for possible interdependence of bilateral observations. This correction has an effect only on the standard errors, not the coefficient estimates. We assumed that pairs of countries within certain clusters (e.g. EU members) were interdependent, but clusters were independent. Clusters had three major categories: both countries belong to an FTA, one of the countries in a pair belongs to an FTA, or neither country belongs to one. We defined 99 clusters. Interdependence of observations within clusters had no significant effect on standard errors and thus was not a major concern. Hence, in the following empirical work, this adjustment was ignored[17].

6.2. Bloc size and bias

The fact that certain countries form a cluster might also introduce bias in coefficient estimates. For instance, Turkey may enter an FTA with the EU not to gain with respect to every member but to gain with respect to members on average. This possibility suggests that the results in specification 7 may be biased by the omission of a variable representing economic characteristics of the 'bloc,' such as the share of world GDP of the bloc's other members. We re-estimated the model adding two variables: the average share of world GDP of the other members of the trading bloc or blocs (if either or both of a country pair were in an FTA) and the absolute difference in these shares. The larger the relative economic size of the other members, the more likely an FTA existed between a country pair. The smaller the difference in these shares, the more likely an FTA existed. The variable representing the relative economic size of other trading bloc members had a positive and statistically significant coefficient estimate, as expected. Also, the variable representing the relative economic size difference had a negative and statistically significant coefficient estimate, as expected. The additional presence of these variables affected the other coefficients' quantitatively, but not qualitatively; the only RHS variable's coefficient estimate that became statistically insignificant—not surprisingly—

[17] We also re-estimated the model correcting for general heteroskedasticity; this had little effect on standard errors.

was the sum of the two countries' GDPs. In fact, the pseudo-R^2 rose from 0.73 to 0.80. The percent of FTAs (No FTAs) correctly predicted rose from 85 to 88% (97–98%).

Thus, the argument that multilateral, not bilateral, characteristics matter has merit; moreover, these empirical results are consistent with our theoretical model. However, we reserve caution about coefficient estimates from this specification due to potential endogeneity. If the econometric model is to 'explain' the likelihood of an FTA between a country pair using economic characteristics, it seems that a RHS variable constructed using a priori knowledge of bloc members (to determine the economic characteristics of the other bloc members) introduces an endogenous RHS variable. To err on the side of caution, we retained specification 7 in Table 1 as the primary specification for later analysis to preclude this potential endogeneity (with the other results available on request).

6.3. Sample bias

One might argue that the importance of bilateral distance and remoteness in explaining the likelihood of an FTA may well be driven by the presence of the EU and the size of the EU (in real GDP and number of countries). Moreover, as just discussed, countries that have obtained an FTA with the EU (say, Turkey) may be driven by the attractive market size of the entire EU, rather than by the economic size of individual EU member countries (say, Denmark). To address these issues, we re-estimated specification 7 for three sub-samples of our entire 1431 observations. The results are qualitatively identical to those in Table 1 (not shown for brevity), and most of the coefficient estimates remain statistically significant at the 1% significance level. Similar results are obtained when the sample excludes any country pair that includes a Western European country or a European country. Thus, results for specification 7 are robust to the exclusion of Europe, the most geographically-clustered country group.

6.4. Tariffs of nonmembers

The net welfare gains (losses) from an FTA should be sensitive to the levels of tariffs among nonmembers. The higher are tariffs in the ROW, the larger will be the volume of trade created within the FTA. We can demonstrate readily (figure not shown) that the net welfare gains (losses) increase (decrease) with higher ROW tariffs. We evaluated the hypothesis that the probability of an FTA increases the higher are tariff levels in the ROW. However, variation in this variable was virtually negligible (coefficient of variation of 0.04) as with ROW's GDP for country pairs; inclusion of ROW's tariffs had an effect only on the intercept's value and statistical significance. The percentage correctly predicted of FTAs (and No FTAs) changed trivially. Hence, we also excluded ROW's tariffs in the remaining analysis.

6.5. Endogeneity of GDPs and capital stocks

As noted earlier, time-varying RHS economic variables were measured using 1960 data to ensure predetermined values; 1996 values of incomes and capital stocks would be potentially endogenous. We implemented the test for endogeneity of the 1996 values of income and capital stocks proposed by Rivers and Vuong (1988). The test for endogeneity is a Wald test. The test statistic is a chi-squared (χ^2) statistic with four restrictions; the critical value is 13.28 at the 1% level. The χ^2 statistic was 51.67. The null hypothesis of exogeneity of 1996 values of incomes and capital stocks was rejected. This is consistent with our theory that trade policy, by influencing terms of trade and other factors, influences income and capital investment. This is consistent with empirical evidence in Frankel and Romer (1999).

6.6. Omitted institutional and political-economy variables

Consistent with our assumption that FTAs are formed by governments maximizing consumer welfare, we have not yet introduced any 'political' variables. In the context of our theory, such variables' inclusion would be ad hoc. However, readers may be concerned that—despite the theory—some political, institutional, social, and cultural factors may be correlated with other RHS variables and with FTA, resulting in biased coefficient estimates of the economic determinants. An exhaustive examination of all such potential non-economic variables is clearly outside our scope.

Nevertheless, we considered several variables. We introduced three measures of 'institutional' characteristics that might affect the likelihood of an FTA: an index of the countries' average degrees of 'market orientation,' a dummy variable to reflect shared legal origins (i.e. British law, etc.), and a dummy for having a common language. Governments also pay attention to national security issues, the environment, and labor standards in deciding on the formation of an FTA. We included, respectively, the share of GDP of the countries in defense expenditures and the (absolute value of the) difference in their shares, the per capita level of CO2 emissions in the countries and the difference in these values, and the (average) fraction of children in a country aged 10–14 in the country's labor force and the difference in these fractions. Of all these nine variables, only one variable was significant; per capita CO2 emissions in a country pair had a negative and statistically significant relationship with the probability of an FTA.

As Trefler (1993) notes, common across many cross-industry endogenous tariff protection studies is the empirical result that protection tends to be higher in industries with greater import penetration. When the bilateral trade between the country pairs was the sole RHS variable in a probit regression, the coefficient estimate was positive and significant; however, the pseudo-R^2 (0.082) was considerably smaller than in any of Table 1's specifications. The addition of the level of trade between a country pair to specification 7—already holding constant the pair's economic size (and other economic determinants)—can be a crude proxy for import 'penetration'; the expected coefficient is negative. In this enhanced specification, the countries' bilateral trade in 1958–1960 had a negative relationship with the FTA probability, consistent with the endogenous protection literature. The coefficient estimate was -0.20 and was significant at 1% ($z=-2.96$). Yet, other coefficient estimates did not change materially.

Finally, Grossman and Helpman (1995) addressed the 'politics' of FTAs. In their theoretical political economy analysis, the formation of an FTA by two governments is more likely when there are substantial economic welfare gains for each country's average voter, similar to our model. Moreover, in their model with specific factors owned by a few concentrated firms, political pressure to prevent an FTA is reduced the more 'balanced' is potential trade between the partner countries, due to offsetting political pressures from exporters and importers. To try to capture the spirit of Grossman–Helpman's analysis, we also re-estimated specification 7 adding the absolute value of the difference in the logarithms of the two countries' average trade flows in 1958–1960. The result was that differences in trade volumes had a negative relationship with the probability of an FTA, but was statistically insignificant. However, with both trade variables included, only the bilateral trade level was significant (at the 1% level).

In sum, the inclusion of CO2 emissions, the level of trade, and the imbalance of trade had no perceptible impact on the coefficient estimates of main specification 7 (or their statistical significance). None of the estimated FTA predictions were altered materially; even with all three additional variables, the model predicted 238, rather than 243, of the existing FTAs, and 1115, rather than 1114, of the 'No FTAs'. This evidence is consistent with the Goldberg and Maggi (1999) result that consumers' welfare had predominant weight in US trade policy. In the interest of parsimony and to focus on 'pure economic' determinants, we ignored including these variables subsequently.

7. Partial effects of RHS variables on response probabilities

As discussed earlier, the probit estimates cannot reveal the quantitative effect of a change in any RHS variable on the probability of an FTA. Given the standard normal cumulative distribution function, G(·), the partial effect on the response probability of FTA (denoted p_{xj}) to a one standard deviation (S.D.) change in any variable x_j, $\hat{\sigma}_{xj}$, is

$$p_{xj} = G\left[\hat{\beta}_o + \sum_{i \neq j} \hat{\beta}_i \bar{x}_i + \hat{\beta}_j(\bar{x}_j \pm \hat{\sigma}_{xj})\right] - G\left[\hat{\beta}_o + \sum_{i \neq j} \hat{\beta}_i \bar{x}_i + \hat{\beta}_j \bar{x}_j\right]$$

where $\bar{x}_i$ denotes the mean level of x_i.

Note that p_{xj} is sensitive to the levels of the elements of x. This accords with our theoretical model. This issue is illustrated most transparently by reconsidering Fig. 1 in Section 5. The net welfare gain from an FTA from being natural rather than unnatural trading partners is sensitive to the level of intercontinental transport costs (b). Analogous nonlinearities arise in our generalization of the FSW model. For instance, we expect a one S.D. increase in economic size to have a larger effect on the probability of an FTA for natural partners than unnatural ones[18]. Similarly, the effects of an increase in economic size disparities, differences in capital–labor ratios, bilateral distance, and remoteness are

[18] Consider how the effect of an increase in economic size on the net welfare gain from FTAs is sensitive to whether the countries are natural or unnatural trading partners. Figs. 2 and 3 in Section 5 illustrate this. In Figs. 2 and 3, assuming $b = 0.10$ and $a = 0.05$, the net welfare gain from a natural or unnatural FTA for the medium-sized countries is negative. Suppose absolute factor endowments increase for each country pair (from 75 to 250). The percentage net welfare gain from an FTA from the increase in the factor endowment rises from − 1.38 to 2.06%, or by 3.44%, for the natural pair. By contrast, the percentage net welfare gain from an FTA from increasing the factor endowment rises from − 1.60 to 1.44%, or by only 3.04%, for the unnatural pair.

Table 2
Response probabilities to a one S.D. (σ) change in RHS variables for natural trading partners (evaluated at the mean level of remote)[a]

Variable	P(FTA = 1|natural partners) = 0.867	
	$-\sigma$	$+\sigma$
NATURAL	0.384 (0.302, 0.472)	0.994 (0.984, 0.998)
REMOTE	0.859 (0.804, 0.903)	0.873 (0.814, 0.911)
RGDP	0.780 (0.693, 0.850)	0.926 (0.873, 0.961)
DRGDP	0.938 (0.895, 0.966)	0.751 (0.663, 0.825)
DKL	0.663 (0.568, 0.749)	0.964 (0.930, 0.983)
DROWKL	0.952 (0.909, 0.977)	0.712 (0.615, 0.796)

[a] Values in parentheses denote the 95% confidence interval for the associated response probability estimate.

sensitive to levels of other variables. Following convention, mean values of the RHS variables are used for levels.

One complication arises in estimating the partial effects on the response probabilities for the particular vector of RHS variables, x, in our model by using mean values for the levels. One of the RHS variables, REMOTE, is the product of a continuous variable and a binary variable. Thus, the variable has the value of two countries' distance from the ROW when the pair share a continent, but 0 if not on the same continent. The mean value of this variable is economically meaningless. To account for this, we estimate the partial effects on the response probabilities for two scenarios, one with the mean value of NATURAL and the mean value of REMOTE when the two countries are on the same continent, and one with the mean value of NATURAL and 0 as the value of REMOTE when they are not.

Tables 2 and 3 present the response probabilities under these two alternative scenarios for a one S.D. change in each of the RHS variables along with (in parentheses) the 95% confidence interval associated with the respective response probability. Table 2 presents the response probabilities for continental trading partners. For ease of reference, we note that at the mean level of all RHS variables the probability of an FTA among natural partners is 0.867[19]. A one S.D. increase (decrease) in the closeness of such partners increases (decreases) this probability by 0.127 (0.483). The differential partial effect is due, of course, to the nonlinear functional relationships. Not surprisingly, a S.D. change in distance has an economically and statistically significant effect on the probability of an FTA among natural partners. A S.D. increase (decrease) in the remoteness of two natural partners from the ROW increases (decreases) the probability of an FTA by 0.006 (0.008).

Geographic proximity is not the only factor influencing the probability of an FTA. Changes in the level of or disparity between countries' real GDPs have economically and statistically significant impacts on $P(\text{FTA}=1)$. For instance, a S.D. increase in the level of real GDPs increases the response probability by 5.9% points, approximately half the effect of a S.D. increase in closeness. S.D. changes in the difference between real GDPs and the differences between capital–labor ratios all have economically and statistically significant impacts of approximately the same magnitudes as real GDP levels.

[19] For NATURAL and REMOTE, we used the means of the variables only for natural partners.

Table 3
Response probabilities to a one S.D. (σ) change in RHS variables for unnatural trading partners (evaluated at remote = 0)[a]

Variable	P(FTA = 1|unnatural partners) = 0.012	
	$-\sigma$	$+\sigma$
NATURAL	0.000014 (0.000001, 0.00010)	0.086 (0.057, 0.126)
RGDP	0.005 (0.002, 0.012)	0.028 (0.015, 0.050)
DRGDP	0.071 (0.045, 0.107)	0.010 (0.004, 0.022)
DKL	0.0009 (0.0002, 0.0033)	0.041 (0.023, 0.069)
DROWKL	0.013 (0.006, 0.028)	0.0007 (0.0002, 0.0024)

[a] Values in parentheses denote the 95% confidence interval for the associated response probability estimate.

Table 3 reports the response probabilities for unnatural country pairs. Not surprisingly, at the mean level of all RHS variables the probability of an unnatural FTA is about 1%[20]. A S.D. increase in closeness causes this probability to rise from 0.012 to 0.086, reinforcing the importance of economic geography in the likelihood of an FTA; this effect is statistically significant. Economic factors still manage a role in influencing the likelihood of an unnatural FTA. A S.D. rise in the level of real GDPs increases the response probability of an FTA by 1.6% points; this effect is economically and statistically significant. A S.D. decrease in the absolute difference between real GDPs of unnatural partners has a similar economically and statistically significant positive effect on the probability of an FTA (6% points). Increases in the differences between capital–labor ratios also have economically and statistically significant effects on P(FTA = 1).

Thus, the response probability estimates confirm that economic characteristics as well as geography have economically and statistically significant impacts on the probability of an FTA.

8. Interpreting the results

> If governments maximized the welfare of their citizens, prospective moves toward regional free trade would almost surely do more good than harm to the members of the free trade areas. (Krugman, 1991b, p. 21)

> This is an empirical question on which Krugman offers little supportive evidence. (Bergsten 1991, p. 48)

The original 'Krugman vs. Krugman' debate yielded unambiguous conclusions. In a world with symmetric economies and no transport costs, bilateralism was bad; in the same world with prohibitive intercontinental transport costs, bilateralism was good. FSW illustrated that the outcome depends upon the degree of intercontinental transport costs.

[20] For REMOTE we used zero, and for NATURAL we used the mean of the variable only for unnatural partners. Response probabilities are not reported for REMOTE in Table 3 since this has a value of zero here.

Drawing upon empirical data for intercontinental transport costs (external to the model), FSW concluded that regionalization may have become excessive.

In a world with asymmetric economies, we cannot make sweeping statements that bilateralism is 'good' or 'bad'. The focus of this paper has been on explaining and predicting FTAs bilaterally based upon pure economic characteristics (of member and nonmember countries). However, as Krugman's quote suggests, we can make limited statements about the net welfare gain or loss for the member countries.

In the context of McFadden's motivation of qualitative choice models, predicted probabilities of an FTA suggest whether particular pairs of countries should have an FTA based upon economic characteristics that—in the context of the theory—enhance welfare. If the predicted probability of an FTA for a country pair exceeds one-half, this suggests—in this framework—that there is a net welfare gain for the country pair. As the empirical results show, the probability of an FTA exceeded one-half for 243 of the 286 country pairs with FTAs, or 84.97%. The results suggest—in the model's context—that bilateralism is good for these pairs (though not necessarily for non-members).

Second, although 243 of the FTAs were predicted, 43 of the remaining 286 country pairs with FTAs were not predicted. In the context of the model, this suggests that 15% of the FTAs in our sample were welfare-reducing for the two countries. One might say, for these country pairs, bilateralism was 'excessive'.

Third, our qualitative choice model also allows us to identify for which country pairs bilateralism might be considered 'insufficient'. Bilateralism is termed 'insufficient' if an FTA is predicted but does not exist (yet). Of 1145 country pairs without an FTA, 1114 pairs were predicted correctly, or 97.29%. We note that 31 country pairs that had no FTA should have such an agreement (according to the model's predictions); these are shown in Table 4 along with each pair's predicted probability in parenthesis[21].

Table 5 shows the 43 cases where bilateralism was 'excessive,' that is, where an FTA existed in 1996 but the model's prediction probability was less than one-half. Five cases involve agreements between Algeria with EC members and ten cases involve agreements between Egypt and EC members; these agreements went into force in 1976 and 1977, respectively, although evidence suggests that Algeria's and Egypt's imports from the EC still face high tariffs. Eight cases involve Turkey with EC members; the EC-Turkey agreement was notified to the GATT/WTO in 1995, legally entered into force January 1996, and is still 'under examination'. Evidence suggests this agreement is effective[22]. Thus, although 15% of the FTAs in existence were not predicted, it is

[21] Of these 31 cases, 11 would become members of an FTA if the Free Trade Agreement of the Americas (FTAA) evolves into an FTA. Six cases involve members of the Asian Pacific Economic Cooperation (APEC) forum. While APEC is not considered an FTA, discussion has centered around members forming an FTA by 2020. Finally, seven cases involve Romania and Bulgaria, which became members of the Central European Free Trade Agreement (CEFTA) in 1997 and 1998, respectively. Thus, 24 of the 31 cases are pairs involved in potential (or, in the 2 years after 1996, actual) FTAs.

[22] We thank Francois Benaroya of the French Trade Ministry for information on Algeria, Egypt and Turkey.

Table 4
Cases of insufficient bilateralism

1	Panama–Venezuela (0.792)
2	Costa Rica–Ecuador (0.539)
3	Costa Rica–Venezuela (0.764)
4	Mexico–Honduras (0.556)
5	Mexico–Guatemala (0.863)
6	Mexico–El Salvador (0.756)
7	Mexico–Nicaragua (0.619)
8	Venezuela–Guatemala (0.604)
9	Venezuela–Brazil (0.645)
10	Peru–Chile (0.948)
11	Peru–Argentina (0.507)
12	Japan–South Korea (0.924)
13	Japan–Philippines (0.728)
14	Hong Kong–Singapore (0.646)
15	Hong Kong–South Korea (0.805)
16	Hong Kong–Philippines (0.716)
17	South Korea–Philippines (0.578)
18	Bulgaria–Czechoslovakia (0.763)
19	Bulgaria–Hungary (0.946)
20	Bulgaria–Poland (0.756)
21	Bulgaria–Romania (0.998)
22	Bulgaria–Turkey (0.514)
23	Romania–Poland (0.756)
24	Romania–Hungary (0.926)
25	Switzerland–Algeria (0.919)
26	Switzerland–Egypt (0.758)
27	Iraq–Turkey (0.711)
28	Iran–Iraq (0.988)
29	Iran–Indonesia (0.557)
30	Iran–Turkey (0.938)
31	Nigeria–South Africa (0.682)

important to note that 23 of the 43 cases of 'excessive' bilateralism can be explained solely by FTAs between the EC and Algeria, Egypt and Turkey.

We close this section addressing three points. First, with the literature on FTAs having been largely a theoretical one, empirical evaluation of FTAs has largely fallen into two camps: CGE models of trade and trade policy, and econometric analyses of the trade flow impacts of FTAs. Common to both approaches—and different from ours—is that FTAs are exogenous. CGE analyses generally focus on the trade creation and trade diversion impacts of an FTA, calculating the impacts in terms of a share of GDP. As is well known, however, CGE studies are essentially, as Baldwin and Venables (1995) note, 'theory with numbers'. Such analyses provide a quantitative articulation of what the underlying theoretical model suggests, but do not explain the formation of FTAs.

Econometric analyses of the impacts of FTA tend largely to explore the ex post effect of an FTA on trade flows, often using 'gravity equations,' such as in Bergstrand, (1985), Bergstrand (1989) and Frankel (1997). While these models have indicated successfully gross trade creation and diversion from an FTA, one still cannot make welfare statements. As with CGE models, gravity equations do not explain the endogenous

Table 5
Cases of excessive bilateralism

1	Algeria–Denmark (0.417)
2	Algeria–Germany (0.275)
3	Algeria–Ireland (0.465)
4	Algeria–Sweden (0.199)
5	Algeria–UK (0.321)
6	Egypt–Iraq (0.031)
7	Egypt–Belgium (0.356)
8	Egypt–Denmark (0.308)
9	Egypt–France (0.497)
10	Egypt–Germany (0.159)
11	Egypt–Ireland (0.164)
12	Egypt–Netherlands (0.364)
13	Egypt–Portugal (0.088)
14	Egypt–Spain (0.224)
15	Egypt–Sweden (0.178)
16	Egypt–UK (0.195)
17	Turkey–Norway (0.125)
18	Turkey–Belgium (0.379)
19	Turkey–Denmark (0.254)
20	Turkey–Germany (0.186)
21	Turkey–Netherlands (0.387)
22	Turkey–UK (0.214)
23	Turkey–Portugal (0.033)
24	Turkey–Spain (0.244)
25	Turkey–Sweden (0.226)
26	Portugal–Hungary (0.336)
27	Portugal–Bulgaria (0.481)
28	Portugal–Romania (0.384)
29	Chile–Mexico (0.022)
30	Chile–Brazil (0.174)
31	Chile–Paraguay (0.318)
32	Chile–Ecuador (0.468)
33	Bolivia–Brazil (0.097)
34	Bolivia–Ecuador (0.334)
35	Bolivia–Colombia (0.163)
36	Bolivia–Mexico (0.004)
37	Colombia–Nicaragua (0.147)
38	Colombia–Mexico (0.194)
39	Argentina–Venezuela (0.484)
40	Brazil–Paraguay (0.248)
41	Philippines–Singapore (0.412)
42	Philippines–Indonesia (0.400)
43	Thailand–Indonesia (0.105)

formation of FTAs. We see our approach as a complement to these alternative approaches in providing quantitative insight about FTAs.

Second, we note that our statements about whether bilateralism is excessive or insufficient abstract from the issue of bilateralism versus multilateralism. Given the model, when all countries are symmetric forming natural FTAs on all continents is welfare inferior to multilateral tariff liberalization. However, one can also show that (for certain transport costs) a natural FTA between a country pair may be welfare superior for that pair to their elimination of tariffs on imports from all countries, or even to world free trade. Our econometric analysis does not address this issue.

Third, we note Leamer's quote, "Give me data or give me death". Leamer (1998) noted that answers to questions such as the one in this paper should "be sought using four different methodologies: theory, calibration, indirect estimation, and direct observation" (p. 149). This paper has attempted intentionally to address the issue of bilateralism using all four methodologies. We have constructed a fairly parsimonious model of international trade with intra-industry trade as well as Heckscher–Ohlin trade in a setting with explicit transportation costs. Despite parsimony, the complexity of the model requires calibration to determine qualitative theoretical relationships. Turning to the qualitative choice framework, we apply observations on FTAs and economic characteristics of countries to determine the predictability of FTAs for particular pairs and to draw inferences about the net welfare gain or loss for these pairs. We find that country pairs that have bilateral FTAs tend to have those economic characteristics that should enhance economic welfare for the pair. Using direct observations, we find evidence that individual cases of 'excessive' bilateralism are constrained to a few plausible pairs of countries.

9. Conclusions

The main purpose of this study was to develop an econometric model that explains the 'pure economic' determinants of FTAs and that also predicts successfully the likelihood of pairs of countries forming FTAs. This is the first econometric model, to our knowledge, that predicts FTAs based upon an explicit general equilibrium model of world trade of multiple countries on multiple continents. It provides a economic benchmark for future political economy models to enhance the explanation of FTA determinants.

The main conclusions of the study are that the potential welfare gains and likelihood of a FTA between a pair of countries are higher: (i) the closer in distance are two trading partners; (ii) the more remote a natural pair is from the ROW; (iii) the larger and more similar economically (i.e. real GDPs) are two trading partners by exploiting economies of scale in the presence of differentiated products; (iv) the greater the difference in capital–labor endowment ratios between two countries due to the gains from traditional comparative advantages (i.e. Heckscher–Ohlin trade); and (v) the less is the difference in capital–labor endowment ratios of the member countries relative to that of the ROW due to less inter-industry trade diversion. These factors have economically and statistically significant effects on the probability of an FTA.

One measure of overall fit of a probit model is how well the model predicts correctly the outcome. Of the 1431 country pairs in our sample, 286 country pairs had an FTA and 1145 pairs did not have an FTA in 1996. We predicted correctly 243 of the 286 FTAs, or 84.97%. Also, 1114 of the 1145 pairs without an FTA are predicted correctly, or 97.29%.

Is bilateralism good? Unlike the restrictive symmetric models of Krugman and FSW, we cannot make any sweeping statement. While we predict 85% of FTAs in our sample in 1996, we find that 43 of the 286 FTAs in 1996 were not predicted, suggesting that 15% of the FTAs in that year were 'excessive' in a strict interpretation of the results. Yet, two important caveats are worth noting. First, of these 43 cases, 23 are agreements between the EC with Algeria, Egypt, and Turkey. Thus, half of the cases of excessive bilateralism are limited to three particular countries (and the Algeria and Egypt agreements may not even be effective). Second, we found 31 cases where agreements should exist (in the model's context) but none did, suggesting for these pairs bilateralism is insufficient.

Acknowledgements

We are grateful for helpful comments from two anonymous referees, Robert Staiger, Richard Baldwin, Francois Benaroya, Daniel Benjamin, William Dougan, Peter Egger, Antoni Estevadeordal, Robert Feenstra, Jeffrey Frankel, Mark Hallerberg, David Hummels, Chris Magee, Emanuel Ornelas, Mika Saito, Dieter Schumacher, Curtis Simon, Ernesto Stein, Ernesto Talvi, Robert Tamura, Jerry Thursby, Shang-Jin Wei, Eduardo Zambrano, and participants at presentations at the Austrian Institute of Economic Research (WIFO) in Vienna, German Institute for Economic Research (DIW) in Berlin, inaugural conference of the Regional Integration Network in Uruguay, second annual European Trade Study Group conference at the University of Glasgow, Midwest International Economics conference at the University of Minnesota, Clemson University, DePaul University, Indiana University, Purdue University, University of Notre Dame, and West Virginia University. Baier thanks the Center for International Trade at Clemson University and Bergstrand thanks the Mendoza College of Business and Kellogg Institute for International Studies at the University of Notre Dame for financial support.

References

Bagwell, K., Staiger, R., 1999. An economic theory of GATT. American Economic Review 89 (1), 215–248.

Baier, S.L., Dwyer, G., Tamura, R., 2000. The Growth and Development of Nations. Clemson University and Federal Reserve Bank of Atlanta, Manuscript.

Baldwin, R.E., Venables, A., 1995. Regional economic integration. In: Grossman, G.M., Rogoff, K. (Eds.). Handbook of International Economics, vol. 3. Elsevier, Amsterdam, pp. 1597–1644.

Bergsten, C.F., 1991. Comment on: Paul Krugman, the move toward free trade Zones. In: Policy Implications of Trade and Currency Zones, proceedings of a Federal Reserve Bank of Kansas City symposium, pp. 43–58.

Bergstrand, J.H., 1985. The Gravity equation in international trade: some microeconomic foundations and empirical evidence. Review of Economics and Statistics 67 (3), 474–481.

Bergstrand, J.H., 1989. The Generalized Gravity equation, monopolistic competition, and the factor-proportions theory in international trade. Review of Economics and Statistics 71 (1), 143–153.

Bergstrand, J.H., 1991. Structural determinants of real exchange rates and national price levels: some empirical evidence. American Economic Review 81 (1), 325–334.

Bond, E.W., Syropoulos, C., 1996. The size of trade blocs: market power and world welfare effects. Journal of International Economics 40 (3/4), 411–437.

Deardorff, A.V., Stern, R.M., 1994. Multilateral trade negotiations and preferential trading arrangements. In: Deardorff, A.V., Stern, R.M. (Eds.), Analytical and Negotiating Issues in the Global Trading System. University of Michigan Press, Ann Arbor, pp. 27–85.

Frankel, J.A., 1997. Regional Trading Blocs. Institute for International Economics, Washington, DC.

Frankel, J.A., Romer, D., 1999. Does trade cause growth? American Economic Review 89 (3), 379–399.

Frankel, J.A., Stein, E., Wei, S.-J., 1995. Trading Blocs and the Americas: the natural, the unnatural, and the super-natural. Journal of Development Economics 47 (1), 61–95.

Frankel, J.A., Stein, E., Wei, S.-J., 1996. Regional trading arrangements: natural or supernatural. American Economic Review 86 (2), 52–56.

Frankel, J.A., Stein, E., Wei, S.-J., 1998. Continental trading blocs: are they natural or supernatural. In: Frankel, J.A. (Ed.), The Regionalization of the World Economy. University of Chicago Press, Chicago, pp. 91–113.

Gawande, K., Bandyopadhyay, U., 2000. Is protection for sale? Evidence on the Grossman–Helpman theory of endogenous protection. Review of Economics and Statistics 82 (1), 139–152.

Goldberg, P.K., Maggi, G., 1999. Protection for sale: an empirical investigation. American Economic Review 89 (5), 1135–1155.

Grossman, G.M., Helpman, E., 1995. The politics of Free-Trade agreements. American Economic Review 85 (4), 667–690.

Haveman, J., 1996. Some welfare effects of sequential customs union formation. Canadian Journal of Economics 24 (4), 941–958.

Haveman, J., 1998. Comment on: Antonio Spilimbergo, Ernesto Stein, the welfare implications of trading blocs among countries with different endowments. In: Frankel, J.A. (Ed.), The Regionalization of the World Economy. University of Chicago Press, Chicago, pp. 145–149.

Krugman, P., 1991a. Is bilateralism bad. In: Helpman, E., Razin, A. (Eds.), International Trade and Trade Policy. MIT Press, Cambridge, pp. 9–23.

Krugman, P., 1991b. The Move Toward Free Trade Zones. In: Policy Implications of Trade and Currency Zones, proceedings of a Federal Reserve Bank of Kansas City symposium, pp. 7–41.

Krugman, P., 1993. Regionalism versus multilateralism: analytical notes. In: de Melo, J., Panagariya, A. (Eds.). New Dimensions in Regional Integration. Cambridge University Press, Cambridge, pp. 58–89.

Krugman, P., 1998. Comment on: Jeffrey A. Frankel, Ernesto Stein, Shang-Jin Wei, continental trading blocs: are they natural or supernatural? In: Frankel, J.A. (Ed.), The Regionalization of the World Economy. University of Chicago Press, Chicago, pp. 114–115.

Lawrence, R.Z., 1996. Regionalism, Multilateralism, and Deeper Integration. Brookings Institution, Washington, DC.

Lawrence, R.Z., 1998. Comment on: Barry Eichengreen, Douglas A. Irwin, the role of history in bilateral trade flows. In: Frankel, J.A. (Ed.), The Regionalization of the World Economy. University of Chicago Press, Chicago, pp. 57–59.

Leamer, E.E., 1998. Comment on: Antonio Spilimbergo, Ernesto Stein, The welfare implications of trading blocs among countries with different endowments. In: Frankel, J.A. (Ed.), The Regionalization of the World Economy. University of Chicago Press, Chicago, pp. 149–151.

Lipsey, R.G., 1960. The theory of customs unions: a general survey. Economic Journal 70 (3), 496–513.

Linnemann, H., 1966. An Econometric Study of International Trade Flows. North-Holland, Amsterdam.

McFadden, D., 1975. The revealed preferences of a government bureaucracy: theory. Bell Journal of Economics 6 (2), 401–416.

McFadden, D., 1976. Quantal choice analysis: a survey. Annals of Economic and Social Measurement 5 (4), 363–390.

Mitchell, B.R., 1992. International Historical Statistics: Europe 1750–1988. Stockton Press, NY.

Mitchell, B.R., 1993. International Historical Statistics: The Americas 1750–1988. Stockton Press, NY.

Mitchell, B.R., 1995. International Historical Statistics: Africa, Asia and Oceania 1750–1988. Stockton Press, NY.

Nitsch, V., 1996. Do three trade blocs minimize world welfare. Review of International Economics 4 (3), 355–363.

Ornelas, E., 2001. Rent Dissipation, Political Viability, and the Strategic Adoption of Free Trade Agreements. University of Wisconsin at Madison, Mimeo.

Panagariya, A., 2000. Preferential trade liberalization: the traditional theory and new developments. Journal of Economic Literature 38 (2), 287–331.

Rivers, D., Vuong, Q.H., 1988. Limited information estimators and exogeneity tests for simultaneous probit models. Journal of Econometrics 39, 347–366.

Road Atlas of Europe, 1988. Rand McNally and Co., Chicago.

Rodrik, D., 1995. Political Economy of Trade Policy. In: Grossman, G.M., Rogoff, K. (Eds.), Handbook of International Economics, vol. 3. Elsevier Science, Amsterdam, pp. 1457–1494.

Roland-Holst, D.W., Reinhart, K.A., Shiells, C.R., 1994. A general equilibrium analysis of North American economics integration. In: Francois, J.F., Shiells, C.R. (Eds.), Modeling Trade Policy: Applied General Equilibrium Assessments of North American Free Trade. Cambridge University Press, Cambridge.

Spilimbergo, A., Stein, E., 1998. The welfare implications of trading blocs among countries with different endowments. In: Frankel, J.A. (Ed.), The Regionalization of the World Economy. University of Chicago Press, Chicago, pp. 121–145.

Srinivasan, T.N., 1998. Comment on: Jeffrey A. Frankel, Ernesto Stein, Shang-Jin Wei, continental trading blocs: are they natural or supernatural. In: Frankel, J.A. (Ed.), The Regionalization of the World Economy. University of Chicago Press, Chicago, pp. 116–120.

Trefler, D., 1993. Trade liberalization and the theory of endogenous protection: an econometric study of US import policy. Journal of Political Economy 101 (1), 138–160.

US Department of the Navy Oceanographic Office, 1965. Distance Between Ports. H.O. Publication No. 15, US Government Printing Office, Washington, DC.

Viner, J., 1950. The Customs Union Issue. Carnegie Endowment for International Peace, New York.

Wooldridge, J., 2000. Introductory Econometrics. South-Western Publishing, Cincinnati.

World Bank, 2000. World Development Indicators. World Bank, Washington, DC.

World Trade Organization, 2002. http://www.wto.org, May.

Yi, S.-S., 2000. Free-trade areas and welfare. Review of International Economics 8 (2), 336–347.

[2]

Why Democracies Cooperate More: Electoral Control and International Trade Agreements

Edward D. Mansfield, Helen V. Milner, and B. Peter Rosendorff

Over the past fifty years, barriers to international trade have decreased substantially. While the decline in protectionism since World War II has stemmed partly from unilateral changes in trade policy by countries, it has also been a result of agreements among countries to liberalize commerce. In this article, we analyze the conditions under which states have concluded such agreements and, more generally, explore the domestic factors affecting interstate economic cooperation. We argue that the likelihood of states cooperating on trade policy depends crucially on their regime type: as states become more democratic, they are increasingly likely to conclude trade agreements.

Our analysis has implications for two broad areas in the field of international relations. First, a large and influential body of research has emerged on the effects of regime type on the outbreak and resolution of interstate conflict, the durability of political-military alliances, the propensity of states to join intergovernmental organizations (IGOs), and various other aspects of foreign policy.[1] Very little of this literature, however, focuses directly on the links between regime type and foreign economic policy. We conduct one of the initial analyses bearing on this important topic.

Earlier versions of this paper were presented at the 1998 Annual Meeting of the American Political Science Association, Boston; the 1999 International Economics Association World Congress, Buenos Aires; the 1999 Latin American Meetings of the Econometric Society, Cancun; the 2000 Southeastern Theory and International Economics Meeting, Houston; the 2000 Latin American and Caribbean Economic Association Annual Meetings, Rio de Janeiro; the 2000 Public Choice Society Annual Meetings, Charleston; and seminars at Brown University, the University of California, Riverside, the University of Michigan, the University of Rochester, the University of Southern California, UCLA, and Yale University. We are grateful to participants in these seminars and David Baldwin, Marc Busch, Peter Gourevitch, Joanne Gowa, David Lake, Lisa Martin, James Morrow, Jon Pevehouse, and Alastair Smith for helpful comments.

1. See, for example, Bueno de Mesquita and Lalman 1992; Bueno de Mesquita et al. 1999; Gaubatz 1996; Mansfield and Snyder 1995; Russett and Oneal 2001; and Russett, Oneal, and Davis 1998.

International Organization 56, 3, Summer 2002, pp. 477–513

Second, this article joins the debate over the causes of international economic cooperation. Many studies attribute variations in cooperation to features of the global system, especially the distribution of capabilities and international institutions.[2] In contrast, much less research addresses the domestic sources of economic cooperation, and virtually none considers the influence of regime type.[3] Furthermore, the few studies that have been conducted on this topic pertain only indirectly to international trade agreements.[4] We help fill this gap in the literature by conducting one of the first direct examinations of the effects of regime type on the establishment of trade agreements. Such agreements embody cooperation among their members because they involve mutual policy adjustments, entailing the reciprocal lowering of trade barriers.

Our analysis shows how international cooperation in trade can be influenced by the control that voters exert over political leaders—a factor that varies starkly between democracies and autocracies. The regular occurrence of fair and competitive elections is fundamental to all democracies.[5] As G. Bingham Powell observes, "There is a widespread consensus that the presence of competitive elections, more than any other feature, identifies a contemporary nation-state as a democratic political system."[6] Such elections vest the public with control over government leaders that is absent in nondemocratic polities.[7] In democracies, political leaders must succeed at the polls to maintain office. To this end, they must gain the support of voters, whose attitudes toward the incumbent tend to depend heavily on their perceptions of recent economic performance.[8] In contrast, elections held in autocracies are much less free and fair; they vest the populace with much less control over public officials and place few (if any) constraints on the autocrat's policy choices. In our analysis, the superior ability of elections in democracies to constrain leaders prompts democratic rulers to be more cooperative internationally than their nondemocratic counterparts.

Elections, however, are not the only domestic constraints leaders face. In any political regime, leaders must balance the policies that enhance their electoral prospects with those that meet the demands of special interest groups.[9] In what follows, we model how this trade-off affects the optimal foreign economic strategy of political leaders operating in different regime types.

It is clear that international trade agreements may stem in part from the associated economic gains that leaders expect to derive. We do not explicitly model these gains

2. See, for example, Keohane 1984; Krasner 1976; and Milner 1992.
3. See, for example, Milner 1997; and Reinhardt 1996. For an exception, see Leeds 1999.
4. See Mansfield, Milner, and Rosendorff 2000; McGillivray and Smith 2000; Remmer 1998; and Verdier 1998.
5. See Dahl 1971, 1–5; and Schumpeter [1942] 1976, 269.
6. Powell 2000, 4.
7. Schumpeter [1942] 1976.
8. See, for example, Fiorina 1981; Kiewiet 1983; and Lewis-Beck 1988.
9. Grossman and Helpman 1994.

here since others have done so.[10] Equally important, but far more poorly understood, however, are the political gains that also motivate state leaders to cooperate in trade. The model we develop focuses on these domestic political incentives. It demonstrates that, as the fate of a government becomes more dependent on free and fair elections, its leaders derive increasing gains from trade agreements, prompting them to engage in greater cooperation with other countries on commercial issues. Hence, the probability of a country concluding an international trade agreement increases as its domestic institutions become more democratic.

This outcome occurs because trade agreements can enhance the utility of both heads of state and voters. Trade agreements convey information to voters about the activities of leaders; in turn, such information helps leaders retain office. This informational role is an important aspect of cooperative agreements, and—although more domestically-oriented—it supports the claims of Robert O. Keohane about the value of information provision in fostering international cooperation.[11]

Voters have heterogeneous preferences about trade policy. Depending on their factor endowments, some prefer higher levels of protection and others prefer freer trade. A purely vote-maximizing representative would therefore choose a tariff level that maximizes the utility of the median voter. However, trade barriers create rents for interest groups whose support policymakers may desire to win. Hence political leaders may seek to raise barriers beyond the level preferred by the median voter to create these rents. Constituents harmed by government rent seeking can threaten to remove the incumbent; politicians trade off increased rents with a decreased vote share at the next election.

Voters, however, face an informational problem in their attempt to monitor politicians; namely, they cannot distinguish perfectly between adverse economic shocks over which leaders have little control and economic adversity stemming from the extractive policies of leaders. Consequently, voters in a democracy may remove a leader from office during economic downturns, even if that individual has not engaged in rent seeking. Leaders in such situations would like to find a way to demonstrate that poor economic performance is not the result of their extractive policies.

Entering into a trade agreement with another country is one way to do so. We argue that such agreements offer a more credible means for leaders to signal voters about their policy choices than do unilateral policy declarations, which leaders may be able to quietly reverse at any time. A trade agreement is defined here as (1) a public commitment by leaders to a less protectionist policy than otherwise would be implemented, and (2) an institutional device that credibly conveys that a state's obligations have been violated in the event of unilateral abrogation. A trade agreement, then, is both a promise and an alarm. It commits each participating

10. See, for example, Bagwell and Staiger 1999.
11. Keohane 1984.

country to lower at least some trade barriers, and countries that violate their international commitments trip an alarm sounded by other participants or the organization monitoring the agreement.

Our model thus emphasizes the signaling function of international agreements. Reporting on the behavior of signatories is a key, although frequently overlooked, function of many commercial agreements. The World Trade Organization (WTO), for example, regularly issues public reports on all of its members' trade policies. These trade policy reviews are an important means by which countries' behavior can be monitored. In addition, its dispute settlement mechanism publicizes suspected violations of the agreement. The European Union (EU) also issues public summaries of the extent to which countries are adopting and implementing its directives.[12] The North American Free Trade Agreement (NAFTA)'s dispute settlement mechanism serves a similar purpose—countries can be publicly accused of violating their international commitments and forced to undergo a long, open process of defending their behavior. We do not claim that voters actually read these documents, but rather that they are more likely to hear about a foreign government's or international organization's complaints regarding their government's violations of a trade agreement than they are to learn about changes in domestic trade policy. Such international accusations of bad behavior are more newsworthy than are unilateral changes in trade policy, as many countries (such as Mexico and Canada during the negotiations over NAFTA) have realized.

Furthermore, publicly exposed cheating on trade agreements can generate domestic "audience costs" for political leaders.[13] Voters become aware that economic downturns may be attributable to leaders' overly protectionist policies and so become more likely to remove them from office. Recent public opinion research, for example, suggests that voters value commercial institutions—like the WTO—and believe they are needed to support an open trading system, implying that leaders may pay a political price for violating the rules of such institutions.[14] These audience costs tend to be higher in democracies than in other regimes because the political survival of democratic leaders hinges more on election outcomes. International economic cooperation can thus help democratic governments boost their chances of re-election, thereby providing a strong inducement for them to pursue such agreements. Autocratic leaders, however, have less reason to worry about voters and consequently face less pressure to solve the informational problems addressed in this article by concluding commercial agreements.

The model we develop demonstrates that leaders have greater political incentives to conclude trade agreements as elections grow in importance. We expect, therefore, the probability of signing an agreement to increase as a country becomes more democratic. To test this hypothesis, we examine whether the regime types of states

12. Martin 2000, chap. 7.
13. Fearon 1994.
14. Herrmann, Tetlock, and Diascro 2001.

have influenced their propensity to form and expand preferential trading arrangements (PTAs) during the period since World War II. Consistent with our model, we find that democratic countries are about twice as likely to form a PTA as autocratic countries, and that pairs of democracies are roughly four times as likely to do so as autocratic pairs. These results provide strong evidence that democracies are more commercially cooperative than other countries.

The Model

We begin by specifying the nature of the underlying economy, which allows us to derive the trade policy preferences of voters. Then we model the structure of the polity, deriving the government's preferences over trade policy. We use an imperfect information model where there is uncertainty about the state of the world. Consequently, voters do not know exactly what policy leaders choose. The extent to which a state is democratic influences how much impact elections have on the probability that a leader retains office, given the voters' choices and the policies adopted. We first derive a Nash equilibrium for the purely domestic game between voters and the government in setting the level of trade barriers. Then we derive the Nash equilibrium for the same game, except that we allow governments to sign trade agreements with other countries. We show that allowing them to make agreements can generate gains for both governments and voters compared to the no-agreement case, and that the gains accruing to governments are directly related to the extent of democracy. Finally, we show that the model indicates that the probability of a trade agreement being signed by two countries increases as either country becomes more democratic. The appendix contains the complete formal derivation of our results.

The Economy

We analyze a small, open Heckscher-Ohlin economy producing two goods with two factors of production, as the appendix further specifies. The domestic price of the imported good (in terms of the export good) in period τ is p_τ, and $p_\tau = \pi_\tau(1 + t_\tau)$ where π_τ is the world price (in period τ) and t_τ is the current period level of trade barriers, modeled here as an ad valorem tariff. Because the economy is small, the world price (π_τ) is given and cannot be affected by states' actions. Without any loss of generality, we normalize the price such that trade ceases at $t_\tau = 1$ (that is, the tariff is prohibitive at 100 percent).

Individuals in the economy maximize the discounted sum of their one-period utilities, which depend on domestic prices and the tariff in two ways. A higher domestic price of the imported good (perhaps due to tariffs) lowers consumption of that good, but if the individual's income rises with protection, consumption (and hence utility) may rise. We can write any individual l's utility as a function solely of domestic prices (which in turn depend on the tariff) as

$$U^l = \sum_{\tau=0}^{\infty} \delta^\tau U^l(p_\tau).$$

Voters differ in their ownership of capital; as such, they differ in the level of protection that each desires most. Since we assume that the imported good is labor-intensive, those individuals who own much capital prefer low or even negative tariffs, whereas those who own little but their labor prefer higher tariffs. We assume that the median voter, indexed by m, owns relatively little capital, and therefore prefers a positive, but moderate, level of trade barriers, denoted t^m.

This assumption about voters' trade preferences is entirely appropriate. In the United States, which is among the least trade-dependent countries, public opinion data show that a vast majority of elites and a majority of the mass public support relatively free trade.[15] In more trade-dependent countries, such sentiment is likely to be even stronger.

The Polity

The executive (also called the incumbent or the government)—whether a democratic or autocratic leader—is a pure rent seeker unconcerned about social welfare.[16] The executive may extract rents either directly via trade tax revenues or indirectly from interest groups in exchange for trade barriers that shield these groups from foreign competition. We adopt a very general objective function for government rents, $G(t)$. It is assumed to be an increasing function of home trade barriers, $G'(t) > 0$. The executive wishes to maximize the sum of the discounted[17] rents collected by the government,

$$G = \sum_{\tau=0}^{\infty} \delta^\tau G(t_\tau).$$

The government is a pure rent seeker, and these rents rise monotonically with the level of protection. This purely venal behavior implies that any predictions we make about the limits on the extractive behavior of leaders stem from the institutional structures within which policies are chosen, rather than from the players' preferences. Furthermore, any variations in policy choice across regimes will be a consequence of institutional variation, not of variations in preferences.

15. See Chittick and Billingsley 1989; and Herrmann, Tetlock, and Diascro 2001.

16. Social or consumer welfare does not enter the government's objective function, making our claims harder to establish.

17. We assume that the discount rates of voters and the government are the same, but that their utility functions are different.

This assumption also ensures that the government will, ceteris paribus, always desire a level of tariffs higher than voters prefer. This tension between voters and leaders—with voters attempting to restrain an extractive leader—is central. Alternatively, we could specify the government's preferences as single-peaked in the tariff. For example, the government may receive a share of the tariff revenues, so that the point at which these are maximized is the preferred level of tariffs of the government. All the same results follow as long as we maintain the assumption that the government's unconstrained, ideal tariff is higher than that of the median voter.

If the government's ideal tariff were to lie below that of the median voter, the political problem facing the voters would be different. No longer would they have to restrain the rent-seeking impulses of their leaders; instead they would encourage leaders to choose higher tariffs. If voters are highly protectionist, and even more so than leaders, the decision to establish trade agreements is itself puzzling. One then has to explain why leaders would negotiate public agreements to adopt policies that are opposed not only by many special interest groups (for example, import-competing groups), but also by a majority of the populace. Our model does not deal with this ordering of preferences.

The voters' problem is informational. Voters are incompletely informed about the exact level of trade barriers, but they do know the domestic price of the goods they produce and consume.[18] We assume that the world price, π_T, is subject to exogenous shocks in each period. The distribution of these shocks is given and known to all.[19] Voters, however, cannot determine exactly how the shocks and government policy combine to affect domestic goods prices.

The sequence of events in each period of our model is as follows: the executive decides on the government's trade policy, t_T, and then the world economy experiences a shock to world prices, π_T. These two events together determine domestic prices, p_T, which are what voters observe. Prices and incomes are then established, and consumption occurs, all of which determine the voters' welfare. At the end of each period, the median voter examines its welfare, U^m, which determines its support for or opposition to the incumbent in the election. If the voter's welfare is above some threshold level, which is determined endogenously, then it votes to re-elect. This one-shot game is repeated ad infinitum.

The executive must commit to a trade policy before the shock has materialized. That is, the government must choose policy in the face of uncertainty about the world price that will be obtained. Once the shock materializes, its magnitude is still unknown to the voters, as is the tariff chosen. In the case of an adverse shock, voters cannot tell if the low utility they experience was caused by an exogenous shock to

18. It is not obvious that voters know the exact policy choices of their representatives. For example, United States voters are much more likely to know the domestic price of sugar than the level of the quota imposed on imported sugar by the government.

19. These shocks to the exogenous world price are identically and independently distributed (i.i.d.) in each period over a finite support.

the economy or by excessive protectionism on the part of the executive. Voters base their electoral decision only on the information available to them, implying that they may reject executives for events that are beyond the executives' control. The executive thus faces the prospect of being ousted from office in every electoral period.

The voters will choose a voting rule conditional on the observed domestic price and hence their current period utility. This simple retrospective voting rule is one in which the voters optimally choose a threshold level of utility, $\underline{U}^l$, such that voter l will choose to reappoint the executive in period τ if l's utility is at least as good as its threshold value, that is, if $U^l(p_\tau) \geq \underline{U}^l$.

We define the (*ex ante*) probability of the median voter recommending reappointment as the probability that actual utility (as a consequence of the policy t_τ and the shock π_τ) is larger than the specified threshold $\underline{U}^m$. That is $\phi(t_\tau, \underline{U}^m) = \Pr[U^m(p_\tau) > \underline{U}^m]$. We assume that $\phi(1, U) = 0$ for all U. That is, when trade barriers are set so high that imports are prohibited, the electorate fails to vote for re-election with certainty.[20]

Political Regime Type

An election is a determination by voters about whether the executive should remain in office. Both democracies and autocracies hold elections. What differs across regimes is the degree to which these contests affect the executive's fate. The more democratic a country, the more important are elections in determining whether the incumbent retains office. If the election's outcome is binding, the regime is a "pure democracy." If, on the other hand, the executive retains office irrespective of the voters' decision, the regime is a "pure autocracy."

We allow a continuum of possibilities for the role of elections and hence for the type of regime: the degree to which the election binds the executive ranges from low to high. That is, the actual probability that the executive keeps office is a weighted average of the probability in a pure democracy and the certainty of keeping office in a pure autocracy. The actual probability of keeping office in any period, τ, is:

$$\rho(t_\tau, \underline{U}^m, \sigma) = \sigma\phi(t_\tau, \underline{U}^m) + (1 - \sigma) \text{ where } \sigma \in [0, 1]. \tag{1}$$

The variable, σ, indicates a country's regime type and takes on higher values in more democratic polities. In a pure democracy, $\sigma = 1$. Only the support of the voting public determines whether a leader retains office. In a pure autocracy, by

20. Equivalently, $U^l[\pi^{\min}(1 + 1)] < U$ for all $U > 0$ and for all individuals, l, where $\pi^{\min}$ is the minimum value in the support of π. That $\phi(1,U) = 0$ for all U is a feature of the political system, not of the preferences of the government. That is, in all systems, complete rent extraction leads the electorate to recommend eviction from office.

contrast, $\sigma = 0$. The incumbent executive keeps office irrespective of the electorate's sentiments.[21]

The Executive's Optimal Level of Trade Barriers

Given that the economy is small, the executive can choose trade barriers without being able to affect world prices and hence other countries' policy decisions, and vice versa. Each executive will choose a level of trade barriers that balances the threat of rejection at the polls with the gains from rent seeking, independent of the foreign country's behavior. Because we are examining the behavior of all countries in the world, it is appropriate to assume that the average country lacks global market power. Very few countries ever have enough market power to affect world prices for any good, let alone for all goods in the economy.

In any period, τ, after choosing domestic trade policy t_τ, the executive gains $G(t_\tau)$. The value of choosing $t_\tau < 1$ at the start of any period, τ, can be written (recursively) as

$$\Gamma_\tau(t_\tau) = G(t_\tau) + \delta\rho(t_\tau, \underline{U}^m, \sigma)\Gamma_{\tau+1}. \tag{2}$$

The executive chooses the current period's trade policy, taking the future play of the game as given ($\Gamma_{\tau+1}$ is the continuation value of the game). The decision reached today affects today's rents and the probability of re-election, but does not affect the level of extraction undertaken tomorrow (because the shocks are i.i.d.). Maximization of equation (2) determines the government's optimal choice of trade policy, which we label t°. The optimal choice of trade barriers exactly balances the gains in rents from higher barriers with the reduced likelihood of re-election. We show in Lemma A.1 (in the appendix) that, as the voter's choice of the threshold level of welfare rises, the optimal tariff rate chosen by the incumbent (t°) must decline. Voters can thus exercise control over their government.

The executive can adopt an alternative strategy, however, which we label the Leviathan strategy. In this course of action, the government maximizes its economic extraction by setting tariffs at their highest level, $t = 1$, and consequently reducing its prospects of re-election. There is still some chance that a maximally extractive government will remain in office in the next period despite the will of the voters

21. It has been suggested that a key distinction between democracies and autocracies is that democratic leaders are less patient (that is, have lower discount factors) and are only concerned about the next election, whereas autocratic leaders have a longer time horizon. See, for example, Haggard and Kaufman 1995, 152. Our model formalizes this intuition by incorporating the role of elections into leaders' decision making. If the election is substantively important, the effect of the election is, in equilibrium, to lower the implied discount factor that leaders use to calculate their future (expected) stream of rents. The leader's effective discount rate is shown endogenously to be lower the more democratic the state.

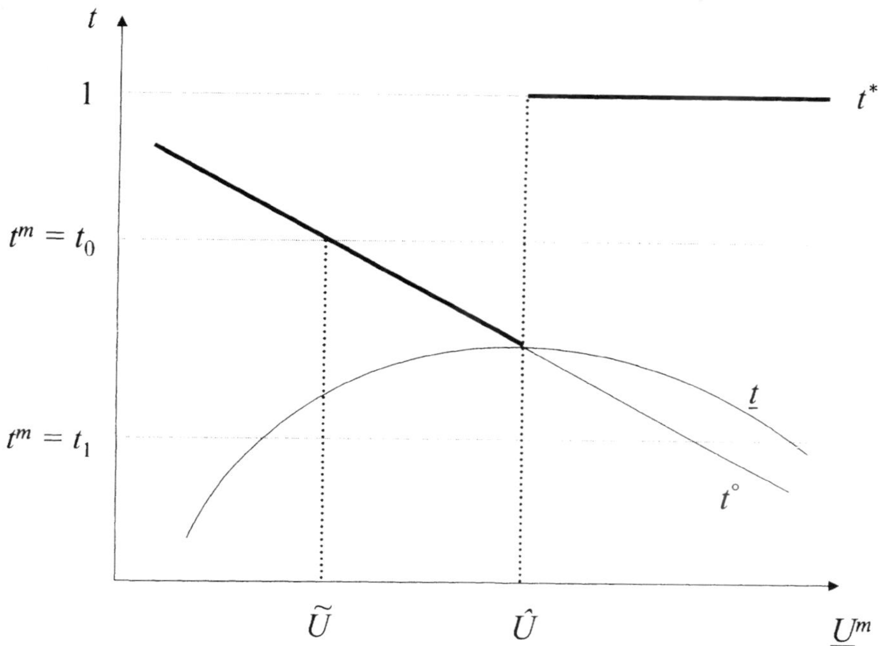

FIGURE 1. *The best response functions*

because the country is not a perfect democracy. This happens with probability $1 - \sigma$. A lower tariff, t—one that balances the rent extraction motive with re-election concerns as in t° above—is preferred by the incumbent over the Leviathan tariff, $t = 1$, when the executive gains more from the lower tariff than from the Leviathan policy. The incumbent's optimal choice between the maximal Leviathan tariff and the moderate tariff then depends on the voters' selection of their welfare threshold, $\underline{U}$. Setting the threshold too high requires the government to choose a very low tariff; in response, the incumbent may choose the Leviathan action, extracting the maximal amount of rents now and risking rejection in the future election. If the threshold is set too low, the government extracts as much as possible, ensuring that the low utility threshold of the voters is still satisfied. Hence the choice of tariff depends crucially on the threshold chosen by the voters. Figure 1 illustrates the government's best response function, indicated in bold.

There is some threshold ($\hat{U}$) that is the highest the incumbent will accept before resorting to the Leviathan action. And since the optimal tariff, t°, falls with the threshold (see Lemma A.1 in the appendix), there is some minimum tariff level, $\underline{t}$, which the incumbent will accept. This tariff, $\underline{t}$, is calculated to be the lowest that the executive will accept instead of adopting the maximally extractive, Leviathan tariff;

the executive is indifferent between the Leviathan and this moderate tariff. Any attempt by the voters to restrict the tariff below this level by raising their welfare threshold induces the government to choose the Leviathan strategy. Any tariff above this minimum level is preferred to the Leviathan tariff by the government. Thus voters have some, but not complete, control over the government through the threat of elections.

Optimizing Voter Behavior

If the government adopts the Leviathan strategy of maximal tariffs, then there is no role for the voters regardless of their welfare threshold. If, instead, the government adopts a more moderate strategy, then the voters (who select their thresholds before the government implements its tariff policy) choose a threshold to maximize their expected utility:

$$EU(p) = EU\{\pi[1 + t^{\circ}(\underline{U}^{m},\sigma)]\}.$$

The Nash Equilibrium

Consider again Figure 1. In the region where t° lies above $\underline{t}$—that is, where $U < \hat{U}$—the optimal response by the government to any U is t°. When U gets too large, the government switches to the Leviathan strategy and adopts the maximal tariff of 1.

The median voter wants a tariff that lies as close as possible to her (*ex ante*) ideal, t^m. If t^m lies everywhere above $\underline{t}$ (as in the case where $t^m = t_0$ in Figure 1), then the voter sets the threshold at $\tilde{U}$ and the government responds with $t^{\circ} = t^m$. Alternatively, when t^m crosses $\underline{t}$, the voter's ideal tariff lies below that which the government can be constrained to provide. Hence, the voters restrict the government to the lowest tariff possible by choosing a threshold at $\hat{U}$. We prove that this pair of strategies is a Nash equilibrium in Lemma A.3 in the appendix.

If the government is perfectly constrained by voters, then t^m is the tariff imposed in response to the threshold of $\tilde{U}$. If, however, the government is imperfectly controlled by the voters, then the government implements a tariff of $\underline{t}(\hat{U})$ in response to $\hat{U}$. The degree of control that the voters exercise depends crucially on whether t^m is larger or smaller than $\underline{t}(\hat{U})$. Now t^m is exogenous; $\underline{t}(\hat{U})$, on the other hand, is the lowest tariff the executive is prepared to accept before switching to the maximally extractive, Leviathan tariff.

The value of the equilibrium tariff, $\underline{t}$, that leaves the executive indifferent between playing it or the Leviathan strategy, depends on the degree of control the voters exercise over the executive, that is, on σ, the level of democracy (see Lemma A.4 in the appendix). However, more democratic polities will not necessarily adopt lower tariffs in the equilibrium to this tariff-setting game. As the polity becomes more democratic, the benefits of the Leviathan tariff fall because the executive becomes more likely to be replaced when selecting this strategy. To maintain the indifference condition between (the payoffs from) $\underline{t}$ and the Leviathan strategy, the benefits generated by a more moderate tariff must fall as well; thus $\underline{t}$ should fall. But a lower $\underline{t}$ also increases the likelihood of re-election in the next period and hence keeps the government in office longer in expectation. This latter effect raises the long-run returns to the government, causing the indifference condition between $\underline{t}$ and the Leviathan tariff to be violated once again. The relative size of these two effects is indeterminate at our level of generality. Hence, it is not necessarily true that more democracy leads to lower unilateral tariffs.

Although the equilibrium tariff, $\underline{t}$, is determined by both the preferences of the players and the domestic institutions that govern the voters' control of the executive, it is *not* necessarily the case that, as domestic institutions become more democratic, the equilibrium tariff, $\underline{t}$, in this game falls. Democracies, in our model, are not unilaterally freer traders than other regime types.[22]

In what follows, however, we show that democracies are more likely to join PTAs than other countries. Moreover, we establish that democracies do not join PTAs solely to lower trade barriers. A more interesting and deeper result related to PTA formation grows out of the model: such arrangements can solve an informational problem that limits the head of state's credibility. In the eyes of the voters, participating in a PTA bolsters the credibility of offers made by the executive to reduce trade barriers, and enhances the leader's prospects of re-election.

In the next section we compare the gains for the executive from the unilateral policy choice described above to those reaped from signing an international trade agreement. We show that both voters and executives can be made better off with an agreement, and that this is increasingly true as a country becomes more democratic.

International Cooperation and Trade Agreements

In addition to setting their own unilateral policies, executives have the capability to negotiate trade agreements with other countries. But an executive will only do so if the gains from an agreement are at least as great as those from setting policy

22. The unilateral, equilibrium tariff (under imperfect control) is the lowest tariff the executive will accept rather than adopt the maximally extractive, Leviathan action; That is, in equilibrium, the executive plays $\underline{t}$ and earns a return identical to the Leviathan payoff, $G(\underline{t})/\{1 - \delta[\sigma\phi(\underline{t},U) + (1 - \sigma)]\} = G(1)/[1 - \delta(1 - \sigma)]$. As the polity becomes more democratic (as σ rises), the benefits of the Leviathan action fall; that is, the right-hand side falls. As the right-hand side falls, so does the left-hand side, but the left falls by less. To maintain the indifference condition, the benefits of a moderate action (the left hand side) must fall even more. A fall in the moderate tariff, $\underline{t}$, reduces the benefits to the government in any period ($G(\underline{t})$ falls). But it also increases the likelihood of re-election ($\phi(\underline{t},U)$ rises) and hence keeps the government in office longer in expectation. This might raise the discounted returns to government, violating the indifference condition. Hence it is not necessarily true that more democracy leads to lower unilateral tariffs. It depends on the particular functional form of the distribution function $\phi(\underline{t},U)$ that captures the uncertainty relative to the shape of government's objective function $G(\underline{t})$. See Lemma A.4 for the implicit differentiation of the equality above.

unilaterally. When can an executive gain from a trade agreement? An agreement is a pair of trade policies and a signaling institution. The signal may be a complaint filed by another country that is party to the agreement or a determination of non-compliance by the international institution monitoring the agreement. That is, an agreement by definition comprises a level of trade barriers lower than the executive's optimal unilateral policy, $t^C < t^*$. It also includes a mechanism for the institution or a foreign country to signal others that the home executive has cheated and raised trade barriers above the agreement level. Consequently, the agreement trips an alarm if $t > t^C$; otherwise, no signal is sent.

The agreement, then, is a level of trade barriers below the government's ideal unilateral level and an alarm mechanism that other governments or a trade institution—such as the General Agreement on Tariffs and Trade (GATT) or the WTO—can use whenever the actual trade policy of a party to the agreement deviates from the one agreed upon. A commercial agreement is public and therefore provides information that voters can use to more closely monitor the executive. In particular, monitors of the trade agreement (such as an independent agency like the WTO or even the participating governments themselves) can announce, just before each election, whether the executive in each country is in compliance with the agreement.[23]

We assume that voters can observe this signal. Moreover, voters have an incentive to pay close attention to it, since the signal improves their welfare. Equally, the trade institution and its members have an incentive to divulge this information and make sure that voters pay attention to it, since this disciplines the government. Our assertion is that voters are more likely to hear about a foreign country's or an international organization's accusations that their government violated a trade agreement than they are to know about a unilateral change in domestic trade policy. We expect that international accusations of violations will be much more newsworthy than marginal, unilateral changes in the tariff code. An international trade agreement, then, both sets policy and provides information.

Under an international trade agreement, the executive will abide by the terms of the agreement whenever the long-term gains from doing so exceed the gains from the Leviathan strategy. The voters reward a compliant executive by setting a zero threshold; that is, they always vote to re-elect the government. If the agreement is violated, the voters set an unreachable threshold and vote to reject the incumbent with certainty. Lemma A.5 establishes that this is equilibrium behavior for both the executive and the voters.

23. As noted earlier, the WTO does indeed issue such reports on all member countries periodically. Its trade policy reviews of member countries are an important aspect of monitoring, as is its dispute settlement system.

Comparing the Regimes: Imperfect Control and Gains for the Executive

When the voters can only imperfectly control the executive, can the executive still gain from the agreement relative to the no-agreement situation? The agreement decreases the tariff below what was the lowest acceptable tariff in the absence of the agreement, that is, $t^C \in [t^m, \underline{t}]$. Since the voters prefer a tariff lower than $\underline{t}$, they obviously gain (or at least no worse off). Does the government gain?

We assume that the voting rule for individuals casting ballots adjusts to the new information the agreement provides. The probability of re-election still depends on their overall utility, but voters also make use of the information embedded in the alarm. If no alarm sounds, it is optimal for the median voter to cast a ballot for the incumbent. After all, the agreed-upon tariff is, by definition, preferred to the tariff absent the agreement. On the other hand, if the alarm sounds, the median voter rejects the incumbent, although there is still the $(1-\sigma)$ chance that the offending government manages to hold onto office.

The value of international cooperation over noncooperation for the executive is the difference between the executive's gains from cooperation and the gains from unilateral policymaking:

$$\Delta(t^C; \sigma) = \frac{G(t^C)}{1-\delta} - \frac{G(1)}{1-\delta(1-\sigma)}. \tag{3}$$

PROPOSITION 1: *Under imperfect voter control, for any $t^C \in [t^m, \underline{t}]$,*

a) *the agreement is preferred by governments that are sufficiently democratic and patient, that is, $\Delta(t^C, \sigma) > 0 \ \forall \ \sigma > \bar{\sigma}(\delta)$;*
b) *the more democratic the polity, the greater the gains from cooperation, that is, $d\Delta/d\sigma > 0$.*

In Proposition 1, we show that the more democratic the country, the more its government prefers the international agreement. Proposition 1 also shows that the gain to the executive from cooperating increases as the state becomes more democratic. As the level of democracy, σ, rises, the probability of being removed from office grows even when the executive is not overly extractive, *ceteris paribus*. Hence, relative to an autocrat, a democratic executive (whose re-election is more dependent on the wishes of voters) has more to gain from making an agreement and thus lowering the chance of eviction from office without a legitimate cause. The executive trades off a greater degree of certainty about re-election when he cooperates in exchange for a lower level of rents because he chooses a lower level of trade barriers.

Notice that any trade agreement, $t^C \in [t^m, \underline{t}]$, yields a gain for the executive. The best possible agreement (for the executive) may be to agree to a tariff as close to $\underline{t}$

as possible. Little would be relinquished in the trade negotiations, but much would be gained in terms of the domestic polity. Recall, of course, that we have abstracted from other motivating factors that induce states to form PTAs, such as the welfare gains from trade creation and the political gains from trade diversion or from deep integration, all of which might induce an executive to lower tariffs even further. But our primary concern here has been to establish the role that an agreement can play in solving the domestic monitoring problem.

Comparing the Regimes: Perfect Control and Gains for the Executive

In the case where the median voter exercises perfect control over the government (that is, $t^* = t^m$), it is also the case that the government will gain from the agreement. The extra information provided by the agreement reduces the chance that the government is unfairly evicted. Consider the case where the agreement sets tariffs equal to those favored by the median voter; that is, $t^C = t^m$. This agreement then merely formalizes pre-existing behavior. Then the gains for the executive from international cooperation relative to noncooperation now are

$$\Delta(t^m; \sigma) = \frac{G(t^m)}{1-\delta} - \frac{G(t^m)}{1-\delta[\sigma\phi(t^m, U) + (1-\sigma)]}.$$

In this case, as Proposition 2 demonstrates, the international agreement is preferred by executives in all regime types, yet it is democratic executives that have the most to gain from these agreements. The executive's gains from signing an agreement rise with the country's level of democracy.

PROPOSITION 2: *Under perfect control, for any agreement* $t^C = t^m$,

a) $\Delta(t^C; \sigma) > 0$ *for all* σ;
b) *the more democratic the polity, the greater the gains from cooperation, that is,* $d\Delta/d\sigma > 0$.

The Voters' Gain from the Cooperative Agreement

Even if the government gains, we need to show that the voters gain as well from an international agreement in all situations. In the case where the government is imperfectly constrained by voters in the absence of a trade agreement, it is balancing two pressures. The first induces the incumbent to extract as much rent as possible by applying a very high tariff, while the second pushes him to limit his extraction so he does not reduce his chances of re-election too much. The net effect is to choose a tariff that is higher than that preferred by the median voter; hence, $t^* > t^m$. Thus any international agreement that lowers the actual tariff below t^* and closer to the median's ideal, t^m, will be preferred by the median voter. As such, the median voter prefers any international agreement $t^C \in [t^m, t^*)$ to the lack of an agreement.

If the government is perfectly constrained by the voters, no improvement with respect to the voters' utility is possible from an international agreement. The agreement at the pre-existing tariff level—the median voter's ideal level—is beneficial to the government but leaves the voters indifferent. (The government will not agree to an international agreement that lowers tariffs below both its and the median voter's ideal level since this will lower its utility and spur its removal from office.) Given these conditions, the median voter weakly prefers the international agreement to the lack of one, as Proposition 3 formally proves.

PROPOSITION 3: *The median voter prefers the trade agreement regime to the no-agreement regime.*

In a world where voters cannot perfectly distinguish between a reduction in utility stemming from an adverse economic shock, on the one hand, and from excessive government rent seeking, on the other, executives and voters will both gain from international trade agreements that provide information about the executive's behavior. Thus we have our central result: the incentives for a leader to sign a trade agreement increase as the country becomes increasingly democratic. As such, the more democratic the polity, the greater the likelihood that the country will sign a trade agreement.

The International Game

For any international trade agreement to be signed, at least two countries must agree. How do both (or all) countries' gains change when the home country becomes more democratic? In this model, because the countries are small, the behavior of each has no impact on the other. An increase in one country's level of democracy has no impact upon the other country's willingness to sign an agreement.

If the probability of signing a trade agreement increases in the gains from such an agreement, then the probability of an agreement depends independently on the level of democracy in each country. As one country becomes more democratic, the other countries' willingness to sign an agreement never falls. Therefore, the probability of an agreement between two or more countries always rises as the level of democracy in any one of them increases. Moreover, the model implies that, although their effects are independent, when each country is very democratic the probability of a trade agreement is highest. It is lowest when each country is very autocratic.

Let F_i and F_j be the probabilities that countries i and j, respectively, sign a trade agreement. Since these probabilities are increasing in the gains from this agreement, we know from Propositions 1 and 2 that the gains from the agreement depend on the tariff levels chosen and the degree of democracy in each country. Thus we have $F_i = F[\Delta(t^C;\sigma_i)]$ and $F_j = F[\Delta(t^C;\sigma_j)]$, with F being a continuous function that takes a value between 0 and 1, and rises with Δ. Then the probability that a PTA forms between i and j is simply the product of these two probabilities: $\Pr(PTA_{ij}) = F_iF_j = F[\Delta(t^C;\sigma_i)]F[\Delta(t^C;\sigma_i)]$. Since both of these depend on the level of democracy, we have the following proposition.

PROPOSITION 4: *The probability that two countries form a PTA rises with the level of democracy in each country. That is,*

$$\frac{d\Pr(PTA_{ij})}{d\sigma_i} > 0 \quad and \quad \frac{d\Pr(PTA_{ij})}{d\sigma_j} > 0.$$

Democracies have a greater incentive to enter into cooperative trade agreements than other polities. There are, of course, other, more standard arguments for trade agreements, especially in the small, open-economy environment assumed here. The economic costs and benefits of joining such arrangements have been extensively studied and are clearly important.[24] We, however, focus on another key determinant of the decision to form a commercial arrangement that has been the subject of remarkably little research to date, namely, the regime types of the member states.

The Empirical Evidence

The preceding analysis indicates that a country is increasingly likely to conclude a cooperative trade agreement as it becomes more democratic and that the probability of two or more countries signing such an agreement rises with the level of democracy in each country. In the remainder of this article, we conduct some preliminary statistical tests of these propositions.

We focus on explaining agreements that establish or expand PTAs—a group of institutions that includes customs unions, common markets, free trade areas, and other commercial agreements. Reductions in reciprocal trade barriers among participants are central to all such arrangements. In fact, Article XXIV of the GATT stipulates that any PTA notified to this body must largely abolish barriers to commerce within the preferential grouping.[25] States making reciprocal trade barrier reductions are engaged in acts of economic cooperation, so it is appropriate to test our model of cooperative trade agreements by focusing on the formation and expansion of PTAs.[26] It is clear that agreements to enter into a preferential trading

24. See Anderson and Blackhurst 1993; Bhagwati 1993; de Melo and Panagariya 1993; Fernández and Portes 1998; Krueger 1999; Pomfret 1988; Panagariya 2000; and Whalley 1998.

25. See Anderson and Blackhurst 1993; Bhagwati 1993, 27; and de Melo and Panagariya 1993.

26. It is important to note that whether such trade barrier reductions adversely affect third parties has no bearing on whether the reductions constitute acts of economic cooperation among the PTA members. As Lisa L. Martin points out, "While cooperation improves the expected welfare of the cooperating states relative to the status quo *ex ante*, it is not necessarily a Pareto-improving (mutually beneficial) move for

arrangement do not constitute the entire universe of trade agreements to which this model could be applied. Nonetheless, PTAs comprise a substantial portion of the commercial agreements concluded since World War II, which is the period analyzed here. Furthermore, comprehensive data on other such agreements are not available for many countries included in our sample.

A Statistical Model of PTAs

Proposition 4 demonstrates that the probability of two countries signing a trade agreement is a positive function of the level of democracy in each country. To test this formal proposition, we estimate the following model of PTA formation:

$$\begin{aligned} PTA_{ij} = {} & \beta_0 + \beta_1 REG_i + \beta_2 REG_j + \beta_3 GDP_i + \beta_4 GDP_j + \beta_5 \Delta GDP_i \\ & + \beta_6 \Delta GDP_j + \beta_7 TRADE_{ij} + \beta_8 DISPUTE_{ij} + \beta_9 COL_{ij} \\ & + \beta_{10} ALLY_{ij} + \beta_{11} DISTANCE_{ij} + \beta_{12} GATT_{ij} \\ & + \beta_{13} HEGEMONY + e_{ij}. \end{aligned} \quad (4)$$

The dependent variable is the log of the odds that a pair of states, i and j, enters a PTA in year $\tau + 1$, where we observe 1 if this occurs and 0 otherwise. We code i and j as entering a PTA if they—either by themselves or in combination with other countries—form a new preferential arrangement, or if one of them joins a PTA in which the other is already a member. Hence, the observed value of PTA_{ij} is 1 in the year i and j enter a preferential arrangement, but not in years when they belong to a pre-existing arrangement. In the following analysis, however, we also briefly consider whether the variables in equation (4) help to explain the existence of a preferential grouping between i and j. Although the PTAs included in our analysis are drawn primarily from those notified to the GATT, they also include other arrangements since there is no reason to limit our model's application to commercial agreements concluded among parties to the GATT.[27]

the world as a whole." Martin 2000, 13; see also Keohane 1984. It is also important to note that, although a large and influential body of literature exists on the economic effects of PTAs, the nature and strength of these effects remain subjects of fierce debate and have little bearing on our analysis. See, for example, Bhagwati 1993; Frankel, Stein, and Wei 1998; Krueger 1999; Krugman 1993; Panagariya 2000; and Pomfret 1988.

27. For a list of PTAs notified to the GATT, see World Trade Organization 1995. In addition to these PTAs—which are limited to arrangements formed by GATT and WTO members—we include the PTAs listed in Hartland-Thunberg 1980. We also include the Council on Mutual Economic Assistance (CMEA), the Southern African Customs Union, the Economic Community of West African States (ECOWAS), the Southern African Development Coordination Conference, and the Eastern and Southern African Preferential Trade Area. On these PTAs, see de Melo and Panagariya 1993; Foroutan 1993, 246–51; Hanlon 1986; Kisanga 1991; Orimalade and Ubogu 1984; and Pomfret 1988.

Each PTA is coded as starting in the year it enters into force. (Note that we do not consider agreements strengthening or superceding an existing PTA to be new preferential arrangements.) The original

To measure each state's regime type, identified as σ in the formal model above, we rely on a widely used index constructed by Keith Jaggers and Ted Robert Gurr.[28] This index combines data on five factors that help to capture the institutional differences between democracies and autocracies that we emphasized earlier: the competitiveness of the process for selecting a country's chief executive, the openness of this process, the extent to which institutional constraints limit a chief executive's decision-making authority, the competitiveness of political participation within a country, and the degree to which binding rules govern political participation within it. Following Jaggers and Gurr, these data are used to create an 11-point index of each state's democratic characteristics (*DEMOC*) and an 11-point index of its autocratic characteristics (*AUTOC*). The difference between these indices, $REG = DEMOC - AUTOC$, yields a summary measure of regime type that takes on values ranging from -10 for a highly autocratic state to 10 for a highly democratic country.

There are three principal reasons we rely on this measure in the following analysis. First, our formal model treats regime type (σ) as a continuous variable, with the competitiveness of elections ranging from perfectly competitive to completely uncompetitive. As noted above, the index developed by Jaggers and Gurr has a range of 21 points, unlike some other measures of regime type.[29] Second, their index highlights a number of institutional dimensions of regime type that we stressed. The ability of voters to choose the chief executive, which is central to our model, is expected to rise as the process for selecting the executive becomes more competitive and more open, and political participation becomes increasingly competitive. Jaggers and Gurr's index captures each of these three institutional elements, whereas various alternative measures do not.[30] Third, their index covers more countries during the period since World War II than any other measure of regime type with which we are familiar.[31]

In equation (4), REG_i is the value of Jaggers and Gurr's measure for state i in year τ and REG_j is the value of this measure for state j in τ. Which state in each pair is

members of every PTA are coded as joining it in this year. A state that enters an existing PTA is coded as having formed a preferential arrangement with each member of the arrangement in the year of its accession. In a few cases, the year when a PTA enters into force or the year a state joins an existing PTA is not available. In those cases, we rely on the year in which the negotiations leading to the arrangement's formation or expansion were completed. The GATT/WTO only lists PTAs whose members are parties to the GATT and only does so when these agreements are officially notified to it. Thus for some PTAs, the date given by the WTO as to when states enter the preferential arrangement differs from the date furnished by the other sources listed above. In these cases, we use the earliest date. For a further explanation of how we code the formation of PTAs, see Mansfield 1998.

28. See Jaggers and Gurr 1995; and Gurr, Jaggers, and Moore 1989.

29. For example, the measure developed by Przeworski et al. treats regime type as dichotomous. Przeworski et al. 2000.

30. For example, Gastil 1980 and 1990.

31. See, for example, Bollen 1980; Gasiorowski 1996; Gastil 1980 and 1990; and Przeworski et al. 2000.

i and which one is j is randomly determined. Recall that our model (Proposition 4) demonstrates that the probability of concluding a trade agreement increases as each participant becomes more democratic. Hence, we expect that both β_1 and β_2 will be positive and that there will be no significant difference between them.

Besides countries' regime types, other factors are likely to influence the formation of PTAs, and we account for their effects as well. As we indicated previously, a number of economic factors may condition a country's decision to join a trade agreement. The size of its domestic market is one such factor. States with larger home markets tend to depend less on trade and may therefore have less reason to conclude agreements that expand their access to foreign markets than economically smaller states. To address this possibility, we include GDP_i and GDP_j in equation (4). These variables are the gross domestic products (GDPs) of states i and j in year τ. Furthermore, economic conditions may affect the probability that countries sign trade agreements. Some observers, for example, have argued that downturns in the business cycle may stimulate the formation of cooperative agreements.[32] Therefore, we analyze the effects of ΔGDP_i and ΔGDP_j, which are the changes in the GDP of i and j from year $\tau - 1$ to τ, and are used here as rough measures of the business cycle in each state.[33] Controlling for such economic factors is important so that we can establish the independent effects of domestic political institutions.

In addition to political and economic conditions within countries, relations between countries are likely to affect their willingness to form a PTA.[34] Many observers, for example, argue that the amount of economic exchange between states influences whether they enter a preferential grouping. Rising economic intercourse may increase the prospects of PTA formation by fostering the growth of coalitions with an interest in developing institutional mechanisms to promote greater economic integration and avert the breakdown of economic relations among the group's members.[35] In the same vein, increasing trade flows can heighten the susceptibility of private traders to opportunistic behavior by foreign governments, prompting firms to press for the establishment of PTAs to reduce the ability of governments to engage in such behavior.[36] We therefore include $TRADE_{ij}$, which is the flow of exports from i to j in year τ, in equation (4).[37]

32. Mattli 1999.

33. Data on GDP and the change in GDP are taken from Summers and Heston 1991; and Maddison 1995. Note that while we measure the change in GDP from year $\tau - 1$ to year τ, we also estimated equation (4) after measuring both ΔGDP_i and ΔGDP_j from τ to $\tau + 1$. These two sets of results are very similar.

34. Note that using country-pairs—rather than individual countries—as the unit of analysis allows us to control for the effects of both domestic and international influences on PTA formation.

35. Nye 1988, 239.

36. Yarbrough and Yarbrough 1992.

37. Data on trade flows are taken from the International Monetary Fund's *Direction of Foreign Trade*, various years. Note that these data and those on GDP are expressed in U.S. dollars and in real terms; they are deflated using the United States wholesale price index and producer price index.

The nature of political relations between i and j is also likely to affect their willingness to form a PTA. It is widely recognized, for example, that various countries have established trade agreements with their former colonies, partly to maintain political influence over colonial possessions once they become independent states.[38] In addition, Cold War dynamics affected international economic relations during the period analyzed here and may have contributed to the establishment of PTAs since World War II. To control for such dynamics—and security relations more generally—we analyze the effects of political-military alliances and military disputes on PTAs.

Countries may be more likely to enter PTAs with their allies than with other states. Trade liberalization yields efficiency gains that enhance the political-military capacity of participants, and alliances help to internalize these security externalities.[39] Since PTAs liberalize commerce among members, alliance politics may influence the likelihood that states will establish such an agreement. It is also important to take account of military disputes since such events obviously might discourage participants from forming a commercial agreement. We therefore include $DISPUTE_{ij}$, COL_{ij}, and $ALLY_{ij}$. The first of these variables equals 1 if i and j are embroiled in a military dispute in τ and 0 otherwise. The second variable equals 1 if i and j had a colonial relationship (ending after World War II) in τ and 0 otherwise. The third variable equals 1 if i and j are allies in τ and 0 otherwise.[40]

The geographical distance between states is another factor that is likely to influence their willingness to enter a PTA. One reason why states form PTAs is to guarantee and expand access to the markets of their key trade partners.[41] Frequently, a country's primary commercial partners are located in relative proximity, since as the distance between states increases, so do transportation costs and various other impediments to commerce.[42] To account for the effects of geographical proximity on the establishment and expansion of commercial agreements, we include $DISTANCE_{ij}$ in equation (4).[43] We mentioned earlier that many of the PTAs in our sample were formed under the auspices of the GATT. To analyze whether members of this organization have been more likely to establish trading arrangements than other states, we include $GATT_{ij}$. This variable equals 1 if both i and j are parties to the GATT in τ and 0 otherwise.

The factors just described pertain to conditions within countries and relations between them, but systemic conditions may affect the formation of PTAs as well. Particularly important in this regard is the influence of hegemony. Since various

38. See Grilli 1993; and Pomfret 1988, 163.

39. See Gowa 1994; and Gowa and Mansfield 1993.

40. Data on military disputes are taken from Jones, Bremer, and Singer 1996. Data on former colonial relations are taken from Kurian 1992. Data on alliances are taken from Small and Singer 1969; and the Correlates of War Project 1993.

41. Whalley 1998.

42. Frankel, Stein, and Wei 1998.

43. Data on distance are taken from Oneal and Russett 1999.

studies have concluded that waning hegemony tends to stimulate the proliferation of PTAs, we analyze *HEGEMONY*, which is the percentage of global trade accounted for by the state that conducts the greatest amount of commerce in a given year.[44] Finally, e_{ij} is a stochastic error term.

Since comprehensive data on both PTAs and the independent variables described above are only available for the period after World War II, we focus our analysis on this era. More specifically, our sample includes all pairs of countries for which complete data on the variables in equation (4) are available for at least part of the period from 1951 to 1992.[45] To estimate this model, we pool the available data across time and country-pairs and then conduct a logistic regression. Following Nathaniel Beck, Jonathan N. Katz, and Richard Tucker, we account for any temporal dependence in the data by including a natural spline function (with three knots) of the number of years that have elapsed (as of year $\tau + 1$) since each pair of states, i and j, last formed a PTA.[46] To conserve space, however, we do not present the estimates of this function.[47] In addition, the tests of statistical significance we report are based on Huber (robust) standard errors, which account for the grouped nature of the data (in the present case, by country-pairs). Recent research indicates that they are superior to logit standard errors in time-series cross-section models with a binary dependent variable.[48]

The Statistical Results

The first column of Table 1 contains our initial results. Consistent with the propositions derived from our formal model, the estimated coefficients of REG_i and REG_j are both positive and statistically significant, indicating that the likelihood of establishing a trade agreement rises as each state in a given dyad becomes more democratic.[49] Moreover, the effects of regime type on commercial cooperation do not vary between states i and j. Indeed, there is no statistically significant difference between the estimates of REG_i and REG_j ($\chi^2 = 0.26$; $p = .61$).

44. See Bhagwati 1993; Gilpin 1987; Krugman 1993; and Mansfield 1998. This measure of hegemony has been used repeatedly in studies of the international political economy. See, for example, Krasner 1976; Lake 1988; Mansfield 1998; and McKeown 1991. Note that global trade is defined as the sum of total global exports and total global imports and that, for each year analyzed below, the United States is the state having the highest percentage of global trade. Data used to construct this variable are taken from the International Monetary Fund's *International Financial Statistics*, various years.

45. Only those countries listed by Singer and Small as members of the international system are included in our sample. Singer and Small 1994.

46. See Beck and Katz 1997; and Beck and Tucker 1996.

47. Note that the base of the spline function and each of the three knots are statistically significant in all of the following analyses.

48. See Beck and Katz 1997; and Beck and Tucker 1996.

49. We also sorted these variables by their size, assigning REG_i the larger annual regime score in each pair and REG_j the lower score. This procedure, which accords with much of the literature on the democratic peace, yields estimates that are very similar to those reported below. See, for example, Russett and Oneal 2001; and Russett, Oneal, and Davis 1998.

TABLE 1. *Effects of regime type, GDP, the change in GDP, trade, military disputes, colonial relations, alliances, distance, the GATT, and hegemony on PTA formation, 1951–1992*

Variable	*(1)*	*(2)*	*(3)*	*(4)*
Intercept	7.315**	7.223**	6.847**	7.212**
	(11.85)	(11.64)	(11.82)	(11.54)
REG_i	0.038**	0.038**	0.035**	0.038**
	(8.89)	(8.80)	(8.84)	(8.93)
REG_j	0.035**	0.035**	0.032**	0.035**
	(8.47)	(8.40)	(8.15)	(8.51)
GDP_i	-4.84×10^{-10}**	-3.29×10^{-10}**	-7.75×10^{-10}**	-4.89×10^{-10}**
	(−3.29)	(−3.47)	(−4.26)	(−3.34)
GDP_j	-3.84×10^{-10}*	-2.26×10^{-10}*	-6.94×10^{-10}**	-3.88×10^{-10}*
	(−2.39)	(−2.16)	(−4.17)	(−2.43)
ΔGDP_i	4.72×10^{-9}		6.41×10^{-9}	4.63×10^{-9}
	(1.28)		(1.55)	(1.26)
ΔGDP_j	4.85×10^{-9}		6.88×10^{-9}*	4.77×10^{-9}
	(1.71)		(2.04)	(1.69)
$TRADE_{ij}$	-1.21×10^{-7}	-1.23×10^{-7}		-1.18×10^{-7}
	(−1.53)	(−1.56)		(−1.52)
$DISPUTE_{ij}$	−0.740	−0.734	−0.620	
	(−1.91)	(−1.89)	(−1.64)	
COL_{ij}	1.338**	1.327**	1.356**	1.324**
	(8.74)	(8.73)	(8.62)	(8.45)
$ALLY_{ij}$	0.665**	0.663**	0.645**	0.673**
	(9.70)	(9.69)	(9.34)	(9.73)
$DISTANCE_{ij}$	−0.731**	−0.730**	−0.681**	−0.717**
	(−17.51)	(−17.47)	(−20.20)	(−16.62)
$GATT_{ij}$	0.391**	0.389**	0.376**	0.396**
	(6.05)	(6.03)	(5.79)	(6.12)
HEGEMONY	−53.75**	−53.07**	−52.29**	−53.84**
	(−14.92)	(−14.73)	(−14.68)	(−14.93)
χ^2	1915.28**	1906.12**	1866.84**	1911.48**
Log likelihood	−7146.54	−7147.73	−7173.51	−7149.97

Note: These parameters are estimated using logistic regression, after including a natural spline function with three knots. Figures in parentheses are asymptotic z-statistics computed using Huber standard errors. In each model, N = 223,568.

$^{**}p \leq .001$. Two-tailed tests are conducted for all estimates.

$^{*}p \leq .05$. Two-tailed tests are conducted for all estimates.

Furthermore, the effects of regime type on PTA formation are quantitatively large. To gauge the magnitude of these effects, we derive the predicted probability of a pair of states establishing a trade agreement if both of them are highly democratic (that is, if $REG_i = REG_j = 10$), if one is highly democratic and the other is highly autocratic (that is, if $REG_i = 10$ and $REG_j = -10$), and if both are highly

TABLE 2. *The influence of regime type on the predicted probability of a dyad forming a PTA and the predicted number of dyads forming a PTA*

Regime types of i and j	*Predicted probability of a dyad forming a PTA*[a]	*Predicted annual number of dyads forming a PTA*[b]
Two democracies	.0057	30.3
One democracy and one autocracy	.0028	14.9
Two autocracies	.0013	6.9

[a]To compute these predicted probabilities, we use the estimates in the first column of Table 1. We assume that i and j are not involved in a military dispute, that they do not have a prior colonial relationship, and that they are neither allies nor parties to the GATT (that is, $DISPUTE_{ij} = COL_{ij} = ALLY_{ij} = GATT_{ij} = 0$). All remaining variables are evaluated at their means.

[b]These figures are computed by multiplying the predicted probability of a dyad forming a PTA by the total number of observations in the sample (223,568) and then dividing that product by the number of years in the sample (42).

autocratic (that is, if $REG_i = REG_j = -10$).[50] Since the modal pair of states in our sample is not involved in a military dispute, did not have a colonial relationship, and is not made up of either allies or parties to the GATT, we set $DISPUTE_{ij}$, COL_{ij}, $ALLY_{ij}$, and $GATT_{ij}$ equal to zero to compute these probabilities. The remaining variables in equation (4) are evaluated at their means.

As Table 2 shows, on average, the probability of a democracy entering a trade agreement is roughly double the probability of an autocracy doing so. Pairs of democracies are about twice as likely to form a PTA as are pairs composed of a democracy and an autocracy. The latter pairs, in turn, are about twice as likely to engage in commercial cooperation as are autocratic pairs. Expressed in terms of the predicted number of dyads forming a PTA, our results indicate that roughly 30 democratic pairs, 15 mixed pairs, and only 7 autocratic pairs are expected to enter into a trade agreement in an average year.

Turning to the remaining variables, there is evidence that the economic size of countries affects their propensity to enter PTAs. The estimates of GDP_i and GDP_j are negative and statistically significant, indicating that the likelihood of a country joining a commercial agreement increases as the size of its home market declines. As expected, political relations between states also influence the likelihood that they will join a cooperative agreement. That the estimates of COL_{ij}, $ALLY_{ij}$, and $GATT_{ij}$ are positive and statistically significant indicates that states with a prior colonial

50. In evaluating the probability of a PTA between a democracy and an autocracy, our decision to consider the case where state i is the democracy and state j is the autocracy is entirely arbitrary. The predicted probability under these conditions is virtually identical to the predicted probability when i is the autocracy and j is the democracy.

relationship, those that are political-military allies, and those that are parties to the GATT are especially likely to enter a PTA. In addition, trade agreements tend to form between states located in proximity to each other and during periods of waning hegemony, since the estimates of $DISTANCE_{ij}$ and *HEGEMONY* are negative and significant.

Equally noteworthy is that the business cycle, trade flows, and military disputes have relatively little influence on whether or not states join the same PTA. The positive estimates of ΔGDP_i and ΔGDP_j imply that economic expansion increases the prospects that states will accede to a commercial agreement, whereas the negative estimates of $TRADE_{ij}$ and $DISPUTE_{ij}$ suggest that heightened trade flows and military disputes discourage the establishment of PTAs. None of these estimates, however, are statistically significant.

Having estimated the effects of regime type on PTA formation, it is important to assess the robustness of our results. To this end, we begin by dropping ΔGDP_i, ΔGDP_j, $TRADE_{ij}$, and $DISPUTE_{ij}$—the variables that are not statistically significant based on our initial findings. As the second, third, and fourth columns of Table 1 show, doing so has little bearing on the remaining estimates.

We also address whether our results depend on the use of Jaggers and Gurr's index of regime type. As noted earlier, there are important reasons to rely on this measure, given our objectives. However, Adam Przeworski, Michael E. Alvarez, José Antonio Cheibub, and Fernando Limongi have developed another measure of regime type that taps the domestic institutions emphasized in our model.[51] They code states in which "those who govern are selected through contested elections" as democratic and all other states as autocratic.[52] The data compiled by Przeworski et al. cover fewer countries and years than are included in our initial analyses, and their dichotomous measure is not as well-suited to testing our model as Jaggers and Gurr's index. But the stress they place on whether or not elections are contested in coding a state's regime type is consistent with our model.

To further assess the robustness of our results, we therefore redefine REG_i and REG_j as dummy variables that equal 1 if Przeworski et al. code states i and j, respectively, as democratic in year τ and 0 otherwise. We then estimate the parameters in equation (4) again. As with the findings presented in Table 1, the estimated coefficients of both REG_i and REG_j are positive and statistically significant.[53] Furthermore, there continues to be no evidence of a significant difference between them. Equally important, the quantitative effects of regime type generated using Przeworski et al.'s data are much the same as those generated using Jaggers and Gurr's data. Based on Przeworski et al.'s measure of regime type, for example, a democracy is roughly three-quarters more likely to enter a PTA than an autocracy,

51. Przeworski et al. 2000.

52. Ibid., 15.

53. More specifically, the estimate of REG_i is .509, the estimate of REG_j is .580, and both estimates are statistically significant at the .001 level.

and democratic pairs are about three times as likely to join a trade agreement as autocratic pairs. Thus our findings are quite robust with respect to the data used to measure regime type.

Next, we include a number of additional factors in equation (4) that might influence the formation of PTAs. First, there is reason to expect that pairs of states belonging to the same PTA will have less incentive to enter (another) one than pairs that are not already party to the same arrangement. We therefore include a variable indicating whether i and j are already members of a common PTA in year τ. Second, it is widely argued that, due to strategic interaction among countries competing in international markets and for other reasons, PTAs tend to form in reaction to one another.[54] This implies that states are especially likely to establish a commercial agreement soon after the creation of other agreements. As such, we include the number of PTAs formed in year $\tau - 1$.

Third, we include a variable indicating whether i and j have command economies in τ. All countries marked by the existence of a command economy are nondemocratic, and such countries rarely have entered preferential groupings. Hence, we need to ensure that the observed relationship between regime type and PTA formation does not stem from the effects of command economies.[55] Fourth, we include a time trend to account for any secular changes in the global economy that might influence the establishment of PTAs. In addition, we estimate equation (4) using conditional logistic regression—a technique that is equivalent to including pair-specific fixed effects in the model—to account for any heterogeneity in the data.[56]

Regardless of whether we include the variables just described separately or together and regardless of whether equation (4) is estimated using conditional logistic regression, the estimates of REG_i and REG_j remain positive and statistically significant.[57] Equally, there is virtually no change in these estimates when we redefine the dependent variable in equation (4) as the existence of a PTA between i and j in year $\tau + 1$, rather than the formation of a preferential grouping between them. Recall that the observed value of PTA_{ij} is 1 if a PTA forms between i and j in $\tau + 1$, and 0 otherwise. When we recode this variable as 1 in all years, $\tau + 1$,

54. See de Melo and Panagariya 1993, 5-6; Fernández and Portes 1998; Mansfield 1998; Oye 1992; and Pomfret 1988.

55. Data on command economies are taken from Kornai 1992.

56. Greene 1993, chap. 16.

57. Estimating our model using conditional logistic regression leads to the omission of roughly 85 percent of the observations in our data, since most country-pairs included in the analysis did not form a PTA during the period since World War II. Furthermore, using this estimation procedure to analyze cross-section time-series data with a binary dependent variable has serious drawbacks. See Beck and Katz 2001; and King 2001. Nonetheless, when equation (4) is estimated using this procedure, the estimate of REG_i is .028, the estimate of REG_j is .023, and both estimates are statistically significant at the .001 level. Of course, factors that are specific to time might also affect the formation of PTAs. A common way of addressing these factors is to include year-specific fixed effects, but these effects are perfectly correlated with *HEGEMONY*, which takes on a different value in each year we examine.

where i and j belong to the same PTA—regardless of whether the arrangement was formed in $\tau + 1$—the results are much the same as those reported in Table 1. In still another analysis, we eliminated all observations for a given country-pair after that pair formed a PTA. Since the probability of states forming a PTA is likely to be lower if they already belong to one than if they do not, this is another useful check on our earlier results. The results are again quite similar to those in Table 1 (although it is interesting that the size of the estimates of both REG_i and REG_j increase by about one-third). These analyses, then, continue to indicate the robustness of our findings.

Finally, the formation of a PTA is a rare event. Gary King and Langche Zeng have recently argued that using logistic regression to estimate the probability of rare events can yield biased results.[58] They have developed methods to correct such biases, and we use these methods to generate another set of estimates of the parameters in equation (4). The resulting estimates and standard errors are very similar to those in Table 1, demonstrating that our findings do not suffer from a rare events bias.[59]

In sum, our statistical results strongly support the propositions developed earlier—particularly the proposition that the likelihood of signing a trade agreement rises with the degree of democracy in each country. During the period since World War II, more democratic states have displayed a greater propensity to enter trade agreements than less democratic states, even after controlling for a host of other economic and political factors. Furthermore, the probability of a pair of countries forming a commercial agreement is highest if both countries are democratic and is lowest if both are autocratic.

Conclusion

We have argued that the regime type of states can strongly affect their propensity to cooperate on economic issues. Leaders in democracies have a greater incentive to pursue international cooperation in trade than do their nondemocratic counterparts. We developed this argument using a formal model of trade policymaking emphasizing the electoral constraints faced by political leaders. Although there are many reasons why countries choose to cooperate, our analysis emphasizes how a country's regime type creates domestic political incentives for leaders that influence this choice.

Our model assumes that both democratic and autocratic leaders would like to maximize the rents stemming from trade barriers, but that both may lose office if their rent seeking becomes excessive. The problem faced by voters and leaders,

58. King and Zeng 2001.

59. This result is not unexpected, since King and Zeng point out that the influence of their methods will be most pronounced when the number of observations being analyzed is less than a few thousand. King and Zeng 2001. Our sample is obviously much larger than that size.

however, is that voters have incomplete information about their leaders' behavior: they do not know exactly what trade policy their leaders have chosen at any point in time. And domestic executives cannot credibly commit to accurately divulge this information. Hence, when exogenous shocks adversely influence the economy, an incumbent executive may be voted out of office not because the executive was too extractive, but rather because voters mistakenly assume that the executive was engaged in protectionist predation. The prospect of losing elections due to factors beyond the incumbent executive's control provides a strong incentive to find ways of reassuring voters that the government is not being too extractive. Trade agreements are one such means.

Commercial agreements can mitigate the executive's informational problem. The monitors of these agreements—either countries that are party to them or the international trade institutions themselves—can credibly signal to voters whether their leader is cheating or abiding by the agreement. Accusations of cheating against one's government by foreign countries or an international institution are newsworthy events that can alert (at least some) voters to the government's behavior. Because of this signal, executives can improve their chances of re-election. In democracies, however, voters have a greater impact on the tenure of leaders than in autocracies, since the democratic electorate can more easily turn incumbents out of office. Since autocratic leaders face fewer worries about re-election, they have fewer incentives to relinquish policy autonomy and sign trade agreements, making them less likely than more democratic leaders to seek commercial cooperation. The greater accountability of leaders to voters in democracies makes a difference. Surprisingly, this result is obtained even though democratic executives discount the future more heavily than their autocratic counterparts.

In our model, international agreements serve a domestic purpose. They allow executives to commit themselves credibly to actions that voters would otherwise find incredible. Unilateral trade barrier reductions are less credible to voters and more easily repealed than are mutually agreed-upon international reductions. Others have argued that international institutions promote cooperation by providing information, but they have been less specific about how this mechanism actually induces leaders to choose cooperation.[60] Here, we identify one mechanism by which cooperative agreements can convey information to voters about the behavior of their leaders, thus allowing voters to better judge their leaders. Other mechanisms might serve this purpose as well, but our claim is that trade agreements do so especially well. The information provided by trade agreements benefits all of the players in our analysis—voters and governments alike. Existing studies rarely acknowledge that international institutions can serve this function. The tendency for such institutions to be created with monitoring and dispute settlement mechanisms suggests their importance in disseminating information domestically as well as internationally.

60. For example, Keohane 1984.

International cooperation can thus generate domestic political benefits for leaders, making them more likely to seek cooperative agreements in the first place.

Our empirical findings strongly support the two central hypotheses stemming from the formal model. Since World War II, more democratic countries have displayed a greater likelihood of concluding trade agreement than other countries, even when holding constant various political and economic influences. Equally, pairs of democratic countries are about twice as likely to form a PTA as are pairs composed of a democracy and an autocracy and roughly four times as likely to form such cooperative agreements as are autocratic pairs. In sum, holding constant Cold War influences, economic variables, and various other factors, we find considerable evidence that democracy promotes commercial cooperation. Clearly, democracy is not alone in promoting such agreements, but our findings indicate that it is a potent impetus to cooperation.

Our study also sheds light on other hypotheses about international cooperation. First, whereas functionalist theories argue that high levels of trade between countries should promote cooperation, we find that trade flows do not have much impact on the probability of signing a commercial agreement. Second, as realist theories suggest, alliances and the existence of a stable hegemon foster cooperation in trade. Somewhat surprisingly, however, military disputes have little bearing on trade agreements. Third, we find that GATT members are especially likely to establish preferential agreements, which accords with the view of neoliberal institutionalists that international institutions can improve the ability of states to cooperate. Even when we account for the effects of these and other potential influences on commercial cooperation, however, domestic politics still affects whether states enter into trade agreements.

Scholars of international relations have displayed a longstanding interest in the sources of economic cooperation. Most research on this topic has been cast at the international level. Far less attention has been paid to the domestic influences on economic cooperation. Our results highlight the drawbacks of ignoring these influences. In addition to systemic and economic factors, the regime types of states strongly condition their likelihood of forging a trade agreement. In commercial matters, democracies are more cooperative than are other states because of the domestic political benefits that can be generated by international trade agreements.

Appendix

In this economy, the export good is the numeraire, and the domestic price of the import good in period τ is $p_\tau = \pi_\tau (1 + t_\tau)$. Both goods require capital and labor for production, which occurs with constant returns to scale. Let the economy-wide aggregate endowment of capital (K) relative to labor (L) be $k = K/L$. Factors are perfectly mobile domestically.

Each individual, l, owns one unit of labor, which is paid a wage $w(p_\tau)$, and each owns k^l units of capital, a unit of which is paid $r(p_\tau)$. Individual preferences for the goods are identical and homothetic in the two goods. An individual l's (one-period) indirect utility can be written as

$$U^l(p_\tau) = V(p_\tau)I^l(p_\tau)$$

where the individual's income is

$$I^l(p_\tau) = w(p_\tau) + r(p_\tau)k^l + \theta^l(p_\tau - \pi_\tau)M(p_\tau)$$

and where $M(p_\tau)$ is the quantity of imports and

$$\theta^l = \frac{w + rk^l}{wL + rK}$$

as in Mayer.[61] The last term implies that tariff revenue is distributed back to individuals in proportion to each individual's share of national factor income.

Voters differ along the single dimension k^l. Assuming no costs to voting, the tariff preferred by the majority of voters is the ideal tariff of the individual with the median capital-labor endowment ratio. This individual, indexed m, is endowed with k^m units of capital (and a single unit of labor). Since the importable is labor-intensive and the median individual owns more labor relative to capital than does society as a whole, that is, $k^m < k$, the median voter prefers a positive level of trade barriers. Given the realization of the world price, π_τ, any voter, including the median voter, has an ideal tariff. Maximization of one period utility with respect to t_τ shows that the utility-maximizing tariff for the median voter, m, is

$$t_\tau^m = -\frac{I}{M'(p_\tau)}\frac{\partial\theta^m/\partial p}{\theta^m}$$

where I is aggregate income. Note first that the quantity of imports decreases with their price, so that $M'(p_\tau) < 0$. Since the economy exports a capital-intensive good, and $k^m < k$, then $\partial\theta^m/\partial p > 0$, so the median voter prefers a positive level of trade barriers.[62]

Each individual has a vote in an election. Unlike in Mayer, where the vote is over a tariff policy in a direct democracy setting, here the voters use the election to indicate their support for the incumbent.[63]

Following Ferejohn, we are interested in equilibria where voters follow a simple retrospective voting rule,[64] in which voter l will choose to reappoint the executive in period τ if their welfare is at least as good as an endogenously determined threshold value, that is, if $\underline{U}^l(p_\tau) \geq \underline{U}^l$. Banks and Sundaram have studied the repeated election game between the voter and the executive in a more general setting (they permit variations in the types of executives [adverse selection] in addition to the moral hazard we study here), and they show the existence of a sequential equilibrium of this threshold-type equilibrium, conditioned on currently available public information.[65]

61. Mayer 1984.
62. Ibid.
63. Ibid.
64. Ferejohn 1986.
65. Banks and Sundaram 1993.

As in Persson et al., we look for an equilibrium in which voters condition their voting decision on their utility in the current period and not on any previous period.[66] A history-dependent rule would require commitment across periods to be optimal; here voters re-optimize at the beginning of every period. Moreover, the action of the executive is not conditioned on any of its past actions but rather on the current state—whether the executive currently is in office or not. Hence the equilibrium strategies of interest will be Markov and stationary.

Unlike Banks and Sundaram, we consider only one type of incumbent—the preferences of the government are common knowledge.[67] An executive removed from office is never reappointed, and there is always another candidate (identical in all respects) available to take over the executive. Moreover, the government moves before the uncertainty is resolved each period. Hence there is nothing to be learned by the voters from the actions of the government.

Recall that $\phi(t_\tau, \underline{U}^m) = \Pr(U^m(p_\tau) > \underline{U}^m)$, and therefore $\phi_t < 0$ and $\phi_{\underline{U}^m} < 0$.

ASSUMPTION: $\phi(1, U) = 0$ for all U.

From equation (2) the executive solves:

$$\frac{\partial \Gamma}{\partial t} = G_t + \delta\sigma\phi_t\Gamma = 0 \tag{5}$$

for the optimal t in any period. From equations (1) and (2) we have, in equilibrium:

$$\Gamma = \frac{G(t)}{1 - \delta[\sigma\phi(t, \underline{U}^m) + (1 - \sigma)]}. \tag{6}$$

Substituting equation (6) into equation (5), we have that the optimal trade policy t° for the executive satisfies:

$$G_t\{1 - \delta[\sigma\phi(t, \underline{U}^m) + (1 - \sigma)]\} + \delta\sigma\phi_t G = 0. \tag{7}$$

LEMMA A.1: *t° falls with $\underline{U}^m$.*

Proof: Totally differentiating equation (5), we have $\Gamma_{tU}dU + \Gamma_{tt}dt = 0$, or $dt^\circ/d\underline{U}^m = -(\Gamma_{t\underline{U}^m}/\Gamma_{tt})$. Now $\Gamma_{t\underline{U}^m} = \delta\sigma\phi_{t\underline{U}^m}\Gamma < 0$ since $\phi_{t\underline{U}^m} < 0$ by Leibniz's rule (the tariff and the threshold are strategic substitutes). $\Gamma_{tt} < 0$ so $dt^\circ/d\underline{U}^m < 0$.

For the Leviathan strategy, where $t = 1$, we assume that the probability that the median voter re-elects the incumbent is zero when incumbent chooses this strategy: $\phi(1,U) = 0$ for all $U > 0$. Then the gains to the incumbent executive from choosing $t_\tau = 1$ at the beginning of any period τ are $\Gamma(1) = G(1) + \delta(1 - \sigma)\Gamma$. A lower tariff t is preferred by the incumbent over the Leviathan tariff when:

66. Persson, Roland, and Tabellini 1997.
67. Banks and Sundaram 1993 and 1998.

$$G(t) + \delta\rho(t, \underline{U}^m, \sigma)\Gamma(t) \geq G(1) + \delta(1 - \sigma)\Gamma(1). \quad (8)$$

Define $\underline{t}$ such that equation (8) is satisfied with equality. Then at $t = \underline{t}(U^m,\sigma)$ the government is exactly indifferent between the lower tariff and the Leviathan strategy.

LEMMA A.2: *Define $\hat{U}$ such that $t^\circ(\hat{U}, \sigma) = \underline{t}(\hat{U}, \sigma)$. Then $d\underline{t}/d\underline{U}^m > 0$ for $U < \hat{U}$, and $d\underline{t}/d\underline{U}^m < 0$ for $U > \hat{U}$.*

Proof: Implicit differentiation of equation (8) taking the continuation values as given yields $d\underline{t}/d\underline{U}^m = -\delta\sigma\Gamma\phi_{U^m}/(G_t + \delta\sigma\Gamma\phi_t)$. Now the numerator is positive, and the denominator is positive for all $t < t^\circ$. So for $U < \hat{U}$ we have $t < t^\circ$ and hence $d\underline{t}/d\underline{U}^m > 0$.

LEMMA A.3: *Let $\tilde{U}$ satisfy $t^m = t^\circ(\tilde{U}, \sigma)$. Then the following pair of strategies is a Nash Equilibrium:* $t^* = \begin{cases} t^\circ(\underline{U}^m, \sigma) & \text{if } \underline{U}^m < \hat{U} \\ 1 & \text{otherwise} \end{cases}$ *and* $\underline{U}^* = \begin{cases} \hat{U} & \text{if } t^m \leq \underline{t}(\hat{U}, \sigma), \\ \tilde{U} & \text{otherwise} \end{cases}$.

Proof: Equations (7) and (8) establish that the government is playing a best response to any threshold $\underline{U}^m$. The median voter wants to get a tariff as close as possible to her (*ex ante*) ideal, t^m. If $t^m > \underline{t}$, then the voter sets the threshold to $\tilde{U}$, given that the government responds with $t^\circ = t^m$. On the other hand, when t^m crosses $\underline{t}$, then the voter's ideal tariff lies below that which the government can be constrained to provide. Hence the voters restrict the government to the lowest tariff possible by choosing a threshold at $\hat{U}$. Hence the voters control the executive as much as is possible; the median voter is playing a best response.

Notice that the voters' strategy here is to choose a threshold, which is effectively equivalent to deciding whether to recommend re-election or not. At the moment at which the voter chooses a threshold, a threshold chosen higher than the utility observed is a recommendation to evict; a lower one, a recommendation to re-elect.

Notice that perfection-type refinements here (such as subgame perfection) are not applicable in a non-trivial way. Subgame perfection requires that the equilibrium strategies be Nash in any proper subgame. But there are no proper subgames in this game. For instance, at the moment at which the voter must choose a threshold in any period (effectively deciding to recommend re-election or not) the voter does not know either the state of the world (π) or the actions of the executive (t) in that period. Hence the decision point is an information set not a single node.

There is a sense, however, that conditional on the publicly available information, the threat to evict (when experienced utility is low) is credible. Consider again the information set where the voter must choose a threshold. Suppose the payoff that period is low—such that the voter is supposed to recommend (in the equilibrium) eviction (by setting high threshold). Suppose they do not. Then in the next period, the government, aware that low payoffs do not imply eviction, will switch from then on to the Leviathan strategy. Such a failure to evict is clearly worse for the voter, and so the voter will continue to evict when called to do so.

LEMMA A.4: *The sign of $d\underline{t}/d\sigma$ is indeterminate.*

Proof: Implicit differentiation of equation (8) and by the definition of $\underline{t}$, we have $d\underline{t}/d\sigma = -\delta[G(1)(\phi - 1) + G(t)]/\{G_t[1 - \delta(1 - \sigma)] + \delta G(1)\sigma\phi_t\}$. Now the first term in the numerator is negative, while the second is positive. In the denominator, the first term is positive, while the second is negative.

LEMMA A.5: *For any international trade agreement* $t^C \in [t^m, \underline{t}]$, *the following strategies constitute a Nash equilibrium:* $t^* = \begin{cases} t^C & \text{if } \sigma > \bar{\sigma}(\delta) \\ 1 & \text{otherwise} \end{cases}$ *and* $\underline{U}^* = \begin{cases} 0 & \text{if no alarm sent} \\ \infty & \text{otherwise} \end{cases}$.

Proof: The optimal deviation for the government is the Leviathan action (since any tariff above t^C leads to rejection by the voters). Then the equilibrium dominates defection whenever $\Delta(t^C; \sigma) > 0$ which is equivalent to the condition $\sigma > [1 - G(t^C)/G(1)](1/\delta - 1) \equiv \bar{\sigma}(\delta)$. As for the voters, once the alarm has (or has not) been sent, changing the threshold will have no effect on their payoffs; hence the equilibrium action is weakly preferred.

Along the equilibrium path, the voter knows more about the actions of the executive than in the unilateral case. However, the state of the world is still unknown—hence perfection refinements are not applicable in a non-trivial way. Nevertheless, at any information set, once reached, it remains optimal for the voters to behave according to the equilibrium strategies—that is, the equilibrium behavior is optimal conditional on the publicly available information.

Proof of Proposition 1: The condition that $\Delta(t^C; \sigma) > 0$ follows directly from Lemma A.5; $\partial\Delta(t^C, \sigma)/\partial\sigma = G(1)/[1 - \delta(1 - \sigma)]^2 \, \delta > 0$.

Proof of Proposition 2: $\Delta(t^C; \sigma) = \delta G(t^C)/(1 - \delta) \, \delta\{1 - [\sigma\phi(t^C, U) + (1 - \sigma)]\}/\{1 - \delta[\sigma\phi(t^C, U) + (1 - \sigma)]\} > 0$ for all σ and $d\Delta(t^C; \sigma)/d\sigma = \delta G(t^C)(\phi - 1)(\delta\{1 - [\sigma\phi(t^C, U) + (1 - \sigma)]\} - 1)/(1 - \delta)\{1 - \delta[\sigma\phi(t^C, U) + (1 - \sigma)]\}^2 > 0$ for all σ.

PROPOSITION 3: $U^m[\pi(1 + t^C)] \geq U^m[\pi(1 + t^*)]$ *for any* $t^C \in [t^m, \underline{t}]$.

Proof: $G_t > 0$ for all t; by inspection of equation (7), it must be that at $t = t^*$, $\phi_t(t) < 0$. Now $\phi_t(t) = 0$ at $t = t^m$ since the voter's utility is maximized, and therefore the probability of re-election is maximized. Therefore $t^* \geq t^m$. After any agreement, $t^C \in [t^m, \underline{t}]$, $\phi(t^C) \geq \phi(t^*)$ since $\phi_t(t) < 0$ for all $t > t^m$ and hence given any realization of π, $U^m[\pi(1 + t^C)] \geq U^m[\pi(1 + t^*)]$.

PROPOSITION 4: $d\Pr(PTA_{ij})/d\sigma_i > 0$ *and* $d\Pr(PTA_{ij})/d\sigma_j > 0$.

Proof: $d\Pr(PTA_{ij})/d\sigma_i = FF' \, d\Delta/d\sigma_i > 0$ since $F' > 0$ by assumption, Propositions 1 and 2 establish the second term, and F lies between 0 and 1. The proof for the second case is identical.

References

Anderson, Kym, and Richard Blackhurst. 1993. Introduction and Summary. In *Regional Integration and the Global Trading System*, edited by Kym Anderson and Richard Blackhurst, 1–15. London: Harvester Wheatsheaf.

Bagwell, Kyle, and Robert Staiger. 1999. An Economic Theory of GATT. *American Economic Review* 89 (1):215–48.

Banks, Jeffrey S., and Rangarajan K. Sundaram. 1993. Adverse Selection and Moral Hazard in a Repeated Elections Model. In *Political Economy: Institutions, Information, Competition, and Representation*, edited by William A. Barnett, Melvin J. Hinich, and Norman J. Schofield, 295–312. Cambridge: Cambridge University Press.

———. 1998. Optimal Retention in Agency Problems. *Journal of Economic Theory* 82 (2):293–323.

Beck, Nathaniel, and Jonathan Katz. 1997. The Analysis of Binary Time-Series Cross-Section Data and/or the Democratic Peace. Paper presented at the 14th Annual Meeting of the Political Methodology Group, Columbus, Ohio.

———. 2001. Throwing Out the Baby with the Bath Water: A Comment on Green, Kim, and Yoon. *International Organization* 55 (2):487–95.

Beck, Nathaniel, and Richard Tucker. 1996. Conflict in Space and Time: Time-Series Cross-Section Analysis with a Binary Dependent Variable. Paper Presented at the 92nd Annual Meeting of the American Political Science Association, San Francisco, Calif.

Bhagwati, Jagdish. 1993. Regionalism and Multilateralism: An Overview. In *New Dimensions in Regional Integration*, edited by Jaime de Melo and Arvind Panagariya, 22–51. New York: Cambridge University Press.

Bollen, Kenneth A. 1980. Issues in the Comparative Measurement of Political Democracy. *American Sociological Review* 45 (3):370–90.

Bueno de Mesquita, Bruce, and David Lalman. 1992. *War and Reason: Domestic and International Imperatives*. New Haven, Conn.: Yale University Press.

Bueno de Mesquita, Bruce, James D. Morrow, Randolph M. Siverson, and Alastair Smith. 1999. An Institutional Explanation of the Democratic Peace. *American Political Science Review* 93 (4):791–808.

Chittick, William, and Keith Billingsley. 1989. The Structure of Elite Foreign Policy Beliefs. *Western Political Quarterly* 42 (2):201–24.

Correlates of War Project. 1993. Alliances Data. Unpublished data set, University of Michigan.

Coughlin, P. J. 1992. *Probabilistic Voting Theory*. Cambridge: Cambridge University Press.

Dahl, Robert. 1971. *Polyarchy: Participation and Opposition*. New Haven, Conn.: Yale University Press.

de Melo, Jaime, and Arvind Panagariya. 1993. Introduction. In *New Dimensions in Regional Integration*, edited by Jaime de Melo and Arvind Panagariya, 3–21. New York: Cambridge University Press.

Fearon, James. 1994. Domestic Audiences and the Escalation of International Disputes. *American Political Science Review* 88 (3):577–92.

Ferejohn, John. 1986. Incumbent Performance and Electoral Control. *Public Choice* 50 (2):5–25.

Fernández, Raquel, and Jonathan Portes. 1998. Returns to Regionalism: An Evaluation of Nontraditional Gains from Regional Trade Agreements. *The World Bank Economic Review* 12 (2):197–220.

Fiorina, Morris. 1981. *Retrospective Voting in American National Elections*. New Haven, Conn.: Yale University Press.

Foroutan, Faezeh. 1993. Regional Integration in Sub-Saharan Africa: Past Experience and Future Prospects. In *New Dimensions in Regional Integration*, edited by Jaime de Melo and Arvind Panagariya, 234–71. New York: Cambridge University Press.

Frankel, Jeffrey A., Ernesto Stein, and Shang-Jin Wei. 1998. Continental Trading Blocs: Are They Natural or Supernatural? In *The Regionalization of the World Economy*, edited by Jeffrey A. Frankel, 189–219. Chicago: University of Chicago Press.

Gasiorowski, Mark. 1996. An Overview of the Political Regime Change Dataset. *Comparative Political Studies* 29 (4):469–83.

Gastil, Raymond D. 1980 and 1990. *Freedom in the World: Political Rights and Civil Liberties*. New York: Freedom House.

Gaubatz, Kurt Taylor. 1996. Democratic States and Commitment in International Relations. *International Organization* 50 (1):109–39.

Gilpin, Robert. 1987. *The Political Economy of International Relations*. Princeton, N.J.: Princeton University Press.

Gowa, Joanne. 1994. *Allies, Adversaries, and International Trade*. Princeton, N.J.: Princeton University Press.

Gowa, Joanne, and Edward D. Mansfield. 1993. Power Politics and International Trade. *American Political Science Review* 87 (2):408–20.

Green, William H. 1993. *Econometric Analysis*, 2d ed. Englewood Cliffs, N.J.: Prentice Hall.

Grilli, Enzo R. 1993. *The European Community and Developing Countries*. Cambridge: Cambridge University Press.

Grossman, Gene, and Elhanan Helpman. 1994. Protection for Sale. *American Economic Review* 84 (4):833–50.

Gurr, Ted Robert, Keith Jaggers, and Will H. Moore. 1989. *Polity II: Political Structures and Regime Change, 1800–1986*. Study no. 9263. Ann Arbor, Mich.: Inter-University Consortium for Political and Social Research.

Haggard, Stephan, and Robert Kaufman. 1995. *The Political Economy of Democratic Transitions*. Princeton, N.J.: Princeton University Press.

Hanlon, Joseph. 1986. *Beggar Your Neighbor*. London: Villiers Publications.

Hartland-Thunberg, Penelope. 1980. *Trading Blocs, U.S. Exports, and World Trade*. Boulder, Colo.: Westview Press.

Herrmann, Richard K., Philip E. Tetlock, and Matthew N. Diascro. 2001. How Americans Think About Trade: Reconciling Conflicts among Money, Power, and Principles. *International Studies Quarterly* 45 (2):191–218.

International Monetary Fund. Various years. *Direction of Foreign Trade*. Washington, D.C.: IMF.

———. Various years. *International Financial Statistics*. Washington, D.C.: IMF.

Jaggers, Keith, and Ted Robert Gurr. 1995. Tracking Democracy's Third Wave with the Polity III Data. *Journal of Peace Research* 32 (4):469–82.

Jones, Daniel M., Stuart A. Bremer, and J. David Singer. 1996. Militarized Interstate Disputes, 1816–1992: Rationale, Coding Rules, and Empirical Patterns. *Conflict Management and Peace Science* 15 (2):163–213.

Keohane, Robert O. 1984. *After Hegemony: Cooperation and Discord in the World Political Economy*. Princeton, N.J.: Princeton University Press.

Kiewiet, Roderick. 1983. *Macroeconomics and Micropolitics*. Chicago: University of Chicago Press.

King, Gary. 2001. Proper Nouns and Methodological Propriety: Pooling Dyads in International Relations Data. *International Organization* 55 (2):497–507.

King, Gary, and Langche Zeng. 2001. Explaining Rare Events in International Relations. *International Organization* 55 (3):693–715.

Kisanga, Eliawony J. 1991. *Industrial and Trade Cooperation in Eastern and Southern Africa*. Hong Kong: Avebury.

Kornai, Janos. 1992. *The Socialist System: The Political Economy of Communism*. Princeton, N.J.: Princeton University Press.

Krasner, Stephen D. 1976. State Power and the Structure of Foreign Trade. *World Politics* 28 (3):317–47.

Krueger, Anne O. 1999. Are Preferential Trading Arrangements Trade-Liberalizing or Protectionist? *Journal of Economic Perspectives* 13 (4):105–24.

Krugman, Paul. 1993. Regionalism versus Multilateralism: Analytical Notes. In *New Dimensions in Regional Integration*, edited by Jaime de Melo and Arvind Panagariya, 58–79. New York: Cambridge University Press.

Kurian, George Thomas. 1992. *Encyclopedia of the Third World*. 4th ed. Vols. 1–3. New York: Facts on File.

Lake, David A. 1988. *Power, Protectionism, and Free Trade: International Sources of U.S. Commercial Strategy*. Ithaca, N.Y.: Cornell University Press.

Leeds, Brett Ashley. 1999. Domestic Political Institutions, Credible Commitments and International Cooperation. *American Journal of Political Science* 43 (4):979–1002.

Lewis-Beck, Michael S. 1988. *Economics and Elections: The Major Western Democracies*. Ann Arbor: University of Michigan Press.

Maddison, Angus. 1995. *Monitoring the World Economy, 1820–1992*. Paris: Organization for Economic Cooperation and Development.

Mansfield, Edward D. 1998. The Proliferation of Preferential Trading Arrangements. *Journal of Conflict Resolution* 42 (5):523–43.

Mansfield, Edward D., Helen V. Milner, and B. Peter Rosendorff. 2000. Free to Trade: Democracies, Autocracies, and International Trade. *American Political Science Review* 94 (2):305–21.

Mansfield, Edward D., and Jack Snyder. 1995. Democratization and the Danger of War. *International Security* 20 (1):5–38.

Martin, Lisa L. 2000. *Democratic Commitments: Legislatures and International Cooperation*. Princeton, N.J.: Princeton University Press.

Mattli, Walter. 1999. *The Logic of Regional Integration: Europe and Beyond*. New York: Cambridge University Press.

Mayer, Wolfgang. 1984. Endogenous Tariff Formation. *American Economic Review* 74 (5):970–85.

McGillivray, Fiona, and Alastair Smith. 2000. Trust and Cooperation Through Agent-Specific Punishments. *International Organization* 54 (4):809–24.

McKeown, Timothy J. 1991. A Liberal Trading Order? The Long-Run Pattern of Imports to the Advanced Capitalist States. *International Studies Quarterly* 35 (2):151–72.

Milner, Helen V. 1992. International Theories of Cooperation: Strengths and Weaknesses. *World Politics* 44 (3):466–96.

———. 1997. *Interests, Institutions, and Information: Domestic Politics and International Relations*. Princeton, N.J.: Princeton University Press.

Nye, Joseph S. 1988. Neorealism and Neoliberalism. *World Politics* 40 (2):235–51.

Oneal, John R., and Bruce Russett. 1999. Assessing the Liberal Peace with Alternative Specifications: Trade Still Reduces Conflict. *Journal of Peace Research* 36 (4):423–42.

Orimalade, Adeyinka, and R. E. Ubogu, eds. 1984. *Trade and Development in Economic Community of West African States*. Delhi: Vikas Publishing.

Oye, Kenneth A. 1992. *Economic Discrimination and Political Exchange: World Political Economy in the 1930s and 1980s*. Princeton, N.J.: Princeton University Press.

Panagariya, Arvind. 2000. Preferential Trade Liberalization: The Traditional Theory and New Developments. *Journal of Economic Literature* 38 (2):287–331.

Persson, Torsten, Gerard Roland, and Guido Tabellini. 1997. Separation of Powers and Political Accountability. *Quarterly Journal of Economics* 112 (4):1163–1202.

Pomfret, Richard. 1988. *Unequal Trade: The Economics of Discriminatory International Trade Policies*. Oxford: Basil Blackwell.

Powell, G. Bingham. 2000. *Elections as Instruments of Democracy*. New Haven, Conn.: Yale University Press.

Przeworski, Adam, Michael E. Alvarez, José Antonio Cheibub, and Fernando Limongi. 2000. *Democracy and Development: Political Institutions and Well-Being in the World, 1950–1990*. New York: Cambridge University Press.

Reinhardt, Eric. 1996. Posturing Parliaments: Ratification, Uncertainty, and International Bargaining. Ph.D. diss., Columbia University, New York.

Remmer, Karen. 1998. Does Democracy Promote Interstate Cooperation? *International Studies Quarterly* 42 (1):25–52.

Russett, Bruce, and John Oneal. 2001. *Triangulating Peace: Democracy, Interdependence, and International Organizations*. New York: Norton.

Russett, Bruce, John Oneal, and David R. Davis. 1998. The Third Leg of the Kantian Tripod for Peace. *International Organization* 52 (3):441–68.

Schumpeter, Joseph. [1942] 1976. *Capitalism, Socialism, and Democracy*. Reprint, New York: Harper Colophon.

Singer, J. David, and Melvin Small. 1994. *Correlates of War Project: International and Civil War Data, 1816–1992*. Study no. 9905. Ann Arbor, Mich.: Inter-University Consortium for Political and Social Research.

Small, Melvin, and J. David Singer. 1969. Formal Alliances, 1816–1965: An Extension of the Basic Data. *Journal of Peace Research* 6 (3):257–82.

Summers, Robert, and Alan Heston. 1991. The Penn World Table (Mark 5): An Expanded Set of International Comparisons. *Quarterly Journal of Economics* 106 (2):327–68.

Verdier, Daniel. 1998. Democratic Convergence and Free Trade. *International Studies Quarterly* 42 (1):1–24.

Whalley, John. 1998. Why Do Countries Seek Regional Trade Agreements? In *The Regionalization of the World Economy*, edited by Jeffrey A. Frankel, 63–83. Chicago: University of Chicago Press.

World Trade Organization. 1995. *Regionalism and the World Trading System*. Geneva: WTO.

Yarbrough, Beth V., and Robert M. Yarbrough. 1992. *Cooperation and Governance in International Trade: The Strategic Organizational Approach*. Princeton, N.J.: Princeton University Press.

[3]

Economic Interests and Regional Trading Arrangements: The Case of NAFTA

Kerry A. Chase

In recent years, there has been a dramatic expansion in the number and scope of regional trading arrangements in the world economy. One study finds that more than one-third of all trading blocs formed since 1948 were established in the past decade.[1] A significant body of work maintains that these arrangements are designed to strengthen protectionist barriers and divert trade.[2] Welfare-based trade models yield only protectionist reasons to form trading blocs—to exercise market power over other countries or blocs. Studies in the political economy of trade emphasize rent-seeking motives to divert trade from outside to within a region.[3]

These approaches suggest that regional trading arrangements tend to evolve in an outwardly protectionist direction, interfering with multilateral trade liberalization. Many analysts point to the disintegration of the trading system during the 1930s as evidence of the pernicious effects of regionalism. Conventional wisdom also links recent regional trade initiatives with protectionist pressures that undermine the multilateral system.[4]

However, there is little systematic empirical work on the political economy factors driving the creation of regional arrangements. One recent review concludes that

I would like to thank the German Marshall Fund for financial support; Stephanie Gray, Christina Marsh, and Amy Swift for research assistance; Benjamin Bishin, James Glaser, and Alan Kessler for advice and suggestions; Durwood Marshall for programming help with data concordances; and the editors of *IO* and two reviewers for their comments. Robert Feenstra and Deborah Swenson graciously shared their data on U.S. trade under the Offshore Assembly Program. I owe special thanks to Jeffry Frieden for his steadfast encouragement and valuable feedback on many prior drafts.

1. Frankel 1997, 4.
2. See Gilpin 2000; Conybeare 1993; Thurow 1992; Garten 1993; Bhagwati 1993; Krueger 1997; and Lal 1993.
3. Grossman and Helpman 1995.
4. Observers note that the pursuit of regional arrangements in U.S. policy coincided with a shift to "aggressive unilateralism" (that is, greater use of contingent protection and strengthened Super 301 provisions for trade retaliation), at a time when the Uruguay Round appeared to have reached a low point. Moreover, many believe the protectionist turn in the United States inspired Canada and Mexico to pursue regional free trade. See Garten 1995; and Cox 1996.

International Organization 57, Winter 2003, pp. 137–174

DOI: 10.1017/S0020818303571053

> There is a lack of empirical evidence indicating which domestic groups support regional trade agreements, whose interests these agreements serve, and why particular groups prefer regional to multilateral trade liberalization. . . [and] we know little about whether, once in place, regional arrangements foster domestic support for broader, multilateral trade liberalization or whether they undermine such support.[5]

This article develops an explanation of domestic lobbying for regional trade liberalization to fill these gaps in the political economy of trading blocs. This framework emphasizes two factors at the industry level that have not received enough attention in the literature: first, economies of scale in production; and second, production sharing across borders in intermediate goods. I then test my expectations in an analysis of lobbying on the North American Free Trade Agreement (NAFTA) in the United States.

Specifying the implications of economies of scale and regional production sharing and evaluating their effects on trade preferences illuminates why particular industry groups in a large, advanced economy such as the United States would seek trading blocs. This approach also explains why business and labor divided over regional free trade in some sectors but united against it in others, a difference that is puzzling for conventional trade models. A closing discussion of the NAFTA case highlights several reasons why many U.S. firms viewed trade discrimination as a prerequisite for reorganizing their manufacturing establishments to operate more efficiently.

I begin with a review of unresolved puzzles in the political economy of trading blocs. The second part of the article presents an explanatory framework to examine the domestic politics of regional trade agreements. The third part tests these expectations on group preferences (lobbying in the United States) and policy outcomes (tariff-phasing schedules in the NAFTA treaty). The fourth part evaluates specific motives in U.S. domestic politics for regionalism and trade discrimination. The final part discusses conclusions and implications.

Trading Blocs: The Economics and the Politics

Jacob Viner's *Customs Union Issue* is the starting point for the modern economic analysis of trading blocs. The purpose of this seminal work was normative: to assess how shifts in the source of supply of goods after regional integration affected national and world welfare. In this exercise, Viner treated customs union formation as an exogenous event.[6] Yet the decision to establish such an arrangement has remained a puzzle for welfare-based trade models because the motives

5. Mansfield and Milner 1999, 604.

6. Viner found that customs unions could have positive or negative welfare effects on members and nonmembers based on the net of "trade creation" and "trade diversion." Viner 1950.

to stop partway along the road to free trade are unclear: eliminating all tariffs is always a better option for governments seeking to maximize social welfare, so regional integration is a "second-best" policy.[7] An exception is the case in which customs union enables members to exploit market power over states left out of the group.[8] Yet neither of these endpoints—global free trade or protectionist regional fortresses—plausibly characterizes the integration process. Thus economists concluded years ago that the motives must be "noneconomic."[9]

As in most normative trade models, customs union theory's focus on consumer surplus (welfare) rather than producer surplus (rents) limits its positive explanatory power. Other work, however, examines rent-seeking motives to form trading blocs. These accounts base their assumption that trading blocs reflect rent-seeking pressure on two generalizations: first, the costs of trade creation are concentrated on a small number of producers while the costs of trade diversion are diffused across a wide range of consumers; second, protectionist groups can form alliances more effectively than antiprotectionist groups.[10] As a result, trading blocs are likely to be weighted in favor of exporters that benefit from enhanced protection, because governments seeking to ensure political support have incentives to grant special exemptions to import-competing sectors that would lose protection.[11] Domestic groups in free trade agreements can also extend trade barriers to the regional level by establishing rules of origin against nonmembers or by abusing dispute settlement provisions.[12]

A minority view counters that trading blocs reduce rent-seeking pressure or strengthen protrade lobbies, which facilitates more extensive trade liberalization. If regional integration establishes a common external tariff or transfers authority to supranational institutions, then protectionist national groups must reorganize at the regional level, where they will be larger, less homogenous, and more susceptible to free riding.[13] Import-competing sectors might also lose political influence at the national level if their output contracts after regional trade liberalization.[14] Third-country exporters injured by trade diversion will lobby to join trading blocs to regain lost markets.[15] For developing countries, regional arrangements provide a commitment device to "lock in" economic reforms, which strengthens exporters and businesses with multinational ties, and weakens import-competing firms and

7. As Kemp and Wan explain, countries *should* have "an incentive to form and enlarge customs unions . . . until the world is one big customs union, that is, until world free trade prevails." Kemp and Wan 1976, 96.

8. Mundell 1964 was the first to analyze the terms-of-trade effects of trading blocs. Recent work includes Krugman 1991; and Saxonhouse 1993.

9. Johnson 1965. Frankel 1997, chap. 10, reviews the extensive literature on the economic theory of customs unions.

10. Bhagwati 1993.

11. See Grossman and Helpman 1995; and Hirschman 1981, chap. 12.

12. See Krueger 1997; and Levy and Srinivasan 1996.

13. Olson 1982.

14. Richardson 1993.

15. Oye 1992.

state-owned enterprises.[16] Finally, regional trade agreements can help to overcome status quo bias when groups are uncertain about the size of the adjustment costs associated with liberalizing trade multilaterally.[17]

However, many "stepping-stone" accounts of regional integration fail to explain why states pursue trade liberalization regionally rather than multilaterally. These arguments present trading bloc formation as an exogenous event that subsequently alters the preferences or organizational abilities of pro-trade and protectionist interests, but most of the approaches lack an endogenous mechanism to explain why groups prefer regionalism in the first place. Owners of locally abundant factors of production and producers of exported goods receive more benefits from multilateral or unilateral trade liberalization; it is not clear why they would prefer a "second-best" policy unless better alternatives are not feasible.[18] At the same time, regional trade liberalization erodes protection for locally scarce factors and import-competing producers, so these actors are likely to prefer trade barriers at the national rather than the regional level. Because regional arrangements involve opportunity costs for competitive producers and adjustment costs for uncompetitive producers, "stumbling bloc" outcomes seem more plausible under neoclassical assumptions (that is, perfect competition and constant returns to scale).

To fill this gap, recent work incorporates imperfect competition and economies of scale into explanations for trading blocs. This research emphasizes incentives to ensure a stable market and to capture excess profits in industries with increasing returns to scale.[19] Barriers to intraregional trade are costly when they deter firms from introducing technologies requiring larger-than-national markets to exploit economies of scale.[20] Regional integration offers especially large benefits to small-country firms, which can move down their cost curves once they gain access to a larger customer base.[21] While some analysts surmise that industries with increasing returns to scale are likely to support protectionism in trading blocs, others argue that the main beneficiaries of regional arrangements tend to be strong advocates for multilateral trade liberalization.[22]

16. Tornell and Esquivel 1997.

17. Wei and Frankel 1996.

18. As a result, some of these accounts add neoliberal assumptions that large numbers and high transaction costs in multilateral negotiations inhibit progress toward global free trade. On this approach, see Haggard 1997; and Yarbrough and Yarbrough 1992.

19. See Froot and Yoffie 1993; Busch and Milner 1994; and Milner 1997.

20. Mattli 1999, 46–47, 77–80.

21. Casella 1996.

22. Froot and Yoffie 1993 find strong incentives to protect industries with increasing returns to scale because, they argue, capital will be less mobile across borders. Busch and Milner counter that "the firms most likely to demand regionalism are also the least likely to favor external protectionism." In this view, firms favorable to free trade seek regional arrangements because multilateral negotiations fail to liberalize trade enough to fully exploit economies of scale (presumably because of high contracting costs). Busch and Milner 1994, 273. Milner's subsequent work, however, suggests that trading blocs are designed to exclude third-country firms. She also predicts that industries with increasing returns to scale will receive more extensive trade liberalization in regional than in multilateral agreements. Milner 1997, 85–86, 100.

These studies offer a promising approach to domestic support for regional arrangements. They also present an alternative way of thinking about the political economy of trade. Recent surveys underscore the growing recognition that factors omitted from standard trade models—economies of scale, product differentiation, and intra-industry trade—are theoretically and empirically important in contemporary trade politics.[23] Yet empirical work to date has not rigorously examined these variables on a large number of cases.[24]

I build on this work by examining the effects of increasing returns to scale and systematically testing their importance in trade lobbying and trade policy. In doing so, I seek both to provide a persuasive account of the formation of trading blocs and to further advance the case for the inclusion of new variables in the political economy of trade.

Domestic Groups and Regional Trade Liberalization

My analytical framework examines how dynamic considerations cause domestic groups to lobby for regional trade liberalization. The static, once-and-for-all effect of trade creation and trade diversion is not a strong motive for regional integration. Rather, it is the opportunity for businesses to reorganize their operations that makes regional trade liberalization politically attractive. The gains from reallocating factors of production are most significant when manufacturing technologies and processes require access to a larger-than-national market to be profitable. Firms will exert political pressure to eliminate barriers to trade and investment that restrict the range of the market available to them if they can subsequently restructure to employ these technologies more effectively. Firms unable to make use of these technologies, however, will be less interested in regional integration; indeed, these firms might have reasons to oppose it.

Examining the dynamic effects of trading blocs helps to explain why some domestic groups lobby for regional trade liberalization while others fight it. I make two specific arguments. First, producers support trading blocs when access to the regional market enables them to take advantage of economies of scale. Firms producing goods with steep cost curves seek regional arrangements because increased production for an enlarged market yields significant reductions in unit costs. If cost curves are flat, however, longer production runs will have little or no effect on unit costs, and businesses will be less interested in a larger market.

Second, producers support trading blocs when an integrated regional market enables them to move stages of production across borders. Because barriers to regional trade and investment restrict opportunities to take advantage of differences between countries in wages, skills, or capital costs, firms seek regional arrange-

23. See Alt et al. 1996, 693–95; and Frieden and Rogowski 1996, 28–30.

24. An exception is Dick 1994. Milner and Yoffie 1989 provide case studies of strategic trade policy and corporate trade preferences.

ments if they can redeploy intermediate production between labor-rich and labor-scarce areas. Firms unable to move production abroad are not affected by these barriers and therefore have less incentive to push for regional trade liberalization.

Studies based on standard trade models ignore these dynamic effects, because they are derived from endowment-based theories of inter-industry trade.[25] However, this type of trade is declining in importance. For one, trade less often follows the conventional pattern of countries with different factor endowments exchanging labor-intensive for capital-intensive goods. Instead, countries with similar endowments frequently exchange similar products. This is inconsistent with the mobile-factors trade model; it also confounds the distinction in the specific-factors approach between export-oriented and import-competing industries. Economies of scale and product differentiation are the factors most commonly adduced to explain this apparent anomaly.

In addition, production is not country-specific: it is subdivided and dispersed across borders, with different stages located where they can be most efficiently performed. Firms engaging in "production sharing" or "outsourcing"[26] across borders transfer intermediate goods between countries, often (though not always) through intrafirm trade. Technological innovation has made this practice increasingly common: 40 percent of U.S. trade involves affiliates of the same multinational firm rather than separate, independent firms.[27] The ease with which owners of capital can move labor-intensive tasks to areas where labor is abundant challenges endowment-based trade models and confounds distinctions between export-oriented and import-competing, because two-way trade occurs as part of an integrated production process within a single firm.

While theoretical accounts of these trends are growing, economics has not yet produced a "new" trade model with the rigor to supplant established approaches.[28]

25. In the "mobile factors" (Heckscher-Ohlin-Samuelson) model, trade divides factors of production, capital versus labor, with the factor of production that is abundant in a given economy experiencing an increase in its income and the scarce factor of production suffering a reduction in its income. This suggests that abundant factors support trade liberalization and scarce factors support trade protection. In the "specific factors" (Ricardo-Viner) model, trade-related domestic cleavages divide sectors, which lobby for trade policies based on whether they are export-oriented or import-competing. Predictions about income distribution in both approaches derive from the Heckscher-Ohlin theory of inter-industry trade (at least in principle). They simply make different assumptions about the ability of factors to move between industries in response to relative price changes. See Rogowski 1989; Magee, Brock, and Young 1989; Frieden 1991; and Hiscox 2001.

26. One study defines outsourcing as "the practice in which firms divide production into stages and then locate each stage in the country where it can be performed at least cost." This includes offshore procurement from affiliated firms as well as unaffiliated suppliers. Feenstra, Hanson, and Swenson 2000, 85. I use outsourcing (or "offshore assembly") specifically to describe the process by which goods sold in the domestic market are first shipped abroad and then returned after value has been added. "Production sharing" more generally refers to linkages in the manufacturing process between producers in different countries, regardless of the market of origin or final sale.

27. Figures for 1994 are 36.3 percent for U.S. exports and 42.7 percent for U.S. imports. Calculated from the sources on intrafirm trade in Appendix 1.

28. Helpman and Krugman 1985 and 1989 attempt to integrate these new approaches into standard trade theory. Also see Krugman 1986; and Grossman 1993. The ensuing discussion draws heavily from these sources.

Efforts to incorporate these factors into empirical work on the political economy of trade therefore rest on a less secure theoretical foundation. Nevertheless, it is possible to draw analytical first principles from this literature to illuminate how domestic actors evaluate their trade preferences when there are opportunities to take advantage of economies of scale or production sharing. Below I discuss the logic underlying my expectations about domestic support for regional trading blocs, before evaluating these hypotheses against the real-world behavior of organized groups.

Economies of Scale

When there are economies of scale, manufacturing costs per unit decline as a firm produces more of a product.[29] Declining unit costs enable firms to earn more "excess profits"[30] the larger their scale of output. This creates a tendency toward concentration and imperfect competition: normally there are few producers, each one an oligopolist or monopolist, with profits commensurate to their scale of production and the number of competitors in the market.

Economies of scale are important to the political economy of trade because trade enlarges the available market, which affects plant size. For example, trade encourages firms to expand production runs, increase capacity utilization, rationalize production facilities, and pursue mergers and acquisitions. As one source puts it, "[s]teady economic expansion . . . tends to reduce the incidence of uneconomically small operations in oligopolistic industries."[31] An enlarged market therefore can trigger a reduction in unit costs and yield larger excess profits.[32]

Recent work on the formation of trading blocs focuses on the size of domestic markets, arguing that producers reap large gains from regional trade liberalization when their home market is small compared to the minimum efficient scale (MES).[33] In its present form, however, this argument is problematic. Both Milner and Casella suggest that the scale firms have attained before regional integration is endogenous to market size: small-country firms produce on a relatively smaller scale than large-country firms because they lack sufficient domestic demand to achieve high-volume production. But this produces a contradiction: on one hand, small-country firms will be more favorable to trading blocs because they experience a

29. In other words, if a firm with economies of scale doubles its inputs of capital and labor, it will more than double its output of finished goods.

30. I use "excess profit" instead of the more conventional "rent" to avoid confusion between motives for protection in alternative trade models. Excess profits exist when price exceeds marginal cost, so producers earn more excess profits the greater their price-cost margin. When there are economies of scale, a firm's scale of production determines its marginal costs; at the same time, markets often are imperfect, so prices tend to exceed marginal costs. Thus each increase in scale reduces a firm's marginal costs and increases its excess profits, all else equal.

31. Bain 1959, 166–67.

32. I assume that firms have not reached the "minimum efficient scale," or the scale of output that minimizes unit costs. In other words, they must remain on the downward sloping portion of their cost curve.

33. See Milner 1997; and Casella 1996.

larger increase in their available market after regional integration; on the other hand, small-country firms will be more resistant to trading blocs because they anticipate competitive pressure from large-country firms in the region after trade liberalization.[34] Thus approaches linking scale and market size cannot explain the formation of trading blocs, as they imply that small-country firms will want national protection and large-country firms will prefer global free trade; neither group has an incentive to lobby for trade liberalization regionally.[35]

Moreover, access to a larger market reduces unit costs and creates excess profits only when the returns to scale are large. If the returns to scale are small, firms limited from reaching MES by small domestic markets will not have higher unit costs than MES firms; they also will not earn excess profits if they expand production. Economies of scale, by definition, require nontrivial returns to larger plant size. Yet the extent of the returns to scale is not captured in home market size or in the MES.

Thus preferences for trading blocs depend on the returns to scale—or, stated technically, the elasticity of unit costs with respect to plant size. The difference in unit costs between producers of different sizes denotes the "penalty," or the "cost in terms of reduced efficiency," when economies of scale are not fully exploited.[36] This suggests that producers gain more from a marginal increase in plant size the steeper the cost curve: each marginal increase in plant size yields more excess profits the larger the returns to scale. When cost curves are steep, producers reap large benefits from the opportunity to trade in a broader market. When cost curves are flat, an increased scale of output yields little reduction in unit costs and few additional excess profits.[37]

If firms benefit more from a marginal increase in plant size the steeper the cost curve, then producer support for regional integration increases with the size of the returns to scale. In this case, trading blocs provide two important benefits. On the one hand, regional trade liberalization opens new markets. This allows firms to reduce unit costs as output increases for export to regional partners.[38] On the other hand, trading blocs retain barriers against outside competition. External protection ensures that firms in the region fully internalize the scale effects of larger markets,

34. For example, Milner argues that firms with large home markets will be less interested in regional arrangements because "they may be close to efficient scale already." Milner 1997, 85. However, she later asserts that "IRS industries which lack competitiveness prior to the [Customs Union] . . . are going to be far more hesitant . . . than are the more competitive ones" and will attempt to "block liberalization . . . [because] these industries intensely prefer and demand protection." See Milner 1997, 97, 99–100.

35. In arguing that the scale firms have attained is not merely a function of home market size, I have not resolved whether firms with unexploited economies of scale might nonetheless oppose regional trade liberalization in anticipation of competitive pressure from larger rivals in the trading bloc. As a result, further empirical testing is needed to determine whether my argument applies only to firms with large domestic markets and to trading blocs with low internal adjustment costs (for example, because of high levels of trade diversion relative to trade creation).

36. Bain 1959, 149.

37. Silberston 1972.

38. Corden 1972.

creating opportunities to leapfrog foreign competitors through "import protection as export promotion."[39]

This analytical approach suggests that regional trade liberalization provides benefits not attainable through multilateral trade liberalization: under most-favored nation rules, external trade barriers must be reduced equally for the imports of all countries; trading blocs, however, allow external protection to remain in place. Particularly when barriers to trade and investment have fragmented production in a region, firms will tend to prefer regional trade liberalization to insulate them against external competition during the transition period while manufacturing facilities are being rescaled for a larger market.

In sum, producers are more likely to seek trading blocs the more they anticipate exploitable gains from trade. These gains are first and foremost a function of the returns to scale. If returns to scale are large, producers will support regional trade liberalization to increase output, reduce unit costs, and earn more excess profits. If returns to scale are small, producers will have little interest in the formation of a trading bloc because they derive no benefits from longer production runs or increased capacity utilization.

Regional Production Sharing

Production sharing involves the subdivision of different stages of manufacturing in different countries. This occurs when cross-national differences—usually disparities in factor endowments—allow certain production processes to be completed more efficiently abroad than at home.[40] In high-wage countries such as the United States, manufactured goods with labor-intensive aspects tend to face competition from developing countries, especially when technology is standardized, production is difficult to automate, and final sales are price-sensitive. In such cases, moving labor-intensive tasks to low-wage areas enables firms to reduce input prices and cut factor costs. When intermediate production moves to a location where it can be performed more efficiently, the capital, skill, and technology-intensive processes remaining in the home country become more profitable.

Firms engaged in production sharing across borders transfer goods between a corporate parent and its foreign affiliates through intrafirm trade, or import these inputs from unaffiliated suppliers.[41] Intermediate components tend to be highly specialized and unique to a production process; many firms invest large sunk costs in products and processes for which no external market exists. Adjusting to any disruption in the flow of inputs across borders requires firms to externalize the market for intermediate goods—in other words, share proprietary technology and informa-

39. Krugman 1993.

40. Differences in institutional, legal, and regulatory environments might also motivate production sharing. For example, restrictions on unionization and lax environmental regimes make export processing zones attractive for firms faced with strict regulatory rules in their home country.

41. Firms rely on intrafirm trade instead of unaffiliated suppliers to retain control over highly specialized capital, technology, and skills. Caves 1996 provides an excellent summary.

tion with local suppliers, which raises the risk of opportunism and market failure—or interrupt the production process altogether. As a result, firms involved in production sharing, especially those that own their suppliers, tend to lack adaptability because their demand for intermediate goods is insensitive to market- or policy-induced changes in price. Measures to reduce the costs and risks associated with cross-border trade, therefore, provide large benefits to firms engaged in production sharing.

Geographic proximity is a key factor in production sharing. Multinationals tend to focus on region-specific sourcing, manufacturing, and marketing because often there are diseconomies of scale in global production networks.[42] Locations closer to the corporate parent offer a number of benefits: lower transport costs in the movement of goods between home and host countries; easier coordination with components suppliers for firms that maintain low inventories and rely on just-in-time delivery systems; and shorter lead times when firms must adapt quickly to changes in demand or consumer tastes. As a result, production sharing primarily crosses borders between neighboring (or nearby) countries.

Most large U.S. businesses have established regionally integrated production networks in North America during the past thirty years. The geographic proximity of these networks to the U.S. market helps to explain why production sharing promotes interest in trading blocs but not multilateral trade liberalization. The most important concern for firms engaged in production sharing is not to liberalize trade worldwide, but to liberalize trade across the borders that link their separate investments. Moreover, free trade in goods alone is not enough to sustain regional production networks; firms also need to have national standards harmonized, trade-related investment measures eliminated, restrictions on equity ownership relaxed, dispute settlement procedures established, and protection of intellectual property enhanced. Multilateral negotiations on these sorts of behind-the-border trade barriers have not fared well to date. If production sharing is internal to a region anyway, regional and bilateral arrangements will be an attractive institutional framework for liberalizing this sort of trade. The potential benefits of liberalization are maximized, and the negotiating costs minimized, when it occurs regionally rather than through multilateral organizations.

Summary of Expectations

Figure 1 summarizes my expectations about the factors that encourage firms to seek trading blocs. First, business groups are more likely to lobby for regional trade liberalization the larger the returns to scale in production. Second, business groups are more likely to lobby for regional trade liberalization the more closely integrated firms are with foreign suppliers through production sharing across borders. Thus I expect Type 1 sectors to exert the most intense pressure for regional trade liberalization, because this creates opportunities to take advantage of economies of scale and to reduce the costs of outsourcing. Types 2 and 4 also derive

42. Wells 1992.

Returns to scale	Regional production sharing: High	Regional production sharing: Low
Large	(1) **Intense** lobbying for trading blocs	(2) **Moderate** lobbying for trading blocs
Small	(4) **Moderate** lobbying for trading blocs	(3) **No** lobbying for trading blocs (opposition likely)

FIGURE 1. *Hypotheses on business group lobbying for trading blocs*

benefits from a trading bloc, either in terms of longer production runs or increased outsourcing, and are expected to show moderate support for regional free trade. Type 3 sectors have few incentives to seek trading blocs because expanding their scale of output does not reduce unit costs, nor can they move production across borders. While sectors with low comparative costs might nonetheless back regional trade liberalization as a "second-best" option, those with high comparative costs will oppose regional free trade.

Trading Blocs and Capital-Labor Cleavages

This framework complements standard trade models, though it is not derived from them.[43] My assumptions about factor mobility are consistent with specific-factors approaches.[44] Work on industrial organization finds that scale effects and entry barriers tend to coexist.[45] Studies of the multinational enterprise also emphasize specific assets, entry barriers, and imperfect competition.[46] While to date these theories have not been formally integrated, they point in the same direction: high levels of factor specificity.[47]

43. Helpman and Krugman 1985 and 1989 emphasize similarities between imperfect competition and standard trade models.

44. My argument differs from studies based on the specific factors model in that it attempts to deduce the trade preferences of sectors from their returns to scale and their involvement in production sharing. These variables, I contend, illuminate elements of trade preferences—lobbying related to trading blocs—that are not fully accounted for by observing levels of import competition and export dependence.

45. See Stigler 1968; and Caves and Porter 1976.

46. Caves 1996.

47. In fact, the framework implies high levels of factor specificity that could produce firm- rather than sector-based lobbying, because these are characteristics internal to firms rather than to sectors as a whole. Hiscox notes that "as economies of scale become more important in production, not only do broad class coalitions become less likely in trade politics, but divisions may also emerge between individual firms within the same sector." Hiscox 2001, 36. At the same time, the analysis below finds predominantly sector-based lobbying, suggesting that firm-specific characteristics are more likely to operate at the associational level than theory would suggest.

It is also possible to develop the implications of this framework for labor unions. Standard trade models predict that capital and labor divide over trade when factors of production are mobile but unite when factors are industry-specific. Evidence of high factor specificity as economies become more specialized suggests that capital and labor are likely to cohere in their trade lobbying.[48]

In addition to the inter-industry mobility of capital and labor, however, international mobility—especially for capital in an era when foreign direct investment is substantial—is also a consideration. When firms are, like most workers, immobile internationally, capital and labor will tend to unite because of factor specificity at the industry level. But firm-specific capital, embodied in the technology, managerial skills, and knowledge base of a company, is not always nation-specific. As a result, the restructuring opportunities some producers anticipate as a favorable effect of regional trade liberalization often impose dislocation costs on labor, especially low-skill workers in high-wage countries, when corporate activities cross borders.

In the case of production sharing, which occurs when producers in labor-scarce markets move labor-intensive tasks to low-wage areas abroad, antagonism between the interests of capital and labor is apparent. Policies that make it easier to move labor-intensive processes offshore create two kinds of unfavorable labor market outcomes for low-skill workers in high-wage countries. First, outsourcing shifts the demand for labor within industries from low-skill to high-skill workers. This in turn generates wage inequality, as Stolper-Samuelson effects reduce the real wages of low-skill labor and raise the real wages of high-skill labor.[49] Second, policies that make it easier for firms to substitute foreign for domestic labor increase the elasticity of demand for low-skill labor, which can create localized unemployment or depress the nonwage aspects of compensation.[50] The prospect that firms are likely to reorganize after regional trade liberalization will cause workers to anticipate changes in wages and benefits favorable to high-skill workers and harmful to low-skill workers. Thus labor unions, which tend to represent low-skill workers, are likely to oppose trading blocs in industries where mobile capital can engage in production sharing.

When specialization is based on economies of scale, labor market outcomes are ambiguous. The gains from trade based on economies of scale are distributed more evenly between capital and labor to the extent that both factors are industry-specific.[51] This suggests that if firms are able to expand output, local labor in the sectors gaining those economies of scale will benefit. In this case, firms and their

48. Magee finds support for the specific-factors model in three empirical tests. Magee, Brock, and Young 1989, chap. 7. Hiscox 2001 suggests these are poor tests, but his evidence of low (and declining) factor mobility and sector-based trade coalitions confirms Magee's preliminary conclusion.

49. This assumes that low-skill foreign workers are substitutes rather than complements for low-skill U.S. labor. If outsourcing increases the demand for low-skill U.S. labor, then the preferences of labor unions are not so clear-cut. Feenstra and Hanson 1996 show that low-skill foreign and U.S. labor are indeed substitutes, not complements.

50. Rodrik 1997.

51. Krugman 1981.

workers will tend to unite in favor of regional trade liberalization—provided that the benefits of liberalization are specific to both sector and location, as they are when firms do not operate factories in multiple countries within a region.

If firms produce at several locations, however, then divisions between capital and labor are likely to emerge.[52] Multinationals can fully internalize the costs and benefits of restructuring as they rationalize facilities in different places to concentrate production for the regional market, expanding product lines in some plants and closing them down in others. But many of the adjustment costs are externalized to low-skill workers. Even if the net effect of these adjustments on industry-level employment turn out to be positive or neutral, workers experience dislocation costs unless they can easily move between contracting and expanding plants. Moreover, when economic activities shift location in response to the new trading environment, it is impossible to predict at the outset which will concentrate in the core and which will move to the periphery.[53] Low-skill workers who might benefit are less likely to organize because it is not known which plants will expand and which will be downsized *ex ante.* Because labor cannot be certain about corporate intentions, unions representing low-skill workers are likely to exhibit a status quo bias against policies that encourage firms to specialize their operations between labor-rich and labor-scarce countries.

In sum, unified support for regional free trade is likely to occur only in industries in which economies of scale are significant and production is country-specific. In industries where offshore manufacturing is common or specialization based on economies of scale crosses borders, cleavages are likely to emerge between capital and labor, and workers will not share the interests of their employers in regional trade liberalization. When production sharing is not an option and economies of scale are absent, capital and labor will tend to join forces *against* regional trade liberalization.

NAFTA Lobbying in the United States: Empirical Analysis

Production sharing and large returns to scale are common in U.S. manufacturing. Yet their importance varies across sectors. It is therefore useful to describe my methods of measurement and to review the data to provide insights into the sectors most likely to benefit from regional trade liberalization.

Economies of Scale: Data and Measurement

Measuring differences across sectors in the size and significance of economies of scale is not easy. "Survivor tests," which observe changes over time in the distribution of plants across size classes, produce crude (and often indeterminate) re-

52. See Helleiner 1977.
53. Krugman and Venables 1990.

sults. Engineering production functions provide valuable information about the MES and the slope of the average cost curve for various products, but data is available for only a handful of cases.[54] Recent empirical work on the political economy of trade measures the MES as the percentage of industry output in the typical plant in the median size class. But this does not capture the critical variable, the size of the returns to scale.[55]

This study estimates the slope of average cost curves by measuring how value added per worker varies in plants of different sizes, a method developed by Hufbauer.[56] In this method, the elasticity of unit costs with respect to plant size is the value of the exponent α in the equation:

$$v = kn^{\alpha}$$

where v is the ratio of value added per worker in plants employing n persons to the average value added per worker for all plants in the sector;[57] k is a constant; n is the average number of employees per plant in the given size class; and α is the scale elasticity parameter. Taking the logarithm of both sides:

$$\log(v) = k + \alpha \log(n)$$

Regressing $\log(v)$ on $\log(n)$ for each establishment size class yields an estimate of α. This estimate produces positive values for economies of scale and negative values for diseconomies of scale.[58]

Table 1 displays the results of these calculations for twenty-four sectors. Returns to scale tend to be largest in chemicals, electrical and industrial machinery, transportation equipment, nonferrous metals, and certain consumer goods such as tobacco and grain products. In contrast, textiles, apparel, rubber, plastic, and leather

54. See Bain 1959; Stigler 1968; Scherer 1970; Pratten 1971; and Scherer et al. 1975.

55. This proxy also suffers from measurement error because it assumes the typical plant in the median size class produces at the same level relative to MES in every sector. Variation across sectors therefore reflects the number of plants, the number of distinct products manufactured, and the degree of industrial concentration—not differences in the minimum efficient scale. Trefler 1993 and Milner 1997 use this measure.

56. My discussion follows the exposition in Hufbauer 1970, 178–79.

57. Value added per worker is a standard measure of industry-level rents in work on rent sharing between capital and labor, such as Katz and Summers 1989.

58. Hufbauer discusses possible sources of measurement error. Because we cannot control for exogenous influences on value added, this method might obtain biased estimates for α when there is a systematic relationship between plant size and (1) product type (for example, if larger plants make higher value-added products); (2) factor inputs (for example, if larger plants employ higher-skill labor and use more machinery); (3) technology (for example, if larger plants are more modern); and (4) monopoly power (for example, if firms with larger plants have more freedom to raise prices). Hufbauer 1970, 179–81. Variation in exogenous influences on profits and costs is a problem for all measures of economies of scale, as no two plants are identical in all respects except for size. (On this issue, see Bain 1959; Stigler 1968; Scherer 1970; Pratten 1971; and Scherer et al. 1975.) Thus there could be some randomly distributed measurement error, but any potential bias is not likely to be systematically correlated with the dependent variables examined below.

TABLE 1. *Returns to scale in U.S. manufacturing*

Economies of scale		*Diseconomies of scale*	
Sector (SIC)	α	*Sector (SIC)*	α
Tobacco products (211)	0.393	Fabricated rubber products (306)	−0.017
Flat glass (321)	0.302	Miscellaneous apparel (238)	−0.027
Grain mill products (204)	0.225	Petroleum refining (291)	−0.027
Agricultural chemicals (287)	0.195	Hats, caps, and millinery (235)	−0.037
Electronic components and accessories (367)	0.184	Men's and boy's suits and coats (231)	−0.050
Special industry machinery (355)	0.175	Footwear cut stock (313)	−0.052
Primary nonferrous metals (333)	0.163	Industrial inorganic chemicals (281)	−0.054
Drugs (283)	0.154	Wool fabrics (223)	−0.061
Computer and office equipment (357)	0.152	Men's and boy's furnishings (232)	−0.093
Photographic equipment and supplies (386)	0.148	Girl's and children's outerwear (236)	−0.171
Farm and garden machinery (352)	0.144	Leather gloves and mittens (315)	−0.172
Motor vehicles and equipment (371)	0.141	Women's and children's undergarments (234)	−0.193

tend to have small or even negative returns to scale. While the former group would benefit from access to a larger market through regional trade liberalization, the latter group would derive little or no gain from the opportunity to increase the scale of output.

Production Sharing: Data and Measurement

Since the mid-1960s, production abroad has expanded U.S. trade in intermediate goods, especially with labor-rich countries. Two factors have encouraged firms to integrate vertically across borders to take advantage of factor price differentials. First, many firms were in sectors that began to experience import competition from Asia. Second, most produced goods with technological characteristics conducive to off-shore manufacturing: production techniques divisible into stages that could be performed at different times and locations; low-skill labor-intensive components and processes that could use cheaper foreign labor; and low weight-to-value ratios for intermediate goods, which create low shipping costs between separate locations.[59]

These characteristics are difficult to measure directly. An alternative is to infer production sharing from trade flows. In this analysis, I employ two alternative measures. The first is intrafirm trade: Table 2 presents intrafirm trade by U.S. firms in 1989 as a percentage of domestic sales (columns 1 and 3) and the proportion of

59. Grunwald and Flamm 1985.

TABLE 2. *Intrafirm trade in U.S. manufacturing*

High intrafirm trade			*Low intrafirm trade*		
Sector (SIC)	*Total (1)*	*Region (2)*	*Sector (SIC)*	*Total (3)*	*Region (4)*
Computer and office equipment (357)	27.6%	19.7%	Paper and allied products (261–67)	1.6%	83.7%
Motor vehicles and equipment (371)	24.3%	95.7%	Leather and leather products (311–19)	1.4%	37.6%
Electronic components and accessories (367)	22.6%	31.3%	Miscellaneous manufacturing (391–99)	1.1%	38.9%
Farm and garden machinery (352)	10.4%	24.7%	Apparel (231–39)	1.1%	27.8%
Construction, mining, and materials-handling machinery (353)	9.3%	45.3%	Stone, clay, and nonmetallic mineral products (324–29)	0.9%	69.1%
Drugs (283)	6.7%	20.5%	Plastics products (308)	0.9%	42.3%
Industrial chemicals and synthetics (281–82, 286)	5.8%	45.8%	Textiles (221–29)	0.6%	61.5%
Communications, audio and video equipment (365–66)	5.7%	45.5%	Furniture and fixtures (251–59)	0.6%	80.8%
Household appliances (363)	5.7%	79.9%	Lumber and wood products (241–49)	0.5%	94.7%
Instruments and related products (381–87)	4.6%	27.7%	Ferrous metals (331–32)	0.2%	62.4%

this trade that is cross-national with Mexico and Canada (columns 2 and 4). The data show that firms producing computer equipment, motor vehicles, and electronic components (for example, semiconductors or integrated circuits) engage in the largest amounts of intrafirm trade. Trade with affiliates abroad is less common in furniture, lumber, paper, nonmetallic minerals, and miscellaneous manufactures. Textiles and apparel recorded large increases in intrafirm trade in the 1980s, but levels remain low relative to total sales.

The second measure is U.S. imports entered under the Offshore Assembly Program (OAP).[60] This measure complements the data on intrafirm trade because it includes subcontracting between unaffiliated parties in addition to trade between affiliated firms. Also, OAP trade is a direct measure of outsourcing for products sold in the U.S. market because these items cross the border twice, as they leave and then reenter the United States. The data is not presented in tabular form because most of the sectors that heavily use the OAP also engage in substantial intrafirm trade—although industries such as apparel, leather, and rubber register moderate levels of OAP trade despite little intrafirm trade. In these industries, many companies outsource abroad, but production processes lack the proprietary capital, technology, and skills that motivate firms to control their suppliers.

Both sets of data show that production sharing, and outsourcing trade more specifically, remains disproportionately within North America. This helps to explain why some firms would be interested in trade liberalization and policy harmonization regionally more than multilaterally. Overall, Mexico and Canada accounted for 60.3 percent of OAP trade in 1987 and 44.0 percent of the foreign content of this trade. Among the industries with above-average levels of offshore assembly, at least one-third of OAP trade occurred in North America in every case except apparel (20.9 percent) and leather (8.9 percent). In addition, 60.5 percent of the intrafirm trade of U.S. firms in 1989 was with Mexico and Canada. As Table 2 illustrates, high levels of intrafirm trade outside the region are prevalent only in computer and office equipment, electronic components, farm and garden machinery, drugs, and instruments—sectors with substantial amounts of trade with North American affiliates as well. While some U.S. firms are closely integrated with affiliates in East Asia, this trade is narrowly concentrated in a few items: computers, consumer electronics, and electronic components.[61] Thus the business constitu-

60. OAP trade is classified under Sections 9802.00.60 and 9802.00.80 of the U.S. Harmonized Tariff System (HTS). Under these chapters, U.S. products exported for processing pay tariffs only on the value added abroad, not on U.S. content, when they are re-imported into the United States. Data from the U.S. International Trade Commission was provided to the author by Robert Feenstra and Deborah Swenson. See Feenstra, Hanson, and Swenson 2000.

61. U.S. firms conducted 7.2 percent of their intrafirm trade with the five principal members of the Association of Southeast Asian Nations (Singapore, Malaysia, Thailand, Indonesia, and the Philippines) and another 3.4 percent with Korea, Taiwan, China, and Hong Kong. In other words, these nine countries amounted to just one-sixth the level of intrafirm trade with Mexico and Canada. Moreover, 93.7 percent of intrafirm trade with ASEAN countries and 71.0 percent of intrafirm trade with Northeast Asia involved machinery and electrical equipment—principally computers, consumer electronics, and electronic components.

ency for agreements to liberalize trade between parent firms and their affiliates outside North America is not as large as the coalition that pushed for free trade with Mexico and Canada.

NAFTA Lobbying: Variables and Data

In this section, I analyze the political debate in the United States over the negotiation and passage of NAFTA to evaluate how well the factors emphasized above explain group preferences toward regional trade liberalization. In 1990, Mexico joined trade negotiations with the United States and Canada. These discussions produced the NAFTA treaty in October 1992. The U.S. Congress ratified NAFTA and its side agreements in November 1993. The treaty was implemented beginning in January 1994.

These three and a half years of negotiation coincided with a lobbying campaign in the United States of equal length, designed to affect the terms of the agreement and then later, its chances for ratification. Because of "fast-track" procedures and the institutional structure of policymaking under the U.S. Constitution, the NAFTA treaty was a product of a three-stage process. In the first stage, interest groups lobbied members of Congress to influence the terms and conditions of delegating trade-negotiating authority to the president. In the second stage, organized interests pressured the U.S. Trade Representative (USTR), the International Trade Commission (ITC), and other executive agencies responsible for formulating trade strategy and conducting negotiations to pursue an agreement favorable to their interests. Proponents of free trade pushed for the elimination of regional tariff and nontariff barriers, as well as other measures relating to intellectual property, foreign investment, and the regulatory treatment of multinationals. Opponents of free trade sought special exemptions for their products and, failing that, the minimum possible trade liberalization. In the third stage, after the treaty and its side agreements were completed, Congress had to approve or reject it.

Congressional committees convened numerous public hearings between June 1990 and November 1993. Many groups testified or provided submissions for the record about their desired objectives for the negotiations and their views of the final treaty. In addition, ITC reports provide information about contacts between organized interests and executive branch agencies. I use this material in Table 3 to evaluate the preferences of sector groups on North American free trade for the dependent variable in an ordered probit analysis. The data are coded at the 3-digit Standard Industry Classification (SIC) level as "1" if representatives of the sector supported regional free trade; "−1" if they opposed regional free trade; and "0" if representatives of the sector did not lobby.[62]

62. I have used two methods for classifying sectors as support (1) or oppose (−1). First, if one or more industry associations testified or submitted material for the record, their position is used to classify the sector's preferences. In rare cases in which industry groups adopted conflicting positions, I have coded preferences based on whether supporters or opponents produced a larger share of industry

TABLE 3. *Definition of variables for NAFTA lobbying*

Variable	*Measurement*	*Sign*
NAFTA LOBBYING	1 if lobbied in support 0 if did not lobby −1 if lobbied in opposition	DV
ECONOMIES OF SCALE	Elasticity of value added per worker with respect to plant size	+
REGIONAL INTRAFIRM TRADE	Intrafirm trade of U.S. corporations with affiliates in Mexico and Canada divided by U.S. sales	+
OFFSHORE ASSEMBLY	Foreign content of imports from Mexico and Canada under HTS Chapter 9802 divided by U.S. sales	+
IMPORT COMPETITION	Imports divided by U.S. consumption	−
LABOR INTENSITY	Wages divided by value added	−
EXPORT DEPENDENCE	Exports divided by U.S. sales	+
INTRA-INDUSTRY TRADE	Index of intra-industry trade	+

If economies of scale and intrafirm trade are important determinants of support for free trade agreements, these variables will be positively signed and statistically significant. To estimate the importance of economies of scale, I use the data on returns to scale discussed previously. For production sharing, I employ (in separate models) both sets of data described above: intrafirm trade with Mexico and Canada divided by U.S. sales; and the foreign content of U.S. imports from Mexico and Canada entered under the OAP divided by U.S. sales.

The ordered probit analysis includes additional variables to estimate a baseline model and to provide statistical controls. These are discussed below.

IMPORT COMPETITION. Empirical tests of endogenous trade models consistently find a positive relationship between import competition and trade protection, as the specific-factors approach predicts. As a result, I expect a negative association between import competition and support for regional trade liberalization. This variable is measured as imports divided by total consumption.

LABOR INTENSITY. Trade in North America reflects, at least in part, wage differentials between the United States and Mexico. While specific-factors approaches assume that trade patterns reflect the comparative cost considerations underlying trade preferences, import competition also depends on a sector's past success at

sales at the 4-digit SIC level. This occurs with SICs 206 (1), 208 (1), and 349 (−1). Second, when only individual firms but not industry associations testified or submitted material for the record, I have used this material to code sector lobbying if there are observed preferences for at least 2 firms responsible for at least 25 percent of industry output. This occurs with SICs 321 (−1), 322 (−1), 323 (−1), 326 (−1), 351 (1), 352 (1), 353 (1), 363 (1), 381 (1), and 386 (1). Industry associations are matched to SIC groups through the "Associations Unlimited" database at ⟨http://infotrac.galenet.com⟩. Firm sales are matched to SIC groups through Gale Research 1990.

securing trade protection and its degree of "natural" protection because of high transport costs or other invisible barriers to trade. Because the NAFTA treaty provoked much debate about labor-cost differences, it is possible that trade preferences responded to the wage structure as well as import competition. Labor intensity, measured as the ratio of wages paid to value added, helps to control for elements of comparative costs not captured in trade patterns. I expect a negative association between labor intensity and support for regional trade liberalization.

EXPORT DEPENDENCE. Specific-factors approaches predict a negative relationship between export dependence and pressure for trade barriers. In addition, case studies establish that groups are more likely to lobby against protection when they have export interests abroad.[63] Thus I expect export-dependent sectors to be more favorable to regional free trade. This variable is measured as the ratio of exports to domestic shipments.[64]

INTRA-INDUSTRY TRADE. Economic models find that intra-industry trade produces fewer adjustment costs than inter-industry trade.[65] In sectors with intra-industry trade, regional trade liberalization allows firms to differentiate their products and specialize for niche markets.[66] As a result, analysts frequently argue that sectors with high levels of intra-industry trade tend to be more favorable to open trade.[67] Others, however, suggest that these sectors are also better able to exert protectionist pressures because they tend to be more concentrated.[68] Thus the effect of intra-industry trade on lobbying for regional trade liberalization is uncertain. This variable is measured as the Grubel-Lloyd index of intra-industry trade.[69]

Statistical Results for NAFTA Lobbying

Statistical results for three ordered probit estimates of NAFTA lobbying appear in Table 4. Model 1 is a baseline version that excludes economies of scale and production sharing. In this model, export dependence is a strong predictor of pro-NAFTA lobbying, as sectors with high export-to-sales ratios were more likely to support regional free trade. Import competition and labor intensity both have a

63. See Milner 1988; and Destler and Odell 1987.

64. An anonymous reviewer has suggested that export dependence and intrafirm trade share variance, because multinational corporations first tend to export before they become involved in intrafirm trade. To alleviate this concern, I regress intrafirm trade on export dependence and enter this variable as the residual.

65. Krugman 1981.

66. Caves 1991.

67. Marvel and Ray 1987.

68. Gilligan 1997.

69. The formula for this index is: $1 - [|\text{exports} - \text{imports}|/(\text{exports} + \text{imports})]$.

TABLE 4. *Ordered probit estimates for NAFTA lobbying*

Variable	*Model 1*	*Model 2*	*Model 3*
ECONOMIES OF SCALE		4.177***	4.228***
		(1.193)	(1.197)
REGIONAL INTRAFIRM TRADE		10.787*	
		(4.299)	
OFFSHORE ASSEMBLY			39.792**
			(15.104)
IMPORT COMPETITION	−2.217*	−2.465**	−2.579**
	(0.889)	(0.949)	(0.953)
LABOR INTENSITY	−3.267**	−2.006	−2.497*
	(1.090)	(1.152)	(1.162)
EXPORT DEPENDENCE	4.339**	3.791*	4.164*
	(1.660)	(1.755)	(1.728)
INTRA-INDUSTRY TRADE	0.224	0.362	0.392
	(0.463)	(0.484)	(0.485)
THRESHOLD 1	−1.894***	−1.215*	−1.476*
	(0.498)	(0.577)	(0.586)
THRESHOLD 2	−0.665	0.110	−0.122
	(0.481)	(0.567)	(0.573)
Log likelihood	−128.28	−119.75	−118.03
Model χ^2	34.10***	51.17***	54.59***
Pseudo R^2	0.117	0.176	0.188

Note: Cell entries are maximum likelihood estimates obtained using ordered probit analysis. Numbers in parentheses are asymptotic standard errors. $N = 134$.
***$p < .001$.
**$p < .01$.
*$p < .05$.

statistically significant negative effect on NAFTA lobbying. Intra-industry trade is positively signed but not significant.

Economies of scale and regional intrafirm trade are added as regressors in Model 2. Both variables are positively signed and statistically significant, suggesting that the desire to concentrate production and expand regional procurement networks was an important consideration for sectors that supported NAFTA. Export dependence also increases support for regional trade liberalization. Import competition continues to be associated with opposition to NAFTA. Labor intensity is negative but is no longer statistically significant. Intra-industry trade remains positive and also nonsigificant.

Model 3 replaces regional intrafirm trade with offshore assembly in Mexico and Canada under the OAP program. The results are nearly identical to Model 2. Offshore assembly, as with regional intrafirm trade, is positive and statistically significant. All other variables maintain the same signs and significance levels, except that labor intensity is now statistically significant.

Returns to Scale	Regional production sharing: High	Regional production sharing: Low
Large	(1) **Intense** lobbying for trading blocs Support: 61.1% Oppose: 5.1%	(2) **Moderate** lobbying for trading blocs Support: 40.6% Oppose: 13.2%
Small	(4) **Moderate** lobbying for trading blocs Support: 28.3% Oppose: 21.8%	(3) **No** lobbying for trading blocs Support: 13.7% Oppose: 39.8%

Note: Cell entries are predicted probabilities from Model 3, Table 4, minus and plus one standard deviation of economies of scale and offshore assembly, holding all other independent variables constant at their mean values.

FIGURE 2. *Business group lobbying for trading blocs: hypotheses and results*

In sum, the baseline version in Model 1 shows that factor-cost considerations reflected in import competition, export dependence, and labor intensity provide a useful first cut in understanding the pattern of support for regional free trade. Nonetheless, Models 2 and 3 confirm that economies of scale and production sharing were significant factors, statistically and substantively, in pro-NAFTA lobbying. Comparing the log likelihood from Model 2 to the restricted version estimated in Model 1, the effect of economies of scale and regional intrafirm trade is significant at the .001 level. A likelihood ratio test for Model 3 and Model 1 also rejects the hypothesis that the coefficients for economies of scale and offshore assembly are simultaneously equal to zero at the .001 level.[70]

To evaluate the substantive effect of intrafirm trade and economies of scale, I translate the maximum likelihood coefficients in Model 3 into predicted probabilities of NAFTA support. These are presented in the interior cells in Figure 2, which returns to the hypotheses presented above. When economies of scale are significant and OAP trade is large, predicted support for NAFTA is 61.1 percent and opposition is only 5.1 percent. This supports the expectation of intense lobbying for regional trade liberalization among sectors with these characteristics. Sectors are still predicted to lobby for NAFTA 40.6 percent of the time when economies of scale are large but regional production sharing is low. This figure falls to 28.3 percent with a high level of OAP trade and small economies of scale. When both of these variables are low, predicted support drops to 13.7 percent and opposition rises to 39.8 percent. Thus the empirical evidence is consistent with my hypotheses about which sectors lobbied for and against free trade in North America.

70. The likelihood ratio test for Model 2 is LR $\chi^2 = 21.49$, $df = 2$, $p < .001$. For Model 3, it is LR $\chi^2 = 24.31$, $df = 2$, $p < .001$.

TABLE 5. *Multinomial logit estimates for NAFTA lobbying*

Variable	*Lobbied no* (−1)	*Did not lobby* (0)	*Lobbied no* (−1)	*Did not lobby* (0)
ECONOMIES OF SCALE	−12.23***	−8.37**	−11.90***	−8.01**
	(3.76)	(3.10)	(3.63)	(2.96)
REGIONAL INTRAFIRM TRADE	−29.96*	−22.36†		
	(12.97)	(11.55)		
OFFSHORE ASSEMBLY			−129.77†	−48.08†
			(72.47)	(28.88)
IMPORT COMPETITION	8.37**	2.20	8.51**	1.84
	(3.25)	(2.55)	(3.16)	(2.39)
LABOR INTENSITY	5.01	2.79	6.20†	3.69
	(3.24)	(2.42)	(3.26)	(2.40)
EXPORT DEPENDENCE	−14.00*	−2.39	−13.83*	−3.79
	(6.75)	(3.45)	(6.37)	(3.37)
INTRA-INDUSTRY TRADE	−0.28	−1.88†	−0.31	−1.90†
	(1.49)	(1.03)	(1.49)	(1.02)
CONSTANT	−1.75	1.20	−2.40	0.67
	(1.83)	(1.24)	(1.80)	(1.21)
Log likelihood	−116.97		−116.04	
Model χ^2	56.71***		58.58***	
Pseudo R^2	0.195		0.202	

Note: Cell entries are maximum likelihood estimates obtained using multinomial logit analysis. Numbers in parentheses are asymptotic standard errors. Lobbying in favor of NAFTA is the comparison group. $N = 134$.
***$p < .001$.
**$p < .01$.
*$p < .05$.
†$p < .10$.

As an additional test of my findings, Table 5 presents multinomial logit results for Models 2 and 3.[71] The purpose is to establish that sectors that lobbied for regional free trade differ in statistically significant ways from both the opponents of regional trade liberalization and groups that did not lobby. In the first model, NAFTA supporters not only have larger economies of scale and more regional intrafirm trade than opponents, they also differ from groups that did not lobby

71. The ordered probit analysis treats sectors that did not lobby as an intermediate outcome between support and opposition. However, it is possible that not lobbying reflects ordering along two dimensions: the intensity of trade preferences and collective action costs. If so, then this coding method assigns the same value on the dependent variable to groups that favored regional free trade but not intensely enough to lobby, groups that opposed regional free trade but not intensely enough to lobby, and groups that had strong preferences for or against regional free trade but faced prohibitive costs of collective action. This can bias the results of ordinal models. The discussion below indicates that the results in nominal models and in ordinal models are no different, which suggests that not lobbying can be regarded as an intermediate outcome in this case. Thus the choice of statistical model amounts to a trade-off between the efficiency and ease of exposition of the ordered probit model and the correction for potential bias in the multinomial logit model. See Long and Freese 2001, chaps. 5–6.

along these two dimensions. The same is true in the second model, where OAP trade substitutes for regional intrafirm trade. In fact, large economies of scale and greater involvement in production sharing with Mexico and Canada appear to be the principal difference between sectors that supported NAFTA and sectors that did not lobby.

These results help to shed light on the motives for groups to lobby in the first place, separate from the question of whether to support or oppose regional trade liberalization. While sectors that did not lobby had smaller economies of scale and less production sharing than sectors that supported NAFTA, their principal difference from sectors that opposed NAFTA is lack of exposure to import competition.[72] Incorporating additional variables shows that while nonlobbying sectors were less concentrated geographically than NAFTA opponents, they were no less concentrated than NAFTA supporters. In addition, industrial concentration is not statistically significant in any multinomial logit specification. This implies that nonlobbying sectors had no unique difficulty organizing for political activity; they merely had less intense preferences than supporters and opponents of NAFTA.

NAFTA Tariff Phasing: Variables and Data

The preceding analysis provides a demand-side model of lobbying on the NAFTA treaty. But it is also important to know how domestic preferences affect policy outcomes. In a second test of my argument, I examine how sector characteristics filter through the political process to affect the supply of trade protection—or in this case, the supply of trade liberalization.

The dependent variable in this analysis is "NAFTA tariff phasing." This variable has two components. First, Annex 302.2 of the NAFTA treaty specifies a staging schedule for the elimination of U.S. tariffs.[73] The timetable for each item is then weighted by U.S. imports of that item from Mexico in 1992.[74] This produces a tariff-phasing value that varies from 0 to 15.[75] Second, the tariff-phasing value is multiplied by the U.S. tariff rate in 1992. The product of tariff phasing and the

72. The results with sectors that did not lobby as the comparison group are not shown, but are available from the author on request.

73. The staging schedule identifies five tariff phase-out categories specifying equivalent annual tariff reductions down to zero: A (immediately); B (five stages, to 1 January 1998); C (ten stages, to 1 January 2003); C+ (fifteen stages, to 1 January 2008); and D (already duty-free). In addition, there are special categories for exceptional items. Those that apply to U.S. manufactures are: C10 (nine stages, with a 20 percent reduction in year one and no reduction in year two); and Sug (special staging schedules for sugar and sugar products).

74. These figures are re-aggregated from 10-digit Harmonized Tariff System (HTS) to 3-digit SIC codes, using files available at ⟨http://www.macalester.edu/research/economics/PAGE/HAVEMAN/Trade.Resources/TradeConcordances.html⟩.

75. "0" means that all imports were free immediately upon implementation of NAFTA (A), or were already free (D); "15" means that all imports were assigned the maximum 15-year phase-out (C+). In practice, this figure varies from 0 to 12.24. The mean number of years to tariff elimination is 1.54, with a standard deviation of 2.76.

tariff rate is NAFTA tariff phasing. It captures how rapidly each sector was to be exposed to free trade under the NAFTA treaty.[76]

All of the independent variables from the previous section are included.[77] The method of analysis is ordinary least squares (OLS) regression. A complete model of trade policy outcomes, however, requires specifying not only what organized groups demand of the political system, but also how effectively these preferences are articulated at the socioeconomic level and then channeled through political institutions. Because trade policy is nonexcludable in that it affects all firms in a sector, it resembles a public good. This gives rise to collective action problems. To control for this, I incorporate two variables to capture the ability of business groups to mobilize a lobbying campaign.

INDUSTRIAL CONCENTRATION. Theories of collective action suggest that small groups of large firms can more easily absorb the costs and internalize the benefits of their political activity. As a result, they are less likely to suffer from free riding.[78] Because political economists commonly assume that protectionist groups tend to be more capable of overcoming collective action problems, I expect industrial concentration to be positively associated with NAFTA tariff phasing. In other words, more concentrated sectors should be able to obtain longer staging periods to delay their exposure to free trade. This variable is measured as the percentage of industry shipments by the twenty largest firms.

GEOGRAPHIC CONCENTRATION. The relationship between geographic concentration and trade policy is less certain. Early empirical work produces inconsistent results for geographic concentration and trade protection.[79] More recent studies suggest that geographic dispersion is more conducive to trade protection in majoritarian systems, especially those with low party discipline such as the United States.[80] However, Busch and Reinhart find a positive association between geographic concentration and nontariff barriers.[81] I use their measure of geographic concentration and, accordingly, expect a positive relationship with NAFTA tariff phasing.

76. A phasing measure for nontariff barriers (NTBs) might be preferable, because tariffs paid on U.S. manufactures averaged only 4.4 percent in 1992. However, NTBs are difficult to quantify and data is not readily available. Most empirical studies (for example, Busch and Reinhart 1999) use binary dependent variables to denote the presence or absence of a nontariff barrier. Coverage ratios—the percentage of imports in each sector covered by an NTB—are not necessarily superior, as NTBs vary widely in their severity. Finally, many NTBs against manufacturing imports into the Untied States were not addressed in the NAFTA treaty. Antidumping and countervailing duties did not change; NAFTA only established trinational review for *future* administrative trade remedies. Because U.S. tariffs and NTBs tend to complement one another at the sector level, I would expect a measure of NTB liberalization, if one were available, to be correlated with NAFTA tariff phasing. See Ray 1981.

77. Note that NAFTA tariff phasing is reverse-ordered from NAFTA lobbying, so I expect these variables to have the opposite sign from the previous analysis.

78. Olson 1965.

79. See Pincus 1975; Caves 1976; and Lavergne 1983.

80. See McGillivray 1997; and Alt and Gilligan 1994.

81. Busch and Reinhart 1999.

Statistical Results for NAFTA Tariff Phasing

Table 6 presents OLS regression results for NAFTA tariff phasing. Import competition is the strongest factor contributing to a delay in exposure to free trade under NAFTA. Industrial concentration and geographic concentration also contribute to long tariff-phasing schedules, though the latter is not statistically significant. Labor intensity, while positively signed, does not appear to have an important effect. Economies of scale, regional intrafirm trade, and offshore assembly, on the other hand, accelerate a sector's exposure to free trade under the NAFTA treaty. Export dependence and intra-industry trade also are associated with shorter tariff-phasing schedules.

To evaluate the substantive effect of these variables, I use a hypothetical sector that is average in all respects except that it is one standard deviation above the mean on one measure. A one-standard-deviation increase in import competition lengthens the tariff-phasing schedule by 81.0 percent (Model 1) and 75.5 percent (Model 2), or from roughly 3.2 to 5.7 years. Alternatively, a one-standard-deviation

TABLE 6. *OLS regression results for NAFTA tariff phasing*

Variable	*Model 1*	*Model 2*
ECONOMIES OF SCALE	−0.606*	−0.620*
	(0.253)	(0.256)
REGIONAL INTRAFIRM TRADE	−2.766***	
	(0.841)	
OFFSHORE ASSEMBLY		−5.280*
		(2.534)
IMPORT COMPETITION	0.704***	0.670***
	(0.200)	(0.202)
LABOR INTENSITY	0.165	0.206
	(0.274)	(0.279)
EXPORT DEPENDENCE	−0.854*	−0.976*
	(0.382)	(0.382)
INTRA-INDUSTRY TRADE	−0.152	−0.171
	(0.105)	(0.106)
INDUSTRIAL CONCENTRATION	0.398**	0.351*
	(0.141)	(0.140)
GEOGRAPHIC CONCENTRATION	0.435	0.449
	(0.231)	(0.235)
Constant	−0.312	−0.317
	(0.199)	(0.203)
F-ratio	9.24***	8.62***
Adjusted R^2	0.332	0.314

Note: Cell entries are ordinary least squares (OLS) regression coefficients, with standard errors in parentheses. N = 134.
***$p < .005$.
**$p < .01$.
*$p < .05$.

increase in economies of scale accelerates exposure to regional free trade by 43.9 percent (Model 1) and 45.1 percent (Model 2), or from 3.2 to 1.8 years. An increase in regional intrafirm trade shortens tariff phasing by 1.9 years (60.0 percent). Stated differently, while the typical sector continued to enjoy some trade protection until 1997, sectors with high levels of regional intrafirm trade were exposed to free trade just one year after the implementation of the treaty. Higher OAP trade causes tariffs to disappear 1.2 years sooner (37.5 percent).

These results demonstrate that sectors with large economies of scale and substantial production sharing had no reason to delay their exposure to free trade. Moreover, the immediate implementation of free trade allowed them to stop paying tariffs on their intrafirm imports into the United States. These sectors therefore sought rapid tariff phaseouts and consented to losing their own trade protection quickly, with little time allowed for adjustment to the free trade environment. Tariff-phasing schedules in the NAFTA treaty clearly reflect these anticipated lobbying patterns.

Business Versus Labor

The preceding analysis focuses on how the trade interests of business groups affected lobbying and policy. But NAFTA also produced cleavages between capital and labor that are not well explained in standard trade models. In one of his "Three Simple Tests of the Stolper-Samuelson Theorem," Magee examined whether capital and labor were united or divided on the 1973 Trade Act. His finding that capital and labor usually lobbied for the same trade policies—nineteen of twenty-one sectors were located along the protection-protection and free trade-free trade diagonal of a two-by-two chart—is often cited as empirical support for the specific-factors model over the mobile-factors model.[82]

Table 7 replicates Magee's test for NAFTA lobbying. It shows that political cleavages were neither factor-based nor sector-based. Every labor union that testified opposed NAFTA, so the bottom half of the chart is empty. Sector associations and labor unions united only against, but never for, regional trade liberalization, as the sectors that lobbied are evenly split between the protection-protection category and the protection—free trade category.

Figures on intrafirm trade as a percentage of U.S. sales (located in the interior cells) suggest that production sharing splits the preferences of business groups and labor unions, while business and labor are more likely to entertain similar trade preferences when production sharing is less important.[83] Capital-labor divi-

82. Magee's other tests examined whether factors were unanimous in their trade preferences and whether these preferences were independent of their trade orientation. Magee, Brock, and Young 1989, chap. 7.

83. I present figures on global intrafirm trade rather than regional intrafirm trade because I would not expect labor unions to respond differently to trade liberalization with any other country; workers appear to respond to overall levels of offshore assembly more than cross-national production sharing.

TABLE 7. *NAFTA preferences of labor and capital*

		Position of business groups			
		Protection		*Free trade*	
Position of labor unions	*Protection*	Glass products	2.9%	Computers and office equipment	27.6%
		Rubber products	2.9%	Motor vehicles	24.3%
		Leather and leather products	1.4%	Electronic components	22.6%
		Miscellaneous manufactures	1.1%	Farm and garden machinery	10.4%
		Apparel	1.1%	Construction and mining machinery	9.7%
		Stone, clay, and nonmetallic minerals	0.9%	Audio, video, and communications equip.	5.7%
		Plastics products	0.9%	Household appliances	5.7%
		Furniture and fixtures	0.6%	Electrical equip. and machinery	2.3%
		Textiles	0.6%	Steel	0.9%
	Free trade				

Note: Cases include industries in which labor unions and sector associations or individual firms testified on NAFTA. SIC groups appear in Table 2 except glass products (321–23), rubber products (302–6), and electrical equipment and machinery (361–62, 364, 369).

sions existed in all but two cases where intrafirm trade exceeds 2.3 percent of U.S. sales. In contrast, business and labor agreed in all but one case with intrafirm trade less than 1.4 percent.[84]

In sectors in which firms engaged in significant production sharing abroad, labor unions emphasized their concern with job losses to foreign countries. In these sectors, workers were particularly apprehensive about H. Ross Perot's "giant sucking sound" of U.S. jobs moving to Mexico. As intrafirm trade declines in importance, however, labor unions and their employers adopted equally protectionist positions. Both suffered from import competition in labor-intensive products, so both benefited from trade restrictions. In these cases, labor unions objected not to the migration of U.S. firms abroad, but to the pain of import competition unleashed through trade liberalization under the General Agreement on Tariffs and Trade (GATT), the Generalized System of Preferences, the Caribbean Basin Initiative, and free trade agreements with Israel, Canada, and Mexico. Business associations in these sectors echoed their complaints.

This suggests that trade-related cleavages have resurfaced between capital and labor when capital can move across borders.[85] Factor specificity facilitates international mobility when businesses can market proprietary assets through foreign investment. Multinational firms producing across all borders in a region will fully internalize the benefits of increased specialization based on production sharing, because resources are transferred among affiliates and remain within the corporate network. Workers, on the other hand, tend to be immobile between sectors. Production sharing therefore reduces the demand for unskilled labor in high-wage countries, which depresses real wages and generates local unemployment.[86]

NAFTA and Trade Discrimination

The preceding analysis demonstrates that sectors with large economies of scale and substantial production sharing supported regional free trade. This helps to illuminate the more specific considerations that caused U.S. firms to seek trade liberalization regionally instead of globally.[87] Before NAFTA, increasing returns to scale production in North America was not already concentrated. The need to rationalize production facilities was most acute for U.S. firms that manufactured

84. Many producers of textiles and apparel shifted to a more neutral or supportive position on NAFTA after the terms of the treaty—notably its long tariff-staging schedule and restrictive rules of origin for these industries—were publicly released in the Fall of 1992.

85. Helleiner 1977.

86. Feenstra and Hanson 1996. Their analysis implies that wage inequality does not, however, depend on labor specificity within sectors: outsourcing reduces demand for low-skill workers in high-wage countries across the board.

87. The following discussion focuses on the incentives for a free trade agreement with Mexico. Chase 2002 provides an extended analysis of the motives for free trade between the United States and Canada.

goods with steep cost curves in Mexican factories. Though U.S. multinationals avoided the "miniature replica" problem in the maquiladora sector, most also owned inefficient plants in Mexico's interior because regional trade barriers compelled production in several locations rather than the optimal level of concentration.[88]

By the 1980s, excess capacity in U.S.-based plants made small-scale factories in Mexico a severe liability. U.S. firms faced intense competitive pressures from Asia and Western Europe. Considerable scope existed to gain economies of scale if manufacturing operations could be streamlined and rescaled for a regional market. But U.S. firms could not specialize their plants in the region and close down inefficient product lines as long as barriers to trade continued to segment the North American market.

Three considerations caused U.S. firms to prefer regional free trade to multilateral liberalization. First, firms with foreign investment in Mexico needed external trade protection to provide "breathing room" while they restructured. These firms especially wanted trade barriers to shelter their Mexican affiliates during this transition. They therefore pushed for gradual movement to free trade to minimize the disruption to their foreign plants. Computer producers IBM, Hewlett-Packard, and Data General, for example, were "strongly supportive" of a free trade agreement, but they wanted "some phase-in of tariff reductions to prevent dislocation to their Mexican operations."[89] Automakers also requested long tariff phaseouts for their affiliates, which operated "at less than maximum scale of efficiency."[90] In home appliances, GE and Whirlpool (which owned factories in Mexico) sought to delay exposure to free trade, while Amana and Maytag (which did not own factories in Mexico) pushed to accelerate the schedule for tariff elimination.[91] These cases suggest that U.S. firms would not have accepted multilateral tariff reductions which would have undercut their affiliates in Mexico.

Second, trade liberalization is less attractive if third-country multinationals can capture the gains from trade creation by investing in the region. If regional integration induces large-scale entry by outsiders, established producers will be pushed up their cost curves. Because U.S. firms were vulnerable to competitive pressure while they reorganized operations in the region, they wanted guarantees that new entrants would not be able to share in the benefits of free trade without having to pay the same restructuring costs. A regional free trade agreement made it possible to impose entry restrictions on foreign firms.

In the NAFTA treaty, rules of origin to limit the benefits of free trade for Asian and European firms were the principal means for imposing entry requirements. Stringent rules offering NAFTA treatment only to textiles, made of North American yarn, and apparel produced from North American yarn and textiles, muted some

88. See Peres 1990; and U.S. International Trade Commission 1990.
89. U.S. International Trade Commission 1990, 2.7.
90. U.S. House of Representatives 1993, 147–50.
91. U.S. International Trade Commission 1993, 16.2 fn.3.

of the opposition to regional free trade among business associations in textiles and apparel. Automakers received a 62.5 percent origin rule to force Japanese multinationals to source inputs locally in return for free trade privileges. Special provisions also required the production of picture tubes in North America to deny duty-free treatment for "snap-together" television receivers assembled by Asian firms.[92] These entry requirements could not have been established in a multilateral treaty. Yet a lobbying campaign to liberalize trade would have been more difficult to mobilize without discrimination to ensure excludable benefits for incumbents.

Third, free trade in North America was necessary, but not sufficient, for the restructuring U.S. multinationals desired to occur. These firms also needed freer access to government procurement markets, fewer equity restrictions on foreign investment, and improved standards for the protection of intellectual property. Most importantly, industrial policies and regulatory rules for foreign investors distorted regional production networks by forcing multinational firms to purchase high-cost local inputs or subsidize unprofitable exports to comply with government mandates. The Uruguay Round and the abortive Multilateral Agreement on Investment did not effectively address foreign investment and trade-related investment measures. Thus regional arrangements facilitate more extensive liberalization than is attainable multilaterally.

Pressure from U.S. multinationals for exclusive provisions in the NAFTA treaty highlights the practical difficulty of liberalizing behind-the-border regulatory measures in multilateral negotiations. Mexico's industrial programs left U.S. multinationals with large sunk costs in poorly specialized, inefficient-scale factories. These firms wanted to rid themselves of the vestiges of import-substituting industrialization but feared that new entrants would build integrated, state-of-the-art production facilities in North America while they attempted to restructure. To prevent foreigners from seizing market shares, they sought discriminatory rules in the NAFTA treaty. For example, computer producers complained that they had "high costs imposed on them by the Computer Decree that would not be borne by new competitors."[93] Likewise, U.S. automakers pushed to delay NAFTA treatment for firms that had not invested in Mexico under its Automotive Decrees.[94] These provisions were designed to provide transitional protection while firms streamlined disorganized operations, eliminated outmoded factories, and integrated production networks in the region. Multilateral arrangements, however, cannot compensate

92. However, producers of computers and integrated circuits defeated strict origin rules that would have inhibited their ability to source inputs from Asia. GM, Ford, and Chrysler also opposed efforts by parts producers and the United Automobile Workers to impose a 75 percent origin requirement on automotive goods. See Hufbauer and Schott 1992; U.S. International Trade Commission 1993.

93. U.S. International Trade Commission 1990, 2.7.

94. The Big Three sought immediate free trade for incumbent firms (themselves plus Volkswagen and Nissan), staged over ten years for new investors; a 50 percent origin requirement for themselves and 60–70 percent for new investors; and compliance by new investors with Mexico's value-added and trade-balancing requirements for five years. "Vehicle Dispute Drives a Wedge Through NAFTA Talks," *Financial Times,* 25 October 1991, 6.

firms for the costs imposed on them by past government intervention, because this would conflict with most-favored nation rules. A small dose of protection is therefore the price of more enduring liberalization when trade-related investment measures applied against specific firms are being phased out.

Conclusion

A number of scholars have discussed the significance of economies of scale and offshore production in the political economy of trade, but to date there have been few systematic empirical explorations of their effects on trade policy. This article explicitly includes these variables in an explanation of trading blocs and demonstrates that they effectively characterize domestic preferences on NAFTA in the United States.

Stated simply, business groups have powerful incentives to seek regional trade liberalization when returns to scale are large and firms engage in production sharing. Economies of scale and cross-border production networks raise a set of issues and problems unique to a particular bilateral (or regional) trading relationship. This makes the creation of trading blocs an attractive framework for liberalizing and regulating this type of trade. The NAFTA treaty is a perfect example: it involved not only free trade, but also rules to govern foreign direct investment, the treatment of foreign corporations, and intellectual property rights.

In finding that economies of scale were a critical factor in industry lobbying in the United States, this study differs from recent studies suggesting that only firms with small domestic markets seek trading blocs. Further empirical testing is required to determine whether economies of scale and production sharing create incentives for regional arrangements in smaller and less advanced countries as well. It is also important to specify the conditions under which firms in trading blocs will seek higher barriers against foreign goods or further trade liberalization. The approach developed here implies that unit costs decline when firms are able to gain economies of scale and outsource more production in a region, reducing the need for protection against outsiders. However, if firms cannot ride down their cost curves and outsourcing remains difficult even after the elimination of barriers to regional trade, then domestic groups are more likely to oppose future liberalization. Whether these considerations strengthen or weaken industry support for global free trade is therefore a question for future research to address.

Appendix 1: Sources of Study Variables

Dependent Variables

NAFTA LOBBYING: Coded from testimony, petitions, and statements in congressional hearings and executive agency reports. In total, thirty-four hearings in the House of Representatives, eighteen hearings in the Senate, and five executive branch reports were consulted. Bibliographic information is available from the author on request.

NAFTA TARIFF PHASING: The tariff phasing schedule appears in "Schedule of the United States," Annex 302.2 of the NAFTA Treaty, at ⟨http://www-tech.mit.edu/Bulletins/Nafta⟩. Import weights and duties are from the U.S. International Trade Commission, available at ⟨http://dataweb.usitc.gov⟩.

Independent Variables

ECONOMIES OF SCALE: Calculated from U.S. Department of Commerce, Bureau of the Census 1989.

REGIONAL INTRAFIRM TRADE: Calculated from U.S. Department of Commerce, Bureau of Economic Analysis 1992; and data files at ⟨http://www.bea.doc.gov/bea/ai/iidguide.htm⟩.

OFFSHORE ASSEMBLY: Feenstra, Hanson, and Swenson 2000, data provided at author's request.

EXPORT DEPENDENCE, IMPORT COMPETITION, INTRA-INDUSTRY TRADE: U.S. Department of Commerce, Bureau of the Census 1991; U.S. International Trade Commission, available at ⟨http://dataweb.usitc.gov⟩.

LABOR INTENSITY, INDUSTRIAL CONCENTRATION: U.S. Department of Commerce, Bureau of the Census 1989.

GEOGRAPHIC CONCENTRATION: Busch and Reinhardt 1999, data file at ⟨http://userwww.service.emory.edu/~erein/research/#geocon⟩.

Appendix 2: Descriptive Statistics

Variable	*Mean*	*Standard deviation*	*Minimum*	*Maximum*
NAFTA LOBBYING	0.073	0.773	−1.000	1.000
NAFTA TARIFF PHASING	0.142	0.335	0.000	2.042
ECONOMIES OF SCALE	0.082	0.098	−0.193	0.393
REGIONAL INTRAFIRM TRADE	0.018	0.031	0.000	0.256
OFFSHORE ASSEMBLY	0.003	0.010	0.000	0.079
IMPORT COMPETITION	0.155	0.160	0.000	0.640
LABOR INTENSITY	0.377	0.099	0.056	0.549
EXPORT DEPENDENCE	0.072	0.078	0.001	0.544
INTRA-INDUSTRY TRADE	0.510	0.291	0.033	1.000
INDUSTRIAL CONCENTRATION	0.669	0.188	0.214	1.000
GEOGRAPHIC CONCENTRATION	0.438	0.102	0.194	0.774
$N = 134$				

Note: Sectors excluded because of missing data are textile finishing (226), public building and related furniture (253), and metal services (347). Cigarettes (211), cigars (212), chewing and smoking tobacco (213), and tobacco stemming and redrying (214) were combined into one SIC group.

Appendix 3: Correlation Matrix

	Economies of scale	*Regional intrafirm trade*	*Offshore assembly*	*Import competition*	*Labor intensity*	*Export dependence*[a]	*Export dependence*[b]	*Intra-industry trade*	*Industrial concentration*
ECONOMIES OF SCALE	1.00								
REGIONAL INTRAFIRM TRADE	0.06	1.00							
OFFSHORE ASSEMBLY	0.02	0.74	1.00						
IMPORT COMPETITION	−0.11	0.25	0.24	1.00					
LABOR INTENSITY	−0.35	−0.10	0.06	0.18	1.00				
EXPORT DEPENDENCE[a]	0.01	0.00	−0.10	0.23	−0.11	1.00			
EXPORT DEPENDENCE[b]	0.03	0.24	0.00	0.27	−0.15	0.96	1.00		
INTRA-INDUSTRY TRADE	−0.06	0.08	−0.03	−0.45	0.06	0.28	0.30	1.00	
INDUSTRIAL CONCENTRATION	0.08	0.29	0.13	0.14	−0.39	0.12	0.20	−0.04	1.00
GEOGRAPHIC CONCENTRATION	−0.12	−0.02	0.06	−0.03	0.07	−0.19	−0.20	−0.07	0.09

Note: [a]Residual from regional intrafirm trade.
[b]Residual from offshore assembly.

References

Alt, James E. and Michael Gilligan. 1994. The Political Economy of Trading States: Factor Specificity, Collective Action Problems, and Domestic Political Institutions. *Journal of Political Philosophy* 2 (2):165–92.

Alt, James E., Jeffry Frieden, Michael J. Gilligan, Dani Rodrik, and Ronald Rogowski. 1996. The Political Economy of International Trade: Enduring Puzzles and an Agenda for Inquiry. *Comparative Political Studies* 29 (6):689–717.

Bain, Joe S. 1959. *Industrial Organization.* New York: John Wiley and Sons.

Bhagwati, Jagdish. 1993. Regionalism and Multilateralism: An Overview. In *New Dimensions in Regional Integration*, edited by Jaime de Melo and Arvind Panagariya, 22–51. New York: Cambridge University Press.

Busch, Marc L., and Helen V. Milner. 1994. The Future of the International Trading System: International Firms, Regionalism, and Domestic Politics. In *Political Economy and the Changing Global Order,* edited by Richard Stubbs and Geoffrey Underhill, 259–76. New York: St. Martin's Press.

Busch, Marc L., and Eric Reinhardt. 1999. Industrial Location and Protection: The Political and Economic Geography of U.S. Non-Tariff Barriers. *American Journal of Political Science* 43 (4):1028–50.

Casella, Alessandra. 1996. Large Countries, Small Countries, and the Enlargement of Trade Blocs. *European Economic Review* 40 (2):389–415.

Caves, Richard E. 1976. Economic Models of Political Choice: Canada's Tariff Structure. *Canadian Journal of Economics* 9 (2):278–300.

———. 1991. Trade Liberalization and Structural Adjustment in Canada: The Genesis of Intra-Industry Trade. In *The Dynamics of North American Trade and Investment: Canada, Mexico, and the United States,* edited by Clark W. Reynolds, Leonard Waverman and Gerardo Bueno, 44–69. Palo Alto, Calif: Stanford University Press.

———. 1996. *Multinational Enterprise and Economic Analysis*, 2d ed. New York: Cambridge University Press.

Caves, Richard E., and Michael E. Porter. 1976. Barriers to Exit. In *Essays on Industrial Organization in Honor of Joe S. Bain,* edited by Robert T. Masson and P. David Qualls, 36–69. Cambridge: Ballinger.

Chase, Kerry A. 2002. From Protectionism to Regionalism: Foreign Investment, Commitment, and the Canada-United States Free Trade Agreement. Unpublished manuscript, Tufts University, Medford, Mass.

Conybeare, John A. C. 1993. 1992, the Community, and the World: Free Trade or Fortress Europe? In *The 1992 Project and the Future of Integration in Europe,* edited by Dale L. Smith and James Lee Ray, 143–63. Armonk, N.Y.: M.E. Sharpe.

Corden, W. M. 1972. Economies of Scale and Customs Union Theory. *The Journal of Political Economy* 80 (3):465–75.

Cox, Ronald W. 1996. Explaining Business Support for Regional Trade Agreements. In *Business and the State in International Relations,* edited by Ronald W. Cox, 109–27. Boulder, Colo.: Westview Press.

Destler, I. M., and John Odell. 1987. *Anti-Protection: Changing Forces in United States Trade Politics.* Washington, D.C.: Institute for International Economics.

Dick, Andrew R. 1994. Does Import Protection Act as Export Promotion? Evidence from the United States. *Oxford Economic Papers* 46 (1):83–101.

Feenstra, Robert C., and Gordon H. Hanson. 1996. Foreign Investment, Outsourcing, and Relative Wages. In *The Political Economy of Trade Policy: Papers in Honor of Jagdish Bhagwati*, edited by Robert C. Feenstra, Gene M. Grossman, and Douglas A. Irwin, 89–127. Cambridge, Mass.: MIT Press.

Feenstra, Robert C., Gordon H. Hanson, and Deborah L. Swenson. 2000. Offshore Assembly from the United States: Production Characteristics of the 9802 Program. In *The Impact of International Trade on Wages,* edited by Robert C. Feenstra, 85–122. Chicago: University of Chicago Press.

Frankel, Jeffrey A., Ernesto Stein, and Shang-Jin Wei. 1997. *Regional Trading Blocs in the World Economic System*. Washington, D.C.: Institute for International Economics.

Frieden, Jeffry A. 1991. *Debt, Development, and Democracy: Modern Political Economy and Latin America, 1965–1985*. Princeton, N.J.: Princeton University Press.

Frieden, Jeffry A., and Ronald Rogowski. 1996. The Impact of the International Economy on National Policies: An Analytical Overview. In *Internationalization and Domestic Politics*, edited by Robert O. Keohane and Helen V. Milner, 25–47. New York: Cambridge University Press.

Froot, Kenneth A., and David B. Yoffie. 1993. Trading Blocs and the Incentives to Protect: Implications for Japan and East Asia. In *Regionalism and Rivalry: Japan and the United States in Pacific Asia*, edited by Jeffrey A. Frankel and Miles Kahler, 125–56. Chicago: University of Chicago Press.

Gale Research. 1990. *Ward's Business Directory of U.S. Private and Public Companies*. Detroit: Gale Research.

Garten, Jeffrey E. 1993. *A Cold Peace: America, Japan, Germany, and the Struggle for Supremacy*. New York: Times Books.

———. 1995. Is America Abandoning Multilateral Trade? *Foreign Affairs* 74 (6):50–62.

Gilligan, Michael J. 1997. Lobbying as a Private Good with Intra-Industry Trade. *International Studies Quarterly* 41 (3):455–74.

Gilpin, Robert. 2000. *The Challenge of Global Capitalism: The World Economy in the 21st Century*. Princeton, N.J.: Princeton University Press.

Grossman, Gene M., ed. 1992. *Imperfect Competition and International Trade*. Cambridge, Mass.: MIT Press.

Grossman, Gene M., and Elhanan Helpman. 1995. The Politics of Free-Trade Agreements. *American Economic Review* 85 (4):667–90.

Grunwald, Joseph, and Kenneth Flamm. 1985. *The Global Factory: Foreign Assembly in International Trade*. Washington, D.C.: Brookings Institution.

Haggard, Stephan. 1997. The Political Economy of Regionalism in Asia and the Americas. In *The Political Economy of Regionalism*, edited by Edward D. Mansfield and Helen V. Milner, 20–49. New York: Columbia University Press.

Helleiner, G. K. 1977. Transnational Enterprises and the New Political Economy of U.S. Trade Policy. *Oxford Economic Papers* 29 (1):102–16.

Helpman, Elhanan, and Paul R. Krugman. 1985. *Market Structure and Foreign Trade: Increasing Returns, Imperfect Competition, and the International Economy*. Cambridge, Mass.: MIT Press.

———. 1989. *Trade Policy and Market Structure*. Cambridge, Mass.: MIT Press.

Hirschman, Albert O. 1981. *Essays in Trespassing: Economics to Politics and Beyond*. New York: Cambridge University Press.

Hiscox, Michael J. 2001. Class Versus Industry Cleavages: Inter-Industry Factor Mobility and the Politics of Trade. *International Organization* 55 (1):1–46.

Hufbauer, Gary Clyde. 1970. The Impact of National Characteristics and Technology on the Commodity Composition of Trade in Manufactured Goods. In *The Technology Factor in International Trade*, edited by Raymond Vernon, 145–231. New York: Columbia University Press.

Hufbauer, Gary Clyde, and Jeffrey J. Schott. 1992. *North American Free Trade: Issues and Recommendations*. Washington, D.C.: Institute for International Economics.

Johnson, Harry G. 1965. An Economic Theory of Protectionism, Tariff Bargaining, and the Formation of Customs Unions. *Journal of Political Economy* 73 (3):256–83.

Katz, Lawrence, and Lawrence Summers. 1989. Industry Rents: Evidence and Implications. *Brookings Papers on Economic Activity: Microeconomics* 1989 (1):209–75.

Kemp, Murray C., and Henry V. Wan Jr. 1976. An Elementary Proposition Concerning the Formation of Customs Unions. *Journal of International Economics* 6 (1):95–97.

Krueger, Anne O. 1997. Problems with Overlapping Free Trade Areas. In *Regionalism versus Multilateral Trade Arrangements*, edited by Takatoshi Ito and Anne O. Krueger, 9–23. Chicago: University of Chicago Press.

Krugman, Paul R. 1981. Intra-Industry Specialization and the Gains from Trade. *Journal of Political Economy* 89 (5):959–73.

———, ed. 1986. *Strategic Trade Policy and the New International Economics.* Cambridge, Mass.: MIT Press.

———. 1991. Is Bilateralism Bad? In *International Trade and Trade Policy*, edited by Elhanan Helpman and Assaf Razin, 9–23. Cambridge, Mass.: MIT Press.

———. 1993. Import Protection as Export Promotion: International Competition in the Presence of Oligopoly and Economies of Scale. In *Imperfect Competition and International Trade*, edited by Gene M. Grossman, 75–86. Cambridge, Mass.: MIT Press.

Krugman, Paul R., and Anthony J. Venables. 1990. Integration and the Competitiveness of Peripheral Industry. In *Unity with Diversity in the European Economy*, edited by Christopher Bliss and Jorge Braga de Macedo, 55–77. New York: Cambridge University Press.

Lal, Deepak. 1993. Trade Blocs and Multilateral Free Trade. *Journal of Common Market Studies* 31 (3):349–58.

Lavergne, Réal P. 1983. *The Political Economy of U.S. Tariffs: An Empirical Analysis.* New York: Academic Press.

Levy, Philip I., and T. N. Srinivasan. 1996. Regionalism and the (Dis)advantage of Dispute-Settlement Access. *American Economic Review* 86 (2):93–98.

Long, J. Scott, and Jeremy Freese. 2001. *Regression Models for Categorical Dependent Variables Using Stata.* College Station, Tex.: Stata Press.

Magee, Stephen P., William A. Brock, and Leslie Young. 1989. *Black Hole Tariffs and Endogenous Policy Theory: Political Economy in General Equilibrium.* New York: Cambridge University Press.

Mansfield, Edward D., and Helen V. Milner. 1999. The New Wave of Regionalism. *International Organization* 53 (3):589–627.

Marvel, Howard P., and Edward John Ray. 1987. Intra-Industry Trade: Sources and Effects on Protection. *Journal of Political Economy* 95 (6):1278–91.

Mattli, Walter. 1999. *The Logic of Regional Integration: Europe and Beyond.* New York: Cambridge University Press.

McGillivray, Fiona. 1997. Party Discipline as a Determinant of the Endogenous Formation of Tariffs. *American Journal of Political Science* 41 (2):584–607.

Milner, Helen V. 1988. *Resisting Protectionism: Global Industries and the Politics of International Trade.* Princeton, N.J.: Princeton University Press.

———. 1997. Industries, Governments, and the Creation of Regional Trade Blocs. In *The Political Economy of Regionalism*, edited by Edward D. Mansfield and Helen V. Milner, 77–106. New York: Columbia University Press.

Milner, Helen V., and David B. Yoffie. 1989. Between Free Trade and Protectionism: Strategic Trade Policy and a Theory of Corporate Trade Demands. *International Organization* 43 (2):239–72.

Mundell, Robert A. 1964. Tariff Preferences and the Terms of Trade. *Manchester School of Economic and Social Studies* 32 (1):1–13.

Olson, Mancur. 1965. *The Logic of Collective Action: Public Goods and the Theory of Groups.* Cambridge, Mass.: Harvard University Press.

———. 1982. *The Rise and Decline of Nations: Economic Growth, Stagflation, and Social Rigidities.* New Haven, Conn.: Yale University Press.

Oye, Kenneth A. 1992. *Economic Discrimination and Political Exchange: World Political Economy in the 1930s and the 1980s.* Princeton, N.J.: Princeton University Press.

Peres, Wilson. 1990. *Foreign Direct Investment and Industrial Development in Mexico.* Paris: OECD Development Center.

Pincus, J. J. 1975. Pressure Groups and the Pattern of Tariffs. *Journal of Political Economy* 83 (4): 757–78.

Pratten, C. F. 1971. *Economies of Scale in Manufacturing Industry.* Cambridge: Cambridge University Press.

Ray, Edward John. 1981. The Determinants of Tariff and Non-Tariff Trade Restrictions in the United States. *Journal of Political Economy* 89 (1):105–21.

Richardson, Martin. 1993. Endogenous Protection and Trade Diversion. *Journal of International Economics* 34 (3–4):309–24.

Rodrik, Dani. 1997. *Has Globalization Gone Too Far?* Washington, D.C.: Institute for International Economics.

Rogowski, Ronald. 1989. *Commerce and Coalitions: How Trade Affects Political Cleavages.* Princeton, N.J.: Princeton University Press.

Saxonhouse, Gary R. 1993. Pricing Strategies and Trading Blocs in East Asia. In *Regionalism and Rivalry: Japan and the United States in Pacific Asia,* edited by Jeffrey A. Frankel and Miles Kahler, 89–119. Chicago: University of Chicago Press.

Scherer, Frederic M. 1970. *Industrial Market Structure and Economic Performance.* Chicago: Rand McNally.

Scherer, Frederic M., Alan Beckenstein, Erich Kaufer, R. Dennis Murphy, and Francine Bougeon-Massen. 1975. *The Economics of Multi-Plant Operation: An International Comparisons Study.* Cambridge, Mass.: Harvard University Press.

Silberston, Aubrey. 1972. Economies of Scale in Theory and Practice. *Economic Journal* 82 (325):369–91.

Stigler, George. 1968. *The Organization of Industry.* Homewood, Ill.: Richard D. Irwin.

Thurow, Lester C. 1992. *Head to Head: The Coming Economic Battle among Japan, Europe, and America.* New York: Morrow.

Tornell, Aaron, and Gerardo Esquivel. 1997. The Political Economy of Mexico's Entry into NAFTA. In *Regionalism Versus Multilateral Trade Arrangements,* edited by Takatoshi Ito and Anne O. Krueger, 25–56. Chicago: University of Chicago Press.

Trefler, Daniel. 1993. Trade Liberalization and the Theory of Endogenous Protection: An Econometric Study of U.S. Import Policy. *Journal of Political Economy* 101 (1):138–60.

U.S. Department of Commerce, Bureau of the Census. 1989. *Census of Manufactures.* Washington, D.C.: U.S. Department of Commerce.

———. 1991. *U.S. Commodity Exports and Imports as Related to Output.* Washington, D.C.: U.S. Department of Commerce.

U.S. Department of Commerce, Bureau of Economic Analysis. 1992. *U.S. Direct Investment Abroad.* Washington, D.C.: U.S. Department of Commerce.

U.S. House. 1993. Committee on Government Operations. *The North American Free Trade Agreement and its Impact on the Textile/Apparel/Fiber and Auto and Auto Parts Industries.* 103d cong., 1st sess. 4 May.

U.S. International Trade Commission. 1990. *Review of Trade and Investment Liberalization Measures by Mexico and Prospects for Future United States-Mexican Relations, Phase I: Recent Trade and Investment Reforms Undertaken by Mexico and Implications for the United States.* Investigation no. 332-282. Washington, D.C.: U.S. International Trade Commission.

———. 1993. *Potential Impact on the U.S. Economy and Selected Industries of the North American Free-Trade Agreement.* USITC Publication 2596. Washington, D.C.: U.S. International Trade Commission.

Viner, Jacob. 1950. *The Customs Union Issue.* New York: Carnegie Endowment for International Peace.

Wei, Shang-Jin, and Jeffrey A. Frankel. 1996. Can Regional Blocs Be a Stepping-Stone to Global Free Trade? A Political Economy Analysis. *International Review of Economics and Finance* 5 (4):339–47.

Wells, Louis T., Jr. 1992. Conflict or Indifference? U.S. Multinationals in a World of Regional Trading Blocs. OECD Technical Paper 57. Paris: OECD Development Center.

Yarbrough, Beth V., and Robert M. Yarbrough. 1992. *Cooperation and Governance in International Trade: The Strategic Organizational Approach.* Princeton, N.J.: Princeton University Press.

[4]

VERTICAL TRADE SPECIALIZATION AND THE FORMATION OF NORTH-SOUTH PTAs

By MARK S. MANGER

REGIONALISM has replaced multilateralism as the principal venue of trade liberalization. While negotiations at the World Trade Organization (WTO) have stalled, the number of preferential trade agreements (PTAs) has grown tremendously since the early 1990s. By 2010, more than 270 PTAs, counting only those dealing with trade in goods, covered a majority of world trade. Remarkably, the most common form of PTA signed since the early 1990s and the majority of those currently under negotiation are highly unequal agreements between a developed country and one or more developing ones, or between a developed country and one transitioning from a formerly communist economy.[1] Since the partners in these agreements are mostly developed-developing country pairs, this article refers to them as North-South PTAs. Although recent research has offered much insight into the factors that promote trade agreements in general, the conspicuous popularity of North-South deals has attracted less scholarly attention.

I argue that a central driving force behind the explosive growth of North-South PTAs is the specialization of manufacturing exports according to the level of economic development of a country. More specifically, when intra-industry trade is shaped by different factor endowments, it creates incentives to form PTAs. By contrast, compara-

* I would like to thank Oana Ciobanu and Swan Yee Ang for excellent research assistance; Eric Neumayer for detailed advice; Jeff Chwieroth, Bob Hancké, Marco Simoni, Ken Shadlen, Lauren Phillips, Andrew Walter, and Stephen Woolcock for comments on the paper; and participants at APSA 2009, IPES 2009, the 2010 Princeton Workshop on PTAs, and the three anonymous reviewers for their helpful suggestions. Matt McKeon deserves special mention for superb data munging and for introducing me to the riveting world of SQL programming. All remaining errors are mine. This research was supported by Grant No. 2007-NP-114251 from the program Établissement de nouveaux professeurs-chercheurs of the Fonds québécois de la recherche sur la société et la culture (FQRSC).

[1] Crawford and Fiorentino 2005, 7.

World Politics 64, no. 4 (October 2012), 622–58

doi: S0043887112000172

tive advantage plays only a minor role in promoting their formation. Although there are large potential gains from trade between countries trading entirely different goods, decades of research in political economy indicate that liberalizing trade between countries with very different endowments should be particularly difficult. Mutual trade liberalization would expose the least competitive sectors to imports, so unless these sectors can retain protection, liberalization may not be politically feasible. The stark asymmetries between developed and developing countries in bilateral negotiations make it even less likely that sunset industries in the North would be forced to shut down.

At the same time, developing countries with low per capita income are often relatively small markets for exporters of goods produced in high-cost locations. Developed-country exporters are therefore often uninterested in joining a political coalition to support trade liberalization in those markets. Such coalitions are essential as a counterweight to protectionist forces.[2] While developed countries may be important markets for individual developing countries, the reverse is rarely the case. Small and sometimes distant economies do not enlarge the export markets of developed-country producers to an extent that allows them to achieve greater economies of scale—an important driving force of regional trade liberalization among economically similar countries.[3] Clearly, countries often "form trade blocs for non-economic reasons, such as national security, peace, and assistance in developing political and social institutions."[4] This, however, leaves a majority of PTAs without an economic rationale. Unsurprisingly, some studies find only a substantively weak and statistically insignificant effect of aggregate bilateral trade on the likelihood of forming a PTA.[5] Could it be that the wave of North-South PTAs has no relation to trade?

I argue that trade does indeed play a central role in motivating North-South PTAs but trade primarily based on comparative advantage does not. The economic interests underpinning North-South PTAs are the result of a mutual specialization of industrial production. The resulting trade is therefore driven by a combination of differences in factor prices and trade in the same industry—in short, vertical intra-industry trade (VIIT). In simplest terms, VIIT is trade in similar goods produced by the same industry but differentiated by the unit value of the goods.

[2] Milner 1988.
[3] Chase 2005; Milner 1997.
[4] Schiff and Winters 2003, 187.
[5] Mansfield, Milner, and Pevehouse 2007.

Such mutual specialization makes North-South liberalization politically much more feasible than eliminating tariffs on interindustry trade based on comparative advantage. Investment in export-oriented manufacturing creates employment in developing countries and generates foreign exchange earnings. At the same time, vertical specialization limits the off-shoring of jobs to developing countries by increasing exports from the North. Yet even in the worst case for workers in developed countries—when net jobs are lost—labor will often be split, since highly paid specialized workers actually benefit as capital-intensive production expands.

The argument presented in this article contributes to several debates. First, it expands on the recently emphasized link between trade liberalization and foreign direct investment (FDI). A growing number of studies show that international agreements can act as commitment devices to help attract foreign investment.[6] Much theorizing in political economy, however, still assumes that trade liberalization is motivated by the gain offered by comparative advantage and pays too little attention to the political interests related to the broader shift of manufacturing industries from the developed to the developing world.

Second, the argument engages the debate over the integration of developing countries into the world economy and the use of PTAs as a developmental policy.[7] Vertical specialization is an essential part of such a developmental strategy. My research shows that vertical specialization promotes the convergence of interests between countries of different income levels, a necessary condition for North-South PTAs to be negotiated.[8] Finally, the argument has implications for whether PTAs should be seen as a substitute for a stalled multilateral liberalization process.[9] Unfortunately, if the reduction of trade barriers in PTAs privileges a relatively narrow range of goods, then the WTO may be left with the intractable issue of agricultural trade liberalization. PTAs may therefore undermine the potential for issue-linkage that has been crucial in achieving agricultural market-opening in the past.[10]

The article begins with a brief survey of the existing literature on PTA determinants and then presents the theoretical foundations of this research. A case study of the Japan-Thailand Economic Partnership

[6] Büthe and Milner 2008; Elkins, Guzman, and Simmons 2006; Kerner 2009; Neumayer and Spess 2005.

[7] Shadlen 2005.

[8] Haggard 1997.

[9] Bhagwati 2008; Freund 2000.

[10] See Davis 2004 for a demonstration of the importance of issue linkage.

Agreement illustrates the causal validity of the argument. The subsequent sections introduce the quantitative research design and discuss the econometric analysis and results, followed by conclusions and an outlook on further avenues of research.

The Political Economy of North-South PTAs

The proliferation of preferential trade agreements since the early 1990s led to a flurry of publications that investigate their determinants, their effects on trade, and their interaction with the multilateral trade regime. The findings indicate that democratic countries are more likely to negotiate trade agreements,[11] although this effect is tempered by the number of veto players in their political systems.[12] Governments may also use trade agreements to overcome domestic resistance to liberalization.[13] Other factors work at the international level, among them worries about a stalled WTO and the breakdown of multilateral negotiations.[14] In the past, countries have also formed trade agreements to strengthen ties with allied states.[15] In addition, PTAs evidently reduce the volatility of the terms of trade and of trade itself and increase foreign direct investment inflows.[16] Finally, recent research indicates that as PTAs multiply, governments increasingly worry about losing markets because others gain better access to them. Countries therefore often form "reactive agreements" because of market-access concerns[17] or because of competition for FDI among countries with similar export profiles.

Given their general thrust, however, these studies do not differentiate between PTAs among developed or developing countries and those that span the North-South divide. This is striking when one considers that in the post–Cold War era, PTAs between countries of different levels of development and per capita income are by far the most common type of agreement, as shown in Table 1. Developed-developing, developed-transition, and transition-transition country PTAs outnumber developed-developed country PTAs.

What explains the convergence of interests between developed and developing countries on North-South PTAs? I argue that mutual ver-

[11] Mansfield, Milner, and Rosendorff 2002.
[12] Mansfield, Milner, and Pevehouse 2007.
[13] Maggi and Rodríguez-Clare 2007.
[14] Dür 2007; Mansfield and Reinhardt 2003; Solís 2003.
[15] Gowa 1995; Mansfield and Reinhardt 2003.
[16] See, respectively, Büthe and Milner 2008; Mansfield and Reinhardt 2008.
[17] Baccini and Dür 2012.

TABLE 1
COUNTRY PAIRS IN PTAS, DURING AND AFTER THE COLD WAR[a]

	Developed/ Developed	*Developed/ Developing*	*Developed/ Transition*	*Developing/ Developing*	*Developing/ Transition*	*Transition/ Transition*	*Total*
1958–89	10	6	0	9	0	0	25
1990–94	3	4	4	5	1	5	22
1995–99	3	7	0	4	2	16	32
2000–05	2	20	4	12	4	21	63
Total Post-Cold War	8	31	8	21	7	42	117

SOURCE: Crawford and Fiorentino 2005, 7.

[a] Developed economies include Canada, the US, EU, the European Free Trade Agreement members, Japan, Australia, and New Zealand. Transition economies are the former Soviet Union, Eastern and Central Europe, the Baltic States, and the Balkans. The rest are classified as developing.

tical specialization of manufacturing trade creates political coalitions that support trade liberalization. Driving the vertical specialization are investment activities that disaggregate production across different locations. The result is vertical intra-industry trade, a form of exchange explained in greater detail below.

VERTICAL INTRA-INDUSTRY TRADE DEFINED

According to neoclassical trade theory, countries ought to specialize in the production and export of those goods in which they have a comparative advantage. Such specialization should result in one-way trade: for example, Australia exports beef to Japan, but imports cars from there. The gains from such trade are evident, its political economy is well understood, and its political implications are the subject of seminal works.[18] However, most global trade is actually the exchange of similar goods produced in countries with comparable factor endowments, something that comparative advantage cannot explain. This observation led to the development of modern trade theory based on increasing returns to scale and monopolistic competition.[19] Drawing on such models, political economists have investigated the implication of scale economies and monopolistic competition for firm lobbying and the demand for protection and liberalization.[20] The focus of these models, however, has been what is sometimes called intra-

[18] See Alt et al. 1996; Rogowski 1989.
[19] Helpman and Krugman 1985.
[20] Chase 2005; Gilligan 1997; Milner 1997.

industry trade by horizontal firms. Horizontal firms aim for economies of scale by replicating their activities in different countries. They produce the same goods in separate plants in different countries if the gains from selling locally, avoiding tariffs, and reducing transport costs outweigh the plant-specific fixed costs. This dynamic is generally the case in countries with similar gross domestic products (GDP) and factor prices.[21] The goods that are traded by these firms are differentiated into varieties to suit the different tastes of consumers so that firms are often not directly competing and reciprocal liberalization is relatively easier than in cases of purely endowment-based trade.[22] Accordingly, these theoretical models have most purchase when explaining the formation of North-North trade agreements and fare less well when applied to North-South trade.[23] The emphasis in the literature on North-North trade and FDI is understandable since it has historically dominated flows of goods and capital.[24] Since the early 1990s, however, developing countries have not only attracted much more FDI, but have also captured a greater share of global manufacturing based on domestic investment. A large portion of such manufacturing activity is export-oriented, and a theory of horizontal intra-industry trade is less useful to explain this development.

If developed and developing countries are trading goods in the same industry, then firms have an incentive to specialize production in countries according to relative factor prices. Relative capital abundance means that capital-intensive production is more profitable in richer countries than in capital-scarce developing countries. Just as in the case of horizontal intra-industry trade, firms differentiate their goods into "varieties," but their choice of variety is determined by relative factor prices. The resulting bilateral trade is referred to as vertical intra-industry trade.[25] As the economic determinants of trade vary significantly, it is essential to distinguish between vertical and horizontal intra-industry trade.[26] VIIT exists at the levels of final products and intermediate goods because firms specialize in the production of inputs

[21] Markusen and Venables 1998; Markusen and Maskus 2002.

[22] But see Gilligan 1997.

[23] Kono 2009 challenges Gilligan's finding that intra-industry trade creates considerable firm-specific adjustment costs, but does not differentiate between horizontal and vertical intra-industry trade in his analysis.

[24] For example, the Baier and Bergstrand 2004 landmark study of PTA formation based on horizontal intra-industry trade in the economics literature tests its model on a data set that consists of 70 percent intra-EU and European Free Trade Association observations.

[25] Falvey 1981.

[26] Abd-el-Rahman 1991; Greenaway 1992; Krugman 1981.

as well as finished goods in different locations. Often, high-end goods are manufactured in developed countries for the home market and exported in small numbers to developing countries, where lower GDP per capita implies that the market for such high unit-value goods is smaller. Mass-market or entry-level goods with a lower individual unit value are produced in developing countries for export to the North as well as for consumption in the South. An example of such trade would be an automotive firm that produces cars in both developed and developing countries that have specialized manufacturing plants. Locally owned parts manufacturers that supply the multinational might produce in the home country and specialize as a firm. The ownership structure is irrelevant because both the locally owned and multinational firms have the same interests regarding trade liberalization (see below). The different characteristics of the three trade types—one way, horizontal intra-industry, and vertical intra-industry—are shown in Table 2.

An alternative case of trade results from regional production sharing[27] by firms referred to as vertical multinationals.[28] Production is shared across borders—in some cases within the firm, in other cases to firms acting as suppliers—by outsourcing intermediate, often labor-intensive, stages to a country with lower wages.

While production sharing within firms has expanded over the last two decades, to be profitable for multinational firms[29] it generally requires geographic proximity, whereas VIIT remains feasible, especially for finished goods, even for geographically distant production locations as long as transport costs remain low. Models that specifically focus on regional production sharing can therefore only explain a small subset of North-South PTAs.[30] Empirical research has generally found that country-specific factors considerably outweigh industry or firm characteristics as determinants of the value of either vertical or horizontal intra-industry trade.[31] Vertical intra-industry trade appears to be determined more by variables such as endowments and relative wealth because they provide the conditions that allow firms to choose different production strategies. In some instances multinational firms expand production and turn a country into an export platform. One such

[27] Chase 2003.

[28] Helpman 1984.

[29] Chase 2003, 146.

[30] Note that the terminology in the literature is by no means uniform. Hummels, Rapoport, and Yi 1998 refer to production-sharing as vertical specialization; others call it outsourcing, fragmentation, multistage production, or disintegration of production, as in the landmark study by Alfaro and Charlton 2009. While those studies are interested in the determinants of FDI, this study and the definition used here focus on the intra-industry rather than intra-firm aspect of the trade, as in Falvey 1981.

[31] Balassa 1986; Greenaway, Hine, and Milner 1994; Loertscher and Wolter 1980.

TABLE 2
CHARACTERISTICS OF TRADE TYPES

	Returns to Scale	*Monopolistic Competition*	*Trade in the Same Goods*	*Varieties*
One way	no	no	no	few
Horizontal intra-industry	yes	yes	yes	many
Vertical intra-industry	sometimes	no	yes	many

case is the auto industry, where developing-country brands have made limited inroads in mature markets. In other examples, such as Apple computers manufactured in Taiwan, multinational firms procure from a developing country goods designed and branded in a developed one. Given the diversity of firm-ownership structures, it is most useful to think of vertical specialization as a country-level rather than firm-level phenomenon, and to analyze the attendant trade using the same degree of aggregation.

VERTICAL TRADE SPECIALIZATION AND PTA FORMATION

This section presents a framework to show how the rise in vertical intra-industry trade contributes to the formation of preferential trade agreements between developed and developing countries. I first describe the interests of economic actors as a result of vertical trade specialization, then I derive predictions that should be observed regarding the coalitions of actors, and finally I show why governments can be expected to respond to demands for PTA formation.

ECONOMIC INTERESTS

Demonstrating the link between trade specialization and PTA formation requires showing that key economic actors, such as firms and workers, can increase their profits and wages, respectively, if such an agreement is concluded, and why they have an interest in bilateral or regional liberalization in particular.

First, when the input of labor per unit produced is identical in developed and developing countries in the same industry, a lower unit-value good is more profitable if it is produced in a country with lower labor costs. For firms, it is therefore more profitable to produce low unit-value goods in a developing country. Higher unit-value goods can be produced in a developed country and will be marketed there. Firms will therefore export the "local goods" to the partner country, which means they have an interest in bilateral tariff reductions with countries in which they produce and sell.

Second, there is a link between different levels of per capita income and economies of scale. Closely related to the relative wealth of the country is the market for goods with different unit values. This implies that specialized production allows firms to achieve greater economies of scale at the plant level in different countries.[32] Goods with a high unit value will sell in greater numbers in the richer country while the market for low-end products will be relatively smaller there. Developing countries will be a market for some high unit-value products, but to a lesser degree than the richer countries. This link also creates an incentive to reduce tariffs between the two countries.

Regarding the interests of workers, textbook economics shows that vertical specialization leads to increased demand for low-skilled labor in the country with a lower capital intensity of production and, intriguingly, increased demand for highly skilled labor in the country with the relatively higher capital intensity.[33] Hence, in this model, wages for both groups will rise. Vertical specialization thus drives a wedge between low-skilled and high-skilled workers in the same country and industry and the two segments of workers will therefore have conflicting interests over trade with the partner country. In the developed country, high-skilled workers benefit from the increased demand while less-skilled workers there lose out. The converse is true in the developing country.

Hence, two simultaneous bargains take place in North-South negotiations. The first is a well-known bargain based on the relative efficiency of firms due to perfect competition and comparative advantage. Import-competing firms will seek protection while export-oriented firms will call for the liberalization of overseas markets.[34] For developed-country firms, a small market in the partner country also means that the firms that are export oriented have little to gain. Consequently, while import-competing firms will lobby for protection, export-oriented firms may not bother to engage in the political process. This dynamic suggests that the export of goods based on comparative

[32] Recall the contrast with horizontal intra-industry trade between countries with similar factor prices. Here, economies of scale are also achieved at the plant level, but firms do not specialize according to unit value cost in response to factor prices.

[33] Feenstra 2003, 386.

[34] Milner 1988; Trefler 1993.

advantage will see less (or no) liberalization in North-South PTAs. In short, it is not where the action is. Without a significant role for vertical specialization, North-South liberalization is unlikely to be politically attractive.

The second bargain revolves around vertical intra-industry trade. With workers split into two groups according to their relative skill level, firms involved in vertical specialization trade scale economies across products with different unit values.[35] Liberalization of low unit-value goods in the North is exchanged for market opening for high unit-value goods in the South. This bargain is essential for North-South PTAs to be politically attractive. It implies first that vertically specialized trade will be the most liberalized in a North-South PTA, and second, that the more important vertical intra-industry trade is to the bilateral trade relationship, the more likely a PTA will be formed. The benefits of establishing a North-South PTA are tariff reductions in both countries for the goods the firms export, which thereby reduce costs and increase profits.

Lobbying Coalitions

This section examines the interest-group coalitions that support or oppose North-South PTAs. Vertically specialized producers are often multinational firms with a local network of suppliers. Such firms are referred to as "lead firms," and the firm and its suppliers as "rent chains."[36] Rent chains are economic actors whose profits are linked because they are part of the same production chain. Trade policies that influence the profit earned on the sale of the final product of the rent chain affect all producers in the chain, who therefore have an incentive to engage in lobbying activities.

Because rent chains are groups of firms with contractual ties, they face less of a collective action problem than firms without such ties. A lead firm can therefore mobilize all the firms in its rent chain to lobby for or against a specific policy. Moreover, the number of competing lead firms is generally small, which makes lobbying efforts among them easy to coordinate.

Rent chains are a common, if underappreciated, feature in many domains of trade policy lobbying.[37] What makes them important in the

[35] The idea of "trading off scale economies" is due to Milner 1997, only that her analysis focuses on horizontal intra-industry trade.

[36] Baron 1995.

[37] Baron 1997.

case of North-South PTAs is that lead firms are able to mobilize them in both the developed and the developing countries. Not only does a lead firm produce vertically specialized final goods in both countries, but some suppliers in its rent chain spread production across both countries as well. Auto parts firms, for example, are often multinational firms with production plants in both developed and developing countries. Accordingly, their interests vis-à-vis a North-South PTA will be strongly influenced by the fact that they form part of a rent chain. Of course, there may be suppliers that are not vertically specialized exporters or traditional export-oriented firms selling finished goods that are nonetheless part of the same rent chain. Consider again auto parts suppliers that sell their products to a lead firm within the same country. Even if they are not exporters themselves, they have contractual ties to such firms, and thus coinciding interests, and may lobby in support of a North-South PTA. Rent chains therefore span international borders and extend deep into the economies of both countries.

A coalition of lead firms and their rent chains will engage in a lobbying contest with those groups opposed to the formation of a North-South PTA. While the constituency in favor of a North-South PTA will be largely determined by vertical specialization, the interests of those opposed will be mostly determined by the well-understood political economy of interindustry trade. In the absence of contractual ties, however, import-competing firms are often at an organizational disadvantage compared to multinational lead firms and their rent chains. This does not imply that they will not lobby, but the costs of organizing and coordinating their efforts are relatively higher and the incentives for free riding are greater.

A necessary corollary of PTAs are rules of origin (ROOs)—regulations designed to prevent goods from being imported via the PTA partner with the lower external tariff and then shipped to the higher-tariff partner. ROOs are the goal of much lobbying because when they act as a local content quota they can provide protection to local producers.[38] Small and medium-sized firms are particularly burdened by the cost of complying with ROOs. But in the case of rent chains that end in a lead firm's final product, such costs will be relatively lower. Vertically specialized production implies that goods are produced in (usually) larger numbers where it is most efficient to do so. Moreover, since lead firms have lobbying power, ROOs will be structured to fit their

[38] Chase 2008; Krishna and Krueger 1995.

products.[39] ROOs in PTAs are therefore likely to be an impediment to broad-based trade promotion. This further illustrates that many North-South PTAs serve a narrow set of interests and do not benefit broad-based trade liberalization.

Government Preferences

Ultimately, governments choose whether to negotiate a PTA and the tariffs to eliminate. Policymakers face demands from numerous actors who offer the usual inducements: direct monetary contributions to parties and campaigns, "consultancy" and other positions for politicians and their followers, and jobs "saved" by promoting exports. The canonical Grossman-Helpman model[40] demonstrates that governments care about voter welfare, direct payments by interest groups, and tariff revenue (although the last point is irrelevant in practice except for least-developed countries). Building on this model, one can assume that governments will liberalize trade if either the payments by the pro-trade groups outweigh those of protectionist groups or if (partial) trade liberalization can be achieved without exposing import-competing groups to foreign competition. Given the rapid increase in the number of North-South PTAs during the last two decades, one can also surmise that country-specific institutional factors (other than the general trend toward democratization)[41] cannot explain a global trend. Accordingly, if the demands (and inducements) of the lobbying coalition around VIIT outweigh those of import-competing groups, governments will support a North-South PTA.

For the government of the developed country, preferential North-South liberalization is almost always possible because the bargaining situation tends to be highly asymmetrical. Unlike in the General Agreement on Tariffs and Trade (GATT) and the WTO where issue-linkage has allowed agricultural liberalization despite strong resistance in Japan and the EU,[42] significant concessions by the richer partner are rarely necessary in a North-South PTA.[43] Import-competing sectors such as agriculture can either be protected for long periods of time or remain fully excluded.

[39] As pointed out by Athukorala and Kohpaiboon 2009, 19, "[n]ormally [l]arge firms and firms with close trade and FDI ties or those located in particular industries where meeting ROO requirements are simple and straightforward use FTAs."

[40] Grossman and Helpman 1994.

[41] Milner and Kubota 2005.

[42] Davis 2004.

[43] See Cameron 1997 for a case study of the North American Free Trade Agreement negotiations. Pekkanen, Solís, and Katada 2007 argue that it is precisely the ability to control the agenda and exclude import-competing sectors from liberalization that makes asymmetrical PTAs attractive.

In addition, labor organizations in the North may not have any objections to mutual trade liberalization if no jobs (or few jobs among high-skilled and, therefore, often better-organized workers) are lost. Instead, the determining factor for the preferences of workers is whether they are part of a rent chain mobilized in favor of a PTA. This means that labor organizations may well be split because some parts of their membership favor a PTA and others are against it. For the developed country's government, the interests of vertically specialized exporters can often be furthered without hurting uncompetitive sectors. While developed countries will often protect their markets from developing-country imports whenever these become particularly competitive, vertically specialized trade is less likely to be hindered by such barriers because the buyers are producers in the North.

Conversely, this implies that the developing country's government cannot hope to achieve significant market-access gains in negotiations. Rather, the main benefit of vertical specialization for the developing country is foreign direct investment in manufacturing and the creation of jobs. In developing countries, low-skilled workers outnumber high-skilled workers, so all else being equal, governments should favor their interests.

Can similar benefits be achieved by pursuing unilateral or multilateral trade liberalization rather than PTAs? In the GATT/WTO, the main tool for tailoring bilateral tariff reductions to the mutual interests of two countries is the "principal supplier rule," but it is not useful if the countries are not actually the foremost exporters of a specific good on a worldwide basis.[44] WTO members can, however, apply lower tariffs unilaterally for specific goods in a nondiscriminatory manner.[45] Yet to a developing country government, such liberalization is less attractive than a preferential agreement for three related reasons.

First, the developing country government trying to unilaterally eliminate tariffs will face resistance from local producers (capital-intensive producers whose products would be replaced by high unit-value imports from the developed country) that are relatively less efficient than their counterparts in the North. Governments can overcome such resistance if low unit-value production will expand. This growth

[44] The principal supplier rule has also been largely replaced by formula approaches to tariff reductions. See Hoekman and Kostecki 2009, 165–66, and Kim 2010, 60–61.

[45] An example of this might be the "de-facto preferential trade agreement" in East Asia, where applied tariffs are lower than bound rates, as shown by Hale 2011. However, even there most of the tariff "binding overhang" between Japan and Korea and their ASEAN partners has been replaced by highly preferential or zero tariffs in PTAs since the time period analyzed in his study.

is much more likely if FDI in these industries is increased after trade liberalization.

Second, promises of FDI from the developed-country partner are far more credible with a PTA. Multinational lead firms from the partner country have already invested in the local producers (recall that VIIT increases precede PTA formation) and are lobbying in support of the PTA in both countries. These lobbying efforts are visible reassurance for the developing country government that preferential trade liberalization will be rewarded with more FDI, jobs, and vertically specialized exports.

Finally, because unilateral liberalization means that foreign manufacturers could source inputs from any competitor country, local firms have no guarantee that they will benefit from vertical specialization in the future. If a competing supplier became more efficient, these inputs would just be imported. Retaining a most-favored-nation tariff prevents this from occurring. Consider the example of the Japan-Mexico Free Trade Agreement. Prior to the opening of negotiations, Japanese firms prodded the Mexican government to unilaterally eliminate tariffs or to offer tariff rebates. The Mexican government was unwilling to offer either because they might have displaced local suppliers' goods with imports from East Asia. Instead, the government offered a preferential trade agreement to address the concerns of Japanese manufacturing firms.[46] Reciprocal liberalization with a developed-country partner is much more politically attractive than unilateral tariff reductions.

North-South PTAs are not the only type of international agreements designed to help attract investment. Bilateral investment treaties (BITs) have grown enormously in number—to over 2,700 such agreements—since 1959.[47] While PTAs address commercial factors, such as the cost of importing parts, that make a country an attractive investment location in the first place, BITs primarily focus on the protection of investor property rights. At times these issues overlap. For example, a government might be tempted to raise tariffs in order to favor local suppliers after an investment has taken place. PTAs help prevent such tariff uncertainty.[48] What's more, BITs and PTAs have converged in recent years and many trade agreements now include investment chapters, so the two policy instruments should not be seen as alternatives.

To summarize, in the negotiation of a North-South PTA, import-competing producers in the developed country will oppose liberal-

[46] Solís 2003, 395–96.

[47] The literature is growing rapidly; see inter alia Allee and Peinhardt 2010; Haftel 2010; Neumayer and Spess 2005.

[48] Athukorala and Kohpaiboon 2009, 16–17.

ization and export-oriented producers of finished goods are unlikely to lobby in favor of it because the partner country's market is small. A PTA's key supporters in both countries will be lead firms and their rent chains centered on vertically specialized trade. The asymmetry of the bargaining situation implies that the developed country will make limited (or no) concessions that would expose its import-competing sectors, so trade based on comparative advantage and different factor endowments will not drive liberalization. Accordingly, governments will respond to these demands by focusing tariff reductions on the vertically specialized share of bilateral trade. The principal implication here is that the greater the importance of such vertically specialized trade in the bilateral trade relationship, the more likely a North-South PTA will be concluded.

Evidence of this can be found by looking at the growing share of vertical intra-industry trade in total North-South trade and the concurrent increase in the number of North-South PTAs as shown in Figure 1.[49] Such averages are, of course, merely suggestive; more stringent tests are required.

A Case Study: The Japan-Thailand FTA

A case that helps illustrate the link between vertical specialization and the subsequent formation of a PTA is the Japan-Thailand Economic Partnership Agreement that entered into force in 2007. Vertical specialization played an essential role in shaping the coalitions in favor of and opposed to a free trade agreement, but the asymmetrical bargaining situation restricted market-access gains for other exports from the developing country.

Since the turn of the millennium, Japan and Thailand have refocused their trade policy on free trade agreements (FTAs). In Thailand, FTAs became the primary trade policy instrument when the Thaksin government took office in 2001. Although the goals were manifold, an important dimension was that the Thai government reacted to FTA initiatives by other countries that possibly would have diverted FDI and affected trade flows to the detriment of Thai export industries.[50] The prior start of FTA negotiations between Japan and the Philippines and

[49] The drop in the number of PTAs and VIIT share in 2004 is the result of several countries joining the EU. These countries had relatively high shares of VIIT with the EU-15, and their individual PTAs ceased to exist once they joined the EU, so that both lines drop that year.

[50] Sally 2007, 13.

VERTICAL TRADE SPECIALIZATION 637

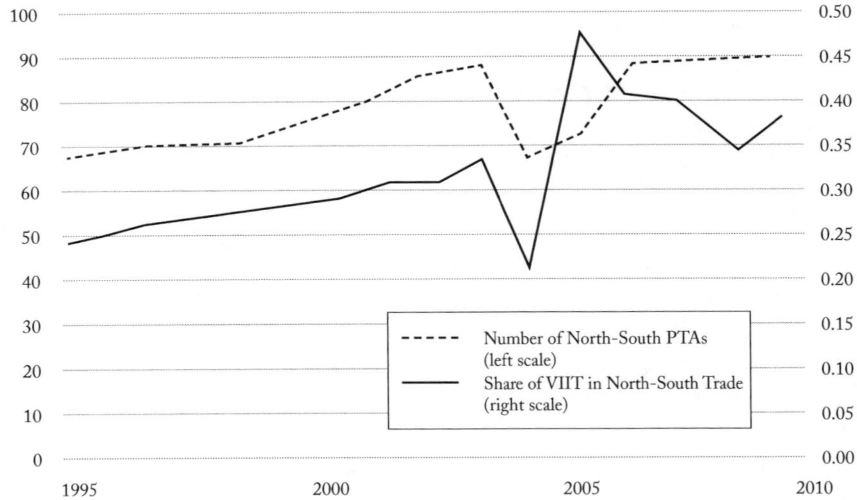

FIGURE 1
TREND IN VIIT SHARE IN NORTH-SOUTH TRADE AND NORTH-SOUTH PTAS, 1995–2009

the concurrent initiation negotiations between Japan and Malaysia may have been particularly important in this regard.

Up until the late 1990s Japanese FDI in Thailand, mostly in the auto and light consumer-goods industries, was oriented toward the domestic market and neighboring Association of Southeast Asian Nations (ASEAN) countries.[51] After the Asian financial crisis in 1997, the rapid depreciation of the Thai baht and the liberalization sought by successive Thai governments turned Thailand into an important export platform for Japanese firms. In a landmark shift from pre-crisis Japanese corporate strategy,[52] finished goods were now exported back to the home market.

Once the restructuring of production was under way, Japanese firms began to lobby the Thai government and the Japanese Ministry of Economy, Trade, and Industry (METI) specifically for the reduction of Thai tariffs on high-value parts and luxury vehicles. The lead firms in the campaign were Isuzu, Honda, Mitsubishi, and Toyota—four Japanese automotive manufacturers with investments in Thailand. In 2004,

[51] Ministry of Economy, Trade, and Industry 2005.

[52] For the comparison with pre-Crisis strategy, see especially Hatch and Yamamura 1996.

Isuzu and Toyota together accounted for 77 percent of local passenger vehicle and 60 percent of commercial vehicle sales by foreign firms. Although Honda and Mitsubishi were less important in terms of total vehicle production in Thailand for that same year, they were particularly effective in their lobbying; together they contributed 34 percent of vehicle exports. All four firms were supported by a rent chain of local suppliers in both countries and upstream producers of machinery and specialized steel with whom they had contractual ties. These Japanese firms had plans for a significant expansion of production in Thailand, and specifically sought to reduce remaining Thai tariffs for inputs they preferred to source from Japan.[53] Such issues had already been raised—prior to any FTA negotiation plans—so that the Japanese government merely needed to translate them into a feasible policy, in this case a North-South PTA.[54] Conveying the requests of these firms became the central lobbying objective for the Japan Automobile Association (JAMA) and the peak industry association, Keidanren.[55] Specialized industry associations, such as the Japan Business Council for Trade and Investment Facilitation, raised specific issues with METI. With reference to Thai tariffs on inputs, the association wrote, "[Regarding electronics parts, ball bearings, and rubber products] it is requested that a further cut in tariff rates be undertaken . . . focusing on those materials that cannot be produced in Thailand. Furthermore, tariffs on cutting tools ought to be reduced rapidly. . . . On auto parts, the duty ranges from 5 to 42%, necessitating a significant reduction."[56] These are exactly the liberalization targets expected from a rent chain based on vertical specialization.

By comparison, METI officials reported that there was virtually no lobbying by other industries and very limited lobbying by auto firms such as Suzuki, which had no significant production facilities in Thailand, and Nissan, which did not majority-own plants or expand production until after the FTA was in place.[57] In line with the expectation of transnational lobbying efforts, the leadership of JAMA and Keidanren also directly addressed the Thai government and emphasized Japanese investment plans.[58] Although vertical specialization in manufacturing played an essential role in nurturing support for the Japan-Thailand

[53] *Kagaku Kōgyō Nippō* 2006.
[54] For detailed discussions of the Japanese shift toward an FTA policy, see Solís 2003.
[55] Yoshimatsu 2005, 2006.
[56] Hideya 2003.
[57] Author interviews with Japanese government officials, December 2003 and June 2008.
[58] *Nikkei Sangyō Shimbun* 2005.

agreement, the import-competing agricultural sector in Japan sought to prevent any significant opening to Thailand's most competitive exports: rice and sugar. Early in the negotiations, Japan's association of agricultural cooperatives obtained a blanket exclusion of these products.[59] In Thailand, suppliers that were partly or wholly owned by Japanese firms or sold primarily to Japanese manufacturers favored a PTA. Suppliers who feared competition from Japanese producers or who primarily supplied European and American producers remained opposed to it. As a result, the toughest bargaining took place over the reduction of tariffs on auto parts and luxury vehicles. European and American auto manufacturers who assembled high-end vehicles in small numbers in Thailand even explicitly opposed the agreement and motivated their suppliers to do the same. Compared to their Japanese competitors who hoped to export comparable vehicles from Japan, they would have faced a higher cost basis because their production could not be vertically specialized.[60] A similar split emerged among textile manufacturers. If fabric producers, either Thai-owned or subsidiaries of Japanese multinationals like Teijin and Toray, supplied Japanese firms and formed part of their rent chain, they joined the coalition in favor of a PTA. In contrast, Thai apparel producers that did not form part of a chain did not lobby.

The liberalization outcomes in the agreement closely reflected the demands of the various lobbying groups and also the considerable asymmetry of the trade relationship between the partners. Thai tariffs on auto parts and specialized steel were gradually reduced from a high base to zero. In Japan, the corresponding imports were tariff free from the time the PTA entered into force. The majority of agricultural exports from Thailand were completely excluded, left for future renegotiation, or retained a tariff-rate quota (a lower tariff for a small amount of exports and a higher tariff—in fact, equal to Japan's most-favored-nation tariff—for the remainder). The few products that were liberalized would only become tariff-free in eleven to sixteen years. Meanwhile, although Thailand's tariff phasing is slower, the country only excluded thirty-two tariff lines from liberalization compared to Japan's 272 lines.

The Japanese did, however, make a few side payments in areas of interest to Thailand, which demonstrated that the Japanese government was willing to incur domestic political and financial costs to pave the

[59] Japan Association of Agricultural Cooperatives 2004.
[60] *Nation* (Bangkok) 2005.

way for the agreement. The payments also facilitated passage of the PTA in Thailand, where agricultural exporters had been largely unsuccessful in achieving their goal of improved access to the Japanese market. In addition, a variety of professionals—including dance and language teachers and Thai cooks—were listed as "instructors," which qualified them for temporary entry to Japan.[61] More importantly, in chapter 13 of the FTA the Japanese government offered to fund a variety of economic cooperation activities to help Thai firms adjust to trade liberalization. Two of these programs related directly to the auto industry and its suppliers. One offered support for the Thai steel industry, an opponent of tariff reductions that would have allowed Japanese specialized steel imports, while the other provided training programs for the auto industry to strengthen human capital.[62] For the Japanese government, ratification of the agreement was unproblematic, since sensitive agricultural imports would only increase minimally. The deal offered few immediate gains for Thai exporters. Rather, the reward came in the form a sizable increase in investment from Japanese firms and the promise of growing exports of Japanese-designed goods from Thailand. Between 2006 and 2008, Japanese FDI into Thailand grew 30 percent, while annual exports of vehicles increased from 400,000 to over 700,000, according to Organization for Economic Cooperation and Development (OECD) statistics.

Although the case study provides evidence of the causal link between vertical intra-industry trade and formation of a North-South PTA, it tells little about how generalizable the argument is. Japanese FDI is clearly dominated by manufacturing, while its agricultural sector is notoriously protected. Moreover, the vertical intra-industry trade between Japan and Thailand is more important than in most trade relationships. The next section therefore presents a broader statistical test.

Quantitative Analysis

This section tests conjectures on the role of VIIT as a determinant of PTA formation using a data set of dyads (pairs) of nine developed and 148 developing and transition economies for the years 1995–2007. To reflect the scope conditions of the argument, the data set only includes North-South dyads matching the WTO classification of developed countries. The dyads sampled are those in which one (and only one)

[61] Ministry of Economy, Trade, and Industry 2010.

[62] See Baccini and Urpelainen forthcoming for an analysis of how such side payments can facilitate the conclusion of PTAs.

of parties is Australia, Canada, the EU, Japan, New Zealand, Norway, Singapore, Switzerland, or the United States. The relatively fine-grained trade data required for the calculation of VIIT shares, based on at least a six-digit disaggregation according to the Harmonized System (HS) of tariffs, are only available from 1995. Nonetheless, the twelve-year span comprises over 75 percent of the PTAs that have entered into force since 1948, and practically all North-South PTAs concluded since then. A total of ninety-eight PTAs are included in the data set.

ESTIMATION

Two problems arise when estimating the effect of vertical intra-industry trade on trade agreement formation. First, VIIT presupposes a selection effect, since only country pairs that have at least some vertically specialized trade can experience any effect on bilateral PTA formation. Second, PTA formation is a binary variable, requiring a dynamic panel estimation. Selection effects are often modeled using the canonical model proposed by James Heckman,[63] but thus far no selection models have been developed for binary dependent variables that take time-dependence into account. A relatively straightforward solution to this problem is a two-stage estimation. For the first stage, I use a gravity-type model to estimate the share of vertical intra-industry trade between two countries.[64] The predicted values from this model then become the independent variable of interest in the second-stage logit estimation with a binary dependent variable. I use a bootstrapping procedure to resample from the individual panels to obtain correct standard errors.[65]

KEY VARIABLES

For the first-stage equation, the dependent variable of interest is the percentage share of vertical intra-industry trade (*VIIT share)* in the bilateral trade of a country dyad in a given year. To measure intra-industry trade and distinguish its vertical and horizontal types, the empirical literature generally uses threshold methods. These methods are based on the assumption that the difference in the unit value of exports and imports of each good provides information about the differences in the quality of the goods traded between the two economies. Quality

[63] Heckman 1979.

[64] The use of a gravity model to estimate intra-industry trade has been theoretically justified by Bergstrand 1989.

[65] A readable introduction to the bootstrap is Efron and Tibshirani 1994. Bischof 2009 provides a careful comparison of the panel bootstrap with more common techniques based on Monte Carlo studies, and finds that it outperforms them when N > T , as in this study. See also Brandt and Schneider 2004 and the Web appendix at www.markmanger.net/published-work for further discussion and references.

characteristics are in turn associated with relative capital intensity and technological level.[66] Accordingly, if goods within a product category differ in unit value, and if this unit value crosses a certain threshold, then the trade is considered vertical intra-industry trade. If the unit value difference stays below this threshold, it is categorized as horizontal intra-industry trade differentiated by variety unrelated to technology or income level. Most studies of intra-industry trade use threshold values of 15 or 25 percent.[67] A refinement of the threshold method as proposed by Lionel Fontagné and Michael Freudenberg[68] decomposes the trade into vertical and horizontal intra-industry trade and the remaining one-way trade.[69] The principal advantage of this method is that it is less likely to overstate the value of intra-industry trade—because very small intra-industry trade values in specific product categories often result from misclassification of imports or exchange rate changes—but still aligns closely with the approach used in much of the empirical literature.

The calculation of the variable is as follows. First, as my theoretical framework applies only to manufacturing trade, I begin by eliminating all trade observations with a six-digit HS tariff code lower than 4XXXXX. I then check if there is significant two-way trade within a particular product category. I define trade as one way (OWT) if the smaller flow in a given category is less than 10 percent of the larger flow in terms of value. Such OWT is fundamentally based on comparative advantage, and the 10 percent cutoff eliminates flows that are not a structural feature of bilateral trade.

The remaining trade is two-way intra-industry trade that is further differentiated into its vertical and horizontal varieties. Horizontal intra-industry trade is defined here as trade in which the unit values differ by less than 25 percent. The trade data for this calculation is drawn from the CEPII's BACI (International Trade Database at the Product Level) database[70] and then aggregated by dyad year.

A concrete example helps to explain the calculation. In 2009, Japan exported 750,309 units of "parts of vacuum pumps, compressors, fans,

[66] Alternative approaches would be to use hedonic pricing like Cooper, Greenaway, and Rayner 1993, or price elasticity like Brenton and Winters 1992, but the necessary data is not available for most developing countries. See Flam and Helpman 1987 for further discussion of the underlying theory.

[67] Abd-el-Rahman 1991; Greenaway, Hine, and Milner 1994. Important applications are Hu and Ma 1999 for China, Durkin Jr. and Krygier 2000 for US trade with OECD economies, and Martin-Montaner and Orts Ríos 2002 for Spanish trade with OECD partners.

[68] Fontagné and Freudenberg 1997.

[69] The decomposition approach has been used by Fukao, Ishido, and Ito 2003, and by Kimura and Ando 2005.

[70] Gaulier and Zignago 2010.

blowers, hoods" (HS code 841490) with a total value of $25,744,523, equal to a unit value of $34.31 each, to Malaysia. Malaysia sold 1,575,113 units worth $20,163,305, equal to a unit value of $12.80, to Japan. Within the same tariff category, the smaller flow by value is more than 10 percent of the larger flow, which indicates intra-industry trade. The products shipped from Japan to Malaysia are more than 25 percent more expensive than the corresponding imports, so the trade is classified as vertical intra-industry trade. The procedure is repeated for each tariff category and the total value of bilateral trade in each category summed up, so that the share in the total trade can be calculated. For these two countries, the VIIT share in manufactured goods ranges from 39 percent in 1997 to 55 percent in 2003.

The dependent variable in the second-stage equation PTA is binary and equals 1 if the two countries form a preferential trade agreement in that year, that is, if a previously negotiated and signed agreement legally enters into force. These dyads subsequently drop out of the analysis, that is, only the first PTA year is included. The definition of PTA encompasses all free trade agreements and customs unions that follow GATT Article 24, as well as any reciprocal trade agreement between WTO members and nonmembers. In line with the existing literature, it excludes partial-scope and unilateral agreements such as the Lomé Convention that only require one side to make concessions. Information on PTAs is drawn from the trade agreement databases of the WTO, the Organization of American States, McGill University, and the Tuck School of Business.[71] In contrast to earlier work, this study considers the European Union as a single actor. Since 1958, the Commission of the European Communities has negotiated all trade agreements on behalf of the EC's member states. Even though member states strongly influence decision making at the community level, the role of the EU as a coherent actor in international trade is well established in the literature.[72] At least legally, EU members have no more of an independent trade policy than US states, and by virtue of single-market directives probably less policy independence than, for example, Canadian provinces.[73] In short, the EU is qualitatively different from a trade agreement.[74]

[71] See rtais.wto.org, ptas.mcgill.ca, www.sice.oas.org/agreements_e.asp, and www.dartmouth.edu/~tradedb/database_home.php.

[72] Meunier 2005; Meunier and Nicolaïdis 1999.

[73] The EU is in this sense unique in international trade. While the members of the European Free Trade Association usually negotiate FTAs as a bloc for example, they sometimes go separate ways, as the 1992 Norway-Faroe Islands FTA and the 2009 Japan-Switzerland EPA show.

[74] Although this fact even today continues to dismay many British conservatives.

INSTRUMENTAL VARIABLES

For the first-stage equation, I use a standard gravity model in log form that includes the products of the GDP of both countries, their GDP per capita, and the total stock of FDI in the countries. In this setup, the products of GDP and FDI function as instruments for the share of vertical intra-industry trade in the bilateral trade. To satisfy the exclusion restriction, these variables need to be strong predictors of the instrumented variable (*VIIT share)*, but uncorrelated with the errors in the second-stage equation.[75] The choice of these instruments is guided by existing work on the determinants of vertical intra-industry trade. Theoretical models predict that differences in factor endowments and income cause VIIT.[76] Empirical studies show that vertical intra-industry trade is primarily influenced by economic size, factor endowments, foreign direct investment (including from third parties), and geographic distance.[77] I rely on GDP and FDI as instruments because there is little theoretical reason to believe that either instrument is correlated with the error term in the second stage or is a predictor of PTA formation more generally, other than indirectly through the effect of vertical intra-industry trade. Countries with sizeable markets should be less inclined to form PTAs among themselves because their industries already achieve sufficient economies of scale in the internal market, and past studies have generally found either a small or no significant effect of GDP on PTA formation.[78] While PTAs are effective policies to attract FDI, the reverse is not true—in fact, countries that already attract much FDI may not see the need to negotiate trade agreements.[79] Finally, although some scholars find that gravity-type models for VIIT work better when predicting the volume of trade in the category than when predicting the share in overall trade,[80] the relative importance of VIIT in the bilateral trade relationship comes closer to the political economy framework in this study and is used henceforth.[81] The measures of the income variables are from the World Development Indicators and Penn World Tables and the measures of FDI are from the United Na-

[75] Greene 2003, 196–97.

[76] Falvey 1981; Falvey and Kierzkowski 1987.

[77] Blanes and Martín 2000; Clark and Stanley 1999; Loertscher and Wolter 1980; Thorpe and Zhang 2005; Torstensson 1996.

[78] See among others Mansfield and Reinhardt 2003, 850.

[79] Büthe and Milner 2008 carefully investigate the possibility of reverse causality (FDI leading to PTA formation) and find no evidence of it.

[80] Fertö 2005.

[81] Using the predicted level of VIIT trade also strongly influences PTA formation, but since VIIT and level of trade are correlated, we cannot know if we are then simply testing whether more trade also predicts PTA formation. Results are available from the author.

tions Conference on Trade and Development (UNCTAD) FDI database.[82] All monetary values are deflated to constant 2000 US dollars using the Bureau of Economic Analysis implied GDP deflator. In addition, the equation includes *Distance*, measured as the great circle distance between the capitals of both countries, except for those countries in which the capital is not identical with the biggest population center.[83]

CONTROL VARIABLES

In the second-stage equation, *Distance* appears again as a key determinant of the likelihood of PTA formation, as does GDP per capita (now as individual terms), since richer countries are better able to shelter affected groups from trade liberalization and hence should have an easier time concluding trade agreements.[84] Past research has shown that allied countries are more likely to form PTAs.[85] I therefore include the variable *Alliance* coded as 1 if two countries have a formal military alliance in that year and 0 otherwise, based on Correlates of War project data,[86] with years after 2000 coded manually.[87] A further important control variable is regime type.[88] I therefore include the variable *Democracy*, measured on a scale from −10 to +10 and based on the Polity IV data set.[89] For several other control variables, the analysis draws on the landmark article on PTA formation by Edward Mansfield and Eric Reinhardt,[90] reproducing their variables for the later time period of this study for all countries in the sample, not just for those in the GATT/WTO as in their study. I include a dummy variable to denote an ongoing WTO negotiating round, *MTN round ongoing*, since PTA formation activity has increased greatly since inception of the Doha Round (the latest round of trade negotiations among WTO members), and a simple count of the number of WTO members, because greater membership may also induce countries to seek alternative arrangements.

Finally, I include the variable *PTA coverage of i and j* (respectively standing for North and South) similar to spatial lags used in recent studies,[91] which captures the notion that states will react to PTAs formed

[82] See stats.unctad.org/fdi/.

[83] Mayer and Zignago 2006.

[84] Mansfield 1998, 526.

[85] Gowa and Mansfield 1993; Mansfield and Milner 1999.

[86] Gibler and Sarkees 2004.

[87] While the EU does not have formal military alliances (since these remain in member state competence), I consider the EU to be in an alliance with a partner country if at least two of Britain, France, and Germany each have such an alliance with that country.

[88] Mansfield, Milner, and Rosendorff 2002.

[89] Marshall and Jaggers 2008.

[90] Mansfield and Reinhardt 2003.

[91] See especially Baccini and Dür 2012.

by their most important commercial partners in other countries. The variable is calculated as the proportion of *i*'s top-ten trade partners, exclusive of *j*, that had a PTA with *j* in the previous year. This should be particularly relevant for developing countries when developed countries conclude trade agreements with other developing economies, because developing countries compete not only for market access to the rich North, but also for FDI. The variable is lagged by one year because it is measured at the end of the time period; not lagging it would mean that some countries could perfectly anticipate their competitors' trade and policy and preempt them with their own PTAs.

THE MODELS

The first-stage equation is specified as

$$VIITshare_{ijt} = \beta_0 + \beta_1 (lnDist_{ij}) + \beta_2 (ln(GDP\,North_t * GDP\,South_t)) + \beta_3(ln(GDPcapNorth_t * GDPcapSouth_t)) + \beta_4(ln(FDI\,North_t * FDI\,South_t) + \gamma_t + \varepsilon_{ijt} \quad (1)$$

where y_t are year-specific fixed effects.

This equation is then used to predict the share of vertical intra-industry trade in the trade between the two countries in a pair in a given year. The predicted value $\hat{z}$ becomes the independent variable of interest in the second-stage equation, in which the dependent variable is 1 if a new PTA enters into force between two countries that do not already have such an agreement:

$$PTA = \beta_0 + \beta_1 \hat{z}_{ij,t} + \beta_3\, lnDist_{ij} + \beta_4 DemocNorth_t + \beta_5 DemocSouth_t + \beta_6\, Alliance_t + \beta_7\, GATTWTOmemb_t + \beta_8 MTNround_t + \beta_9 lnGDP capNorth_t + \beta_{10} lnGDPcapSouth_t + \beta_{11}\, PTACoverageNorth_{t-1} + \beta_{12}\, PTACoverageSouth_{t-1} + \varepsilon_{ijt}. \quad (2)$$

The only common variables in the two stages are *Distance* and *GDP-percapita.*

RESULTS

Table 3 presents the parameter estimates. Wald tests show that the instruments are all individually and jointly significantly different from zero (probability $>X^2 = 0.000$). Including them in the second stage, however, does not produce statistically significant estimates of their coefficients.

To reiterate, the central expectation is that ceteris paribus, a greater share of VIIT in the bilateral trade increases the probability that two countries will form a preferential trade agreement. The second-stage estimation (column 2) shows the expected result: the coefficient of $\hat{z}$, the predicted share of VIIT between two countries, is positive and significant. Moreover, it is substantively important. To show this, the relative risk contribution for each variable can be calculated by dividing the predicted probability of PTA formation when the variable is at its mean value plus one standard deviation, by the predicted probability of PTA formation when the variable is at its mean.[92] For negative coefficients, this ratio is inversed. For dichotomous variables, the relative risk is the ratio of predicted probabilities at 0 and 1. The relative risk contribution for each variable is shown in Figure 2. As $\hat{z}$ moves from its mean (5.25 percent) to one standard deviation above the mean (10.86 percent) with all other variables held at their mean, the predicted probability of PTA formation becomes 2.63 times larger. This effect is substantively more important than all others except *MTN round ongoing*, and slightly bigger in magnitude than the effect of *Democracy* in the developing country.[93] Marginal effects with a 95 percent confidence interval are shown to the right of the bars; as is typical with logit models predicting rare events, the marginal effects are quite small.

In Table 3, most control variables have the expected signs and correspond to previous results in the literature. The threat of exclusion from the markets of important trade partners, as captured by the measure of PTA coverage of the top-ten trade partners, is another important motivation for developed and developing countries alike. *GDP per capita North*, *GDP per capita South*, and *Democracy South* have the correctly signed coefficients, although only the last is significant in all specifications.[94] The only variables that change signs and lose significance in some specifications are *Number of WTO members* and *MTN round ongoing*. The results show no statistically significant effect of *Alliance* ties.[95] These findings are robust to a variety of checks. First, there is a possibility of simultaneity bias. Column 3 shows the second stage of the model with

[92] Given the two-stage setup, this implies recalculating the predicted mean in the first equation that is due to the shift in the second stage. I thank the anonymous reviewer who alerted me to this fact.

[93] The model correctly predicts 99.34 percent of the observations, but this is a typically exaggerated value when applying logit models to relatively rare events.

[94] Not much should be made of the coefficient on Democracy North, since the only developed country in the sample that is not a full democracy—Singapore—is probably exceptional in many respects. The estimated coefficient may capture the relative ease with which Singapore negotiates PTAs, given that it has no tariff barriers to eliminate.

[95] Note that the sample of this study is much smaller than usual, with between 1 and 10 percent of the observations of other dyadic studies that consider the whole international system post-WWII. This naturally yields lower significance levels for the control variables.

TABLE 3
ESTIMATION RESULTS, 25 PERCENT UNIT-VALUE DIFFERENCE THRESHOLD[a]

	1		2		3		4	
	Coeff.	*S.E.*	*Coeff.*	*S.E.*	*Coeff.*	*S.E.*	*Coeff.*	*S.E.*
Predicted VIIT share			.180***	.041				
Predicted VIIT share, *t–1*					.145***	.041		
ln VIIT share							.016*	0.008
Distance	–2.297***	.574	–1.196***	.231	–.679	.399	–1.654***	.198
Product of GDPs	1.154***	.183						
Product of GDP/cap	–.310	.242						
Product of FDI	.880***	.155						
Democracy North			–.155***	.039	–.150***	.043	–.114***	.032
Democracy South			.136***	.029	.084*	.034	.127***	.024
Alliance			.234	.448	.553	.548	.704	.393
Number WTO members			–.255***	.058	.112	.072	–.894***	.238
MTN round ongoing			2.648***	.876	–.620	.873	3.450***	1.044
GDP/cap North			–.072	.157	–.082	.211	.378**	.130
GDP/cap South			.335	.180	.470	.201	.480**	.167
PTA coverage North, *t–1*			1.953**	.596	2.304**	.846	2.564***	.466
PTA coverage South, *s*			2.728***	.762	2.161*	1.100	1.537*	.658
Constant	–28.872***	7.336	35.464***	8.474	–19.329	11.890	116.073***	30.523
Observations	12623		12623		11490		12623	
R^2	.21							
Pseudo-R^2			.39		.23		.40	

* $p < 0.05$, ** $p < 0.01$, *** $p < 0.001$

[a] Two-tailed tests are conducted for all estimates. Standard errors (S.E.) are bootstrapped by resampling from panels with 1,000 repetitions, except for column 4, which provides robust standard errors clustered over country dyads.

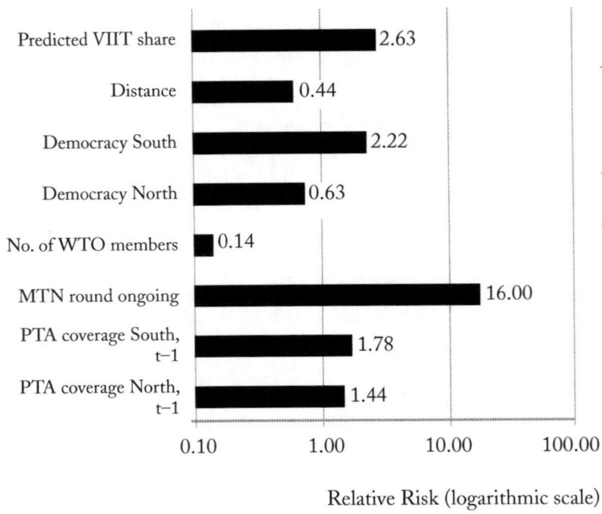

dy/dx	95% CI	
0.00014	0.00006	0.00023
−0.00095	−0.00164	−0.00025
0.00011	0.00004	0.00018
−0.00012	−0.00021	−0.00004
−0.00020	−0.00034	−0.00007
0.00284	−0.00013	0.00580
0.00216	0.00070	0.00362
0.00155	0.00027	0.00282

FIGURE 2
ESTIMATED CONTRIBUTION TO RELATIVE RISK OF PTA FORMATION, MODEL 2

the predicted *VIIT share* variable lagged by a year. The lagged variable retains its significance, positive sign, and substantive importance. The overall model fit is worse than in the case of a nonlagged variable. For comparison purposes, column 4 shows the estimation ignoring the selection effect described above and including the natural cubic splines.[96] The coefficient estimate for the share of VIIT remains clearly significant, but given the selection effect, its estimation is biased.

Second, the results do not depend on different threshold values (see Table 4). Columns 5 and 6 reproduce the same analysis for a VIIT unit-value difference of 35 percent, showing the first and second stages respectively. Columns 7 and 8 show the results for a 15 percent unit-value difference. At both threshold values, the predicted VIIT values remain significant and substantively important. The principal difference is that as the threshold moves closer to horizontal intra-industry trade with a relatively low difference in unit value of only 15 percent, the coefficient loses substantive importance. This finding is in accord with with the theoretical understanding that horizontal intra-industry trade is less relevant in North-South trade. Alternatively, horizontal intra-industry

[96] Beck, Katz, and Tucker 1998.

TABLE 4

ROBUSTNESS CHECKS, 35 PERCENT AND 15 PERCENT UNIT-VALUE DIFFERENCE THRESHOLD[a]

	5 (35%)		6 (35%)		7 (15%)		8 (15%)	
	Coeff.	*S.E.*	*Coeff.*	*S.E.*	*Coeff.*	*S.E.*	*Coeff.*	*S.E.*
VIIT share, 35% threshold			.194***	.042				
VIIT share, 15% threshold							.163***	.035
Distance	−2.307***	.516	−1.167***	.229	−2.738***	.636	−1.169***	.229
Product of GDPs	1.078***	.166			1.269***	.207		
Product of GDP/cap	.602*	.253			−.128	.276		
Product of FDI	.862***	.148			1.002***	.170		
Democracy North			−.155***	.038			−.154***	.038
Democracy South			.136***	.029			.136***	.029
Alliance			.218	.448			.226	.448
Number WTO members			−.261***	.059			−.264***	.059
MTN round ongoing			2.717**	.898			2.733**	.904
GDP/cap North			−.258	.178			−.112	.160
GDP/cap South			.152	.185			.294	.180
PTA coverage North, *t–1*			1.950**	.597			1.959**	.596
PTA coverage South, *s*			2.741***	.749			2.718***	.746
Constant	−42.485***	7.391	39.377***	8.734	−34.604***	8.261	37.208***	8.707
Observations	12339		12623		12339		12623	
R^2	.25				.23			
Pseudo-R^2			.40				.40	

* $p < 0.05$, ** $p < 0.01$, *** $p < 0.001$

[a] Two-tailed tests are conducted for all estimates. Standard errors (S.E.) are bootstrapped by resampling from panels with 1,000 repetitions.

trade may motivate some firms to lobby trade liberalization because under it they would have to bear adjustment costs individually.[97]

Third, we can compare the results of the *VIIT share* model with a model that uses aggregate bilateral trade flows as a predictor of PTA formation with the help of Akaike information criterion (AIC) and Bayesian information criterion (BIC). Both provide strong support for the choice of *VIIT share* rather than aggregate bilateral trade flows, with an AIC*N of 719.8 for *VIIT share* versus 743.7 for aggregate trade, and a BIC difference of 23.9 in favor of the *VIIT share* model.[98] A number of additional robustness checks are available in a Web appendix,[99] among them subsamples that alternatively drop the EU; the US; developed-country resource exporters such as Australia, Canada, New Zealand and Norway; and industrialized countries classified as developing by the WTO. The Web appendix also includes results for regressions with trade volumes instead of an instrumental-variable approach, fixed-effects models, and with the date of entry-into-force replaced by the date of signature of the PTA. None of these change the substantive finding.

Conclusion

Preferential trade agreements between countries of different levels of economic development have come to dominate the international trade regime in the post-Cold War era. Although the novelty of this phenomenon is widely acknowledged, much less research has been devoted to investigating its causes and effects than to the spread of trade agreements in general. I argue that the mutual specialization of manufactured-goods trade represents an important driving force behind PTA formation. While a number of studies have focused on the link with horizontal intra-industry trade, this article is among the first to specifically investigate the role played by vertically specialized trade.

Vertical specialization leads to the emergence of a political coalition in support of trade liberalization within the context of a preferential agreement. The governments of less-developed countries often seek PTAs as a policy to attract export-oriented FDI. Multinational firms from developed countries relocate the production of less-capital-intensive goods to these countries. The interests of countries with different per capita incomes therefore converge on preferential liberalization, al-

[97] Gilligan 1997.

[98] A BIC difference > *20* is classified as "very strong support" by Raftery 1995.

[99] www.markmanger.net/published-work.

beit with particular focus on the goods produced and exported by these firms and their suppliers.

The case study of the Japan-Thailand FTA illustrates how vertical specialization is linked to the formation of a political coalition led by a small number of lead firms. These lead firms mobilize their chain of suppliers to lobby for a relatively narrow liberalization effort in a PTA. As a result, the quickest gains are made in the reduction of trade barriers for these firms. By contrast, liberalization of trade that is based on comparative advantage and where the greatest gains could be made tends to be delayed. When these exports threaten import-competing industries in the North, they are at times completely excluded from tariff reductions. The statistical analysis presented in this article shows that the greater the share of vertical intra-industry trade in a North-South dyad, the more likely the countries are to form a preferential trade agreement. The result is robust to a variety of checks. Other variables identified in the literature likewise contribute to an increased probability, but the character of the bilateral trade relation clearly plays a central role and helps explain the growing popularity of PTAs in the post-Cold War era.

These findings have implications for the study of preferential trade agreements and economic integration in general. In particular, they suggest that preferential trade liberalization may negatively affect the prospects of trade liberalization in multilateral negotiation rounds. If the political constituents, that is, if multinational firms that have in the past counterbalanced protectionist sectors[100] are satisfied with preferential deals, then they are less likely to commit resources to support multilateral liberalization efforts. This means that manufactured-goods tariff reductions by less-developed countries can no longer be traded off against agricultural liberalization by richer partners. Given these political implications, PTAs driven by vertical specialization are (at the very least) unlikely to give multilateral efforts a boost.

This research can be extended in several directions. The case study suggests that in the context of a PTA, a high share of vertical trade in a particular tariff category should predict faster tariff liberalization for those goods than for manufactured goods that reflect comparative advantage—and far more quickly than for agricultural exports from the developing country. More generally, countries with very different natural factor endowments should be less likely to form PTAs than those with more similar endowments. An open empirical question is whether

[100] Milner 1988.

developing countries that have concluded such PTAs remain active supporters of WTO-centered liberalization or if they are content with the gains they have achieved. As PTAs remain popular, more research into their determinants, design, and effects is needed.

References

Abd-el Rahman, Kamal. 1991. "Firms' Competitive and National Comparative Advantages as Joint Determinant of Trade Composition." *Weltwirtschaftliches Archiv* 127, no. 1: 83–97.

Alfaro, Laura, and Andrew Charlton. 2009. "Intra-Industry Foreign Direct Investment." *American Economic Review* 99, no. 5: 2096–119.

Allee, Todd, and Clint Peinhardt. 2010. "Delegating Differences: Bilateral Investment Treaties and Bargaining over Dispute Resolution Provisions." *International Studies Quarterly* 54, no. 1: 1–26.

Alt, James E., Jeffry A. Frieden, Michael Gilligan, Dani Rodrik, and Ronald Rogowski. 1996. "The Political Economy of International Trade: Enduring Puzzles and an Agenda for Inquiry." *Comparative Political Studies* 29, no. 6: 689–717.

Athukorala, Prema-chandra, and Archanun Kohpaiboon. 2009. "East Asian Exports in the Global Economic Crisis: The Decoupling Fallacy and Post-crisis Policy Challenges." Working Paper 2009/13. Canberra: The Arndt-Corden Division of Economics, Australian National University, College of Asia and the Pacific.

Baccini, Leonardo, and Andreas Dür. 2012. "The New Regionalism and Policy Interdependence." *British Journal of Political Science* 42, no. 1: 57–79.

Baccini, Leonardo, and Johannes Urpelainen. Forthcoming. "Strategic Side Payments: Preferential Trading Agreements, Economic Reform, and Foreign Aid." *Journal of Politics*.

Baier, Scott L., and Jeffrey H. Bergstrand. 2004. "Economic Determinants of Free Trade Agreements." *Journal of International Economics* 64, no. 1: 29–63.

Balassa, Bela A. 1986. "The Determinants of Intra-Industry Specialization in United States Trade." *Oxford Economic Papers* 38, no. 2: 220–33.

Baron, David P. 1995. "The Nonmarket Strategy System." *Sloan Management Review* 37, no. 1: 73–85.

———. 1997. "Integrated Strategy and International Trade Disputes: The Kodak-Fujifilm Case." *Journal of Economics and Management Strategy* 6, no. 2: 291–346.

Beck, Nathaniel, Jonathan N. Katz, and Richard Tucker. 1998. "Taking Time Seriously: Time-series-cross-section Analysis with a Binary Dependent Variable." *American Journal of Political Science* 42, no. 4: 1260–88.

Bergstrand, Jeffrey H. 1989. "The Generalized Gravity Equation, Monopolistic Competition, and the Factor-Proportions Theory in International Trade." *Review of Economics and Statistics* 71, no. 1: 143–53.

Bhagwati, Jagdish N. 2008. *Termites in the Trading System: How Preferential Agreements Undermine Free Trade*. Oxford: Oxford University Press.

Bischof, Jonathan M. 2009. "A Bootstrap Approach to Time Invariance in Panel

Data." Paper presented at the American Political Science Association annual conference, Chicago, September 1–4.
Blanes, José V., and Carmela Martín. 2000. "The Nature of Causes of Intra-Industry Trade: Back to the Comparative Advantage Explanation? The Case of Spain." *Review of World Economics* 136, no. 3: 423–41.
Brandt, Patrick T., and Christina J. Schneider. 2004. "So the Reviewer Told You to Use a Selection Model? Selection Models and the Study of International Relations." Manuscript, University of Texas at Dallas.
Brenton, Peter A., and L. Alan Winters. 1992. "Estimating the International Trade Effects of '1992': West Germany." *JCMS: Journal of Common Market Studies* 30, no. 2: 143–56.
Büthe, Tim, and Helen V. Milner. 2008. "The Politics of Foreign Direct Investment into Developing Countries: Increasing FDI through International Trade Agreements." *American Journal of Political Science* 52, no. 4: 741–62.
Cameron, Maxwell A. 1997. "North American Trade Negotiations: Liberalization Games between Asymmetric Players." *European Journal of International Relations* 3, no. 1: 105–39.
Chase, Kerry A. 2003. "Economic Interests and Regional Trading Arrangements: The Case of NAFTA." *International Organization* 57, no. 1: 137–74.
———. 2005. *Trading Blocs: States, Firms, and Regions in the World Economy.* Ann Arbor, Mich.: University of Michigan Press.
———. 2008. "Protecting Free Trade: The Political Economy of Rules of Origin." *International Organization* 62, no. 3: 507–30.
Clark, Don P., and Denise L. Stanley. 1999. "Determinants of Intra-Industry Trade between Developing Countries and the United States." *Journal of Economic Development* 24, no. 2: 79–95.
Cooper, Douglas, David Greenaway, and Anthony J. Rayner. 1993. "Intra-Industry Trade and Limited Producer Horizons: An Empirical Investigation." *Review of World Economics* 129, no. 2: 345–66.
Crawford, Jo-Ann, and Roberto V. Fiorentino. 2005. "The Changing Landscape of Regional Trade Agreements." Discussion Paper 8, Secretariat of the World Trade Organization. Geneva, Switzerland: World Trade Organization.
Davis, Christina L. 2004. "International Institutions and Issue Linkage: Building Support for Agricultural Trade Liberalization." *American Political Science Review* 98, no. 1: 153–69.
Dür, Andreas. 2007. "EU Trade Policy as Protection for Exporters: The Agreements with Mexico and Chile." *Journal of Common Market Studies* 45, no. 4: 833–55.
Durkin Jr., John T., and Markus Krygier. 2000. "Differences in GDP Per Capita and the Share of Intra-Industry Trade: The Role of Vertically Differentiated Trade." *Review of International Economics* 8, no. 4: 760–74.
Efron, Bradley, and Robert J. Tibshirani. 1994. *An Introduction to the Bootstrap.* New York, N.Y.: Chapman & Hall/CRC.
Elkins, Zachary, Andrew T. Guzman, and Beth Simmons. 2006. "Competing for Capital: The Diffusion of Bilateral Investment Treaties." *International Organization* 60, no. 4: 811–46.
Falvey, Rodney E. 1981. "Commercial Policy and Intra-Industry Trade." *Journal of International Economics* 11, no. 4: 495–511.

Falvey, Rodney E., and Henryk Kierzkowski. 1987. "Product Quality, Intra-Industry Trade and (Im)Perfect Competition." In Henryk Kierzkowski and Rodney E. Falvey, eds., *Protection and Competition in International Trade*. New York, N.Y.: Basil Blackwell.

Feenstra, Robert C. 2003. *Advanced International Trade: Theory and Evidence*. Princeton, N.J.: Princeton University Press.

Fertö, Imre. 2005. "Vertically Differentiated Trade and Differences in Factor Endowment: The Case of Agri-Food Products between Hungary and the EU." *Journal of Agricultural Economics* 56, no. 1: 117–34.

Flam, Harry, and Elhanan Helpman. 1987. "Vertical Product Differentiation and North-South Trade." *American Economic Review* 77, no. 5: 810–22.

Fontagné, Lionel, and Michael Freudenberg. 1997. "Intra-Industry Trade: Methodological Issues Reconsidered." CEPII Working Paper 1997-01. Paris, France: Centre d'études prospectives et d'informations internationals.

Freund, Caroline. 2000. "Different Paths to Free Trade: The Gains from Regionalism." *Quarterly Journal of Economics* 115, no. 4: 1317–41.

Fukao, Kyoji, Hikari Ishido, and Keiko Ito. 2003. "Vertical Intra-Industry Trade and Foreign Direct Investment in East Asia." Tokyo, Japan: Research Institute of the Ministry of Economy, Trade and Industry.

Gaulier, Guillaume, and Soledad Zignago. 2010. "BACI: International Trade Database at the Product Level: The 1994–2007 Version." CEPII Working Paper 2010-23. Paris: Centre d'études prospectives et d'informations internationals.

Gibler, Douglas M., and Meredith Sarkees. 2004. "Measuring Alliances: The Correlates of War Formal Interstate Alliance Data Set, 1816–2000." *Journal of Peace Research* 41, no. 2: 211–22.

Gilligan, Michael J. 1997. "Lobbying as a Private Good with Intra-Industry Trade." *International Studies Quarterly* 41, no. 3: 455–74.

Gowa, Joanne S. 1995. *Allies, Adversaries, and International Trade*. Princeton, N.J.: Princeton University Press.

Gowa, Joanne, and Edward D. Mansfield. 1993. "Power Politics and International Trade." *American Political Science Review* 87, no. 2: 408–20.

Greenaway, David. 1992. "Trade-Related Investment Measures and Development Strategy." *Kyklos* 45, no. 2: 139–59.

Greenaway, David, Robert Hine, and Chris Milner. 1994. "Country-Specific Factors and the Pattern of Horizontal and Vertical Intra-Industry Trade in the UK." *Weltwirtschaftliches Archiv* 130, no. 1: 77–100.

Greene, William H. 2003. *Econometric Analysis*, 5th ed. Upper Saddle River, N.J.: Prentice Hall.

Grossman, Gene M., and Elhanan Helpman. 1994. "Protection for Sale." *American Economic Review* 84, no. 4: 833–50.

Haftel, Yoram Z. 2010. "Ratification Counts: US Investment Treaties and FDI Flows into Developing Countries." *Review of International Political Economy* 17, no. 2: 348 –77.

Haggard, Stephan. 1997. "Regionalism in Asia and the Americas." In Edward D. Mansfield and Helen V. Milner, eds., *The Political Economy of Regionalism*. New York, N.Y.: Columbia University Press.

Hale, Thomas. 2011. "The De Facto Preferential Trade Agreement in East Asia." *Review of International Political Economy* 18, no. 3: 299–327.

Hatch, Walter, and Kozo Yamamura. 1996. *Asia in Japan's Embrace: Building a Regional Production Alliance*. Cambridge, UK: Cambridge University Press.

Heckman, James J. 1979. "Sample Selection Bias as a Specification Error." *Econometrica* 47, no. 1: 153–61.

Helpman, Elhanan. 1984. "A Simple Theory of International Trade with Multinational Corporations." *Journal of Political Economy* 92, no. 3: 451–71.

Helpman, Elhanan, and Paul R. Krugman. 1985. *Market Structure and Foreign Trade: Increasing Returns, Imperfect Competition, and the International Economy*. Cambridge, Mass.: MIT Press.

Hideya, Taida. 2003. *Issues and Requests Relating to Trade and Investment in 2003*. Tokyo, Japan: Japan Business Council for Trade and Investment Facilitation.

Hoekman, Bernard, and Michel M. Kostecki. 2009. *The Political Economy of the World Trading System: The WTO and Beyond*, 3rd ed. Oxford, UK: Oxford University Press.

Hu, Xiaoling, and Yue Ma. 1999. "International Intra-Industry Trade of China." *Review of World Economics* 135, no. 1: 82–101.

Hummels, David, Dana Rapoport, and Kei-Mu Yi. 1998. "Vertical Specialization and the Changing Nature of World Trade." *Economic Policy Review* 4, no 2: 79–99.

Japan Association of Agricultural Cooperatives (JA Group). 2004. "Kankoku, tai, fuiripin, indoneshia to no FTA ni kan suru JA gurūpu no kihonteki na kangaekata [JA Group's Basic View of the FTAs with Korea, Thailand, Indonesia, and the Philippines]." *Nihon Nōgyō Shimbun*. February 11: 2.

Kagaku Kōgyō Nippō. 2006. "Ajia no jidōsha, zairyō sangyō (2) [The Asian Car, Materials Industries, Part 2]." August, 2: 2.

Kerner, Andrew. 2009. "Why Should I Believe You? The Costs and Consequences of Bilateral Investment Treaties." *International Studies Quarterly* 53, no. 1: 73–102.

Kim, Soo Yeon. 2010. *Power and the Governance of Global Trade: From the GATT to the WTO*. Ithaca, N.Y: Cornell University Press.

Kimura, Fukunari, and Mitsuyo Ando. 2005. "Two-Dimensional Fragmentation in East Asia: Conceptual Framework and Empirics." *International Review of Economics & Finance* 14, no. 3: 317–48.

Kono, Daniel Yuichi. 2009. "Market Structure, Electoral Institutions, and Trade Policy." *International Studies Quarterly* 53, no. 4: 885–906.

Krishna, Kala, and Anne O. Krueger. 1995. "Implementing Free Trade Areas: Rules of Origin and Hidden Protection." In Alan Deardorff, James Levinsohn, and Robert Stern, eds., *New Directions in Trade Theory*. Ann Arbor: University of Michigan Press.

Krugman, Paul R. 1981. "Intra-Industry Specialization and the Gains from Trade." *Journal of Political Economy* 89, no. 5: 959–73.

Loertscher, Rudolf, and Frank Wolter. 1980. "Determinants of Intra-Industry Trade: Among Countries and across Industries." *Review of World Economics* 116, no. 2: 280–93.

Maggi, Giovanni, and Andrés Rodríguez-Clare. 2007. "A Political-Economy Theory of Trade Agreements." *American Economic Review* 97, no. 4: 1374–406.

Mansfield, Edward D. 1998. "The Proliferation of Preferential Trading Arrangements." *Journal of Conflict Resolution* 42, no. 5: 523–43.

Mansfield, Edward D., and Helen V. Milner. 1999. "The New Wave of Regionalism." *International Organization* 53, no. 3: 589–627.

Mansfield, Edward D., Helen V. Milner, and B. Peter Rosendorff. 2002. "Why Democracies Cooperate More: Electoral Control and International Trade Agreements." *International Organization* 56, no. 3: 477–513.

Mansfield, Edward D., Helen V. Milner, and Jon C. Pevehouse. 2007. "Vetoing Co-Operation: The Impact of Veto Players on Preferential Trading Arrangements." *British Journal of Political Science* 37, no. 3: 403–32.

Mansfield, Edward D., and Eric Reinhardt. 2003. "Multilateral Determinants of Regionalism: The Effects of GATT/WTO on the Formation of Preferential Trading Arrangements." *International Organization* 57, no. 4: 829–62.

———. 2008. "International Institutions and the Volatility of International Trade." *International Organization* 62, no. 4: 621–52.

Markusen, James R., and Keith E. Maskus. 2002. "Discriminating among Alternative Theories of the Multinational Enterprise." *Review of International Economics* 10, no. 4: 694–707.

Markusen, James R., and Anthony J. Venables. 1998. "Multinational Firms and the New Trade Theory." *Journal of International Economics* 46, no. 2: 183–203.

Marshall, Monty G., and Keith Jaggers. 2008. *Polity IV Data Set*, 2008 ed. College Park, Md.: Center for International Development and Conflict Management, University of Maryland.

Martin-Montaner, Joan A., and Vicente Orts Ríos. 2002. "Vertical Specialization and Intra-Industry Trade: The Role of Factor Endowments." *Review of World Economics* 138, no. 2: 340–65.

Mayer, Thierry, and Soledad Zignago. 2006. *CEPII Distance Data*. Paris, France: Centre d'études prospectives et d'informations internationals.

Meunier, Sophie. 2005. *Trading Voices: The European Union in International Commercial Negotiation*. Princeton, N.J.: Princeton University Press.

Meunier, Sophie, and Kalypso Nicolaïdis. 1999. "Who Speaks for Europe? The Delegation of Trade Authority in the EU." *JCMS: Journal of Common Market Studies* 37, no. 3: 477–501.

Milner, Helen V. 1988. *Resisting Protectionism: Global Industries and the Politics of International Trade*. Princeton, N.J.: Princeton University Press.

———. 1997. "Industries, Governments, and the Creation of Regional Trade Blocs." In Edward D. Mansfield and Helen V. Milner, eds., *The Political Economy of Regionalism*. New York, N.Y.: Columbia University Press.

Milner, Helen V., and Keiko Kubota. 2005. "Why the Move to Free Trade? Democracy and Trade Policy in the Developing Countries." *International Organization* 59, no. 1: 107–43.

Ministry of Economy, Trade, and Industry. 2005. "Dai-sanjūkai Heisei jūgo nendo kaigai jigyō katsudō kihon chōsa [2003 Basic Study of Overseas Firm Activities: The Overseas Activities of Japanese Enterprises.]" Tokyo, Japan: Ministry of Economy, Trade, and Industry (METI) Economic and Industrial Policy Bureau, Research and Statistical Studies Division, Industrial Statistics Office and METI Trade and Economic Cooperation Bureau, Trade Division.

———. 2010. "2010 Report on Compliance by Major Trading Partners with Trade Agreements." Tokyo, Japan: Ministry of Economy, Trade and Industry.

Nation (Bangkok). 2005. "Warning from Carmakers." April 8: 12.

Neumayer, Eric, and Laura Spess. 2005. "Do Bilateral Investment Treaties Increase Foreign Direct Investment to Developing Countries?" *World Development* 33, no. 10: 1567–85.

Nikkei Sangyō Shimbun. 2005. "Kōzai neage de jikōkai kaichō: 'kakaku tenka muzukashii' [Steel Price Increase Not To Blame for Rising Costs, Says JAMA Chairman]." June 20: 13.

Pekkanen, Saadia M., Mireya Solís, and Saori N. Katada. 2007. "Trading Gains for Control: International Trade Forums and Japanese Economic Diplomacy." *International Studies Quarterly* 54, no. 4: 945–70.

Raftery, Adrian E. 1995. "Bayesian Model Selection in Social Research." *Sociological Methodology* 25, no. 1: 111–64.

Rogowski, Ronald. 1989. *Commerce and Coalitions*. Princeton, N.J.: Princeton University Press.

Sally, Razeen. 2007. "Thai Trade Policy: From Non-discriminatory Liberalisation to FTAs." *The World Economy* 30, no. 10: 1594–620.

Schiff, Maurice W., and L. Alan Winters. 2003. *Regional Integration and Development*. Washington, DC: World Bank.

Shadlen, Kenneth C. 2005. "Exchanging Development for Market Access? Deep Integration and Industrial Policy under Multilateral and Regional-Bilateral Trade Agreements." *Review of International Political Economy* 12, no. 5: 750–75.

Solís, Mireya. 2003. "Japan's New Regionalism: The Politics of Free Trade Talks with Mexico." *Journal of East Asian Studies* 3, no. 3: 377–404.

Thorpe, Michael, and Zhaoyang Zhang. 2005. "Study of the Measurement and Determinants of Intra-Industry Trade in East Asia." *Asian Economic Journal* 19, no. 2: 231–47.

Torstensson, John. 1996. "Can Factor Proportions Explain Vertical Intra-Industry Trade?" *Applied Economics Letters* 3, no. 5: 307–309.

Trefler, Daniel. 1993. "Trade Liberalization and the Theory of Endogenous Protection—An Econometric Study of United States Import Policy." *Journal of Political Economy* 101, no. 1: 138–60.

Yoshimatsu, Hidetaka. 2005. "Japan's Keidanren and Free Trade Agreements: Societal Interests and Trade Policy." *Asian Survey* 45, no. 2: 258–78.

———. 2006. "The Politics of Japan's Free Trade Agreement." *Journal of Contemporary Asia* 36, no. 4: 479–99.

[5]

Multilateral Determinants of Regionalism: The Effects of GATT/WTO on the Formation of Preferential Trading Arrangements

Edward D. Mansfield and Eric Reinhardt

Abstract Preferential trading arrangements (PTAs) have spread widely over the past fifty years. During the same era, multilateral openness has grown to unprecedented heights, spurred by the General Agreement on Tariffs and Trade (GATT) and its successor, the World Trade Organization (WTO). If the cornerstone of the manifestly successful multilateral regime is nondiscrimination, why have its members increasingly resorted to preferential liberalization? We argue that developments at the heart of GATT/WTO encourage its members to form PTAs as devices to obtain bargaining leverage within the multilateral regime. Specifically, the growth in GATT/WTO membership, the periodic multilateral trade negotiation rounds, as well as participation and, especially, losses in formal GATT/WTO disputes, have led its members to seek entrance into PTAs. Conducting the first statistical tests on the subject, we find strong evidence in support of this argument.

What are the problems of the GATT that lead countries to turn to their neighborhood instead?

Paul Krugman (1993, 73)

During the past fifty years, the international trading system has been marked by the rapid proliferation of preferential trading arrangements (PTAs). During the same era, multilateral openness has grown to unprecedented heights, spurred by the General Agreement on Tariffs and Trade (GATT) and its successor, the World Trade Organization (WTO). That these developments have occurred in tandem is somewhat surprising. Whereas the norm of nondiscrimination in trade is the corner-

For helpful comments, we are grateful to Marc Busch, Peter Gourevitch, David Lake, Lisa Martin, Joy Mazumdar, Helen Milner, Thomas Oatley, Çaglar Özden, Francisco Parodi, Jon Pevehouse, Jay Smith, Jeffrey Stacey, Chris Zorn, and two anonymous reviewers. For research assistance, we thank Yoram Haftel, Jesse Hamner, and Jon Pevehouse. Earlier versions of this article were presented at the 2000 Annual Meeting of the American Political Science Association, Washington, D.C.; the 2001 Annual Meeting of the Midwest Political Science Association, Chicago; and seminars at Emory University, the University of Chicago (PIPES), the University of Illinois, and the University of Wisconsin.

International Organization 57, Fall 2003, pp. 829–862

DOI: 10.1017/S0020818303574069

stone of GATT/WTO, PTAs vest each member with preferential access to the other participants' markets. Equally surprising is that most preferential groupings are composed of GATT/WTO members. It is not clear why states form preferential economic blocs when they belong to a successful multilateral regime. How the spread of PTAs will affect the GATT/WTO system has been widely studied and fiercely debated.[1] Remarkably little research, however, has addressed how, if at all, the multilateral regime has conditioned the spread of PTAs.

We argue that GATT/WTO has played a large role in stimulating the formation of PTAs. A central reason why states enter PTAs is to increase their bargaining power. Preferential arrangements serve this purpose by furnishing states with insurance against the emergence of conditions within GATT/WTO that could threaten their economic interests, as well as by giving states a greater voice in multilateral trade talks and increasing their market power. Developments within the multilateral regime can create incentives for states to enhance their bargaining power, thereby triggering the establishment of preferential groupings. These developments include the growth of GATT/WTO membership, which has reduced each participant's leverage over the pace and path of multilateral liberalization. Such growth has also heightened collective action problems within the regime, making it progressively more difficult to conclude new multilateral agreements, monitor members' behavior, and enforce the regime's rules. Forming a PTA composed of a small group of members with similar economic interests can help states insure against the adverse consequences stemming from these problems.

In addition, the central vehicles used to promote an open global trading system—the periodic multilateral trade negotiations (MTNs) sponsored by GATT/WTO—can prompt members to enter PTAs as a means of guaranteeing they will not be left behind if the MTN stalls and of boosting their bargaining position in the multilateral talks. Therefore, states have reasons to establish a PTA during multilateral negotiating rounds. Trade disputes among GATT/WTO members are also likely to influence whether and when states accede to a preferential arrangement. A country embroiled in a GATT/WTO dispute may seek PTAs with third parties in the hopes of improving its leverage in the conflict. Likewise, losing a GATT/WTO dispute can impel a state to form preferential arrangements with third parties to obtain countervailing market access, insurance against future GATT/WTO enforcement failures, or additional bargaining leverage.

To test these arguments, we conduct one of the first systematic analyses of PTA formation within GATT/WTO. The evidence strongly supports our claims. Countries are more likely to form a PTA when (1) GATT/WTO membership rises, (2) a multilateral negotiating round is taking place, and (3) they have recently participated in a GATT/WTO dispute, especially when (4) they obtained an unsatisfactory outcome in the dispute. More generally, our results indicate that while

1. See Bhagwati 1993; Bhagwati and Panagariya 1996; Krugman 1993; Lawrence 1996; Mansfield and Milner 1999; Oye 1992; Pomfret 1997; and WTO 1995a.

GATT/WTO has made considerable headway in liberalizing foreign trade, it has also had various unintended consequences. Particularly important is that developments and institutional features associated with the growth of multilateral liberalization—such as rising GATT/WTO membership, MTNs, and active dispute settlement—create incentives for states to seek bilateral commercial arrangements in hopes of obtaining the greatest possible benefits from the multilateral regime.

Discrimination in a 'Nondiscriminatory' System

The central feature of all PTAs is the special market access that each member grants the other participants. Members set lower trade barriers on goods produced within the preferential grouping than on those produced elsewhere. These institutions—which include agreements that partially liberalize commerce, free trade areas (FTAs), customs unions, and common markets—have dotted the international landscape for centuries, but they have become increasingly pervasive in the past fifty years. Dozens have formed since the conclusion of World War II, and the concentration of trade flows has risen substantially within many PTAs, leading to widespread agreement that these groupings have become key elements of the international political economy.[2]

Because PTAs are generally made up of countries located in the same geographical region, the spread of these arrangements has led many observers to conclude that commercial regionalism is on the rise. As shown in Figure 1, two distinct waves of regionalism took place during the second half of the twentieth century.[3] The first occurred from the late 1950s through the 1970s; the second occurred in the 1990s.

Most PTAs formed since World War II have been composed of parties to GATT and the WTO; and, at present, virtually every WTO member belongs to some type of preferential arrangement.[4] From its inception, GATT attempted to regulate these arrangements.[5] Article XXIV of the 1947 General Agreement on Tariffs and Trade—GATT's founding document—stipulates that member-states are permitted to form a PTA only if it eliminates barriers to "substantially all the trade" among its mem-

2. Serra et al. 1997, 8.

3. See Bhagwati 1993; and Mansfield and Milner 1999.

4. WTO 1995a. In this article, we are only concerned with "reciprocal" PTAs. Nonreciprocal agreements, such as the Generalized System of Preferences, are ones in which advanced industrial states unilaterally grant preferential market access to developing countries without requiring any trade concessions in return. The consequences for the trading regime are profoundly different than when preferences are reciprocal. Özden and Reinhardt 2003. While virtually every party to the WTO belongs to some PTA, only about half of them belong to a reciprocal PTA, as shown in Figure 2.

5. Provisions for forming PTAs were made at the time of GATT's establishment because it was apparent that this body would be hard pressed to forbid states from doing so. In addition, some decision makers seemed to believe that Article XXIV's requirement that PTAs remove all trade barriers among members would complement GATT initiatives to promote multilateral openness. Bhagwati 1993, 35–36.

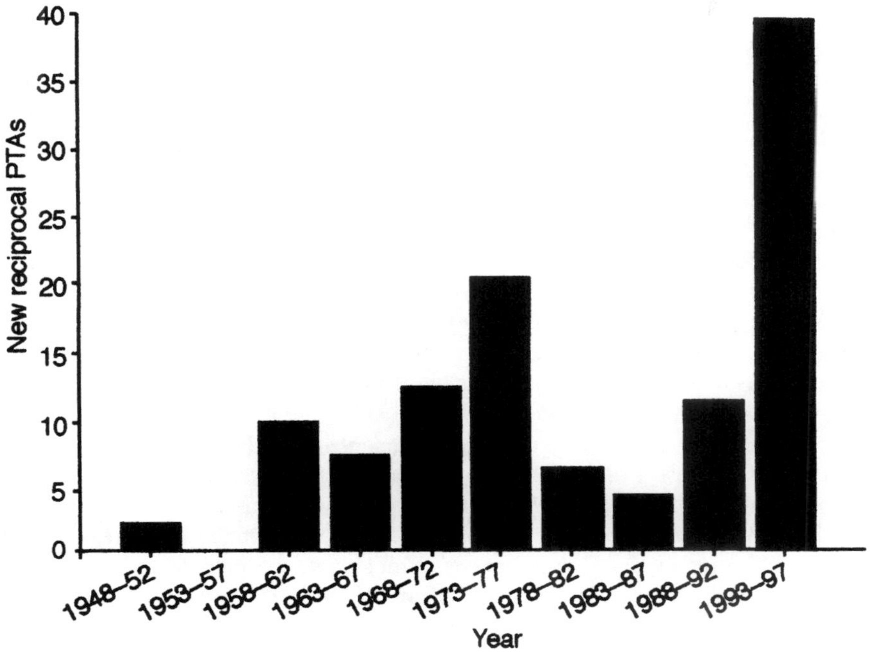

Note: Year indicates the date that PTAS entered.

FIGURE 1. *Number of new reciprocal PTAs notified to GATT/WTO, 1948–98*

bers and does not "on the whole" increase protectionism against nonmembers.[6] Further, the Enabling Clause, which was adopted by GATT in 1979, permits developing countries to furnish preferences to one another through the creation of PTAs that do not adhere to Article XXIV.[7]

These efforts to regulate the formation of PTAs, however, have met with little success. As Jagdish Bhagwati points out, with respect to such arrangements, the multilateral regime "is so full of holes in its discipline that almost anything goes."[8] Members have been required to notify new preferential groupings to GATT working parties (before 1995) and to the WTO's Committee on Regional Trade Agreements (since 1995). These bodies—which assess the degree of compliance by PTAs with GATT/WTO rules—have failed to reach judgment on all but one of the 118 PTAs submitted for review, mostly because of differences among members about

6. See Bhagwati 1993; and WTO 1995b, 791.
7. WTO 1995a, 18–19.
8. Bhagwati 1993, 44.

what constitutes compliance.[9] As a WTO staff member observes, "history has proved this to be one of the most unsatisfactory of all GATT procedures." [10] Consequently, a former GATT Deputy Director General concluded, "Of all the GATT articles, this [Article XXIV] is one of the most abused. [New PTA members] have little fear that they will be embarrassed by some GATT body finding them in violation of their international obligations and commitments and recommending that they abandon or alter what they are about to do." [11]

In fact, GATT/WTO members joining a PTA routinely violate Article XXIV. Trade barriers within preferential arrangements are almost never completely eliminated and members frequently raise trade barriers on nonmembers' products. Germany's average tariff on third parties, for example, nearly doubled after its accession to the European Economic Community in 1958.[12] To align with the European Union's (EU) textile and apparel import regime, Turkey increased its quantitative restrictions against outside states after signing an FTA with the EU in 1995.[13] Similarly, Mexico, Israel, and the members of the *Mercado Común del Cono Sur* (Mercosur) increased their external trade barriers after joining PTAs.[14] Even preferential groupings whose members have not raised their external trade barriers often inflict some damage on third parties, if for no other reason than because the preferential access granted to members' products degrades the competitiveness of nonmembers' products within the PTA.[15]

To be clear, we are not claiming that PTAs generally have been economically harmful. Although the available evidence indicates that some PTAs—especially those composed of developing countries—have had adverse economic consequences, various studies conclude that other arrangements—particularly those formed in recent years—have promoted economic welfare.[16] Regardless, the welfare implications of PTAs do not directly bear on the issues addressed here.

Nonetheless, the fact that GATT/WTO has been unable to prevent PTAs from enacting policies that place third parties at a competitive disadvantage in international markets suggests that, contrary to the view of some observers, GATT/WTO has not "made the world safe for regionalism." [17] Rather, we argue that

9. See Crawford and Laird 2001; Sampson 1996, 90; and WTO 1995a, 63, and 1999a.
10. Sampson 1996, 90.
11. WTO 1995a, 63.
12. Ibid., 47.
13. Hudec and Southwick 1999, 72–74.
14. Panagariya 2000, 317.
15. See Frankel 1997, 112–13; Freund and McLaren 1999; Sapir 2001; and Winters and Chang 2000.
16. See Bhagwati 1993; Bhagwati and Panagariya 1996; Frankel 1997; Panagariya 2000; and Pomfret 1997. Central to assessing the global welfare implications of a PTA is whether it creates more trade among members than it diverts from efficient producers located outside the arrangement. Viner 1950. However, it should be noted that in addition to this factor, PTAs affect members' welfare by influencing foreign direct investment, the governance of international economic relations, and other issues. See Lawrence 1996; and Yarbrough and Yarbrough 1992.
17. *New York Times*, 19 December 1993, D4.

states form PTAs to ensure the greatest possible gains from the multilateral regime itself.

How the Multilateral Trade Regime Induces PTA Formation

Much research concludes that states form PTAs to obtain the economic gains stemming from preferential access to members' markets (although it is worth reiterating that whether states actually benefit from such arrangements remains the subject of substantial controversy). A growing body of literature, however, focuses on the incentives for states to establish PTAs as a means of increasing their bargaining power within the multilateral regime.[18] We focus on two ways that states entering preferential groupings enhance such power.

First, establishing a preferential arrangement can strengthen a state's bargaining position vis-à-vis nonmembers by furnishing it with insurance against developments within the multilateral regime that threaten its interests. Developments such as the failure to reach agreement in multilateral trade talks become less costly because the state has already secured open access to its PTA partners' markets. An Australian government official illustrated this point nicely. Speaking about two proposed FTAs, he remarked that "Australia's clout in the WTO talks depends on holding the line in our bilateral trade negotiations with Japan [and] the U.S. . . ."[19]

Safeguarding access to crucial overseas markets by forming a PTA is particularly useful if the enforcement mechanisms in the multilateral trade regime, designed to minimize discrimination and new protectionism, prove weak.[20] Under these conditions, a preferential arrangement furnishes members with insurance against the prospect of their key trade partners unilaterally raising trade barriers in the future. Even if GATT/WTO enforcement mechanisms are strong, however, halting progress in achieving multilateral liberalization can stimulate fears of losing competitiveness in international markets, especially on the part of smaller states. For instance, at a time when the Uruguay Round had stalled and was threatening to end in failure, an Inter-American Development Bank official declared, "The Caribbean is in danger of becoming a backwater. Small countries will be wiped out unless they integrate."[21] Referring to the unsuccessful efforts to jumpstart multilateral liberalization at the WTO's 1999 Seattle Ministerial meeting and China's looming accession to the WTO, Singapore's Foreign Minister expressed concerns

18. See, for example, Bhagwati 1993; Bhagwati and Panagariya 1996; Fernández and Portes 1998; Krueger 1999; Krugman 1993; Ludema 1996; Mansfield 1998; Oye 1992; Perroni and Whalley 2000; and Whalley 1998.

19. *Australian*, 29 April 2002, 4.

20. Bagwell and Staiger 2001, 321.

21. *Journal of Commerce*, 3 September 1991, 5A.

that Southeast Asia was "being left behind economically while North Asian countries raced ahead." [22]

By insuring states against the loss of competitiveness in international markets and any future disruption in trade that developments within the multilateral regime could precipitate, PTAs promote the bargaining power of their members. The claim that preferential arrangements vest states with insurance against shocks to the international trading system has gained increasing currency in recent years.[23] To date, however, no effort has been made to analyze how events within GATT/WTO might lead member-states to seek the insurance that PTAs provide. This gap in the literature is surprising because it is widely acknowledged that even the United States has considered using PTAs to help offset the effects of any failures at the multilateral level.[24] In 1993, for example, U.S. Trade Representative Mickey Kantor explicitly argued that trade liberalization within the Asia-Pacific Economic Cooperation (APEC) and the proposed Free Trade Agreement of the Americas (FTAA) would be viable means to expand U.S. market access in the event that the Uruguay Round faltered.[25]

Second, PTAs may also boost bargaining power by giving states a greater voice in international trade forums and enhancing their market power. Many developing countries have considerable difficulty maintaining sufficient expertise on the multitude of covered issues and policies to participate effectively in multilateral trade negotiations. In fact, many of them have no delegation at the WTO whatsoever.[26] To help resolve these problems, various PTAs pool members' resources to improve how they research, articulate, and represent their common interests in trade talks with nonmembers. For example, observers agree that a primary goal of the Caribbean Community and Common Market (CARICOM) was to "strengthen the region's external position through the coordination of member states' [trade] policies." [27] Indeed, CARICOM has sometimes negotiated as a group at the WTO.[28] Likewise, Prime Minister Said Musa of Belize justified the proposed Central American-Caribbean FTA by saying, "we need to establish a common strategy so that we can obtain special treatment in international trade negotiations." [29] Even larger countries have incentives to use PTAs to coordinate on the best ways to pursue their mutual interests vis-à-vis third parties. For instance, Malaysian Prime Minister Mahathir Mohamad's 2002 proposal for an East Asian Economic Group,

22. *Financial Times*, 25 July 2000, 10.

23. See Fernández and Portes 1998; Mansfield 1998; Perroni and Whalley 2000; Whalley 1998; and Yarbrough and Yarbrough 1992.

24. Whalley 1998.

25. *Irish Times*, 29 October 1993, 14.

26. See Michalopoulos 1999; and Reinhardt 2002.

27. IADB 2000, 31; see also Andriamananjara and Schiff 2001.

28. WTO 2001.

29. James Canute, "Caribbean and Central America Press for Co-Operation," *Financial Times*. Available at ⟨www.ft.com⟩. Accessed 12 February 2002.

a revival of a Uruguay Round-era plan, was intended to help its potential members "be more effective in protecting their collective interests."[30]

Further, PTAs may increase leverage by accumulating the market power of individual members, giving them a greater ability to influence their terms of trade and to negotiate favorable settlements with outsiders.[31] On this score, Pascal Lamy—the EU's Commissioner for External Trade—conceded that "consolidating Mercosur will give Brazil and its partners . . . more political weight in international negotiations."[32] Anticipating the formation of Mercosur, a Brazilian official similarly remarked, "Dealing directly with the U.S. on international trade issues is like getting into a cage with a tiger. Only if we have others in with us do we stand a better chance of getting some satisfactory results."[33]

The ability of a PTA to heighten the market power of members is especially pronounced for states in a customs union—such as the European Community (EC) and Mercosur—because these institutions erect a common external tariff (CET) and thus bargain over tariff levels with third parties as a unit.[34] However, states need not form a customs union to enhance their negotiating position. It is widely argued that states have tried to influence the outcome of multilateral negotiations by threatening to form or actually establishing various types of PTAs.[35] Further, regardless of whether a PTA imposes a CET, its members accrue bargaining power insofar as the arrangement improves their reversion point in negotiations with third parties and promotes collective action among them. In any case, Rodney Ludema has identified a fairly broad set of conditions under which the external bargaining power of customs unions and other PTAs is quite similar.[36] Hence, we focus on PTAs as a group, rather than distinguishing among different types of them, in the following analysis.

Central to our argument is that developments within GATT/WTO have influenced when member-states have sought the bargaining power offered by PTAs. As we explain below, the existence of a GATT/WTO multilateral negotiating round, fluctuations in its membership, and its mechanisms to settle commercial disputes between members are particularly important in this regard.

Multilateral Trade Negotiations

Since its creation, GATT/WTO has sponsored eight rounds of MTNs: Geneva (1947), Annecy (1949), Torquay (1950–51), Geneva (1955–56), Dillon (1961–62),

30. *Business Times (Malaysia)*, 23 May 2002, 2.
31. See Fernández and Portes 1998, 201; Krugman 1993, 73; Lawrence 1996, 37; and Oye 1992.
32. European Commission, Trade DG, Information Unit, 10 July 2001.
33. *Financial Times*, 2 July 1985, 5. See also Lawrence 1996, 37.
34. However, FTAs routinely level asymmetries in external tariffs using rules of origin. WTO 1995a, 48–49.
35. See Fernández and Portes 1998; Krueger 1999; and Whalley 1998.
36. Ludema 1996.

Kennedy (1963–67), Tokyo (1973–79), and Uruguay (1986–94), plus the Doha Development Agenda, launched in November 2001. Participants in MTNs that enter a PTA may be able to strengthen their bargaining position in these negotiations.[37] Heightened market power enhances the ability of members to use protectionist instruments to improve their terms of trade, thereby dampening their incentive to liberalize trade and bolstering their bargaining position in multilateral negotiations.[38] Further, by vesting each member with preferential access to the markets of other participants, PTAs can help firms in member-states to achieve economies of scale. States entering a preferential grouping thus face a reduced need for multilateral liberalization to generate such economies, bolstering their leverage in multilateral negotiations.[39] In this vein, it is noteworthy that the definitive accounting shows that countries such as Bolivia, India, Australia, South Africa, and Ecuador were granted significantly fewer Uruguay Round market access concessions than, respectively, Uruguay, Brazil, Austria, Turkey, and Honduras.[40] At the time, the latter five countries were members of more preferential arrangements than the former five, suggesting that participation in these arrangements did indeed increase their bargaining power in the Uruguay Round. If PTAs boost bargaining power in MTNs, as this illustrative evidence suggests, then MTNs should provide an impetus for states to enter PTAs.

Moreover, by forming a PTA with key trade partners during a multilateral negotiating round, parties to GATT/WTO can obtain insurance against the round stalling or failing to produce results in the specific areas they deem most important.[41] A deadlocked MTN would place pressure on the multilateral regime and could threaten the stability of commercial relations between important trade partners. Such partners can minimize the severity of this threat by entering a PTA, because the grouping liberalizes commerce among members and limits their ability to raise trade barriers in the future. In addition, entering a PTA helps a state attract foreign investment: overseas firms are often drawn to the expanded market access offered by preferential groupings, especially when the outcome of multilateral talks is uncertain or delayed.

Although each of the eight MTNs sponsored by GATT/WTO yielded accords that liberalized global trade, nearly every MTN has been marked by intense disagreement while being fashioned. Ministers and observers often asserted that the round was in a state of crisis and teetering on the brink of failure until the final text was inked. The desire for insurance and bargaining power more generally is thus paramount throughout an MTN. We therefore hypothesize that PTAs are more likely to form during an MTN than when no such negotiation is underway.

37. See Bhagwati and Panagariya 1996; and Whalley 1998.
38. See Mansfield 1998, 527; and Oye 1992.
39. See Bhagwati 1993; and Fernández and Portes 1998, 201–2.
40. Finger, Ingco, and Reincke 1996, 201.
41. See Fernández and Portes 1998, 212; Krugman 1993, 74; Mansfield 1998, 535–36; Perroni and Whalley 2000; Whalley 1998; and WTO 1995a, 52.

Anecdotal evidence is consistent with this hypothesis. The WTO, for example, officially attributed the wave of regionalism during the past decade to events in the Uruguay Round, such as the failed Brussels Ministerial meeting in December 1990.[42] In the same vein, economic ministers of the Association of Southeast Asian Nations (ASEAN) launched an FTA in 1993, an initiative that was widely viewed as "a sign [of] . . . concern about the inability to achieve a successful conclusion to the Uruguay Round."[43] Equally, many observers point to the stalled multilateral negotiations as a critical catalyst for the U.S.-Canada FTA, arguing that the United States conceived of this arrangement as "a prod to recalcitrant nations to join in the GATT effort to make sure they weren't cut out of the action."[44] More recently, the United States has proposed an extensive series of bilateral trade accords, with the explicit purpose of leveraging more concessions from nonmembers during the Doha round of WTO talks.[45]

Growing GATT/WTO Membership

Membership in GATT/WTO has grown more than sixfold since its inception, from twenty-two states in 1948 to 137 in 2000.[46] It is widely recognized that as the multilateral system adds members, each member's leverage declines.[47] Especially for smaller states, which have relatively little bargaining power to begin with, there are clear incentives to respond to a decrease in leverage by banding together to enhance their influence through the formation of a PTA. Consistent with this hypothesis, a number of formal models have shown that rising GATT/WTO membership decreases the leverage of each participant and stimulates the establishment of preferential groupings.[48] To date, however, this issue has not received much systematic empirical scrutiny.

There are a number of related reasons to expect growth in the size of GATT/WTO to precipitate PTA formation. As the number of parties to the multilateral regime has increased, so have the severity of collective action problems and the heterogeneity of preferences within the institution.[49] An expanded membership reduces each participant's ability to monitor the trade practices of its counterparts. States also face rising incentives to cheat: because the actions of any single mem-

42. See Dryden 1995, 370; and WTO 1995a, 54.

43. *Far Eastern Economic Review*, 5 November 1992, 50.

44. Dryden 1995, 340; see also Preeg 1995, 80.

45. For example, upon the completion of the U.S.-Singapore FTA negotiations, U.S. Trade Representative Robert Zoellick declared, "I firmly believe that a process of . . . competitive liberalization will enhance our ability to get Doha done." See *Washington Post*, 20 November 2002, E3; and *Financial Times*, 1 November 2002, 14.

46. Chile signed the 1947 GATT agreement but did not accede formally until 1949. WTO 1995b, 1136.

47. See, for example, Koremenos, Lipson, and Snidal 2001, 791–92; and McCalman 2002, 154.

48. See Freund 2000, 373–74; and McCalman 2002, 154.

49. See Fernández and Portes 1998, 205; and Krugman 1993, 74.

ber are likely to have relatively little bearing on the performance of the multilateral regime, cheating is less likely to weaken the GATT system.[50]

Further, increased membership tends to introduce greater heterogeneity of preferences, as well as trade and business practices, within GATT/WTO. For example, when there are more negotiating partners, trade liberalization tends to influence more goods and adversely affect a greater number of potent interest groups.[51] Adding developing countries to the multilateral regime creates further complications, because the trade barriers these states most want removed (for example, those on textiles and agriculture) have long been the sacred cows of protectionist interests in the advanced industrial states. The accession of developing states to GATT/WTO also has intensified North-South divisions on intellectual property and labor and environmental standards. The WTO Director General admitted after the failed Seattle Ministerial meeting in 1999 that "the reason we had problems was the diversity of our members."[52] Even the addition of a single member can hamper efforts to promote multilateral liberalization. For example, the EU Trade Commissioner recently stated that "a round with China in is going to be much more difficult than a round without China in."[53] Because of China's WTO accession, Prime Minister Junichiro Koizumi has proposed a dramatic shift away from Japan's historical aversion to regionalism, starting with a PTA involving Singapore.[54]

Faced with heightened difficulty arriving at any overarching agreement on economic matters as the number of members grows,[55] parties to GATT/WTO may find it advantageous to form smaller, preferential arrangements composed of states with common interests on trade policy.[56] Such arrangements provide insurance against future disruptions of trade that might occur if multilateral negotiations buckle under the weight of a large number of participants with disparate commercial preferences, thereby enhancing the members' bargaining power within the regime.

GATT/WTO Disputes

While MTNs and membership growth are two of the most obvious achievements of the multilateral regime, the daily business—indeed, the "jewel"[57] or

50. Krugman 1993, 74.
51. Ethier 1999, 136.
52. *New Straits Times (Malaysia)*, 30 January 2000, 19.
53. *Financial Times*, 25 May 2000, 14.
54. See *International Trade Reporter*, 6 September 2001, 1389; and *Australian Financial Review*, 24 April 2002, 4.
55. The first MTN, in 1947, took six months to complete, whereas the last one took nine years.
56. See Ethier 1999; and Westhoff, Yarbrough, and Yarbrough 1994. In the same vein, Downs, Rocke, and Barsoom argue that PTAs have an easier time achieving deep integration than GATT/WTO because they generally have a more homogeneous set of members. Downs, Rocke, and Barsoom 1998.
57. Hudec 1993, 9.

"backbone"[58]—of the GATT/WTO system is settling commercial disputes among its members.[59] Formal GATT/WTO disputes occur with striking frequency and are another factor likely to affect the establishment of PTAs.[60] In a dispute, one state—the "complainant"—notifies GATT of its objections to trade practices of a counterpart—the "defendant." The disputants consult bilaterally and may request an independent legal judgment by a GATT/WTO-appointed panel of experts. Enforcement, however, is left to the complainant alone. Accordingly, a disputant is more likely to prevail—that is, to induce concessions from a defendant or withstand a complainant's retaliatory threats, as appropriate—if it possesses significant market power.[61] Because PTAs possess more market power than any constituent member, states may enhance their leverage in trade disputes by entering a preferential grouping.[62]

Of course, the stakes involved in any single dispute—while often surprisingly large—are small compared to those involved in forming a PTA.[63] It is therefore unlikely that, by itself, participating in a single GATT/WTO dispute would be sufficient to prompt a state to seek a preferential arrangement. Involvement in a dispute, however, dramatically raises a state's chances of participating in other future disputes.[64] Consequently, the costs of forming a PTA are at least partially offset by what are likely to be a long stream of improved dispute outcomes.

Further, many disputes concern policies, such as export subsidies, aimed at increasing competitiveness in a third party's market. An unsatisfied disputant may seek a PTA with that third party as a way of bypassing the dispute process. For instance, one of Argentina's primary motives for entering and deepening its commitment to Mercosur was to secure preferential access to the Brazilian wheat market. Brazil was Argentina's leading export market for wheat, and its competitiveness in that market was threatened by Canadian and U.S. export subsidy programs, which Argentina had challenged ineffectually in a GATT dispute.[65] In some disputes, third parties also face the possibility that disputants will arrive at a settlement that discriminates against them, thereby increasing the incentives for third parties to form a PTA with either disputant (separately) to ensure that their market access is not jeopardized.[66] Thus, we hypothesize that if either of a pair of countries has recently participated in a GATT/WTO dispute with a third party, the two will be more likely to form a PTA with each other.[67]

58. Moore 2000.
59. Reinhardt forthcoming, chap. 1.
60. From 1948 through 1998 there were over 600 GATT/WTO trade disputes.
61. See Hudec 1993, 318, 324, 326; and Mavroidis 2000.
62. See Bagwell and Staiger 2001; and WTO 1995a, 53.
63. On the size of the stakes involved in GATT/WTO disputes, see Reinhardt forthcoming.
64. Busch and Reinhardt 2002.
65. See *Los Angeles Times*, 9 December 1994, D3; and GATT 1994, 24.
66. Busch and Reinhardt 2002.
67. A good part of the U.S. emerging interest in regionalism in the 1980s derived from its frequent GATT disputes (often incompletely resolved) with the EU. Indeed, in February 1988, Treasury Secretary James Baker publicly chastised the EC's recalcitrance on several outstanding disputes and threat-

The incentives to form a PTA are greater still if a state ends up losing its dispute as well. Whether a state "wins" or "loses" a dispute is not defined by any multilateral legal judgment, but rather by practical policy consequences. A complainant loses for our purposes if it fails to induce the target to change the disputed policies fully; a defendant loses if it fails to maintain the status quo (protectionist) policy in the face of foreign pressure. Losing a dispute constitutes a proven bargaining failure. For a complainant, a loss is firsthand evidence that GATT's enforcement system is weak. The lesson may be that market access for its exports is best insured through bilateral rather than multilateral means. For a defendant, a loss is proof of its weakness, which is particularly galling when other states are sometimes able to resist foreign challenges against their protectionist practices. The lesson may be that the reciprocity underpinning the regime is only enforced at the convenience of more powerful members. Hence, we hypothesize that a state that has lost a recent GATT/WTO dispute will be especially likely to enter a preferential arrangement with a third party, to insure itself against future defeats and to bolster its position henceforth in such conflicts.

Research Design

Despite the widespread interest expressed in commercial regionalism, little systematic empirical research has analyzed the influences on PTA formation, let alone the role of GATT/WTO.[68] To address the hypotheses advanced earlier, we examine each pair of GATT/WTO members, i and j, that do not already share a PTA in every year, t, from GATT's creation in 1948 until 1998.[69] Our dependent variable, PTA, is the log of the odds that i and j form a PTA entering into force in t, given that the pair did not belong to the same PTA in year $t - 1$. We observe 1 if this occurs and 0 otherwise. We consider all PTAs (that is, partially-liberalizing agreements, FTAs, customs unions, and common markets) formally notified to GATT/WTO, as long as they are "reciprocal," meaning that each party grants the others preferential market access.[70] The annual number of GATT/WTO members entering reciprocal PTAs is shown in Figure 2. Out of all pairs of GATT/WTO members not already in the same PTA, a little more than 6 percent joined together in new PTAs at some point from 1948 through 1998.

ened that the United States was considering FTA talks with Japan, South Korea, and Taiwan, which took shape later as APEC. See Hudec 1993; and Preeg 1995, 80.

68. For some exceptions, see Mansfield 1998; and Mansfield, Milner, and Rosendorff 2002.

69. A state is included in the sample during year t if it was a member of GATT/WTO on any day in that year. The EC/EU is the only PTA that itself is a member of GATT/WTO; we do not include it but do count its member states. See Jackson 1969, 898–900; GATT 1990, 139; and WTO 1998.

70. See Smith 2000, 151; and WTO 1995a, 77–91 and 1999b. Note that PTA "upgrades" (for example, Sweden, Finland, and Austria, were in an FTA with the EU and then acceded to the EU proper in 1995) are not included in the following analysis, because the participants were already PTA members in $t - 1$.

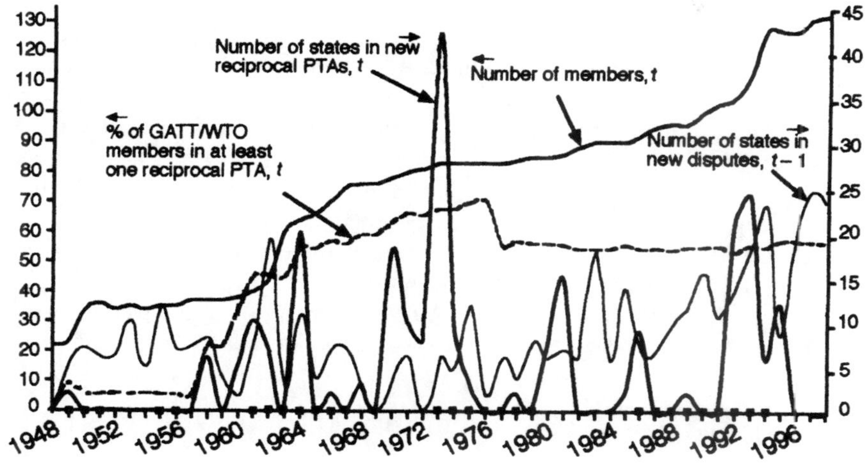

Note: Small arrows point to relevant vertical axis. Squares on horizontal axis show years in which an MTN was underway. "Number of states in new disputes" counts EU as one state.

FIGURE 2. *Trends in GATT/WTO membership, disputes, and reciprocal PTAs, 1948–98*

Explanatory Variables

To test our arguments, we focus on four explanatory variables. First, NUMBER OF MEMBERS is the number of contracting parties to GATT/WTO in $t - 1$.[71] Second, MTN ROUND UNDERWAY equals 1 if a formal multilateral trade negotiation occurred in t, 0 otherwise. Third, NEW DISPUTE WITH THIRD PARTY equals 1 if either i or j participated as a complainant or defendant in a GATT/WTO dispute with a third party in $t - 1$ (not counting third parties in PTAs with the other state in the pair), 0 otherwise.[72] Based on the arguments advanced earlier, we expect to find positive associations between PTA formation, on the one hand, and NUMBER OF MEMBERS, MTN ROUND UNDERWAY, and NEW DISPUTE WITH THIRD PARTY, on the other. Trends in these variables are shown in Figure 2. For the full population of GATT/WTO member-pairs, MTN ROUND UNDERWAY and NEW DISPUTE WITH THIRD PARTY equal 1 in 53 percent and 31 percent of the observations, respectively.

The final explanatory variable, DISPUTE LOSS WITH THIRD PARTY, indicates the performance of i and j in GATT/WTO disputes with third parties. It draws on an

71. The EC itself is not included in this count.

72. We include all complaints formally filed, not just those in which GATT/WTO adjudication panels were established or issued rulings. Disputes lodged against or by the EC/EU are assigned to every one of its contemporary members. The list of disputes is from Busch and Reinhardt 2002, which draws on Hudec 1993; and WTO 1995b, 620, 623–28, 772–87, and 1999c.

existing measure of the extent of concessions—none, partial, or full—made by a defendant to the initial demands of the complainant in a GATT/WTO dispute, regardless of whether a ruling was ultimately issued.[73] We define a participant as "losing" if it fails to meet its primary objectives in the conflict. The complainant loses if it fails to induce full concessions from the defendant; the defendant loses if it makes any concessions. DISPUTE LOSS WITH THIRD PARTY equals 1 if either i or j lost a dispute with a third party (again, excluding disputes where the third party belongs to a PTA with the other state in the pair) that started in year $t-3$, 0 otherwise. We lag the effects of this variable by three years because the average length of GATT disputes is roughly two to three years. This variable equals 1 in 20 percent of the population of GATT/WTO dyad-years. We anticipate a positive relationship between DISPUTE LOSS WITH THIRD PARTY and PTA formation.

Control Variables

To adequately assess the effects of these explanatory variables, it is important to control for various other factors that previous studies have identified as likely influences on PTA formation. First, open trade generates efficiency gains that can be used to enhance states' political-military capability. Preferential trading arrangements—all of which liberalize commerce among participants—thereby generate a security externality. States can help internalize this externality by trading more freely with political-military allies than with neutral countries or adversaries.[74] As such, PTAs are more likely to form between allies than between other states.[75] Hence, we analyze ALLIANCE, which equals 1 if i and j maintained a formal military alliance in $t-1$, 0 otherwise.[76]

Second, it is widely recognized that PTAs tend to form among states located in close geographical proximity to one another. A state's primary trade partners tend to be neighbors because of the reduction in transportation and transaction costs stemming from close proximity.[77] We therefore assess the effects of DISTANCE, which is the mileage (in thousands) between the capital cities of i and j, set to 0 if the pair is contiguous.[78] Third, recent research indicates that the likelihood of i and j forming a PTA rises as each country becomes more democratic.[79] We thus include DEMOCRACY, a 21-point measure of each state's regime type in $t-1$ that ranges from -10 for highly autocratic countries to 10 for highly democratic ones.[80]

Fourth, as a state's domestic market grows larger, it typically depends less on foreign trade and has less need to increase its market power for bargaining pur-

73. See Busch and Reinhardt 2002 and 2003; Hudec 1993; and Reinhardt 2001 and forthcoming.
74. See Gowa 1994; and Gowa and Mansfield 1993.
75. See Mansfield 1993; and Mansfield and Milner 1999.
76. Data on alliances are taken from Correlates of War Project 1993; and Lai and Reiter 2000.
77. See Deardorff 1998; and Frankel 1997, chap. 3.
78. Data on distance are obtained from Bennett and Stam 1999.
79. Mansfield, Milner, and Rosendorff 2002.
80. Data for this variable are found in Gurr and Jaggers 1999.

poses. Further, the expanded market access furnished by PTAs can help firms in member-states to realize economies of scale, but the corresponding gains tend to be greater for firms located in small countries. Hence, we expect the probability of PTA formation to be greater for economically small states than for their larger counterparts. To address this hypothesis, we analyze the gross domestic product (GDP) (in trillions of constant 1995 international dollars, expressed in terms of purchasing power parity) of each state in $t - 1$. Fifth, because many observers have noted that rich states tend to form PTAs more frequently than poor ones, we control for both states' PER CAPITA GDP (in thousands of constant 1995 international dollars, expressed in terms of purchasing power parity) in year $t - 1$. Sixth, it has been argued that downturns in the business cycle can prompt states to enter PTAs.[81] Because PTAs discriminate against third parties, joining a preferential grouping is one way that governments can respond to the domestic pressures for protection that often accompany recessions without contravening GATT/WTO rules. Joining a PTA also attends to a country's export-oriented firms, which have particular reason to press for preferential access to foreign markets in the face of depressed demand for their products. We therefore include GROWTH, the annual percentage change in each state's real GDP for year $t - 1$.[82]

We have argued that strategic interaction guides the formation of PTAs, as states seek to augment their bargaining position within GATT/WTO. Moreover, we have argued that developments within GATT/WTO influence the nature of strategic interaction across dyads and across time, thereby affecting which states form PTAs and when states do so. However, it is obvious that other factors also influence strategic interaction in the international trading system. These factors, too, are likely to affect the establishment of preferential groupings, and it is therefore important to account for them in our analysis.

To this end, we include TRADE, which is the sum of *i*'s imports from and exports to *j* (in trillions of constant 1995 U.S. dollars) in $t - 1$.[83] Because preferential arrangements provide states with insurance against being locked out of the participants' markets, we expect GATT/WTO members to form PTAs with their most important trade partners. PTAs liberalize commerce among members and restrict their ability to increase trade barriers in the future, creating an incentive for those economic partners that would suffer most if commerce was disrupted to create such groupings.[84]

81. See Mansfield 1998, 526; and Mattli 1999, 81.

82. Data on GDP, per capita GDP, and growth are taken from IMF 1998b; Summers and Heston 1991; and World Bank 2001.

83. Data on bilateral trade flows are obtained from IMF 1999a. Nominal values of trade are adjusted by changes in the U.S. producer price index, which is found in United States 2000.

84. Furthermore, as neofunctionalists have long argued, international commerce promotes the development of coalitions with an interest in creating institutional mechanisms to increase economic integration and avert the breakdown of economic relations between the trade partners. Integration also increases the vulnerability of private traders to opportunistic behavior by foreign governments, which in turn gives them a motive to constrain governments' behavior using a PTA. See Mattli 1999, 23–28, 46–50; and Yarbrough and Yarbrough 1992.

Not only do we expect GATT members to establish PTAs with their most important trade partners, we also expect them to form PTAs with states that belong to the same preferential groupings as these partners. Doing so further reduces the prospect of being closed out of vital foreign markets, for example, if groupings involving a state's key commercial partners—but excluding this state itself—raise trade barriers against third parties. As such, we include TRADE PARTNER PTA COVERAGE. This variable is the proportion of *i*'s top ten GATT/WTO trade partners, exclusive of *j*, which maintained a reciprocal PTA with *j* in $t - 1$.

Within GATT/WTO, preferential groupings often form in reaction to each other.[85] As an increasing number of GATT/WTO members establish PTAs, those states left uncovered by an arrangement have a growing incentive to join one. Such states have reason to fear that they will be placed at a competitive disadvantage vis-à-vis participants in PTAs, generating pressure on them to enter a trade bloc. Furthermore, the perception that PTAs are spreading because participants are reaping economic benefits can prompt states that do not belong to a preferential grouping to join one.[86] Equally, existing PTAs can provide templates for states that are considering forming one, furnishing "institutional models" that can be duplicated or altered and thereby decreasing the costs associated with establishing such an arrangement.[87] Consequently, as PTAs proliferate, it may become easier to set up new groupings.

In addition, we mentioned earlier that PTAs generally are vested with greater bargaining power than their constituent members. As the number of states covered by a PTA grows larger, the bargaining power of states that remain uncovered by such an arrangement degrades. Thus, states that do not belong to a preferential grouping have reason to enter one as PTAs spread. We therefore include PTA DENSITY—the portion of GATT/WTO dyads that belong to a reciprocal PTA in $t - 1$, excluding those in which either *i* or *j* is a member.

We also consider the possibility that the relationship between PTA DENSITY and the likelihood of PTA formation is characterized by a saturation or ceiling effect.[88] When enough dyads belong to preferential groupings, it is likely that relatively few pairs with an interest in forming a PTA will be left uncovered by one. If so, there may be a quadratic relationship between PTA DENSITY and the likelihood of PTA formation. To address this possibility, we add PTA DENSITY^2.

Two of our four key explanatory variables concern participation in and the outcomes of *i*'s and *j*'s GATT/WTO disputes with third parties. To verify that the effects of these two variables do not stem from the bilateral dispute record between *i* and *j*, we add a dummy variable, NEW DISPUTE BETWEEN *i* AND *j*, which equals 1 if either state filed a GATT/WTO dispute against the other in year $t - 1$. Our argument does not speak to the likely impact of this variable on PTA forma-

85. See Pomfret 1997; and Serra et al. 1997.
86. See Pomfret 1997; and Yarbrough and Yarbrough 1992.
87. Yarbrough and Yarbrough 1997, 158.
88. Mansfield 1998.

tion. A record of disputes may, on the one hand, indicate intense conflicts of interest that reduce the probability of *i* and *j* forming a PTA. On the other hand, *i* and *j* may seek to avoid the costs of these confrontations by embedding a solution in a new joint PTA, much as Canada sought with the U.S.-Canada FTA to tie the hands of the United States on a series of unfair trade actions (on lumber, etc.) recently disputed under GATT. Finally, we include YEAR, which is *t*, to capture any secular trend in PTA formation between GATT/WTO members.

Statistical Models

A number of the aforementioned control variables—DEMOCRACY, GDP, PER CAPITA GDP, GROWTH, and TRADE PARTNER PTA COVERAGE—are "monadic," meaning that they measure properties of each state in a pair, not the pair itself. Thus, each of these variables should be entered in the model twice, with one variable corresponding to country *i* and a second variable corresponding to country *j*. Yet arbitrarily determining which state in a pair is *i* and which one is *j* could influence our results, so we estimate a "directed dyad" model in which each dyad-year is analyzed twice. For example, in the case of the U.S.-Canada dyad in 1990, we include one observation where the United States is *i* and Canada is *j*, and a second observation where Canada is *i* and the United States is *j*. Each monadic variable is included in this model only once, for the country listed as *i* in each particular observation. Of course, analyzing directed dyads doubles the number of observations in the sample, thereby producing standard errors that are too small. To correct this problem, we cluster the standard errors over the *un*directed dyad. As a result, this test is more conservative than one based on the 151,912 undirected dyad-years in the population. Rather than doubling the sample size, clustering the standard errors over the undirected dyad effectively reduces it by a factor of 17 (to 8,799 dyads), yielding estimated standard errors that are about four times larger than would otherwise be the case.

Nevertheless, for comparison, we also estimate a more typical undirected dyad model that includes each monadic variable twice. Which state is *i* and which one is *j* is determined by random assignment. Descriptive statistics for the variables included in the basic directed dyad and undirected dyad models—labeled models (1) and (3) and models (4) and (6), respectively—are shown in Table 1.

Because a number of independent variables are missing a considerable amount of data, these models include a little less than half the universe of the yearly dyadic observations from 1948 to 1998. To assess whether our results are sensitive to these missing data, we also estimate directed and undirected dyad models (labeled (2) and (5), respectively) without GROWTH, ALLIANCE, and TRADE, raising the sample size to about 85 percent of the population (for directed dyads). Whereas our initial analyses exclude the first and last few years of the sample due to missing data, omitting these variables allows us to analyze the entire period from 1948 to 1998.

TABLE 1. *Descriptive statistics*

Variable	Directed dyad years Models 1 and 3				Undirected dyad years Models 4 and 6			
	Mean	*SD*	*Min.*	*Max.*	*Mean*	*SD*	*Min.*	*Max.*
PTA, t	0.006	0.076	0	1	0.006	0.077	0	1
NUMBER OF MEMBERS, $t-1$	85.255	14.823	23	105	86.195	13.406	23	105
DETRENDED # OF MEMBERS, $t-1$	−2.104	7.070	−10.573	12.446	−2.177	7.074	−10.574	12.446
MTN ROUND UNDERWAY, t	0.652	0.476	0	1	0.656	0.475	0	1
NEW DISPUTE WITH 3RD PARTY, $t-1$	0.381	0.486	0	1	0.394	0.489	0	1
DISPUTE LOSS WITH 3RD PARTY, $t-3$	0.302	0.459	0	1	0.315	0.465	0	1
NEW DISPUTE BETWEEN i AND j, $t-1$	0.016	0.124	0	1	0.017	0.131	0	1
ALLIANCE, $t-1$	0.094	0.292	0	1	0.098	0.297	0	1
DISTANCE, t	4.866	2.701	0	12.363	4.935	2.687	0	12.363
TRADE, $t-1$	0.0004	0.0032	0	0.1878	0.0004	0.0034	0	0.1790
PTA DENSITY, $t-1$	0.004	0.032	−0.075	0.080	0.004	0.031	−0.075	0.080
PTA DENSITY^2, $t-1$	0.001	0.002	0	0.006	0.001	0.002	0	0.006
DEMOCRACY i, $t-1$	2.423	7.755	−10	10	2.236	7.782	−10	10
DEMOCRACY j, $t-1$	—	—	—	—	2.165	7.777	−10	10
GDP i, $t-1$	0.250	0.770	0.0001	6.440	0.251	0.782	0.0001	6.440
GDP j, $t-1$	—	—	—	—	0.242	0.758	0.0001	6.440
PER CAPITA GDP i, $t-1$	7.438	9.156	0.114	45.951	7.349	9.157	0.114	45.951
PER CAPITA GDP j, $t-1$	—	—	—	—	7.267	9.173	0.114	45.951
GROWTH i, $t-1$	3.564	4.846	−24.049	39.487	3.513	4.893	−24.049	39.487
GROWTH j, $t-1$	—	—	—	—	3.570	4.870	−24.049	39.487
TRADE PARTNER PTA COVERAGE i, $t-1$	0.132	0.233	0	0.9	0.140	0.238	0	0.9
TRADE PARTNER PTA COVERAGE j, $t-1$	—	—	—	—	0.140	0.237	0	0.9
YEAR, t	1980.42	9.473	1950	1993	1980.93	8.969	1950	1993
POSTCOMMUNIST, t	0.025	0.157	0	1	0.025	0.155	0	1
FORMER COLONIAL RELATIONSHIP, t	0.029	0.169	0	1	0.032	0.177	0	1
Number of observations		149,308				65,153		

Note: Shaded rows identify the variables that are central to our argument. SD = standard deviation.

Results

Because the observed value of the dependent variable is dichotomous, we use a logit specification to estimate these models. To account for any duration dependence in the data, we include a natural cubic spline function of the number of years i and j have been without a PTA, as of t.[89]

As reported in Tables 2 and 3, the models fit the data well.[90] Further, the results of these analyses strongly support our argument about the impact of the multilateral regime on PTA formation. The estimates of NUMBER OF MEMBERS, MTN ROUND UNDERWAY, NEW DISPUTE WITH THIRD PARTY, and DISPUTE LOSS WITH THIRD PARTY are positive as well as both statistically (at the .001 level) and substantively significant.[91] Equally, the coefficient estimates are quite similar regardless of whether we use the directed or undirected dyad approach—see models (1) and (4)—or whether we use the larger-sample specification without ALLIANCE, GROWTH, and TRADE—see models (2) and (5).

To address the substantive effects of these factors as well as some selected control variables, Figure 3 reports the "relative risk" of states i and j forming a PTA, based on the results in model (1). For each dummy variable shown in Figure 3, this risk is the probability of establishing an arrangement when the variable equals 1 divided by the probability when it equals 0 (since the coefficient estimate of each dummy variable in the figure is positive), holding constant the remaining variables in the model. For every other variable with a positive (negative) coefficient estimate in model (1), the relative risk is the predicted probability of PTA formation when the variable is one standard deviation above its mean (at the mean) divided by this probability when the variable is evaluated at its mean (one standard deviation above the mean).

Our results clearly indicate that rising GATT/WTO membership has increased the probability of states creating a PTA. Figure 3 shows that shifting NUMBER OF MEMBERS from its sample mean by one standard deviation yields more than a forty-fold increase in the predicted probability of PTA formation, a far larger impact than any other variable considered here. In addition, during a multilateral trade negotiation, the likelihood of any two states establishing a preferential grouping increases by roughly a factor of six. If either state in the pair participated in a new GATT/WTO dispute with a third party in $t - 1$, the prospect of entering a PTA

89. Beck, Katz, and Tucker 1998, 1270–71. Wald tests of the joint significance of the terms in this spline function (which yield $p < .001$ for all models) confirm that they should be included.

90. Estimates were produced using *Stata* 7.0's *logit, robust cluster* command. Note that there is little evidence of collinearity in this analysis. The exceptions include PER CAPITA GDP with DEMOCRACY, DISTANCE with YEAR and NUMBER OF MEMBERS, and PTA DENSITY with its square, which all exhibit no more than moderate ($r < .6$) bivariate correlations. Only NUMBER OF MEMBERS and YEAR are highly correlated. Their estimates are nonetheless statistically significant.

91. Wald tests lead us to reject the null hypothesis that NUMBER OF MEMBERS, MTN ROUND UNDERWAY, NEW DISPUTE WITH THIRD PARTY, and DISPUTE LOSS WITH THIRD PARTY jointly equal zero, with $p < .001$ for all models.

TABLE 2. *Duration dependent logit models of PTA formation, directed dyads*

Variable	*Model 1 (1950–93)*		*Model 2 (1948–98)*		*Model 3 (1950–93)*	
Prob(PTA) = 1	*Coefficient*	*SE*	*Coefficient*	*SE*	*Coefficient*	*SE*
NUMBER OF MEMBERS, $t-1$	0.251**	0.030	0.155**	0.012	—	—
DETRENDED # OF MEMBERS, $t-1$	—	—	—	—	0.235**	0.024
MTN ROUND UNDERWAY, t	1.848**	0.154	1.900**	0.155	1.730**	0.159
NEW DISPUTE WITH 3RD PARTY, $t-1$	0.527**	0.133	0.629**	0.118	0.587**	0.133
DISPUTE LOSS WITH 3RD PARTY, $t-3$	1.183**	0.115	1.073**	0.102	1.270**	0.114
NEW DISPUTE BETWEEN i AND j, $t-1$	−0.933	0.643	−0.922	0.619	−0.809	0.640
ALLIANCE, $t-1$	0.270*	0.116	—	—	0.453**	0.117
DISTANCE, t	−0.627**	0.027	−0.665**	0.026	−0.545**	0.027
TRADE, $t-1$	14.304**	3.129	—	—	16.826**	3.459
PTA DENSITY, $t-1$	−37.658**	3.971	−23.331**	2.636	−32.651**	3.263
PTA DENSITY^2, $t-1$	−364.91**	83.59	−690.87**	70.01	−455.14**	82.62
DEMOCRACY, $t-1$	0.065**	0.006	0.047**	0.005	0.059**	0.005
GDP, $t-1$	−0.273**	0.059	−0.133*	0.054	−0.311**	0.061
PER CAPITA GDP, $t-1$	0.010*	0.004	0.016**	0.004	0.018**	0.004
GROWTH, $t-1$	−0.022**	0.008	—	—	0.006	0.008
TRADE PARTNER PTA COVERAGE, $t-1$	3.040**	0.135	2.765**	0.128	3.073**	0.142
YEAR, t	−0.503**	0.042	−0.395**	0.025	−0.040*	0.018
POSTCOMMUNIST, t	—	—	—	—	2.772**	0.209
FORMER COLONIAL RELATIONSHIP, t	—	—	—	—	1.511**	0.197
CONSTANT	968.966**	79.678	763.259**	48.358	73.128*	35.361
Number of observations	149,308		259,267		149,308	
Model χ^2	2661.9**, 22 d.o.f.		3069.4**, 19 d.o.f.		2768.6**, 24 d.o.f.	
Pseudo-R^2	0.390		0.360		0.414	

Note: Shaded rows identify the variables that are central to our argument. Two-tailed tests are conducted for all estimates. Robust standard errors (SEs) clustered over dyads. Six duration dependence splines omitted from table. PTA DENSITY is "centered" by subtracting .075 to reduce collinearity without other effects. d. o. f. = degrees of freedom.

$^{**}p < .01$.

$^{*}p < .05$.

TABLE 3. *Duration dependent logit models of PTA formation, undirected dyads*

Variable	Model 4 (1950–93)		Model 5 (1948–98)		Model 6 (1950–93)	
Prob (PTA) = 1	*Coefficient*	*SE*	*Coefficient*	*SE*	*Coefficient*	*SE*
NUMBER OF MEMBERS, $t-1$	0.289**	0.046	0.142**	0.012	—	—
DETRENDED # OF MEMBERS, $t-1$	—	—	—	—	0.258**	0.034
MTN ROUND UNDERWAY, t	1.911**	0.179	1.827**	0.160	1.652**	0.181
NEW DISPUTE WITH 3RD PARTY, $t-1$	0.546**	0.161	0.573**	0.127	0.595**	0.159
DISPUTE LOSS WITH 3RD PARTY, $t-3$	1.415**	0.146	1.098**	0.112	1.534**	0.145
NEW DISPUTE BETWEEN i AND j, $t-1$	−0.700	0.739	−0.920	0.633	−0.492	0.735
ALLIANCE, $t-1$	0.170	0.138	—	—	0.434**	0.145
DISTANCE, t	−0.566**	0.037	−0.605**	0.031	−0.431**	0.036
TRADE, $t-1$	33.070**	5.482	—	—	43.086**	5.980
PTA DENSITY, $t-1$	−45.103**	5.833	−22.836**	2.971	−38.741**	4.364
PTA DENSITY^2, $t-1$	−203.29*	93.98	−621.78**	69.53	−281.46**	85.06
DEMOCRACY i, $t-1$	0.063**	0.010	0.039**	0.009	0.059**	0.009
DEMOCRACY j, $t-1$	0.041**	0.010	0.027**	0.009	0.038**	0.010
GDP i, $t-1$	−0.171	0.119	0.020	0.118	−0.301*	0.136
GDP j, $t-1$	−0.188	0.193	−0.021	0.101	−0.311	0.220
PER CAPITA GDP i, $t-1$	−0.031**	0.007	−0.009	0.006	−0.024**	0.007
PER CAPITA GDP j, $t-1$	−0.007	0.007	0.006	0.006	−0.002	0.007
GROWTH i, $t-1$	−0.045**	0.015	—	—	−0.017	0.014
GROWTH j, $t-1$	−0.042**	0.014	—	—	−0.019	0.014
TRADE PARTNER PTA COVERAGE i, $t-1$	3.458**	0.248	2.591**	0.192	3.907**	0.260
TRADE PARTNER PTA COVERAGE j, $t-1$	3.528**	0.244	2.673**	0.202	4.007**	0.261
YEAR, t	−0.573**	0.064	−0.374**	0.026	−0.049*	0.023
POSTCOMMUNIST, t	—	—	—	—	3.088**	0.225
FORMER COLONIAL RELATIONSHIP, t	—	—	—	—	2.030**	0.255
CONSTANT	1103.07**	121.91	723.037**	50.786	89.410	46.433
Number of observations	65,153		115,846		65,153	
Model χ^2	1414.0**, 27 d.o.f.		2276.0**, 23 d.o.f.		1449.2**, 29 d.o.f.	
Pseudo-R^2	0.465		0.388		0.493	

Note: Shaded rows identify the variables that are central to our argument. Two-tailed tests are conducted for all estimates. Robust standard errors (SEs) clustered over dyads. Six duration dependence splines omitted from table. PTA DENSITY is "centered" by subtracting .075 to reduce collinearity without other effects. d. o. f. = degrees of freedom.
$^{**}p < .01$.
$^{*}p < .05$.

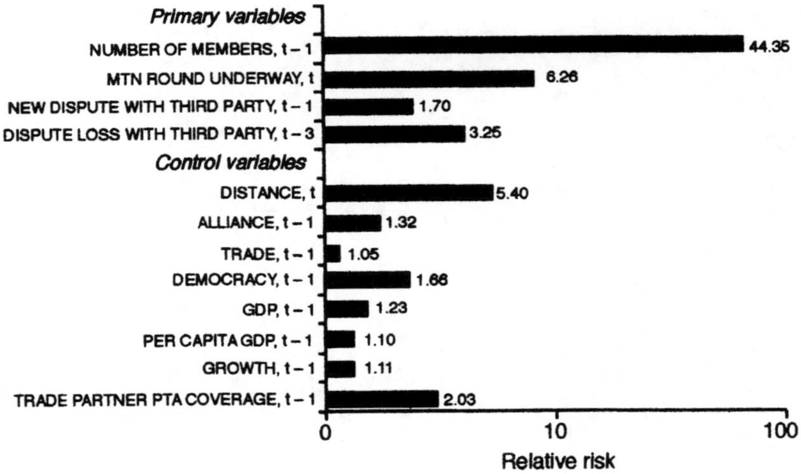

Note: Horizontal axis is in logarthmic scale. For all variables that are not dichotomous and that have a positive (negative) coefficient, "relative risk" is the predicted probability of PTA formation when the variable in question equals its sample mean plus one standard deviation (sample mean), divided by the predicted probability of PTA formation when it equals its sample mean (sample mean plus one standard deviation) holding other variables at their sample means. For dichotomus variables, the comparison is between values of 1 and 0. (The ratios are inverted for GDP and DISTANCE, whose coefficients are negative.)

FIGURE 3. *Estimated substantive significance of selected variables in model (1), in terms of relative risk*

almost doubles. If either state recently lost a GATT/WTO dispute with a third party, the probability of a new preferential grouping between them more than triples. Even if none of these variables add more than 0.1 percent to the chance of any two states entering a PTA, as many as eight additional bilateral PTAs would form in a single year as a result (since there were more than 8,000 GATT/WTO dyads by the end of the period we analyze). Clearly, the multilateral trading system has played a substantively important role in shaping PTA formation.

Moreover, these results are quite robust. For instance, as shown in models (2) and (5), the reduction in sample size that occurs when ALLIANCE, GROWTH, and TRADE are included has little discernible effect on the estimates of the variables pertaining to the multilateral trading regime. Nor do these estimates change if we add a number of omitted variables that seem likely to influence the formation of PTAs. For example, we include a measure of hegemony in the international trading system,[92] a variable indicating whether i and j were antagonists in a milita-

92. Gilpin 1987.

rized interstate dispute in year $t - 1$,[93] a measure of trade dependence between i and j, and country-specific fixed effects.[94] Finally, we exclude all observations including the United States, an outlier in terms of GATT/WTO dispute participation,[95] or the founding members of the EC, which are outliers in terms of PTA formation. Each of these analyses yields estimates quite similar to those in Tables 2 and 3.

A related issue that merits consideration is whether our findings about the effects of the multilateral regime might really stem from the wave of postcolonialism in the 1960s or the wave of postcommunism in the 1990s. Members of the same imperial system are probably more likely to establish PTAs than other states once colonialism ends, and the states of Eastern Europe have demonstrated a remarkable zeal for regional trade arrangements since the Berlin Wall's collapse. Also, it is well known that the waves of postcolonialism and postcommunism took place at roughly the same time as the two waves of regionalism we discussed earlier. Likewise, how much of the proliferation in PTAs can we attribute to heightened GATT/WTO membership given that its growth is highly correlated with time? To address these issues, we add one dummy variable to the model that equals 1 if either i or j has transitioned from a communist regime (POSTCOMMUNIST) and another indicating whether both states were members of the same colonial system at some point after World War II (FORMER COLONIAL RELATIONSHIP). We also detrend NUMBER OF MEMBERS, replacing this variable with the residuals of a regression of NUMBER OF MEMBERS on YEAR.

The results are reported in the columns labeled models (3) and (6) in Tables 2 and 3, respectively. Not surprisingly, the results show that postcommunist states and those that were in the same imperial system are much more likely to form PTAs than other countries. Particularly important for present purposes, however, is that the estimates of our four key variables (with NUMBER OF MEMBERS now detrended) are virtually identical to those in models (1) and (4), still positive and statistically significant.[96] Thus, we continue to find strong evidence that develop-

93. Jones, Bremer, and Singer 1996.

94. We measure hegemony two ways: (1) using the U.S. portion of total world imports plus exports, based on data taken from IMF 1999a, and (2) using the ratio of U.S. GDP to the GATT/WTO member with the next highest GDP in year $t - 1$. We measure trade dependence using the value of bilateral trade divided by the GDP of i and j, respectively.

95. Reinhardt forthcoming.

96. We conducted a number of additional robustness tests as well. PTA formation is a rare event. King and Zeng have recently argued that using a logit model to analyze rare events can yield biased results. King and Zeng 2001. We therefore estimate models (1) and (4) using a method they developed to correct such bias. The results are virtually identical to those in Tables 2 and 3, indicating that our findings are not undermined by any rare-events bias. If we reestimate the models coding TRADE as 0 when the IMF records an annual trade flow as missing, the results are effectively identical. The same is true if we use the natural log of GDP, PER CAPITA GDP, DISTANCE, and TRADE (substituting the minimum non-zero sample value of DISTANCE and TRADE when they are exactly 0). Further, the coefficients of our key variables remain positive and significant even if we (1) estimate heteroskedastic probit variants of models (1) and (4) (*Stata* 7.0's *hetprob, robust*) with variance functions conditioned

ments within the multilateral regime are important forces shaping the proliferation of PTAs.[97]

It is important to reiterate that the pronounced effect of the GATT/WTO system on PTA formation is observed even after accounting for the influence of alliances, market size, national income, the business cycle, regime type, distance, the flow of trade, and various other factors shaping strategic interaction in the international trading system. The effects of these control variables largely accord with our expectations, although a few of them depend on the model's specification. For example, economically larger states are less likely to join PTAs than their smaller counterparts, but this influence is much stronger when we focus on directed rather than undirected dyads. In addition, preferential groupings are unlikely to form between countries that are geographically distant, poor, or enjoy high levels of economic growth. Again, though, the effects of economic development and growth depend somewhat on which model is considered. Democracies tend to form PTAs, as do allies and states that trade extensively. PTAs are also a product of "bandwagoning" insofar as a country is more likely to enter a preferential arrangement with other states that already belong to groupings with its primary trade partners. Finally, there is evidence of a saturation or ceiling effect in the formation of preferential arrangements. Because we "centered" PTA DENSITY to reduce collinearity, the negative and statistically significant estimates of PTA DENSITY and PTA DENSITY^2 indicate that there is an inverted U-shaped relationship between the proportion of country-pairs in preferential groupings and the odds of a given pair of states establishing a new PTA.

It is also important to point out that the features of the GATT/WTO system that we have emphasized tend to have larger substantive effects on PTA formation than the control variables in our model. As shown in Figure 3, the effects of DISTANCE, TRADE PARTNER PTA COVERAGE, and DEMOCRACY are relatively sizeable, ranging from about a fivefold decrease in the predicted probability of forming a PTA if the mean distance between states i and j rises by one standard deviation to a two-thirds increase in this probability if the average regime score experiences a similar rise. The remaining control variables, however, have much smaller effects on the likelihood of entering a preferential grouping.

on TRADE, GDP, YEAR, DISTANCE, NUMBER OF MEMBERS, and TRADE PARTNER PTA COVERAGE; or (2) use a nonproportional hazards specification by including the interaction of all variables with the (logged) number of years the pair has gone without a PTA.

97. Still another possibility is that our findings about the strong direct effects of GATT/WTO membership might stem from an underlying demand for greater trade, stimulating participation in all international trade organizations, both preferential and multilateral. However, we have controlled for many of the economic factors that are likely to influence such demand, including GDP, growth, and per capita income. We also controlled for time, which may proxy for any secular increase in the demand for greater foreign commerce. Finally, we took account of the flow of trade as well as various features of the international trading system (for example, the existence of a multilateral negotiating round and the portion of GATT/WTO dyads that belong to a PTA), additional factors that are likely to be related to the demand for trade. Consequently, there is little reason to worry that our findings reflect the influence of such demands.

Interpretation of the Results

One of our core findings is that participation and undesirable outcomes in GATT/WTO disputes induce countries to seek PTAs with third parties. Once formed, do PTAs actually insure against future losses and improve a state's bargaining position in such conflicts, as our argument implies? Leaders seem to believe so. For example, Malaysian Prime Minister Mahathir's reaction to the U.S. steel safeguard tariffs, which were imposed in spring 2002 and subsequently challenged under WTO dispute rules, was to renew his push for trade integration in Southeast Asia.[98] No statistical study has yet examined the impact of PTA membership on GATT/WTO dispute outcomes. However, we can offer some preliminary evidence on this score by adding our data on each disputant's participation in PTAs to an existing statistical model of GATT dispute outcomes.[99]

Specifically, to tap the bargaining power and insurance provided by preferential groupings for any given state, we sum the GDP of all its PTA partners with its own national income. The logged value of this variable is statistically significant for both state i and state j when we include it in the model of dispute outcomes, indicating that greater GDP increases the likelihood of a favorable outcome.[100] If, however, we subtract the PTA partners' GDPs from this variable, leaving just the disputant's GDP, it is no longer significant.[101] For a small complainant (say, with a GDP of $10 billion), joining a PTA with partners possessing $500 billion of GDP boosts its ability to leverage full concessions from a typical GATT/WTO defendant by a third (increasing the predicted probability from 0.27 to 0.36). The effect of such a change would of course be compounded over numerous future disputes. What is more, this finding is not driven by PTAs with a common external tariff, because the sample includes few customs union members.[102] Instead, the bargaining benefits of PTAs in GATT/WTO disputes are due almost entirely to FTAs, which make up most of the groupings considered here. It is thus quite plausible to attribute the finding that GATT/WTO disputes are associated with PTA formation to states' motivation to seek extra insurance and bargaining power because of such disputes.

As a more specific illustration of the links between GATT disputes and PTA formation, consider Venezuela's free trade areas with Mexico and Colombia. These preferential arrangements were formed in 1995, on the heels of Venezuela's first

98. *Business Times (Malaysia)*, 23 May 2002, 2.

99. To this end, we use model (2) from Reinhardt 2001, 178, and the updated data from Reinhardt forthcoming.

100. This model controls for whether a GATT panel is formed, how the panel rules (if at all), and several features of the measure in dispute.

101. Results available on request. The correlation between a disputant's GDP and the sum of its PTA partners' GDP plus its own is too high to include both in the same model.

102. Because the EC, by far the most frequent customs union disputant, acted as a unit in GATT disputes, its GDP is already counted as the sum of its members' GDP. Our variable thus only contributes the GDPs from the EC's external PTA partners, which did not share the same external tariff.

experiences as a GATT complainant in disputes against the EU and United States. Further, the United States and Canada both were involved in rapidly increasing numbers of GATT/WTO disputes, many against the EU, in the years immediately preceding the establishment of their free trade area. Chile participated in just five disputes between 1949 and 1987, but was embroiled in thirteen high-stakes conflicts with the United States and the EU from 1988 to 1997. It is no coincidence that Chile completed (separate) talks aimed at creating free trade areas with Mexico, Canada, Mercosur, Bolivia, Colombia, Ecuador, and Venezuela in the second half of the 1990s.[103] In a similar vein, all of the ASEAN members together participated in just one GATT dispute before 1987. By contrast, they participated in seven during the years leading up to the 1993 AFTA accord, which the prime ministers of Singapore and Malaysia claimed would "give ASEAN a bigger voice . . . in talks with the European Community."[104] This evidence is obviously anecdotal, but—consistent with our quantitative results—it suggests that the GATT/WTO dispute settlement system has contributed to the proliferation of PTAs.

Anecdotal evidence also lends support to our hypothesis that multilateral trade negotiations induce PTA formation. For instance, in the midst of the Uruguay Round, the difficulty of reaching agreement among such a heterogeneous group of countries prompted Singapore's foreign minister to "question the usefulness" of GATT and to endorse an ASEAN-based free trade area.[105] APEC ministers resolved to "use their combined strength as leverage against Europe" to bring a quick end to the Uruguay Round in 1993.[106] Equally, the Caribbean states formed the Caribbean Free Trade Association (CARIFTA) during the Kennedy Round and then CARICOM during the Tokyo Round at least partly to boost their collective negotiating leverage in these multilateral trade negotiations.[107]

Conclusions

Central to the GATT/WTO system are efforts to liberalize trade on a multilateral basis, expand the number of parties to this organization, and enforce compliance with its rules through a reliable dispute settlement procedure. GATT/WTO has been remarkably successful in meeting these objectives. At the same time, however, such efforts have contributed greatly to the rise of PTAs, institutions that pose a challenge to GATT/WTO's principle of nondiscrimination. Although it is widely recognized that PTAs have proliferated rapidly among GATT/WTO members, there has been little systematic research addressing how developments within the multilateral regime have contributed to their spread.

103. Smith 2000, 152.
104. *Straits Times*, 23 October 1993, 1.
105. *Daily Telegraph*, 10 February 1993, 13.
106. *Straits Times*, 3 November 1993, 4.
107. Andriamananjara and Schiff 2001.

We argue that GATT/WTO members form preferential groupings to improve their bargaining position in trade negotiations with third parties. Heightened bargaining power is especially useful during multilateral trade negotiations, when GATT/WTO adds members, and during commercial disputes. Specifically, adding members to the MTN regime reduces each participant's leverage, creating incentives for states to pool their influence by establishing a PTA. Increasing the regime's size can also render multilateral negotiations more contentious and harder to conclude by expanding the range of interests that need to be accommodated. Faced with greater difficulty arriving at any multilateral solution to commercial issues as the size of GATT/WTO grows, its members may find it useful to enter smaller, preferential groupings composed of states with common economic interests.

In the same vein, preferential arrangements also provide participants with insurance against future disruptions of commerce that might arise if multilateral negotiations stall or the system weakens as a growing number of states with heterogeneous commercial preferences accede to GATT/WTO. Furthermore, in the course of striking MTNs or resolving ongoing disputes, states may enter PTAs to solidify important trade relations or to bolster their market power in the hopes of leveraging greater concessions from third parties. States also look to the success of the MTN regime's enforcement system for cues. If too many disputes end in nascent trade wars, members lose confidence in the multilateral trading system. To secure their market access and to obtain the greatest possible benefits from the multilateral regime, states have reason to lock open key markets by forming PTAs with crucial trade partners. Our results, therefore, indicate that not only have GATT/WTO rules done little to constrain the emergence of PTAs, developments within the multilateral trade regime have actually contributed to the rise of these arrangements.

Our findings have implications for the study of both economic regionalism and international relations. Scholars of international relations have devoted considerable attention to identifying the factors leading to the establishment of multilateral institutions. Far less effort, however, has been devoted to addressing whether and, if so, how these institutions influence state behavior.[108] In addition, too little effort has been made to address how changes within multilateral institutions affect the actions of members. Our analysis bears heavily on these issues. That GATT/WTO has influenced the behavior of its members is no surprise. After all, it is widely understood that this institution has generated substantial trade liberalization. More surprising, though, is that developments within it have systematically contributed to the formation of discriminatory commercial groupings. In ways not previously recognized, core features of the multilateral trading regime—such as its growing membership, dispute settlement system, and periodic negotiating rounds—have prompted states to enter preferential arrangements that clash with the regime's fundamental norm of nondiscrimination.

108. See Keohane 1984; and Martin and Simmons 1998, 743.

Of course, this situation does not imply that PTAs are welfare-degrading or that they will undermine the multilateral trading system. On the one hand, parties to GATT/WTO with protectionist interests may set up PTAs to countervail multilateral trade liberalization. Unlike unilateral measures such as raising tariffs, forming a preferential grouping allows states to discriminate against third parties without breaching GATT/WTO rules.[109] On the other hand, however, parties to GATT/WTO with an especially liberal orientation may set up PTAs because doing so allows them to achieve greater openness than could otherwise be realized in a multilateral setting.[110] Either possibility is consistent with our analysis, which is silent on the global welfare implications of preferential groupings.

During the past decade, a considerable amount of interest has been expressed in whether PTAs will be "building blocks" or "stumbling blocks" to greater multilateral liberalization.[111] Regardless of whether PTAs will bolster or undermine the WTO, our results point out the problems associated with ignoring the reverse line of causation, namely, how multilateral liberalization bears on the formation of PTAs. Furthermore, many studies have analyzed the conditions influencing whether states choose multilateral or bilateral strategies.[112] Our analysis suggests some conditions under which a multilateral approach is likely to grow less attractive, prompting states to pursue PTAs with greater intensity. But whereas existing studies often assume that states choose either bilateral or multilateral strategies, our findings also indicate that these strategies are not mutually exclusive. States frequently rely on both types of strategies simultaneously, for example, engaging in multilateral trade negotiations and establishing a PTA at the same time.[113]

In addition, the preceding results show that the determinants of PTA formation are not limited to developments within GATT/WTO. For instance, there is considerable evidence that the creation of preferential groupings is guided by strategic interaction.[114] As more country-pairs become covered by these groupings, the odds increase that those pairs that do not belong to the same PTA will establish one in response. As Alan Winters puts it, PTAs resemble street gangs: "you may not like them, but if they are in your neighborhood, it is safer to be in one."[115] PTA formation, however, is also marked by a saturation or ceiling effect. Once most dyads that could benefit by creating a preferential grouping have done so,

109. Pomfret 1997.

110. See Kahler 1992; and Westhoff, Yarbrough, and Yarbrough 1994. Westhoff, Yarbrough, and Yarbrough present a framework that helps to explain why PTAs might allow subsets of GATT/WTO members to generate more trade liberalization than is possible in the GATT/WTO setting, especially as the preferences of its members become more heterogeneous.

111. See Bhagwati 1993; and Lawrence 1996.

112. Yarbrough and Yarbrough 1992.

113. Kahler 1992. In U.S. Trade Representative Zoellick's words, "We can walk and chew gum at the same time." *Washington Post*, 20 November 2002, E3.

114. See Baldwin 1997; Fernández and Portes 1998; Mansfield 1998; Oye 1992; Pomfret 1997; and Yarbrough and Yarbrough 1992.

115. Quoted in Crawford and Laird 2001, 201.

the likelihood of PTA formation declines. Further, allies are more likely to enter into a PTA than other states, which accords with the argument that alliances help to internalize the security externalities stemming from arrangements that liberalize trade among participants. We also find some support for functionalist claims that international economic institutions tend to form in response to increasing interdependence and rising levels of economic exchange. The flow of trade is directly related to the establishment of PTAs, although its effect is substantively small.

Finally, domestic conditions influence whether states enter preferential arrangements. Democracies are more likely to join such arrangements than autocracies, economically smaller states are generally more likely to do so than their larger counterparts, and economic downturns tend to promote PTA formation. These findings highlight the obvious, but important, point that preferential trading arrangements are caused by various factors operating at different levels of analysis. As such, no single theoretical approach will suffice to explain their proliferation fully.

While our results shed new light on the links between the multilateral trade regime and PTAs, they also raise various questions for future research. For example, the form, trajectories, and duration of preferential trading agreements vary widely.[116] What determines the institutional form of a PTA—particularly whether it is a common market, a customs union, an FTA, or a different type of arrangement? Why are some PTAs—such as the Latin American Free Trade Association—never fully implemented, while others—like Mercosur—experience rapid consolidation?[117] Why do some FTAs ultimately evolve into customs unions (such as when former EFTA members joined the EU), while others do not? What explains whether a PTA "broadens" by adding new members, "deepens" its scope by covering policies and issues not previously included (such as labor or capital mobility, monetary policy, etc.), strengthens its implementation and enforcement mechanisms, or simply dies a quiet death? Answering these questions is sure to promote an improved understanding of regionalism, as well as the international political economy.

During the past half-century, GATT/WTO has met with considerable success in fostering multilateral trade liberalization. At the same time, however, its success has had various unintended consequences.[118] Here, we have identified one especially important consequence that has been largely overlooked. The very instruments of GATT/WTO's progress—its growing membership, active dispute settlement, and frequent trade negotiations—encourage states to seek bilateral options to secure the greatest possible benefits from the multilateral regime.

116. Smith 2000.

117. WTO 1995a, 34–35.

118. For discussion of the unintended—and often unwelcome—consequences of international institutions, see Martin and Simmons 1998, 749–51; and Barnett and Finnemore 1999.

References

Andriamananjara, Soamiely, and Maurice Schiff. 2001. Regional Cooperation Among Microstates. *Review of International Economics* 9 (1):42–51.

Bagwell, Kyle, and Robert W. Staiger. 2001. Reciprocity, Non-Discrimination, and Preferential Agreements in the Multilateral Trading System. *European Journal of Political Economy* 17 (2):281–325.

Baldwin, Richard E. 1997. The Causes of Regionalism. *World Economy* 20 (7):865–88.

Barnett, Michael N., and Martha Finnemore. 1999. The Politics, Power, and Pathologies of International Organizations. *International Organization* 53 (4):699–732.

Beck, Nathaniel, Jonathan N. Katz, and Richard Tucker. 1998. Taking Time Seriously: Time-Series–Cross-Section Analysis with a Binary Dependent Variable. *American Journal of Political Science* 42 (4):1260–88.

Bennett, D. Scott, Jr., and Allan C. Stam, III. 1999. *EUGene: Expected Utility Generation and Data Management Program*, version 1.18. Pennsylvania State University. Available at ⟨www.eugenesoftware.org⟩.

Bhagwati, Jagdish. 1993. Regionalism and Multilateralism: An Overview. In *New Dimensions in Regional Integration*, edited by Jaime de Melo and Arvind Panagariya, 22–51. New York: Cambridge University Press.

Bhagwati, Jagdish, and Arvind Panagariya. 1996. Preferential Trading Areas and Multilateralism—Strangers, Friends, or Foes? In *The Economics of Preferential Trade Agreements*, edited by Jagdish Bhagwati and Arvind Panagariya, 1–78. Washington, D.C.: AEI Press.

Bowles, Paul. 1997. ASEAN, AFTA and the "New Regionalism." *Pacific Affairs* 70 (2):219–33.

Busch, Marc L., and Eric Reinhardt. 2002. Testing International Trade Law: Empirical Studies of GATT/WTO Dispute Settlement. In *The Political Economy of International Trade Law: Essays in Honor of Robert E. Hudec*, edited by Daniel L. M. Kennedy and James D. Southwick, 457–81. New York: Cambridge University Press.

———. 2003. Transatlantic Trade Conflicts and GATT/WTO Dispute Settlement. In *Dispute Prevention and Dispute Settlement in the Transatlantic Partnership*, edited by Ernst-Ulrich Petersmann and Mark Pollack. New York: Oxford University Press.

Correlates of War Project. 1993. Alliances Data. Unpublished manuscript, University of Michigan, Ann Arbor.

Crawford, Jo-Ann, and Sam Laird. 2001. Regional Trade Agreements and the WTO. *North American Journal of Economics and Finance* 12 (2):193–211.

Deardorff, Alan V. 1998. Determinants of Bilateral Trade: Does Gravity Work in a Neoclassical World? In *The Regionalization of the World Economy*, edited by Jeffrey A. Frankel, 7–22. Chicago: University of Chicago Press.

Downs, George W., David M. Rocke, and Peter N. Barsoom. 1998. Managing the Evolution of Multilateralism. *International Organization* 52 (2):397–419.

Dryden, Steve. 1995. *Trade Warriors: USTR and the American Crusade for Free Trade*. New York: Oxford University Press.

Ethier, Wilfred J. 1998. Regionalism in a Multilateral World. *Journal of Political Economy* 106 (6):1214–45.

———. 1999. Multilateral Roads to Liberalization. In *International Trade Policy and the Pacific Rim*, edited by John Piggott and Alan Woodland, 131–52. New York: St. Martin's.

Fernández, Raquel, and Jonathan Portes. 1998. Returns to Regionalism: An Evaluation of Non-traditional Gains from RTAs. *World Bank Economic Review* 12 (2):197–220.

Finger, J. Michael, Merlinda D. Ingco, and Ulrich Reincke. 1996. *The Uruguay Round: Statistics on Tariff Concessions Given and Received*. Washington, D.C.: World Bank.

Frankel, Jeffrey A. 1997. *Regional Trading Blocs in the World Economic System*. Washington, D.C.: Institute for International Economics.

Freund, Caroline L. 2000. Multilateralism and the Endogenous Formation of Preferential Trade Agreements. *Journal of International Economics* 52 (2):359–76.

Freund, Caroline L., and John McLaren. 1999. On the Dynamics of Trade Diversion: Evidence from Four Trade Blocs. International Finance Discussion Paper 637. Washington, D.C.: Board of Governors of the Federal Reserve System.

General Agreement on Tariffs and Trade (GATT). 1990. *GATT Activities, 1989: An Annual Review of the Work of the GATT*. Geneva: General Agreement on Tariffs and Trade.

———. 1994. Council of Representatives—Held in the Centre William Rappard on December 17, 1993. C/M/268. Geneva: General Agreement on Tariffs and Trade.

Gilpin, Robert. 1987. *The Political Economy of International Relations*. Princeton, N.J.: Princeton University Press.

Gowa, Joanne. 1994. *Allies, Adversaries, and International Trade*. Princeton, N.J.: Princeton University Press.

Gowa, Joanne, and Edward D. Mansfield. 1993. Power Politics and International Trade. *American Political Science Review* 87 (2):408–20.

Gurr, Ted Robert, and Keith Jaggers. 1999. *Polity 98: Regime Characteristics, 1800–1998*. Center for International Development and Conflict Management. College Park, Md.: University of Maryland. Available at ⟨www.cidcm.umd.edu/inscr/polity/⟩. Accessed 7 July 2003.

Hudec, Robert E. 1993. *Enforcing International Trade Law: The Evolution of the Modern GATT Legal System*. Salem, N.H.: Butterworth Legal Publishers.

Hudec, Robert E., and James D. Southwick. 1999. Regionalism and WTO Rules: Problems in the Fine Art of Discriminating Fairly. In *Trade Rules in the Making: Challenges in Regional and Multilateral Negotiations*, edited by Miguel Rodríguez Mendoza, Patrick Low, and Barbara Kotschwar, 47–80. Washington, D.C.: Organization of American States and Brookings Institution Press.

Inter-American Development Bank (IADB). 2000. *Periodic Note on Integration and Trade in the Americas*. Washington, D.C.: Inter-American Development Bank.

International Monetary Fund (IMF). 1998a. *Direction of Trade Statistics*. Washington, D.C.: IMF.

———. 1998b. *International Financial Statistics*. Washington, D.C.: IMF.

Jackson, John H. 1969. *World Trade and the Law of GATT*. Indianapolis: Bobbs-Merrill.

Jones, Daniel M., Stuart A. Bremer, and J. David Singer. 1996. Militarized Interstate Disputes, 1816–1992: Rationale, Coding Rules, and Empirical Patterns. *Conflict Management and Peace Science* 15 (2):163–213.

Kahler, Miles. 1992. Multilateralism with Small and Large Numbers. *International Organization* 46 (3):681–708.

Keohane, Robert O. 1984. *After Hegemony: Cooperation and Discord in the World Political Economy*. Princeton, N.J.: Princeton University Press.

King, Gary, and Langche Zeng. 2001. Explaining Rare Events in International Relations. *International Organization* 55 (3):693–715.

Koremenos, Barbara, Charles Lipson, and Duncan Snidal. 2001. The Rational Design of International Institutions. *International Organization* 55 (4):761–99.

Krugman, Paul. 1993. Regionalism Versus Multilateralism: Analytical Notes. In *New Dimensions in Regional Integration*, edited by Jaime de Melo and Arvind Panagariya, 58–79. New York: Cambridge University Press.

Lai, Brian, and Dan Reiter. 2000. Democracy, Political Similarity, and International Alliances, 1816–1992. *Journal of Conflict Resolution* 44 (2):203–27.

Lawrence, Robert Z. 1996. *Regionalism, Multilateralism, and Deeper Integration*. Washington, D.C.: Brookings Institution.

Ludema, Rodney D. 1996. On the Value of Preferential Trade Agreements in Multilateral Negotiations. Working Paper 97-22. Washington, D.C.: Georgetown University.

Mansfield, Edward D. 1993. Effects of International Politics on Regionalism in International Trade. In *Regional Integration and the Global Trading System*, edited by Kym Anderson and Richard Blackhurst, 199–217. New York: Harvester Wheatsheaf.

———. 1998. The Proliferation of Preferential Trading Arrangements. *Journal of Conflict Resolution* 42 (5):523–43.

Mansfield, Edward D., and Helen V. Milner. 1999. The New Wave of Regionalism. *International Organization* 53 (3):589–627.

Mansfield, Edward D., Helen V. Milner, and B. Peter Rosendorff. 2002. Why Democracies Cooperate More: Electoral Control and International Trade Agreements. *International Organization* 56 (3):477–513.

Martin, Lisa L., and Beth A. Simmons. 1998. Theories and Empirical Studies of International Institutions. *International Organization* 52 (4):729–57.

Mattli, Walter. 1999. *The Logic of Regional Integration: Europe and Beyond*. New York: Cambridge University Press.

Mavroidis, Petros C. 2000. Remedies in the WTO Legal System: Between a Rock and a Hard Place. *European Journal of International Law* 11 (4):763–813.

McCalman, Phillip. 2002. Multi-Lateral Trade Negotiations and the Most Favored Nation Clause. *Journal of International Economics* 57 (1):151–76.

Michalopoulos, Constantine. 1999. The Developing Countries in the WTO. *World Economy* 22 (1): 117–43.

Moore, Michael. 2000. WTO's Unique System of Settling Disputes Nears 200 Cases in 2000. PRESS/ 180. Geneva: World Trade Organization.

Oye, Kenneth A. 1992. *Economic Discrimination and Political Exchange: World Political Economy in the 1930s and 1980s*. Princeton, N.J.: Princeton University Press.

Özden, Çaglar, and Eric Reinhardt. 2003. The Perversity of Preferences: GSP and Developing Country Trade Policies, 1976–2000. Working Paper No. 2955. Washington, D.C.: World Bank.

Panagariya, Arvind. 2000. Preferential Trade Liberalization: The Traditional Theory and New Developments. *Journal of Economic Literature* 38 (2):287–331.

Perroni, Carlo, and John Whalley. 2000. The New Regionalism: Trade Liberalization or Insurance? *Canadian Journal of Economics* 33 (1):1–24.

Pomfret, Richard. 1997. *Unequal Trade: The Economics of Regional Trading Arrangements*. New York: Oxford University Press.

Preeg, Ernest H. 1995. *Traders in a Brave New World*. Chicago: University of Chicago Press.

Reinhardt, Eric. 2001. Adjudication Without Enforcement in GATT Disputes. *Journal of Conflict Resolution* 45 (2):174–95.

———. 2002. Tying Hands Without a Rope: Rational Domestic Response to International Institutional Constraints. In *Locating the Proper Authorities*, edited by Daniel Drezner, 75–102. Ann Arbor: University of Michigan Press.

———. Forthcoming. *Legislative Politics and GATT Trade Disputes, 1948–1994*. New York: Cambridge University Press.

Sampson, Gary P. 1996. Compatibility of Regional and Multilateral Trading Agreements: Reforming the WTO Process. *American Economic Review (Papers and Proceedings)* 86 (2):88–92.

Sapir, André. 2001. Domino Effects in Western European Regional Trade, 1960–1992. *European Journal of Political Economy* 17 (2):377–88.

Serra, Jaime, Guillermo Aguilar, José Córdoba, Gene Grossman, Carla Hills, John Jackson, Julius Katz, Pedro Noyola, and Michael Wilson. 1997. *Reflections on Regionalism: Report of the Study Group on International Trade*. Washington, D.C.: Carnegie Endowment for International Peace.

Smith, James McCall. 2000. The Politics of Dispute Settlement Design: Explaining Legalism in Regional Trade Pacts. *International Organization* 54 (1):137–80.

Summers, Robert, and Alan Heston. 1991. The Penn World Tables (Mark 5): An Expanded Set of International Comparisons, 1950–1988. *Quarterly Journal of Economics* 106 (2):327–68.

United States. 2000. *Economic Report of the President*. Washington, D.C.: Government Printing Office.

Viner, Jacob. 1950. *The Customs Union Issue*. New York: Carnegie Endowment for International Peace.

Westhoff, Frank H., Beth V. Yarbrough, and Robert M. Yarbrough. 1994. Preferential Trade Arrangements and the GATT: Can Bilateralism and Multilateralism Coexist? *Kyklos* 47 (2):179–95.

Whalley, John. 1998. Why Do Countries Seek Regional Trade Agreements? In *The Regionalization of the World Economy*, edited by Jeffrey A. Frankel, 63–83. Chicago: University of Chicago Press.

Winters, L. Alan, and Won Chang. 2000. Regional Integration and Import Prices: An Empirical Investigation. *Journal of International Economics* 51 (2):363–77.
World Bank. 2001. *World Development Indicators 2001 CD-ROM*. Washington, D.C.: World Bank.
World Trade Organization (WTO). 1995a. *Regionalism and the World Trading System*. Geneva: WTO.
———. 1995b. *Guide to GATT Law and Practice*, vol. 2. Geneva: WTO.
———. 1998. Membership of the World Trade Organization. WT/INF/6/Rev.4. Geneva: WTO.
———. 1999a. Report (1999) of the Committee on Regional Trade Agreements to the General Council. WT/REG/8. Geneva: WTO.
———. 1999b. Regional Trade Agreements Notified to the GATT/WTO and in Force in April 1999. Geneva: WTO.
———. 1999c. Overview of the State-of-Play of WTO Disputes. Geneva: WTO. Available at ⟨www.wto.org/english/tratop_e/dispu_e/stplay_e.doc⟩. Accessed 7 July 2003.
———. 2001. Negotiating Proposal on Behalf of Members of the Caribbean Community (CARICOM). G/AG/NG/W/100. Geneva: WTO.
Yarbrough, Beth V., and Robert M. Yarbrough. 1992. *Cooperation and Governance in International Trade: The Strategic Organizational Approach*. Princeton, N.J.: Princeton University Press.
———. 1997. Dispute Settlement in International Trade: Regionalism and Procedural Coordination. In *The Political Economy of Regionalism*, edited by Edward D. Mansfield and Helen V. Milner, 134–63. New York: Columbia University Press.

[6]

Journal of International Economics 88 (2012) 1–16

Contents lists available at SciVerse ScienceDirect

Journal of International Economics

journal homepage: www.elsevier.com/locate/jie

Are Free Trade Agreements contagious?

Richard Baldwin [a,*], Dany Jaimovich [b,1]

[a] Graduate Institute of International and Development Studies, Centre for Trade and Economic Integration, P.O. Box 136, 1211 Geneva 21 Switzerland
[b] Faculty of Economics and Business Administration, Goethe University Frankfurt, RuW Postbox 46, Grüneburgplatz 1, D-60323 Frankfurt am Main, Germany

ARTICLE INFO

Article history:
Received 21 June 2010
Received in revised form 22 February 2012
Accepted 26 March 2012
Available online 1 April 2012

JEL codes:
F13
F53

Keywords:
Contagion index
Free Trade Agreements
International trade
Regionalism
Domino theory of regionalism

ABSTRACT

This paper tests the hypothesis that the domino-like spread of regionalism is partly driven by 'defensive' FTAs, i.e. FTAs signed to reduce discrimination created by third-nation FTAs. A theory-based measure is used to test contagion against alternative determinants of regionalism. The main finding is that contagion is present in our data and robust to various econometric specifications, samples, and inclusions of various economic and political controls including the Baier–Bergstrand controls. Some support is found for political theories that stress 'political distance' but none for those that stress 'slow multilateralism'.

1. Introduction

Regionalism is sweeping the world trade system like wildfire while WTO talks advance at a glacial rate – an unconditional correlation that is often used to suggest that regionalism is a threat to the multilateral trading system (Bhagwati 2008). This concern has prompted a wave of research on why nations are so eager to remove barriers bilaterally.

The most common theoretical explanation in recent decades is "slow multilateralism", i.e. the assertion that regionalism is spreading because multilateral talks are progressing so slowly (Krugman 1991,1993; Bhagwati 1993, 2008). Other explanations turn on idiosyncratic events, such as the US's opening of the US–Canada FTA talks in 1986 (Bhagwati 1991 p.71), the breakup of the USSR in 1991 (Lester and Mercurio 2009 p.3), and the Asian Crisis of 1997 (Harvie et al., 2006 p.3). More institutional explanations for regionalism's popularity include the global spread of democracy (Mansfield et al., 2002; Wu 2004), and the quest for geopolitical stability (Mansfield and Pevehouse 2000; Martin et al. 2008, 2010, and Vicard 2008).

One lacuna in these hypotheses is the lack of recognition of third-nation effects, i.e. FTA interdependence. This angle is stressed by the so-called bandwagon or emulation arguments that posit a link between FTAs signed by the 'trade giants' (US, EU and Japan) and the attitudes of other nations. The giant FTAs create "a sense elsewhere that regionalism is the order of the day and others must follow suit" (Bhagwati 1991 p.73, and, more recently, Solis et al., 2009). The political economy logic of this assertion has not been fully worked out but the idea seems a general 'demonstration effect'. A related line of thinking for which the political economy links have been worked out is the domino theory of regionalism formalized in Baldwin (1993).[2] This argues that the signing or deepening of one FTA can induce excluded nations to sign new FTAs that were previously shunned. The logic turns on the way that trade diversion creates new political economy forces in excluded nations. Specifically, excluded nations seek to sign FTAs as a means of redressing the new discrimination. The FTAs thus signed create their own trade diversion that may lead to more FTAs. Using an obvious metaphor, the domino theory explains why FTAs seem to be 'contagious'.

Our paper uses a broad panel of countries to empirically test the various hypotheses for spreading regionalism, especially the notion that FTAs are contagious in the sense that a new FTA between nations A and B increases the likelihood that nation C will sign a new FTA with A or B.

* Corresponding author. Tel.: +41 22 9085933.
E-mail addresses: Baldwin@graduateinstitute.ch (R. Baldwin), jaimovich@econ.uni-frankfurt.de (D. Jaimovich).
[1] Tel.: +49 69 79834844.

0022-1996/$ – see front matter © 2012 Elsevier B.V. All rights reserved.
doi:10.1016/j.jinteco.2012.03.009

[2] There are precedents to the domino/contagion effect. Whalley (1993) informally argues that Western Hemispheric regionalism was largely defensive, focusing on fears of US aggressive unilateralism instead of trade diversion; he also does not posit a circular causality between bloc size and the strength of inclusionary pressures. Hufbauer (1989) uses the term "FTA magnetism" which captures the first step (idiosyncratic deepening sparks membership requests) but does not relate the strength of the magnetism to the bloc size. See Baldwin (1994, 1997, 2008) for applications to, respectively, the waves of regionalism in Europe, the Western Hemisphere, and East Asia.

The value added of our paper is primarily empirical. First, while the empirical linkages have already been established in a more reduced form setting by Egger and Larch (2008) using spatial econometric methods, we use a broader sample of FTAs than previous studies. Moreover, our method allows us to test the contagion/domino effect against alternative hypotheses using a theory-based measure of contagion. This measure captures asymmetries in the dyads, and reflects trade dependencies. As such it goes beyond the earlier literature that uses measures based solely on geographical distance.

The rest of the paper is organized as follows. The next section presents an overview of relevant literature and the subsequent one presents our model. Section 4 presents our empirical strategy and Section 5 our data and results. The final section presents our concluding remarks.

2. Previous literature[3]

2.1. Theoretical work on FTA formation

A wide range of theory articles have studied the incentive to form customs unions (CUs) and FTAs. The first paper to consider endogenous CU formation seems to be Riezman (1985). He works in a 3-nation Walrasian setting where nations have an incentive to manipulate their terms of trade unilaterally or as members of a two-nation CU. International transfers are not allowed, so the external tariff is assumed to be set unilaterally by the "dominant" CU member. There are eight possible coalitions and he numerically calculates national utility levels for all eight assuming Cobb–Douglas preferences and three different endowment allocations. With these numbers he determines which coalition structures (i.e. trade arrangements) are blocked in the sense that at least one of the nations would prefer some other allocation. The trade arrangements that survive this elimination process thus have a chance of appearing through voluntary agreements.

Real-world multilateral constraints are ignored in the model; governments are allowed to violate their GATT/WTO commitments both unilaterally (by breaking their tariff binding commitments) and in pairs (by raising the CU's common external tariff). In this sense, this line of research asks what sort of regionalism would have been observed if GATT/WTO rules had not been respected in the postwar period. Implicitly, this provides a rationale for why such rules were actually respected. The issue of CU contagion never arises in Riezman (1985) given his use of the concept of the 'core' to evaluate which trade arrangements are most likely to occur. Riezman (1999) uses a similar model to ask whether banning FTAs and/or CUs would result in higher or lower Nash tariffs, when participation in such arrangements is endogenous.

Melatos and Woodland (2007) use a similar set up to consider the links between the nature of nations (similarities of endowments and preferences) and the nature of the core when FTAs, CUs, and non-cooperative outcomes are possibilities. They show that global free trade is in the core only when nations are sufficiently similar. CUs are in the core when nations are dissimilar; in this case, the selection of CU members tends to involve members that are similar in terms of preferences or endowments. When nations are very dissimilar, FTAs are preferred to CUs.

A different approach is the domino theory of regionalism (Baldwin 1993). Working with a monopolistic competition trade model, he shows that the trade-diversion effects of CU formation can induce nations that were previously against membership to join. Moreover, the economic incentive to join rises with the CU's size. If the CU enlargement is spread over time for practical reasons, a single event of regionalism may appear to spark a domino-like chain reaction where each enlargement triggers another. The result may be global free trade if nations' intrinsic resistance to joining is not too great.

[3] A comprehensive review of the literature on FTA formation is provided by Freund and Ornelas (2010).

Yi (1996), working with a version of the Brander–Krugman model, studies the domino effect more formally by analyzing coalition structures. He shows that the global free trade outcome is stable when membership is open, but not necessarily when incumbents can veto enlargement. Krishna (1998) and Freund (2000) also work with the Brander–Krugman model. Krishna (1998) assumes governments' FTA choices are only affected by their firms' operating profit and shows that nations of similar size are likely to gain from an FTA — especially when it produces trade diversion. Freund (2000) shows that nations can gain from forming an FTA as long as their MFN tariffs are below the optimal tariff level.

Aghion et al. (2007) use cooperative game theory to analyze CU formation. Assuming that one nation is the undisputed agenda setter and that unlimited transfers among nations are possible and costless (transferable utility), they show that almost anything can happen — including an outcome that resembles the domino effect.

2.2. Empirical studies of FTA formation

Empirical studies of FTA formation are rarer as FTA membership is typically taken as exogenous by empirical researchers. The seminal article in the empirical FTA formation literature is Baier and Bergstrand (2004). However, they do not consider any of the hypotheses discussed above — focusing purely economic determinants. Using cross-section data, they estimate the impact of economic factors on the probability that an FTA is signed. They find that the likelihood of an FTA is higher when the partners are: closer geographically, more distant from the rest of the world, larger, more similar in economic size, and further apart in terms of per capita incomes.

Several empirical studies have focused on aspects beyond the economic determinants. Mansfield and Reinhardt (2003) offer a political explanation, providing empirical support for the "slow multilateralism" argument. Mansfield et al. (2002) find that pairs of democratic countries are more likely to form an FTA, a result confirmed by Wu (2004), who also claims that economic and trade uncertainty matter. Holmes (2005) shows "mercantile interests" are also important determinants. The first test of the 'geopolitical stability' hypothesis is by Mansfield and Pevehouse (2000). They show that countries with an FTA are less likely to go to war — a result in conformity with the theory of Martin et al. (2008) and tested by Martin et al. (2010) and Vicard (2008).

FTA interdependence has received little empirical attention. The first efforts tested the domino theory on European data. Sapir (1997) estimates year-by-year gravity equations to identify the trade diversion effect of the EU on non-members. He finds that trade diversion estimates tend to spike just in advance of EU enlargements; he suggests that the enlargements were caused by the heightened trade diversion. Baldwin and Rieder (2007) undertake a similar procedure as a first stage to identify trade diversion and add a second stage that estimates a linear probability model linking the likelihood of joining the EU to contemporaneous trade diversion. This procedure, however, is plagued by the endogeneity of the membership.

Manger (2006) introduced spatial econometric techniques into the literature by using a weighting matrix based on distances. Egger and Larch (2008), using a similar weighting strategy, extend the spatial econometric analysis to the study of dynamic FTA formation and enlargement, incorporating long-term implications of interdependence in a cross-section analysis estimated with Bayesian techniques. Bergstrand et al. (2010) use survival analysis and a distance-based weighting matrix to predict the timing of FTA formation.

3. Theoretical considerations

This paper's main contribution is empirical but our empirical strategy depends upon a 'contagion index' that gauges the extent to which an FTA between nation-j and nation-k changes nation-i's interest in signing a new FTA with either j or k. To inform the calculation of our contagion index, we present a simple political economy model that parsimoniously captures our two core beliefs about the nature of FTA contagion: the key economic channel is the profit-depressing effect that trade diversion has on third-nation exporters, and the key political-economy channel is the desire of governments to offset these fresh losses.

3.1. The economic model

We work in a world of N countries, each with two sectors: a manufacturing sector (the M-sector) and a numeraire sector (the A sector), and two factors (labor L and capital K). Tastes of all consumers are given by the quasi-linear utility function:

$$U = c_A + \mu \ln(C_M), C_M \equiv \left(\int_{i \in \Gamma} c_i^{1-1/\sigma} di\right)^{1/(1-1/\sigma)}; \sigma > 1. \mu > 0 \tag{1}$$

where c_A is consumption of A, C_M is a CES aggregate of the consumption of individual varieties, c_j, and Γ is the set of such varieties; $\sigma > 1$ is the constant elasticity of substitution among varieties.

The M-sector is marked by Dixit–Stiglitz monopolistic competition with firms facing a sunk set-up cost (comprised only capital with one unit of K per variety) and a constant marginal cost (comprised only labor with a_M units of L per unit of output). The A-sector is marked by perfect competition, constant-returns, and production that requires a_A units of L per unit of output. A-sector goods are homogeneous and traded costlessly. We take A as the untaxed numeraire.

Given (1), the demand functions are:

$$c_A = E - \int_{i \in \Gamma} p_i c_i di. c_j = \left(p_j^{-\sigma}/P_M^{1-\sigma}\right)\mu; P_M^{1-\sigma} \equiv \int_{i \in \Gamma} p_i^{1-\sigma} di \tag{2}$$

where $p_A = 1$ by choice of numeraire, E is the nation's total consumer expenditure, p_i is the consumer price of variety-i, μ is the nation's total expenditure on all M varieties (given (1)), and P_M is the CES price index.

Costless trade equalizes p_A globally and thus equalizes wages as long as the nations are sufficiently similar in size to ensure that some A-good is made in all nations (an assumption maintained throughout). By choice of numeraire then, we have $1 = p_A = a_A w$ in all nations. Choosing units such that $a_A = 1$ yields $w = 1$ for all nations.

Dixit–Stiglitz competition implies 'mill pricing' with a constant price to marginal-cost mark-up equal to $1/(1-1/\sigma)$. Choosing units so $a_M = (1-1/\sigma)$ and using $w = 1$, the consumer price of a variety produced in origin nation 'o' and sold in destination nation 'd' is:

$$p_{od} = (1 + t_{od}) \tag{3}$$

where t_{od} is the ad valorem tariff on goods sold from nation-o to nation-d; as usual $t_{oo} = 0$.

With Mill pricing, a firm's operating profit – namely its pure profit gross of the fixed costs – is $1/\sigma$ times its revenue, so using Eqs. (2) and (3):

$$\pi_o + f = \frac{1}{\sigma} \sum_{d=1}^{N} \phi_{od} B_d; B_d \equiv \mu_d / \left(\sum_{i=1}^{N} \phi_{id} n_i\right); 0 \le \phi_{od} \equiv (1 + t_{od})^{1-\sigma} \le 1 \tag{4}$$

where π_o is the pure profit of a typical nation-o firm, *f* is the sunk cost, ϕ_{od} is the 'free-ness' of trade between nations o and d (i.e. ϕ is zero with an infinite tariff, and unity with a zero tariff), μ_d is nation-d's expenditure on M-varieties, and n_i is the mass of identical M-firms producing in nation-i. The long-run, free-entry equilibrium is defined by the set of ns that satisfy the N free entry conditions:

$$\pi_i \le 0, \forall i = 1, \ldots, N \tag{5}$$

where this holds with complementary slackness, i.e. $n_i \pi_i = 0$ for all i. [4]

[4] See Baldwin and Jaimovich (2010) for a fuller presentation of the model that includes discussion of the short and long run equilibriums.

3.1.1. Equilibrium economic features

The short term profit effects of tariffs (i.e. when the *ns* are fixed) are very simple. From Eq. (4), operating profit is proportional to revenue; from Eqs. (2) and (3), revenue is proportional to sales, and sales are inversely proportional to relative prices. Keeping track of profits therefore boils down to tracking the impact of tariffs on relative prices in various markets. When we allow entry, the *ns* are found by solving the Bs in terms of ϕs, σ, and *f*, and then solving the Bs for the *ns* – see Eq. (5). The equilibrium *ns* are linear in the parameters, but the solutions are too unwieldy to be revealing in the general case. However, when the ϕs are all identical, the solutions are very simple. See Theory appendix (Appendix 1) for details.

3.2. The political economy model

Our political economy model is designed to reflect the policymaking processes that we believe generated our dataset. As such, it focuses on four features that we feel were important in actual policy decisions. First, some FTAs are 'political' in the sense that they are signed for non-economic reasons, e.g. the EEC, or the US–Israel FTA. In our story, such 'shock FTAs' trigger the domino/contagion effect. Second, many FTAs are 'defensive' in the sense that they are signed to offset discrimination created by FTAs among their trade partners. Third, governments are mercantilists; they place disproportionate weight on the interests of trading firms when setting trade policy. Fourth, nations sign FTAs slowly.

We capture the first feature by introducing bilateral 'political' parameters that indicate the intrinsic political cost or benefit of signing a particular FTA. These parsimoniously capture the vast complexity of actual bilateral trade-policy formulation.

The second feature is well captured by the often-observed 'loser's paradox', i.e. the fact that special interest groups tend to fight harder to avoid losing a dollar than they do to win a dollar (Tovar 2009). In the presence of the loser's paradox, a third-party FTA that forces losses on domestic firms (via trade diversion) will generate especially strong, *de novo* political-economy efforts by domestic firms. These new efforts can explain why a government finds it optimal to sign an FTA that it shunned before the shock. There are many ways of modeling this 'losers lobby harder' phenomenon. The most famous is the "conservative social welfare function" of Corden (1974). The modeling approach we adopt turns on sunk market-entry costs, namely that of Baldwin and Robert-Nicoud (2007).

Specifically, we assume that firms enter quickly but exit slowly. The quick entry means that incumbent manufacturing firms cannot benefit from lobbying for new gains. The reason is that these gains would be instantly arbitraged away by new entrants leaving the incumbents with the lobbying cost and zero benefit. Incumbents can, by contrast, benefit from lobbying when faced with pure losses. The reason is that the slow exit creates quasi-rents that can be raised to the zero-profit level without inducing entry.

Apart from the bilateral political parameters, our political economy model is standard. As in Grossman and Helpman (1994), the government chooses trade arrangements to maximize a weighted objective function, where the weights apply to, respectively, social welfare (i.e. utility of citizens) and pure profits which are, on the margin, fully paid to the government in the Grossman–Helpman story. The typical government's objective function is:

$$G_i = aW + (1-a) n_i \pi_i - \sum_{j \in J} Z_{ij} - K \tag{6}$$

where 'a' is the weight on welfare, Z_{ij} is government-is idiosyncratic political cost of signing an FTA with nation-j, K is a constant (related to the Grossman-Helpman game between firms and the government), and J is the set of FTA partners. When $Z_{ij} > 0$, FTAs create political costs; when $Z_{ij} < 0$, they create political benefits.

To capture the third feature (mercantilism) we join Krishna (1998) in assuming that $a = 0$ in Eq. (6), so governments care only about their firms' pure profits when considering the economic impact of trade policy. (In the Theory appendix (Appendix 1), we show that our main results go through if instead we assume $a=1$, but the critical role of trade diversion comes through much less clearly.)

A first-order feature of our data is that nations sign FTAs slowly, rarely negotiating more than a few at a time. While there may be many reasons for this, we capture it parsimoniously by assuming that each nation can only sign one FTA per period.[5]

As we are trying to capture first-order aspects of actual FTA choices – and FTAs in our dataset were signed in a particular multilateral setting – we embrace two additional assumptions. First, the initial tariff levels are not chosen according to some optimization process. Rather, we assume that they are the outcome of a decades-long process of GATT/WTO negotiations that occurs outside of our model. Tariff levels are thus taken as an initial condition; for simplicity, we assume that they are all equal. Second, we assume that all tariffs are "bound" in the WTO sense of the word, and that all nations respect their WTO obligations. (We consider the implication of relaxing this constraint in the Theory appendix (Appendix 1).)

3.2.1. Equilibrium political economy features

The equilibrium is marked by a number of useful features. First, the initial equilibrium is stable (in a Nash sense) with respect to MFN tariffs for any initial condition. That is, starting from the zero-profit equilibrium, no government will want to unilaterally raise or lower its MFN tariff; instant entry obviates any pure profit gain from higher tariffs, while slow exit means that lower tariffs harm profits.

As we shall see, the initial equilibrium is also stable with respect to FTAs as long as nations have some political resistance to forming an FTA (i.e. the Zs are all positive). For example, an FTA between nations 1 and 2 leads to an incipient rise in profits that is eliminated by instant entry. With all pure profits gone, the changes in the governments' objective functions are minus Z_{12} and minus Z_{21} respectively (see Eq. (6)). As a consequence, nation-1 would reject an FTA with nation-2, or any other nation when Zs are positive. The same logic holds for all nations, so the initial equilibrium is stable with respect to bilateral trade agreements. Our task is to investigate the evolution of FTAs after an 'FTA shock' occurs.

3.3. Contagion

Contagion means that a government, which initially opposes a particular trade agreement, changes its mind due to a trade agreement signed by other nations. We illustrate the key roles that asymmetric entry and negative-profits play in creating FTA contagion by first distinguishing sharply between FTAs and CUs.

3.3.1. Contagion for customs union versus FTAs

As Melatos and Woodland (2007) point out, there are important differences between FTAs and CUs that are not always clear in the endogenous trade-block literature. In our model, however, the difference is critical. Our asymmetric-entry assumption is not essential to contagion stemming from CU enlargements, but it is for contagion stemming from FTAs. This is the key feature that distinguishes our model from Baldwin (1993), which considered only CU contagion.

To see this, note that if a nation joins a CU that already has M members, Eq. (4) implies that the change in its profit – assuming no entry or exit of firms – is equal to:

$$\left(\frac{\mu}{\sigma n}\right)\frac{M\phi(1-\phi)\left(M(1-\phi)(N-1)+\phi(N-1)^2-1\right)}{((1-\phi)(M+1)+\phi N)(1+\phi(N-1))((1-\phi)M+\phi N))} \qquad (7)$$

where we have assumed all nations are symmetric in terms of μ, ϕ, and n to keep the formula simple. This difference is increasing in M, so the profit gain from joining a CU – as opposed to staying out – rises with the CU's size. In this way, an exogenous CU enlargement tends to produce contagion. Non-member nations view membership more favorably after the exogenous enlargement, so some may change their mind and join. This is the political logic of the standard contagion/domino effect.[6]

While the contagion logic is extremely direct in the case of CU enlargements, CUs are rare in our data. The most common events are bilateral FTAs. As it turns out, the CU-contagion logic does not carry over to bilateral FTAs. This is for one simple reason – preference erosion. The profit gain from signing an FTA with a given partner is decreasing in the number of FTAs the partner already has – not increasing as in the CU case.

With N nations, there are $N(N-1)/2$ possible FTAs, and a very large number of permutations of these, so we focus on a particular example where the role of preference erosion is particularly clear – that of a 'hub and spoke' arrangement. To be concrete, suppose the 'shock FTA' gets formed between nations 2 and 3 (e.g. it gets signed for political reasons), and take nation-2 as the hub and nation-3 as the first spoke. We denote F_2 as the number of FTAs that the 'hub' (nation-2) has with other nations (the spokes); we assume there are no other FTAs.[7] While this is not a general solution, it has the advantage that it is the type of contagion that happens in the three-nation case that is so common in the literature.

We show that the shock-FTA will not create contagion by showing that the gain to nation-1 of signing an FTA with nation-2 is reduced by the shock-FTA (rather than increased as in the CU-enlargement case). Holding the number of firms constant, the change in profits of a firm in a nation with and without an FTA is, from Eq. (4):

$$\left(\frac{\mu}{\sigma n}\right)\left(\frac{(1-\phi)\left((1+\phi(N-1))^2-(1-\phi)^2F_2\right)}{((1+(1-\phi)F_2+\phi(N-1))(2+\phi(N-2))(1+\phi(N-1))}\right) \qquad (8)$$

By inspection, this is decreasing in F_2. This confirms that contagion does not happen for FTAs when the number of firms is fixed. If nation-1 does not find it politically optimal to sign an FTA with nation-2 to start with (i.e. when $F_2=0$), an FTA between nations 2 and 3 will make nation-1 less interested – not more interested – in signing an FTA with nation-2. By symmetry of nations, no contagion will happen.

3.3.2. Asymmetric entry, negative profits, and defensive FTAs

The asymmetric-entry aspect of our model restores FTA contagion in a very direct manner. Fast entry renders improvements in market access uninteresting to governments. As mentioned above, starting from symmetric MFN tariffs and no FTAs, any proposed FTA will be rejected as long as one of the governments has some political resistance to the FTA. Instant entry eliminates any potential economic gain from the FTA, and this leaves only the political costs.

However if a shock-FTA appears then slow exit makes other governments interested in redressing the profit losses that comes with the new discrimination. Thus nation-1 can be uninterested in signing an FTA with nation-2 before the shock-FTA, but could be interested in signing afterwards. This is the basic political-economy logic behind our contagion index. The goal is to capture the extent to which an FTA between nation-j and k harms the profits of firms in nation-i.

While the basic logic of this FTA contagion is simple, the fact that governments may anticipate the contagion raises a number of issues that need to be addressed. Given that the aim of the paper is to

[5] There is no absolutely natural definition of period here, but we note that it often takes several years to move from the start of FTA negotiations to actual implement.

[6] A domino-like effect can occur since each enlargement increases the attractions of membership for the remaining outsiders (Baldwin 1993).

[7] In a schematic diagram of this FTA arrangement, nation-2 would look like a hub in an old-fashioned wheel and the FTAs would be the spokes.

provide empirical evidence of the contagion effect in FTAs formation, these concerns are discussed in the Theory appendix (Appendix 1).

3.3.3. Deriving a contagion index

The preceding discussion makes it clear that the linchpin of the FTA contagion effect is the way an FTA between a nation's partners harm its exporters' profit. More precisely, the fundamental trade-off balances the reduction of profit losses that an FTA would bring by reducing discrimination on the one hand against the political cost of signing an FTA on the other hand. The reduction in profit losses required us to know two things: the present value of profit losses with the FTA and the present value without the FTA. In the simple example elaborated in the Theory appendix (Appendix 1) (perfect foresight, one FTA signed per period, and three symmetric nations), these are simple to characterize.

In our dataset, however, such magnitudes would be difficult to calculate for many reasons. The most practical one is that the present value would require knowledge of the full path of FTAs. Even looking retrospectively, this would only make sense if we believed that government had perfect foresight, or at least a good idea of evolution of FTAs for many years in the future – an assumption that is more heroic than we are willing to make. For example, the US and Korean governments decided they wanted a bilateral FTA in 2005, talks started in 2006 and finished in 2007, but it was still not ratified as of September 2011. Meanwhile, the EU and Korea started, completed and implemented an FTA. In characterizing the US decision to sign the FTA there is a real question as to whether we should assume that they knew that the EU–Korea FTA would enter into force before the Korea–US FTA. Moreover, Korea is now talking about FTAs with Japan and China. It is not at all clear how one should implement this observation into an empirical measure of the US's evaluation in 2005. The usual assumption of perfect foresight with white noise is problematic given that FTAs are rare and contagion is path-dependent.

A second, more practical problem concerns the availability of data. Even if we knew what nations had assumed about the evolution of FTAs, it would be impossible to calculate the full impact on profits analytically for general patterns of bilateral tariffs; we are missing bilateral tariff data for too many years for too many trade pairs.

The solution we propose returns to the source of the FTA contagion effect – namely the negative profit effect of third-nation FTAs. We operationalize this using a first-order approximation of the negative profit effect arising from any given FTA. Differentiating the definition of operating profit for nation-1 with respect to reciprocally freer trade between nation-j and nation-k, and then multiplying this by the tariff change (which is the initial level of the bilateral tariff since we are considering FTAs), this yields:

$$d\pi_1 = (1-\sigma)\frac{\mu E^w}{\sigma n^w}\left(\frac{s_{Ej}\phi_{1j}}{P_{Mj}^{1-\sigma}}\left(\frac{-s_{nk}}{P_{Mj}^{1-\sigma}}\right)d\phi_{kj}t_{kj} + \frac{s_{Ej}\phi_{1k}}{P_{Mk}^{1-\sigma}}\left(\frac{-s_{nj}}{P_{Mk}^{1-\sigma}}\right)d\phi_{jk}t_{jk}\right). \quad (9)$$

While the preferential liberalization between nations j and k is reciprocal in the case of an FTA, we can think of it as two separate changes in trade policy – lower tariffs charged by j on imports from k (this is reflected in the rise of ϕ_{kj}) and the lower tariff charged by k on imports from j (this is reflected in the rise of ϕ_{jk}). This allows us to consider the 'contagion' coming to nation 1 from nation j and, separately, from nation-k. Separating the effects and forming proportional changes for the first, we have:

$$\frac{d\pi_1/\pi_1}{d\phi_{kj}/\phi_{kj}} = \left(\frac{\pi_{1j}}{\pi_1}\right)\left(\frac{-s_{nk}\phi_{kj}t_{kj}}{P_{Mj}^{1-\sigma}}\right).$$

Note that the first right-hand term is the proportion of operating profit that a typical nation-1 firms earns on sales to nation-j. Because operating profits in this model are proportional to sales, we can take the share of nation-1's total exports that go to nation-j as a proxy for the first right-hand term. The second right-hand term is the market share of firms from nation-k in nation-j's market. We can take j's import share from k as a proxy for this. Finally, as the annual, bilateral tariff data are so incomplete, we are obliged to ignore bilateral tariffs in the construction of the index. Instead, we consider interactions of the contagion index with tariffs in some regressions (see Table 4 column 3).

Putting these together, and noting that the bilateral ϕ goes to unity under the FTA, we can approximate the contagion effect from nation-j's FTAs on nation 1 by:

$$\text{Contagion}_{1kj} \cong \left(\frac{\text{bilateral exports}_{1j}}{\text{total exports}_1}\right)\left(\frac{\text{bilateral exports}_{kj}}{\text{total imports}_j}\right)FTA_{kj}. \quad (10)$$

Here the first subscript indicates that nation-1 is subject to contagion when nation-j offers tariff preferences to imports from nation-k. Intuitively this says that: (i) the more important is market-j in nation-1's export pattern the greater will be nation-1's concern over discrimination in nation-j, and (ii) the larger is the importance of nation-1's competitor in market-j (i.e. nation-k who is signing the FTA with nation j) the larger will be the discriminatory impact on nation-1 of the FTA between k and j. The variable FTA_{kj} is a binary variable that is zero when there is no FTA between k and j, and unity otherwise.

4. Empirical strategy

4.1. Spatial definition of the contagion index

The index in Eq. (10) measures the contagion from a single FTA. However, as a given prospective FTA partner, say nation-j, may have several FTAs, we sum over all of nation-j's FTAs, namely:

$$\text{Contagion}_{ij,t} \equiv \sum_{k\in\Omega_{j,t}}\left(\frac{\text{bilateral exports}_{1j}}{\text{total exports}_1}\right)\left(\frac{\text{bilateral exports}_{kj}}{\text{total imports}_j}\right)FTA_{jk} \quad (11)$$

where $\Omega_{j,t}$ is the set of nations with which nation-j has FTA in year t. The index can be interpreted as the sum of FTA signed by nation- j up to year t weighted by the relevance of market-j for the exporters in nation-i (export share of j in i) and the importance of exports of nation-k in market-j (import share of k in j).

In the empirical specification, we will follow the spatial econometrics literature and represent the structure of the spatial interdependence in the contagion index as an N by N weighting matrix (**W**), where each element w_{pq} is a measure of the 'distance' between the dyads p and q, with dyad p formed by country-pair i, j and dyad q by country-pair k,l.

Previous studies that use spatial econometrics to analyze FTA interdependence (e.g., Manger (2006), Egger and Larch (2008) and Bergstrand et al. (2010)) use symmetric weighting matrices where the element w_{pq} is defined as the inverse of the average geographical distance (D). For example, in Egger and Larch (2008) $w_{pq} = e^{-D_{pq}/500}$ with $D_{pq} = (D_{ik} + D_{il} + D_{jk} + D_{jl})/4$. [8]

Following Eq. (11), we will derive a weighting matrix version of the contagion index with the following characteristics:

[8] Egger and Larch (2008) show an alternative weighting that uses natural bilateral trade flows.

i. The definition of 'distance' comes from our model, specifically, a typical element in W is:

$$w_{pq} = \left(\frac{\text{bilateral exports}_{ij}}{\text{total exports}_i}\right)\left(\frac{\text{bilateral exports}_{kj}}{\text{total imports}_j}\right).$$

ii. The matrix **W** is not symmetric, since generally $w_{pq} \neq w_{qp}$ (except when both are zero), reflecting the fact that the threat of trade diversion will be different for each country in the pair.

iii. The matrix **W** is (theoretically) sparse, since $w_{pq} = 0 \ \forall \ 1 \neq j$, meaning the country-pair's probability to sign an FTA will not be affected by FTA signed by countries outside the dyad.[9]

Apart from these particularities, all the traditional properties of the spatial weighting matrices hold, namely a zero diagonal and rows normalized to sum up to unity.

For the empirical part, we will define a spatial weighting matrix $\mathbf{W_t}$, where the sub index indicates that a different matrix will be created for each period. Nevertheless, as can be seen from Eq. (11), the export and import share measures are time-invariant. This empirical choice is meant to reduce the simultaneity between FTAs and market shares. For example, if nation-i signs an FTA with a third nation, then it is likely that the export share to nation-j will be reduced, and with it the contagion index from j to i. To avoid this sort of problems, we estimate the shares as the first observation in the sample of predicted shares from a simple gravity equation estimated with fixed effects and the log GDP of nations in the dyad as regressors (data details in Appendix 3).[10]

In Fig. 1 we present a graphical exploration of the contagion index, dividing the observations in two groups: those country-pairs that signed an FTA and those that do not. It is possible to see that the growth of the average contagion index for the first group in the years previous to the signature of the FTA is faster than for the rest of the sample.[11]

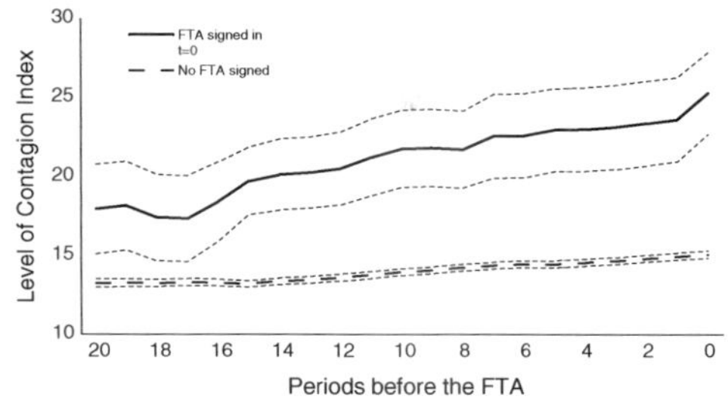

Fig. 1. Evolution of the average contagion index. Note: 90% confidence intervals. 199 observations for FTA signed data and 25,255 observations for no FTA signed data.

4.2. Econometric specification

The empirical specification aims to identify the variables that affect the probability that a given FTA will be signed, with special emphasis on the possibility that contagion plays a role. We will follow the empirical literature summarized above in having a dummy variable reflecting the existence of a particular FTA (unity if yes and zero if no) as the dependent variable. Our main explanatory variables are the Contagion Index from Eq. (11) and controls for several economic, institutional and geographic determinants of FTAs.[12]

Given the dynamic nature of the contagion/domino effect, panel data is most appropriate.[13] For this, we will follow Mansfield and Reinhardt (2003), and Egger and Larch (2008) in using the following specification:

$$\Pr(\text{switch}) = G\left(\beta_0 + \rho W_{t-1} FTA_{jk,t-1} + \beta_1 X_{ij,t-1} + \beta_2 X_{i,t-1} + \beta_3 X_{t-1}\right) \tag{12}$$

where the probability to switch status from non-FTA to FTA is determined by the logistic cumulative distribution function G(•) of a linear vector of lagged explanatory variables X at different levels (country-pair-year, country-year and year) and the spatial lag, which is $W_{t-1}FTA_{jk,t-1}$ with W_{t-1} being the one-period lagged weighting matrix described above and $FTA_{jk,t-1}$ the vector of all FTAs signed by the nation j with third countries up to period t − 1. In other words, $W_{t-1}FTA_{jk,t-1}$ is the empirical representation of our Contagion Index, and ρ is the coefficient that will capture its effect.

When estimating Eq. (12), we include only not-yet-switched dyads, i.e. pairs that could adopt an FTA but have not yet. A dyad stays in the panel until an FTA is signed; after that it is dropped from the panel.[14] This reduces simultaneity problems between the components of the Contagion Index and the dependent variable. In other words, the use of a time-lagged spatial lag avoids the usual complications of spatial econometric techniques to deal with endogeneity; this relies on the assumption that FTAs cannot affect the probability of FTAs retroactively.

Estimating a panel data model with a limited dependent variable raises the problem of incidental parameters, namely inconsistency in the estimation of fixed effects being 'transmitted' to inconsistency in the estimation of parameters. Our first approach to deal with this is to exclude country-pair fixed effects relying instead on dyad-level time invariant control variables (like geographical distance, common border, common language, etc.).

In order to control for unobservable heterogeneity at country-pair level, we will present an alternative estimation method using conditional logit estimation, as proposed by Chamberlain (1980). If the conditional probability is different from 1, the logit function does not involve the fixed effect parameters and conventional maximum likelihood estimation can be performed. In this case, conditional logit will provide unbiased estimates of the parameters, but only for the sub-sample of dyads that switch FTA status during the observed period. The conditional likelihood function will take the following form:

$$L = \prod_{ij=1}^{N} \Pr\left(\frac{FTA_{ij,1}, \ldots, FTA_{ij,T}}{\sum_{t=1}^{T} FTA_{ij,t}}\right), \forall FTA_{ij,T-1} = 0, FTA_{ij,T} = 1. \tag{13}$$

---

[9] Giving this characteristic, it is possible to say that the type of contagion considered by Manger (2006), Egger and Larch (2008) and Bergstrand et al. (2010) belongs to undirected dyad contagion class in the classification recently proposed by Neumayer and Plumper (2010), while the one we use in the present study is classified as specific target contagion.

[10] One possible concern with the total export shares as weight is the fact that some FTAs cover just a number of industries, so only these sectors are threatened by the potential trade diversion, and only the export share of these industries might be used as the weight in the contagion indexes. Even this concern is true, our database do not have information on the specific sectors covered by the FTA. Moreover, our prior is that even if a sector is not included in the original FTA, the fact that the agreement was signed creates the threat that the sector can be included in the future.

[11] The sample used to create the figure is limited to data with enough observations available where the contagion index for previous periods was recorded, keeping the sample constant in time.

[12] Each agreement enters the database twice, one per each member of the dyad, since there is contagion from i to j, but also (and with a different magnitude) from j to i, same for other country-pair time variant control variables.

[13] Jaimovich (2012) estimates contagion effects with cross-sectional data using Bayesian spatial probit models.

[14] This means FTAs signed before the beginning of our sample will not be included, e.g. the original EU customs union and the EEC–EFTA bilateral FTAs.

In the robustness check section we present alternative methodologies that also deal with the unobserved heterogeneity issue.

Another concern with this empirical specification relates to serial correlation. Because observations are likely to be temporally correlated due to duration dependence, the use of traditional probit or logit techniques poses problems. To address this, we include, in all estimations, a natural cubic spline function of the number of years a dyad have been without an FTA, a solution proposed by Beck et al. (1998). A different strategy to deal with serial correlation is the use of duration models. To pursue this alternative, we estimate a Cox proportional hazard model, where the length of time before the 'failure event' (FTA signature in our specification) is considered in the estimation using a baseline hazard function.

Finally, the inference in dyadic regressions is problematic because observations are not independent (Fafchamps and Gubert, 2007). We first correct for this by clustering standard errors at the dyad level. We also perform a robustness check using a two-way clustering of errors at the country level proposed by Cameron et al. (2011).

5. Data and results

5.1. Free Trade Agreements

Our data on FTAs comes from the recently released Preferential Trade Agreements Database developed by Hufbauer and Schott (2009). This source is the most extensive and detailed currently available to our knowledge; it is more comprehensive than the WTO database which lists only agreements that have been officially notified to the WTO. The Hufbauer-Schott database has 570 agreements recorded from 1948 to 2007; of these, 329 agreements were still force in 2007. We limit the period of investigation to 1976–2005 due to lack of comprehensive data on our 'right hand side' variables.

In the original database, a cumulative total of 1319 country-pair trade deals are registered up to 2005, but just 1134 are still in force or signed for later implementation. This means that around 17% of country pairs are covered by some sort of trade agreement in 2005. Among these agreements, 65% are classified as 'pure' Free Trade Agreements, 21% as partial scope or preferential agreements (i.e. Free Trade Agreements among developing nations where GATT/WTO rules allow tariffs to be preferential without going to zero); the rest as CUs, CU accessions, and consultative frameworks. Nevertheless, to avoid linguistic infelicities, we refer to all of them as FTAs and, more importantly, for our analysis we will use all types of registered agreements, since our prior is that the contagion effect is produced at the moment the agreement is created. The idea is that the threat of trade diversion is as important as actual trade diversion. Nevertheless, we will also explore if the results change when we limit our panel to "pure FTAs" and CUs.

Appendix 2 presents the number of FTAs signed by each country in our database during the period 1976–2005 for a total of 358 country-pairs with FTAs; 422 when only "pure FTA" and CUs are considered. The fact that the latter are more numerous than the former means that some partial scope agreements signed before 1976 were converted into deeper agreements afterwards.

5.2. Sample and controls

Our sample is limited by data availability arising from calculation of the contagion index as well as controls used. The final sample includes 113 countries over the period 1977–2005 (the full list of countries is in Appendix 2). Thus we have a total of 105,927 observations representing 4609 country-pairs. Descriptive statistics for the variables are presented in Table 1 and the details about sources and data construction in Appendix 3.

As mentioned above, previous studies have investigated the hypothesis of interdependence of FTA using undirected spatial lags.

Table 1
Descriptive statistics.

Variable	Mean	Std. Dev.	Min	Max
FTA	0.007	0.083	0	1
PURE FTA	0.008	0.086	0	1
CONTAGION INDEX	13.285	17.210	0	76.375
GENERAL INTERDEPENDENCE	33.906	14.542	0.001	90.019
WTO MEMBERS	0.368	5.072	−11.020	9.607
WTO ROUND	0.605	0.489	0	1
WTO DISPUTE	0.581	0.493	0	1
WTO LOST	0.243	0.429	0	1
GDP SUM	49.610	2.419	39.572	59.222
GDP DIFFERENCE	2.465	1.771	0	10.150
GDPPC DIFFERENCE	1.951	1.314	0	5.864
DISTANCE	8.876	0.671	4.710	9.892
REMOTE	0.935	2.737	0	9.405
BILATERAL TRADE	0.505	2.213	0	76.743
GDP GROWTH	3.602	3.740	−24.049	20.266
RELATIVE GROWTH	3.146	0.813	1.043	4.643
FTA COVERAGE	39.255	30.488	0	98.193
POLITICAL DISTANCE	6.662	6.190	0	20
DEMOCRACY	0.598	0.490	0	1
COMMUNIST TRANSITION	0.177	0.381	0	1
MILITARY ALLIANCE	0.070	0.255	0	1
COMMON LANGUAGE	0.115	0.318	0	1
COMMON COLONIZER	0.051	0.219	0	1
FORMER COLONY	0.029	0.167	0	1
COMMON BORDER	0.007	0.082	0	1
FTA DENSITY	0.012	0.032	−0.039	0.061

Number of observations: 105,927 (112,995 in the case of PURE FTA).

In order to show that our contagion index is capturing a different form of spatial dependence, we will include the variable GENERAL INTERDEPENDENCE, which is the time-lagged spatial lag calculated using a weighting matrix based on geographical distance, as described in Section 4.1.

Baier and Bergstrand (2004) show the importance of gravity-like variables and the difference in relative factor endowments to predict FTA formation. To control for these influences, we include GDP SUM, the sum of the logs of real GDP and GDP DIFFERENCE, the absolute value of the difference in the logs of real GDP of countries in the dyad for each year, DISTANCE, the geographical distance between the countries and its relative distance to the rest of the world, REMOTE. To proxy the difference in factor endowments, we follow Egger and Larch (2008) and use the absolute value of the log difference in real GDP per capita as a proxy, labeled as GDPPC DIFFERENCE.

In testing the effects of multilateral trade liberalization on regionalism, we follow Mansfield and Reinhardt (2003) in including four explanatory variables: (i) WTO ROUND, a dummy equal 1 if a trade round is on-going in a given year, to test if FTAs are used as a way to gain bargaining power during multilateral talks; (ii) WTO MEMBERS, the detrended number of GATT/WTO members, since a larger number of members implies lower leverage power within the system that can induce bilateralism; (iii) WTO DISPUTE, a dummy equal 1 if one country in the dyad was in a GATT/WTO dispute in t-1, since countries can be more willing to sign FTAs in order to enhance their leverage in the quarrel; and (iv) a country losing a dispute can be more willing to form an FTA that mitigates the negative impacts of the lost, then we include a dummy equal 1, WTO LOST, if one country in the pair lost a dispute that started three years before.

Taking advantage of the panel nature of our data, we can include other important economic determinants that cannot be present in the cross-section analysis of Baier and Bergstrand (2004). A crucial determinant is the level of trade integration between the countries before the FTA. We therefore include the variable BILATERAL TRADE measured as the sum of exports to and imports from the partner in the dyad as a ratio to the country's own GDP. Also, when a country has already signed many FTAs, it has greater expertise in negotiating agreements, so we expect it to be more likely to sign new FTAs. To capture this, we include FTA COVERAGE, the percentage of total exports covered by previous FTAs. The idea that crisis and economic downturns can promote trade reforms as a way to improve the performance is captured by the variable GDP GROWTH, the country's real GDP variation and RELATIVE GROWTH, the relative real GDP growth with respect to the average of the rest of the world in the same year.

We include other political determinants. DEMOCRACY – a dummy equal to 1 if the country has a positive level in the POLITY IV index (an index that ranges from −10 to 10, increasing in democratic level, details in Appendix 3). We also test the related idea that countries with political regimes that are more similar will be more likely to sign an agreement including the dyad-year level variable POLITICAL DISTANCE, namely the absolute difference in the POLITY IV values. The quest for geopolitical stability is captured by the variable MILITARY ALLIANCE, which is a dummy variable equal to 1 if the countries concerned are in a military alliance (we get this from the Correlates of War database). To control for the opening of Central and Eastern nations to the world trade system, another dummy, COMMUNIST TRANSITION, is unity if one of the countries is a former communist economy.

Some other country-pair common characteristics are included in the regressions but not reported for the sake of space: border, language, colonizer and former colonial relation. Also, we add a time trend and the (detrended) proportion of total dyads covered by FTAs in a given year.

5.3. Estimation results

The main results of our empirical exercises are presented in Table 2. In column 1, we estimate Eq. (12) using the traditional distance-linked weight matrix, as indicated by GENERAL INTERDEPENDENCE, to account for FTA interdependence, together with the other control variables. The result reproduces the finding of previous studies as the coefficient associated to that variable is positive and significant (but just at the 10% level).

Column 2 presents one of our main results, i.e. where CONTAGION INDEX is also included. Importantly, we obtain a positive coefficient on the index that is significant at the 1% level. Moreover, the coefficient on the GENERAL INTERDEPENDENCE index becomes insignificant, suggesting that a distance-based weighting matrix does not have an impact on FTA contagion once trade diversion effects are controlled for with CONTAGION INDEX. Column 3 presents that same regression on data that includes only "pure FTAs" and CUs in the Hufbauer–Schott database. Here we get the same encouraging results for the CONTAGION INDEX. The traditional distance-linked contagion indicator is also positive and significant.

In column 4 we address the issue of unobservable heterogeneity using the conditional likelihood function described in Eq. (13), so the sample is limited to switchers. This entails a dramatic reduction in the number of observations. Again the CONTAGION INDEX has the expected sign and is statically significant at any conventional level of confidence, but this is not the case for the alternative spatial lag, GENERAL INTERDEPENDENCE. In the last column, the Cox duration model confirms the results related to the CONTAGION INDEX and provides some support for the undirected spatial lag measure.

Taken together, these results provide support for the notion that FTAs are contagious when this effect is measured by our theoretically motivated contagion index. By contrast, we find that the significance of the undirected measure of spatial dependence (GENERAL INTERDEPENDENCE) is not robust.

All the economic and geographical determinants have the expected sign and significance. In terms of the dyad level DISTANCE, GDP DIFFERENCE and GDPPC DIFFERENCE are always negative and significant (except in the conditional logit for the last two), the opposite for REMOTE and GDP SUM. For the country level variables, BILATERAL TRADE indicates that previous trade level with the partner is a significant predictor of FTAs. Also, the more FTAs a country has, the more likely it is

Table 2
Main empirical results.

	(1) Indirect dyad contagion	(2) Spatial contagion index	(3) Pure FTA	(4) Conditional logit	(5) Duration model
Contagion index		0.017^{***}	0.020^{***}	0.190^{***}	0.014^{***}
		(0.002)	(0.002)	(0.037)	(0.002)
General interdep.	0.001^{*}	0.004	0.010^{**}	0.007	0.017^{***}
	(0.005)	(0.005)	(0.005)	(0.024)	(0.003)
GDP sum	0.229^{***}	0.219^{***}	0.209^{***}	10.02^{***}	0.182^{***}
	(0.025)	(0.026)	(0.024)	(1.833)	(0.019)
GDP Difference	-0.235^{***}	-0.231^{***}	-0.152^{***}	6.390^{***}	-0.197^{***}
	(0.040)	(0.041)	(0.037)	(1.600)	(0.030)
GDPpc difference	-0.112^{**}	-0.09^{*}	-0.089^{*}	5.934^{***}	-0.051
	(0.050)	(0.052)	(0.049)	(2.017)	(0.040)
Distance	-1.417^{***}	-1.351^{***}	-1.196^{***}		-1.306^{***}
	(0.079)	(0.083)	(0.075)		(0.054)
Remote	0.005	0.016	0.031^{*}		0.046^{***}
	(0.017)	(0.017)	(0.016)		(0.012)
Bilateral trade	0.0357^{***}	0.043^{***}	0.032^{***}	0.135	0.035^{***}
	(0.013)	(0.013)	(0.009)	(0.134)	(0.013)
GDP growth	-0.026^{**}	-0.033^{***}	-0.050^{***}	-0.084^{***}	-0.020^{**}
	(0.011)	(0.011)	(0.011)	(0.024)	(0.010)
Relative growth	-0.626^{***}	-0.632^{***}	-0.422^{***}	-0.639^{***}	
	(0.098)	(0.098)	(0.093)	(0.156)	
WTO members	-0.019	-0.017	-0.025	0.022	
	(0.023)	(0.023)	(0.020)	(0.041)	
WTO round	-0.152	-0.137	-0.184	-0.083	
	(0.170)	(0.172)	(0.174)	(0.332)	
WTO dispute	0.211	0.219	0.404^{***}	0.475	0.097
	(0.141)	(0.142)	(0.135)	(0.305)	(0.092)
WTO lost	0.039	-0.007	-0.369^{*}	-0.125	-0.146
	(0.182)	(0.183)	(0.193)	(0.470)	(0.136)
FTA coverage	0.008^{***}	0.009^{***}	0.011^{***}	0.082^{***}	0.007^{***}
	(0.001)	(0.002)	(0.002)	(0.023)	(0.001)
Political distance	-0.117^{***}	-0.113^{***}	-0.049^{**}	-0.169^{**}	-0.117^{***}
	(0.020)	(0.020)	(0.021)	(0.083)	(0.014)
Democracy	-0.511^{**}	-0.506^{**}	-0.164	16.65^{***}	-0.820^{***}
	(0.229)	(0.241)	(0.270)	(0.629)	(0.168)
Communist transit.	-0.722^{***}	-0.563^{***}	-0.903^{***}	-2.119	0.054
	(0.150)	(0.150)	(0.144)	(1.381)	(0.100)
Military alliance	-0.063	0.035	-0.279	1.578	-0.200
	(0.210)	(0.213)	(0.179)	(0.966)	(0.123)
Observations	105,972	105,972	112,995	7476	105,660
Pseudo R^2	0.320	0.327	0.323	0.604	

Standard errors clustered at dyad level in parentheses. Six duration dependence splines, time trend and FTA density used in the estimation but not displayed in the table.

*** $p<0.01$.
** $p<0.05$.
* $p<0.1$.

to sign others, since the variable FTA COVERAGE is also positive and significant. The variables GDP GROWTH and RELATIVE GROWTH are both negative and significant, providing some preliminary evidence to the idea that trade reforms are more likely in economic downturns.

We find little evidence that developments at the multilateral level have an impact on FTA formation. The four variables from the Mansfield and Reinhardt (2003) study are almost always insignificant and often with unexpected signs. Also, we find weak support for the idea that democracy influences regionalism, since the variable DEMOCRACY is usually negative and not always significant, except in the case of the conditional logit estimation, where the associated coefficient is positive and significant. On the other hand, it seems similarity in political regimes encourages FTAs, because the coefficient on POLITICAL DISTANCE is always negative and significant. As for the Eastern bloc hypothesis, the variable COMMUNIST TRANSITION has a negative sign but is not always significant, a result that should be interpreted with caution since various former communist countries are excluded from our sample due to lack of data. The other political variable, MILITARY ALLIANCE, is never significant.

R. Baldwin, D. Jaimovich / Journal of International Economics 88 (2012) 1–16 9

5.4. Quantification of the results

The nature of our empirical strategy makes quantification a difficult task. The dependent variable is a switch from non-FTA status to FTA status — a rare event in our data set, just 0.7% of the observations classified as non-zeros for all type of agreements and 0.8% for pure agreements (Table 1). This implies that the traditional "correct classification ratio" that assigns a value 1 to all predicted values over 0.5 and zero otherwise is uninformative in our case. An alternative is to use the sample mean of the dependent variable as a cut-off when classifying correctly predicted values. If we do so, we find that the model in column 1 of Table 2 correctly predicts 85.22% of the cases, while the model in column 2, that includes the contagion index, correctly predicts 85.48%.

One different way to quantify the results is to take advantage of the fact that logit estimates can be interpreted in terms of changes in the odds. In Table 3 we calculate the change in the odds-ratio of a one standard deviation increase in a given variable keeping the value of all the others constant. We report results for the model using all FTAs and just pure FTAs (corresponding to columns 2 and 3 of Table 2, respectively).[15] In the model with all FTAs, a one standard deviation increase in the CONTAGION INDEX leads to a 30.6% increase in the odd of signing an FTA. In the case of pure FTAs, the positive change in the odd is 51.9%. It is interesting to note that, apart from the CONTAGION INDEX, the only variables that produce statistically significant changes in the odds ratio of more than 30% are: GDP SUM, GDP DIFFERENCE, DISTANCE, RELATIVE GROWTH, FTA COVERAGE and POLITICAL DISTANCE.

In terms of the goodness of fit of the different models, there is a small improvement (0.8%) from column 1 to column 2 in Table 2 using Pseudo-R^2 (similar results are obtained using adjusted McFadden R^2). A more accurate way of comparing the two models is the Bayesian information criterion (BIC), which provides an indication on how likely the model generates the observed data. The difference in BIC between the two models is 50.04. Using the Raftery (1995) guidelines, it is possible to say that there is a "very strong" support for the inclusion of the contagion index. The Akaike's information criterion (AIC), with a decrease of 59.56 in the model that includes the contagion index, also supports this conclusion. For the other specifications, the information measures yield similar results. In the model for pure FTA, the difference in BIC is 10.51, while in the conditional logit it is 35.08.

Table 3
Change in odds associated to the main explanatory variables.

Variable	All FTA	Pure FTA
	% change in odd	% change in odd
Contagion index	30.6	34.8
General interdependence	8.8	20.7
GDP sum	54.6	54.6
GDP difference	−40.1	-44.2
GDPpc difference	−11.7	−6.7
Distance	−89.8	−77.9
Bilateral trade	9.4	9.7
GDP growth	−11.7	−22.3
Relative growth	−50.2	−38.4
FTA coverage	30.1	38.5
Political distance	−66.3	−51.6
Democracy	−21.7	−17.7
Communist transition	−21.6	−29.0

Note: The percentage change in odds is related to a one standard deviation increase in each variable in the model when all the others are hold in their mean values. For "all FTA" the results are based in column 2 of Table 2, for "pure FTA" in column 3 of the same table.

5.5. Robustness checks

In Table 4 we present various modifications of the original specification to check that our results are not driven by the characteristics of a particular model or sample composition. We will use the specification with all FTAs (column 2 of Table 2) as the baseline model for comparison, unless an alternative specification is mentioned.

We first explore the possibility of non-linearities in the functional form, adding a squared term for the measures of spatial dependence (column 1), namely the contagion index and the GENERAL INTERDEPENCE variable. The variables are orthogonalized using a modified Gram–Schmidt procedure to avoid multicollinearity between the linear and the square terms. While the linear coefficient for the contagion index is still positive, its quadratic term is negative and significant, indicating a possible threshold effect, with decreasing marginal values for of the contagion from third trade partners.

In order to show that our results are sensitive to the configuration of weights of the spatial matrix, we create a "RANDOM CONTAGION INDEX" that is calculated in the same way as the CONTAGION INDEX, but using random exports and import shares instead of the actual ones. The results are presented in column 2. The random contagion variable is not significant while the contagion index keeps its value and inference does not change. We take this result as evidence that the definition of weights for the spatial lag is important.

In order to analyze how the contagion effect changes with the level of tariff, we include the bilateral tariff level (obtained from the WITS database) and its interaction with the contagion index as additional explanatory variables. If contagion increases with the level of tariff, as to be expected, the interaction term will be positive. Given the lack of availability of tariff data, the sample is reduced to 33,675 observations. The results are presented in column 3. It is possible to see that the coefficient for the contagion index is unchanged and still very significant. Moreover both the tariff variable and its interaction with the contagion index are insignificant. This suggests that the contagion effect is independent of the level of bilateral tariffs, a result that must be taken with caution given the reduced sample for which bilateral tariff data are available. In particular, the nations dropped are systematically developing countries. Moreover, as Eq. (9) indicates, the perfect measure would have included the bilateral tariffs of all the FTAs signed by all the prospective nation's FTA partners. Once better bilateral tariff data becomes available, it would be useful to revisit this conclusion.

Table 2 showed that the contagion effect holds both in the sample with all FTAs and the sample with only "pure FTAs" and CUs. What about impure FTAs? If the agreements are never effectively implemented it should be unlikely to observe any contagion from them. In order to test this hypothesis, we create an alternative dependent variable "impure FTAs", defined as agreements that are neither "pure FTAs" nor CUs or were not ratified as such after 5 years of the initial partial agreement. In our database there are just 38 "impure FTAs" (mainly between Latin-American, African and South Asian countries), reflecting that most of the "dead on arrival" agreements date back to before the start of our sample in 1976.[16]

We re-calculate the contagion index and the GENERAL INTERDEPENDENCE variable based on these impure agreements and present the logit estimation in column 4 of Table 4. The "impure" contagion index is not significant at any conventional level (p-value = 0.35); this supports the idea that it is the credible threat of trade diversion that is causing the contagion; agreements that are unlikely to create much trade diversion do not seem to have a contagion effect. In the case of GENERAL INTERDEPENDENCE, the coefficient is negative and

[15] A similar exercise can be produced using the survival model estimations in the last Column of Table 2. The results (available upon request) are in line to those summarized in Table 3.

[16] We thank an anonymous referee for suggesting this specification.

Table 4
Robustness check.

	(1)	(2)	(3)	(4)	(5)	(6)	(7)	(8)	(9)	(10)	(11)
	Quadratic terms	Random contagion	Tariff	Impure FTA	Trade partners	Balanced panel	Balanced clogit	Two way cluster	Rare events	MundlakRE	LPM
Contagion index	0.020***	0.018***	0.015**	0.019	0.017***	0.017***	0.297***	0.017***	0.017***	0.009***	0.048***
	(0.003)	(0.004)	(0.006)	(0.018)	(0.002)	(0.004)	(0.104)	(0.006)	(0.002)	(0.001)	(0.009)
General interdep.	-0.001	−0.002	0.006	−0.065***	0.005	0.022***	−0.138***	0.004	0.004	−0.035***	−0.036***
	(0.005)	(0.005)	(0.008)	(0.023)	(0.005)	(0.008)	(0.043)	(0.008)	(0.005)	(0.005)	(0.011)
Contagion index²	−0.071**										
	(0.032)										
General interdep.²	0.293***										
	(0.083)										
Random contagion		0.006									
		(0.006)									
Contagion × tariff			0.036								
			(0.031)								
Tariff			0.013								
			(0.008)								
Observations	105,972	105,972	33,675	116,255	101,928	36,884	2806	105,972	105,972	105,972	105,972
Pseudo R^2	0.331	0.331	0.345	0.472	0.325	0.242	0.719	0.331	0.331	0.392	
R^2											0.173

Standard errors clustered at dyad level in parentheses.
Six duration dependence splines, time trend, FTA density and all the controls in Table 2 are included in the regressions but not displayed in the table.
*** p<0.01.
** p<0.05.
* p<0.1.

significant, showing that, if anything, the impure FTAs will deter neighboring countries from signing similar agreements.[17]

One common problem with trade data is the difficulty of distinguishing between a missing value and a true zero when it comes to trade flows. A consequence of this fact may be that our results could be driven by countries with few data. The idea is that the shares (of both exports of i to j and imports of j from third nations) used to build the contagion index could be over-evaluated for such countries. To address this concern, we include an additional specification that present the results just for countries with at least 50 reported trade partners (Table 4, column 5). The main results are unchanged.

Another potential problem with our sample composition is that having countries with few observations in the time dimension or entering the sample at different years can create problems in the estimation. Acknowledging the issue, we have run two additional estimations where the sample is limited to the period 1990–2005 and we just include observations for which we have data for the whole period, reducing the sample to 36,884 observations. The result for this balanced subsample, in column 6, show the same pattern as before for the contagion index, but the variable GENERAL INTERDEPENDENCE is now also positive and significant. In column 7, we present results for the conditional logit estimation for the balanced subsample, finding similar results to those for the full sample (Table 2, column 4). The contagion index is positive and statistically significant. In the case of GENERAL INTERDEPENDENCE, the coefficient is also statistically significant, but negative.

Inference with dyadic data imposes additional complications given that observations are not independent. Taking $u_{ij,t}$ as the standard errors from our estimating equation, we will have that $E[u_{ij,t}, u_{ik,t}] \neq 0$ and $E[u_{ij,t}, u_{kj,t}] \neq 0$ for all k. Similarly, $E[u_{ij,t}, u_{jk,t}] \neq 0$ and $E[u_{ij,t}, u_{ki,t}] \neq 0$. We follow Fafchamps and Gubert (2007) and Cameron et al. (2011) in implementing adjusted standard errors by two-way clustering that correct for non-independent errors as well as potential heteroscedasticity. While the standard errors for the contagion index are now about double the previous size (column 8 of Table 4), the inference analysis is basically unchanged.

FTAs are very rare events in our data. As mentioned above, less than 1% of the country-pairs in our sample actually have one. The consequence of this structure of the dependent variable can be a loss of power and bias in the estimation. In order to address this problem, we re-estimate our main regression using the rare-event adjusted logit proposed by King and Zeng (2001) in column 9. This adjustment leaves the results qualitatively unchanged.

In Table 2, we presented conditional logit estimations as a way to control for unobserved heterogeneity at the country-pair level, a difficult problem to deal with in panel data with limited dependent variable given the incidental-parameter problem. The problem of conditional logit is that the sample gets dramatically smaller. In the last two columns of Table 4, we present results using alternative methodologies. In column 10 we present results when estimating the Mundlak–Chamberlain's random effects probit model (Wooldridge 2002), where averages of the time variant variables are included in the estimation. Some results change, notably the GENERAL INDEPENDENCE variable becomes negative, but the contagion index keeps its positive and significant value. In the last column we present the estimation of a linear probability model with country-pair fixed-effects, where these results are confirmed.

6. Concluding remarks

The rapid proliferation of FTAs is one of the more remarkable developments of the world trade system over the past decades. As it involves more than a hundred nations and many different types of agreements, the driving force behind this trend is surely quite complex. Our paper is an effort to understand the empirical determinants of this proliferation.

Our basic hypothesis is that much of the spread of regionalism is driven by "defensive" FTAs. That is, nations sign FTAs to reduce the discrimination created by FTAs signed among their trade partners. As each new FTA creates additional discrimination, FTAs can spread in a domino-like pattern. Putting it roughly, FTAs are contagious and the degree of contagion is related to the importance of the partners' markets.

We believe our paper contains two elements of value-added. First, it provides a theory-based, empirical measure of FTA contagion. Second, we use this measure, the 'contagion index', to test for contagion/domino

[17] On the other hand, the coefficient for the variable DISTANCE (not displayed in Table 4) is negative and highly significant, showing that those impure FTAs are actually signed by countries in the same region.

effects as well as to test these against alternative hypotheses. Our main finding is that the contagion phenomenon is present in our data and is robust to various econometric specifications and samples. The finding is also robust to the inclusion of variables that capture other explanations such as the bandwagon effect, slow-multilateralism, spread of democracy, etc.

Our theoretical model and the design of our empirics are focuses on tariffs since these have been the focus of trade liberalization for most of the last 60 years (including the years covered by our data sample, 1977–2005). Recent unpublished work, however, suggests that the most recent trends in regionalism may have less to do with tariff preferences and more to do with competition for supply-chain-linked foreign direct investment (Baldwin 2011).[18] This conjecture suggests that FTA contagion may either be less marked in coming decades, or driven by different political-economy mechanisms. Following up on these points may prove to be a fruitful avenue for future research.

Acknowledgments

We would like to thank the editor, Giovanni Maggi, and two anonymous referees for useful comments and suggestions as well as Jean-Louis Arcand, Patricio Aroca, Peter Egger, Sebastian Krautheim, Pierre-Louis Vezina, and participants of seminars organized by the Swiss Trade Economist Cooperative (STEC), Graduate Institute (Geneva), Rigotnomics (Geneva), World Trade Organization (Geneva), Hitotsubashi University (Tokyo), European Economic Association (Barcelona), Latin American and Caribbean Economic Association (Rio de Janeiro), Universidad de Chile (Santiago), and Universidad Catolica del Norte (Antofagasta).

Appendix 1. Theory appendix

This appendix shows the political economy logic of FTA contagion is robust to (i) strategic behavior by nations when governments care only about profits and Zs, and (ii) switching the government objective function to the polar opposite of the assumed mercantilism, namely welfare maximization.

A.1. Strategic behavior by governments

The spillovers stemming from contagion raise issues with forward-looking agents. This section shows that – due to such considerations – some FTAs will not create contagion although many will.

Before turning to specifics, we note that the source of all the forward-looking issues concerns the fact that the preference erosion triggered by contagion may eventually create pure losses. Such losses create the possibility that the present value of profits might be negative when a nation signs an FTA. Since governments care about negative profits in our model, a forward-looking government might either not sign the FTA, or it might sign the FTA and then lower its MFN tariff to deter contagion (more on this below). For such FTAs, the initial FTA will not produce contagion.

When the present value of profits is positive, however, no such issues arise. Instant entry in the initial signatories restores the present value to zero, so the governments have no interest in reducing any possible losses in the future; if they did do so, the only impact would be more first-period entry that left the government's objective function unaltered. Moreover, such entry worsens the profit loses in third nations, so again forward-looking behavior changes nothing qualitative concerning contagion.

This preliminary discussion reveals that contagion goes through as discussed in the text for those initial FTAs that imply a positive present value of profits for the signatories. In this sense, strategic issues do not alter our basic assertion that a few 'politically motivated' FTAs can generate many 'defensive' FTAs. More importantly, forward-looking issues do not alter the logic underpinning our contagion index. The primary driver of the contagion – when it happens – is still the negative profit effects of trade diversion. This preliminary discussion also suggests that not all FTAs can trigger contagion. The goal of this section is to characterize the constellation of parameters where contagion does and does not occur and to explain how unilateral reductions in MFN tariffs may be used to deter contagion in certain cases.

A.2. Conflicted and consensual FTAs

We distinguish two classes of initial FTAs according to the present value of profits (holding the number of firms constant). We label those with positive present values as "consensus FTAs", and those with negative present values as "conflicted FTAs". In the former, economic and political interests inside each nation pull in the same direction. In the latter, industry in one of the signatories opposes the FTA, but the FTA gets signed because the political gain to the government outweighs the present value of the profit losses.

To be more precise and to keep the reasoning concrete, we focus on the hub-and-spoke contagion discussed in the text. While this is not a general solution, it has the advantage that it is the type of contagion that happens in the three-nation case that is so common in the literature. It also has the advantage of making it more likely that the contagion will eventually produce negative pure profits and thus make it more likely that strategic issues arise. Formally we ensure that only hub-and-spoke regionalism occurs by assuming that the political cost of signing any other type of bilateral FTA is infinite for non-hub nations; all Zs of hub nation are assumed to be negative.

As in the text we suppose, for the moment, that the initial FTA is signed between nations 2 and 3, and we refer to this as FTA23. We start by evaluating the present value of profit when there is no entry or exit.[19] With n constant, pure profit of firms in nation-2 (the hub), nation-3 (the first spoke), and nation-1 (the second potential spoke) are, from (4):

$$\begin{aligned}
\pi_3 &= \left(\frac{\mu}{\sigma n}\right)\left(\frac{1}{1+(1-\phi)F_2+\phi(N-1)}+\frac{1+\phi(F_2-1)}{2+\phi(N-2)}+\frac{\phi(N-F_2-1)}{1+\phi(N-1)}\right)-f\\
\pi_2 &= \frac{\mu}{\sigma n}\left(\frac{1}{1+(1-\phi)F_2+\phi(N-1)}+\frac{F_2}{2+\phi(N-2)}+\frac{\phi(N-F_2-1)}{1+\phi(N-1)}\right)-f\\
\pi_1 &= \frac{\mu}{\sigma n}\left(\frac{\phi}{1+(1-\varphi)F_2+\phi(N-1)}+\frac{\phi F_2}{2+\phi(N-2)}+\frac{1+\phi(N-F_2)}{1+\phi(N-1)}\right)-f.
\end{aligned} \tag{14}$$

Here the three terms in the parentheses capture, in order, sales to the hub, to spoke economies (including nation-3), and to other markets (including nation-1). The 'n' here is the free-entry n with symmetric MFN tariffs maintained by all nations.

It can easily be shown that π_2 is positive for all F_2 and increasing in F_2; π_3 is positive for $F_2=1$ but decreasing in F_2; and π_1 is negative for $F_2=1$, and decreasing in F_2.This tells us that nation-1 suffers pure losses while nations 2 and 3 enjoy pure profits in the first period. If F_2 rises, things get worse for nation-1 and nation-3, while they get better for the hub.

As the present value of hub profit is positive in all cases, a 'conflicted' FTA case comes about only when the present value of π_3 is negative. Close inspection of Eq. (14) shows that π_3 becomes negative if F_2 rises high enough. Specifically, solving $\pi_3=0$ from

[18] This point was suggested by one of our referees.

[19] This tells us the direction of entry and exit, when fast entry and slow exit are allowed.

Eq. (14) for F_2 identifies the threshold F_2 beyond which π_3 becomes negative; this is:

$$F'_2 = \frac{1+\phi+2(N-1)\phi^2-\sqrt{4\phi^3N^2+12\phi^2(1-\phi)N+(1+8\phi)(1-\phi)^2}}{2\phi(1-\phi)}. \tag{15}$$

For example, if N = 20, and $\phi = 0.7$, π_3 turns negative when the hub has at least 10 agreements. In our model this would take 10 periods (assuming political resistance is sufficiently small in all nations). Note that common case of three-nations is marked by a highly unusual feature – there can be no contagion without pure losses; for N = 3, F'_2 is less than 2 for any ϕ in the economically relevant range.

In short, a necessary condition for negative present values is that contagion continues long enough for $F_2 > F'_2$. Implicitly, this tells us that that contagion can occur without the threshold being crossed (except in the N = 3 example). In particular, it is perfectly possible that contagion would induce nation-1 to change its mind on an FTA with nation-2, without all other countries following suit. For example, other governments might face much higher political costs of signing with the hub.

Even if the necessary condition is met, the present value of π_3 needs not be negative – the pure profit gains in the periods running up to period F'_2 could result in a positive present value. In our model the natural length of a period is the time it takes to negotiate and implement an FTA. In many cases, this is a matter of years. Thus it may take many years, perhaps decades, for F_2 to rise from 1 to the threshold in Eq. (15). Obviously, the longer this takes, the more likely it is that the present value is positive. We also note that F'_2 rises with the number of potential trade partners (N), so more nations make a negative present value less likely. Again, this suggests that the standard N = 3 example is somewhat special.

A.3. Deterring contagion with unilateral MFN liberalization

In cases where the initial FTA is conflicted, the government of nation-3 would like to deter contagion to avoid the negative present value of its firm's profits. As it turns out, nation-3 can deter contagion by unilaterally lowering its MFN tariff. Although this reduces the pure profits arising from its FTA with nation-2, these profit gains do not matter to the government; instant entry eliminates them. Specifically, if we re-calculate profits for all three nations in the FTA23 situation allowing nation-3 to charge a lower MFN tariff, we see that nation-1's profit loses are reduced as nation-3 lowers its tariffs. Indeed, solving $\pi_1 = 0$, for ϕ_3 gives us the MFN trade freeness that eliminates the negative profits that are the only reason nation-1 wants to sign an FTA with nation-2. This threshold ϕ_3 is:

$$\frac{\phi(3+\phi(N-3))}{1+\phi^2(N-2)+\phi}.$$

By symmetry, this unilateral action by nation-3 eliminates losses in all potential spokes, so no contagion occurs. As it turns out, the level of trade freeness also pushes π_3 to zero; thus the unilateral liberalization raises nation-3's present value of profits from a negative number to zero. The hub nation will be harmed by this erosion of its preference in nation-3, but it still gains, so it is still interested in signing the initial FTA. To summarize, our model predicts that a 'conflicted FTA' will produce no FTA contagion. Rather it produces unilateral liberalization by one of the initial FTA signers.

A.4. The three-nation example

To make these points more formally, we consider that standard example of a three nation world where the extensive form of the FTA game is simple. The analysis begins with a political shock in nations 2 and 3 that may induce them to sign an FTA. Specifically, all the Z_{2i}s and Z_{3i}s change sign, so these nations flip from viewing bilateralism negatively to viewing it positively (i.e. all Z_{2i} and Z_{3i} become negative). The game is illustrated in Fig. 2.

One possibility is that FTA23 is not signed in period zero, so the MFN status quo is maintained and no contagion occurs. If, however, FTA23 is signed in period zero, government-1 has three choices in period one: do nothing, or sign an FTA with nation 2 or 3 (symmetry allows us to focus on the former without loss of generality). If doing nothing is preferable, there is no contagion from FTA23; this is 'Path A' in the diagram. If signing an FTA with nation-2 is preferable, and government-2 agrees, the game moves to FTA2312, and we have a hub-and-spoke arrangement with nation-2 as the hub. Government-1's next decision is whether to sign and FTA with 3. If doing so is preferable to doing nothing, and government-3 agrees, we move to MFN free trade (i.e. full contagion, marked as 'Path C' in the diagram), otherwise we move to 'Path B' (partial contagion).

To build intuition and determine the direction of entry, we evaluate the profit impact holding the number of firms constant for the moment. The pure profits earned by the three nations in the three combinations of FTAs are shown in Fig. 3; the superscripts indicate the relevant case with an obvious notation. We have placed the expressions vertically to reflect their sign and relative magnitude. For example, $\pi_2^{FTA2312}$ is greater than π_2^{FTA23} and both are positive. We note that this ranking holds when tariffs are not too high to start with. The specific regularity condition is that $\phi > 1/4$ and we maintain this assumption throughout.[20]

Working backwards, we consider the decision facing nations 1 and 3 at the node FTA2312 in Fig. 2. From Fig. 3, we see that both nations 1 and 3 would gain economically from signing FTA13. Since nation-3 also gains politically as well (recall that $Z_{31} < 0$), we know that if the political cost to government-1 are not too great – i.e. the magnitude of Z_{13} is sufficient small – FTA13 will be signed. While nation-2's profits are harmed by FTA13 (see Fig. 3), FTA13 does not require approval of government-2.

Backing up to the FTA23 node, we see that governments 1 and 2 both gain economically, and government-2 gains politically by assumption, so FTA12 will be signed as long as the political costs to nation-1 are not too great, i.e. the magnitude of Z_{12} is sufficient small. Observe that government-3 would like to oppose FTA12 in period two (see Fig. 3), but its approval is not necessary for FTA12.

Finally, backing up to the initial state, we ask whether nations 2 and 3 actually sign FTA23 in period zero, knowing that it will cause contagion?

Plainly FTA23 requires approval of both nations. It is plain that nation-2 will gain economically from FTA23 along all three paths (see Fig. 2). Since it also gains politically, nation-2 will be interested in signing FTA23. But will nation-3 agree? When considering FTA23, government-3 faces an ambiguous economic situation. If Path A is the equilibrium, it gains economically in all periods. If Path B is the equilibrium, it gains economically in the first period, and loses in all subsequent periods. If Path C is the equilibrium, the second period losses are extinguished from period three onwards. Thus whenever contagion occurs (Paths B and C), government-3 faces a trade-off between economics losses and political gains.

[20] When tariffs are very high, nation-1 will not raise profits by signing FTA12 and so contagion will never occur. Interestingly, the number of FTA proliferated in the mid 1990s when tariffs were already quite low and moving lower due to the Uruguay Round liberalization. Recall that $\phi = (1+t)^{1-\sigma}$, so if $\sigma = 2$, $\phi > 1/4$ means tariffs must be less than 300%; for $\sigma = 4$, the threshold is about 58%.

R. Baldwin, D. Jaimovich / Journal of International Economics 88 (2012) 1–16 13

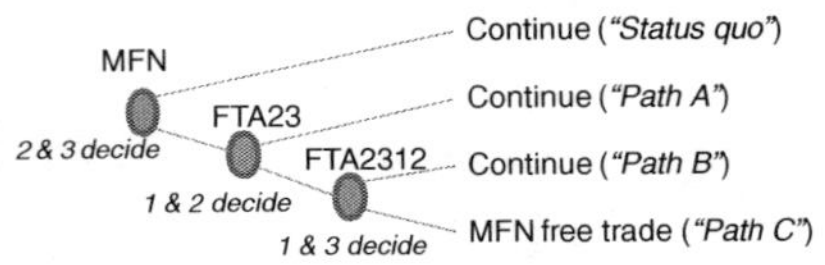

Fig. 2. Simple game of contagion.

Two forms of sufficient conditions can resolve the ambiguity. First, if politically gains are sufficiently large for government-3, it will sign FTA23 regardless of the equilibrium path (e.g. this happens if the present value of Z_{23} exceeds the present value of any profit losses). Second if the discount rate is high enough (i.e. agents are impatient or the periods are long), the present value of profits will be positive in period zero, so government-3 will sign FTA23 (recall that the Z_{2i}s are positive).

Now consider what happens when we allow fast entry and slow exit. For nation-2, the answer is easy. Regardless of the equilibrium path, its firms see a rise in the present value of profits, so entry occurs up to the point where their present value is zero. Thus all that remains for government-2 is the present value of the political gains from signing FTAs (which are positive in all cases). For nation-3, the same holds for Path A. It also holds for Paths B and C if the discount rate is high enough (or the periods long enough) to ensure a positive present value of profits. If the present value of profits is not positive along PATHs B and C (the 'conflicted' FTA case), no new nation-3 firms will enter and indeed, slow exit will commence. In either case, the shock FTA, namely FTA23, is a politically motivated FTA.

Finally, nation-1 faces an unambiguously negative present value of profits along all three equilibrium paths, so slow exit begins for nation-1 firms immediately. Importantly, considerations of entry do not qualitatively change the nature of the trade-off facing nation-1. The entry of new nation-2 firms and (possibly) nation-3 firms exacerbate nation-1 profit losses (the extra competition adds to the losses coming from discrimination per se). Thus even with asymmetric entry, the basic trade-off facing government-1 is the economic gain from signing FTAs versus the political costs.

A.5. Incentives to break tariff bindings

The analysis so far has limited the strategy space to FTAs and unilateral tariff liberalization. What about tariff rises? As we shall see, non-spoke nations do have an incentive to violate their GATT/WTO commitments. For example, at node FTA23 and FTA2312, nation-1 profits are negative, so government-1 would gain from unilaterally raising tariffs. Government-3 faces as similar situation at node FTA2312.

What this suggests is that our data might have looked very different if it had been generated in an alternative world where multilateral disciplines were absent. In this alternative world, FTA contagion might have been less prevalent and unilateral protection might have been more prevalent. The recent unilateral reduction of applied rates – a trend that has gained traction among developing nations in the last ten years – does open the possibility of unilateral tariff rises from applied rates to bound rates. Incorporating this into the domino logic would require the theorist to explain why unilateral tariff cuts were politically optimal in the first place. Whatever the explanation, it is likely that the forces that led to the cuts in the first place would continue to make the option of unilateral tariff hikes unattractive.

A.6. When governments care only about welfare

Here we show that the qualitative nature of the equilibrium trade policy paths derived in the text is unaltered if we make the alternative assumption that governments care only about social welfare.

The contagion we illustrated in the text was driven by two pairs of decisions. The first was that of nations 1 and 2 signing an FTA when FTA23 is already in place. The second was nations 1 and 3 signing an FTA when FTA23 and FTA12 were already in place. We also have to identify conditions under which both 2 and 3 would agree to FTA23 after the political shock.

When the government cares only about welfare, two additional factors enter the political economy decisions: tariff revenue, and local prices. Pure profits still matter just as before since they enter total expenditure and expenditure enters the indirect utility function linearly. Specifically, the indirect utility function that corresponds to Eq. (1) is:

$$V = E - \mu + \mu \ln\left(\frac{\mu}{P_M}\right); \quad E = L + n\pi + R \tag{16}$$

where R is tariff revenue. When governments care only about welfare this becomes the government objective function with the political costs of FTAs – the Zs – added.

In the simple case above (three symmetric sized nations with the number of firms held constant), tariff revenue and price indices are simple to calculate. The symmetric tariff rate 't' is charged on all imports in the initial MFN situation. The rate is applied to the border price, which equals unity in all situations in our simple model. Thus tariff revenue per variety equals 't' times consumption, which itself is

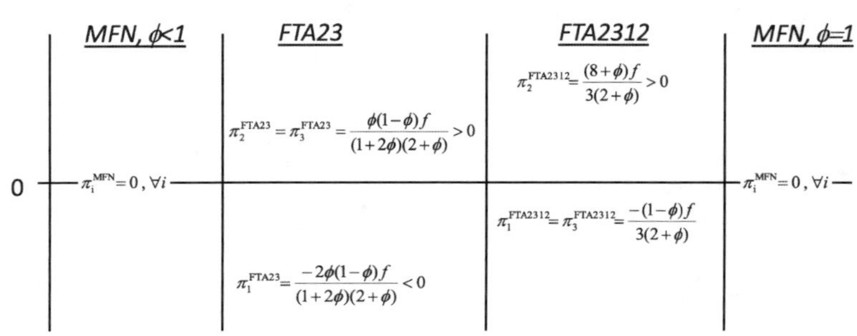

Fig. 3. Stage payoffs, no entry/exit.

given by Eqs. (2) and (3). For the three nations in the three situations, the revenue equals:

$$R_i^{MFN} = \frac{2t\mu}{1+2\phi}, \forall i; R_1^{FTA23} = R_i^{MFN}; R_i^{FTA23} = \frac{t\mu}{2+\phi}, i = 2;3$$
$$R_i^{FTA2312} = \frac{t\mu}{2+\phi}, i = 1,3; R_2^{FTA2312} = 0. \tag{17}$$

R is zero under MFN free trade for all nations. The corresponding price indices are:

$$P_{Mi}^{MFN} = ((1+2\varphi)n)^{1/(1-\sigma)}, \forall i, \quad P_{M1}^{FTA23} = P_{Mi}^{MFN} \; ; \quad P_{Mi}^{FTA23} = ((2+\varphi)n)^{1/(1-\sigma)}, \; i = 2;3$$
$$P_{Mi}^{FTA2312} = ((2+\varphi)n)^{1/(1-\sigma)}; \; i = 1,3 \; ; \quad P_{M2}^{FTA2312} = (3n)^{1/(1-\sigma)}. \tag{18}$$

Under MFN free trade, all price indices equal $(3n)^{1/(1-\sigma)}$.

As usual, we start with the last possible move, i.e. from FTA2312 to MFN free trade. At this point, the decision turns on the signs of the change in the Vs of nations 1 and 2. These changes are:

$$\Delta V_i^{FTA2312} = \frac{(1-\phi)f}{3(2+\phi)} - \frac{t\mu}{2+\phi} + \left(\frac{\mu}{\sigma-1}\right) \ln \frac{3}{2+\phi}, i = 1,3. \tag{19}$$

While the economic considerations in this situation are identical for nations 1 and 3, nation-3 views FTA13 as a political benefit, while nation-1 views it as a political cost. We know therefore that if nation-1 wants FTA13 so too will nation-3. For nation-1 to want FTA13, Eq. (19) must be positive and the political cost of FTA13 must not be too large. Thus the crucial issue is the set of situations where Eq. (19) is positive.

Moving up the extensive form, the second key decision point is when nations 1 and 2 decide whether to sign FTA12 after FTA23 is already in place. As before, the addition of tariff revenue renders the sign of the economic effect ambiguous for both nations. However, we can always define sufficient conditions on the initial political shock to ensure that nation-2 wants FTA12; we just assume the magnitude of Z_{21} is sufficient to overcome any reduction in V_2. We cannot do the same for nation-1, however, since it views FTA12 as a political cost. Thus, as with the previous decision-point, the critical issue is whether the change in V_1 is positive. If it is, we can say that FTA12 will be signed, if the political costs to nation-1 are sufficiently small. The change in V_1 when moving from the FTA23 situation to the FTA2312 situation is:

$$\Delta V_1^{FTA23} = \frac{(4\phi-1)(1-\phi)f}{3(1+2\phi)(\phi+2)} - \frac{3t\mu}{(1+2\phi)(\phi+2)} + \left(\frac{\mu}{\sigma-1}\right) \ln \frac{2+\phi}{1+2\phi}. \tag{20}$$

The signs of Eqs. (19) and (20) are not simple to characterize fully since 't' enters them both linearly and raised to the non-integer power $1-\sigma$. However inspection reveals one simple sufficient condition; if 't' is sufficiently low, both Eqs. (19) and (20) are positive. Thus we can say, as in the text, that contagion will happen if the political costs to nation-1 are not too high. When governments care only about welfare instead of only about profits, we add an additional sufficient condition, i.e. that the initial MFN tariff level is not too high. The thrust of this sufficient condition is to ensure that the tariff revenue loss from the FTA is not very important.

Appendix 2. Countries in the sample

Country	Number of observations	First year	FTA (1976–2005)	Pure FTA (1976–2005)
Albania	150	2002	3	4
Algeria	306	1999	12	21
Argentina	1495	1976	0	5
Armenia	215	2000	0	0
Australia	1914	1976	3	4
Austria	1476	1976	18	19
Azerbaijan	237	1999	0	0
Bahrain	206	1993	3	4
Bangladesh	1395	1976	1	0
Belarus	429	1999	0	0
Belgium	306	2000	3	6
Belize	360	1996	2	0
Bolivia	657	1990	0	8
Brazil	1684	1976	0	5
Bulgaria	544	1996	13	9
Burkina Faso	29	1997	0	0
Cambodia	192	2001	1	0
Canada	1920	1976	5	5
Chile	1335	1976	22	28
China	569	1999	11	6
Colombia	1192	1981	3	4
Congo, Dem. Rep.	137	1976	0	0
Costa Rica	793	1990	5	8
Cote d'Ivoire	1272	1976	0	0
Croatia	351	1999	25	6
Cyprus	1374	1976	15	24
Czech Republic	694	1994	9	8
Denmark	1348	1976	10	16
Dominican Republic	1063	1976	7	5
Ecuador	548	1996	0	0
Egypt, Arab Rep.	1326	1976	22	27
El Salvador	624	1991	2	8
Estonia	365	1999	5	5
Finland	1461	1976	18	17
France	1366	1976	8	15
Gabon	399	1978	0	0
Georgia	270	1999	1	1
Germany	1367	1976	8	15
Ghana	955	1976	0	0
Greece	1772	1976	8	8
Guatemala	740	1991	1	6
Guinea	381	1996	0	0
Guyana	118	1976	0	0
Haiti	124	1976	0	0
Honduras	582	1994	1	6
Hungary	1466	1976	26	24
Iceland	1045	1976	13	18
India	1750	1976	4	3
Indonesia	1625	1976	3	5
Iran, Islamic Rep.	403	1999	0	0
Ireland	1317	1976	10	16
Israel	1321	1976	19	18
Italy	1371	1976	8	15
Jamaica	1273	1976	4	0
Japan	2075	1976	2	2
Jordan	345	1999	11	20
Kazakhstan	368	1999	0	0
Kenya	1385	1976	6	0
Korea, Rep.	1769	1976	2	1
Kuwait	513	1976	0	0
Kyrgyz Republic	240	1999	0	0
Latvia	273	1999	5	5
Lithuania	320	1999	5	5
Luxembourg	232	2000	3	6
Macedonia, FYR	252	1999	22	22
Madagascar	1016	1976	1	0
Malawi	579	1976	4	0
Malaysia	1758	1976	3	5
Mali	167	1997	0	0
Mexico	925	1986	19	29
Moldova	210	1999	2	3
Morocco	874	1987	12	19
Netherlands	1363	1976	8	15

(*continued overleaf*)

Appendix 2 (*continued*)

Country	Number of observations	First year	FTA (1976–2005)	Pure FTA (1976–2005)
New Zealand	1796	1976	3	3
Nicaragua	747	1976	1	6
Norway	1471	1976	15	16
Pakistan	1678	1976	4	1
Panama	516	1997	0	1
Paraguay	467	1994	0	5
Peru	1376	1976	0	4
Philippines	1485	1979	1	5
Poland	858	1991	24	21
Portugal	1433	1976	18	19
Romania	947	1988	24	19
Russian Federation	527	1999	0	0
Singapore	1691	1976	12	14
Slovak Republic	621	1995	7	6
Slovenia	589	1994	13	22
South Africa	1514	1976	14	12
Spain	1622	1976	27	30
Sri Lanka	1393	1976	2	2
Sweden	1480	1976	20	20
Switzerland	1556	1976	15	16
Syrian Arab Republic	310	1999	0	0
Tanzania	484	1996	1	0
Thailand	1495	1982	4	8
Togo	336	1990	0	0
Trinidad and Tobago	1290	1976	3	0
Tunisia	772	1990	13	20
Turkey	1378	1976	21	19
Turkmenistan	78	1999	1	0
Uganda	332	1995	0	0
Ukraine	395	1999	1	1
United Arab Emirates	203	1994	3	4
United Kingdom	1375	1976	10	16
United States	2022	1976	6	7
Uruguay	1019	1976	0	5
Uzbekistan	165	2000	0	0
Venezuela, RB	695	1990	1	4
Vietnam	514	1999	0	0
Yemen, Rep.	272	1999	0	0
Zambia	440	1985	1	0
Zimbabwe	498	1980	2	0

Note: The FTA data come from Hufbauer and Schott (2009). The table shows FTAs signed from the first year a country is in the sample until 2005. In "pure FTA" also CUs and CU accessions are considered.

Appendix 3. Data sources

Variable	Source
Distance, common language, common colonizer, colony	CEPII gravity database.
FTA	We use the newly built database described in Hufbauer and Schott (2009). The data are based on historical notifications of the date the agreements entered into force and their contemporary participants.
Trade and tariffs	UN Comtrade database (using the World Integrated Trade Solution of the World Bank), at the 1-digit Standard International Trade Classification (SITC) level. Whenever a country did not report data on exports, we use the import image from the partner.
GDP, GDP growth, GDP per capita	World Bank's World Development Indicators (WDI).
Democracy	Polity IV project.
Military alliance	Correlates of War (COW) database. Since the variable is just available up to 2000, we assumed that the values of the last year were the same for the missing period 2001–2004.
Transition from communism	We updated the variable in Mansfield and Reinhardt (2003) database, incorporating former Soviet republics and other countries not included in their sample.
GATT/WTO disputes	We updated the variable used by Mansfield and Reinhardt (2003).

References

Aghion, Philippe, Antràs, Pol, Helpman, Elhanan, 2007. Negotiating free trade. Journal of International Economics 73, 1–30.

Baier, Scott, Bergstrand, Jeffrey, 2004. Economic determinants of Free Trade Agreements. Journal of International Economics 64, 29–63.

Baldwin, Richard, 1993. A domino theory of regionalism. In: Haaparanta, Kiander (Eds.), NBER Working Paper 4465. Eventually published in Baldwin. : Expanding Membership of the European Union. Cambridge University Press. 1995.

Baldwin, Richard, 1994. Towards an Integrated Europe. CEPR, London.

Baldwin, Richard, 1997. The causes of regionalism. The World Economy 20 (7), 865–888.

Baldwin, Richard, 2008. Managing the Noodle Bowl: the fragility of East Asian Regionalism. Singapore Economic Review 53 (3), 449–478.

Baldwin, Richard, 2011. 21st Century Regionalism: filling the gap between 21st century trade and 20th century trade rules. CEPR Policy Insight 56. .

Baldwin, Richard, Jaimovich, Dany, 2010. Are Free Trade Agreements contagious? NBER Working Paper 16084. .

Baldwin, Richard, Rieder, Roland, 2007. A test of endogenous trade bloc formation theory on EU data. Journal of International Economic Studies 11 (2), 77–111.

Baldwin, Richard, Robert-Nicoud, Frédéric, 2007. Entry and asymmetric lobbying: why governments pick losers. Journal of the European Economic Association 5 (5), 1064–1093.

Beck, Nathaniel, Katz, Jonathan, Tucker, Richard, 1998. Taking time seriously: time-series–cross-section analysis with a binary dependent variable. American Journal of Political Science 42 (4), 1260–1288.

Bergstrand, Jeffrey, Egger, Peter, Larch, Mario, 2010. Economic Determinants of the Timing if Preferential Trade Agreement Formations and Enlargements. Unpublished manuscript, University of Notre Dame.

Bhagwati, Jagdish, 1991. The World Trading System at Risk. Princeton University Press, Princeton, New Jersey.

Bhagwati, Jagdish, 1993. Regionalism and multilateralism: an overview. In: de Melo, J., Panagariya, A. (Eds.), Dimensions in Regional Integration. Cambridge University Press, Cambridge, pp. 22–51.

Bhagwati, Jagdish, 2008. Termites in the Trading System: How Preferential Agreements Undermine Free Trade. Oxford University Press.

Cameron, Colin, Gelbach, Jonah, Miller, Douglas, 2011. Robust inference with multi-way clustering. Journal of Business and Economic Statistics 29 (2), 238–249.

Chamberlain, Gary, 1980. Analysis of covariance with qualitative data. Review of Economic Studies 47 (1), 225–238.

Corden, W. Max, 1974. Trade Policy and Economic Welfare. Clarendon Press, Oxford.

Egger, Peter, Larch, Mario, 2008. Interdependent preferential trade agreement memberships: an empirical analysis. Journal of International Economics 76 (2), 384–399.

Fafchamps, Marcel, Gubert, Flore, 2007. Risk sharing and network formation. American Economic Review Papers and Proceedings 97 (2), 75–79.

Freund, Caroline, 2000. Different paths to free trade: the gains from regionalism. Quarterly Journal of Economics 115 (4), 1317–1341.

Freund, Caroline, Ornelas, Emanuel, 2010. Regional trade agreements. Annual Review of Economics 2, 139–166.

Grossman, Gene, Helpman, Elhanan, 1994. Protection for sale. The American Economic Review 84 (4), 833–850.

Harvie, Charles, Kimura, Fukunari, Lee, Hyun-Hoon, 2006. New East Asian regionalism: causes. Progress And Country Perspectives. Edward Elgar Publishing, Northampton.

Holmes, Tammy, 2005. What drives regional trade agreements that work? HEI Working Paper 07/2005. Graduate Institute of International Studies, Geneva.

Hufbauer, Gary, 1989. Background Paper for the Free Trade Debate: Reports of the Twentieth Century Fund Task Force on the Future of American Trade Policy. Priority Press, New York.

Hufbauer, Gary, Schott, Jeffrey, 2009. Fitting Asia-Pacific agreements into the WTO system. In: Baldwin, R., Low, P. (Eds.), Multilateralising Regionalism: Challenges for the Global Trading System. Cambridge University Press, pp. 554–635.

Jaimovich, Dany, 2012. A Bayesian spatial probit estimation of Free Trade Agreement contagion. Applied Economics Letters 19 (6), 579–583.

King, Gary, Zeng, Langche, 2001. Explaining rare events in international relations. International Organization 55 (3), 693–715.

Krishna, Pravind, 1998. Regionalism and multilateralism: a political economy approach. Quarterly Journal of Economics 113 (1), 227–250.

Krugman, Paul, 1991. The move toward free trade zones. Economic Review. Federal Reserve Bank of Kansas City. issue November 5-25.

Krugman, Paul, 1993. Regionalism versus multilateralism: analytic notes. In: De Melo, J., Panagariya, A. (Eds.), New Dimensions in Regional Integration. Cambridge University Press, Cambridge, pp. 58–84.

Lester, Simon, Mercurio, Bryan, 2009. Bilateral and Regional Trade Agreements: Commentary and Analysis. Cambridge University Press, Cambridge.

Manger, Mark, 2006. The political economy of discrimination: modelling the spread of preferential trade agreements. Working Paper Department of Political Science. McGill University.

Mansfield, Edward, Pevehouse, Jon, 2000. Trade blocs, trade flows, and international conflict. International Organization 54 (4), 775–808.

Mansfield, Edward, Reinhardt, Eric, 2003. Multilateral determinants of regionalism: the effects of GATT/WTO on the formation of preferential trade agreements. International Organization 57 (4), 829–862.

Mansfield, Edward, Milner, Helen, Rosendorff, Peter, 2002. Replication, realism, and robustness: analyzing political regimes and international trade. American Political Science Review 96 (1), 167–169.

Martin, Philippe, Mayer, Thierry, Thoenig, Mathias, 2008. Make trade not war? Review of Economic Studies 75 (3), 865–900.

Martin, Philippe, Mayer, Thierry, Thoenig, Mathias, 2010. The geography of conflicts and Free Trade Agreements. CEPR Discussion Paper 7740. .
Melatos, Mark, Woodland, Alan, 2007. Endogenous trade bloc formation in an asymmetric world. European Economic Review 51 (4), 901–924.
Neumayer, Eric, Plumper, Thomas, 2010. Spatial effects in dyadic data. International Organization 64, 145–166.
Raftery, Adrian, 1995. Bayesian model selection in social research. Sociological Methodology 25, 111–196.
Riezman, Raymond, 1985. Customs unions and the core. Journal of International Economics 19 (3–4), 355–365.
Riezman, Raymond, 1999. Can bilateral trade agreements help induce free trade. Canadian Journal of Economics 32 (3), 751–766.
Sapir, André, 1997. Domino effects in Western European Trade, 1960–1992. European Journal of Political Economy 17, 377–386.
Solis, Mireya, Stallings, Barbara, Katada, Saori, 2009. Competitive Regionalism: FTAs in the Pacific Rim. Palgrave, MacMillan: New York.
Tovar, Patricia, 2009. The effects of loss aversion on trade policy: theory and evidence. Journal of International Economics 78 (1), 154–167.
Vicard, Vincent, 2008. Trade, conflicts and political integration: explaining the heterogeneity of regional trade agreements. CES Working Papers 2008.22. .
Whalley, John, 1993. Regional trade arrangements in North America: CUSTA and NAFTA. In: De Melo, J., Panagariya, A. (Eds.), New Dimensions in Regional Integration. Cambridge University Press, Cambridge.
Wooldridge, Jeffrey, 2002. Econometric Analysis of Cross Section and Panel Data. MIT Press.
Wu, J. Pedussel, 2004. Measuring and explaining levels of regional economic integration. ZEI Working Paper B12/2004. Centre for European Integration Studies, Bonn.
Yi, Sang-Seung, 1996. Endogenous formation of customs unions under imperfect competition: open regionalism is good. Journal of International Economics 41 (1–2), 153–177.

Part II
What Does the Public Think about Trade?

[7]

Journal of International Economics 54 (2001) 267–292
Journal of INTERNATIONAL ECONOMICS
ELSEVIER
www.elsevier.nl/locate/econbase

What determines individual trade-policy preferences?

Kenneth F. Scheve[a], Matthew J. Slaughter[b,*]

[a]*Department of Political Science, Yale University, 77 Prospect Street, New Haven, CT 06520, USA*
[b]*Department of Economics, Dartmouth College and NBER, 309 Rockefeller Hall, Hanover, NH 03755, USA*

Received 2 September 1999; received in revised form 30 December 1999; accepted 30 June 2000

Abstract

This article provides new evidence on the determinants of individual trade-policy preferences using individual-level survey data for the United States. There are two main empirical results. First, we find that factor type dominates industry of employment in explaining support for trade barriers. Second, we find that home ownership also matters for individuals' trade-policy preferences. Independent of factor type, home ownership in counties with a manufacturing mix concentrated in comparative-disadvantage industries is correlated with support for trade barriers. This finding suggests that, in addition to current factor incomes driving preferences as in standard trade models, preferences also depend on asset values.

Keywords: Trade; Policy preferences; Political economy

JEL classification: F13

1. Introduction

A complete political-economy model of trade policymaking must somehow characterize individuals' preferences over trade policy. Rodrik (1995, p. 1458) claims this is the first essential element of modeling: "In principle a political-

*Corresponding author. Tel.: +1-603-646-2939; fax: +1-603-646-2122.
E-mail address: slaughter@dartmouth.edu (M.J. Slaughter).

0022-1996/01/$ – see front matter
PII: S0022-1996(00)00094-5

economy model of trade policy must have four elements. First, it must contain a description of individual preferences over the domain of policy choices available to policymakers."

These preferences surely depend on how trade policy affects income for factors of production, as current factor income is a major determinant of individual economic welfare. It is well known from standard trade theory that trade's effect on current factor income depends crucially on the degree of intersectoral factor mobility, i.e. on the degree of factor specificity. In a Ricardo–Viner (RV) framework where some or all factors cannot move to other sectors, factor incomes tend to vary by industry of employment. In contrast, in a Heckscher–Ohlin (HO) framework where factors move costlessly across sectors, factor incomes tend to vary by factor type. But beyond factor income, standard trade theory does not focus on intertemporal consumption choices in which current factor income can be saved and invested for future periods. In reality, people do save and invest in a wide range of assets. Accordingly, trade-policy preferences may hinge not just on factor income but on asset ownership as well.

In this article we provide new empirical evidence on the determinants of individual trade-policy preferences. To date, there is only a small empirical literature on this question, and our work aims to improve on it significantly. We organize our data analysis around the basic HO and RV models, supplemented by a consideration of asset ownership. Our direct measure of trade-policy preferences comes from the National Election Studies (NES, 1993) survey, an extensive survey of current political opinions based on an individual-level stratified random sample of the U.S. population. Our measure is responses to a question asking about support for new U.S. trade barriers. The survey also reports each respondent's occupation, industry of employment, home-ownership status, and county of residence. We construct a data set with several plausible measures of "exposure" to freer trade across factor types, industries, asset ownership, and counties. Merging this information with the NES survey, we generate an individual-level data set identifying both trade-policy preferences and potential trade exposure through several channels. We then evaluate how these preferences vary with individual characteristics that trade theory predicts might matter.

We present two main empirical results. First, we find that factor type dominates industry of employment in explaining support for trade barriers. Lower skill, measured by education or average occupation earnings, is strongly correlated with support for new trade barriers. In contrast, employment in industries more exposed to trade, measured by tariff rates or net exports, is not strongly correlated with support for new trade barriers. Our second main empirical result is that, in addition to factor incomes, home ownership also matters for individuals' trade-policy preferences. Assets like housing do not fit into standard trade theory because they are neither currently employed factors nor currently produced goods. We find that independent of factor type or industry of employment, home ownership in counties with a manufacturing mix concentrated in comparative-disadvantage industries is strongly correlated with support for trade barriers. Both these findings are robust to including in our analysis a large number of other possible determinants of trade-policy preferences.

We do not consider these results to be direct tests among various trade models, but we do think the findings can be interpreted in light of these models. Our first result is consistent with the distributive conflict predicted in a Heckscher–Ohlin model in which the United States is well endowed with skilled labor relative to the rest of the world. It is also consistent with there being relatively high intersectoral labor mobility in the United States over the time horizons relevant to individuals when evaluating trade policy. Our second finding suggests that, in addition to current factor incomes driving preferences, as in standard trade models, in reality preferences also depend on asset values.

There are five additional sections to this article. Section 2 surveys the literature on trade-policy preferences and relates our work to this literature. Section 3 summarizes the trade theory underpinning our empirical work. The following section discusses the data and our model specifications. Section 5 presents the empirical results, while Section 6 concludes.

2. Literature survey

In the political-economy literature, this article is related to work focusing on actual political cleavages over trade policy and what those cleavages imply about the sector-specificity of assets.

Irwin (1994, 1996) and Magee (1978) find evidence consistent with trade-policy preferences being determined primarily by industry. Using county-level data to regress county votes on measures of county factor and industry mix, Irwin (1996) finds that industry interests rather than factor interests best explain voting in the 1923 British general election, an election that hinged primarily on the issue of whether Britain should implement new trade barriers. In a similar paper, Irwin (1994) finds the same result for the 1906 British general election. Magee (1978) reports that of 21 industries testifying before the House Ways and Means Committee on the Trade Reform Act of 1973, in 19 cases trade unions representing labor's interests took the same position as management and industry trade associations representing capital's interests. Magee also documents that neither capital nor labor shared a uniform lobbying position across sectors.

In contrast, Beaulieu (1996, 1998), Balistreri (1997), Rogowski (1987, 1989), Midford (1993), and Kaempfer and Marks (1993) find support for factor types explaining trade-policy preferences. Using an individual-level survey of Canadian voters, Beaulieu (1996) finds that factor type rather than industry of employment best explains votes in the 1988 Canadian federal election, an election widely regarded as a national referendum on the Canadian–U.S. Free-Trade Agreement (CAFTA). Beaulieu (1998) finds similar results using stated preferences rather than votes. Balistreri (1997) concludes that the same data are consistent with the generalized Stolper–Samuelson theorem. Using data on Canada's relative endowments measured in terms of occupations, he finds that people employed in occupations abundant in Canada relative to the United States — thus the people likely to gain from freer trade — were more likely to favor the CAFTA. Rogowski (1987, 1989) explains several national political coalitions with respect to groups' exposure to international trade as predicted by the Stolper–Samuelson theorem. Midford (1993) expands Rogowski's framework from just three factors — capital, labor, and land — by disaggregating labor and land more finely and by introducing raw materials as well; this allows him to explain some additional real-world political coalitions. Analyzing 1991 Congressional votes on granting presidential "fast track" trade-negotiating authority, Kaempfer and Marks (1993) find House votes significantly correlated with the average wage in House districts (but not so for Senate votes and average state wages).

All these studies provide valuable information on trade-policy preferences and political behavior. However, our work improves upon them in at least three important ways.

First, and perhaps most importantly, our study uses a direct measure of individual trade-policy preferences. In contrast, all studies cited here (except Balistreri, 1997; Beaulieu, 1998) draw inferences about trade-policy preferences from some observed political actions — coalition formation, lobbying, or voting. These indirect preference measures face the important limitation of being endogenous outcomes of the interaction between trade-policy (and possibly other) preferences and political institutions. Policy preferences and institutions together determine policy actions, so the mapping from preferences to actions is not unambiguous.

Rodrik (1995, p. 1459) makes this distinction between preferences and actions when commenting that a complete political-economy model of trade policy "must contain a description of how these individual [trade-policy] preferences are aggregated and channeled, through pressure groups, political parties, or grass-roots movements, into 'political demands' for a particular policy or another." Similarly, Alt et al. (1996, p. 707) highlight the problem with reference to Magee's analysis of Congressional testimony: "the difficulty in taking this approach beyond a qualitative comparison of patterns into measuring the extent of participation across industries is that one is measuring the dependent variable rather than the independent variable to some extent. That is, this testimony is the behavior that a measure of [factor] specificity should help you predict; therefore, if one is trying to explain policy outcomes, then there is a big risk of rendering one's conclusions circular." We avoid this risk by measuring trade-policy preferences directly.

A second important improvement of our study is we consider trade-policy preferences not only in terms of individual income but more broadly in terms of asset ownership as well. Standard trade theory usually assumes that individual welfare depends only on individual factor income. As will be discussed, we analyze the empirical relevance of assets, too, particularly assets like housing that are neither currently employed factors nor currently produced goods.

Our study's third major improvement is in data quality. We briefly highlight three strengths of our data. First, as just discussed, this study is one of the first to measure trade-policy preferences directly rather than indirectly through policy actions. Second, our units of observation are individuals, not more-aggregated geographic units such as counties or Congressional districts. This accords with many political-economy models where individuals are the basic units whose preferences ultimately motivate any trade policies. Third, we have sufficient data to examine the alternative predictions of both the RV and the HO models. Factor type, industry of employment, and county of residence are all directly measured in our data. In contrast, many of the papers cited above do not have direct measures on factor type and/or industry. Balistreri (1997), Rogowski (1987, 1989), and Midford (1993) all examine whether the data are consistent with an HO story, but they do not benchmark this against the performance of an RV story. Beaulieu (1996, 1998) and Irwin (1994, 1996) infer both factor type and industry from data on occupation alone. These inferences almost surely create substantial measurement error (particularly for industry of employment) which is not systematically accounted for.

Overall, this study contributes to the existing literature in at least three important ways: by measuring trade-policy preferences directly rather than indirectly; by analyzing trade's effect on assets as well as income; and by using higher-quality measures of factor type and industry.

3. Theoretical framework

In the literature on the political economy of trade policy, it is commonly assumed that individuals evaluate trade policy based on how their current factor incomes are affected without regard for aggregate national welfare. In this article we follow the general spirit of this convention by assuming that individuals' policy preferences are determined by how policy affects their personal welfare. Our theory discussion considers two dimensions of welfare: factor income and asset ownership. We intend this discussion to guide our empirical analysis. We do not consider it to be a lead-in for directly testing alternative trade theories. We also do not consider it to exhaust all possible influences on trade-policy preferences; in our data analysis, we will examine influences other than factor income and asset ownership in our robustness checks.[1]

[1] In our analysis we assume that individuals know with certainty the effects of trade policies on individual incomes and asset holdings. This is a common but not universal assumption. Fernandez and Rodrik (1991) model trade-policy formation in an environment where people do not know ex ante how trade policy affects their welfare.

3.1. Trade's effect on factor incomes

The RV and HO models are the two most commonly used models for characterizing trade-policy preferences. In both, changes in trade policy affect the incomes of factors by changing the country's relative product prices. The key difference between the two models is their different assumptions about intersectoral factor mobility. Different degrees of factor mobility imply very different factor-income changes from — and thus preferences about — trade liberalization.

We use the basic predictions of these two models to organize our data analysis of preferences. In doing this, however, we emphasize that preferences may be consistent with both models, not just one. The RV model can be characterized as a short-run version of the more long-run HO model. For example, Mayer (1974) and Mussa (1974) compare wage changes in the two models, and Mussa (1978) formalizes how with intersectoral mobility costs an RV short-run gradually becomes an HO long-run. In reality, each model might be relevant over different time horizons. If individuals evaluate both short-run and long-run effects of trade liberalization, then trade-policy preferences might depend on both factor type and industry of employment.[2]

The HO model assumes that factors can move costlessly across sectors. Trade liberalization which changes relative product prices changes relative (and possibly real) factor prices according to the Stolper–Samuelson theorem: returns tend to rise (fall) for the factors employed relatively intensively in the sectors whose relative product price rises (falls). In this model it is usually assumed that protection is received by the sectors which employ relatively intensively the factors with which the country is poorly endowed relative to the rest of the world. Thus a country's abundant factors support freer trade while its scarce factors oppose it.

At the opposite extreme from the HO model, the RV model assumes that some or even all factors cannot move across sectors. Here, the income of specific factors is linked to their sector of employment. Trade-liberalization-induced changes in relative product prices redistribute income across sectors. Sectors with price declines — presumably comparative-disadvantage sectors — realize income losses for their specific factors while sectors with prices increases — presumably comparative-advantage sectors — realize income gains for their specific factors. So trade-policy preferences are determined by sector of employment. Factors

[2]Another way both models might accurately describe the economy is that within some time frame specificity might vary across units in the economy (such as industries or factor types). Alt et al. (1999) find support for this perspective in their study of firm lobbying behavior in Norway.

employed in sectors with product prices elevated (lowered) by trade protection oppose (support) trade liberalization.[3]

To summarize, in HO models factors evaluate trade policy based on their factor type while in RV models factors evaluate trade policy based on their industry of employment. What do these two models predict about trade-policy preferences in the United States? Many studies (e.g., Leamer, 1984) have documented that the United States is well endowed with more-skilled labor relative to the rest of the world. According to the HO model, then, in the United States more-skilled workers should support freer trade while less-skilled workers should oppose it. In contrast, the RV model predicts that U.S. workers employed in comparative-advantage sectors should support freer trade while those in comparative-disadvantage sectors should oppose it.

An important caveat to the theory just summarized is nontraded industries. By definition, trade barriers cannot be granted for these industries. Does this matter for the predictions of the HO and RV models? The HO reasoning still applies if there remains costless interindustry factor mobility among all sectors. For the RV model, however, we need to clarify how trade policies affect the product prices of nontraded sectors. Because freer trade tends to raise national income, if we assume positive income elasticities of demand for nontraded goods then freer trade should raise nontraded prices by raising demand for nontraded goods. Thus we predict that in an RV model workers in nontraded sectors should support freer trade. However, because trade policy's effect on nontraded prices works indirectly through nontraded demand, it might be the case that nontraded workers support freer trade less strongly than do comparative-advantage-sector workers. We return to this issue when discussing our industry trade-exposure measures.

3.2. Trade's effect on asset values

In standard trade models individuals spend all current factor income on consumption. In reality, people can have current factor income differ from current consumption by accumulating or decumulating assets. To understand the links between trade-policy preferences and asset ownership, this section discusses how trade affects asset values.

Many kinds of assets fit easily into standard trade models. Some assets are currently employed by firms as factors of production; for example, machine tools and office buildings. These assets earn rates of return determined by the economy's set of zero-profit conditions and, in some cases, the economy's

[3] If some factors remain mobile across sectors in a Ricardo–Viner model, their factor prices are not so clearly linked to product-price changes. Changes in real wages for these mobile factors are ambiguous: it depends on the consumption basket of these mobile factors. In the above discussion we focus only on the specific factors.

endowments as well. In turn, these rates of return are an important determinant of asset prices. There is a well-developed literature analyzing how these productive assets accumulate over time within open economies (e.g., Findlay, 1984; Smith, 1984). Another kind of asset which fits into standard trade models is currently produced goods such as automobiles. Their domestic prices are set just like those of other non-asset products, as some combination of world prices and domestic trade barriers.

Some assets, however, are neither currently employed factors nor currently produced goods. Residential housing is a major example. Firms do not employ houses as factors of production. And at each point in time, nearly all of a region's housing stock is not produced: it is the (appropriately depreciated) accumulation of all previous housing construction in earlier periods. Construction adds a very small amount to the current housing stock both because of the time lags involved and because the flow is very small relative to the housing stock.[4]

Some assets, then, are not clearly linked to the production side of standard trade models. We focus on housing because it is the only asset of this kind reported in the NES data. But it is important to note that housing constitutes a very large share of people's total wealth holdings. For the average U.S. household in 1990, the gross value of the primary residence accounted for nearly 90% of total household assets (Caplin et al., 1997). Among all U.S. homeowners in 1986, for the median homeowner in all age groups housing equity accounted for more than half of his/her total wealth (Skinner, 1994).[5] Though our data cover only housing, this is the single most important asset for a big share of the U.S. population.

To understand how trade policy can affect housing prices, consider a simple supply-and-demand framework. A country has many distinct regional housing markets, each of which faces a perfectly inelastic supply schedule at each point in time. Prices are then set by regional housing demand. Demand depends on considerations such as tax differentials between renting and owning. As discussed by Caplin et al. (1997), it also depends on the level of economic activity in a region. Greater economic activity means more employment, more housing demand.

Trade policy is one of the forces affecting the level of regional economic activity. Freer trade tends to shrink comparative-disadvantage industries and expand comparative-advantage ones. Accordingly, regions with a higher concentration of activity in sectors with a comparative disadvantage are more

[4]The Census Bureau (1997, 1998) estimates that on July 1, 1996 the total U.S. housing stock was 110 million housing units. For all of 1996 approximately 1.3 million new homes were constructed, with approximately 0.3 million existing homes becoming uninhabitable due to demolition, disasters, and other causes. Thus, 1996 net construction was about 1 million new homes — 0.9% of the existing stock. Also that year, an average of 8.33 months passed between issuing a residential permit and construction completion.

[5]Skinner reports median housing equity-to-net worth ratios for six different age groups within the population. These ratios range from 54.5 to 61.3%.

vulnerable to adverse housing-demand shocks from freer trade. As regional economic output declines people leave the local labor force, either for work elsewhere or, at least temporarily, unemployment. This reduces housing demand and thus housing prices. Note this trade-housing linkage operates whether the underlying factor markets are HO or RV.

To summarize: in regions with a high concentration of activity in comparative-disadvantage sectors, homeowners should oppose freer trade because its contractionary effects in the region tend to reduce homeowners' welfare by lowering housing demand and thus housing values.[6]

This link between trade and asset values operates independently of trade's effect on labor incomes. People's economic welfare depends on both income and asset holdings, and freer trade might affect these two channels differently. Consider a more-skilled homeowner in Gary, Indiana, a city with production very concentrated in a comparative-disadvantage sector, steel. This person might support freer trade through the income channel, but oppose it through the asset channel. We will examine both these links in the data analysis.

4. Data description and empirical specification

A convincing empirical analysis of the determinants of individual trade-policy preferences requires measures of policy preferences and trade exposure, consistent with the hypotheses outlined above, all at the level of the individual. We develop such an analysis by combining individual-level data from the 1992 NES survey (1993) with data on average wages, tariffs, trade flows, and county manufacturing activity. Using these data we examine how various measures of trade exposure affect individual trade-policy preferences.

4.1. Data description

We measure policy preferences by responses to this question from the 1992 NES survey:

> "Some people have suggested placing new limits on foreign imports in order to protect American jobs. Others say that such limits would raise consumer prices and hurt American exports. Do you favor or oppose placing new limits on imports, or haven't you thought much about this?"

[6]Research in the regional-economics literature has documented an empirical link between local industry mix and local housing prices. For the Boston area during the 1980s, Case and Mayer (1996) find that average house prices rose less in housing jurisdictions with a larger share of residents employed in manufacturing in 1980. They hypothesize "displaced manufacturing workers ... [were] reducing their demand for housing" (p. 391).

By coding responses 1 for those individuals favoring protection and 0 for those opposing it we constructed the dichotomous variable *Trade Opinion*. This question requires respondents to reveal their general position on the proper direction for U.S. trade policy. Our theoretical framework hypothesizes that trade policy can affect both individuals' factor income, either based on skill levels or on industry of employment, and the value of their housing assets. To apply our framework to this question, we assume that respondents think that import limits will be placed on comparative-disadvantage sectors. This assumption allows us to construct measures of factor and industry trade exposure which follow closely from the theory. The assumption seems reasonable relative to alternatives such as import limits on comparative-advantage sectors.

One of this question's strengths is that it does not refer to a specific country or a particular trade agreement. Consequently, a respondent's answer should reflect trade-policy preferences rather than preferences on other issues such as human-rights violations in China, competition regulation in Japan, or migration controls in Mexico.

To see whether skill levels are a key determinant of trade-policy preferences, for each individual in the 1992 NES survey we construct two measures of skill. First, respondents report their occupation coded according to 1980 Census Occupation Code classifications. We obtained BLS data on 1992 U.S. average weekly wages for these occupations (US Department of Labour, 1992). If the average market returns for each occupation are determined primarily by the skills required for it, these average wages, called *Occupation Wage*, measure respondents' skill levels. As a second skill measure, the NES survey also records the years of education completed by each respondent, *Education Years*. Educational attainment is another commonly used measure of skills. For both measures, by the HO model U.S. less-skilled workers are more likely to benefit from trade restrictions on comparative-disadvantage sectors and thus are more likely to support new trade barriers.

To examine the hypothesis that sector of employment is a key determinant of trade-policy preferences, for each individual in the NES survey we construct two measures of industry trade exposure. Each measure is based on respondents' reported industry of employment coded according to the three-digit 1980 Census Industry Code classification.

Our first industry trade-exposure measure, *Sector Net Export Share*, is the industry's 1992 net exports as a share of output. This variable follows the common assumption that an industry's comparative advantage is "revealed" by its net exports: industries with positive (negative) net exports are assumed to be comparative-advantage (disadvantage) industries and thus likely to realize income gains (losses) for their employed factors from trade liberalization. To construct this variable we obtained through the NBER Feenstra's (1996) data on 1992 manufacturing exports, imports, and value of shipments at the four-digit Standard Industrial Classification (SIC, revision two) level. To cover all truly tradable sectors, we obtained similar data for agriculture and tradable services from various

BEA sources (US Department of Commerce). All data were concorded to 1980 CIC industries, and then for each industry we calculated *Sector Net Export Share* as exports minus imports divided by value of shipments. For all nontradable sectors we set this variable equal to zero.

For this industry measure, according to the Ricardo–Viner model individuals employed in industries with greater revealed comparative disadvantages (i.e., more negative *Sector Net Export Shares*) are more likely to support trade protection for these industries. Notice that this measure matches the continuum across sectors of support for trade barriers discussed in Section 3.1: strong opposition for comparative-advantage sectors, possibly weaker opposition for nontraded sectors, and strong support for comparative-disadvantage sectors.

The second measure is of the industry's 1992 U.S. tariff rate. To construct this variable, *Sector Tariff*, from the ITC (United States International Trade Commission, 1997) we obtained data on 1992 tariff duties collected and customs-value imports at the four-digit SIC (revision three) level.[7] We concorded these tariff and import values to the 1980 CIC industries, and then for each industry we calculated an effective tariff rate by dividing tariffs value by imports value. These tariff data cover all tradable industries in agriculture and manufacturing. For all other sectors we set the tariff rate equal to zero.

To use this industry measure we assume that industries with higher current protection have more of a comparative-disadvantage. Given this, according to the Ricardo–Viner model individuals employed in industries with higher tariffs are more likely to support trade barriers for the comparative-disadvantage sectors. Notice that by assigning the same value to both zero-tariff tradables and nontradables, this measure restricts workers in the two groups to have the same trade-policy preference on this margin.

Finally, to examine the hypothesis that housing values are a key determinant of trade-policy preferences, for each individual in the NES survey we construct two measures of how exposed homeowners are to trade liberalization reducing local economic activity. To construct these measures we exploit two dimensions of the NES survey.

One is that the NES reports whether each respondent or his/her family owns his/her home of residence. From this information we create the dichotomous variable *House* coded 1 to indicate ownership and 0 otherwise. The other survey dimension we use is that each respondent reports his/her county of residence. We used the 1992 Census of Manufactures (COM) from the Census Bureau (1992) to construct two measures of county-level trade exposure. Both measures are based upon the COM's disaggregation of county employment and other economic-activity variables into the 20 two-digit SIC manufacturing industries.[8] First, using

[7]We thank Michael Ferrantino for helping us obtain these data.

[8]Unfortunately, comparably disaggregated county-level data for non-manufacturing industries are not readily available. We thank Clark Bensen for providing these data.

the ITC tariff data described above, we identified the 10 two-digit SIC manufacturing industries with above-median tariff rates in 1992.[9] We then calculated *County Exposure 1*, the share of county employment accounted for by these high-tariff industries. Second, using the Feenstra data described above, we identified the net-import industries in 1992 (14 total).[10] We then calculated *County Exposure 2*, the share of county employment accounted for by these net-import industries. These two variables measure each county's comparative-disadvantage employment.

We create our measure of homeowners' exposure to international trade by multiplying the county-exposure measures with *House* to construct two interaction variables, *County Exposure 1*House* and *County Exposure 2*House*. According to the theory presented earlier, homeowners living in counties with a larger share of employment in comparative-disadvantage sectors are more likely to oppose trade liberalization because regional housing values depend, among other things, on the amount of regional economic employment in trade-exposed sectors.

Table 1 reports the summary statistics of our trade-opinion measure and our trade-exposure variables. These estimates and all the statistical analyses in this article rely on multiple imputation to deal with missing-data problems.[11] Notice that about 67% of respondents favored trade restrictions while 33% were opposed. This split is very similar to margins found in many other surveys of American opinions about trade.

4.2. Econometric model

Our empirical work aims to see how different types of trade exposure affect the probability that an individual supports trade restrictions. Again, *Trade Opinion*

[9]These 10 high-tariff industries were 21, 22, 23, 28, 30, 31, 32, 34, 38, and 39.

[10]The 14 net-import sectors were 22, 23, 24, 25, 26, 29, 30, 31, 32, 33, 34, 36, 37, and 39.

[11]A complete description of the imputation procedures is available in the unpublished appendix to this article at http://www.fas.harvard.edu/~scheve. The missing-data problems in the analysis ranged from modest to substantial. Overall, when we simply dropped observations with any missing data we lost between 4.4 and 73.4% of all observations, depending on which model was estimated. This listwise-deletion approach to inference with incomplete data is always inefficient and risks bias unless the data are missing completely at random. Multiple imputation (King et al., 2000; Schafer, 1997; Little and Rubin, 1987; Rubin, 1987) is consistent and generates correct uncertainty estimates under the less-restrictive assumption that the data are missing randomly conditional on the data included in the imputation procedures. The imputation model used in this application was multivariate normal and was implemented using the data augmentation method known by the acronym "IP" because it involves two key iterative steps: the imputation step and the posterior step. The imputation procedures generated 10 completed data sets each containing 1736 observations equal to the actual number of individuals in the 1992 NES survey either supporting or opposing more trade restrictions. Each data set was analyzed using the logit specifications described in Section 4.2, with the results across the datasets combined using the standard multiple imputation formulas. All the main findings reported in this article are qualitatively the same for the case where imputations are also made by treating as missing data the fact that some respondents did not express a trade-policy opinion. In addition, all main results are qualitatively the same using the listwise-deletion method.

Table 1
Summary statistics[a]

Variable	Mean	Standard error
Trade Opinion	0.671	0.470
Occupation Wage	0.532	0.187
Education Years	13.288	2.610
Sector Tariff	0.006	0.019
Sector Net Export Share	−0.004	0.091
County Exposure 1	0.096	0.093
County Exposure 2	0.191	0.334
House	0.679	0.467

[a] These summary statistics are multiple imputation estimates based on the 10 imputed data sets with 1736 observations for each variable in each data set. The variable *Occupation Wage* reports the actual wage divided by 1000.

equals 1 when an individual supports trade restrictions and 0 when opposed. Then $E(Trade\ Opinion_i) = \Pr(Trade\ Opinion_i = 1|\pi_i) = \pi_i$ where i indexes each observation and π_i equals the probability that an individual supports trade restrictions. We model the variation in π_i according to the logistic form with $\pi_i = 1/(1 + \exp(-x_i\beta)$. In this expression, x_i is a vector of individual-specific explanatory variables hypothesized to affect the probability of supporting trade restrictions and β is a vector of effect parameters. We estimate these effect parameters using logistic regressions.

The theory discussed in Section 3 suggests alternative sets of explanatory variables to include in the x_i vector. Altogether we estimate 16 different models. The first four models include just the factor-income regressors individually. Models 5 through 8 include pairs of explanatory variables, one measuring skills and the other industry. Finally, the last eight specifications, Models 9 through 16, replicate the specifications in Models 5 through 8 but also include our asset regressors. Specifically, we include a homeowner interaction variable and its related county-exposure variable. We include the county-exposure variable itself to

Table 2
Hypothesized sign for the regressors

Regressor	Hypothesized sign
Occupation Wage	Negative
Education Years	Negative
Sector Tariff	Positive
Sector Net Export Share	Negative
*County Exposure 1*House*	Positive
County Exposure 1	Zero
*County Exposure 2*House*	Positive
County Exposure 2	Zero

verify that it is not living in a trade-exposed county per se that matters: only homeowners should care about industry mix and its effect on housing values. Overall, Models 1 through 8 examine the role of factor income only in explaining trade-policy preferences. These specifications follow the previous literature most closely. Models 9 through 16 examine both factor-income and asset-value effects as well. All 16 models also include a constant. Table 2 shows the hypothesized sign for the regressors in x_i.

5. Empirical results

5.1. Factor type, industry of employment, and trade-policy preferences

The results of our logistic regressions for Models 1 through 8 strongly support the hypothesis that individuals' skill levels determine trade-policy preferences. Little evidence is found consistent with the hypothesis that industry of employment influences policy preferences.

The actual coefficient estimates and standard errors from Models 1 through 8 using the multiple-imputation methodology are reported in Table 3 (listwise-deletion estimates yielding qualitatively similar results are available from the authors). But these coefficient estimates alone do not answer our key substantive question of how *changes* in skill levels and industry trade exposure affect the probability that an individual supports trade restrictions. To answer this question we used the estimates of Models 1 through 8 to conduct simulations calculating the effect of changing one variable of interest from average to above-average values while holding the other variables constant at their means.

Our simulation procedure is best described with reference to a specific model and variable of interest. Consider Model 5 and *Occupation Wage* (this model's other regressor is *Sector Tariff*). Recognizing that the parameters reported for this model are estimated with uncertainty, we drew 1000 simulated sets of parameters from their sampling distribution defined as a multivariate normal distribution with mean equal to the maximum likelihood parameter estimates and variance equal to the variance–covariance matrix of these estimates. For each of the 1000 simulated sets of coefficients we then calculated two probabilities. First, we calculated the estimated probability of supporting trade restrictions when *Occupation Wage* and *Sector Tariff* are equal to their means. Second, we calculated the estimated probability of supporting trade restrictions when *Occupation Wage* is one standard deviation above its mean while *Sector Tariff* is held at its mean. The difference between these two estimated probabilities is the estimated difference in the probability of supporting trade restrictions between an individual with average skills and someone with (one standard deviation) above-average skills. We calculated this difference 1000 times, and then to show the distribution of this

Table 3
Determinants of individual opinion on international-trade restrictions: factor-income models[a]

Explanatory variable	Model 1	Model 2	Model 3	Model 4	Model 5	Model 6	Model 7	Model 8
Constant	1.642	3.648	0.696	0.711	1.625	1.642	3.651	3.650
	(0.168)	(0.350)	(0.054)	(0.051)	(0.170)	(0.168)	(0.355)	(0.351)
Occupation Wage	−1.716				−1.711	−1.720		
	(0.288)				(0.288)	(0.288)		
Education Years		−0.217					−0.217	−0.217
		(0.025)					(0.025)	(0.025)
Sector Tariff			2.730		2.420		−0.137	
			(2.994)		(3.089)		(2.976)	
Sector Net Ex Share				−0.697		−0.720		0.027
				(0.612)		(0.614)		(0.615)
# of observations	1736	1736	1736	1736	1736	1736	1736	1736

[a] Notes: these results are multiple-imputation estimates of logistic regression coefficients based on the 10 imputed data sets. Each cell reports the coefficient estimate and (in parentheses) its standard error. The dependent variable is individual opinions about U.S. trade policy. The measure is coded a 1 for those individuals favoring new restrictions and 0 for those opposed.

difference we calculated its mean, its standard error, and a 90% confidence interval around the mean.

Table 4 reports the results of this simulation for Models 1 through 8. Each column reports a different model. Within each column, each row reports the estimated effect on the probability of supporting trade restrictions of increasing that row's variable from its sample mean to one standard deviation above its mean, holding fixed all other variables at their means. For example, Model 1 indicates that increasing *Occupation Wage* from its mean to one standard deviation above its mean reduces the probability of supporting trade restrictions by 0.074 on average. This estimated change has a standard error of 0.012 and a 90% confidence interval of [−0.095, −0.053].

Models 1 through 4 present these results one regressor at a time. Models 5 through 8 examine directly the factor-type versus industry-of-employment hypotheses. This second group of models aims to determine whether one hypothesis better explains the data. In evaluating these results, however, it is important to recall from Section 3 that if individuals evaluate both short-run and long-run effects of trade liberalization then their trade-policy preferences might be explained by both factor type and industry of employment.

Across all models in Table 4, higher skills is strongly correlated with lower probabilities of supporting trade restrictions. The mean estimates of probability changes are much larger than those for the industry measures. These mean estimates are virtually identical whether the specification includes just a skill measure or a skill measure and an industry measure. Moreover, they all are precisely estimated: all have 90% confidence intervals strictly less than zero.

In contrast, higher industry trade exposure has much more ambiguous effects. In Models 3 and 4, greater industry trade exposure is correlated with the hypothesized increase in probability of supporting trade restrictions. But neither of these changes is precisely estimated: both 90% confidence intervals bracket zero. In Models 5 and 6 these results are basically unaffected by including *Occupation Wage*. However, in Models 7 and 8 the inclusion of *Education Years* both reverses the estimated change in probabilities and makes these estimated changes much less precise. Comparing the industry results for Models 5 and 6 with Models 7 and 8, we cannot even conclude with a high degree of confidence that individuals employed in relatively trade-exposed sectors are more likely to support trade restrictions once we control for skill levels.

The key message of Table 4 is that an individual's skill level rather than industry of employment is strongly correlated with the probability of supporting trade restrictions. The effects of skill trade exposure are large and precise; the effects of industry trade exposure are small and uncertain. This suggests that individuals care about trade policy in a manner consistent with the HO model, and that there is relatively high intersectoral labor mobility in the United States over time horizons relevant to individuals evaluating trade policy.

Table 4
Determinants of respondent opinion on international trade restrictions: factor-income models[a]

Variable	Change in probability of supporting trade restrictions as a result of a one standard deviation increase in the independent variable for each model[b]							
	Model 1	Model 2	Model 3	Model 4	Model 5	Model 6	Model 7	Model 8
Occupation Wage	−0.074 (0.012) [−0.095, −0.053]				−0.074 (0.012) [−0.094, −0.055]	−0.074 (0.013) [−0.097, −0.054]		
Education Years		−0.132 (0.015) [−0.158, −0.107]					−0.132 (0.016) [−0.158, −0.106]	−0.133 (0.016) [−0.161, −0.106]
Sector Tariff			0.012 (0.012) [−0.010, 0.032]		0.011 (0.013) [−0.011, 0.032]		−0.001 (0.012) [−0.021, 0.019]	
Sector Net Export Share				−0.014 (0.013) [−0.035, 0.008]		−0.014 (0.013) [−0.035, 0.008]		0.000 (0.013) [−0.021, 0.021]

[a] For each of the eight factor only models, we estimated using multiple imputation with a logit specification the effect of factor and industry exposure to international trade on individuals' trade policy opinions. The parameter estimates from this analysis are reported in Table 3. Here we interpret those results by presenting the impact of a one standard deviation increase in each independent variable, holding other variables constant, on the probability that the respondent supports trade restrictions.

[b] Each triple of entries in the table begins with the mean effect from 1000 simulations of the change in probability of supporting trade restrictions due to an increase of one standard deviation from the independent variable's mean, holding all other variables constant at their means. The standard error of this estimate is reported in parentheses. Finally, a 90% confidence interval for the probability change is presented in brackets.

5.2. Asset ownership and trade-policy preferences

Tables 5 and 6 report results for the hypothesis that individuals care about how trade liberalization affects housing values independent of how it affects factor incomes. Similar to the earlier set of results in Table 3, Table 5 reports the multiple-imputation coefficient estimates from Models 9 through 16. Table 6 reports the results from simulations calculating the effect of changing one variable of interest from average to above-average values while holding the other variables constant at their means. Before discussing the housing results, we note that the results in Table 6 for skills and industry of employment are substantially the same as the results in Table 4. Even with the inclusion of housing regressors our key conclusion that factor type dominates industry of employment remains unchanged.

In all eight models reported in Table 6, our estimates of the effect of county trade exposure on individual homeowners' trade preferences are consistent with our theoretical expectations. We estimate that, for homeowners, an increase in county trade exposure from its sample mean to one standard deviation above its mean increases the probability of supporting trade restrictions by between 0.029 and 0.039. The results are very similar whether we use *County Exposure 1* or *County Exposure 2*. And in all eight models the probability changes are precisely estimated, with 90% confidence intervals all above zero. These results support our hypothesis that homeowners living in counties with a larger share of employment in comparative-disadvantage sectors are more likely to oppose trade liberalization because regional housing values depend, among other things, on the amount of regional economic employment in trade-exposed sectors.

5.3. Robustness checks

We checked the robustness of the empirical results in several ways. First, the theory motivating our analysis assumes all individuals work and earn factor income. Accordingly, we limited our data set to individuals currently in the labor force (either working or unemployed but actively seeking work). Like the United States overall in 1992, in the NES survey only about two-thirds of respondents were in the labor force. The results for the working-only sample were qualitatively similar to the full-sample results.[12]

Similar to this, we considered the possibility that the proper unit of observation is the household rather than the individual. The NES survey reports education, occupation, and industry of employment for spouses of respondents, so in some specifications we used regressors reporting a combination of respondent and

[12] Sixty-five percent of the sample reported being in the labor force, versus the 1992 actual national share of 66.6%. Respondents not currently in the labor force are asked in the NES survey to report as "industry of employment" the industry last worked in.

Table 5
Determinants of individual opinion on international-trade restrictions: factor-income and asset-ownership models[a]

Variable	Model 9	Model 10	Model 11	Model 12	Model 13	Model 14	Model 15	Model 16
Constant	1.567	1.552	1.596	1.578	3.586	3.590	3.594	3.593
	(0.174)	(0.176)	(0.172)	(0.174)	(0.355)	(0.358)	(0.355)	(0.359)
Occupation Wage	−1.766	−1.759	−1.746	−1.738				
	(0.292)	(0.292)	(0.291)	(0.290)				
Education Years					−0.218	−0.218	−0.216	−0.216
					(0.025)	(0.025)	(0.025)	(0.025)
Sector Tariff		1.828		2.275		−0.573		−0.128
		(3.189)		(3.132)		(3.056)		(3.004)
Sector Net Ex Share	−0.624		−0.653		0.084		0.044	
	(0.609)		(0.609)		(0.615)		(0.615)	
County Exposure 1	−0.334	−0.301			−0.570	−0.567		
	(0.849)	(0.852)			(0.881)	(0.880)		
*County Exp 1*House*	2.195	2.182			2.183	2.185		
	(0.951)	(0.951)			(0.966)	(0.964)		
County Exposure 2			−0.146	−0.136			−0.183	−0.184
			(0.296)	(0.298)			(0.311)	(0.311)
*County Exp 2*House*			0.780	0.779			0.675	0.676
			(0.375)	(0.376)			(0.392)	(0.391)
# of observations	1736	1736	1736	1736	1736	1736	1736	1736

[a] These results are multiple-imputation estimates of logistic regression coefficients based on the 10 imputed data sets. Each cell reports the coefficient estimate and (in parentheses) its standard error. The dependent variable is individual opinions about U.S. trade policy. The measure is coded a 1 for those individuals favoring new restrictions and 0 for those opposed.

Table 6

Determinants of respondent opinion on international trade restrictions: factor-income and asset ownership models[a]

Variable	Change in probability of supporting trade restrictions as a result of a one standard deviation increase in the independent variable for each model[b]							
	Model 9	Model 10	Model 11	Model 12	Model 13	Model 14	Model 15	Model 16
Occupation Wage	−0.074 (0.013) [−0.095, −0.052]	−0.075 (0.012) [−0.095, −0.055]	−0.074 (0.012) [−0.094, −0.053]	−0.074 (0.013) [−0.094, −0.052]				
Education Years					−0.130 (0.016) [−0.156, −0.104]	−0.131 (0.017) [−0.158, −0.104]	−0.130 (0.016) [−0.157, −0.105]	−0.131 (0.016) [−0.157, −0.103]
Sector Tariff		0.008 (0.013) [−0.015, 0.029]		0.010 (0.012) [−0.011, 0.030]		−0.003 (0.013) [−0.024, 0.017]		−0.001 (0.013) [−0.022, 0.020]
Sector Net Export Share	−0.013 (0.012) [−0.033, 0.008]		−0.013 (0.012) [−0.034, 0.008]		0.002 (0.012) [−0.019, 0.021]		0.001 (0.012) [−0.020, 0.021]	
Cty Exp 1	0.034	0.034			0.029	0.030		
*Cty Exp 1*House*[c]	(0.013) [0.011, 0.055]	(0.014) [0.012, 0.057]			(0.013) [0.007, 0.051]	(0.013) [0.006, 0.051]		
Cty Exp 2 *Cty Exp 2*House*[c]			0.039 (0.015) [0.014, 0.063]	0.038 (0.016) [0.012, 0.064]			0.029 (0.017) [0.000, 0.056]	0.029 (0.017) [0.001, 0.056]

[a] For each of the eight factor and asset models, we estimated using multiple imputation with a logit specification the effect of factor, industry, and asset exposure to international trade on individuals' trade policy opinions. The parameter estimates from this analysis are reported in Table 5. Here we interpret those results by presenting the impact of a one standard deviation increase in each independent variable, holding other variables constant, on the probability that the respondent supports trade restrictions.

[b] Each triple of entries in the table begins with the mean effect from 1000 simulations of the change in probability of supporting trade restrictions due to an increase of one standard deviation from the independent variable's mean, holding all other variables constant at their means. The standard error of this estimate is reported in parentheses. Finally, a 90% confidence interval for the probability change is presented in brackets.

[c] The one-standard-deviation increase for the county-exposure variable is calculated assuming the individual is a homeowner. This means that the change affects two independent variables: the county variable itself and its interaction with homeownership.

spousal information. These household results were generally consistent with the individual ones.

To verify the strength of our data we tried other measures of factor type, industry exposure, and county exposure. For factor type we tried the respondents' reported 1991 annual income. The results were qualitatively similar to those obtained for average occupation wages and education. For industry trade exposure we tried imports as a share of output. Although imports do not measure revealed comparative advantage, so often imports are considered to be harmful that we thought many individuals might focus on imports only when evaluating trade policy. This import measure did not work as hypothesized, however. To examine the robustness of our county-exposure measures, we tried wage bill instead of employment as the indicator of county economic activity. The wage-bill results were qualitatively similar to those for employment.

Similar to this, we also estimated specifications including both *Occupation Wage* and *Education Years* and then specifications including both *Sector Tariff* and *Sector Net Export Share*. This allowed us to check whether each regressor has explanatory power independent of its substitute. When regressed together, both *Occupation Wage* and *Education Years* are significantly less than zero. In contrast, when regressed together both *Sector Tariff* and *Sector Net Export Share* are not significantly different from zero.

Finally, we controlled for many other possible determinants of trade-policy preferences that are not derived from trade theory but that might bias our estimates. First, we reran Models 9 through 16 including *House*, the other separate component of our interaction term. Like *County Exposure 1 (2)*, *House* never entered significantly. Most importantly, with either or both separate regressors the results for our interaction term were qualitatively unchanged (although with *House* the significance of our interaction term fell slightly). This suggests that neither home ownership alone nor residence in a trade-exposed county alone is sufficient to affect trade-policy preferences: it is the combination of the two that matters. Note that the insignificance of *County Exposure 1 (2)* is inconsistent with altruistic stories in which people oppose trade liberalization because of its perceived negative effects on their local community overall.

In addition to robustness checks involving homeownership and geography, we also tried a number of other demographic, political, and economic variables. For example, we reestimated Models 1 through 8 adding in the following regressors: age, gender, race, party identification, and union membership. In these specifications, age and race have no consistently significant effect while women, those who identify more strongly with the Democratic party, and union members are significantly more likely to support trade barriers. Controlling for all these variables, however, does not significantly change our key result that factor exposure explains trade preferences much more than sector exposure. In other similar robustness checks, we also found that our home ownership result holds up to the inclusion of additional regressors. Finally, we estimated Models 1 through

16 adding a variable indicating the average 1992 unemployment rate in the state in which the respondent lives. Including this variable had no systematic effect on our substantive inferences. If anything, including the unemployment measure tends to strengthen the magnitude of the estimated factor-type effects. Average state unemployment is positively correlated with restrictionist trade opinions in most specifications.[13]

5.4. Relating our empirical results to the political-economy literature

One may ask how our findings relate to the existing theory literature on trade policy. Many important political-economy models have assumed, by construction, an RV economy in which individual preferences fall along industry lines. Examples of this modeling strategy include Findlay and Wellisz (1982), Hillman (1982), and Grossman and Helpman (1994). Our finding that factor type, not industry of employment, is robustly correlated with trade-policy preferences suggests there is a high degree of intersectoral factor mobility over time horizons relevant to individuals when evaluating trade policies. This is more consistent with an HO perspective than an RV perspective (again, with the caveat that these results are not direct tests of various trade models, and that nothing in our analysis ruled out both factor and industry interests mattering).

One message of our findings is that important political-economy models like these could be re-worked with an HO assumption about the underlying economic structure. This would follow the example of Mayer (1984), who solves his full political-economy equilibrium for both HO and RV economies. It would also be consistent with the central empirical conclusion of Baldwin (1985, p. 176) that the trade-policy actions of U.S. government officials are explained by many types of political-economy models. Indeed, Breecher's (1982, p. 236) suggested extensions of Findlay and Wellisz (1982) call for precisely this kind of re-working: "Although the [Findlay–Wellisz] paper draws the battle lines between owners of land and of capital [specific factors], other sorts of conflict are worth considering. For example, ... the familiar division between capital and labor ... with no sector-specific factors." And the Grossman and Helpman (1994) analysis could be re-worked for an HO setting. Their introduction (p. 834) states, "In our model, lobbies represent industry interests." It seems the model could be recast for factor lobbies.

[13] Might the estimated effects of *Occupation Wage* and *Education Years* on trade-policy preferences reflect something other than returns to skill? One empirical result supporting our interpretation is our robustness check that both *Occupation Wage* and *Education Years* are significant when regressed together. If one variable captures something other than returns to skill, the significance of the other variable conditional on the first supports our interpretation. A second empirical finding supporting our interpretation is that our main results are attenuated when we analyze the sub-sample of individuals not currently in the labor force. If our variables were not measuring skills then presumably their explanatory power would not be attenuated among non-working individuals.

In suggesting that standard political-economy models could be reworked from an HO economic structure, it does not follow that equilibrium policy actions cannot fall along industry lines. Again, we regard as very important Rodrik's (1995) argument that policy actions are the equilibrium outcome of preferences interacting with political institutions. Mayer (1984, p. 983) is a classic reference on this point, arguing that a full model contains both an "economic link" and a "political link." He endogenizes tariffs as the outcome of economic preferences channeled into some domestic voting structure, and different voter eligibility rules and participation costs lead to different tariff equilibria from the same preferences. Both Epstein and O'Halloran (1996) and McGillivray (1997) provide theoretical and empirical analyses of how political parties can affect the aggregation of interests. More generally, Alt and Gilligan (1994) analyze how given trade-policy preferences can lead to a wide range of political cleavages based on the institutional framework within which preferences are aggregated. Given the appropriate set of political institutions, preferences falling on factor lines could lead to actions taken on industry lines.

The other message of our empirical analysis is that political-economy modelers might consider asset ownership. Our empirical analysis suggests that individuals care about trade's effect on the price at which their homes can be transacted. In the standard models discussed in this section, the "assets" of sector-specific inputs are always assumed to be nontradable across individuals. Additional insights might be gained by extending these models to consider intertemporal considerations with ownership of tradable assets (for example, individuals might trade off short-run welfare declines from trade liberalization for long-run welfare increases).

6. Conclusion

In the literature on the political economy of trade policy it has been long known that individuals' preferences over trade policy play a central role. Theory shows quite clearly that different preferences can lead to different trade-policy outcomes. But a major limitation of this literature has been the small number of empirical studies of these preferences.

In this article we have provided some new evidence on the determinants of individual trade-policy preferences. To do this we constructed a new data set covering the United States in 1992. This is an individual-level data set identifying both stated trade-policy preferences and potential trade exposure through several channels. The data's comprehensiveness allowed us to organize our data analysis around the factor-income predictions of the Heckscher–Ohlin and Ricardo–Viner models. We were also able to go beyond the factor-income focus of these models to examine whether asset ownership matters as well. We generated two main empirical results.

First, we found that factor type dominates industry of employment in explaining support for trade barriers. Lower skill is strongly correlated with support for new trade barriers; employment in industries more exposed to trade is not. This result is consistent with a Heckscher–Ohlin model in which the United States is well endowed with skilled labor relative to the rest of the world. It suggests there is high intersectoral labor mobility over the time horizons relevant to individuals when evaluating trade policy. Our second main result is that home ownership also matters for individuals' trade-policy preferences. Independent of factor type or industry, home ownership in counties with a manufacturing mix concentrated in comparative-disadvantage industries is strongly correlated with support for trade barriers. This finding suggests that, in addition to current factor incomes, preferences also depend on asset values.

Our findings are based on people's opinions about trade policy. But many other government policies such as exchange-rate and antitrust policies also affect citizens by changing relative product prices. As with trade policy, precisely how individuals form preferences over these other policies has long been a subject of controversy. Our findings suggest preferences over these other policies might also vary with factor type and asset ownership.

Acknowledgements

For helpful comments we thank two anonymous referees and Jim Alt, John Freeman, Jim Harrigan, James Honaker, Doug Irwin, Ed Leamer, Jim Levinsohn, Jonathan Nagler, Sharyn O'Halloran, Ron Rogowski, Charles Stewart, and seminar participants at Brandeis University, Dartmouth College, Harvard University, Oxford University, the University of Warwick, and the ITI Program Meetings at the National Bureau of Economic Research. For generous assistance with data we thank Clark Bensen, Karolyn Bowman, Gary Engelhardt, Michael Ferrantino, Annamaria Lusardi, and Jonathan Skinner. For financial support Scheve thanks the National Science Foundation for a Graduate Research Fellowship. Slaughter thanks the Russell Sage Foundation and the Rockefeller Center for Public Policy at Dartmouth College.

References

Alt, J., Carlsen, F., Heum, P., Johansen, K., 1999. Asset specificity and the political behavior of firms: lobbying for subsidies in Norway. International Organization 53, 99–116.

Alt, J., Gilligan, M., 1994. The political economy of trading states. Journal of Political Philosophy 2, 165–192.

Alt, J., Frieden, J., Gilligan, M., Rodrik, D., Rogowski, R., 1996. The political economy of international trade: enduring puzzles and an agenda for inquiry. Comparative Political Studies 29, 689–717.

Baldwin, R., 1985. The Political Economy of U.S. Import Policy. MIT Press, Cambridge.

Balistreri, E., 1997. The performance of the Heckscher–Ohlin–Vanek model in predicting endogenous policy forces at the individual level. Canadian Journal of Economics 30, 1–17.

Beaulieu, E., 1996. Who supported the Canada–U.S. free trade agreement: factor or industry cleavages in trade policy? Unpublished manuscript.

Beaulieu, E., 1998. Factor or industry cleavages in trade policy? An empirical test of the Stolper–Samuelson theorem. Unpublished manuscript.

Breecher, R., 1982. Endogenous tariffs, the political economy of trade restrictions, and welfare. In: Bhagwati, J. (Ed.), Import Competition and Response. The University of Chicago Press, Chicago, pp. 234–238.

Caplin, A., Chan, S., Freeman, C., Tracy, J., 1997. Housing Partnerships: A New Approach To A Market at A Crossroads. MIT Press, Cambridge.

Case, K., Mayer, C., 1996. Housing price dynamics within a metropolitan area. Regional Science and Urban Economics 26, 387–407.

Epstein, D., O'Halloran, S., 1996. The partisan paradox and the U.S. tariff, 1877–1934. International Organization 50, 301–324.

Feenstra, R., 1996. U.S. imports: data and concordances. NBER Working Paper #5515 plus data CD (data also available on-line at the NBER's web site).

Fernandez, R., Rodrik, D., 1991. Resistance to reform: status quo bias in the presence of individual-specific uncertainty. American Economic Review 81, 1146–1155.

Findlay, R., 1984. Growth and development in trade models. In: Jones, R.W., Kenen, P.B. (Eds.). Handbook of International Economics, Vol. 1. Elsevier, Amsterdam, pp. 185–236.

Findlay, R., Wellisz, S., 1982. Endogenous tariffs, the political economy of trade restrictions, and welfare. In: Bhagwati, J. (Ed.), Import Competition and Response. The University of Chicago Press, Chicago, pp. 223–234.

Grossman, G., Helpman, E., 1994. Protection for sale. American Economic Review 84, 833–850.

Hillman, A., 1982. Declining industries and political-support protectionist motives. American Economic Review 72, 1180–1187.

Irwin, D., 1994. The political economy of free trade: voting in the British general election of 1906. Journal of Law and Economics 37, 75–108.

Irwin, D., 1996. Industry or class cleavages over trade policy? Evidence from the British general election of 1923. In: Feenstra, R., Grossman, G., Irwin, D. (Eds.), The Political Economy of Trade Policy: Papers in Honor of Jagdish Bhagwati. MIT Press, Cambridge, pp. 53–75.

Kaempfer, W., Marks, S., 1993. The expected effects of trade liberalization: evidence from US congressional action on fast-track authority. The World Economy 16, 725–740.

King, G., Honaker, J., Joseph, A., Scheve, K., 2000. Analyzing incomplete political science data: an alternative algorithm for multiple imputation. In: Paper prepared for the presentation at the 1998 Annual Meetings of the American Political Science Association, Boston, MA.

Leamer, E., 1984. Sources of International Comparative Advantage. MIT Press, Cambridge.

Little, R.J.A., Rubin, D., 1987. Statistical Analysis With Missing Data. Wiley, New York.

Magee, S., 1978. Three simple tests of the Stolper–Samuelson theorem. In: Oppenheimer, P. (Ed.), Issues in International Economics. Oriel Press, Stockfield.

Mayer, W., 1974. Short-run and long-run equilibrium for a small open economy. Journal of Political Economy 82, 955–967.

Mayer, W., 1984. Endogenous tariff formation. American Economic Review 74, 970–985.

McGillivray, F., 1997. Party discipline as a determinant of the endogenous formation of tariffs. American Journal of Political Science 41, 584–607.

Midford, P., 1993. International trade and domestic politics: improving on Rogowski's model of political alignments. International Organization 47, 535–564.

Mussa, M., 1974. Tariffs and the distribution of income: the importance of factor specificity. Substitutability, and intensity in the short and long run. Journal of Political Economy 82, 1191–1203.

Mussa, M., 1978. Dynamic adjustment in the Heckscher–Ohlin–Samuelson model. Journal of Political Economy 86, 775–791.

National Election Studies, Miller, W., Kinder, D., Rosenstone, S., 1993. American National Election Study, 1992: Pre- and Post-Election Survey (enhanced with 1990 and 1991 data), Computer File, Conducted by University of Michigan, Center for Political Studies, ICPSR (editor), Ann Arbor, MI: University of Michigan, Center for Political Studies, and Inter-university Consortium for Political and Social Research (producers), 1993. Ann Arbor, MI: Inter-university Consortium for Political and Social Research (distributor).

Rodrik, D., 1995. Political economy of trade policy. In: Grossman, G., Rogoff, K. (Eds.). Handbook of International Economics, Vol. 3. Elsevier, Amsterdam, pp. 1457–1494.

Rogowski, R., 1987. Political cleavages and changing exposure to trade. American Political Science Review 81, 1121–1137.

Rogowski, R., 1989. Commerce and Coalitions. Princeton University Press, Princeton.

Rubin, D., 1987. Multiple Imputation For Nonresponse in Surveys. Wiley, New York.

Schafer, J., 1997. Analysis of Incomplete Multivariate Data. Chapman & Hall, London.

Skinner, J., 1994. Housing and saving in the United States. In: Noguchi, Y., Poterba, J. (Eds.), Housing Markets in the United States and Japan. The University of Chicago Press, Chicago, pp. 191–213.

Smith, A., 1984. Capital theory and trade theory. In: Jones, R.W., Kenen, P.B. (Eds.). Handbook of International Economics, Vol. 1. Elsevier, Amsterdam, pp. 289–324.

United States Census Bureau, 1992. 1992 Census of Manufactures. United States Government Printing Office, Washington, DC.

United States Census Bureau, 1997. Estimates of housing units, households, households by age of householder, and persons per household. Available on the Census Bureau Web Page at http://www.census.gov/population/www/estimates/housing.html.

United States Census Bureau, 1998. Census Bureau Web Page, http://www.census.gov/hhes/www/-housing/hvs/q497tab5.html.

United States Department of Commerce, Bureau of Economic Analysis. Survey of Current Business and Trade and Employment. United States Government Printing Office, Washington, DC, various years.

United States Department of Labor, Bureau of Labor Statistics, 1992. Unpublished tabulations from the current population survey, Table A-26, 1992 Annual Averages.

United States International Trade Commission, 1997. Unpublished data file on U.S. tariffs collected in 1992.

[8]

KEVIN H. O'ROURKE
Trinity College Dublin
RICHARD SINNOTT
University College Dublin

The Determinants of Individual Trade Policy Preferences: International Survey Evidence

What determines trade policy? While this may seem to be mainly a question for political scientists, it is of increasing concern to international trade theorists, faced with the obvious disjunction between the free trade prescriptions of standard trade models and the protectionist policies pursued by so many governments.[1] The intellectual stakes for economists have increased further with the advent of endogenous growth models, which predict that policies can have important, long-run growth effects, as opposed to the fairly trivial deadweight losses implied by static constant returns models. Clearly it is not sufficient to take these policies as exogenous and examine their implications. To understand growth, the theory seems to be telling us, we need to understand why some countries pursue appropriate policies and others inappropriate ones.

When faced with such questions, the instinct of economists is to eschew state-centered or cognitive theories and to reach for the rational choice approach: politicians supply policies; voters and interest groups demand them; the institutional environment helps determine the ways in which these demands

The authors thank Elva Hannon for able research assistance. We also thank Ken Benoit, Susan Collins, Kevin Denny, Colm Harmon, Patrick Honohan, Gary King, David Madden, Anthony Murphy, Dani Rodrik, Mike Tomz, Paul Walsh, and participants at the Dublin Economics Workshop, ERWIT 2001, the Brookings Trade Policy Forum, and seminars at Queen's University Belfast and Trinity College Dublin for valuable comments, suggestions, and econometric advice.

1. Rodrik (1995).

and supplies interact with each other, and thus the eventual equilibrium. In these models, a key consideration is the determination of individual voter preferences, which in turn depends on the structure of the economy in question. In an environment in which factors are stuck in particular sectors, as in the specific factors model, factors have a direct stake in those particular sectors. Thus, management and labor in each sector will agree with each other that their sector deserves protection (if it is an import-competing sector), or that free trade is the best policy (if it is an exporting sector). On the other hand, if factors are mobile between sectors, as in the Heckscher-Ohlin model, then unskilled workers everywhere will have the same interest (since they all earn the same wage), as will skilled workers, as well as capital and all other relevant, mobile factors of production. In this case, abundant factors will favor free trade, and scarce factors will favor protection.[2] Classic economic contributions to the literature, such as Findlay and Wellisz; Mayer; Magee, Brock, and Young; and Grossman and Helpman all assume such a rational choice world, with some adopting a specific factors specification and others a Heckscher-Ohlin one.[3]

On the other hand there are powerful empirical reasons for believing that interests alone may not provide a complete explanation for the evolution of trade policy. Ideas (or ideology) may matter too. Sometimes the ideology is socialist, as in the case of COMECON, while the case of late nineteenth century Britain arguably provides an example of the power of liberal ideology.[4] In this paper we take seriously a third possibility, that a preference for economic protectionism among voters is a function of strong feelings of national identity and an associated set of patriotic and nationalist attitudes that include pride in country, sense of national superiority, and, at the extreme, antagonistic attitudes toward those who are not part of the nation. Of course nationalist ideology may have its origins in a conjuncture between identity and group interests, and particularly in a conjuncture between identity and perceptions of inequality. The point here, however, is that whatever their origins, nationalist attitudes are likely to have a certain autonomy and may exercise an independent influence on the way in which individuals react to the opening up of trade and to other globalization issues.[5]

2. Rogowski (1989).

3. Findlay and Wellisz (1982), Mayer (1984), Magee, Brock, and Young (1989), and Grossman and Helpman (1994).

4. A controversial claim, to be sure. See Irwin (1989) for one view, and Schonhardt-Bailey (1991) for another.

5. Gellner (1983). One should be wary of oversimplifying the implications of nationalist

These competing explanations have radically different policy implications. If support for economic protectionism is a function of the material interests of individuals, it can in principle be dealt with by offering side payments that compensate for the losses that result from liberalization. For example, in a specific factors framework workers who have been displaced from declining industries can be given help in relocating to other sectors.[6] In a Heckscher-Ohlin framework, the problems faced by unskilled workers in rich countries can be reduced by education and training schemes that, in principle, lower unskilled labor supply. If, on the other hand, protectionist policy preferences are rooted in nationalist attitudes, the strategy to alter them will have to be very different, and the strategist may have to be less sanguine about the prospects of success. Of course, the truth may well lie somewhere between these alternatives, with both interests and ideology reinforcing opposition to free trade. In this case it becomes necessary to tease out the relative effects of each, and to identify the conditions under which such effects operate.

In pursuing these questions, this paper starts with rational choice models of policy formation, and asks to what extent does the Heckscher-Ohlin model provide a useful guide to predicting trade policy preferences. This question has often been addressed in the empirical economics literature. Typically, authors have used aggregate data to ask whether factor interests or sectoral interests are more important in determining policy preferences. For example, Magee looked at industry testimony before the U.S. Congress in 1973, and found that labor and capital seemed to have the same interests within each sector, suggesting that a specific factors model is appropriate.[7] More typically, voting behavior has been related to constituency characteristics, either in the context of U.S. congressional votes on trade-related issues, or in the context of national elections that are assumed to have been fought largely on such issues.[8]

This paper pursues a different strategy. The inquiry is pitched, not at the level of interest groups (where, almost by definition, interests are likely to be

ideology for foreign economic policy. Shulman, for example, shows that Quebec, Hindu, and Ukrainian nationalists experience both integrationist and protectionist incentives and that policy choices depend on a number of situational factors (Shulman 2000). One could cite the Republic of Ireland's decision to abandon protectionism in the late 1950s and its subsequent pursuit of European integration as another case in point. However, the main thrust of nationalist ideology, particularly at the mass level, probably remains autarkic. At any event, this is the hypothesis tested in this paper.

6. See, for example, several contributions to Bhagwati (1982).

7. Magee (1978).

8. See, for example, Irwin (1994), or Kaempfer and Marks (1993).

determining), or at the level of the electoral constituency (where data on ideological and political variables are likely to be missing), but at the level of individuals or mass public opinion. In so doing, we are following in the footsteps of Balistreri, and Scheve and Slaughter, both of whom use survey data to tackle the question of who is in favor of free trade, and why.[9] As Scheve and Slaughter point out, individual-level preferences regarding trade must lie at the heart of any rational choice account of policy formation, but using aggregate data provides only indirect information on agents' preferences, since "policy preferences and institutions together determine policy actions, so the mapping from preferences to actions is not unambiguous."[10]

Of course, using survey data has its own limitations. If the Heckscher-Ohlin trade model accurately describes the world, then that has profound (and negative) implications for the impact of global North-South trade on Northern wage inequality, and equally profound, but positive, implications for the impact of that same trade on Southern wage inequality. It might well have political implications for the ease with which the transition economies of Eastern Europe can be integrated into the European Union. Finally, it would clearly have intellectual implications for the way in which theorists should specify their models of endogenous tariff formation. Leaving aside measurement problems in attitude research (to which we return below), survey data on their own cannot tell us whether the Heckscher-Ohlin model in fact describes reality. All that they can tell us is that agents' preferences are consistent, or inconsistent, with the predictions of the model. Our claim is that findings of the latter, more cautious variety are useful, since the determinants of preferences matter in themselves, both intellectually and politically.

Our paper provides a brief discussion of what theory has to say about the impact of trade on skilled and unskilled wages, since it is this link that leads us to expect a relationship between skill and trade policy preferences. We introduce the data, including our measures of nationalist attitudes, and discuss the strengths and weaknesses of our evidence relative to the data used by previous authors. This paper provides an ordered probit analysis of the determinants of individual trade preferences in twenty countries, including both "economic" and "ideological" determinants. Finally, we conclude by drawing some preliminary inferences and outlining an agenda for future research.

9. Balistreri (1997), and Scheve and Slaughter (2001, p. 270).

10. Scheve and Slaughter (2001, p. 4, citing Rodrik (1995)). Since beginning this project, we have become aware of the simultaneous and independent work being pursued by Anna Maria Mayda and Dani Rodrik (2001), who use the same International Social Survey Program (ISSP) survey data as we do, and who reach many of the same conclusions.

Trade and Wages: A Theoretical Digression

In a simple two country, two commodity, two factor (skilled and unskilled labor) framework, the links between trade and wage gaps are clear. Assume that Mexico is abundant in unskilled labor, and that the United States is abundant in skilled labor. Let NAFTA reduce the barriers to trade between the two economies. Mexico will export and produce more unskilled-labor-intensive products, and the demand for unskilled labor will increase. The country will import more skill-intensive goods, which will lead to a reduced demand for skilled workers, and a fall in the skilled wage. Wage inequality in Mexico will thus fall. Unskilled Mexican workers should favor free trade, while skilled workers should oppose it. Of course precisely the opposite scenario will occur in the United States. Skilled wages will rise and unskilled wages will fall. Thus in the United States it is the unskilled who should be protectionist, and the skilled who should favor free trade.

There have been several recent trade-theoretic papers exploring the ways in which the links between trade and income distribution become more complicated once we move away from simple two-by-two-by-two models. These contributions have been largely motivated by the fact that, while simple Heckscher-Ohlin logic might seem to suggest that globalization should lower skill differentials in the South, in fact differentials have widened in several developing countries (DCs) during the past twenty years (Wood, 1997). One possibility is that FDI, associated with trade liberalization, might lead to new skill-intensive activities being introduced into DCs.[11] Under such circumstances, the relative demand for skilled labor could rise in the South. Alternatively, if skilled labor and capital are complementary to some natural resource (for example, minerals), then liberalization in a resource-rich DC might increase skill premiums and inequality overall.[12] Clearly, allowing for more than two factors of production, or for links between trade and factor flows, or between trade and technology transfers, leads to theoretical ambiguity regarding the relationship between trade and wages. Nonetheless, it is interesting to ask whether the predictions of simple two-by-two models help to shed light on policy preferences generated in the admittedly complicated real world.

Even within a simple two-factor framework, however, there is another set of complications that has to be faced. Not all DCs are homogeneous. Instead,

11. Feenstra and Hanson (1996).
12. Kanbur (1999).

they differ greatly in their endowments of capital, labor, and skills. Davis points out that in a two-factor (capital and labor) world, a country may be globally labor abundant, but locally capital abundant, in the sense that it is capital abundant relative to other countries in the same "production cone." For such a country, liberalization lowers wages.[13] By implication, a middle-income country such as Mexico might be skill abundant relative to countries like China and India. It might therefore protect its unskilled-labor-abundant sectors and might thus see skill premiums rising on liberalization.[14] There is, in fact, evidence that unskilled-labor-intensive sectors received the most protection in countries such as Mexico and Morocco prior to liberalization.[15]

The argument may have some relevance for this study. With the exception of the Philippines, our data set does not include any third world countries (see below). Rather it contains data for rich countries and for the transition economies of Eastern Europe. We will be interested to see whether there are different determinants of trade policy preferences in the latter group of economies than in the former, but the Davis article reminds us that while these countries may be poor relative to the West, they are rich and skill abundant relative to most of the rest of the world. In that sense, our sample is a truncated one, and the results need to be interpreted in that light.

In particular the Heckscher-Ohlin theory predicts that the highly skilled will favor free trade in the most skill-abundant countries (such as the United States). In these countries, a regression explaining protectionist attitudes should find a negative coefficient on skills. Whether the coefficient on skills in the least skill-abundant country in our sample should be positive or negative depends entirely on where that country fits in terms of the worldwide hierarchy of skill abundance. The sign of the coefficient is thus a priori unclear. In order to test the Heckscher-Ohlin theory, therefore, we will pursue two strategies. First, we will estimate models (for the entire sample of countries) of the form

$$PROTECT_{ij} = \alpha_i + \beta_1 \mathrm{SKILL}_j + \beta_2 SKILL_j{*}GDPCAP_i + \beta_3 X_{ij} + \varepsilon_{ij}. \quad (1)$$

where

$PROTECT_{ij}$: the extent to which individual j in country i is protectionist

$SKILL_j$: a measure of the individual's skill

$GDPCAP_i$: the GDP per capita of country i

X_{ij}: a vector of control variables.[16]

13. Davis (1996).

14. Slaughter (2000); Wood (1997).

15. Currie and Harrison (1997); Hanson and Harrison (1999).

16. Equations (1) and (2) are used for expositional purposes. However, because of the nature

In this setup, the test of whether the Heckscher-Ohlin theory holds is the sign of the interaction term, β_2, which should be negative, since in richer countries high-skilled workers should be more in favor of free trade (that is, less protectionist).[17]

Second, we run country-specific regressions of the form

$$PROTECT_j = \alpha + \beta_1 SKILL_j + \beta_2 X_j + \varepsilon_{j,} \quad (2)$$

and compare the β_1 coefficients across countries. Again, the test of the Heckscher-Ohlin theory is whether these coefficients are systematically lower (that is, more negative) in richer, more skill-abundant countries.

Data

What do we need to accomplish our objectives? We need a data set that provides information on individuals' trade preferences, socioeconomic position, sociodemographic characteristics, and political attitudes. Since the Heckscher-Ohlin model predicts that skill levels will have different implications for trade policy preferences in different countries, the data should be cross-national in scope.

What we have are data provided by the 1995 International Social Survey Program (ISSP) module on national identity. The ISSP is an international consortium of survey research agencies that conducts comparative public opinion research on economic, social, and political issues across a wide range of countries on a regular basis. The sample in each country is a national representative random sample of the adult population designed to achieve a norm of 1,400 cases and, in any event, not less than 1,000 cases. Questionnaires are designed to be completed in fifteen minutes (not including a standard set of sociodemographic questions). Questionnaires are also designed to be suitable for self-administration.[18] The ISSP national identity survey was conducted in twenty-four countries in 1995–96. The countries concerned were: Australia,

of the data, we actually estimate nonlinear ordered probit models, as explained below. As shown the specification incorporates country dummies, but we also experiment by running regressions without these country fixed effects.

17. We used country GDP per capita rather than educational attainment variables for reasons given later in this paper. This amounts to assuming that GDP per capita is highly correlated with country endowments of human capital.

18. Full details on the ISSP consortium, including details on membership, rules and procedures, and availability of data sets and technical reports can be obtained at www.issp.org/info.htm.

West Germany, East Germany, Great Britain, the United States, Austria, Hungary, Italy, Ireland, the Netherlands, Norway, Sweden, the Czech Republic, Slovenia, Poland, Bulgaria, Russia, New Zealand, Canada, the Philippines, Japan, Estonia, Latvia, and Slovakia. The questionnaire (as implemented in the Republic of Ireland) is available on request.

Our dependent variable is the scaled response to a question that asked respondents how much they agreed or disagreed with the statement that their country "should limit the import of foreign products in order to protect its national economy" (question six in the survey). While in an ideal world one would like to have a battery of questions on trade policy preferences, we take this to be a reasonable operationalization of protectionist sentiment.[19] The data set also provides individual-level measures of a range of demographic, socioeconomic, and political variables. Among the socioeconomic variables, the most valuable from the point of view of testing the implications of trade theory is the respondent's skill level. This is arrived at by coding the answers to questions on respondents' occupation using the International Labour Organisation's (ILO) ISCO88 (International Standard Classification of Occupations) coding scheme. ISCO88 is a radical revision of the ILO's previous occupational coding scheme (ISCO68). The main thrust of the revision makes ISCO88 particularly relevant for our purposes. As Ganzeboom and Treiman put it, "the logic of the classification is mostly derived from skill requirements at the expense of industry distinctions" and the overall effort may "be seen as an attempt to introduce more clear-cut skill distinctions into ISCO88." They go on to illustrate this point by noting that "whereas in ISCO68 all 'textile workers' were organized in a single minor group, irrespective of their skill level (thereby precluding distinctions based on skill), textile workers are now spread out over three different minor groups, depending on whether they do elementary labor, operate machines, or perform craft work."[20] Similar changes were implemented for other manual occupations and, analogously, for nonmanual occupations. While a complex coding scheme of this sort allows for very fine distinctions between different occupations, we are interested in the four main skill categories provided by ISCO88. In brief, these are:

19. One might argue that the inclusion of the phrase 'in order to protect its national economy' is unfortunate in that it could bias responses in a protectionist direction by assuming that limiting imports is in some sense good for the economy. On the other hand, this is the way protectionist measures are defended in political discourse. Furthermore, we are interested in the relationships between this variable and our independent variables, not in estimating the absolute levels of support for protectionism. This objective is much less vulnerable to any response bias that may exist.

20. Ganzeboom and Treiman (1996, p. 206).

—Elementary occupations (that is, "simple and routine tasks, involving...with few exceptions, only limited personal initiative").

—Plant and machine operators and assemblers, craft and related trades workers, skilled agricultural and fishery workers, service workers and shop and market sales workers, clerks.

—Technicians and associate professionals.

—Professionals.[21]

A fifth group, "legislators, senior officials, and managers," does not have a skill coding under this four-step skill classification and were included as a separate, fifth skill category. Finally, we excluded members of the armed forces, since it was unclear what their skill levels were.

Unfortunately our use of the occupational coding in the 1995 ISSP survey created a complication which had to be faced. The survey that we are using coded occupation in three different ways, depending on the country in question. The ISCO88 coding scheme was used in twelve cases: Australia, Hungary, Ireland, East Germany, West Germany, Czech Republic, Poland, Slovenia, Canada, Russia, Slovakia, and Latvia. The earlier ISCO68 scheme was used in five countries: Norway, New Zealand, Bulgaria, Austria, and the United States. Finally, a further six countries (Britain, Italy, Netherlands, Sweden, Japan, and the Philippines) used a variety of national coding schemes. Estonia provided no occupational coding. It was, however, possible to reclassify the ISCO68 countries' occupation codes according to the ISCO88 classification. We were also able to derive an approximation to the ISCO skill classification from the country-specific occupational codes used in Britain, the Netherlands, and the Philippines. This left us with skill data for twenty of our twenty-four countries. We have had to omit the other four (Estonia, Italy, Sweden, and Japan) when estimating models involving skill.[22]

In addition to the foregoing reasonably objective economic variables, we will make use of a subjective economic variable, namely the stated willingness of people to move from one location to another in order to improve their standard of living or their work environment. Respondents were asked: "If you could improve your work or living conditions, how willing or unwilling would you be to move to another neighborhood or village; another town or city within this county or region; another county or region; outside [named country]; outside [named continent]?" Based on the responses to these ques-

21. ILO (1990, p.7).

22. We checked whether our results are dependent on our recoding schemes, by running separate regressions for our twelve ISCO88 countries, and the other eight countries for which we were able to obtain skill data. The results (available on request) were reassuringly similar.

tions, we derived two binary variables, indicating whether or not individuals were nationally mobile and internationally mobile.[23] Arguably those willing to relocate within the country should be more sanguine about the dislocation implied by free trade than those who are immobile. The rationale behind including the international mobility variable is to test Rodrik's argument that globalization is currently favoring internationally mobile factors of production (physical and human capital) over immobile factors such as unskilled labor.[24] By the same token, we also make use of a question which asks whether the respondent had ever lived abroad, on the basis that previous experience of living abroad may provide a signal regarding willingness to move again.

The ISSP national identity data set includes a wide range of indicators of nationalist attitudes. Rather than focusing on just one or two of these as indicators of what is, after all, a complex phenomenon, the approach taken here is to seek to identify an underlying dimension (or dimensions) of nationalism that would be measured by a subset (or subsets) of the items. An added advantage of this approach is that using multiple items to measure the same basic concept should improve the reliability of measurement. Factor analysis provides a statistical means of identifying the hypothesized dimension or dimensions.[25] A combination of a priori assessment of the individual items and exploratory factor analysis suggested a strategy of focusing on the following seven items (versions implemented in Ireland, other country/nationality labels substituted as appropriate):

—"Generally speaking, Ireland is a better country than most other countries."

—"The world would be a better place if people from other countries were more like the Irish."

—"I would rather be a citizen of Ireland than of any other country in the world."

—"It is impossible for people who do not share Irish customs and traditions to become fully Irish."

23. Details available on request.

24. Rodrik (1997). Although immigration to the United States, for example, has become increasingly unskilled in recent decades (Borjas, 1999).

25. Factor analysis is a generic term often used to cover both principal components analysis and factor analysis strictly speaking. Both are techniques that can be applied to a set of variables "when the researcher is interested in discovering which variables in the set form coherent subsets that are relatively independent of one another. Variables that are correlated with one another but largely independent of other subsets of variables are combined into factors. Factors are thought to reflect underlying processes that have created the correlations among variables" (Tabachnick and Fidell, 2001, p. 582).

Table 1. Factor Analysis of Nationalist Items in ISSP National Identity Survey 1995[a]

Questions	*Factor 1*	*Factor 2*
[Country] better country than most other countries	0.86	0.02
World better place if people from other countries more like the [nationality]	0.78	0.2
Rather be citizen of [country] than of any other country in world	0.61	0.29
Impossible for people who do not share [nationality] traditions to be fully [nationality]	-0.01	0.71
People should support their country even if country is wrong	0.20	0.63
Importance of having been born in [country] to be fully [nationality]	0.16	0.63
[Country] should follow own interests, even if conflicts with other nations	0.23	0.55
Percent variance	26.34	24.50

Source: Authors' calculations using data from ISSP National Identity Survey 1995.
a. Extraction method: Principal component analysis. Rotation method: Varimax with Kaiser normalization.

—"People should support their country even if the country is in the wrong."

—"Ireland should follow its own interests, even if this leads to conflicts with other nations."

—"How important do you think each of the following is for being truly Irish?"... "to have been born in Ireland?"

In each case, respondents were asked to rank their responses along a scale, in the case of the first six items, from one (strongly disagree) to five (strongly agree) and, in the case of the seventh item, from one (very important) to four (not at all important). The seventh item was reordered to make it consistent with the other six. Principal components analysis of these responses yielded two factors or underlying dimensions of nationalist attitudes. As can be seen from the rotated factor loadings in table 1, the first factor is a straightforward preference for and sense of the superiority of one's own country (here labeled patriotism). The second factor identifies a narrow or exclusive sense of nationality combined with a degree of chauvinism of the "my country right or wrong" variety (here labeled chauvinism). On the basis of this analysis, patriotism and chauvinism scores have been calculated by averaging responses across the relevant subsets of items identified in the factor analysis.[26]

Appendix table A-1 provides summary statistics for our key variables. As mentioned, "Protect" ranges from one to five, as do "patriotism" and "chauvinism."

26. The Cronbach's alpha reliability coefficient for the three-item patriotism scale is .68 and the item-total correlations vary from .41 to .57. The four-item ethnic chauvinism scale is somewhat less satisfactory in this regard: an alpha of .53 and inter-item correlations ranging from .31 to .36.

"Skill" also ranges from one to five, reflecting the fivefold classification above. Note, however, that we do not include such a variable in our regression analyses, since there is no reason to believe that the gap between the first and second skill levels, say, is equivalent in its effects to the gap between the second and third levels. For this reason, we incorporate skill into the analysis by introducing a variety of dummy variables. The mobility variables are both categorical. Zero denotes immobility and one, mobility. As table A-1 makes clear, there is a lot of variation both between and within countries, which is exploited later in this paper.

This brings us to the advantages and disadvantages of our data set compared to the data used by other authors and in particular those used by Scheve and Slaughter.[27] The big disadvantage is that we do not have data on the sector in which respondents are employed. Thus, we cannot directly confront the Heckscher-Ohlin and specific factors world views, as other authors have done.[28] The big advantage is that we have data for not just one country, but twenty. Scheve and Slaughter find that low-skill workers in the United States favor protection, which is useful evidence consistent with the Heckscher-Ohlin model. But such a finding on its own does not preclude the possibility that low-skill workers everywhere have the same attitudes (which would be completely at variance with the predictions of such a model).[29] Our data set allows us to explore whether skill has a differential impact on attitudes across countries, and thus allows for a cleaner test of the Heckscher-Ohlin predictions. Finally, our data allow us to test these "economic" relationships while controlling for the effect of variations along two dimensions of nationalist ideology.

Determinants of Attitudes toward Protection

We begin by looking at some crude country-level correlations. Table 2 takes the country means of seven variables (the six given in table A-1 and GDP per capita), and calculates the cross-country correlations between these variables. While this ignores the vast range of variation in attitudes within countries, the data are nonetheless instructive. Richer countries have higher skill levels and

27. Scheve and Slaughter (2001).

28. Nor do we have data on home ownership, another variable which Scheve and Slaughter (2001) found to be important.

29. For example, it might be the case that better-educated people everywhere are more flexible and able to cope with the rigors of the market, or even that they are more likely to understand the intellectual case for free trade.

Table 2. Cross-Country Correlations

	Protect	*Patriotism*	*Chauvinism*	*Skill*	*National mobility*	*International mobility*	*GDP per capita*
Protect	1.000						
Patriotism	0.127	1.000					
Chauvinism	0.691	0.105	1.000				
Skill	-0.271	0.223	-0.590	1.000			
National mobility	-0.376	0.126	-0.572	0.468	1.000		
International mobility	-0.151	0.012	-0.120	0.003	0.633	1.000	
GDP per capita	-0.482	0.383	-0.582	0.672	0.664	0.080	1.000

Source: Authors' calculations using data from ISSP National Identity Survey 1995 and World Bank (1999).

rates of internal mobility than poorer countries, and they also show more patriotism and less chauvinism. There is a strong positive correlation (+.691) between protectionism and chauvinism, but only a weak correlation between protectionism and patriotism. Skill, mobility, and income per capita are all associated across countries with pro-free-trade sentiments, rather than with protectionism.

However, our interest is in the determinants of protectionism at the individual level and table 3 provides some exploratory analysis. In all cases, the dependent variable is "protect," which as already mentioned is an ordered variable running from one to five. We therefore used ordered probit methods in estimating our relationships.[30] In each case, there is assumed to be a latent variable, $PROTECT^*$, related to the independent variables as in equation (1):

$$PROTECT_{ij}^* = \alpha_i + \beta_1 SKILL_j + \beta_2 SKILL_j{*}GDPCAP_i + \beta_3 X_{ij} + \varepsilon_{ij}. \quad (3)$$

There are also four cutoff points, μ_1–μ_4, such that protect takes the value:

—One if $PROTECT^*$ lies below μ_1

—Two if $PROTECT^*$ lies between μ_1 and μ_2

—Three if $PROTECT^*$ lies between μ_2 and μ_3

—Four if $PROTECT^*$ lies between μ_3 and μ_4

—Five if $PROTECT^*$ lies above μ_4.

The disturbance term is assumed to be normally distributed.

In this model, the probability that protect will take on the value one, say, is the probability that

$$PROTECT^* = \beta' Y + \varepsilon < \mu_1, \quad (4)$$

30. For an introduction, see Greene (2000, chap. 19).

Table 3. Exploratory Regressions: Ordered Probit[a]

	(1)	*(2)*	*(3)*	*(4)*	*(5)*	*(6)*	*(7)*	*(8)*	*(9)*
Country dummies	*Yes*	*Yes*	*Yes*	*Yes*	*Yes*	*Yes*	*Yes*	*No*	*Yes*
GDPCAP								-0.0163	0.0034
								(-13.2)	(1.47)
Patriotism		0.1946	0.1722	0.1750	0.1734	0.1864	0.1527	0.2077	0.1750
		(20.35)	(17.34)	(17.14)	(12.55)	(14.05)	(11.34)	(22.04)	(17.14)
Chauvinism		0.3369	0.3293	0.3301	0.3183	0.3594	0.3176	0.3382	0.3301
		(36.45)	(34.8)	(33.85)	(23.7)	(28.96)	(23.43)	(36.27)	(33.85)
Skill345	-0.0816	-0.0169	0.0070	-0.0204	-0.0913	-0.0713	0.0558	-0.0353	-0.0204
	(-2.16)	(-0.44)	(0.18)	(-0.51)	(-1.81)	(-1.28)	(1.04)	(-0.92)	(-0.51)
Skill345*GDPCAP	-0.0137	-0.0104	-0.0109	-0.0095	-0.0055	-0.0074	-0.0115	-0.0039	-0.0095
	(-6.36)	(-4.75)	(-4.88)	(-4.16)	(-1.74)	(-2.50)	(-3.30)	(-1.80)	(-4.16)
National mobility			-0.0174	-0.0048	0.0181	-0.0113	0.0095	0.0313	-0.0048
			(-1.18)	(-0.31)	(0.86)	(-0.56)	(0.45)	(2.05)	(-0.31)
International mobility			-0.1325	-0.1179	-0.1174	-0.1218	-0.0890	-0.1025	-0.1179
			(-7.22)	(-6.2)	(-4.68)	(-4.97)	(-3.47)	(-5.46)	(-6.2)
Never lived abroad			0.1132	0.1043	0.1141	0.1015	0.0848	0.0234	0.1043
			(6.35)	(5.64)	(4.67)	(4.46)	(3.29)	(1.31)	(5.64)
Age				0.0014	0.0027	0.0022	0.0008	0.0022	0.0014
				(2.98)	(3.51)	(3.55)	(1.21)	(4.72)	(2.98)
Woman				0.2222	0.2243	0.2592	0.1863	0.2251	0.2222
				(15.96)	(11.66)	(14.48)	(9.72)	(16.31)	(15.96)
Married				0.0333	0.0002	0.0233	0.0446	0.0156	0.0333
				(2.24)	(0.01)	(1.21)	(2.23)	(1.07)	(2.24)
Catholic				0.0667	0.0469	0.0652	0.1155	0.1302	0.0667
				(3.36)	(1.72)	(2.66)	(4.47)	(9.06)	(3.36)
Rural					0.1326				
					(5.84)				

Unemployed					0.0653				
					(1.12)				
Public sector					0.0363				
					(1.58)				
Self-employed					-0.0834				
					(-2.76)				
Trade union					0.0074				
					(1.62)				
Right-wing						-0.0706			
						(-7.47)			
Familiar with regional association (RA)							-0.0239		
							(-1.17)		
No benefit from RA							0.1364		
							(8.97)		
Stay independent from RA							0.0883		
							(6.15)		
Cut1	-1.7205	-0.2570	-0.2796	-0.0497	-0.2597	-0.2467	0.2368	0.0086	0.0260
Cut2	-0.8396	0.6801	0.6610	0.9021	0.7886	0.7804	1.1959	0.9344	0.9258
Cut3	-0.1743	1.3880	1.3734	1.6196	1.4807	1.4728	1.8647	1.6238	1.6433
Cut4	0.7632	2.3855	2.3719	2.6212	2.5015	2.5335	2.8431	2.5851	2.6449
No. obs.	26827	26365	25273	24278	13009	14737	13282	24278	24278
LR chi^2	3258.61	6151	6038.6	6065.92	3116.12	4320.99	3483.05	4488.98	6065.92
Prob > chi^2	0.0000	0.0000	0.0000	0.0000	0.0000	0.0000	0.0000	0.0000	0.0000
Pseudo R^2	0.0407	0.0781	0.0799	0.0835	0.0804	0.0979	0.0873	0.0618	0.0835
Log likelihood	-38412.2	-36294.3	-34784.6	-33281.2	-17815.5	-19904.5	-18216.6	-34069.7	-33281.2

Source: Authors' calculations using data from ISSP National Identity Survey 1995 and World Bank (1999).
T statistics are in parentheses.
a. Dependent variable is protect. Country dummy coefficients not reported.

(where Y is the vector of all independent variables), which is equivalent to the probability that:

$$\varepsilon < \mu_1 - \beta' Y, \tag{5}$$

or

$$\varphi(\mu_1 - \beta' Y), \tag{6}$$

where φ is the standard normal distribution. The probabilities that protect will take on any of the other possible values are similarly constructed. They depend on the respondent's characteristics, Y; the vector of estimated coefficients, β; the cutoff points, which are parameters to be estimated alongside β; and the standard normal distribution.

It follows that the marginal effect of changing an independent variable on the probability of a given outcome depends not only on β but on the standard normal density function evaluated using a particular choice of Y. A significant positive coefficient implies that changing the relevant independent variable increases the probability that protect takes on the value five, and reduces the probability that protect takes on the value one. The marginal effect of changing such a variable on the probability that protect takes on the values two–four is, however, a priori unclear. Initially we will simply estimate ordered probit models and will loosely speak of variables being either positively or negatively related to protectionism. Marginal effects will be estimated later.

In nearly all cases we include a full set of country dummy variables, to take account of country-level effects operating on all individuals within a country (coefficients not reported). Each column in table 3 indicates whether these dummies have been included or not. For all other variables the table reports the coefficient, with the t statistic in parentheses below.

Equation (1) provides a preliminary examination of the impact of skill. *Skill345* is a binary variable which takes the value one if the respondent's skill level is either three, four, or five, and zero if his or her skill level is one or two.[31] In what follows, we will loosely speak of the variable as indicating whether a respondent is high-skilled or not. The equation relates protectionism not only to this variable, but to *Skill345* interacted with the country's GDP per capita (measured in thousands of U.S. dollars).[32] The results indicate that the high-skilled are more predisposed toward free trade than the low-skilled, and the interaction term suggests that this effect is greater in rich countries

31. We will explore other skill-related specifications later.

32. These are the World Bank's data for 1995 PPP-adjusted GDP per capita, in 1995 international dollars.

than in poor countries, just as Heckscher-Ohlin theory predicts. Equations (2) through (9) indicate that the latter finding is quite robust to the inclusion of other variables (although the former is not). Since it is the interaction term which is crucial in testing Heckscher-Ohlin theory, it seems that, so far, preferences are entirely consistent with that theory.

Equation (2) in table 3 establishes that patriotism and chauvinism are both positively related to protectionism, as expected, with chauvinism having a larger impact. A glance across the table confirms that these findings are also extremely robust to the choice of specification: the hypothesis that nationalism is an important determinant of attitudes toward trade policy is, on the basis of these results, confirmed. However, nationalist attitudes are not all-important. Taking them into account still leaves scope for skill differentials to have an effect in ways that, as noted above, are consistent with economic theory.

National mobility has no consistent effect on attitudes, which is perhaps a surprise, but those who consider themselves to be internationally mobile, as well as those who have lived abroad in the past, are more positively disposed toward trade, supporting Rodrik's arguments.[33] Older people tend to be more protectionist, as are rural dwellers, women, Roman Catholics, and those in marital relationships (although the latter finding is not robust across specifications). There is a statistically weak but positive link between trade union membership and public sector employment and protectionism, while the self-employed are more likely to be free traders, as are those who can be identified as right wing on the basis of the political party they support.[34] The last three variables measure familiarity with, and attitudes toward, relevant regional associations (for example, the European Union, in Ireland's case). There was a negative but statistically insignificant relationship between familiarity with the association and protectionism. But those who felt that their country did not benefit from the association, as well as those who felt that their country should be protecting its independence, were more likely to be protectionist.[35]

Finally we experimented with our specification by including country GDP per capita, with and without country dummies.[36] With country dummies omitted, richer countries tend to be associated with a higher preference for free trade, but this relationship goes away (and indeed the sign of the coefficient is reversed) when country dummies are introduced. More importantly for our

33. Rodrik (1997).

34. Data on these variables are not available for all countries.

35. Again these regional integration questions were only asked in a subset of our countries.

36. An additional country dummy is of course dropped in the specification involving both country dummies and GDP per capita.

purposes, the sign of the interaction term between high skills and GDP per capita remains negative and significant in both these specifications. Another noteworthy feature of these regressions is that when country dummies are excluded, the coefficient on Roman Catholicism becomes much larger and more statistically significant, suggesting that variation in religious beliefs might be explaining cross-country differences in protectionist attitudes, as well as within-country differences. Roman Catholic social teaching has traditionally been more skeptical of the market than some brands of Protestantism, so these correlations make intuitive sense. On the other hand, Catholicism could be proxying across our set of countries for the Mediterranean region, which might have more protectionist attitudes for reasons unrelated to religion.

Table 4 explores the links between skill levels and preferences in greater detail.[37] The first regression in table 4 uses five dummy variables reflecting the five skill categories, rather than the single high-skill variable used in table 3, and as before introduces them into the regression both on their own, and interacted with GDP per capita. Using this finer grid does reveal several relationships consistent with Heckscher-Ohlin theory. Most importantly the coefficient on Skill1 is negative, suggesting that the lowest skilled are in favor of free trade. But the interaction term is positive, suggesting that the association between being low skilled and having protectionist preferences rises with incomes. The coefficients imply that in countries with per capita incomes below $11,942 in 1995 (roughly $1,000 more than incomes in Slovenia), belonging to the lowest skill category is associated with a preference for free trade, but that in countries with incomes higher than that amount those in the lowest category are more likely to be protectionist. We take this to be strong evidence in favor of the Heckscher-Ohlin hypothesis. A similar sign pattern emerges for *Skill2*, although the coefficient on *Skill2* itself (as opposed to its interaction term) is statistically insignificant. For *Skill3* and *Skill4* (but not *Skill5*), the sign of the interaction term becomes negative, again consistent with the theory, although the coefficients are statistically insignificant.

The second regression drops the interaction terms, but allows the coefficient on the high-skill variable to vary, depending on whether the economy is western, a transition economy, or the Philippines. In the West, high skills are strongly associated with a preference for free trade. They are also strongly associated with such a preference in the transition economies, although the coefficient is only about half the size as in the West. Finally the relationship

37. Country dummies were included for all regressions in tables 4 through 6.

Table 4. Different Specifications of Skill[a]

Variable	*(1)*	*(2)*
Patriotism	0.175	0.175
	(17.16)	(17.12)
Chauvinism	0.329	0.331
	(33.73)	(33.92)
Skill1	-0.162	
	(-1.90)	
Skill1*GDPCAP	0.0136	
	(2.67)	
Skill2	-0.068	
	(-0.90)	
Skill2*GDPCAP	0.0087	
	(2.02)	
Skill3	-0.019	
	(-0.21)	
Skill3*GDPCAP	-0.0031	
	(-0.63)	
Skill4	-0.098	
	(-1.12)	
Skill4*GDPCAP	-0.0017	
	(-0.36)	
Skill5	-0.300	
	(-2.80)	
Skill5*GDPCAP	0.0056	
	(0.96)	
Skill345*DWEST		-0.212
		(-9.99)
Skill345*DEAST		-0.104
		(-3.80)
Skill345*DPHILIPPINES		-0.013
		(-0.09)
National mobility	-0.005	-0.005
	(-0.35)	(-0.33)
International mobility	-0.117	-0.118
	(-6.16)	(-6.20)
Never lived abroad	0.102	0.104
	(5.50)	(5.61)
Age	0.002	0.001
	(3.37)	(2.90)
Woman	0.220	0.222
	(15.69)	(15.97)
Married	0.031	0.033
	(2.07)	(2.25)
Catholic	0.065	0.067
	(3.29)	(3.36)
Cut1	-0.063	-0.055
Cut2	0.890	0.897
Cut3	1.608	1.615
Cut4	2.610	2.616
Number of observations	24,278	24,278
LR chi^2	6097.800	6059.440
Prob > chi^2	0.000	0.000
Pseudo R^2	0.084	0.083
Log likelihood	-33265.257	-33284.436

Source: Authors' calculations using data from ISSP National Identity Survey 1995 and World Bank (1999).
T statistics are in parentheses.
a. Dependent variable is protect. Country dummies included (coefficients not reported).

Figure 1. Skill, Protectionism, and GDP

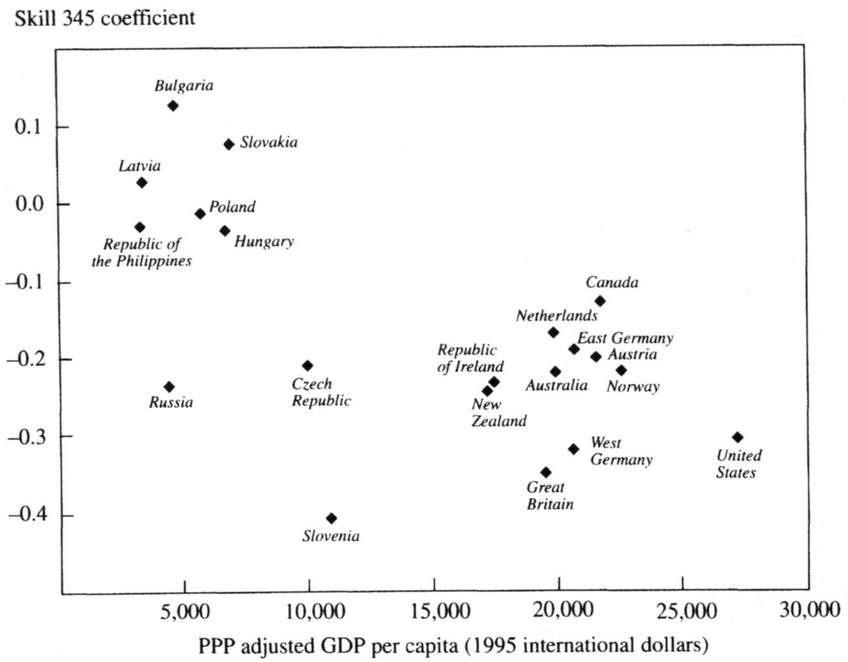

Source: Authors' calculations using data from ISSP National Identity Survey 1995 and World Bank (1999).

in the Philippines is insignificant. Again this is suggestive evidence in favor of the Heckscher-Ohlin world view.

Table A-2 pursues the same issue in a different way, again using the single "high-skill" dummy variable. It runs identical regressions (data permitting) for each country individually. While interesting patterns emerge for several of the other variables, our focus here is on the skill variable. Figure 1 plots the "high-skill" coefficient, for each country, against that country's GDP per capita. A clear negative association appears between the two variables (the correlation coefficient is -.634). That is, the richer the country, the more negative (less positive) is the association between high skills and protectionist attitudes. To the left of the picture, there is a cluster of poorer countries for which the coefficient on high skills is either close to zero or positive, while to the right of the picture are the rich countries in which high skills are clearly associated with a preference for free trade, rather than protection.[38]

38. We also ran a regression over the entire sample which included country dummies, the high-skill variable, and the high-skill variable interacted with country dummies (one country

Again, we take figure 1 to be strong evidence in favor of the Heckscher-Ohlin perspective. Of course, it might be objected that high skills are only associated with protectionism in three countries, and that the *t* statistics fall below conventional levels in all three cases (see table A-2). But we think that there is a convincing counter-argument (already suggested earlier in this paper), which, however, we are unable to provide evidence for given our current data set. Our sample of countries, while twenty times bigger than the samples used in previous studies, only contains twenty countries. There are many, poorer countries in which the high-skilled might be even more protectionist than in Bulgaria and Slovakia. One could imagine the negatively sloped relationship in figure 1 extending further to the left, with the countries of the world as a whole more evenly divided between those where skills are associated with protectionism, and those where skills are associated with liberal attitudes toward trade. Of course, this is pure speculation on our part. Nonetheless, the results we are able to obtain from these data seem entirely consistent with the insights of Eli Heckscher and Bertil Ohlin.

The evidence in figure 2, which plots the same coefficients against the average years of schooling in each country,[39] is less compelling. The correlation is much weaker (-.0993), and this is disturbing, since theory says that attitudes should be related to factor endowments, rather than income per capita. (The rationale for using income per capita is thus that it is correlated with the skill level of the population.) As can be seen from the figure, however, the Barro-Lee figures for schooling in several transition countries are very high. For example, average schooling is higher in Slovakia, Bulgaria, Latvia, and Poland than in the Netherlands, Ireland, and Austria. We doubt whether these figures provide a genuine reflection of the economically relevant human capital endowments of these economies, and thus doubt the usefulness of figure 2 as a test of the Heckscher-Ohlin theory.

Leaving aside the testing of trade theory for a moment, what other insights can be gleaned from table A-2? Patriotism and chauvinism are significantly related to protectionist attitudes in virtually all countries, with the size of the coefficients being fairly consistent throughout. Clearly, our findings regarding nationalism and trade policy preferences reflect a quite general phenomenon (at least in this sample of countries), rather than depending on

was of course omitted). The interaction terms were jointly highly statistically significant (and several individual interaction terms were also statistically significant), indicating that the skill coefficients are indeed significantly different across countries.

39. Taken from Barro and Lee (2000).

Figure 2. Skill, Protectionism, and H/L

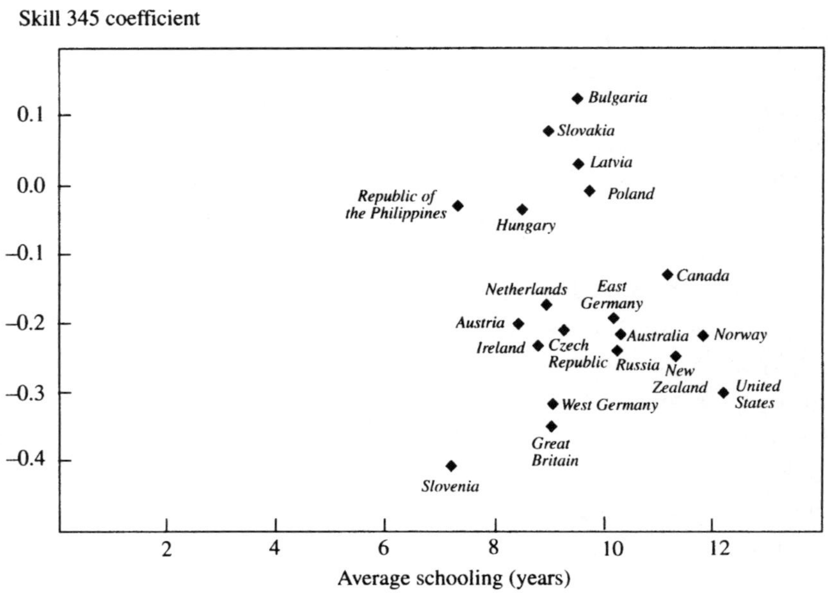

Source: Authors' calculations using data from ISSP National Identity Survey 1995 and Barro and Lee (2000), available at (www.cid.harvard.edu/ciddata/ciddata.html).

strong correlations in a few countries. There are several exceptions to the general rule that the old are more protectionist. They are significantly more likely to favor free trade in East Germany, Poland, and Estonia, all former Communist countries, and coefficients are statistically insignificant in several countries. The finding that women tend to be more protectionist than men is, however, a fairly general one.

Table 5 investigates the data further, by estimating models separately for various sub-samples of the data. The first four columns take a further look at cross-country variations in the data by splitting the sample into its western and former Communist components.[40] The high-skill coefficient in column 2 is positive (and statistically significant at the 10 percent level) in the east, and the interaction term between skills and GDP per capita is negative and significant, consistent with both Heckscher-Ohlin theory and figure 1. The results in column 2 suggest that in countries with per capita incomes below $4,215 (slightly lower than the Russian income) high-skilled workers are more likely to be protectionist, whereas they are more likely to support free trade

40. The Philippines is not included in either sample.

Table 5. Sensitivity Analysis[a]

Equation *Sample*	*(1)* *West* *only*	*(2)* *East* *only*	*(3)* *West* *only*	*(4)* *East* *only*	*(5)* *Men* *only*	*(6)* *Women* *only*	*(7)* *Immobile* *only*	*(8)* *Mobile* *only*
Patriotism	0.1672	0.1809	0.1699	0.1670	0.1772	0.1793	0.1760	0.1710
	(13.08)	(10.18)	(9.42)	(7.20)	(12.36)	(12.26)	(11.45)	(12.42)
Chauvinism	0.3692	0.2766	0.3463	0.2938	0.3340	0.3250	0.3240	0.3350
	(30.64)	(16.01)	(20.17)	(12.85)	(24.37)	(23.33)	(22.61)	(25.07)
Skill345	-0.1647	0.1037	-0.6101	0.1192	-0.0840	0.0517	0.0240	-0.0640
	(-1.01)	(1.66)	(-1.83)	(1.24)	(-1.41)	(0.96)	(0.44)	(-1.08)
Skill345*GDPCAP	-0.0027	-0.0246	0.0205	-0.0329	-0.0110	-0.0079	-0.0128	-0.0067
	(-0.35)	(-3.33)	(1.24)	(-2.53)	(-3.26)	(-2.55)	(-3.74)	(-2.08)
National mobility	-0.0089	-0.0080	0.0260	-0.0071	-0.0111	-0.0003		
	(-0.46)	(-0.29)	(0.96)	(-0.20)	(-0.50)	(-0.02)		
International mobility	-0.1150	-0.1380	-0.1380	-0.1195	-0.0936	-0.1476	-0.1510	-0.1230
	(-5.01)	(-3.78)	(-4.47)	(-2.43)	(-3.54)	(-5.37)	(-3.55)	(-5.69)
Never lived abroad	0.1200	0.0861	0.1501	0.0574	0.1483	0.0646	0.1090	0.1010
	(5.63)	(2.19)	(5.24)	(1.12)	(5.85)	(2.38)	(3.82)	(4.14)
Age	0.0003	0.0038	0.0015	0.0052	0.0027	0.0008	0.0010	0.0020
	(0.50)	(4.28)	(1.51)	(3.85)	(3.80)	(1.22)	(2.06)	(2.32)
Woman	0.2810	0.1187	0.3143	0.1041			0.1970	0.2490
	(16.42)	(4.70)	(12.74)	(3.11)			(9.61)	(13.03)
Married	0.0282	0.0487	-0.0242	0.0275	0.0125	0.0349	0.0610	0.0040
	(.54)	(1.82)	(-0.91)	(0.74)	(0.54)	(1.74)	(2.76)	(0.20)
Catholic	0.0472	0.0887	0.0593	0.0217	0.0852	0.0478	0.0680	0.0610
	(1.84)	(2.70)	(1.64)	(0.48)	(3.06)	(1.68)	(2.24)	(2.33)
Rural			0.1528	0.1496				
			(5.02)	(3.98)				
Unemployed			0.1067	0.0189				
			(1.48)	(0.19)				
Public sector			0.0035	0.0773				
			(0.13)	(1.71)				
Self-employed			-0.0432	-0.1055				
			(-1.18)	(-1.52)				
Trade union			0.0069	0.0100				
			(1.40)	(0.75)				
Cut1	0.0053	0.1404	-0.4000	-0.1878	0.0844	-0.4003	-0.0110	-0.0910
Cut2	1.0338	0.9306	0.7877	0.6078	1.0380	0.5692	0.8790	0.9080
Cut3	1.8017	1.5632	1.5314	1.2312	1.6756	1.3776	1.6260	1.6040
Cut4	2.9218	2.3338	2.6924	2.0111	2.6575	2.4011	2.5560	2.6810
Number of obs.	15977	7671	7887	4492	11811	12467	11499	12779
LR chi^2	4556.3	1381.3	2058.3	833.9	3134.7	2822.2	2658.9	3280.1
Prob > chi^2	0.0000	0.0000	0.0000	0.0000	0.0000	0.0000	0.0000	0.0000
Pseudo R^2	0.0957	0.0610	0.0885	0.0632	0.0866	0.0782	0.0780	0.0850
Log likelihood	-21523.6	-10640.3	-10595.9	-6176.5	-16522.4	-16631.2	-15622.3	-17579.1

Source: Authors' calculations using data from ISSP National Identity Survey 1995 and World Bank (1999).
T statistics are in parentheses.
a. Dependent variable is protect. Country dummies included (coefficients not reported).

in countries with higher incomes. The interaction term is insignificant within the West, which is again consistent with figure 1. There may be too little variation in the western data to pick up any relationship here.

The impact of gender appears to be much stronger in the West, although it is still strong in the East (consistent with Blanchflower, who finds that women are less satisfied with democracy). But age appears only to affect attitudes in the East.[41] Unemployment is weakly associated with protectionist attitudes in the west, but not at all in the east. Attitudes toward being unemployed may be quite different in a society undergoing rapid structural change than in a typical western economy. Interestingly, the impact of being rural appears to be almost identical in East and West. This is at odds with the intuition that western farmers should be more protectionist, since they are less competitive and more dependent on protection than their eastern counterparts. Of course agriculture is not the only rural industry, but it is the main one. The data are consistent with other rural characteristics of a sociological or even cultural nature driving these correlations.

We estimated the model for men and women separately. The results are given in columns 5 and 6. The most notable difference to our mind is that while age appears to matter for men, it does not matter for women. We were also interested in whether the gender effect was due to the fact that women are less likely to be in the labor force than men. We therefore estimated the model separately for those in the labor force and those outside it. The results (given in table 6) suggest that the gender effect is not due to lower female labor force participation, since the gender effect is actually stronger for those in the labor force than for those outside it.[42]

The last two columns in table 5 address the issue of whether those reporting themselves to be immobile (within the country) are less influenced by their skill type than those who are mobile. The reason for the question is that, arguably, the immobile should care more about their sector of employment (assuming that regions are largely dominated by particular industries). The hypothesis is rejected in that the interaction between skills and GDP per capita (the test of the Heckscher-Ohlin theory) is even stronger for the immobile than

41. Blanchflower (2001).

42. Moreover the gender effect remains unchanged when a labor force dummy variable is included in the model, estimated over the full sample (results available on request). We counted those in full-time and part-time work, as well as the unemployed, as being in the labor force. We could also have included those working less than fifteen hours a week and relatives assisting, but there were too few respondents in these categories (less than 500 across all countries) for this to be worthwhile.

Table 6. Sensitivity Analysis: Labor Force Participation and Age[a]

In labor force? *Sample*	*(1)* *In LF* *West* *only*	*(2)* *In LF* *East* *only*	*(3)* *Not in* *LF West* *only*	*(4)* *Not in* *LF East* *only*	*(5)* *Both* *West* *only*	*(6)* *Both* *East* *only*	*(7)* *Both* *West* *only*	*(8)* *Both* *East* *only*
Patriotism	0.1521	0.2029	0.2019	0.1239	0.1672	0.1812	0.1663	0.1811
	(9.43)	(9.64)	(9.53)	(3.68)	(13.07)	(10.19)	(12.99)	(10.18)
Chauvinism	0.3718	0.2776	0.3605	0.2789	0.3692	0.2772	0.3690	0.2767
	(24.69)	(13.58)	(17.75)	(8.57)	(30.62)	(16.04)	(30.61)	(15.01)
Skill345	-0.1692	0.0337	0.1633	0.3667	-0.1647	0.0948	-0.0717	-0.0697
	(-0.87)	(0.50)	(0.50)	(1.86)	(-1.01)	(1.52)	(-0.41)	(-0.67)
Skill345*age							-0.0020	0.0038
							(-1.55)	(1.99)
Skill345*GDPCAP	-0.0029	-0.0193	-0.0167	-0.0498	-0.0027	-0.0244	-0.0029	-0.0246
	(-0.31)	(-2.48)	(-1.07)	(-1.99)	(-0.35)	(-3.31)	(-0.38)	(-3.33)
National mobility	0.0098	-0.0283	-0.0467	0.0364	-0.0089	-0.0105	-0.0085	-0.0117
	(0.40)	(-0.87)	(-1.49)	(0.65)	(-0.46)	(-0.38)	(-0.44)	(-0.42)
International mobility	-0.1321	-0.0955	-0.0801	-0.2897	-0.1150	-0.1345	-0.1160	-0.1351
	(-4.76)	(-2.33)	(-1.94)	(-3.55)	(-5.01)	(-3.68)	(-5.05)	(-3.70)
Never lived abroad	0.1481	0.1278	0.0758	0.0240	0.1199	0.0856	0.1191	0.0892
	(5.56)	(2.64)	(2.12)	(0.35)	(5.63)	(2.18)	(5.59)	(2.26)
Age	0.0000	0.0062	0.0001	0.0032	0.0001	0.0148	0.0003	0.0136
	(0.03)	(4.18)	(0.08)	(2.19)	(0.05)	(3.13)	(0.09)	(2.86)
Age-squared					0.0000	-0.0001	0.0000	-0.0001
					(0.05)	(-2.37)	(0.14)	(-2.30)
Woman	0.3059	0.1497	0.2316	0.0587	0.2810	0.1173	0.2793	0.1213
	(13.78)	(4.91)	(7.89)	(1.26)	(16.42)	(4.64)	(16.29)	(4.79)
Married	-0.0023	-0.0143	0.0903	0.1340	0.0286	0.0243	0.0287	0.0264
	(-0.09)	(-0.42)	(3.09)	(2.89)	(1.44)	(0.85)	(1.45)	(0.92)
Catholic	0.0441	0.0928	0.0605	0.0707	0.0472	0.0882	0.0465	0.0888
	(1.42)	(2.31)	(1.31)	(1.22)	(1.84)	(2.68)	(1.81)	(2.70)
Cut1	-0.2033	0.3189	0.0707	-0.2083	0.2035	0.3440	0.0135	0.3059
Cut2	0.8476	1.1260	1.0620	0.5484	1.2319	1.1342	1.0419	1.0961
Cut3	1.5838	1.7013	1.8914	1.3419	1.9999	1.7670	1.8099	1.7290
Cut4	2.6954	2.4932	3.0286	2.0781	3.1200	2.5382	2.9302	2.5006
Number of obs.	9808	5242	6169	2429	15977	7671	15977	7671
LR chi^2	2719.3	965.1	1749.5	386.0	4556.3	1386.9	4558.7	1390.9
Prob > chi^2	0.0000	0.0000	0.0000	0.0000	0.0000	0.0000	0.0000	0.0000
Pseudo R^2	0.0921	0.0611	0.0977	0.0572	0.0957	0.0612	0.0958	0.0614
Log likelihood	-13403.0	-7412.3	-8083.3	-3179.0	-21524	-10637	-21522	-10635

Source: Authors' calculations using data from ISSP National Identity Survey 1995 and World Bank (1999).
T statistics are in parentheses.
a. Dependent variable is protect. Country dummies included (coefficients not reported).

for the mobile. (We also experimented by including interaction terms between skill and mobility in various models, but these interaction terms are always insignificant.)

Finally, table 6 explores the effect of age on protectionist attitudes in greater detail. Consistent with our expectations, age squared has a negative coefficient in the East, suggesting that the marginal effect of age declines as respondents get older. Age remains insignificant in the West, but important in the East. Could it be that the overall correlation between age and attitudes is simply being driven by the length of time over which East-bloc respondents were exposed to Communist ideology? Two pieces of evidence suggest not. First, columns 7 and 8 in table 6 introduce an interaction term between skill and age. In the West the term is negative (and significant, at the 12.5 percent level), suggesting that the high-skilled become more pro-free trade the older they get. If respondents' human capital increases with age, as the labor economics literature suggests, then this is precisely what one would expect. On the other hand, in the East the high-skilled become more protectionist the older they get. This is consistent with the skills acquired under communism being largely irrelevant to a modern economy, and to these individuals' position in society being threatened by liberalization.[43] The second piece of evidence suggesting that age is influencing attitudes through economic channels is given in columns 2 and 4 of table 6. These show that the impact of age on protectionist attitudes is much larger for those in the labor force than for those not in it.

So much for statistical significance. What about the quantitative impact of these variables on attitudes toward protection? In order to answer this question, we began by estimating the model in column 4 of table 3, and then set all right-hand-side variables equal to their median values. Having done that, we calculated the impact of changing each individual independent variable on the probabilities that "protect" would take on each of the values one to five. For binary variables, we considered the impact of changing the variable from zero to one; for other variables we explored more complicated changes, as discussed below.

Our point estimates of the coefficients and cutoff points, together with the assumption that other variables are set equal to their median values, produce a point estimate of the impact of changing a given independent variable on the dependent variable. On the other hand, our coefficients are estimated with uncertainty. We therefore estimated our impact effects with 95 percent confidence intervals, to reflect the fact that different samples would have produced

43. Indeed labor economists have found that the "return to experience obtained under communism fell during the transition" (Svejnar 1999, p. 2839).

Table 7. Simulating the Impact of Changing Dependent Variables

Variable	*Pr(protect=1)*	*Pr(protect=2)*	*Pr(protect=3)*	*Pr(protect=4)*	*Pr(protect=5)*
Benchmark (simulated probability, equation 4, table 3)	0.0148	0.0954	0.1954	0.3833	0.3111
Impact of changing patriotism					
from 40th to 60th percentile	-0.0023	-0.0090	-0.0093	+0.0004	+0.0203
from 20th to 80th percentile	-0.0117	-0.0451	-0.0464	+0.0022	+0.1011
Impact of changing chauvinism					
from 40th to 60th percentile	-0.0062	-0.0249	-0.0267	-0.0005	+0.0582
from 20th to 80th percentile	-0.0247	-0.0901	-0.0894	+0.0065	+0.1977
Impact of being high-skilled					
when GDP per capita = $5,000	+0.0027	+0.0103	+0.0106	-0.0007	-0.0229
when GDP per capita = $15,000	+0.0072	+0.0263	+0.0253	-0.0042	-0.0547
when GDP per capita = $25,000	+0.0128	+0.0436	+0.0390	-0.0109	-0.0844
Impact of					
being female	-0.0106	-0.0372	-0.0342	+0.0080	+0.0739
being internationally mobile	+0.0050	+0.0188	+0.0186	-0.0021	-0.0402
never having lived abroad	-0.0044	-0.0166	-0.0166	+0.0017	+0.0359

Source: Authors' calculations using data from ISSP National Identity Survey 1995 and World Bank (1999).

different coefficient estimates.[44] Full results, including confidence intervals, are given in table A-3. Table 7 provides a summary of the most important results (point estimates only).

The first row simply presents the simulated probabilities that an observation will take on any of the five values of the dependent variable, protect. As can be seen, there is nearly a 20 percent probability that protect takes on the value three, a 38 percent probability that it takes on the value four, and a 31 percent probability that it takes on the value five. The rows immediately below give the impact of changing our nationalism variables on all five probabilities. In the following discussion we focus on the probability that protect takes on the value five. Increasing patriotism from its fortieth to sixtieth percentile increases the probability that protect takes on the value five by two percentage points, with a 95 percent confidence interval of 1.79 to 2.28 percentage points (table A-3). Changing chauvinism from its fortieth to sixtieth percentile increases the probability that protect takes on its highest value by 5.8

44. All results were produced using *Clarify*, as described in Tomz, Wittenberg, and King (1999) and King, Tomz, and Wittenberg (2000).

percentage points. If these two variables are changed from their twentieth to their eightieth percentiles, the impact on protect is enormous. The probability of the most protectionist response occurring increases by 10.1 percentage points in the case of patriotism, an increase of 32 percent over the benchmark simulated probability. In the case of chauvinism, the impact is to increase the probability that protect equals five by 19.8 percentage points, an increase of 64 percent (with a 95 percent confidence interval of 18.4 to 21.2 percentage points). These are huge effects by any standards.

No other variable has an impact as big as chauvinism, although some come close. The interaction term between high-skill and GDP per capita in the equation indicates that the effect of being high-skilled on protectionist attitudes depends on how rich the country is. The next three rows therefore indicate the impact of being high-skilled in economies with GDPs per capita of $5,000, $15,000, and $25,000, respectively. As the regression results (and Heckscher-Ohlin logic) suggest, the impact on protectionism is much greater in the richer countries. Thus, the probability that protect is five declines by only 2.3 percentage points in the poorest country, but by 5.5 percentage points in the middle-income country, and by 8.4 percentage points in the rich country (a fall of 27 percent). Clearly skill has a large effect on preferences in rich countries.

The only other variable to matter to this extent was gender. Being a woman increases the probability of the most protectionist response by 7.4 percentage points, or 24 percent. This is clearly a large effect. Being internationally mobile reduces the probability that protect takes on the value five by 4 percentage points, while never having lived abroad increases that probability by almost the same amount (3.6 percentage points). The other variables do not have a particularly large effect on attitudes (table A-3).

We then generated the simulated probabilities implied by the model given in column five of table 3. This allowed us to explore the impact of further variables, not available for all countries, on preferences (all results are given in table A-3). The simulated probability that protect would take on the value five was equal to nearly 26 percent. Being a rural dweller increases this probability by 4.4 percentage points, quite a large effect, but being unemployed only increases it (surprisingly, it might be argued) by 2.1 percentage points. Belonging to a trade union has almost no impact on attitudes, which again seems surprising. But being self-employed reduces the probability of an extreme protectionist response by some 2.6 percentage points.

What Have We Learned?

There are a number of key results from this study.

First protectionist attitudes are strongly related to both patriotism and chauvinism. This is a quite general result across countries, and the effect is quantitatively as well as statistically significant. To that extent it would appear that trade policy preferences are heavily influenced by noneconomic—in this case cultural or ideological—factors. Nationalism is, of course, a complex phenomenon with many roots, including, as noted above, adverse economic experiences and conditions. A totally economic-determinist or reductionist explanation of nationalism is, however, implausible. It seems safe, therefore, to conclude that nationalist attitudes exercise some autonomous influence and are a significant factor in the genesis of protectionist policy preferences.

The second result is that even when cultural or ideological factors are taken into account, skill matters for policy preferences, and the effect that skill has on those preferences varies across countries in ways which are consistent with Heckscher-Ohlin theory. Roughly speaking, in countries with per capita incomes below $12,000, the lowest skilled tend to be more in favor of free trade, while they tend to be more protectionist in countries above that income threshold. Belonging to one of the higher skill categories only shifts attitudes in a slightly more liberal direction in poor countries. The effect is a large one in rich countries. Finally, there seems to be a strong negative relationship between the impact of skills on protectionist attitudes, on the one hand, and income per capita on the other. That is, high skills are generally associated with a preference for free trade, and this effect is stronger in richer countries than in poorer countries. Indeed, in some of the poorest countries in our truncated sample, high skills are, albeit weakly, associated with a preference for protection.

Third we have found evidence of a pronounced gender gap regarding trade policy preferences, which is quantitatively important and apparently consistent across countries. We have no explanation for this phenomenon, though we note that it is consistent with findings regarding the persistence of gender differences in support for European integration even after controlling for the effects of a wide range of other variables.[45]

45. Wessels (1995, pp. 111–14). Similarly Carol Graham and Stefano Pettinato find that Latin American men are more likely to have pro-market attitudes (Graham and Pettinato, 2000), and to agree with the proposition that trade is "very important" to their country's prosperity (Graham and Pettinato 2002).

In terms of the economic debates surrounding the determinants of protectionist attitudes, we have, as stated, found evidence broadly consistent with the Heckscher-Ohlin viewpoint. What we have not been able to do, given the data we are currently working with, is to compare the impact of skills on protectionist attitudes with the impact of the sector of employment. Nor have we been able to follow Scheve and Slaughter in exploring the impact of home ownership. We will shortly have access to a data set from the Republic of Ireland that includes both these variables, and we intend to pursue these questions via this avenue. Unfortunately, that analysis, like that of Scheve and Slaughter, will lack a cross-country comparative dimension. However, it is our intention in the future to organize the collection of relevant data across a broad range of countries that will allow us to address all these issues on an appropriate comparative scale.

Table A-1. Summary Statistics, Selected Variables

Country	Variable	Protect	Patriotism	Chauvinism	Skill	National mobility	International mobility
Australia	Obs	2398	2398	2339	2181	2407	2404
	Mean	3.997	3.956	2.952	2.934	0.619	0.204
	Std.dev.	0.988	0.677	0.862	1.262	0.486	0.403
W.Germany	Obs	1255	1248	1234	709	1171	1193
	Mean	3.083	3.089	2.672	2.677	0.638	0.220
	Std.dev.	1.232	0.922	0.960	1.074	0.481	0.415
E. Germany	Obs	604	596	589	306	569	577
	Mean	3.563	3.136	2.818	2.699	0.571	0.125
	Std.dev.	1.189	0.900	0.957	1.063	0.495	0.331
Britain	Obs	1043	1029	1016	1006	974	982
	Mean	3.723	3.535	3.322	2.613	0.574	0.231
	Std.dev.	1.004	0.817	0.830	1.174	0.495	0.422
United States	Obs	1343	1348	1281	1300	1336	1340
	Mean	3.707	3.972	3.113	2.746	0.738	0.166
	Std.dev.	1.016	0.705	0.841	1.204	0.440	0.373
Austria	Obs	1007	1007	1007	505	1007	1007
	Mean	3.873	3.871	3.422	2.638	0.393	0.127
	Std.dev.	1.163	0.820	0.888	1.256	0.489	0.333
Hungary	Obs	998	995	996	913	997	1000
	Mean	4.047	3.285	3.430	2.318	0.311	0.094
	Std.dev.	1.075	0.779	0.805	1.082	0.463	0.292
Italy	Obs	1093	1090	1090	0	1091	1094
	Mean	3.571	3.067	3.112	...	0.630	0.224
	Std.dev.	1.216	0.873	0.778	...	0.483	0.417
Ireland	Obs	991	994	988	908	987	986
	Mean	3.650	3.729	3.342	2.439	0.421	0.173
	Std.dev.	1.128	0.684	0.709	1.171	0.494	0.379
Netherlands	Obs	2071	2070	2052	1702	2035	2048
	Mean	2.912	3.065	2.881	2.791	0.639	0.250
	Std.dev.	0.992	0.789	0.812	1.018	0.480	0.433
Norway	Obs	1494	1492	1458	1280	1485	1491
	Mean	3.144	3.537	3.144	2.665	0.602	0.192
	Std.dev.	1.038	0.739	0.846	1.121	0.490	0.394
Sweden	Obs	1284	1274	1265	0	1245	1265
	Mean	3.228	3.290	3.042	...	0.590	0.288
	Std.dev.	1.081	0.800	0.869	...	0.492	0.453
Czech Republic	Obs	1109	1111	1099	970	1068	1104
	Mean	3.415	3.110	3.129	2.533	0.488	0.121
	Std.dev.	1.294	0.806	0.817	1.041	0.500	0.327
Slovenia	Obs	1036	1035	1035	823	1036	1036
	Mean	3.465	3.229	3.292	2.350	0.378	0.125
	Std.dev.	1.174	0.792	0.791	0.992	0.485	0.330
Poland	Obs	1582	1573	1556	1454	1094	1564
	Mean	3.787	3.456	3.458	2.221	0.441	0.187
	Std.dev.	1.083	0.731	0.714	0.914	0.497	0.390
Bulgaria	Obs	1102	1098	1095	996	1097	1099
	Mean	4.190	3.582	3.998	2.228	0.418	0.257
	Std.dev.	1.090	0.865	0.750	1.130	0.493	0.437
Russia	Obs	1585	1585	1585	807	1585	1585
	Mean	3.670	3.297	3.517	2.530	0.218	0.107
	Std.dev.	1.282	0.831	0.805	1.067	0.413	0.310

(continued overleaf)

Table A-1 (continued)

Country	*Variable*	*Protect*	*Patriotism*	*Chauvinism*	*Skill*	*National mobility*	*International mobility*
New Zealand	Obs	1019	1015	996	633	1018	1021
	Mean	3.406	3.798	3.060	2.866	0.623	0.245
	Std.dev.	1.147	0.693	0.798	1.263	0.485	0.430
Canada	Obs	1525	1527	1496	923	1519	1519
	Mean	3.264	3.831	2.707	3.115	0.722	0.286
	Std.dev.	1.135	0.823	0.809	0.963	0.448	0.452
Philippines	Obs	1200	1200	1198	633	1200	1200
	Mean	3.624	3.613	3.430	1.790	0.469	0.279
	Std.dev.	0.918	0.633	0.564	0.897	0.499	0.449
Japan	Obs	1252	1252	1247	0	1256	1256
	Mean	2.919	3.931	2.890	...	0.318	0.076
	Std.dev.	1.282	0.740	0.950	...	0.466	0.265
Estonia	Obs	1221	1221	1221	0	1221	1221
	Mean	3.813	3.260	3.362	...	0.498	0.215
	Std.dev.	0.906	0.760	0.692	...	0.500	0.411
Latvia	Obs	1041	1026	1026	434	1027	1035
	Mean	4.042	3.146	3.252	2.816	0.251	0.135
	Std.dev.	1.180	0.831	0.828	1.136	0.434	0.342
Slovakia	Obs	1388	1388	1388	1222	1359	1388
	Mean	3.488	3.029	2.851	2.265	0.531	0.241
	Std.dev.	1.273	0.906	0.926	0.982	0.499	0.428

Source: Authors' calculations using data from ISSP National Identity Survey 1995.

Table A-2. Country-Specific Models[a]

Variable	*Australia*	*West Germany*	*East Germany*	*Great Britain*	*United States*	*Austria*	*Hungary*	*Italy*
Patriotism	0.240	0.128	0.246	0.159	0.286	0.057	0.053	0.174
	(5.63)	(2.07)	(2.52)	(2.78)	(5.39)	(1.09)	(0.98)	(3.91)
Chauvinism	0.344	0.425	0.433	0.510	0.419	0.454	0.225	0.299
	(9.76)	(7.12)	(4.85)	(9.18)	(9.54)	(8.97)	(4.62)	(6.01)
Skill345	-0.216	-0.318	-0.191	-0.352	-0.300	-0.201	-0.035	...
	(-4.04)	(-3.59)	(-1.40)	(-4.38)	(-4.58)	(-2.20)	(-0.41)	...
National mobility	0.029	-0.215	-0.338	0.089	0.056	-0.158	-0.052	0.069
	(0.51)	(-2.23)	(-2.38)	(1.08)	(0.74)	(-1.94)	(-0.62)	(0.94)
International mobility	-0.119	-0.187	-0.123	-0.124	0.001	-0.154	-0.160	-0.027
	(-1.76)	(-1.77)	(-0.63)	(-1.28)	(0.01)	(-1.33)	(-1.22)	(-0.31)
Never lived abroad	0.102	0.188	0.443	0.073	0.099	0.174	-0.103	0.271
	(1.81)	(1.66)	(1.47)	(0.84)	(1.31)	(1.77)	(-0.73)	(2.64)
Age	0.003	-0.002	-0.013	0.003	0.002	-0.003	0.005	0.000
	(1.66)	(-0.37)	(-1.96)	(1.08)	(1.18)	(-1.38)	(1.90)	(0.19)
Woman	0.333	0.405	0.680	0.191	0.155	0.311	0.074	0.215
	(6.29)	(4.53)	(5.06)	(2.54)	(2.44)	(4.34)	(0.98)	(3.28)
Married	-0.060	-0.199	0.125	0.005	0.113	0.180	0.010	0.152
	(-0.99)	(-2.06)	(0.82)	(0.07)	(1.79)	(2.44)	(0.14)	(2.09)
Catholic	0.083	0.014	-0.166	0.077	-0.031	-0.076	-0.033	-0.130
	(1.33)	(0.16)	(-0.46)	(0.61)	(-0.42)	(-0.83)	(-0.42)	(-0.84)
Cut1	-0.321	-0.177	0.047	-0.100	0.529	-0.173	-0.961	0.228
Cut2	0.863	0.971	1.255	1.228	1.431	0.750	-0.291	1.050
Cut3	1.401	1.728	1.912	2.040	2.223	1.267	0.468	1.567
Cut4	2.679	2.716	2.888	3.325	3.546	2.226	1.172	2.535
Number of obs.	1827	648	285	906	1225	985	930	1084
LR chi^2	313.120	179.890	104.600	243.020	276.110	226.380	50.160	124.830
Prob > chi^2	0.000	0.000	0.000	0.000	0.000	0.000	0.000	0.000
Pseudo R^2	0.067	0.091	0.120	0.098	0.083	0.083	0.021	0.039
Log likelihood	-2164.910	-899.460	-385.137	-1113.125	-1535.116	-1255.603	-1188.651	-1553.800

Source: Authors' calculations using data from ISSP National Identity Survey 1995. *T* statistics are in parentheses.
a. Dependent variable is protect.

(*continued overleaf*)

Table A-2. Country-Specific Models[a] (continued)

Variable	*Ireland*	*Netherlands*	*Norway*	*Sweden*	*Czech Republic*	*Slovenia*	*Poland*	*Bulgaria*
Patriotism	0.197	0.073	0.218	0.337	0.154	0.254	0.171	0.103
	(3.33)	(2.01)	(4.51)	(7.26)	(3.12)	(4.59)	(2.94)	(2.14)
Chauvinism	0.335	0.480	0.281	0.352	0.318	0.357	0.231	0.397
	(5.63)	(12.71)	(6.83)	(8.39)	(6.82)	(6.57)	(3.99)	(7.41)
Skill345	-0.233	-0.170	-0.217	...	-0.212	-0.407	-0.009	0.128
	(-2.81)	(-3.19)	(-3.56)	...	(-2.85)	(-4.97)	(-0.11)	(1.50)
National mobility	-0.038	-0.036	-0.098	-0.113	-0.068	-0.090	-0.009	0.017
	(-0.44)	(-0.65)	(-1.52)	(-1.62)	(-0.94)	(-1.09)	(-0.11)	(0.21)
International mobility	-0.110	-0.087	-0.281	-0.275	-0.125	-0.109	-0.034	-0.219
	(-1.01)	(-1.35)	(-3.43)	(-3.45)	(-1.10)	(-0.90)	(-0.35)	(-2.29)
Never lived abroad	0.139	0.123	0.160	0.135	0.034	0.069	0.142	0.161
	(1.72)	(1.78)	(2.21)	(1.79)	(0.33)	(0.77)	(1.29)	(1.43)
Age	-0.002	0.001	0.000	0.006	0.010	-0.001	-0.005	0.002
	(-0.88)	(0.69)	(-0.16)	(2.68)	(4.23)	(-0.21)	(-2.11)	(0.87)
Woman	0.371	0.335	0.235	0.506	0.217	0.109	0.034	0.019
	(4.96)	(6.59)	(4.11)	(8.00)	(3.17)	(1.48)	(0.47)	(0.27)
Married	-0.035	0.111	0.038	-0.070	0.032	-0.082	-0.102	0.139
	(-0.45)	(2.07)	(0.59)	(-1.02)	(0.44)	(-0.97)	(-1.30)	(1.74)
Catholic	0.051	0.061	-0.923	-0.164	0.095	0.064	0.057	-0.573
	(0.35)	(0.95)	(-2.27)	(-0.46)	(1.32)	(0.72)	(0.54)	(-0.97)
Cut1	-0.149	0.097	-0.150	0.783	0.563	-0.071	-0.724	0.454
Cut2	1.147	1.551	1.072	1.769	1.315	1.171	0.198	0.750
Cut3	1.510	2.503	2.050	2.885	1.929	1.873	0.894	1.445
Cut4	2.679	3.794	3.228	3.990	2.709	2.702	1.838	2.181
Number of obs.	866	1827	1391	1186	994	876	951	1050
LR chi^2	126.500	372.290	263.010	383.120	177.000	186.410	58.420	132.090
Prob > chi^2	0.000	0.000	0.000	0.000	0.000	0.000	0.000	0.000
Pseudo R^2	0.053	0.074	0.067	0.110	0.057	0.071	0.022	0.053
Log likelihood	-1133.695	-2325.767	-1845.643	-1547.066	-1461.511	-1214.625	-1320.243	-1192.092

Table A-2. Country-Specific Models[a] (continued)

Variable	*Russia*	*New Zealand*	*Canada*	*Philippines*	*Japan*	*Estonia*	*Latvia*	*Slovakia*
Patriotism	0.201	0.120	0.117	0.127	0.142	0.135	0.140	0.288
	(3.96)	(2.12)	(2.24)	(1.79)	(2.96)	(2.67)	(1.90)	(6.94)
Chauvinism	0.323	0.400	0.354	0.103	0.312	0.295	0.237	0.171
	(6.31)	(8.05)	(6.47)	(1.31)	(8.16)	(5.22)	(3.22)	(4.46)
Skill345	-0.237	-0.246	-0.129	-0.030	...	...	0.030	0.078
	(-2.96)	(-3.04)	(-1.48)	(-0.19)	...	...	(0.26)	(1.11)
National mobility	0.182	-0.035	0.121	0.205	-0.004	0.162	0.012	0.025
	(1.97)	(-0.44)	(1.27)	(2.18)	(-0.06)	(2.14)	(0.10)	(0.39)
International mobility	-0.165	0.005	-0.142	0.030	-0.124	0.083	-0.217	-0.137
	(-1.34)	(0.06)	(-1.54)	(0.29)	(-1.03)	(0.91)	(-1.39)	(-1.81)
Never lived abroad	-0.187	0.140	0.028	-0.091	0.091	-0.153	0.162	0.120
	(-1.05)	(1.86)	(0.33)	(-0.58)	(0.66)	(-1.53)	(1.21)	(1.20)
Age	0.013	0.007	-0.005	0.000	-0.003	-0.005	0.014	0.004
	(3.53)	(2.88)	(-1.31)	(-0.13)	(-1.46)	(-2.58)	(2.70)	(2.03)
Woman	0.201	0.242	0.169	0.083	0.389	0.127	0.003	0.133
	(2.58)	(3.37)	(2.12)	(0.89)	(6.32)	(1.96)	(0.03)	(2.25)
Married	0.218	-0.177	0.090	0.071	-0.070	0.138	-0.179	0.038
	(2.58)	(-2.27)	(1.03)	(0.68)	(-0.99)	(2.00)	(-1.43)	(0.62)
Catholic	...	-0.070	0.187	-0.053	0.415	0.433	0.376	0.087
	...	(-0.69)	(2.24)	(-0.45)	(1.09)	(3.72)	(2.47)	(1.44)
Cut1	0.653	0.222	-0.305	-1.653	0.619	-0.770	0.124	0.285
Cut2	1.486	1.285	0.767	-0.121	1.127	0.375	0.786	1.050
Cut3	2.053	1.931	1.536	0.442	2.099	1.107	1.264	1.651
Cut4	2.774	3.001	2.591	1.968	2.718	2.543	1.834	2.455
Number of obs.	821	893	727	630	1228	1184	418	1346
LR chi^2	127.990	159.410	81.440	14.850	166.810	107.660	47.200	204.910
Prob > chi^2	0.000	0.000	0.000	0.138	0.000	0.000	0.000	0.000
Pseudo R^2	0.052	0.060	0.038	0.010	0.044	0.036	0.041	0.049
Log likelihood	-1177.318	-1252.144	-1034.937	-775.849	-1817.111	-1425.143	-546.282	-1970.547

Source: Authors' calculations using data from ISSP National Identity Survey 1995. T statistics are in parentheses.
a. Dependent variable is protect.

Table A-3. Simulating the Impact on Preferences of Changing RHS Variables

A. Equation (4), table 3

Simulated Probability	*Mean*	*Std. Dev.*	*[95% Conf. Interval]*	
Pr(protect=1)	.014755	.0014167	.0121608	.0177452
Pr(protect=2)	.0954396	.0055841	.0846833	.1061769
Pr(protect=3)	.195409	.0062344	.1829937	.2076478
Pr(protect=4)	.3832816	.0036822	.376044	.390276
Pr(protect=5)	.3111148	.0128818	.286102	.3362912

First Difference: Change Patriotism from 40th to 60th percentile

Change in Probability	*Mean*	*Std. Dev.*	*[95% Conf. Interval]*	
dPr(protect=1)	-.0023152	.0002286	-.0027948	-.001922
dPr(protect=2)	-.0090372	.0006171	-.0102836	-.0079466
dPr(protect=3)	-.0093477	.0005717	-.0105066	-.0082473
dPr(protect=4)	.0004353	.0007389	-.0010632	.001884
dPr(protect=5)	.0202647	.0012482	.0178992	.0227651

First Difference: Change Patriotism from 20th to 80th percentile

Change in Probability	*Mean*	*Std. Dev.*	*[95% Conf. Interval]*	
dPr(protect=1)	-.0117189	.0011616	-.0141546	-.0097234
dPr(protect=2)	-.045126	.0030677	-.051317	-.0397028
dPr(protect=3)	-.0463831	.0028001	-.0520588	-.0409887
dPr(protect=4)	.0021564	.0036593	-.0052714	.0093273
dPr(protect=5)	.1010716	.0061935	.0893281	.1134693

First Difference: Change Chauvinism from 40th to 60th percentile

Change in Probability	*Mean*	*Std. Dev.*	*[95% Conf. Interval]*	
dPr(protect=1)	-.0061805	.0005189	-.0072785	-.0051952
dPr(protect=2)	-.0248769	.001137	-.0270738	-.0226583
dPr(protect=3)	-.0266989	.0009393	-.0285721	-.0249653
dPr(protect=4)	-.0004574	.0020837	-.0047143	.0036249
dPr(protect=5)	.0582136	.0020582	.0541598	.0622817

First Difference: Change Chauvinism from 20th to 80th percentile

Change in Probability	*Mean*	*Std. Dev.*	*[95% Conf. Interval]*	
dPr(protect=1)	-.0247046	.0020259	-.0289362	-.0207627
dPr(protect=2)	-.0900888	.0039576	-.097731	-.0822445
dPr(protect=3)	-.0894131	.0031579	-.0956985	-.083667
dPr(protect=4)	.0065264	.0070095	-.0078236	.0199749
dPr(protect=5)	.1976801	.0069093	.1840308	.2115107

First Difference: Impact of high-skill when GDP per capita = $5000

Change in Probability	Mean	Std. Dev.	[95% Conf. Interval]	
dPr(protect=1)	.0026699	.0012682	.0001494	.0052034
dPr(protect=2)	.0103182	.004741	.0006345	.0194862
dPr(protect=3)	.0105686	.0047525	.0006773	.0195221
dPr(protect=4)	-.0006657	.0010204	-.0030787	.0010019
dPr(protect=5)	-.0228909	.0102694	-.0420419	-.0014672

First Difference: Impact of high-skill when GDP per capita = $15000

Change in Probability	Mean	Std. Dev.	[95% Conf. Interval]	
dPr(protect=1)	.0072067	.0009877	.0053957	.0093273
dPr(protect=2)	.0263177	.002958	.0206797	.0324438
dPr(protect=3)	.025299	.0026539	.0202207	.0305039
dPr(protect=4)	-.0041574	.0021097	-.0083383	-.0003163
dPr(protect=5)	-.0546661	.0057117	-.0655149	-.0436477

First Difference: Impact of high-skill when GDP per capita = $25000

Change in Probability	Mean	Std. Dev.	[95% Conf. Interval]	
dPr(protect=1)	.0127708	.0020405	.0090668	.0170057
dPr(protect=2)	.0436224	.0054026	.0330583	.0541702
dPr(protect=3)	.0389498	.003894	.0312127	.0462664
dPr(protect=4)	-.0109429	.004037	-.019564	-.0036387
dPr(protect=5)	-.0844001	.008483	-.1006383	-.0677581

First Difference: Impact of national mobility

Change in Probability	Mean	Std. Dev.	[95% Conf. Interval]	
dPr(protect=1)	.0001647	.000602	-.0009862	.0013277
dPr(protect=2)	.0006607	.0024323	-.0039293	.0052194
dPr(protect=3)	.0007024	.002618	-.004298	.0055967
dPr(protect=4)	-3.03e-06	.0002122	-.0004342	.0004178
dPr(protect=5)	-.0015247	.0056915	-.0121468	.0094165

First Difference: Impact of international mobility

Change in Probability	Mean	Std. Dev.	[95% Conf. Interval]	
dPr(protect=1)	.0049903	.0009142	.0032012	.0068706
dPr(protect=2)	.0187507	.0030806	.0125397	.0248353
dPr(protect=3)	.0185949	.0029016	.0125033	.024531
dPr(protect=4)	-.0021242	.0015527	-.0053734	.0007657
dPr(protect=5)	-.0402116	.0062809	-.0528894	-.0271189

(continued overleaf)

(*continued*)

First Difference: Impact of never having lived abroad

Change in Probability	*Mean*	*Std. Dev.*	*[95% Conf. Interval]*	
dPr(protect=1)	-.0043958	.0009459	-.0064719	-.0026324
dPr(protect=2)	-.0166275	.0031617	-.0230548	-.0104391
dPr(protect=3)	-.016615	.0029039	-.0221301	-.010629
dPr(protect=4)	.0017006	.0015057	-.0010203	.0051738
dPr(protect=5)	.0359378	.006238	.0227924	.0476815

First Difference: Impact of changing age from 30 to 60

Change in Probability	*Mean*	*Std. Dev.*	*[95% Conf. Interval]*	
dPr(protect=1)	-.0015981	.0005331	-.0026549	-.0005986
dPr(protect=2)	-.0064954	.002123	-.010649	-.0024426
dPr(protect=3)	-.007031	.0023066	-.0115803	-.0026377
dPr(protect=4)	-.0001971	.0005872	-.0014513	.0008854
dPr(protect=5)	.0153217	.0050335	.0057954	.025114

First Difference: Impact of being female

Change in Probability	*Mean*	*Std. Dev.*	*[95% Conf. Interval]*	
dPr(protect=1)	-.0105906	.0009866	-.0127733	-.0087948
dPr(protect=2)	-.0371693	.0025282	-.0422877	-.0322484
dPr(protect=3)	-.0341823	.0023486	-.0386092	-.0295846
dPr(protect=4)	.0080248	.0027035	.0025342	.0136012
dPr(protect=5)	.0739175	.0049386	.0640913	.0829416

First Difference: Impact of being married or living as married

Change in Probability	*Mean*	*Std. Dev.*	*[95% Conf. Interval]*	
dPr(protect=1)	-.0013144	.0005919	-.002546	-.0002151
dPr(protect=2)	-.0051992	.0022952	-.009917	-.0009015
dPr(protect=3)	-.0054664	.0023992	-.01021	-.0009952
dPr(protect=4)	.0001146	.0004661	-.0008027	.0011273
dPr(protect=5)	.0118654	.0052007	.0021536	.0223169

First Difference: Impact of being a Roman Catholic

Change in Probability	*Mean*	*Std. Dev.*	*[95% Conf. Interval]*	
dPr(protect=1)	-.0023132	.0007333	-.0038933	-.0009683
dPr(protect=2)	-.0097175	.0029776	-.0159036	-.0042047
dPr(protect=3)	-.0109054	.0033224	-.0176632	-.0046724
dPr(protect=4)	-.0009572	.0008932	-.0029647	.0005849
dPr(protect=5)	.0238934	.0072726	.0102972	.0384006

B. Equation (5), table 3

Simulated Probability	*Mean*	*Std. Dev.*	*[95% Conf. Interval]*	
Pr(protect=1)	.0174649	.002789	.0127167	.0233261
Pr(protect=2)	.1264871	.0114484	.1065978	.1500246
Pr(protect=3)	.2110957	.009337	.1925624	.2294772
Pr(protect=4)	.3859744	.0055172	.3751257	.3963836
Pr(protect=5)	.2589779	.0198112	.2198795	.2959962

First Difference: Impact of being rural

Change in Probability	*Mean*	*Std. Dev.*	*[95% Conf. Interval]*	
dPr(protect=1)	-.0049403	.0010727	-.0071378	-.0030334
dPr(protect=2)	-.0228495	.0041677	-.0308445	-.0147179
dPr(protect=3)	-.0199502	.0036924	-.0268114	-.0128275
dPr(protect=4)	.0033016	.0028547	-.0020696	.0091907
dPr(protect=5)	.0444383	.0082096	.0288076	.0594362

First Difference: Impact of being unemployed

Change in Probability	*Mean*	*Std. Dev.*	*[95% Conf. Interval]*	
dPr(protect=1)	-.0023965	.0022055	-.0065941	.0020396
dPr(protect=2)	-.0109467	.0099035	-.0300374	.008259
dPr(protect=3)	-.0094249	.0085891	-.0270617	.006401
dPr(protect=4)	.0017947	.0024421	-.00296	.0070637
dPr(protect=5)	.0209735	.0191444	-.0142154	.060015

First Difference: Impact of working in public sector

Change in Probability	*Mean*	*Std. Dev.*	*[95% Conf. Interval]*	
dPr(protect=1)	-.0015352	.0009784	-.0034262	.0003988
dPr(protect=2)	-.0067115	.0042186	-.0146584	.0016643
dPr(protect=3)	-.0054888	.0034838	-.0121543	.0013485
dPr(protect=4)	.0015316	.0012789	-.0004131	.0044134
dPr(protect=5)	.0122039	.0077459	-.0029597	.0272057

First Difference: Impact of being self-employed

Change in Probability	*Mean*	*Std. Dev.*	*[95% Conf. Interval]*	
dPr(protect=1)	.003982	.0015977	.0011853	.0072821
dPr(protect=2)	.0159954	.0059724	.0050317	.0280853
dPr(protect=3)	.0118232	.0043245	.0040024	.0206445
dPr(protect=4)	-.0053709	.0028221	-.0116064	-.0010744
dPr(protect=5)	-.0264298	.0096174	-.0462615	-.0088937

(*continued overleaf*)

(*continued*)

First Difference: Impact of belonging to a trade union

Change in Probability	*Mean*	*Std. Dev.*	*[95% Conf. Interval]*	
dPr(protect=1)	-.0003211	.0002013	-.0007417	.0000625
dPr(protect=2)	-.0013806	.00085	-.003074	.0002784
dPr(protect=3)	-.0011037	.0006855	-.0024854	.000232
dPr(protect=4)	.0003517	.0002788	-.0000952	.0010108
dPr(protect=5)	.0024536	.0015179	-.0005132	.0055294

Source: Authors' calculations using data from ISSP National Identity Survey 1995 and World Bank (1999).

Comments and Discussion

J. David Richardson: This paper is a treasure trove of fascinating patterns. It charts the correlates of answers to a question about whether a government "should limit the import of foreign products in order to protect its national economy" across a diverse array of individuals and countries of residence. Robust and memorable patterns from ordered probit regressions with elaborate and rich controls include the ways that:

—individual skills correlate negatively with protectionist sentiment, but the correlation weakens and even reverses as a country's average standard of living falls,

—extreme, but not more moderate nationalism, correlates positively with protectionist sentiment, and

—union status hardly correlates at all with protectionist sentiment.

But I have two broad complaints. The first is about the paper's repeated claim that its empirical patterns correspond to Heckscher-Ohlin theory. The second is about the authors' seeming omission of sensible econometric approaches to interpreting their patterns and perhaps to uncovering new ones.

I find the authors' attempt to root their specification and interpret their results using Heckscher-Ohlin trade theory to be intriguing, but not very compelling. They use the theory rhetorically—heuristically at best. There are two problems in how they argue. The more severe problem is that in a world with more than two inputs, Heckscher-Ohlin theory loses its sharp intuitive predictions about what happens to the returns to any single input when border liberalization occurs. It is no longer intuitively clear whether skilled or unskilled labor gains when other inputs (for example, physical capital) are in the background. A worker's stake in liberalization is determined by "friendship/rival" relations between the multiple inputs—and these are in turn determined by input substitution and complementarity relationships.[1] The second and less severe problem is that there are alternative trade theories to Heckscher-Ohlin that would explain why skilled workers are less protectionist in richer countries. One recent example (associated with Marc Melitz) is the theory that border liberalization increases the implicit scope of input markets and amplifies the dispersion of the rewards to every input group's heterogeneous membership. A more traditional example is one in which Ricardian technology differences across countries are associated with hard-to-measure quality-and-productivity differences in inputs that go by the same name (with "skilled labor" in rich countries being more productive than in poor countries).

In a similar vein, I applaud the authors' wide spectrum of econometric approaches, and suspect indeed that their empirical results are robust. But I think they neglected some potentially illuminating variations. For one example, though they report separate regressions by country, gender, and labor-force participation, they do not report separate regressions by age group (old-young, say, or old-young women, then men). Since age is important as a freestanding variable in determining Eastern European import-protection preferences, it seems natural to me to ask whether the skill coefficients or the patriotism-chauvinism coefficients differ significantly between old and young. Alas, I can't tell. Or for a second example, the estimated properties of the disturbance term in such split-sample regressions are intrinsically interesting. The estimated error variance is a measure of how diffuse the unexplained preferences are—are western preferences more "inexplicable" than eastern? Alas, I can't tell. More generally, the authors' assumption about the stochastic properties of the disturbance term seems always at the natural extreme—the stochastic properties are always common across observations, both in the full sample and in the various split samples. However I would like to know the effect of maintaining that assumption, but allowing the coefficients to differ across sample splits, testing for significant differences between the entire regressions over the various subsamples using something like standard F tests for probit regres-

1. Nor do the authors fully answer the implicit criticism of the multicountry models they cite in one paragraph. Even when the number of inputs is conveniently and intuitively two, say skilled and unskilled labor, the position of each toward border liberalization is determinate only in the two countries of the "world" that are most and least skill abundant, not in the "middle-abundance" countries. Nor is there any a priori theoretical reason to rank those middle-income countries by their proximity to either input-abundance extreme. Yet such ranking is precisely what the authors use to justify the key interaction term in their fundamental equation (1).

sions. Do Canadians determine protectionist sentiment "differently" than the British? Alas, I can't tell.

But I can tell a lot more at the end of the paper than when I started. And that's a fine commendation.

Dani Rodrik: Before I begin, a disclaimer. I stand in an awkward position vis-à-vis this paper as I have just completed (jointly with Anna Maria Mayda) a very similar paper.[1] We too use the ISSP 1995 survey, and focus on both the economic and noneconomic determinants of preferences over trade. Reassuringly many of our key conclusions coincide with those of O'Rourke and Sinnott, even though we have made somewhat different methodological choices. Since this compromises my status as a dispassionate critic of the present paper, I shall content myself with elaborating some of the striking features of this line of research.

As O'Rourke and Sinnott emphasize, there are two irresistible advantages of the ISSP data set. First, it is rich enough in content that we can look for the influence on trade attitudes of not just material self-interest, but of values, attachments, and identities. Second, the data have a cross-national dimension, allowing us to check for the validity of, say, the Stolper-Samuelson theorem in novel ways.

Indeed the evidence that emerges in favor of Stolper-Samuelson is strong and (in view of my own priors, at least) surprising. Previous studies, such as those of Scheve and Slaughter, have shown that higher-skilled individuals are more likely to be pro-trade in an advanced country such as the United States that is well-endowed with human capital.[2] This does not constitute direct evidence in favor of Stolper-Samuelson because it could well be that higher skilled individuals prefer free trade for other reasons than its anticipated distributive effect: they could simply be better informed about its efficiency benefits, for example. The evidence in favor of Stolper-Samuelson would be more compelling if we were to find that the relationship between an individual's skill and his attitude to trade weakens or reverses in countries that are poorly endowed with human capital. This paper, along with ours, are the first papers that present evidence of this kind.

Let me note here that in Mayda and Rodrik we use a different measure of skill, which is based on years of education.[3] O'Rourke and Sinnott use an

1. Mayda and Rodrik (2001). A third recent paper that uses the same survey is Beaulieu, Benarroch, and Gaisford, (2001).

2. Scheve and Slaughter (2001).

3. Mayda and Rodrik (2001).

occupation-based measure. Regardless of measure used, the pattern is the same, which is reassuring. Individuals with higher levels of human capital are in favor of trade, but only in countries that are well endowed with human capital. When we use education as a measure of human capital (as in our paper), the results are stronger in that we find one case where the relationship between pro-trade views and skills is reversed: the Philippines (the poorest country in our sample), where better-educated individuals are significantly less likely to be in favor of trade. Had the ISSP sample contained more low-income, low-skill countries, perhaps we would have had more such cases.

In Mayda and Rodrik we also test for the implications of the sector-specific factors model. We do that by establishing a concordance between detailed occupational codes (included in ISSP) and manufacturing industries. As mentioned above, O'Rourke and Sinnott use the occupational codes to infer skills instead, and therefore do not test separately for the sector-specific factors model. We find that individuals employed in import-competing industries are more likely to be in favor of trade restrictions (compared to individuals in nontraded sectors). Individuals in export-oriented sectors tend to be in favor of import restrictions as well (compared again to individuals in nontraded sectors), if less so than individuals in import-competing industries. In other words, controlling for preferences in nontraded industries, individuals in export-oriented sectors are on average more likely to be pro-trade than individuals in import-competing sectors. This finding can be rationalized within the sector-specific model by appealing to the presence of intra-industry (two-way) trade: individuals in export-oriented sectors still feel the pressure of imports and thus their attitudes to trade are intermediate: they do not favor trade as much as individuals in nontraded sectors, but neither are they as protectionist as individuals in import-competing sectors.

The fact that Stolper-Samuelson and the sector-specific factors model both find support in the data can in turn be interpreted as the result of differing time horizons or perceptions of mobility among the respondents. Individuals with long time horizons and greater mobility act in accordance with Stolper-Samuelson, while the others act in accordance with the sector-specific factors model. When we run a horse race between the two models, both survive.

O'Rourke and Sinnott's treatment of the noneconomic determinants of trade attitudes is particularly insightful. They usefully distinguish between patriotism and chauvinism, and find that both are powerful determinants of anti-trade attitudes (the latter somewhat more than the former). To the extent that protectionist attitudes are tied up with deep-seated values and norms, the economist's usual trick of compensating losers is unlikely to be effective in fostering open trade. In Mayda and Rodrik we show that a large part of the cross-country variation in average protectionist attitude is explained by differences in feelings of patriotism/nationalism.[4] We also show that such protectionist attitudes are somewhat moderated when individuals have greater confidence in the working of domestic political and economic institutions.

The last point is an important one. Trade policy is often an arena where domestic political conflicts play out in full force—at the expense of other countries. The better the quality of conflict-management institutions, the more conducive the environment to compromise, and the more vibrant the level of economic activity, the less likely that purely protectionist forces will prevail. Relative income disparities and perceived social injustices are an important motivation behind protectionist pressures. As the O'Rourke and Sinnott paper shows, the narrow, materialist perspective of our trade models is a useful first step in understanding the determinants of protectionist attitudes, but it goes only so far.

General discussion: Barry Eichengreen pointed out that free trade is a subtle concept and education may show up differently than a skill variable as a determinant of pro-trade attitudes. He also suggested that whether or not there is an accountable government that can compensate the losers will matter both for attitudes toward trade as well as for how powerfully the Heckscher-Ohlin-Samuelson logic operates. He was concerned about regressing attitudes on attitudes, as it is not clear what are the primitive variables. Whether one is born Catholic is presumably exogenous. But if one feels good about one's nation and wants to protect the national industry from imports, which is the causal variable and the other the result? Frederic Pryor reported the results of an exercise he had carried out, looking at 200 or so questionnaires about protectionism in the United States from 1950 to about 1998. He expected to find attitudes toward protection declining as U.S. tariffs had declined, but attitudes toward protectionism have not changed very much over the last fifty years. He also found that the answers varied greatly depending on how the question was phrased and presumably what the people being questioned understood. For instance, 45 percent of the American population that was questioned did not know what a tariff was, so their answers to "do you favor tariffs?" are a bit difficult to interpret. This may account for the low pseudo-R-squares in the paper.

4. Mayda and Rodrik (2001).

Edwin Truman asked what the policy implications of the paper were, particularly with respect to the chauvinism/nationalism variable. He also wanted to know if the authors had uncovered any evidence of the sort that had been mentioned by Dani Rodrik in his comments, that greater confidence in a country's social security institutions moderates anti-trade feelings. Along the same lines, Gordon Hanson suggested that the data set may allow taking into account the fact that the institutions that mediate between preferences and policies vary systematically across countries, and that it may be possible therefore to say something about when individuals are going to be more concerned about import competition. Referring to his earlier work on the United States, Matthew Slaughter suggested that the reason less-skilled workers do not like freer trade may be because they have had really bad labor market outcomes, in real and relative terms. He wondered if the same was going on in many of the countries in the sample. He suggested caution in interpreting the results as a horse race between the Heckscher-Ohlin and the specific-factors models, because it may be the case that people think both about the very short run and the very long run, in which case industry and factor type may both matter. It seemed, from figure 1, that a lot of the countries in which the skill coefficients are around zero are in Eastern Europe, where, given the turmoil that has been going on in recent years, people discount the future a lot more heavily than they do in other countries.

With respect to the gender difference, Daniel Tarullo suggested looking at the psychology literature on differences in moral reasoning, which contains fairly robust findings for a different approach to these kinds of issues among men and women of similar education and economic backgrounds. He also echoed others' concern that the particular question being analyzed was somewhat loaded, crying for a nationalist response in those who have a tendency in that direction anyway.

Moreover, perceptions of what is at stake with trade almost surely vary with what is happening in the policy realm at the time that they are asked the question. At the time the database for the paper was put together, NAFTA was the issue in the United States, and so almost everything was surely seen through that lens. Carol Graham pointed out the only real developing country in the sample is the Philippines, which is fairly different. In her own work on Latin America, Graham had found the opposite result, at least in terms of support for an index of market-oriented policies, of which trade is one of the three: skilled or more educated people are much more in favor of market-oriented policies than unskilled workers. Susan Collins suggested that the gender difference might be accounted by the fact that women are perhaps more concentrated in import-competing industries, as they are in the United States.

Kevin O'Rourke responded that it would be a good idea to add more interactions with country-level variables such as institutions or cross-industry dispersion of tariffs as well as looking at correlations between their skill variables and patriotism and chauvinism variables. With regard to the question being loaded, he reiterated Rodrik's point that the analysis could not shed light on the average levels of protectionism, but on the dispersion around the mean. On Latin America, he pointed out, referring to work by Hanson and Harrison, that if those countries have been protecting the labor-intensive sectors, if skill differentials have widened, and if the high-skilled are in favor of reform, that would all be consistent with Heckscher-Ohlin.

References

Balistreri, Edward J. 1997. "The Performance of the Heckscher-Ohlin-Vanek Model in Predicting Endogenous Policy Forces at the Individual Level." *Canadian Journal of Economics* 30 (February): 1–17.

Barro, Robert J., and Jong-Wha Lee. 2000. "International Data on Educational Attainment: Updates and Implications." Working Paper 42. Cambridge, Mass.: Center for International Development at Harvard University (April). Data available at www.cid.harvard.edu/ciddata/ciddata.html.

Beaulieu, Eugene, Michael Benarroch, and James Gaisford. 2001. "Intra-Industry Trade Liberalization: Why Skilled Workers Everywhere Resist Protectionism." University of Calgary, Department of Economics. (June).

Bhagwati, Jagdish N., ed. 1982. *Import Competition and Response*. University of Chicago Press.

Blanchflower, David G. 2001. "Unemployment, Well-Being and Wage Curves in Eastern and Central Europe." Mimeo (January). Dartmouth College, Department of Economics.

Borjas, George J. 1999. *Heaven's Door: Immigration Policy and the American Economy*. Princeton University Press.

Currie, Janet, and Ann Harrison. 1997. "Sharing the Costs: The Impact of Trade Reform on Capital and Labor in Morocco." *Journal of Labor Economics* 15 (July): S44–S72.

Davis, Donald R. 1996. "Trade Liberalization and Income Distribution." Working Paper 5693. Cambridge, Mass.: National Bureau of Economic Research (August).

Feenstra, Robert C., and Gordon H. Hanson. 1996. "Foreign Investment, Outsourcing, and Relative Wages." In *The Political Economy of Trade Policy: Papers in Honor of Jagdish Bhagwati*, edited by Robert C. Feenstra, Gene M. Grossman, and Douglas A. Irwin, 89–127. MIT Press.

Findlay, Ronald, and Stanislaw Wellisz. 1982. "Endogenous Tariffs, the Political Economy of Trade Restrictions, and Welfare." In *Import Competition and Response*, edited by Jagdish Bhagwati, 223–34. University of Chicago Press.

Ganzeboom, Harry B. G., and Donald J. Treiman. 1996. "Internationally Comparable Measures of Occupational Status for the 1988 International Standard Classification of Occupations." *Social Science Research* 25 (September): 201–39.

Gellner, Ernest, 1983. *Nations and Nationalism*. Cornell University Press.

Graham, Carol, and Stefano Pettinato. 2000. "Happiness, Markets, and Democracy: Latin America in Comparative Perspective." Working Paper 13. Center on Social and Economic Dynamics (August) and forthcoming in *Journal of Happiness Studies*.

———. 2002. *Happiness and Hardship: Opportunity and Insecurity in New Market Economies*. Brookings Institution.

Greene, William H. 2000. *Econometric Analysis*, fourth ed. Upper Saddle River, N.J.: Prentice-Hall.

Grossman, Gene M., and Elhanan Helpman. 1994. "Protection for Sale." *American Economic Review* 84 (September): 833–50.

Hanson, Gordon H., and Ann Harrison. 1999. "Trade Liberalization and Wage Inequality in Mexico." *Industrial and Labor Relations Review* 52 (January): 271–88.

International Labor Office. 1990. *International Standard Classification of Occupations: ISCO-88*. Geneva: International Labor Organization.

Irwin, Douglas A. 1989. "Political Economy and Peel's Repeal of the Corn Laws." *Economics and Politics* 1 (Spring): 41–59.

———. 1994. "The Political Economy of Free Trade: Voting in the British General Election of 1906." *Journal of Law and Economics* 37 (April): 75–108.

Kaempfer, William H., and Stephen V. Marks. 1993. "The Expected Effects of Trade Liberalization: Evidence from U.S. Congressional Action on Fast-Track Authority." *World Economy* 16 (November): 725–40.

Kanbur, Ravi. 1999. "Income Distribution Implications of Globalization and Liberalization in Africa." Working Paper 99–04. Cornell University (March).

King, Gary, Michael Tomz, and Jason Wittenberg. 2000. "Making the Most of Statistical Analyses: Improving Interpretation and Presentation." *American Journal of Political Science* 44 (April): 347–61.

Magee, Stephen P. 1978. "Three Simple Tests of the Stolper-Samuelson Theorem." In *Issues in International Economics*, edited by Peter Oppenheimer, 138–53. Stocksfield: Oriel Press.

Magee, Stephen P., William A. Brock, and Leslie Young. 1989. *Black Hole Tariffs and Endogenous Policy Theory: Political Economy in General Equilibrium.* Cambridge University Press.

Mayda, Anna Maria, and Dani Rodrik. 2001. "Why Are Some People (and Countries) More Protectionist Than Others?" Working Paper 8461. Cambridge, Mass.: National Bureau of Economic Research (September).

Mayer, Wolfgang. 1984. "Endogenous Tariff Formation." *American Economic Review* 74 (December): 970–85.

Rodrik, Dani. 1995. "Political Economy of Trade Policy." In *Handbook of International Economics*, vol. 3, edited by Gene M. Grossman and Kenneth Rogoff, 1457–94. Amsterdam: Elsevier.

———. 1997. *Has Globalization Gone Too Far?* Washington: Institute for International Economics.

Rogowski, Ronald. 1989. *Commerce and Coalitions: How Trade Affects Domestic Political Arrangements.* Princeton University Press.

Scheve, Kenneth F., and Matthew J. Slaughter. 2001. "What Determines Individual Trade-Policy Preferences?" *Journal of International Economics* 54 (August): 267–92.

Schonhardt-Bailey, Cheryl. 1991. "Specific Factors, Capital Markets, Portfolio Diversification, and Free Trade: Domestic Determinants of the Repeal of the Corn Laws." *World Politics* 43 (July): 545–69.

Shulman, Stephen. 2000. "Nationalist Sources of International Economic Integration." *International Studies Quarterly* 44 (September): 365–90.

Slaughter, Matthew J. 2000. "Trade and Labor-Market Outcomes: What About Developing Countries?" Paper prepared for National Bureau of Economic Research Inter-American Seminar on Economics, Cambridge, Mass., July 22, 2000.

Svejnar, Jan. 1999. "Labor Markets in the Transitional Central and East European Economies." In *Handbook of Labor Economics,* vol. 3B, edited by Orley Ashenfelter and David Card, 2809–57. Amsterdam: Elsevier.

Tabachnick, Barbara G., and Linda S. Fidell. 2001. *Using Multivariate Statistics, Fourth Edition*. Boston: Allyn and Bacon.

Tomz, Michael, Jason Wittenberg, and Gary King. 1999. "CLARIFY: Software for Interpreting and Presenting Statistical Results. Version 1.1.1." Harvard University, June 1.

Wessels, Bernhard. 1995. "Development of Support: Diffusion or Demographic Replacement." In *Public Opinion and Internationalized Governance*, edited by Oskar Niedermayer and Richard Sinnott, 105–36. Oxford University Press.

Wood, Adrian. 1997. "Openness and Wage Inequality in Developing Countries: The Latin American Challenge to East Asian Conventional Wisdom." *World Bank Economic Review* 11 (January): 33–57.

World Bank. 1999. *World Development Indicators.* CD-ROM. Washington: World Bank.

[9]

Available online at www.sciencedirect.com
SCIENCE DIRECT
ELSEVIER
European Economic Review 49 (2005) 1393–1430
EUROPEAN ECONOMIC REVIEW
www.elsevier.com/locate/econbase

Why are some people (and countries) more protectionist than others?

Anna Maria Mayda[a], Dani Rodrik[b,*]

[a] *School of Foreign Service and Department of Economics, Georgetown University, Washington, DC 20057, USA*
[b] *Kennedy School of Government, Harvard University, Cambridge, MA 02138, USA*

Received 1 April 2002; accepted 7 December 2003

Abstract

We analyze two cross-country data sets that contain information on attitudes toward trade as well as a broad range of socio-demographic and other indicators. We find that pro-trade preferences are significantly and robustly correlated with an individual's level of human capital, in the manner predicted by the factor endowments model. Preferences over trade are also correlated with the trade exposure of the sector in which an individual is employed: individuals in non-traded sectors tend to be the most pro-trade, while individuals in sectors with a revealed comparative *dis*advantage are the most protectionist. Third, an individual's relative economic status has a very strong positive association with pro-trade attitudes. Finally, non-economic determinants, in the form of values, identities, and attachments, play an important role in explaining the variation in preferences over trade. High degrees of neighborhood attachment and nationalism/patriotism are associated with protectionist tendencies.

JEL classification: F1

Keywords: Trade; Policy preferences; Political economy

1. Introduction

Economists disagree intensely on many public policy issues. What is the best way to deal with poverty? What is the appropriate role of the government in providing health insurance? Is it good anti-trust policy to break up Microsoft? Does counter-cyclical macroeconomic policy make sense? Should social security be privatized? Should we

* Corresponding author. Tel.: +1-617-495-9454.
E-mail addresses: amm223@georgetown.edu (A.M. Mayda), dani_rodrik@harvard.edu (D. Rodrik).

0014-2921/$ - see front matter © 2004 Elsevier B.V. All rights reserved.
doi:10.1016/j.euroecorev.2004.01.002

tax international capital flows? Is the minimum wage desirable? In these and many other areas, economists are engaged in lively controversies that reflect broader public debates on social problems.

International trade poses an interesting contrast. Here the debates remain largely technical, even among policy-oriented economists: Which theory is more appropriate in explaining the patterns of trade? How much, if at all, has trade contributed to the rise in the skill premium in the U.S.? Why are "border effects" so large? On the important policy questions that excite the public, there is virtually no difference of views. In particular, there exists near-universal consensus among mainstream economists on the desirability of free trade (see for example Alston et al., 1992).

It is striking how little this consensus resonates with public opinion. When asked about their views on trade, approximately 60% of respondents in opinion polls express anti-trade views. [1] While there are some interesting differences across countries, which we shall document and analyze later, a majority of respondents tend to be in favor of restricting trade in most countries. Our purpose in this paper is to shed light on this phenomenon, by undertaking a systematic analysis of individual attitudes towards trade and their underlying determinants. We make use of two cross-country surveys of individual opinions. The first of these comes from the International Social Survey Programme (ISSP), and it allows us to perform a comparative analysis covering more than 28,000 individuals in 23 countries. We use as our dependent variable a question in the ISSP data set that asks whether the respondent favors restricting trade. The data set also contains a wealth of information on demographics, socio-economic status, and values, which we use to test a number of hypotheses about the formation of attitudes. To ascertain the robustness of our findings, we also run parallel tests whenever possible with the third wave of the World Values Survey (WVS), which covers a larger sample of countries.

The standard workhorse models of international trade have well-defined implications for the distributive consequences of trade and hence for individual attitudes (see Rodrik (1995) for a review of the literature). Under the factor-endowments model, which assumes costless inter-sectoral mobility of productive factors, trade benefits individuals who own the factors with which the economy is relatively well endowed, and hurts the others. This is the well-known Stolper–Samuelson theorem. Under the specific-factors model, trade benefits individuals who are employed in the export-oriented sectors and hurts those who are employed in the import-competing sectors. To the extent that individuals are motivated by material self-interest, these models provide important hints about an individual's likely attitude to trade depending on his/her factor type or sector of employment.

Our first set of results directly relates to these economic models. Most strikingly, we find strong support for the factor-endowments view of the world in both the ISSP and WVS data sets. Individuals with higher levels of human capital (proxied by educational attainment or occupational categories) oppose trade restrictions, but only in countries that are well endowed with human capital. In the ISSP data set, higher

[1] The fraction of individuals who are against trade (i.e., in favor of limiting imports of foreign products) ranges from 55% in the ISSP data set to 60% in the WVS data set.

levels of education are associated with pro-trade views in advanced countries such as Germany and the United States, but with anti-trade views in the Philippines (the poorest country in the ISSP sample). We find a very similar pattern in the WVS data set, which has the advantage for this purpose that it covers many more developing countries (including very poor countries such as Nigeria and Bangladesh). Regardless of whether skill is measured by educational attainment or occupation-based skill levels, the estimated impact of skill on pro-trade attitudes in the WVS data set is strongly positive in the richest countries, but weak or negative in the poorest. That individual trade opinions interact with country characteristics in exactly the manner predicted by the factor-endowments model in both data sets may be considered surprising, but it is a robust result and perhaps our strongest single finding.

We find support for the specific-factors model as well. In particular, individuals employed in import-competing industries are more likely to be in favor of trade restrictions (compared to individuals in non-traded sectors). Individuals in export-oriented sectors are not significantly more likely to oppose import restrictions (compared again to individuals in non-traded sectors). This finding can be rationalized within the specific-factors model by appealing to the presence of intra-industry (two-way) trade and myopic behavior on the part of individuals in CA sectors (given how the trade question is phrased in the surveys).

The fact that the factor-endowments and specific-factors models both find support in the data suggests that individuals may differ in the time horizon they use to evaluate trade policy. We find evidence that some think in terms of the long run (and express trade opinions in line with the factor-endowments model), while others think in terms of both the long run and the short run (and express trade opinions in line with both the factor-endowments and the specific-factors model).

While the implications of conventional economic models are borne out by the data, these models go only part of the way in explaining the formation of attitudes. We find that social status, relative incomes, values, and attachments play, if anything, a more important role. For example, individuals who consider themselves part of the upper classes tend to be more favorable to trade than those who consider themselves to be from the lower classes. Individuals with higher relative incomes are more likely to favor trade than those with low relative incomes. Also, protectionist attitudes go together with a well-defined set of normative attributes. Individuals who favor trade restrictions tend to have high attachments to their neighborhood and community, have a high degree of national pride, and believe that national interest should be paramount in making trade-offs. At the same time, individuals who have confidence in their country's democracy are less likely to favor trade protection. In other words, communitarian-patriotic values tend to foster protectionist attitudes, but this tendency is moderated when the broader institutions of society are perceived to be working well.

Our bottom line is that both economic and non-economic considerations are important in determining attitudes towards trade. Once we take the myriad factors discussed above into account, we are reasonably successful in explaining the variation in trade opinions in our sample. Our preferred "combined" model accounts for about a fifth of the sample variance. Moreover, we are also reasonably successful in explaining the differences in mean attitudes across countries. Our preferred model does a good job in explaining why respondents in Poland, for example, are more protectionist on average than those in Germany.

The empirical literature on the political economy of trade policy is not small, but it has focused largely on testing the implications of the factor-endowments and specific-factors models in a single country. Studies that have found support for the factor-endowments model include Rogowski (1987, 1989), Midford (1993), Beaulieu (1996), Balistreri (1997), and Scheve and Slaughter (2001a, 2001b). Studies that have found support for the specific-factors model include Magee (1978) and Irwin (1994, 1996). Some have found support for both views of the world (Baldwin and Magee, 1998; Beaulieu and Magee, 2001). With the exception of Balistreri (1997) and Scheve and Slaughter (2001a), none of these studies analyze individual attitudes directly. Instead they infer trade positions from aggregated information on voting, campaign-contributions, or policy outcomes. [2]

Since we began our work with the ISSP data set we have become aware of two other related, but independent papers: O'Rourke and Sinnott (2001) and Beaulieu et al. (2003). Both of these papers only use the ISSP survey to explore the determinants of trade attitudes. Thus, they mainly focus on countries at the high end of the world income and skill distribution. In addition, neither paper tests the specific-factors model. The O'Rourke and Sinnott paper is closest to ours, and many of its conclusions parallel to our own findings.

Our paper is also related to a growing literature within economics that examines survey data to analyze the formation of individual preferences. See for example Luttmer (2001) and Alesina and La Ferrara (2001) on preferences for redistribution, and Blanchflower and Oswald (2000) and Alesina et al. (2001) on the determinants of "happiness", and Caplan (2001) on the sources of differences in policy preferences of the lay public and of economists.

The plan of the paper is as follows. In the next section, we briefly describe the data and the methods we have used. Next, we present a series of empirical models highlighting different types of determinants of trade attitudes. In a final section, we put all our results together and comment on the overall fit of our explanatory framework.

2. Description of the data and empirical approach

The International Social Survey Programme (ISSP) collects cross-national data on topics that are important for social science research. In this paper we use data from the 1995 ISSP National Identity module (ISSP). The data set covers information at the individual level on some 28,456 respondents from 23 countries, including the United States, Canada, Japan, many Western and Eastern European countries, and one developing country (the Philippines). [3] For each individual, the data set contains responses on

[2] For example, Irwin (1994, 1996) looks at the outcomes of the 1906 and 1923 British general elections and interprets them as proxies for voters' opinions on new trade barriers.

[3] See Table 1 for the full list of countries. We consider Germany West and East separately, even though the survey was carried out after their unification, in order to see whether there are important differences between the two.

a variety of topics, ranging from opinions on trade and immigration policy to feelings of patriotism and regional attachment. In addition, the ISSP data set contains information on several economic and demographic variables. Thus the survey allows us to identify both stated attitudes towards trade and individual characteristics that explain trade positions in standard economic models.[4]

In order to measure individual trade-policy attitudes, we focus on survey answers to the following question: "Now we would like to ask a few questions about relations between (respondent's country) and other countries. How much do you agree or disagree with the following statement: (Respondent's country) should limit the import of foreign products in order to protect its national economy."[5] After deleting the "can't choose, don't know" and "NA, refused" responses, we transformed survey questions into the dependent variable *Trade Opinion* (with answers ranging from 1 = agree strongly to 5=disagree strongly). Higher values of *Trade Opinion* therefore correspond to attitudes that are more pro-trade and less protectionist.

We also created two binary variables, which we label *Pro-Trade Dummy* and *Against-Trade Dummy*. *Pro-Trade Dummy* is set equal to unity for individuals opposing trade protection (i.e., for those replying "disagree" or "disagree strongly" to the question), and to zero for the rest. *Against-Trade Dummy* is set equal to unity for individuals favoring trade protection (i.e., for those replying "agree" or "agree strongly" to the question), and to zero for the others.[6] Since the results based on *Pro-Trade Dummy* and *Against-Trade Dummy* are very similar to those with the ordered logits using *Trade Opinion*, we will present the results based on *Pro-Trade Dummy*.[7]

Table 1 presents summary statistics for *Trade Opinion*, *Pro-Trade Dummy* and *Against-Trade Dummy*, by country. Several results stand out. First, the ISSP data set shows that protectionist sentiment runs high on average. Taking the 23 countries as a whole, more than half of the respondents agree with the proposition that trade should be restricted (average *Against-Trade Dummy* = 0.55), while fewer than a quarter disagree (average *Pro-Trade Dummy* = 0.22). Second, there is quite a large variation in trade attitudes across countries. Netherlands emerges as the country that is the most pro-trade (*Pro-Trade Dummy* = 0.37) while Bulgaria is the most protectionist (*Pro-Trade Dummy* = 0.08), regardless of the indicator used. Third, as the last comment indicates, the rankings of the countries are not very sensitive to the measure of trade attitudes.

Are these findings truly reflective of underlying attitudes towards trade? It is well known that survey responses tend to be highly sensitive to framing – the phrasing of the question and the context and order in which it is asked. In this particular case, there

[4] Since not all questions are covered in individual country surveys, our regressions will typically not include all 23 countries.

[5] The possible answers to this question are as follows: (1) agree strongly, (2) agree, (3) neither agree nor disagree, (4) disagree, (5) disagree strongly, (8) can't choose, don't know, (9) NA, refused.

[6] Note that these two alternative formulations of the dependent variable do not require us to drop observations corresponding to "can't choose, don't know" or "NA, refused" answers (which are coded as zeros).

[7] Our results are unchanged when we drop "can't choose, don't know" or "NA, refused" observations in the definition of *Pro-Trade Dummy*.

Table 1
Summary data on individual attitudes towards trade (ISSP data set)

Country	Trade Opinion						Average Trade Opinion		Pro-Trade Dummy		Against-Trade Dummy	
	Agree strongly (1)	Agree (2)	Neither agree nor disagree (3)	Disagree (4)	Disagree strongly (5)	Can't choose (8) NA, refused (9)						
Germany West	0.1513	0.2371	0.1849	0.2683	0.0952	0.0632	2.9134	3	0.3635	2	0.3885	20
Germany East	0.2598	0.3039	0.1699	0.1732	0.0474	0.0458	2.4178	11	0.2206	13	0.5637	13
Great Britain	0.2316	0.4017	0.1853	0.1238	0.0142	0.0435	2.2549	16	0.1380	18	0.6333	10
USA	0.2129	0.4309	0.1602	0.1039	0.0293	0.0629	2.2592	16	0.1331	19	0.6437	9
Austria	0.3784	0.3198	0.1092	0.1261	0.0387	0.0278	2.1021	20	0.1648	15	0.6981	5
Hungary	0.4540	0.2580	0.1580	0.0690	0.0260	0.0350	1.9171	21	0.0950	22	0.7120	3
Italy	0.2578	0.3473	0.1453	0.1609	0.0658	0.0229	2.4163	12	0.2267	11	0.6051	11
Ireland	0.2425	0.4135	0.1087	0.1962	0.0272	0.0121	2.3442	14	0.2233	12	0.6559	7
Netherlands	0.0512	0.2393	0.2824	0.3193	0.0551	0.0527	**3.0925**	1	**0.3743**	1	**0.2906**	23
Norway	0.0910	0.2849	0.2737	0.2279	0.0491	0.0733	2.8481	4	0.2770	5	0.3759	21
Sweden	0.1242	0.2809	0.2924	0.1752	0.0640	0.0633	2.7586	5	0.2392	10	0.4051	19
Czech Republic	0.2556	0.2655	0.1773	0.1719	0.0954	0.0342	2.5713	8	0.2673	6	0.5212	15
Slovenia	0.2403	0.2683	0.1795	0.2046	0.0396	0.0676	2.5010	9	0.2442	9	0.5087	17
Poland	0.3004	0.3486	0.1270	0.1176	0.0263	0.0801	2.1531	18	0.1439	17	0.6489	8
Bulgaria	0.5357	0.2380	0.0498	0.0326	0.0452	0.0986	**1.6837**	23	**0.0778**	23	**0.7738**	1
Russia	0.3558	0.2448	0.1174	0.1502	0.0681	0.0637	2.2844	15	0.2183	14	0.6006	12
New Zealand	0.1764	0.3423	0.1937	0.1985	0.0499	0.0393	2.5868	7	0.2483	7	0.5187	16
Canada	0.1413	0.3169	0.2158	0.2184	0.0603	0.0473	2.7265	6	0.2787	4	0.4582	18
Philippines	0.1275	0.5375	0.1633	0.1517	0.0083	0.0117	2.3685	13	0.1600	16	0.6650	6
Japan	0.1409	0.1680	0.2954	0.1497	0.1903	0.0557	3.0852	2	0.3400	3	0.3089	22
Spain	0.2121	0.5012	0.1097	0.0925	0.0098	0.0745	2.1212	19	0.1024	21	0.7133	2
Latvia	0.5019	0.2079	0.0987	0.0900	0.0412	0.0603	1.8940	22	0.1312	20	0.7098	4
Slovak Republic	0.2666	0.2875	0.1599	0.1614	0.0857	0.0389	2.4925	10	0.2471	8	0.5540	14
Mean	0.2357	0.3122	0.1780	0.1666	0.0548	0.0526	2.4643		0.2214		0.5480	
Standard deviation	0.4245	0.4634	0.3825	0.3727	0.2275	0.2233	1.2021		0.4152		0.4977	

Notes: *Trade Opinion* gives responses to the following question: "How much do you agree or disagree with the following statement: (respondent's country) should limit the import of foreign products in order to protect its national economy." The six columns under *Trade Opinion* present the fraction of individuals in a country giving each of the six possible answers. Average Trade Opinion is the average of Trade Opinion excluding can't choose (8) and NA, refused (9) answers. *Pro-Trade Dummy* is coded as follows: Pro-Trade Dummy = 1 if Trade Opinion = 4 or 5; 0 if Trade Opinion = 1, 2, 3, 8, or 9. *Against-Trade Dummy* is coded as follows: Against-Trade Dummy = 1 if Trade Opinion = 1 or 2; 0 if Trade Opinion = 3, 4, 5, 8, or 9. The second column of each variable gives the ranking of countries according to that variable. Bold numbers correspond to highest and lowest values. Mean and standard deviation are across individuals in the full sample.

is especially cause to worry because the question in the ISSP survey refers to possible benefits of restricting imports ("protecting national economy") without mentioning any drawbacks. One would suspect that this imparts a strong protectionist bias to the responses. There are two countervailing considerations. First, there is ample evidence from the U.S., which suggests that the precise phrasing of the question on imports does not greatly affect the average responses provided (see the review in Scheve and Slaughter (2001b)). Second, in our empirical work, we will be interested in identifying the determinants of the differences in attitudes across individuals. Even though the responses on trade may be biased in one direction, our results will not be affected as long as the bias is uniform across individuals (i.e., each individual in a given country expresses a less pro-trade view than otherwise by an equal amount).

A related question concerns the bias that may arise from the fact that individuals in the various countries face different policy environments and economic contexts. Cross-country differences in attitudes towards trade may be shaped by these variations. [8] We will include a full set of country dummies in our regressions to pick up any spurious correlation between the regressors and the dependent variable. To the extent that such contextual effects affect all individuals in a country in a similar manner, the country dummies will sweep them up. For example, if a given country is caught in a recession and respondents tend to be more protectionist than in normal times, this will be reflected in the estimated coefficient of the country fixed effect. With few exceptions, the inclusion of country fixed effects did not affect the results. On occasion, there may be reason to believe that country characteristics will affect individuals differentially. When such concerns arise, we shall also interact relevant country characteristics with individual attributes.

We might wonder whether protectionist sentiment, as captured by surveys of this kind, has any relationship to actual trade policies. There are of course good reasons to believe that in any political system there would be considerable slippage between individual preferences on any specific issue and policy outcomes. The "supply" side of policy can be as important as the "demand" side. Moreover, the institutional structures of government and of political representation mediate between individual voters and policy makers (Rodrik, 1995). Nonetheless, it is interesting to know whether trade attitudes broadly correlate with trade policies.

Fig. 1 shows that the answer is broadly yes. The correlation between average values of *Trade Opinion* and average levels of trade duties across countries is negative and statistically significant (robust t-statistic $= -2.13$, significant at 5% level). [9] The point estimate suggests that a one-point increase in *Trade Opinion* on our 5-point scale is accompanied by a 3.6 percentage point reduction in average duties. At the same time, it is clear from the figure that the relationship is quite a loose one: the average values

[8] Luttmer (2001), for example, shows that individual preferences for redistribution are shaped in part by an "exposure" effect – the extent of welfare recipiency in the respondent's own community.

[9] Trade duties refer to combined import and export duties (t_m and t_x, respectively) over the 1992–1998 period, calculated as $[(1 + t_m)^*(1 + t_x)] - 1$. The source for duties is the World Development Indicators CD-Rom of the World Bank. Two countries, Slovenia and Slovak Republic, are not included in Fig. 1 because the World Bank does not provide data on duties for them.

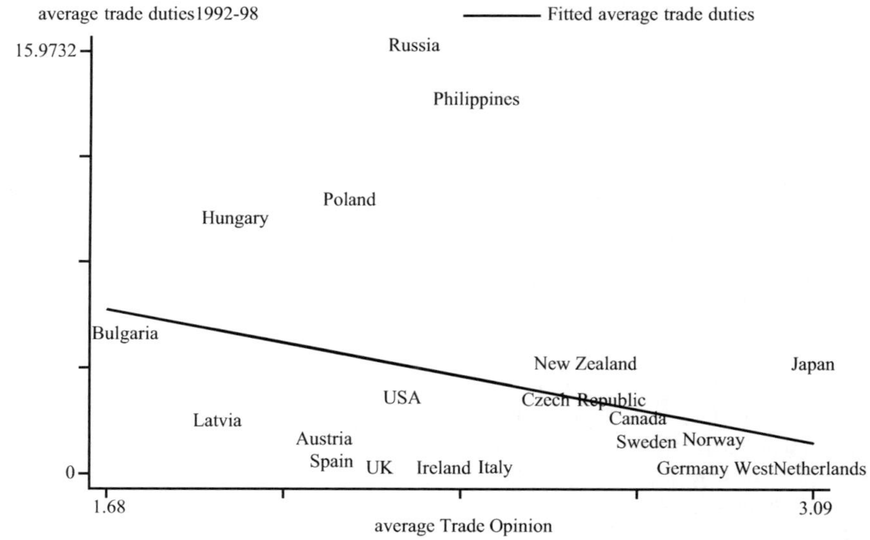

Fig. 1. Relationship between trade opinion and average trade duties (ISSP data set).

of *Trade Opinion* accounts for no more than 8 percent of the cross-country variation in tariffs.

As mentioned in the introduction, we use the third wave of the WVS data set (Inglehart, 1997), carried out in 1995–1997, to complement our findings based on the ISSP data set. While the WVS contains information on trade attitudes for more countries than the ISSP survey (47 countries, versus 23), its question on trade allows only a binary response: "Do you think it is better if: (1) Goods made in other countries can be imported and sold here if people want to buy them; or that: (2) There should be stricter limits on selling foreign goods here, to protect the jobs of people in this country; or: (9) Don't Know." In coding the responses, we followed the same procedures as with the ISSP survey. We constructed a binary variable, *Pro-Trade Dummy* (*WVS*), set equal to 1 if the individual answered (1), and equal to 0 if the individual answered (2) or (9). Missing values (no answer) were kept as missing values.[10] Across countries that are covered in both the ISSP and WVS data sets, the simple correlation between average values of pro-trade attitudes is 0.72 (significant at the 95% level).[11] One important shortcoming of the WVS is that it does not contain the information that would allow the matching of respondents to sectors of employment in the way that the ISSP data set does. This means that we cannot use the WVS for purposes of testing the implications of the specific-factors model.

[10] We found that our analysis remains unaffected if we count "don't knows" as missing values instead.

[11] See Tables 2 and 3 for summary statistics of *Pro-Trade Dummy* (*WVS*) and for a comparison of the two data sets in terms of trade attitudes.

Table 2
Summary data on individual attitudes towards trade (WVS)

Country	Pro-Trade Dummy (WVS)	Country	Pro-Trade Dummy (WVS)
Uruguay	0.0720	S. Korea	0.3483
Venezuela	0.1209	Bulgaria	0.3517
Brazil	0.1297	Switzerland	0.3639
Argentina	0.1395	Germany East	0.3647
Mexico	0.1523	Macedonia	0.3697
Peru	0.1528	Finland	0.3850
India	0.1667	Sweden	0.4143
Turkey	0.1747	Estonia	0.4251
Bangladesh	0.1856	Taiwan	0.4554
Pakistan	0.1951	Latvia	0.4583
Puerto Rico	0.2109	Croatia	0.4676
Chile	0.2170	Norway	0.4685
Poland	0.2350	Bosnia	0.4700
Australia	0.2366	Nigeria	0.4745
China	0.2414	Serbia	0.4922
Dominican Republic	0.2566	Armenia	0.5075
Spain	0.2601	Ukraine	0.5240
USA	0.2705	Azerbaijan	0.5280
Philippines	0.2833	Belarus	0.5378
Lithuania	0.2864	Germany West	0.5428
Slovenia	0.2982	Georgia	0.5547
Russia	0.3034	Montenegro	0.5708
Moldova	0.3130	Japan	0.7170
S. Africa	0.3431		
Mean	0.3490		
Standard deviation	0.4766		

Notes: Trade Opinion (WVS) gives responses to the following question: "Do you think it is better if: 1. Goods made in other countries can be imported and sold here if people want to buy them; or that: 2. There should be stricter limits on selling foreign goods here, to protect the jobs of people in this country; or: 9. Don't Know." Pro-Trade Dummy (WVS) is coded as follows: Pro-Trade Dummy (WVS) = 1 if Trade Opinion (WVS) = 1; 0 if Trade Opinion (WVS) = 2 or 9.

In most of our tests, we shall use *Pro-Trade Dummy* from the ISSP data set and *Pro-Trade Dummy* (*WVS*) from the WVS as our dependent variables and estimate a series of probit models. We have checked the robustness of our results to alternative econometric models, estimating ordered logit specifications as well as OLS regressions with *Trade Opinion* as the dependent variable. We find very few substantive differences so we shall not present the results from these different specifications.[12] When we present probit results, we report the marginal effect of each variable, i.e. the estimated change in the probability of being pro-trade ("disagree" and "disagree strongly" with trade restrictions) given a marginal increase in the value of the relevant regressor,

[12] See the working paper version (NBER Working Paper 8461) for ordered-logit results.

Table 3
Comparison between ISSP and WVS data sets

Country	Pro-Trade Dummy (WVS)	Pro-Trade Dummy (ISSP)
Poland	0.2350	0.1439
Spain	0.2601	0.1024
USA	0.2705	0.1331
Philippines	0.2833	0.1600
Slovenia	0.2982	0.2442
Russia	0.3034	0.2183
Bulgaria	0.3517	0.0778
Germany East	0.3647	0.2206
Sweden	0.4143	0.2392
Latvia	0.4583	0.1312
Norway	0.4685	0.2770
Germany West	0.5428	0.3635
Japan	0.7170	0.3400

Notes: In both data sets, Pro-Trade Dummy is set equal to 1 if an individual is in favor of imports, 0 if he is not in favor of imports. The correlation coefficient between the country average values of Pro-Trade Dummy in the two data sets is 0.7226, significant at the 5% level (only countries for which data is available in both data sets were considered).

holding all other regressors at their mean value. These marginal effects represent the estimated impact that each regressor has on the probability that an "average" individual will be pro-trade. [13]

3. A first pass: The naïve demographic model

As a first pass through the data, we ignore economic theory and present some estimates that relate trade attitudes to a list of standard demographic characteristics. We use information from ISSP questions regarding age, gender, citizenship, years of education, real income, area of residence (rural vs. urban), subjective social class, trade union membership, and political party affiliation. [14] The results are shown in the first two columns of Table 4. The WVS data yield very similar results, which we do not present to save space. [15]

We find evidence of a strong gender effect on trade attitudes, which survives virtually all specifications we have tried. Column (1) in Table 4 shows that being male increases the probability of replying either "disagree" or "disagree strongly" with trade restrictions by 7.7 percentage points (significant at the 1% level). This is quite a

[13] As is mentioned above, in each specification we include a full set of country dummy variables that capture unobserved additive country-specific effects. We also cluster standard errors by country, to account for correlation across individuals within the same country.

[14] See definitions of variables at the end of Table 4.

[15] Some control variables are defined differently in regressions using the WVS due to differences in the questions posed: country of birth (in WVS) instead of citizenship (in ISSP), highest education level attained (in WVS) instead of years of education (in ISSP), town size (in WVS) instead of rural vs. urban (in ISSP).

Table 4
Factor endowments model (ISSP data set)

Probit with country dummy variables	1	2	3	4	5	6	7	8	9
Dependent variable	Pro-trade dummy								
Age	−0.0008 0.0004+	−0.0007 0.0006	−0.0008 0.0004+	−0.0008 0.0005+	−0.0005 0.0004	−0.0010 0.0004*	−0.0010 0.0004*	−0.0007 0.0005	−0.0008 0.0004+
Male	0.0766 0.0087**	0.0688 0.0151**	0.0760 0.0092**	0.0801 0.0089**	0.0950 0.0077**	0.0719 0.0089**	0.0719 0.0089**	0.0730 0.0098**	0.0734 0.0093**
Citizen	−0.0751 0.0332*	−0.2003 0.0423**	−0.0743 0.0328*	−0.0769 0.0337*	−0.1146 0.0381**	−0.0819 0.0323*	−0.0819 0.0322*	−0.0652 0.0329*	−0.0662 0.0325*
Education (years of education)	0.0200 0.0024**	0.0157 0.0031**	−0.1157 0.0308**	−0.0766 0.0206**	−0.1086 0.0534*	−0.0966 0.0308**	−0.0963 0.0335**	−0.1207 0.0384**	−0.1142 0.0327**
Education∗gdp			0.0142 0.0032**	0.0102 0.0021**	0.0135 0.0054*	0.0121 0.0032**	0.0120 0.0035**	0.0146 0.0039**	0.0140 0.0033**
Log of real income		0.0380 0.0115**				0.0542 0.0070**	0.0478 0.1305		
Log of real income∗gdp							0.0007 0.0140		
Education∗import duties								0.0002 0.0005	
Education∗(imports/gdp)									0.0000 0.0001
Rural		−0.0095 0.0083							
Upper social class		0.0314 0.0059**							
Trade union member		−0.0110 0.0207							
Political affiliation with the right		0.0375 0.0122**							
Number obs	24025	4834	24025	22874	18719	16611	16611	21692	23023
Pseudo R^2	0.08	0.09	0.08	0.08	0.09	0.09	0.09	0.08	0.08

Notes: The table contains the estimated marginal effect on the probability of being pro-trade, given an increase in the value of the relevant regressor, holding all other regressors at their mean value. The standard errors of the marginal effect of each relevant regressor – adjusted for clustering on country – are presented under each marginal effect. + significant at 10%; * significant at 5%; ** significant at 1%. In regression (4) we drop the Philippines. In regressions (5), we drop low-income countries (Poland, Bulgaria, Russia, Latvia and the Philippines). *Pro-Trade Dummy* is coded as follows: Pro-Trade Dummy = 1 if Trade Opinion = 4 or 5; 0 if Trade Opinion = 1, 2, 3, 8, or 9. *Education* refers to years of education, with a maximum top-coding (introduced by us) of 20. *gdp* is the log of per capita GDP in 1995, PPP (current international dollars). *Rural* is coded as follows: 1 = urban, 2 = suburbs/city-town, 3 = rural. *Log of real income* is calculated using data in local currency on individual yearly income from the ISSP data set and purchasing power parity conversion factors from the WDI (World Bank). *import duties* are average import duties (as % of imports) in 1990–1995. *imports/gdp* is the average imports-to-GDP ratio in 1990–1995. *Upper social class* is coded as follows: 1 = lower, 2 = working, 3 = lower middle, 4 = middle, 5 = upper middle, 6 = upper. *Trade union member* equals 1 if the individual is a member of a trade union, 0 if he is not. *Political affiliation with the right* is coded as follows: 1 = far left, 2 = centre left, 3 = centre, 4 = right, 5 = far right.

striking difference given that only 22% of the ISSP sample overall is pro-trade. This gender-based difference in trade attitudes provides us with an early glimpse into the important role played by values in shaping attitudes.[16] Older individuals appear to be more protectionist, but the estimates are not always significant.[17] Citizenship in the country is negatively associated with pro-trade sentiments, while political affiliation with the right has a positive and significant impact on pro-trade attitudes.[18] Finally, self-evaluations of high social status (*upper social class*) have a positive effect on pro-trade attitudes, i.e. individuals who identify themselves as belonging to one of the upper classes are more likely to oppose protection.

Column (2) in Table 4 shows that an individual's real income is positively associated with pro-trade attitudes, even after controlling for education and other socio-demographic attributes. Given that a full set of country dummy variables is included in the specification, this marginal effect captures the impact of the variation of individual income within each country, i.e. the effect of relative income. Thus trade is generally perceived to be a good thing for individuals at the high end of a country's income distribution, and a bad thing for those at the bottom. This result survives various robustness checks, including embedding the income variable in the economic frameworks we discuss below. We are not aware of any simple economic theory that would explain this finding, and we leave the development of such a theory to further research. Whatever the underlying story, one interesting implication of the relationship between relative income and pro-trade attitudes is worth noting. Consider a political-economy model in which trade policies are determined by the preferences of the median voter (as in Mayer, 1984). In countries with greater income inequality the median voter will normally have a lower relative income than in countries with greater equality. Consequently, greater inequality will be associated with higher levels of trade protection across countries.

When we modify the naïve demographics specification below, we shall drop some of the socio-demographic variables (area of residence, subjective social class, political party affiliation and trade union membership) because we would be losing too many observations to missing values otherwise. We shall keep age, gender, citizenship and education as controls in all specifications.

4. Economic determinants of individual attitudes: The factor-endowments model

Moving towards free trade, a country that is well endowed with skilled labor will experience an increase in the relative price of skill-intensive goods and correspond-

[16] An alternative hypothesis is that gender differences arise from the significantly lower levels of labor-market participation of women or from differences in the labor-market positions of women relative to men. We do not find evidence of such effects when we control for whether an individual is in the labor market or not, or when we control for comparative-advantage (comparative-disadvantage) status of the individual's sector of employment.

[17] We do not find evidence of non-linear effects of age on pro-trade attitudes.

[18] Trade union membership is associated with protectionist attitudes, but the effect is not significant in the simple probit specification.

ingly specialize in the production of those goods. According to the Stolper–Samuelson theorem, skilled workers in all sectors of the economy will gain and unskilled workers will lose. A key assumption of the factor-endowments model – of which the Stolper–Samuelson theorem is an implication – is that factors of production can move costlessly across economic sectors. This is an extreme assumption. However, as long as the time horizon individuals use to evaluate trade policy is a long-run one – in which rates of return to factors are equalized across sectors – their attitudes over trade policy will be informed by the underlying logic of the Stolper–Samuelson theorem. In this section, we test this idea.

We first focus on the analysis of the ISSP data set. We use as our theoretical backdrop a world in which skilled and unskilled labor are the only relevant factors of production. We do not have information on capital ownership, so we shunt it aside by assuming that it plays an insignificant role in shaping comparative advantage, perhaps because it is internationally mobile. Our measure of skill is years of education (*education*), which we have already used above.

According to the factor-endowments model, an individual's trade policy attitudes will depend both on his skill level and on his country's relative factor endowment. A skilled individual will be pro-trade in an economy that is well endowed with skilled labor, but anti-trade in an economy that is well endowed with low-skill labor. So we need information also on an economy's relative abundance in skilled labor. As a proxy for relative factor endowments, we shall use per-capita GDP (in 1995, PPP-adjusted). Table 14 in Appendix B presents per capita GDP values for the countries included in the two data sets. It is reasonable to suppose that countries with higher values of GDP per capita are also better endowed with skilled labor.[19]

Before we present regression results, it is instructive to examine whether the estimated effect of *education* varies systematically across countries in the manner predicted by the Stolper–Samuelson theorem. So we first ran a series of probit regressions on individual countries, with *Pro-Trade Dummy* as the dependent variable. In each case, we regressed *Pro-Trade Dummy* on *education* (along with *age* and *male*). In Fig. 2a, we plot the estimated marginal effects we obtained on *education* alongside each country's per-capita GDP. The result is striking: there is a very strong and tight relationship between a country's per-capita GDP and the magnitude of the corresponding estimated marginal effect of *education* (the coefficient of per capita GDP is 1.53 percentage points per US$10,000, robust t-statistic = 4.97, significant at 1% level). The richer a country, the more positive is the impact of a marginal increase of *education* on the probability of pro-trade attitudes. The Philippines lies at the low end of the spectrum, and is without question the country with the lowest skill endowment in the ISSP sample. The marginal effect of *education* we obtained for the Philippines is not only the smallest among all countries in the ISSP data set, it is actually negative (and

[19] We could have also used the Barro and Lee (1996,2000) data sets, but these suffer from some clear defects where the countries in our sample are concerned. For example, when we construct a measure of relative human capital endowment (high-skilled vs low-skilled labor) by considering no schooling and primary schooling attainment in the low-skilled labor measure and secondary schooling and higher schooling attainment in the high-skilled labor measure, we obtain that West Germany and Spain rank lower than the Philippines in 1990.

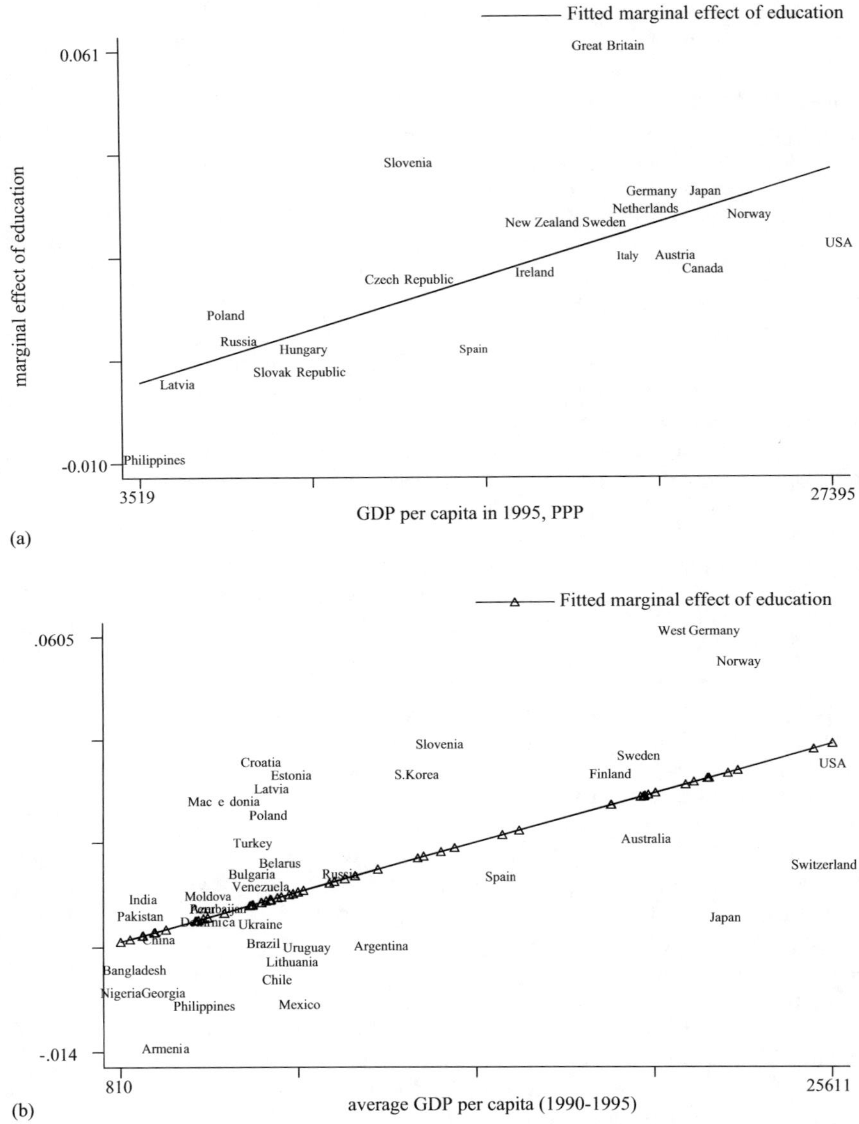

Fig. 2. Relationship between per-capita GDP and the estimated marginal effect of: (a) education on pro-trade attitudes (ISSP data set) and, (b) occupational skill on pro-trade attitudes (WVS data set).

statistically significant at the 1% level). Greater education is associated with more protectionist views in the Philippines – the only such case in the ISSP sample. These findings are quite in line with the Stolper–Samuelson theorem.

In columns (3)–(9) of Table 4 we show pooled regressions, with a full set of country dummies, where we take into account the cross-country heterogeneity with respect to the effect of *education*. In regression (3), we interact *education* with log per-capita GDP, *education∗gdp*, and enter the main effect of education separately.[20] The previous exercise on individual countries suggests that the impact of *education* should depend on the level of per-capita GDP; that is, we should get a negative coefficient on *education* but a positive coefficient on the interaction term *education∗gdp*. This is exactly what we get.[21] Both terms are highly significant. Columns (4) and (5) confirm that the pattern continues to hold when we drop the Philippines and the other lower-income countries from the sample.[22] This is important evidence, suggesting that the non-linearity in *education* is present for the entire range of countries; it is not an artifact driven by either the Philippines or a small number of low-income countries. Column (6) confirms that the result is robust to controlling for an individual's real income. Finally, in regression (7), we introduce an additional interaction term between individual income and per-capita GDP, *log of real income∗gdp*, to confirm that what we are capturing is a non-linearity in the impact of education, and not with respect to income/earnings.

We also take into consideration the possibility that different levels of trade policy may affect individuals within a country not uniformly. In particular, international differences in trade openness may impact the interaction coefficient of individual skill and country factor-endowments. We are worried about the possibility that richer countries are more open to trade and that the distributive implications are therefore more evident there. To guard against this, we interact *education* with both a country's average import-tariff level and its import/GDP ratio (columns (8) and (9), Table 4). However, we find that the coefficients on these interaction terms, which are insignificant, are not supportive of this possibility. And more important, in neither case are the findings on the Stolper–Samuelson effect altered.[23]

Since the WVS covers more countries, including many more low-income countries, it is important to check whether these results carry over to the WVS data set. This is done in Table 5. The WVS allows us to use four different measures of skill: the highest education level attained by the individual (*education*), the age at which the individual finished school (*education age*), the skill of the individual according to an occupation-based classification (*individual skill*), and the skill of the chief wage earner in the household according to the same occupation-based classification (*cwe skill*). Depending on the measure of skill used, the number of countries included is either 37 or 40, which is a significant improvement over 23. As before, we use the log of per capita GDP (in 1995, PPP-adjusted) to measure each country's endowment of skilled labor.

Table 5 reveals the same non-linear pattern with respect to the impact of skill on pro-trade attitudes that we uncovered with the ISSP data set. Regardless of the

[20] Notice that the main effect of per capita GDP is captured by the country dummy variables.

[21] O'Rourke and Sinnott (2001) have independently replicated this result, even though their measure of skill is different from ours. These authors use an occupational measure, in contrast to our educational measure.

[22] The countries dropped are Poland, Bulgaria, Russia, Latvia and the Philippines.

[23] Regressions (7) and (8) in Table 5 show parallel results using the WVS data: again, the findings of the Stolper–Samuelson effect are not altered.

Table 5
Factor endowments model (WVS data set)

Probit with country dummies	1	2	3	4	5	6	7	8
Dependent variable	Pro-Trade Dummy (WVS)							
Age	−0.003	−0.0026	−0.0039	−0.0034	−0.004	−0.0034	−0.0025	−0.003
	0.0001**	0.0002**	0.0002**	0.0002**	0.0002**	0.0002**	0.0002**	0.0001**
Male	0.0365	0.0721	0.0385	0.0344	0.044	0.0239	0.0464	0.037
	0.0043**	0.0078**	0.0046**	0.0047**	0.0050**	0.0072**	0.0049**	0.0043**
Country of birth	−0.0463	−0.1037	−0.0469	−0.0419	−0.0535	−0.0294	−0.0767	−0.0418
	0.0094**	0.0159**	0.0099**	0.0101**	0.0103**	0.0152+	0.0116**	0.0095**
Education (educational attainment)	−0.1004	−0.1399					−0.1184	−0.106
	0.0090**	0.0248**					0.0166**	0.0096**
Education∗gdp	0.014	0.0185					0.0156	0.0143
	0.0011**	0.0026**					0.0018**	0.0011**
Education age (age at which education completed)			−0.0232	−0.057				
			0.0043**	0.0054**				
Education age∗gdp			0.0031	0.0077				
			0.0005**	0.0006**				
Individual skill (occupation-based individual skill)					−0.0831			
					0.0086**			
Individual skill∗gdp					0.0115			
					0.0010**			
Cwe skill (chief wage earner's occupation-based skill)						−0.0446		
						0.0105**		
Cwe skill∗gdp						0.0066		
						0.0013**		
Education∗import duties							0.0006	
							0.0002**	
Education∗(imports/GDP)								0.0001
								0.0001+
Number obs	50771	15166	46143	44495	40068	22962	35413	49789
Pseudo R^2	0.1	0.07	0.1	0.1	0.1	0.11	0.09	0.1

Notes: The table contains the estimated marginal effect on the probability of being pro-trade, given an increase in the value of the relevant regressor, holding all other regressors at their mean value. The standard errors of the marginal effect of each relevant regressor – adjusted for clustering on country – are presented under each marginal effect. + significant at 10%; ** significant at 1%. *Education* (the highest education level attained by the individual) is coded as follows: 1=no formal education; 2 = incomplete primary school; 3 = complete primary school; 4 = incomplete secondary school (technical/vocational type); 5 = complete secondary school (technical/vocational type); 6 = incomplete secondary (university/preparatory type); 7 = complete secondary (university/preparatory type); 8 = some university-level education, without degree; 9 = university level education, with degree. *Education age* is the age at which the individual finished school. *Individual skill* is coded as follows: 1 = agricultural worker; 2 = farmer (own farm); 3 = unskilled manual worker; 4 = semi-skilled manual worker; 5 = skilled manual worker; 6 = foreman and supervisor; 7 = non manual-office worker (non-supervisory); 8 = supervisory-office worker; 9 = professional worker (lawyer, accountant, teacher, etc.); 10 = employer/manager of establishment with less than 10 employees; 11 = employer/manager of establishment with 10 or more employees. *cwe* (chief wage earner in the household) skill is coded in the same way as individual skill. Regression (2) is the same as (1) but it only considers observations from the countries in common between the ISSP and the WVS data sets (see Table 3). Regression (4) is the same as regression (3) but it excludes individuals who finished school when they were more than 30 years old. *import duties* are average import duties (as % of imports) in 1990–1995. *imports/gdp* is the average imports-to-GDP ratio in 1990–1995.

measure of skill used, the estimated marginal effect of skill is negative (and significant), while the estimated marginal effect of skill interacted with per-capita GDP is positive (and also significant). As we did with the ISSP data, we also plot the estimated marginal effect of individual skill against a country's per-capita GDP. Fig. 2b shows the scatter plot for the occupation-based skill measure (the others are quite similar). The relationship has a distinctly positive slope: the associated regression slope has a robust t-statistic of 3.85. The poorest countries in the sample – Bangladesh, Nigeria, Armenia, Georgia – are those where more skill is associated with less pro-trade views. None of the richer countries exhibits this reversal.

Overall, these findings are strikingly supportive of the implications of the factor-endowments model and of the Stolper–Samuelson theorem. Education and skill are very strongly correlated with support for free trade in countries that are well endowed with human capital. It is either weakly or negatively correlated with support for free trade in countries that are poorly endowed with human capital. No other theory that we are aware of can explain this pattern. In particular, these findings are hard to square with the hypothesis that better educated people prefer more trade simply because they have a better understanding of comparative advantage or because they get more out of contact with foreign countries/products.

5. Economic determinants of individual attitudes: The specific-factors model

If individuals are on average immobile across industries, attitudes towards trade should be determined by their sector of employment, rather than their factor type. Respondents working in sectors where the home economy has a comparative advantage should be pro-trade; respondents employed in comparative-disadvantage sectors should be protectionist; and individuals in non-traded sectors on balance indifferent or pro-trade. This is the central insight of the specific-factors model.

In taking this insight to our data, we face an immediate problem. The ISSP survey contains no direct question about sector of employment. But it does provide very detailed information on occupation (based on the 4-digit International Standard Classification of Occupations [ISCO] or national classifications). We do our best to infer sector of employment from this data on occupation. Since our goal is to establish a correspondence between these sectors and international trade data, we recode the occupation variables according to the industry classification used in the World Trade Analyzer (WTA) data set. In particular, we end up reorganizing the data on the basis of a breakdown into 34 manufacturing industries (plus one – non-manufacturing) as defined by the U.S. Bureau of Economic Analysis (BEA). Since the occupation codes used in the ISSP data set are not always detailed enough to be matched with any single BEA code, we create in addition new codes as combinations of the original codes. This results in a total of 54 (partly overlapping) sectors. The details of our procedures and the sectoral breakdown we use are discussed in Appendix A. In some cases, the mapping is straightforward, as many occupational codes (e.g., "dairy and livestock producers", "chemical-processing-plant operators", or "aircraft engine mechanics and fitters") are directly indicative of sectors. In other cases, it is impossible to assign an individual to a specific sector, and this results in either a less precise recoding or in missing values.

We determine a sector's revealed comparative advantage (or comparative disadvantage) by looking at the sign of adjusted net imports in that sector (averaged over the years 1990–1995). The adjustment is meant to "correct" for the existence of overall trade imbalances. Hence, we define an adjustment factor, λ, as follows:

$$\lambda = \frac{\sum_i (M_i - X_i)}{\sum_i M_i}.$$

The indicator λ is positive for countries that have a trade deficit and negative for countries with a trade surplus. In particular, λ tells us by what fraction imports in each sector would have to be reduced in order to balance the trade account. Our measure of adjusted net imports in each sector is the difference between $(1 - \lambda)M_i$ and X_i. We then define the two sector-specific variables, CA_{ik} (comparative-advantage sector) and CD_{ik} (comparative-disadvantage sector) for each sector i in country k as follows:

$$CA_{ik} = \begin{cases} 1, & \text{if } M_{ik} - X_{ik} - \lambda M_{ik} < 0, \text{ for sector}_{ik} = 1,\ldots,54, \\ 0, & \text{if } M_{ik} - X_{ik} - \lambda M_{ik} > 0, \text{ for sector}_{ik} = 1,\ldots,54 \text{ or if non-tradable sector,} \end{cases}$$

$$CD_{ik} = \begin{cases} 1, & \text{if } M_{ik} - X_{ik} - \lambda M_{ik} > 0, \text{ for sector}_{ik} = 1,\ldots,54, \\ 0, & \text{if } M_{ik} - X_{ik} - \lambda M_{ik} < 0, \text{ for sector}_{ik} = 1,\ldots,54 \text{ or if non-tradable sector.} \end{cases}$$

A sector is defined as a comparative-advantage sector if its adjusted net imports are less than zero and as a comparative-disadvantage sector if its adjusted net imports are greater than zero. Each individual is therefore assigned to one of three types of sectors: (a) a comparative-advantage sector; (b) a comparative-disadvantage sector; or (c) a non-tradable sector.[24]

The sector classification based on the occupation variables delivers a fairly good measure of the comparative-advantage (comparative-disadvantage) status of each individual. We use external data from another ISSP data set, Social Inequality II (1992), which contains information on both individuals' sector of employment and occupation for the United States, Germany, and Austria. For approximately 85% of individuals in these three countries for whom both sector and occupation data is available, our reclassification on the occupation data produces the same information on comparative-advantage and comparative-disadvantage status as if direct data on sector had been used.[25]

The first regression in Table 6 shows the results of our test of the sector-specific model. An individual in a comparative-disadvantage sector is significantly less likely to be pro-trade (by 2.5 percentage points), compared to an individual in a non-traded sector. This is highly supportive of the specific-factors model. Perhaps surprisingly, an individual in a comparative-advantage industry is not more likely to be pro-trade than

[24] This is true unless the individual has not reported his occupation or there is no data on imports and exports for his sector of employment, in which case the individual is assigned a missing value.

[25] A separate appendix describing this analysis along with the analysis of attenuation bias arising from misclassification (see Card, 1996) is available upon request. We thank Jörn-Steffen Pischke and an anonymous referee for suggestions that prompted these analyses.

Table 6
Sector specific model (ISSP data set)

	Probit with country dummy variables				
	1	2	3	4	5
Dependent variable	Pro-Trade Dummy				
Age	−0.0004	−0.0004	−0.0005	−0.0005	−0.0004
	0.0004	0.0004	0.0004	0.0004	0.0005
Male	0.0802	0.0805	0.0811	0.0808	0.0846
	0.0129**	0.0125**	0.0130**	0.0128**	0.0131**
Citizen	−0.0695	−0.0691	−0.068	−0.0678	−0.0693
	0.0390+	0.0387+	0.0396+	0.0392+	0.0413+
Education (years of education)	0.019	0.0189	−0.1332	−0.1303	−0.124
	0.0028**	0.0030**	0.0238**	0.0254**	0.0241**
Education*gdp			0.016	0.0157	0.0154
			0.0025**	0.0027**	0.0026**
CA sector	−0.0133		−0.0207		0.0115
	0.0239		0.0187		0.0358
CD sector	−0.0252		−0.0204		−0.0168
	0.0116*		0.0122+		0.0311
Exports		−271.602		−242.337	
		408.5989		416.4975	
Imports		−1,807.68		−1,567.50	
		721.0540*		703.3980*	
Education*willingness to move					−0.0336
					0.0308
Education*gdp*willingness to move					0.0027
					0.003
Willingness to move					0.126
					0.0671+
CA*willingness to move					−0.0454
					0.0574
CD*willingness to move					0.002
					0.0449
Number of obs	12432	12432	12432	12432	11473
Pseudo R^2	0.07	0.07	0.07	0.07	0.07

Notes: The table contains the estimated marginal effect on the probability of being pro-trade, given an increase in the value of the relevant regressor, holding all other regressors at their mean value. The standard errors of the marginal effect of each relevant regressor – adjusted for clustering on country – are presented under each marginal effect. + significant at 10%; * significant at 5%; ** significant at 1%. *Pro-Trade Dummy* is coded as follows: Pro-Trade Dummy = 1 if Trade Opinion = 4 or 5; 0 if Trade Opinion = 1, 2, 3, 8, or 9. *gdp* is the log of per capita GDP in 1995, PPP (current international dollars). *Willingness to move*, which varies between 0 and 1, measures the stated willingness to move to another city/town, in order to improve work or living conditions. A sector is defined as a *CA* (comparative-advantage) sector if its adjusted net imports are less than zero and as a *CD* (comparative-disadvantage) sector if its adjusted net imports are greater than zero. *Exports* refers to the value of exports in the respondent's sector of employment, normalized by GDP. *Imports* refers to the value of imports in the respondent's sector of employment, normalized by GDP.

an individual in a non-traded sector: the marginal effect of *CA sector* is negative but not significant.[26]

The latter result can be rationalized by considering the original survey question, which is meant to elicit attitudes related to restrictions on imports only. In the presence of two-way (intra-industry) trade, myopic individuals may oppose import restrictions in their sectors, even when those sectors are large exporters on balance. Additionally, our sectoral classification and aggregation procedures may have resulted in the lumping together of comparative-advantage and comparative-disadvantage sectors. Whatever the reason, the bottom line that emerges from this regression is that the main cleavage in preference formation over trade lies not between the two tradable sectors but between tradables and non-tradables.

An alternative specification, which takes into account the presence of two-way trade, is shown in column (2). Now we enter separately the actual volumes of exports and imports (normalized by GDP) of the sector in which an individual is employed. The logic of the specific-factors model (augmented by the possibility of two-way trade) is that the estimated coefficient on imports should be negative. The estimated coefficient on exports should be positive to the extent that individuals fear retaliation from abroad or see through the Lerner symmetry theorem. We do indeed find the negative (and significant) effect on the imports term. The estimated coefficient on exports, however, is insignificant. We interpret this as mildly supportive of the specific-factors model.

In columns (3) and (4), we carry out a joint test of the factor-endowments and specific-factors models. Both models survive, though the significance level of the comparative-disadvantage variable drops to 10%. We also compare the two competing models, in their linear specification, using a non-nested test, the *J* test proposed by Davidson and MacKinnon (Greene, 1997, p. 365). First, we estimate the two models separately: we regress *Trade Opinion* on age, gender and citizenship plus, respectively, *education* and *education∗gdp* (for the factor-endowments model) and *CA sector* and *CD sector* (for the specific-factors model). Next, we augment each of the two specifications with the fitted values from the other model. We find that the coefficients on the fitted values are significant in both cases (but only at the 10% level for the specific-factors fitted values).[27] Thus, the results based on the non-nested test – in favor of the factor-endowments model and marginally in favor of the sector-specific model – are consistent with what we found in column (3), Table 6.

It is important to emphasize that our analysis of misclassification – due to the use of the occupation-based sector classification – suggests that the attenuation factors of the specific-factors coefficients are of a very small magnitude (approximately 0.5). This implies that the coefficients of *CA sector* and *CD sector* could be substantially underestimated.

---

[26] In the ordered logit results, using as a common benchmark individuals in non-traded sectors, respondents in comparative-disadvantage industries are on average less likely to be pro-trade than respondents in export-oriented sectors: the coefficients on *CA sector* and *CD sector* are significantly different at the 10% level.

[27] In particular, we find that H_0: *factor-endowments model* should be rejected in favor of H_1: *sector-specific model* at a 90% level of significance. When we reverse the roles of H_0 and H_1, we find that H_0: *sector-specific model* should be rejected in favor of H_1: *factor-endowments model* at a 99% level of significance.

The horse-race analysis between the factor-endowments model and the specific-factors model gives us information regarding the time-horizon individuals use to assess trade policy, i.e. whether they are thinking about the long-run (as in the factor-endowments model) or the short-run (as in the specific-factors model) or both. The variation across individuals in terms of the relative importance of the two time frameworks is likely to depend on mobility. A plausible interpretation is that a certain fraction of individuals in our sample view themselves as intersectorally mobile over the time horizon that is relevant to them, and a certain fraction think of themselves as stuck in their present line of employment. The first group's trade attitudes would be in accordance with the factor-endowments model, while the second group's attitudes would be in accordance with both the specific-factors model and the factor-endowments model. [28]

The ISSP data set contains some questions on mobility. In particular, individuals are asked: "If you could improve your work or living conditions, how willing or unwilling would you be to move to another town or city?" Answers to the questions range from "very unwilling" (1) to "very willing" (5). The question relates to geographical mobility rather than inter-sectoral mobility, but may still be indicative of the latter. This gives us an opportunity to check whether willingness to move relates to trade attitudes in the manner consistent with our interpretation.

Our discussion suggests a specification of the form $E + (1 - mobile)*S$, where E are the regressors that capture the factor-endowments model, and S are the regressors reflecting the specific-factors model (we include the education main effect as part of the E set). If we estimate a regression with all the main effects (E, S and *mobile*) and interactions ($E*mobile$ and $S*mobile$), we should find that the coefficient on $E*mobile$ is not significant and that the coefficients on S and $S*mobile$ are equal in absolute value and with opposite signs. According to this model, the coefficient on the main effect *mobile* should not be significant. However, we would not be surprised to find a positive coefficient, since high mobility allows more flexibility in terms of other side-effects of trade liberalization not analyzed in the paper. [29] We test these restrictions in regression (5), Table 6.

First, the sign on the comparative advantage variable (*CA sector*) now becomes positive, in line with the original expectations from the specific-factors model (but the marginal effect is insignificant). Second, individuals in comparative-advantage sectors are less pro-trade (but not significantly) if their willingness to move is high. Third, individuals in comparative-disadvantage sectors express less protectionist sentiments when their stated willingness to move is high, although the interaction term in this case is nowhere near significant. [30] These results are all consistent with our interpretation,

[28] The implicit assumption is that the economy behaves as in the specific-factors model in the short-run (i.e., the average mobility rate is low in the short run) and as in the factor-endowments model in the long-run (i.e., the average mobility rate is high in the long run). A mobile individual is not concerned about the short run, because he can move from sector to sector, but he cares about the long run.

[29] For example, trade liberalization may affect the value of assets in a certain area.

[30] Notice that the marginal effects of *CA sector* and *CA* willingness to move*, in absolute value, are not significantly different from each other. The same is true for the marginal effects of *CD sector* and *CD* willingness to move*.

but the insignificance of the estimates prevents us from reading too much support into them.

6. The role of values, identity, and attachments

We have drawn attention to the importance of non-economic determinants of trade attitudes in the introduction. Indeed, some of our most interesting results pertain to the role of values, identity, and attachments in shaping individual attitudes on trade policy. These attributes are particularly significant in explaining differences in average trade attitudes across countries. We consider three different specifications in Table 7.

First, we look at the impact of community and regional attachments (column (1)). We focus on answers to the following questions: "How close do you feel to respondent's neighborhood?" (*neighborhood attachment*); respondent's town/city?" (*town attachment*); respondent's county/region?" (*county attachment*); respondent's country?" (*national pride* (1)); respondent's continent?" (*continent attachment*).[31] The results show a clear pattern. Individuals with strong attachments to their neighborhood, county/region, or nation tend to be less pro-trade.[32] The second set of issues we look at relates directly to patriotism, nationalism, and chauvinism. In addition to *national pride* (1), we focus on the following questions: "How much do you agree or disagree with the following statements? I would rather be a citizen of respondent's country than of any other country in the world." (*national pride* (2)); Generally respondent's country is a better country than most other countries." (*national pride* (3)); respondent's country should follow its own interests, even if this leads to conflicts with other nations." (*national pride* (4)).[33] On the one hand, national pride entails feelings of patriotism, i.e. genuine attachment to one's own country. On the other, national pride can be associated with feelings of nationalism – or, in its extreme form, chauvinism – i.e. sentiments of superiority of one's own country (Smith and Jarkko, 1998). We interpret answers to *national pride* (1) and (2) as reflecting both feelings of patriotism and nationalism. *National pride* (3) matches perfectly Smith and Jarkko's (1998) definition of nationalism as a feeling of superiority of one's own country. *National pride* (4) applies this nationalistic stand to a practical situation.

In a world where there are gains from trade at the national level, we would expect patriotism to be positively correlated with pro-trade attitudes. Regardless of distributional implications, individuals who care about the country as a whole should be in favor of free trade. On the other hand, patriotic individuals might lean towards protection if trade is viewed as a zero-sum game between nations or its social consequences are judged as adverse. The results in column (2) of Table 7 are more in line with the latter interpretation. There is a particularly strong negative relationship between

[31] The four possible answers to these questions range from "not close at all" (1) to "very close" (4).

[32] Such attachments tend to be particularly strong in countries like Japan and Spain, and weak in Britain and the U.S. (see Table 12 in Appendix B).

[33] The five possible answers to these questions range from "disagree strongly" (1) to "agree strongly" (5).

Table 7
Community/national attachment model (ISSP data set)

	Probit with country dummy variables			
	1	2	3	4
Dependent variable	Pro-Trade Dummy			
Age	−0.0003	−0.0001	−0.0007	0.0001
	0.0005	0.0004	0.0005	0.0004
Male	0.0805	0.0832	0.0785	0.088
	0.0089**	0.0097**	0.0081**	0.0089**
Citizen	−0.0759	−0.0582	−0.0846	−0.0704
	0.0379*	0.0249*	0.0284**	0.0237**
Education (years of education)	0.019	0.0157	0.0196	0.0143
	0.0025**	0.0024**	0.0027**	0.0025**
Neighborhood attachment	−0.0174			−0.0157
	0.0052**			0.0051**
Town attachment	0.0069			0.0091
	0.0056			0.0062
County attachment	−0.0213			−0.0167
	0.0051**			0.0043**
Continent attachment	0.0259			0.018
	0.0081**			0.0083*
National pride (1)	−0.0232	0.002		−0.0045
	0.0089**	0.0066		0.0078
National pride (2)		−0.0379		−0.0381
		0.0042**		0.0042**
National pride (3)		−0.0224		−0.0203
		0.0051**		0.0068**
National pride (4)		−0.0527		−0.0551
		0.0044**		0.0046**
Pride in democracy			0.0134	0.0183
			0.0061*	0.0053**
Pride in political influence			−0.0311	−0.0172
			0.0077**	0.0091+
Economic pride			0.0023	0.0097
			0.007	0.0072
Pride in social security system			0.0004	0.0034
			0.0072	0.0078
Number of obs	18993	20472	19867	15091
Pseudo R^2	0.08	0.11	0.08	0.12

Notes: The table contains the estimated marginal effect on the probability of being pro-trade, given an increase in the value of the relevant regressor, holding all other regressors at their mean value. The standard errors of the marginal effect of each relevant regressor – adjusted for clustering on country – are presented under each marginal effect. + significant at 10%; * significant at 5%; ** significant at 1%. *Pro-Trade Dummy* is coded as follows: Pro-Trade Dummy = 1 if Trade Opinion = 4 or 5; 0 if Trade Opinion = 1, 2, 3, 8, or 9. See Appendix B, Tables 12 and 13 for definitions of *neighborhood attachment*, *town attachment*, *county attachment*, *continent attachment*, *national pride* (1) – (4), *pride in democracy*, *pride in political influence*, *economic pride*, and *pride in social security system*.

national pride (2) and pro-trade views. This is significant in explaining the cross-country variation in trade attitudes, as *national pride* (2) varies greatly among countries. [34]

At the more explicitly nationalistic end of things, the results are as one would have expected. Feelings of superiority of one's own country presumably encourage thoughts of national isolationism, and abstention from political alliances and other international economic relations. Individuals who agree with the statement that their country "should follow its own interests, even if this leads to conflicts with other nations" (*national pride* (4)) are significantly less likely to be pro-trade. [35] These individuals clearly perceive trade as a zero-sum game. [36]

Finally, we turn to pride in specific national achievements. We focus on the following questions: "How proud are you of respondent's country in each of the following? The way democracy works." (*pride in democracy*); Political influence in world." (*pride in political influence*); Economic achievements." (*economic pride*); Social security system." (*pride in social security system*). [37] As shown in column (3) of Table 7, pride in a country's democracy is positively correlated with pro-trade attitudes. We take this to indicate that trade is less threatening to individuals who have confidence in their country's political institutions. On the other hand, pride in a country's political influence in the world (where the U.S. tops the list) is negatively associated with pro-trade attributes.

7. Concluding remarks

In Table 8 we present our preferred specification, based on the models we have considered so far. The main constraint in formulating a "summary" model is that missing values for specific questions result in a reduction in the sample size as more explanatory variables are added. The specification in Table 8 represents our compromise. It is meant to capture the essential insights of all the approaches we have used in explaining the formation of trade attitudes, with one exception: we have had to exclude regressors that relate to the specific-factors model, because the sample size would become unacceptably low otherwise. [38]

[34] The percentage of respondents that would "rather be citizen of own country than of any other country" varies from 91% in the U.S. to only 50% in the Netherlands (Table 12 in Appendix B).

[35] The percentage of respondents who agree with the proposition that their own country's interests should be followed even at the cost of conflict with others ranges from 73% in Bulgaria to 19% in Japan (Table 12 in Appendix B).

[36] Where similar questions exist in the WVS, the results are very similar to those reported in the text for the ISSP data set. We do not present these results with the WVS to save space.

[37] As might be expected, levels of pride are generally quite low in the former socialist economies: only 9% of respondents are proud of the economic achievements of their country in Hungary, compared to 83% in Germany and 82% in the U.S. (Table 13).

[38] We tested the robustness of our results to changes in the size of the sample (for example, we estimated various specifications in previous tables restricting the sample to observations without missing values for the regressors in our preferred specification ($n = 9696$)). We don't find substantive differences relative to our previous results.

Table 8
Preferred specification (ISSP data set)

	OLS	
	1	2
	Without country DV	With country DV
Dependent variable	Trade opinion	
Age	−0.0022	−0.0023
	0.0014	0.0013+
Male	0.2603	0.2252
	0.0320**	0.0339**
Education (years of education)	−0.1953	−0.3798
	0.0903*	0.0932**
Education∗gdp	0.023	0.0425
	0.0094*	0.0097**
Log of real income	0.0872	0.1114
	0.0332*	0.0269**
Upper social class	0.1212	0.077
	0.0213**	0.0133**
Neighborhood attachment	−0.0614	−0.0743
	0.0305+	0.0193**
Town attachment	0.0628	0.0629
	0.0211**	0.0206**
County attachment	−0.0767	−0.0767
	0.0336*	0.0217**
Continent attachment	0.0216	0.048
	0.0239	0.0170*
National pride (2)	−0.1518	−0.1403
	0.0256**	0.0184**
National pride (3)	−0.0697	−0.0895
	0.0235**	0.0179**
National pride (4)	−0.1969	−0.1623
	0.0199**	0.0139**
Constant	2.6136	2.5462
	0.4037**	0.2420**
Number of obs	9696	9696
Adj. R^2	0.19	0.22

Notes: Standard errors – adjusted for clustering on country – are presented under each estimated coefficient. + significant at 10%; * significant at 5%; ** significant at 1%. See definitions of the variables at the end of Tables 4, 6 and 7.

The basic specification is shown with and without country dummies. Note that the inclusion of country dummies does not greatly improve the overall fit of the regression. (The models in Table 8 are OLS specifications, so that we can interpret the R^2 in the usual fashion.) Even without the country dummies, our preferred specification explains almost a fifth (19%) of the variation in trade attitudes in our sample. Inclusion of the country dummies raises the adjusted R^2 only to 22%. In view of the complex nature of the issue at hand and the imperfections of our data, we consider this to be a fair level of success at explaining attitudes towards trade.

At the beginning of the paper, we highlighted the important differences that exist across countries in average pro-trade orientation. How well does our preferred specification do in explaining these cross-country differences? One way of getting at this question is to compute the standard deviation of the country dummy variables estimated without controls and, next, with all the variables in our preferred specification. As in Krueger and Summers (1988), we adjust the raw standard deviations, which are upwardly biased due to sampling variation.[39] We find that the adjusted standard deviation decreases from 0.9642 to 0.6775 when we switch from the specification with no controls (only country dummy variables) to the specification with both economic and non-economic determinants (regression (2), Table 8). What this indicates is that our preferred specification is fairly successful in explaining average differences in trade attitudes across countries.

Consider two specific cases, Poland and Sweden. In Poland's case, the average value of Trade Opinion is 0.90 points lower (on a 5-point scale) than in Germany.[40] What accounts for the difference? We can apply the coefficient estimates in column (2) of Table 8 to country-level averages of the regressors to arrive at an approximate decomposition. Our results indicate that some 65% of the difference is explained by differences in comparative advantage – i.e., more individuals associate themselves with skill-based gains from trade in Germany than in Poland – more than 20% by greater nationalism/patriotism in Poland, and about 6% by the greater incidence of perceptions of low social status in Poland. In Sweden's case, the average value of Trade Opinion is 0.33 points smaller than in Germany. Since the patterns of comparative advantage and the skill distribution do not differ greatly in these two countries, the bulk (roughly 60%) of the difference between Germany and Sweden is accounted for by greater cosmopolitanism in Germany and greater nationalism/patriotism in Sweden.

Non-economic determinants, in the form of socio-demographic background, values, identities, and attachments, play a very important role in explaining the variation in attitudes over trade. Using a linear specification (as in regression (2), Table 8), if we first consider a model with only economic variables (*education*, *education∗gdp*, (*log*) *real income*) and dummy variables, and we next introduce the non-economic variables (*age*, *male*, *upper social class*, *neighborhood attachment*, *town attachment*, *county attachment*, *continent attachment*, *national pride* (2), *national pride* (3), and *national pride* (4)) the increase in the R^2 is equal to 0.0667 (from a value of 0.1536). If we repeat the same steps reversing the order (first the non-economic variables plus dummy variables, next the economic ones), the R^2 increases by 0.0218 (from a value of 0.1985).

To conclude, attitudes to trade are shaped by a complex set of determinants, both economic and non-economic ones. Values and narrow self-interest both matter.

[39] We use Krueger and Summers (1988)'s formula $SD(\delta) \approx \sqrt{\text{var}(\hat{\delta}) - \sum_{k=1}^{n} \hat{\sigma}_k^2/n}$, where δ are the true country effects, $\hat{\delta}$ are the estimated ones, $\hat{\sigma}_k^2$ is the standard error of $\hat{\delta}_k$ and n is the number of countries. As in Krueger and Summers (1988), we do not adjust for covariance terms.

[40] The average values of *Trade Opinion* are calculated restricting the sample to observations without missing values for the regressors in our preferred specification.

Acknowledgements

The authors thank Pippa Norris for acquainting us with the ISSP data set, and the Ford and Rockefeller Foundations for financial support. Seminar participants at Harvard, Stanford, and Cornell have provided very useful comments. They also thank Gary Chamberlain and Jack Porter for valuable econometric advice, and Zoë McLaren for editorial assistance. Suggestions made by two anonymous referees and especially by Jörn-Steffen Pischke have substantially improved the paper.

Appendix A. Sector classification: Description of the reclassification procedure

Since in the ISSP survey there is no direct question about industry, we infer sector of employment from data on occupation. We use individual answers to two questions in the data set, one asking for occupation according to an international code (the 4-digit International Standard Classification of Occupations (ISCO) from 1968 and from 1988) and another one asking for occupation in terms of national codes. Individuals in each country give information about own occupation according to only one of the classifications (either ISCO 1968 or ISCO 1988 or according to a national classification). In particular, individuals' occupations from the following countries are coded according to ISCO 1968: Germany West, Germany East, USA, Austria, Norway, Bulgaria, New Zealand, Spain, Slovak Republic. The occupation codes of this group of countries are recoded all together. Respondents' occupations from the following countries are instead coded according to ISCO 1988: Hungary, Ireland, Czech Republic, Poland, Slovenia, Canada, Russia, Latvia. Again, we recode the occupation codes of this group of countries all together. Finally, respondents' occupations for Great Britain, Sweden, the Philippines, Italy, Netherlands and Japan follow national occupation codes. Data from Great Britain, Sweden and the Philippines are recoded individually. The national occupation codes for Italy, Netherlands and Japan cannot be reclassified, since they are not detailed enough.

We reclassify the occupation variables from the ISSP data set in order to match the coding in the World Trade Analyzer (WTA) data set, containing world trade flows from 1980 to 1997. To classify industries, the WTA uses a slightly modified version of the Standard International Trade Classification (SITC), Revision 2. However, in the WTA CD-ROM, information is also available in a different format. Data is organized according to the 34 manufacturing industry basis used by the U.S. Bureau of Economic Analysis (BEA). This coding is quite similar to the U.S. Standard Industrial Classification. The WTA CD-ROM includes the annual bilateral trade values between all countries in the world in 1980–1997 according to this 34-industry classification. We use the BEA classification to recode the occupation variables in the ISSP data set and construct a new variable indicating the individual sector of employment. The 34 industries (plus one – Non-manufacturing – recoded as 35) are listed in Table 9. In order to obtain a more precise match between the ISSP occupation data and the BEA industry codes, we base the recoding on a very detailed description of the correspondence between BEA codes and SITC Revision 2 (four-digit level) codes (we used "Appendix

Table 9
BEA (Bureau of Economic Analysis) 34 manufacturing industry codes

1.	Grain, Mill and Bakery Products
2.	Beverages
3.	Tobacco Product
4.	Other Food and Kindred Products
5.	Apparel and Other Textile Products
6.	Leather and Leather Products
7.	Pulp, Paper and Board Mills
8.	Other Paper and Allied Products
9.	Printing and Publishing
10.	Drugs
11.	Soaps, Cleaners, and Toilet Goods
12.	Agricultural Chemicals
13.	Industrial Chemicals and Synthetics
14.	Other Chemicals
15.	Rubber Products
16.	Miscellaneous Plastic Products
17.	Primary Metal Industries, Ferrous
18.	Primary Metal Industries, Nonferrous
19.	Fabricated Metal Products
20.	Farm and Garden Machinery
21.	Construction, Mining, etc.
22.	Computer and Office Equipment
23.	Other Nonelectric Machinery
24.	Household Appliances
25.	Household Audio and Video, etc.
26.	Electronic Components
27.	Other Electrical Machinery
28.	Motor Vehicles and Equipment
29.	Other Transportation Equipment
30.	Lumber, Wood, Furniture, etc.
31.	Glass Products
32.	Stone, Clay, Concrete, Gypsum, etc.
33.	Instruments and Apparatus
34.	Other Manufacturing
35.	Non-Manufacturing (natural resources, etc.)

D: SITC Revision 2 codes used by Statistics Canada, WTA, and the corresponding BEA 34 manufacturing industry codes", from "World Trade Flows, 1980–1997", by Feenstra (2000)).

In addition to the 35 BEA industry codes, we create new codes as combinations of the original 35 codes. This is necessary since the occupation codes used in the ISSP data set are not always detailed enough to be matched to any single BEA code. See an extract from the 1968 ISCO classification in Table 10 and corresponding BEA codes, assigned by us, as an example of the reclassification.

For each of the 35 original BEA industries, we consider sector-specific exports and imports. For each new code, exports (imports) are obtained as sum of exports (imports) of the sectors used in the combination (so, for example, exports of sector 36, which is the combination of sectors 17 and 18, are set equal to the sum of exports of sectors 17 and 18). We then average both exports and imports over the years 1990–1995.

Table 10
Extract from 1968 International Standard Classification of Occupations

1968 ISCO	BEA code
Agricultural, animal husbandry and forestry workers, fishermen and hunters	
60 Farm managers and supervisors	
6000 Farm managers and supervisors	1, 4
6001 Farm managers and supervisors (general)	1, 4
6009 Farm managers	1, 4
61 Farmers	
6100 Farmers	1, 4
6110 General farmers	1, 4
6112 General farmers (general)	1, 4
6115 Collective farmers	1, 4
6120 Specialised farmers	1, 4
62 Agricultural and animal husbandry workers	
6200 Agricultural and animal husbandry worker	1, 4
6210 General farm workers	1, 4
6211 Farm helpers (general)	1, 4
6219 Farm hand	1, 4
6220 Field crop and vegetable farm workers	1, 4
6230 Orchard, vineyard and related tree and shrub crop workers	4
6240 Livestock workers	4
6250 Dairy farm workers	4
6260 Poultry farm workers	4
6270 Nursery workers and gardeners	4
6280 Farm machinery operators	1, 4
6290 Agricultural and animal husbandry workers, n.e.c.	1, 4
63 Forestry workers	
6300 Forestry workers	30
6310 Loggers	30
6319 Logger	30
6320 Forestry workers (except logging)	NT
64 Fishermen, hunters and related workers	
6400 Fishermen, hunters and related workers	4
6410 Fishermen	4
6490 Fishermen, hunters and related workers, n.e.c.	4
Production and related workers, transport equipment operators and labourers	
70 Production supervisors and general foremen	
7000 Production supervisors and general foremen	m.v.
7001 Production supervisors and general foremen (general)	m.v.

(*continued overleaf*)

Table 10 (*Continued*)

1968 ISCO	BEA code
71 Miners, quarrymen, well drillers and related workers	
7100 Miners, quarrymen, well drillers	35
7110 Miners and quarrymen	35
7111 Quarrymen (general)	35
7112 Cutting machine operators (mine)	35
7119 Miners and related workers n.e.c.	35
7120 Mineral and stone treaters	35
7130 Well drillers, borers and related workers	35
72 Metal processors	
7200 Metal processors	17,18
7210 Metal smelting, converting and refining furnacemen	17,18
7220 Metal rolling-mill workers	17,18
7230 Metal melters and reheaters	17,18
7240 Metal casters	17,18
7250 Metal moulders and coremakers	17,18
7260 Metal annealers, temperers and case-hardeners	17,18
7270 Metal drawers and extruders	17,18
7280 Metal platers and coaters	17,18
7290 Metal processers, n.e.c.	17,18
73 Wood preparation workers and paper makers	
7300 Wood preparation workers	30
7310 Wood treaters	30
7320 Sawyers, plywood makers and related wood-processing workers	30
7321 Sawmill sawyers (general)	30
7330 Paper pulp preparers	7
7340 Paper makers	7
74 Chemical processers and related workers	
7400 Chemical processers and related workers	13
7410 Crushers, grinders and mixers	13
7420 Cookers, roasters and related heat-treaters	13
7430 Filter and separator operators	13
7440 Still and reactor operators	13
7450 Petroleum-refining workers	13
7490 Chemical processers and related workers, n.e.c.	13
75 Spinners, weavers, knitters, dyers and related workers	
7500 Spinners, weavers and related workers	5
7510 Fibre preparers	5
7520 Spinners and winders	5
7530 Weaving- and knitting-machine setters and pattern-card preparers	5
7540 Weavers and related workers	5
7550 Knitters	5
7560 Bleachers, dyers and textile product finishers	5
7590 Spinners, weavers, knitters, dyers and related workers, n.e.c.	5
76 Tanners, fellmongers and pelt dressers	
7600 Tanners, fellmongers and pelt dressers	6
7610 Tanners and fellmongers	6
7620 Pelt dressers	6

Table 10 (*continued*)

1968 ISCO	BEA code
77 Food and beverage processers	
7700 Food and beverage processers	2,4
7710 Grain millers	1
7720 Sugar processers and refiners	4
7730 Butchers and meat preparers	4
7740 Food preservers	4
7750 Dairy product processors	4
7760 Bakers, pastrycooks and confectionery makers	4
7770 Tea, coffee and cocoa preparers	2
7780 Brewers, wine and beverage makers	2
7790 Food and beverage processers, n.e.c.	2
78 Tobacco preparers and tobacco product makers	
7810 Tobacco preparers	3
7820 Cigar makers	3
7830 Cigarette makers	3
7890 Tobacco preparers and tobacco product makers, n.e.c.	3
79 Tailors, dressmakers, sewers, upholsterers and related workers	
7900 Tailors, dressmakers, sewers and rel. workers	5
7910 Tailors and dressmakers	5
7919 Tailor	5
7920 Fur tailors and related workers	5
7930 Milliners and hatmakers	5
7940 Patternmakers and cutters	5
7950 Sewers and embroiderers	5
7960 Upholsterers and related workers	5
7990 Tailors, dressmakers, sewers, upholsterers and related workers, n.e.c.	5
80 Shoemakers and leather goods makers	
8000 Shoemakers and leather good makers	6
8010 Shoemakers and shoe repairers	6
8020 Shoe cutters, lasters, sewers and related workers	5
8030 Leather goods makers	6
81 Cabinetmakers and related woodworkers	
8100 Cabinetmakers and related woodworkers	30
8110 Cabinetmakers	30
8120 Woodworking-machine operators	30
8190 Cabinetmakers and related woodworkers, n.e.c.	30
82 Stone cutters and carvers	
8200 Stone cutters and carvers	32

Appendix B

For ISSP data sets see Tables 11–14.

Table 11
Demographic variables (ISSP data set)

Country	Number of observations in the sample	Age	Average years of education	Male	Rural	Trade union membership	Upper social class						Political affiliation with the right				
							Lower	Working	Lower middle	Middle	Upper middle	Upper	Far left	Centre left	Centre	Right	Far right
Germany West	1282	46	10.93	0.54	—	0.36	2.03	0.00	16.15	56.40	16.54	1.25	0.31	48.99	5.46	35.96	2.57
Germany East	612	48	10.93	0.50	—	0.78	8.99	0.00	33.50	43.14	4.25	0.33	15.20	43.46	5.07	25.49	1.31
Great Britain	1058	47	11.34	0.40	—	0.21	—	—	—	—	—	—	0.57	42.91	14.56	26.28	0.00
USA	1367	45	13.43	0.44	1.59	0.10	5.85	45.79	0.00	44.33	0.00	3.29	0.00	34.31	36.06	27.65	0.00
Austria	1007	46	10.39	0.45	—	0.46	3.67	0.00	15.49	61.77	12.51	0.79	0.00	36.15	4.47	29.89	0.00
Hungary	1000	48	10.50	0.43	1.97	0.15	12.70	35.20	25.30	22.20	1.20	0.00	—	—	—	—	—
Italy	1094	43	11.03	0.48	1.98	0.12	1.37	0.00	11.52	71.30	13.35	2.47	—	—	—	—	—
Ireland	994	46	12.26	0.49	2.02	0.26	1.61	35.31	14.29	38.73	4.33	0.50	0.00	2.41	35.41	0.91	0.00
Netherlands	2089	44	12.69	0.46	1.72	0.21	—	—	—	—	—	—	6.46	18.00	25.99	15.65	2.73
Norway	1527	43	12.68	0.50	2.09	0.44	0.00	30.39	6.48	39.49	8.32	0.52	0.65	38.11	18.60	19.71	0.00
Sweden	1296	45	11.43	0.49	1.23	0.71	2.39	35.19	0.00	45.06	9.18	0.69	5.79	33.33	13.97	17.98	0.00
Czech Republic	1111	43	12.91	0.51	1.65	0.21	4.14	27.27	21.24	35.01	6.39	1.26	5.13	10.80	39.33	22.59	9.00
Slovenia	1036	43	10.68	0.44	2.03	0.35	3.28	34.07	0.00	47.49	6.18	0.19	0.00	4.54	9.56	17.37	1.93
Poland	1598	47	10.29	0.45	1.72	0.13	7.38	41.24	0.00	39.55	4.44	2.19	0.00	24.16	9.26	4.69	0.00
Bulgaria	1105	49	—	0.48	1.92	0.19	14.57	51.67	0.00	26.24	0.00	1.00	5.97	15.02	8.05	8.96	2.71
Russia	1585	45	11.19	0.45	1.50	0.32	12.81	29.72	14.64	25.11	2.90	0.69	18.30	3.15	8.08	35.84	4.35
New Zealand	1043	46	14.33	0.47	1.50	0.15	3.36	18.98	10.64	40.94	11.79	0.96	0.00	4.22	55.23	4.89	0.00
Canada	1543	42	14.78	0.49	1.16	0.20	2.59	16.40	10.17	31.82	13.09	1.49	0.91	20.03	30.07	14.58	0.00
Philippines	1200	40	9.38	0.50	1.75	0.01	25.08	61.33	0.00	10.83	0.00	2.75	—	—	—	—	—
Japan	1256	46	11.87	0.46	—	0.13	4.46	0.00	19.27	48.65	17.20	3.50	1.67	5.18	6.21	24.12	0.00
Spain	1221	45	10.13	0.48	1.48	0.08	6.14	41.28	17.61	28.75	3.77	0.33	11.47	31.37	0.25	28.58	0.00
Latvia	1044	47	11.64	0.39	0.39	0.19	11.88	43.30	20.98	0.00	9.77	0.57	—	—	—	—	—
Slovak Republic	1388	41	11.83	0.48	—	0.32	8.65	30.98	21.97	26.59	6.63	1.66	4.90	13.18	35.81	12.68	6.41
Mean	28,456	44.77	11.69	0.47	1.69	0.31	7.29	30.77	12.45	40.15	7.90	1.44	6.07	33.16	28.97	29.28	2.52
Standard Deviation		16.88	3.58	0.50	0.90	0.46											

Rural is coded as follows: 1 urban, 2 suburbs/city-town, 3 rural.

Male is coded as follows: 1 male, 0 otherwise (i.e., 0 includes m.v.).

Trade Union Membership is coded as follows: 1 member, 0 otherwise (i.e., 0 includes m.v.).

Both *Upper Social Class* and *Political Affiliation with the Right* give percentages of individuals belonging to each category, over the whole national sample (i.e., including m.v.).

Table 12
Attachment to own neighborhood, town/city and county/region and national pride variables (ISSP data set)

Country	% in each nation declaring													
	Attachment to own neighborhood (neighborhood attachment)		Attachment to own town/city (town attachment)		Attachment to own county/region (country attachment)		Attachment to own country (national pride (1))		"rather be citizen of own country" (national pride (2))		Own country better than others (national pride (3))		In favor of country's interests at any cost (national pride (4))	
Germany	0.74	12	0.72	7	0.68	7	0.80	4	0.69	3	0.37	8	0.29	5
Great Britain	0.64	3	**0.56**	1	0.51	2	0.71	2	0.73	8	0.56	13	0.52	16
USA	0.57	2	0.60	2	0.62	4	0.81	5	**0.91**	22	0.81	21	0.44	13
Austria	0.83	16	0.84	16	0.89	20	0.91	13	0.86	15	0.69	17	0.62	20
Hungary	0.80	14	0.84	15	0.86	18	**0.96**	22	0.87	17	0.26	3	0.41	10
Italy	0.68	8	0.82	12	0.80	16	0.87	10	0.62	2	0.37	7	0.30	6
Ireland	0.84	17	0.83	14	0.81	17	0.93	15	0.86	16	0.71	18	0.63	21
Netherlands	0.71	10	0.71	5	**0.49**	1	0.87	9	**0.50**	1	0.46	11	0.28	4
Norway	**0.51**	1	0.70	4	0.79	15	0.94	20	0.78	11	0.67	16	0.38	9
Sweden	0.65	4	0.66	3	0.66	6	0.83	7	0.70	5	0.48	12	0.44	12
Czech Republic	0.81	15	0.87	19	0.69	9	0.92	14	0.73	7	**0.22**	1	0.31	7
Slovenia	0.77	13	0.82	13	0.78	14	0.93	17	0.78	13	0.28	4	0.28	3
Poland	0.73	11	0.75	9	0.64	5	0.94	19	0.88	19	0.39	9	0.48	15
Bulgaria	0.88	21	0.89	21	0.86	19	0.93	16	0.88	20	0.57	14	**0.73**	22
Russia	0.67	6	0.72	6	0.62	3	0.82	6	0.75	9	0.42	10	0.61	19
New Zealand	0.65	5	0.76	10	0.71	11	0.94	18	0.81	14	0.78	20	0.52	17
Canada	0.69	9	0.76	11	0.74	13	0.74	3	0.78	12	0.77	19	0.43	11
Philippines	0.86	19	0.73	8	0.68	8	**0.68**	1	0.88	18	0.59	15	0.37	8
Japan	**0.91**	22	0.88	20	0.89	21	0.95	21	0.89	21	**0.84**	22	**0.19**	1
Spain	0.88	20	**0.92**	22	**0.90**	22	0.89	12	0.73	6	0.36	6	0.61	18
Latvia	0.68	7	0.85	18	0.69	10	0.86	8	0.76	10	0.32	5	0.44	14
Slovak Republic	0.84	18	0.85	17	0.73	12	0.89	11	0.69	4	0.23	2	0.23	2
Mean	0.74		0.78		0.73		0.87		0.78		0.51		0.43	
Standard deviation	0.11		0.10		0.12		0.08		0.10		0.20		0.15	

(*continued overleaf*)

Table 12. (*Continued*)

Notes: The second column of each variable gives the ranking of countries according to that variable. Bold numbers correspond to highest and lowest values. *Neighborhood attachment* gives responses to the following question: "How close do you feel to (respondent's neighbourhood)?" *Town attachment* gives responses to the following question: "How close do you feel to (respondent's town/city)?" *County attachment* gives responses to the following question: "How close do you feel to (respondent's county)?" *National pride* (1) gives responses to the following question: "How close do you feel to (respondent's country)?". *National pride* (2) gives responses to the question: "How much do you agree or disagree with the following statements? I would rather be a citizen of (respondent's country) than of any other country in the world." *National pride* (3) gives responses to the question: "How much do you agree or disagree with the following statements? Generally (respondent's country) is a better country than most other countries." *National pride* (4) gives responses to the question: "How much do you agree or disagree with the following statements? (respondent's country) should follow its own interests, even if this leads to conflicts with other nations."

Table 13
Pride in specific achievements (ISSP data set)

Country	% in each nation declaring							
	Proud of national democracy		Proud of political influence in the world		Proud of economic achievements		Proud of social security system	
Germany	0.57	12	0.61	16	**0.83**	22	0.62	17
Great Britain	0.68	15	0.55	15	0.44	12	0.48	12
USA	0.83	20	**0.80**	22	0.82	19	0.50	13
Austria	0.71	16	0.63	17	0.82	21	**0.84**	22
Hungary	**0.20**	1	**0.18**	1	**0.09**	1	**0.07**	1
Italy	0.26	6	0.23	3	0.40	9	0.28	8
Ireland	0.75	18	0.79	21	0.82	20	0.65	19
Netherlands	0.84	21	0.49	13	0.78	16	0.83	21
Norway	0.80	19	0.78	19	0.80	18	0.62	16
Sweden	0.64	13	0.41	11	0.17	3	0.65	18
Czech Republic	0.35	8	0.51	14	0.42	11	0.19	6
Slovenia	0.21	3	0.29	4	0.34	8	0.30	9
Poland	0.24	5	0.36	6	0.28	6	0.17	4
Bulgaria	0.31	7	0.36	7	0.26	5	0.18	5
Russia	**0.20**	1	0.32	5	0.16	2	0.08	2
New Zealand	0.73	17	0.71	18	0.72	15	0.39	10
Canada	**0.84**	22	0.79	20	0.62	14	0.81	20
Philippines	0.53	10	0.39	9	0.50	13	0.52	14
Japan	0.66	14	0.45	12	0.80	17	0.47	11
Spain	0.54	11	0.40	10	0.41	10	0.53	15
Latvia	0.40	9	0.38	8	0.21	4	0.12	3
Slovak Republic	0.22	4	0.19	2	0.31	7	0.22	7
Mean	0.52		0.48		0.50		0.43	
Standard deviation	0.24		0.20		0.26		0.25	

Notes: The second column of each variable gives the ranking of countries according to that variable. Bold numbers correspond to highest and lowest values. *Pride in democracy* answers the following question:: "How proud are you of (respondent's country) in each of the following? The way democracy works." *Pride in political influence* answers the following question: : "How proud are you of (respondent's country) in each of the following? Political influence in world." *Economic pride* answers the following question: : "How proud are you of (respondent's country) in each of the following? Economic achievements." *Pride in social security system* answers the following question: : "How proud are you of (respondent's country) in each of the following? Social security system."

Table 14
Per capita GDP of the countries in the ISSP and WVS samples

Country	Per capita GDP in 1995 (PPP-adjusted)	Log of per capita GDP in 1995 (PPP-adjusted)
Nigeria	824.990	6.715
Bangladesh	1280.880	7.155
Ghana	1709.830	7.444
Pakistan	1765.360	7.476
India	1871.220	7.534
Armenia	1938.330	7.570

(*continued overleaf*)

Table 14 (*continued*)

Country	Per capita GDP in 1995 (PPP-adjusted)	Log of per capita GDP in 1995 (PPP-adjusted)
Azerbaijan	1982.220	7.592
Georgia	2016.160	7.609
Moldova	2403.020	7.784
China	2681.390	7.894
Philippines	3633.240	8.198
Ukraine	3811.710	8.246
Macedonia	4299.560	8.366
Dominican Republic	4350.740	8.378
Peru	4419.710	8.394
Latvia	5037.370	8.525
Belarus	5217.670	8.560
Lithuania	5626.700	8.635
Bulgaria	5679.510	8.645
Croatia	5905.530	8.684
Turkey	5924.610	8.687
Colombia	6012.530	8.702
Venezuela	6019.300	8.703
Romania	6543.390	8.786
Estonia	6558.690	8.789
Brazil	6726.440	8.814
Poland	6794.980	8.824
Russia	7206.220	8.883
Mexico	7221.970	8.885
Chile	7733.390	8.953
Uruguay	8017.480	8.989
S. Africa	8631.180	9.063
Slovakia	8667.670	9.067
Hungary	9577.070	9.167
Argentina	10940.100	9.300
Czech Republic	12414.290	9.427
Slovenia	13191.210	9.487
S. Korea	13758.830	9.529
Portugal	13774.940	9.531
Spain	15412.220	9.643
Ireland	17844.910	9.789
Finland	19204.450	9.863
Britain	19880.390	9.897
Sweden	20449.570	9.926
Italy	20888.240	9.947
France	21065.020	9.955
Netherlands	21087.570	9.956
Australia	21562.500	9.979
Germany	22029.480	10.000
Austria	22672.040	10.029
Belgium	22892.860	10.039
Iceland	23305.430	10.056
Canada	23487.480	10.064
Denmark	23527.680	10.066
Japan	23725.340	10.074
Norway	25336.920	10.140
Switzerland	25964.120	10.164
USA	28173.420	10.246

Source: World Development Indicators CD-ROM (World Bank).

References

Alesina, A., La Ferrara, E., 2001. Preferences for redistribution in the land of opportunities. NBER Working Paper W8267.

Alesina, A., Di Tella, R., MacCulloch, R., 2001. Inequality and happiness: Are Europeans and Americans different? NBER Working Paper W8198.

Alston, R.M., Kearl, J.R., Vaughan, M.B., 1992. Is there a consensus among economists in the 1990's? The American Economic Review 82 (2); Papers and Proceedings of the Hundred and Fourth Annual Meeting of the American Economic Association, pp. 203–209.

Baldwin, R.E., Magee, C.S., 1998. Is trade policy for sale? congressional voting on recent trade bills. NBER Working Paper W6376.

Balistreri, E.J., 1997. The performance of the Heckscher–Ohlin–Vanek model in predicting endogenous policy forces at the individual level. Canadian Journal of Economics 30 (1), 1–17.

Barro, R., Lee, J., 1996. International data on educational attainment. Data set.

Barro, R., Lee, J., 2000. International data on educational attainment. Data set.

Beaulieu, E., 1996. Who supported the Canada–U.S. free trade agreement: Factor or industry cleavages in trade policy? University of Calgary.

Beaulieu, E., Magee, C.S., 2001. Campaign contributions and trade policy: New tests of Stolper-Samuelson, University of Calgary.

Beaulieu, E., Benarroch, M., Gaisford, J., 2003. Intra-industry trade liberalization: Why skilled workers resist protectionism, University of Calgary.

Blanchflower, D.G., Oswald, A.J., 2000. Well-Being over Time in Britain and the USA.

Caplan, B., 2001. Systematically biased beliefs about economics. Center for the Study of Public Choice, George Mason University.

Card, D., 1996. The effect of unions on the structure of wages: A longitudinal analysis. Econometrica 64 (4), 957–979.

Feenstra, R.C., 2000. World Trade Flows. 1980–1997 plus data CD.

Inglehart, R., 1997. World Value Surveys and European Values Surveys, 1981–1984, 1990–1993, and 1995–1997 [computer file], ICPSR version, Institute for Social Research [producer], Interuniversity Consortium for Political and Social Research [distributor].

International Social Survey Programme, 1995. National Identity.

Irwin, D.A., 1994. The political economy of free trade: Voting in the British general elections of 1906. Journal of Law and Economics 37, 75–108.

Irwin, D.A., 1996. Industry or class cleavages over trade policy? Evidence from the British general election of 1923. In: Feenstra, R.C., Grossman, G.M., Irwin, D.A. (Eds.), The Political Economy of Trade Policy: Papers in Honor of Jagdish Bhagwati. The MIT Press, Cambridge, MA, pp. 53–75.

Krueger, A.B., Summers, L.H., 1988. Efficiency wages and the inter-industry wage structure. Econometrica 56 (2), 259–293.

Luttmer, E.F.P., 2001. Group loyalty and the taste for redistribution. Journal of Political Economy 109 (3), 500–528.

Magee, S.P., 1978. Three simple tests of the Stolper–Samuelson theorem. In: Oppenheimer, P. (Ed.), Issues in International Economics. Oriel Press, Stockfield.

Mayer, W., 1984. Endogenous tariff formation. American Economic Review 74, 970–985.

Midford, P., 1993. International trade and domestic politics: Improving on Rogowski's model of political alignments. International Organization 47 (4), 535–564.

O'Rourke, K.H., Sinnott, R., 2001. What determines attitudes towards protection? Some cross-country evidence. In: Collins, S.M., Rodrik, D. (Eds.), Brookings Trade Forum 2001. Brookings Institute Press, Washington DC, pp. 157–206.

Rodrik, D., 1995. Political economy of trade policy. In: Grossman, G., Rogoff, K. (Eds.), Handbook of International Economics, Vol. 3. Elsevier Science Publishers, Amsterdam, pp. 1457–1494.

Rogowski, R., 1987. Political cleavages and changing exposure to trade. American Political Science Review 81 (4), 1121–1137.

Rogowski, R., 1989. Commerce and Coalitions. Princeton University Press, Princeton, NJ.

Scheve, K.F., Slaughter, M.J., 2001a. What determines individual trade policy preferences? Journal of International Economics 54 (2), 267–292.

Scheve, K.F., Slaughter, M.J., 2001b. Globalization and the Perceptions of American Workers. Institute for International Economics, Washington DC.

Smith, T.W., Jarkko, L., 1998. National pride: A cross-national analysis. GSS Cross-national Report 19.

[10]

Government Spending and Public Support for Trade in the OECD: An Empirical Test of the Embedded Liberalism Thesis

Jude C. Hays, Sean D. Ehrlich, and Clint Peinhardt

Abstract According to the embedded liberalism thesis, governments committed to free trade provide insurance and other transfers to compensate those who lose economically from expanded trade. The goal of this spending is to maintain public support for trade liberalization. We provide a micro-level test of the critical assumption behind the embedded liberalism thesis that government programs designed to protect individuals harmed by imports reduce opposition to free trade. Our micro results have important implications for the macro relationship between trade and government spending, which we also test. We find empirical support for the embedded liberalism thesis in both our micro- and macro-level analyses.

According to Ruggie, the international community learned two important lessons from the collapse of the gold standard and interwar global economy. First, the international economy would break down if states pursued unilateral, beggar-thy-neighbor trade policies. As a result, postwar governments around the Organization for Economic Cooperation and Development (OECD), by and large, have committed themselves to pursuing free trade through multilateralism. Second, governments could not ignore the internal costs of adjusting to external economic shocks. Because trade causes economic dislocations and exposes workers to greater risk, it generates political opposition that democratically elected leaders ignore at their peril. Thus, one important implication of the commitment to free trade is that political leaders have had to be aware of and actively manage public support for

Earlier versions of this article were presented at the Midwest Political Science Association's 2002 Meeting and at the University of Illinois during summer 2003. We thank the respective panel and seminar participants for their feedback. In addition, we want to acknowledge valuable comments from William Bernhard, Rebecca Blank, Kerwin Charles, Alan Deardorff, John DiNardo, John Freeman, Brian Gaines, Jim Granato, Nathan Jensen, William Keech, Layna Mosley, Robert Pahre, Ken Scheve, Marina Whitman, two anonymous reviewers, and Lisa Martin. They, of course, are not responsible for any errors.

International Organization 59, Spring 2005, pp. 473–494

DOI: 10.1017/S0020818305050150

economic openness. To do this, governments have exchanged welfare state policies that cushion their citizens from the vagaries of the international economy in return for public support for openness.

Ruggie has termed this exchange the bargain of embedded liberalism.[1] According to this story of postwar reconstruction, a link between trade and welfare state spending was established soon after World War II ended. Of course, the specific form this bargain takes is both geographically and historically contingent. The Keynesianism that emerged in the United States, for example, differed from the social democratic corporatism that developed in Sweden and Austria, and the demand management policies of the Bretton Woods era have given way to the active (supply-side) labor market policies of the so-called Third Way. But the idea that there is a more or less universal expectation held by citizens in the developed democracies that their governments will limit the costs and distribute the benefits of open markets through some kind of government intervention and spending, and that public support for liberalism depends on the willingness and ability of governments to do this successfully, is the core of the embedded liberalism thesis. This is what distinguishes the embedded liberalism of the postwar period from the ideology of pure laissez-faire that guided economic policy under the gold standard.[2]

Recently, the argument that trade and government spending go hand in hand because governments have to compensate market losers has come under attack. Several studies claim that the relationship between trade and spending is weak at best and largely attributable to omitted variable bias. We have three criticisms of this research, which has focused almost entirely on the macro-level (country) empirical relationship. First, this research rarely distinguishes between imports and exports. Most studies use the summed value of imports and exports as a percentage of gross domestic product (GDP)—trade openness—as an independent variable in their respective regression analyses. This constrains the effects of imports and exports on government spending to have the same sign. We suspect these flows should have opposite signs. Second, it fails to consider the varying degrees of labor market exposure to international trade. We argue the postindustrial shift in production from tradables to nontradables should reduce the effect that trade has on government spending, because it reduces the number of workers employed in import-competing sectors of the economy.

Our final and most important criticism is that no one has tested the microfoundations of the embedded liberalism thesis. The key assumption is that government policies can build public support for trade. We believe macro-empirical studies that put spending on the left-hand-side of regression models will always be vulnerable to claims of omitted variable bias and that to make a convincing empirical case for the free trade–welfare state linkage, it is necessary to examine data at a

1. Ruggie 1982, 1994, 1997, and 2003.

2. See Blyth 2002. Blyth argues that liberal capitalism has become less embedded since the Ronald Reagan and Margaret Thatcher period, but the changes, in his view, do not amount to a return to pre–World War I policies. Others argue that the significance of the Reagan and Thatcher "revolutions" has been exaggerated—for example, Pierson 1994.

lower level of aggregation. In this article, we provide a micro-level test of the embedded liberalism thesis. Our results have important and testable implications for the relationship between aggregate trade and government spending.

The article is organized as follows. In the first section, we briefly review and critique the literature on trade and government spending. In the second section, we present an empirical examination of the determinants of individual support for protectionism. Our results show that individuals employed in import competing industries are the strongest opponents of trade, but unemployment insurance and active labor market programs can moderate their opposition. Based on these findings we argue that (1) politicians respond to surges in imports and not necessarily to expanding trade if it is balanced, and (2) the extent to which politicians respond to rising imports will be a function of how many workers are employed in tradable industries. We test these two macro-level hypotheses in the third section of the article as a way to check the significance of our micro-level results for the trade–welfare state debate. We conclude in the final section.

Trade and Government Spending in the Developed Democracies

It is well known that countries with open economies have bigger governments.[3] It is also true that OECD countries have increased both their levels of trade and government spending during the post–World War II period. However, the debate remains unresolved as to whether these strong cross-national and over-time correlations reflect a causal relationship between trade and government spending, a politically conditioned relationship, or a completely spurious one. In addition to Ruggie, those who have argued government policies, by neutralizing the negative effects of trade, can deliver protrade majorities are Rodrik, Adserà and Boix, Swank, and Mares.[4] These scholars argue there is a short-term causal relationship between trade and government spending.[5]

This position has been challenged in two ways. First, Garrett and Mitchell argue the relationship between trade and welfare state effort is long-term and historically contingent.[6] For the small economies of Western Europe, trade dependence facilitated unionization, which, in turn, created strong social democratic parties that built large welfare states when they came to power. They distinguish this argument from Ruggie's:

> With respect to trade, for example, Cameron (1978) and Katzenstein (1985) both argue that there is a historical relationship between trade and welfare

3. See, for example, Cameron 1978; Katzenstein 1985; and Rodrik 1998.
4. Rodrik 1997, 1998; Adserà and Boix 2002; Swank 2002a; and Mares 2004.
5. By short-term we mean changes in trade at time $t-1$ have a discernible effect on government spending at time t.
6. Garrett and Mitchell 2001.

> state effort. . . . This is a very different argument from another perspective with which it is often conflated—Ruggie's (1983) notion of embedded liberalism. For Ruggie, the American welfare state expanded immediately after World War II because the government chose to liberalize trade, and realized they had to compensate market losers directly for the dislocations liberalization generated.[7]

Garrett and Mitchell contend that when country dummies (fixed-country effects) are added to regression models, the analyst can distinguish between the long-term historical argument of Cameron and Katzenstein and Ruggie's notion of embedded liberalism. In Garrett and Mitchell's analysis, the positive relationship between trade openness and government spending disappears.[8]

The strongest challenge to the embedded liberalism thesis, however, has come from Iversen and Cusak, who argue the post–World War II growth of the welfare state is a product of deindustrialization not globalization.[9] They posit that workers who move from manufacturing and agriculture to services cross significant skill boundaries that make the transition difficult and uncertain. These problems, in turn, create demands for government spending. Iversen and Cusak show that the relationship between trade and spending is either statistically or substantively insignificant after controlling for deindustrialization. Moreover, they claim that deindustrialization and globalization are largely independent processes.

Garrett and Mitchell and Iversen and Cusak raise serious questions about the validity of the embedded liberalism thesis. Thus the causal mechanisms identified by Ruggie and others deserve closer empirical scrutiny. We believe it is difficult to do this effectively by working only with data at the country level, and so in the next section, we test the microfoundations of the embedded liberalism argument using survey data. However, before moving on, we note two important criticisms of the research described in this section.

First, the research fails to adequately distinguish between imports and exports. Most studies use trade openness—the summed value of exports and imports as a percentage of GDP—as the key independent variable.[10] This variable constrains the effect of imports and exports on government spending to have the same sign. Yet theory tells us increasing imports and exports should have opposite effects on government spending.[11] Rising imports create losers—displaced workers in import

7. Ibid., 163. We believe both short-term and long-term historical forces are operating. Our empirical analysis bears this out.

8. In fact, they find that the relationship is negative and statistically significant.

9. Iversen and Cusak 2000.

10. In addition to trade openness, Garrett and Mitchell, 169–70, include the value of imports from low-wage countries in their analysis. They find these imports are weakly positively correlated with higher government spending and transfers. They do not examine the effects of total imports on spending and transfers.

11. This is true unless one is interested in measuring a country's exposure to external risk. To do this, one would interact a country's trade openness—a measure of how exposed it is to the international economy—with a measure of external risk like its terms of trade volatility. See Rodrik 1997, 1998. By itself, trade openness is not a good measure of risk.

competing industries—that may have to be compensated, rising exports do not. Similarly, falling exports are harmful to domestic employment in a way that declining imports are not.

Second, the research also fails to recognize that the impact of trade flows on government spending depends on the underlying structure of the economy, in particular how many workers are employed in vulnerable traded industries. Because democratically elected governments are sensitive to numbers of votes, ceteris paribus, their response will be conditioned by the scope of threatened industries. If imports displace a large number of workers/voters, governments will have little choice but to provide compensation. If a small number of workers are displaced, politicians will face less pressure to respond.[12]

In the next section, we test whether government policies can build support for economic openness among groups that oppose it. If government spending on programs such as unemployment insurance and active labor market programs successfully reduces the level of opposition, there is micro-level evidence that the embedded liberalism compromise is a viable solution to the political problems faced by democratically elected leaders who commit their countries to free trade.

Unemployment Benefits and Individual Attitudes Toward Trade

A flurry of research on the determinants of individual support for trade has been published in the last couple of years. Most of it, drawing on international trade theory, focuses on how skill level and sector of employment determine an individual's support for protectionism. Examples include studies by Scheve and Slaughter, O'Rourke and Sinnot, and Mayda and Rodrik.[13] The main conclusion of this research is that groups adversely affected by international economic competition are less likely to support policies of free trade. If government spending is driven partly by the need to generate public support for economic openness, this micro-level research has significant implications for the macro debate over trade and government spending. Yet none of these studies examine the impact of government programs on support for trade. It is surprising that few scholars have tried to bridge the micro-macro divide.

The exception is new work being done by Aldrich, Lange, and others at Duke University, who, picking up where the economists leave off, show that objective conditions of vulnerability translate into subjective feelings of insecurity and strong policy preferences that then determine an individual's party identification and

12. The ceteris paribus condition is important. We are assuming that the ability of those employed in traded industries to organize remains constant. Because small groups may find it easier to engage in collective action, they are often able to exert political influence that is disproportionate to their numbers. For a discussion of the importance of collective action issues in trade policy politics, see Alt and Gilligan 1994.

13. See Scheve and Slaughter 2001; O'Rourke and Sinnot 2002; and Mayda and Rodrik 2002.

ideology, variables that significantly affect vote choice.[14] In other words, if it is true that globalization produces economic losers and anxiety, citizens will demand insurance and/or compensation and vote for politicians who are likely to provide these policies. In democracies, this situation should pressure politicians to respond. While this important research looks at the relationship between globalization and government spending, it focuses almost entirely on the "demand side" of the political bargain.

We focus much more on the "supply side" of the welfare state/trade openness nexus. We suspect that those adversely affected by trade are more likely to demand tariff protection than welfare state compensation. Governments that want to maintain free trade policies supply compensation as a compromise solution. Our "supply side" focus leads us to ask: If governments provide compensation in the form of unemployment insurance or active labor market programs, will it effectively build support for free trade among those who are likely to oppose it otherwise? This relationship between government spending and support for trade is essential to the embedded liberalism thesis, and it has yet to be tested directly.

Before turning to our empirical analysis, we note another strength of the Duke project—its attention to the role of institutions in shaping individual policy preferences. Drawing on important insights from the varieties of capitalism literature, the Duke project examines the effects of different national production regimes on policy attitudes.[15] Because these regimes determine the underlying nature of an economy's factor markets, they shape the political cleavages over trade, determine how vulnerable workers are to economic downturns, and influence whether or not firms will support or oppose welfare state policies. For example, coordinated market economies rely more heavily on labor with sector-specific skills. Skill specificity makes workers more vulnerable to unemployment during economic downturns increasing political pressure for social insurance. In general, firms tend to be more supportive of welfare state policies in the coordinated economies as well. Moreover, because of the low levels of intersectoral mobility, trade politics is likely to divide along sector lines. In these ways, national production regimes affect how individuals perceive globalization.

We do not doubt that a country's institutional structure plays an important role in shaping individual attitudes toward trade, but we believe there are more general forces at work as well. We begin with these and leave the effects of production regimes and other important national differences (beyond welfare state policies) for future research. Institutions also constrain how governments respond to changes in the policy preferences of organized interests and voters. We return to this topic in our conclusion.

14. For a summary of this research, see Aldrich et al. 2002. One of the underlying motivations behind this project is that the macro-level literature on globalization rests on simple micro-level assumptions that have not been tested.

15. See Hall and Soskice 2001 for an exposition of the varieties of capitalism argument.

Data and Methods

The data we use is from the International Social Survey Program's (ISSP) 1995 survey on national identity. This data set, used by both Mayda and Rodrik and O'Rourke and Sinnot, provides information about individuals' attitudes toward free trade. The countries in our sample are Australia, Germany, the United Kingdom, the United States, Austria, Hungary, Norway, Sweden, the Czech Republic, Poland, New Zealand, Canada, and Spain.[16] The dependent variable (FREETRADE) is constructed from respondents' answers to the following question asked in the survey:

How much do you agree or disagree with the following statement: (Respondent's Country) should limit the import of foreign products in order to protect its national economy.

1. Agree strongly
2. Agree
3. Neither agree nor disagree
4. Disagree
5. Disagree strongly

We assigned a value of 1 to respondents who answered, "agree strongly," a 2 to those who answered, "agree," etc. Thus, high values of FREETRADE reflect pro-trade attitudes whereas low values reflect support for protectionism.

Our baseline regression is grounded in trade theory.[17] The specific factors (Ricardo-Viner) model from international economics identifies sector of employment as crucial to determining an individual's attitudes toward trade. Individuals employed in export industries are likely to benefit from trade whereas individuals employed in import industries are likely harmed. This contrasts with the mobile factors (Stolper-Samuelson) model, which highlights the importance of one's factor endowment. Regardless of their industry of employment, the owners of relatively abundant factors of production benefit from trade. For the countries in our sample, the abundant factors are highly skilled labor and capital.[18]

In our analysis, we use an income dummy variable as a proxy for one's capital endowment. We gave everyone in our sample whose annual family income was

16. We included all countries reporting occupational categories that allowed us to determine a respondent's industry of employment.

17. See Alt and Gilligan 1994; and Hiscox 2002.

18. These models tell us the direct effect of trade on income earned from employing different factors of production. It is also possible that trade affects the wealth and (unearned) income of asset owners. For example, Scheve and Slaughter 2001 find that home owners who live in import competing regions of the United States are, ceteris paribus, more likely to oppose trade than renters. Unfortunately, the data that we would need to test this and similar hypotheses on a cross-national basis is not readily available.

greater than $35,000 a score of one and everyone else a score of zero.[19] Following Mayda and Rodrik and Scheve and Slaughter, we use one's level of education as a proxy for skill endowment. We identify a respondent's (or spouse's) industry of employment by their occupation using the reported four-digit code from the International Labor Organization's *International Standard Classification of Occupations*. We created a dummy variable indicating whether the respondent or respondent's spouse was employed in one of fourteen tradable industries identified in the OECD's Industry Structural Analysis (STAN) database.[20] We then used the STAN database to create an export and import variable using each industry's ratio of exports and imports to value added. The export variable ranges from a low of zero for nontraded industries to a high of 3.28 for the transportation equipment industry in Austria. The denominator in this ratio, value added, represents each sector's contribution to the country's GDP. The ratio can be greater than one for industries with costly inputs. The import variable ranges from zero for all nontraded industries to 7.47 for the textile industry in Norway.

To this list we add several demographic and ideological variables used by Hiscox and Burgoon.[21] They identify gender, age, employment status, and marital status as important determinants of trade preferences. They also focus on an individual's political ideology and whether or not the respondent self-identifies with a particular religious faith. For ideology we use a five-point party affiliation scale provided in the ISSP data set that ranges from far left (1) to far right (5). For our religion variable, we use a dummy that takes a value of one for individuals who self-identify with a religious denomination and zero for everyone else. We also include whether one holds nationalist attitudes, which was found by both Mayda and Rodrik and O'Rourke and Sinnott to be an important determinant of trade policy preferences. In their analysis, Mayda and Rodrik use four separate questions that gauge whether one holds patriotic, nationalistic, and/or chauvinistic attitudes. Using factor analysis, we extract a single component from the answers to these four questions that measures the degree to which an individual holds nationalist attitudes.

Finally, we include three policy variables in our analysis. Two of the three variables are objective measures of government policy: the net replacement rate for unemployment insurance (NRR) and the amount of government spending on active labor market programs per unemployed worker (ALM). The former measure varies

19. Local currencies were converted into dollars using the appropriate exchange rate; monthly income was converted to annual income when necessary. This is the same income measure used by Hiscox and Burgoon 2003.

20. The industries are (1) agriculture, hunting, forestry, and fishing; (2) mining and quarrying; (3) food products, beverages, and tobacco; (4) textiles, textile products, leather, and footwear; (5) wood and products of wood and cork; (6) paper and paper products; (7) publishing, printing, and reproduction of recorded media; (8) chemical, rubber, plastics, and fuel products; (9) other nonmetallic mineral products; (10) basic metals; (11) fabricated metal products, except machinery and equipment; (12) machinery and equipment; (13) transport equipment; and (14) manufacturing not elsewhere classified.

21. Hiscox and Burgoon 2003.

across individuals within countries while the latter does not. We also include a subjective evaluation of the social security system (SOCIAL SECURITY). This variable is based on a question that asks respondents how proud they are of the social security system in their country. Respondents can answer "very proud," "somewhat proud," "not very proud," or "not proud at all." We scored these responses from 1 to 4, giving those who were not proud at all a 1 and those who were very proud a 4. We included a subjective measure out of concern that respondents might not be aware of the details of the unemployment insurance and active labor market policies in their countries. We assume that respondents who are "very proud" of their social security system feel that they are well protected by it, and those who are "not proud at all" feel that they are not.[22]

Turning to the objective measures, we calculated each country's spending on active labor market programs per unemployed worker (ALM) using data from the OECD's Social Spending and Labor Force databases. These active labor market programs, which are designed to improve job seekers' prospects of finding employment and increase the earning potential of workers, include spending on public employment, labor market training, and other policies intended to promote employment among the unemployed. We include the net replacement rate of each respondent's government-provided unemployment benefits (NRR). The 1998 OECD's *Benefit Systems and Work Incentives* calculates net replacement rates for four family types at two income levels.[23] The family types are single, married couple, couple with two children, and lone parent with two children. The income levels are average and two-thirds the average income level. This gives up to eight different net replacement rates for each country in the sample.

We used SINGLE, NUMBER OF PERSONS IN HOUSEHOLD, and the HOUSEHOLD CYCLE variables from the ISSP data set (v202, v293, and v294 respectively) as well as the family income dummy variable (INCOME) to identify each survey respondent's net replacement rate. The HOUSEHOLD CYCLE variable indicates whether there are children in the household. There are no problems identifying singles and married couples without children. In many instances it is not difficult to identify lone parents and married couples with children because these family types are included in the HOUSEHOLD CYCLE variable. The difficult cases arise when singles live in households with more than one adult and couples live in households with more than two adults. In these cases, parental status is unknown. We gave all identified married respondents with children the married two-child net replacement rate. Similarly, we gave all lone parents the lone parent two-child net replacement rate. When we could not identify parental status, we gave the respondent the average value of their no dependent and two-child net replacement rate.

22. We realize that this measure has its limitations. Political conservatives, for example, might not say they are proud of their country's social security system even if it offers generous protection. However, if conservatives are more supportive of trade, this will bias against finding a positive relationship between this subjective evaluation and support for free trade.

23. OECD 1998. See tab. 3.1, 30, for these net replacement rates.

The HOUSEHOLD CYCLE variable was not available for the United Kingdom, Austria, the Czech Republic, and Poland. For the respondents in these countries, we used the NUMBER OF PERSONS IN HOUSEHOLD variable to identify cases where there are no children living in the household (for example, a single respondent living in a household with only one person). When we could not determine whether or not children were living in the household, we used an average net replacement rate. In most countries net replacement rates are higher for low-income individuals. We used our existing income dummy variable (INCOME) to assign average income and below average net replacement rates. The main advantage of our NRR variable is that, with eight replacement rates, it provides substantial within country variation in unemployment insurance coverage.[24] (See the Appendix Tables A1 and A2 for summary statistics.)

We estimate ordered probits because the dependent variable, FREETRADE, is ordinal. Ordinal dependent variables can create problems for linear models because these models assume that the intervals between adjacent categories are equal. If this assumption does not hold, the estimated coefficients will be biased and misleading.[25] Also, because many individuals in each country are exposed to the same "treatment" (for example, the same active labor market programs) and cannot be considered independent trials, we have to be careful estimating the standard errors for our regression coefficients.[26] We reported robust "clustered" standard errors as a way to address the "duplication" problem.[27]

Results

The regression results are presented in Table 1.[28] Model 1 includes the baseline controls and the respondent's net replacement rate variable (NRR). All of the variables are correctly signed and statistically significant. Individuals employed in high import industries are more likely to support tariffs to protect the economy than individuals who are employed in either high export or nontradable industries. Moreover, individuals with high levels of education (skills) and income (capital) are less likely to support protectionism. Finally, the higher an individual's net replacement rate the less likely they are to support protectionism. This confirms an important element of the embedded liberalism argument: government policies that remedy the negative effects of trade increase support for economic openness. In

24. In terms of research design, this variable is an improvement over countrywide measures of unemployment protection because it allows the analyst to incorporate fixed country effects into the regressions. The fixed-effects model allows us to control for unobservable or otherwise omitted country-level factors that correlate with a country's average net replacement rate.

25. McKelvey and Zavoina 1975.

26. Moulton 1990.

27. For a discussion of this problem, see Steenbergen and Jones 2002, 219–20. In calculating our standard errors, we assume respondents are clustered by country.

28. The cut-point estimates are omitted from the table to save space.

TABLE 1. *Models of individual support for trade*

Variables	*Model 1*	*Model 2*	*Model 3*	*Model 4*	*Model 5*	*Model 6*
TRADABLE	−.281***	−.239***	−.233***	−.248**	−.241***	−.220***
	(.080)	(.081)	(.085)	(.097)	(.080)	(.082)
EXPORTS	.234***	.211**	.248***	.171***	.174***	.236***
	(.087)	(.087)	(.049)	(.052)	(.050)	(.050)
IMPORTS	−.052*	−.049*	−.067***	−.030**	−.027**	−.063***
	(.029)	(.028)	(.024)	(.014)	(.012)	(.022)
EDUCATION	.145***	.160***	.117***	.142***	.150***	.138***
	(.032)	(.030)	(.025)	(.021)	(.023)	(.026)
INCOME	.282***	.138***	.367***	.231***	.165***	.177***
	(.047)	(.042)	(.057)	(.037)	(.038)	(.045)
MALE	–	–	.284***	.268***	.246***	.250***
			(.048)	(.049)	(.046)	(.045)
AGE	–	–	−.002*	−.002	−.002	−.002*
			(.001)	(.001)	(.001)	(.001)
SINGLE	–	–	.152***	.081**	.031	.039
			(.058)	(.036)	(.040)	(.028)
UNEMPLOYED	–	–	−.226**	−.198**	−.201**	−.240***
			(.096)	(.091)	(.079)	(.078)
IDEOLOGY	–	–	.045	.072**	.085***	.072**
			(.031)	(.030)	(.025)	(.032)
RELIGIOUS	–	–	−.024	−.130**	−.139**	−.095
			(.079)	(.066)	(.062)	(.069)
NATIONALISM	–	–	−.279***	−.260***	−.277***	−.291***
			(.050)	(.035)	(.033)	(.040)
NRR	.768**	–	.871**	.597***	–	
	(.361)		(.367)	(.186)		
ALM	–	.043***	–	–	–	.046***
		(.009)				(.008)
SOCIAL SECURITY	–	–	–	–	.097***	–
					(.023)	
Fixed-country effects	no	no	no	yes	yes	no
Observations	8768	9780	4975	4975	5619	5772
Log likelihood	−12469.4	−13759.0	−6724.8	−6595.0	−7397.8	−7683.5
Pseudo R^2	.029	0.034	.059	.078	.077	.066

Note: Robust standard errors are in parentheses. Respondents are clustered by country. ALM = active labor market; NRR = net replacement rate. *** significant at 1%; ** significant at 5%; * significant at 10%.

the second regression (Model 2), we include each country's active labor market spending per unemployed worker. Again, the coefficient is correctly signed and statistically significant. Next, we add the demographic and ideological variables to the net replacement model rate (Model 3). The coefficient on NRR remains positive and statistically significant. Then we add fixed-country effects (Model 4)—that is, we include country dummies in the regression. This allows us to control for any omitted or unobservable variables at the national level that are correlated with the generosity of a country's unemployment insurance benefits. The results do not change.[29] In Model 5 we switch the variable NRR for the subjective measure of an individual's satisfaction with the variable SOCIAL SECURITY. Again, the results are consistent with our expectations. In Model 6 we include active labor market spending in a model with the full set of individual-level controls.[30] The coefficient on the variable ALM is statistically significant and correctly signed.

In order to demonstrate the size of the effects that the key variables have on individual support for free trade, we conduct several counterfactual experiments using simulation methods.[31] The results are reported in terms of predicted probabilities and changes in predicted probabilities in Table 2. As our benchmark, we use an individual with median scores on all of the variables included in the analysis. This individual is not employed in a tradable sector of the economy, comes from a family with a combined annual income of less than $35,000, has the equivalent of a high school education, and supports protectionism as a means to bolster the domestic economy with an approximate probability of 0.60. This representative respondent opposes protection with an approximate probability of 0.20. If this respondent were employed in an export-oriented sector of the economy, the probability of support for protectionism would be similar. In our counterfactual, where the sector's exports are about 118 percent of value added, we cannot reject the hypothesis of no change. If this respondent were employed in an import-competing sector of the economy, the probability of supporting protection rises by about 0.13 from 0.60 to 0.73.[32] If the respondent had a college degree instead of a high school diploma, support for protectionism would drop by approximately 0.11. Increasing

29. We get similar results when we interact our measures of trade exposure with the social protection variables. For example, in Model 4, if we make the effect of trade exposure on support for trade dependent on the level of social protection, we continue to find that employment in import competing sectors of the economy has a large negative impact. The size of this effect declines, however, as the level of social protection rises.

30. Because this variable is constant across individuals within countries, we cannot include it in a model with fixed country effects.

31. These experiments were conducted using the software developed by Tomz, Wittenberg, and King 1999.

32. This number is calculated by totaling the first two columns of Table 2. In our experiment, we define import competing as a sector with imports worth 184 percent of value added. The two percentages—118 percent (exports) and 184 percent (imports)—are at the 95th percentile in our sample. Note that this percentile is for our entire sample and most respondents are employed in nontraded industries. These numbers are more representative for the subsample of respondents employed in tradable industries.

TABLE 2. *Simulated effects of key variables on individual support for free trade*

	Pr(freetrade=1) (support protection)	*Pr(freetrade=2)*	*Pr(freetrade=3) (indifferent)*	*Pr(freetrade=4)*	*Pr(freetrade=5) (oppose protection)*
Benchmark (predicted probability)	.218	.377	.203	.163	.038
	(.033)	(.022)	(.027)	(.022)	(.010)
1. Impact of changing from nontradable to export industry	−.000	.002	−.000	−.001	−.001
	(.023)	(.008)	(.008)	(.016)	(.007)
2. Impact of changing from nontradable to import industry	.126**	.007	−.047**	−.065**	−.021**
	(.043)	(.019)	(.016)	(.016)	(.006)
3. Impact of changing from high school to college graduate	−.073**	−.040**	.022**	.060**	.031**
	(.012)	(.018)	(.006)	(.015)	(.012)
4. Impact of changing from low income to high	−.072**	−.038**	.023**	.058**	.029**
	(.010)	(.014)	(.006)	(.012)	(.007)
5. Impact of raising NRR from 72% to 88%	−.032**	−.015**	.011**	.025**	.012**
	(.013)	(.011)	(.004)	(.012)	(.008)
6. Impact of raising ALM from $4,180 to $12,730	−.091**	−.051**	.030**	.074**	.038**
	(.019)	(.014)	(.009)	(.015)	(.009)

Note: Standard errors are in parentheses. For each experiment, we report the change in predicted probabilities.
** significant at 5% (based on simulated 95% confidence interval using Model 1 except for the sixth counterfactual that uses Model 2). ALM = active labor market; NRR = net replacement rate; Pr = probability.

this respondent's unemployment insurance from the median net replacement rate of 72 percent to 88 percent would lower the probability of supporting protection by 0.05 and raise the probability of opposing it by 0.04. Finally, raising the level of active labor market spending from the median of $4,180 to $12,730 would decrease support for protectionism by 0.14.

Overall, our results are very supportive of the embedded liberalism thesis. The strongest opposition to trade comes from individuals employed in sectors of the economy that have the highest levels of imports. Yet, these results demonstrate that politicians can, in fact, build support for trade, even among these sectors. Politically feasible policy reforms can offset declines caused by increased exposure to international competition.

Imports and Government Spending in Postindustrial Economies

Our micro results confirm the significance of the tradable/nontradable and import/export distinctions. Politicians who want to maintain support for trade will have to respond to surges in imports. This is particularly true if there are a large number of individuals employed in tradable sectors of the economy. However, as individuals move out of tradable industries it becomes less important for politicians to respond to increased imports. Thus, our micro results suggest that the movement of workers from tradable to nontradable sectors will increase support for trade. Therefore, globalization and deindustrialization should have interdependent effects on government spending.[33] In postindustrial economies, the effect of imports on spending should be smaller in magnitude. We test this hypothesis below.

Data and Methods

Our sample, which spans from 1960 to 2000, includes seventeen OECD countries: Australia, Austria, Belgium, Canada, Denmark, Finland, France, Germany, Ireland, Italy, Japan, the Netherlands, New Zealand, Norway, Sweden, the United Kingdom, and the United States. The key independent variable is the natural log of imports measured in millions of 1995 U.S. dollars.[34] The size of the effect that imports will have on spending depends on how many workers are employed in

33. Many believe that globalization and deindustrialization are interdependent processes in the sense that expanding trade explains the decline of manufacturing among the OECD economies. Iversen and Cusak reject this argument. See Iversen and Cusak 2000, 339–45. We are not arguing that trade causes deindustrialization but rather deindustrialization conditions the effect of trade on government spending. A similar argument is made by Mares 2004.

34. OECD's Economic Outlook Database. See OECD 2003b.

tradable industries. We use Iversen and Cusak's measure of deindustrialization as a measure of the number of workers exposed to import competition.[35]

We include three separate dependent variables in our analysis. The first two are common in the literature: government consumption as a percentage of GDP (GOVCON) and social benefits as a percentage of GDP (SOCBEN).[36] The third is based on the NRR measure from our micro analysis. We use spending on unemployment insurance per unemployed worker divided by the average level of compensation per employee as a proxy for each country's NRR.[37] The first two measures are less specific to the causal argument being made—we might expect changes in these variables to be driven by a number of other factors—but there is almost twenty additional years of data available for them. Moreover, it is possible that the NRR measure is too limited in its scope. Constrained governments might respond in less direct ways to demands for insurance. For example, in the United States, much of the insecurity associated with losing one's job comes from the fear of losing one's health insurance. In theory, the U.S. government could respond to globalization pressures by providing better health care for its poorest citizens, and this would not show up in the NRR measure.

We add five control variables to our analysis: GDP per capita; the percentage of the population above the age of sixty-five; the percentage of cabinet seats held by left-wing parties; union density; and exports.[38] The first variable controls for Wagner's law, which predicts that governments will spend a higher proportion of GDP as per-capita real income rises. Pierson and others have identified an aging population as the key demographic change driving government spending in the OECD today.[39] (For the NRR variable, by contrast, we would expect a negative relationship because retired individuals do not benefit from unemployment insurance.) One would expect government spending to be higher where the political left and/or organized labor is strong. Because imports and exports are highly correlated, the log of exports is also included as a control variable. We expect the coefficients on imports and exports to have opposite signs. (See the Appendix for summary statistics.)

We estimate six panel regressions, two for each of our dependent variables. One model includes the controls; the other does not. As do many political scientists, we include the lag of the dependent variable and country dummies in all of our

35. Their measure is 100 minus the workers employed in manufacturing and agriculture as a percentage of the working age population.

36. This data is from OECD's Economic Outlook Database. See OECD 2003b.

37. The variables used to construct NRR are from the OECD's Social Spending, Labor Force, and Economic Outlook Databases. See OECD 2001, 2003a, and 2003b. For a critique of the research using government consumption and social benefits as dependent variables, see Burgoon 2001; and Mares 2004. Mares argues that all expenditure-based measures are problematic because they do not reflect politically salient aspects of policy design. We disagree because expenditures are directly related to the generosity of benefit payments, and the generosity of benefits is as politically salient as (if not more salient than) any other feature of welfare state policy.

38. The sources are OECD 2003b; Franzese 2002, and Swank 2002b.

39. See, for example, Pierson 2001.

models to control for persistence and unit heterogeneity respectively. In other words, we estimate a dynamic panel model using the least squares with dummy variables (LSDV) estimator.[40] For this purpose, the LSDV estimator performs well against some of the more sophisticated alternatives.[41] All of our right-hand-side variables are lagged one period to address potential problems of endogeneity.

Results

The regression estimates are reported in Table 3. In short, we find that the effect of imports on a country's level of government spending depends on how exposed the domestic labor market is to trade.[42] The estimated coefficients on the imports and deindustrialization interaction variables are correctly signed in all six of the regressions.[43] An increase in a country's imports is associated with an increase in government spending. This effect is magnified when a large portion of the working-age population is employed in tradable industries. As for the controls, real GDP per capita is correctly signed and statistically significant in all three regressions. The coefficients on union density in the government consumption and social benefits regressions are correctly signed and statistically significant. The coefficient on the percentage of the population over sixty-five years of age is correctly signed and statistically significant in the net replacement rate regression: the greater the percentage of retirees, the lower the benefits for unemployed individuals.

To demonstrate the implications of the regressions, we conduct a set of counterfactual experiments that compare the effects of increasing imports on government spending in a hypothetical industrial and postindustrial economy.[44] To do this, we extend the first difference procedure described in King, Tomz, and Wittenberg.[45] The change in government spending caused by a simulated increase in imports is called the first difference. We simulate the effects of an increase in imports for both types of economy. Thus we record two first differences for each trial in our experiments.[46] Because we are interested in whether the responses (that

40. For a good introduction to the LSDV estimator, see Hsiao 2003, chap. 3.

41. Judson and Owen 1999.

42. This is similar to Mares's finding for the interwar period that both terms-of-trade and unemployment volatility have a larger impact on the coverage of unemployment insurance when the percentage of the workforce employed in manufacturing is high. See Mares 2004.

43. We do not include deindustrialization as a stand-alone regressor in Model 5 because it is highly collinear with the interaction term and we have a small sample. Our estimates of the other coefficients are much more precise when deindustrialization is omitted from the model. We feel comfortable dropping the variable because its coefficient is not statistically significant. In other words, we cannot reject the hypothesis that deindustrialization does not have a direct effect on net replacement rates. Excluding deindustrialization as a stand-alone regressor does not change the results in a qualitative sense though it does make them stronger.

44. For the experiments, we use regressions 1, 3, and 5.

45. King, Tomz, and Wittenberg 2000.

46. Each trial involves drawing a new vector of parameters from the multivariate sampling distribution defined by the coefficient estimates and the estimated variance-covariance matrix.

TABLE 3. *Imports, deindustrialization, and government spending*

Variables	GOVCON		SOCBEN		NRR	
	Model 1	*Model 2*	*Model 3*	*Model 4*	*Model 5*	*Model 6*
LAGGED DV	.954***	.914***	.972***	.940***	.781***	.669***
	(.030)	(.029)	(.034)	(.034)	(.063)	(.068)
IMPORTS	1.329***	2.106***	1.772***	2.560***	8.566***	28.927*
	(.372)	(.487)	(.638)	(.667)	(1.708)	(15.266)
DEINDUSTRIALIZATION	.084*	.066	.168**	.131*	–	3.711
	(.046)	(.053)	(.084)	(.078)		(2.219)
imports × DEINDUSTRIALIZATION	−.013***	−.011**	−.019**	−.015**	−.041***	−.387*
	(.004)	(.004)	(.008)	(.007)	(.013)	(.203)
EXPORTS	–	−1.747***	–	−1.760***	–	.172
		(.372)		(.466)		(2.984)
RGDP PER CAPITA	–	2.272***	–	1.238***	–	21.763***
		(.465)		(.375)		(6.472)
OLD AGE	–	−.054	–	.052	–	−.813**
		(.035)		(.035)		(.390)
LEFT GOVERNMENT	–	.001	–	−.000	–	.017
		(.001)		(.001)		(.012)
UNION DENSITY	–	.016***	–	.013**	–	.047
		(.005)		(.007)		(.158)
R^2	.976	.979	.982	.984	.962	.966
Joint Wald test	17.77***	33.46***	12.35***	31.00***	25.70***	11.23**
Observations	639	599	575	535	280	262
Number of countries	17	17	17	17	17	17

Note: Panel-corrected standard errors are in parentheses. GOVCON = government consumption; NRR = net replacement rate; RGDP = real gross domestic product; SOCBEN = social benefits. *** significant at 1%; ** significant at 5%; * significant at 10%.

TABLE 4. *Effect of increasing imports on government spending*

	Government consumption	*Social benefits*	*Net replacement rate (unemployment insurance)*
High exposure (industrial economy)	0.237**	0.252**	2.636**
first difference standard deviation	(.068)	(.088)	(.542)
95% confidence interval	[.104, .383]	[.076, .416]	[1.661, 3.709]
Low exposure (postindustrial)	0.137**	0.097	2.308**
first difference standard deviation	(.054)	(.058)	(.510)
95% confidence interval	[.028, .247]	[−.014, .212]	[1.347, 3.318]
Difference in difference	0.100**	0.155**	0.328**
standard deviation	(.032)	(.059)	(.100)
95% confidence interval	[.037, .163]	[.041, .263]	[.126, .532]

Note: ** Significant at 5% (based on a simulated 95% confidence interval using the robust Beck-Katz variance-covariance matrix. All values held at the sample median unless noted otherwise).

is, first differences) differ systematically across our two hypothetical economies, we also record the difference in the size of the changes across our two cases. This comparison is the difference in the first differences, which we record for each trial. We can then use this distribution to put a confidence interval around the mean difference in expected changes in government spending for our industrial and post-industrial economies.

We set the deindustrialization variable to its sample values at the 10th (62.32) and 90th percentiles (80.32) to simulate our industrial and postindustrial economies respectively. In each experiment we increase the logged level of imports from $9.111 to $9.551. This is the size of the import surge New Zealand experienced between 1973 and 1974.[47] All other variables are held at the sample median. We conducted one thousand trials for each experiment.

The results, which are reported in Table 4, are similar for all three types of government spending. The short-term effect of increasing a country's imports is larger for industrial than postindustrial economies. The difference in first differences is statistically and politically significant for each measure of government spending. The short-term effect of an import surge on government consumption is 0.100 higher for our hypothetical industrial economy when compared to its post-industrial counterpart. If the increase in imports were sustained, after three years the gap would increase to 0.287 (0.679–0.392). The differences for social benefits and net replacement rates are 0.155 and 0.328 respectively. Again, these differences would grow over time with a sustained increase in imports.

Our macro results demonstrate the significance of our individual-level findings for the trade/welfare state debate. Previous research has concluded that the short-

47. This is the largest one-period increase in imports experienced by a country in our sample. We prefer to use this within country change rather than, for example, the difference from the 25th to 75th percentile, which is a much larger difference but one that is only observed across countries in our sample.

term relationship between trade and government spending is an artifact (caused by omitted variable bias) that disappears when fixed-country effects and deindustrialization are taken into account. Our results show that this is not the case. The relationship between trade and government spending is robust when imports and exports are distinguished and the interactive effects of trade and deindustrialization are recognized.

Conclusion

Ruggie's embedded liberalism involves a political compromise in which leaders commit their countries to freer trade while managing the dislocations that follow. Our empirical tests—the first of the microfoundations of this theory—demonstrate that this compromise is a politically feasible one. Citizens' attitudes toward trade are malleable and well informed by their self-interest according to the predictions of trade theory. Workers who compete against imports tend to oppose free trade, but their opposition can be reduced with policies designed to protect them like unemployment insurance and active labor market programs.

We suspect many readers will be persuaded by our statistical results. Others will be skeptical because our results do not square with their previous beliefs about the importance of trade in determining government spending. If it is such a good idea politically to compensate those who lose from trade, why does it not happen more often? We have three responses to this query. First, it happens more often than many realize. The bargain of embedded liberalism is alive and well even in countries where we might not expect to find it. In the United States, for example, the Bush administration and free trade proponents in the Congress recently bought off opposition to Trade Promotion Authority by increasing the size of trade adjustment assistance and providing wage insurance for older workers displaced by trade.

Second, our results suggest that governments are less responsive to imports today than in the past. As OECD countries have moved more toward service economies, the effect of import surges on spending has declined because fewer citizens work in import-competing sectors. Having made this point, we want to stress that this situation is unlikely to persist. There is every reason to believe those employed in services sectors of the economy will become increasingly exposed to international competition over time, especially if trade in services is effectively incorporated into the General Agreement on Tariffs and Trade (GATT) and the World Trade Organization (WTO). Some of the recent U.S. backlash against Indian phone centers, for instance, shows that service industries are increasingly competitive across borders. Therefore, it is likely that the bargain of embedded liberalism will remain politically significant well into the twenty-first century.

Finally, even though our analysis in this article largely avoids institutions, we believe national institutions play an important role in determining if, when, and how the bargain of embedded liberalism is implemented in different countries. Cross-national variation in a number of political and economic institutions ranging from national production regimes to electoral systems is likely to be important. Welfare state policies are likely to be more attractive to politicians in coordinated market economies and majoritarian political institutions can insulate politicians from the pressures of trade losers. Future research should focus on how these and other institutions shape individual attitudes toward trade and constrain policy responses to economic globalization.

Appendix

TABLE A1. *Summary statistics for micro-level data*

Variable	*Observations*	*Mean*	*Standard deviation*	*Median*	*Minimum*	*Maximum*
FREETRADE	16,222	2.418	1.150	2	1	5
TRADABLE	11,476	0.2390	0.427	0	0	1
EXPORTS	11,476	0.176	0.431	0	0	3.282
IMPORTS	11,476	0.283	0.815	0	0	7.472
EDUCATION	17,007	4.604	1.401	5	1	7
INCOME	14,873	0.348	0.476	0	0	1
MALE	16,991	0.479	0.500	0	0	1
AGE	16,881	45.618	16.868	44	14	98
SINGLE	16,897	0.371	0.483	0	0	1
UNEMPLOYED	16,699	0.051	0.220	0	0	1
IDEOLOGY	13,119	2.861	0.936	3	1	5
RELIGIOUS	16,356	0.781	0.414	1	0	1
NATIONALISM	13,242	0.085	0.985	0.127	−3.315	1.759
SOCIAL SECURITY	16,070	2.516	0.920	3	1	4
NRR	13,503	0.693	0.099	0.72	0.37	0.88
ALM	17,103	4.707	3.960	4.18	0.49	12.73

Note: ALM = active labor market; NRR = net replacement rate.

TABLE A2. *Summary statistics for macro-level data*

Variable	*Observations*	*Mean*	*Standard deviation*	*Median*	*Minimum*	*Maximum*
GOVCON	681	19.143	4.104	18.905	9.838	31.329
SOCBEN	615	12.496	4.490	12.568	2.681	23.890
NRR	299	37.130	23.181	30.546	7.111	133.582
IMPORTS	667	11.250	1.167	11.189	8.591	13.965
DEIND	662	71.902	7.044	72.255	48.31	84.53
EXPORTS	667	11.260	1.193	11.201	8.431	13.743
RGDPPC	675	9.634	0.326	9.684	8.469	10.368
OLDAGE	680	12.368	2.609	12.374	5.970	18.282
LEFTC	680	31.176	38.193	0	0	100
UNDENS	632	43.987	17.189	42.782	9.867	85.483

Note: DEIND = deindustrialization; GOVCON = government consumption; LEFTC = left-wing government; NRR = net replacement rate; RGDPPC = real gross domestic product per capita; SOCBEN = social benefits; UNDENS = union density.

References

Adserà, Alicia, and Carles Boix. 2002. Trade, Democracy, and the Size of the Public Sector: The Political Underpinnings of Openness. *International Organization* 56 (2):229–62.

Aldrich, John H., Claire Kramer, Peter Lange, Renan Levine, Jennifer Merolla, Laura Stephenson, and Elizabeth Zechmeister. 2002. In Pursuit of the Missing Link: Do Voters Make the Connection Between Macroeconomic Change and Welfare State Growth? Paper presented at the 98th Annual Meeting of the American Political Science Association, August–September, Boston.

Alt, James, and Michael Gilligan. 1994. The Political Economy of Trading States: Factor Specificity, Collective Action Problems and Domestic Political Institutions. *Journal of Political Philosophy* 2 (2):165–92.

Blyth, Mark. 2002. *Great Transformations: Economic Ideas and Institutional Change in the Twentieth Century*. Cambridge: Cambridge University Press.

Burgoon, Brian. 2001. Globalization and Welfare Compensation: Disentangling the Ties that Bind. *International Organization* 55 (3):509–51.

Cameron, David. 1978. The Expansion of the Public Economy: A Comparative Analysis. *American Political Science Review* 72 (4):1243–61.

Franzese, Robert J. 2002. *Macroeconomic Policies of Developed Democracies*. Cambridge: Cambridge University Press.

Garrett, Geoffrey, and Deborah Mitchell. 2001. Globalization, Government Spending and Taxation in the OECD. *European Journal of Political Research* 39 (2):145–78.

Hall, Peter, and David Soskice, eds. 2001. *Varieties of Capitalism: The Institutional Foundations of Comparative Advantage*. New York: Oxford University Press.

Hiscox, Michael. 2002. *International Trade and Political Conflict: Commerce, Coalitions, and Mobility*. Princeton, N.J.: Princeton University Press.

Hiscox, Michael, and Brian Burgoon. 2003. Trade Openness and Political Compensation: Explaining Labor Demands for Adjustment Assistance. Unpublished manuscript. Cambridge, Mass.: Harvard University.

Hsiao, Cheng. 2003. *Analysis of Panel Data*. 2d ed. Cambridge: Cambridge University Press.

Iversen, Torben, and Thomas R. Cusack. 2000. The Causes of Welfare State Expansion: Deindustrialization or Globalization? *World Politics* 52 (3):313–49.

Judson, Ruth A., and Ann L. Owen. 1999. Estimating Dynamic Panel Data Models: A Guide for Macroeconomists. *Economic Letters* 65 (7):9–15.

Katzenstein, Peter. 1985. *Small States in World Markets: Industrial Policy in Europe*. Ithaca, N.Y.: Cornell University Press.

King, Gary, Michael Tomz, and Jason Wittenberg. 2000. Making the Most of Statistical Analyses: Improving Interpretation and Presentation. *American Journal of Political Science* 44 (2):347–61.

Mares, Isabela. 2004. Economic Insecurity and Social Policy Expansion: Evidence from Interwar Europe. *International Organization* 58 (4).

Mayda, Anna M., and Dani Rodrik. 2002. Why Are Some People (and Countries) More Protectionist than Others? Unpublished manuscript. Cambridge, Mass: Harvard University.

McKelvey, Richard, and William Zavoina. 1975. A Statistical-Model for Analysis of Ordinal Level Dependent Variables. *Journal of Mathematical Sociology* 4 (1):103–20.

Moulton, Brent R. 1990. An Illustration of a Pitfall in Estimating the Effects of Aggregate Variables on Micro Units. *Review of Economics and Statistics* 72 (2):334–38.

Organization for Economic Cooperation and Development (OECD). 1998. *Benefit Systems and Work Incentives*. Paris: OECD.

———. 2001. Social Spending Database. Paris: OECD.

———. 2003a. Labor Force Database. Paris: OECD.

———. 2003b. Economic Outlook Database. Paris: OECD.

O'Rourke, Kevin H., and Richard Sinnott. 2002. The Determinants of Individual Trade Policy Preferences: International Survey Evidence. In *Brookings Trade Forum: 2001*, edited by Susan M. Collins and Dani Rodrik, 157–206. Washington, D.C.: Brookings Institution.

Pierson, Paul. 1994. *Dismantling the Welfare State? Reagan, Thatcher, and the Politics of Retrenchment.* Cambridge: Cambridge University Press.

———. 2001. The Dynamics of Welfare State Expansion: Trade Openness, De-industrialization, and Partisan Politics. In *The New Politics of the Welfare State*, edited by Paul Pierson, 80–104. New York: Oxford University Press.

Rodrik, Dani. 1997. *Has Globalization Gone Too Far?* Washington, D.C.: Institute for International Economics.

———. 1998. Why Do More Open Economies Have Bigger Governments? *Journal of Political Economy* 106 (5):997–1032.

Ruggie, John G. 1982. International Regimes, Transactions, and Change: Embedded Liberalism in the Postwar Economic Order. *International Organization* 36 (2):195–231.

———. 1994. Trade, Protectionism, and the Future of Welfare Capitalism. *Journal of International Affairs* 48 (1):1–11.

———. 1997. Globalization and the Embedded Liberalism Compromise: The End of an Era? Working Paper 97/1. Cologne, Germany: Max Planck Institut für Gesellschaftsforschung.

———. 2003. Taking Embedded Liberalism Global: the Corporate Connection. In *Taming Globalization: Frontiers of Governance*, edited by David Held and Mathias Koenig-Archibugi, 93–129. Oxford: Polity Press.

Scheve, Kenneth, and Matthew Slaughter. 2001. *Globalization and the Perceptions of American Workers.* Washington, D.C.: Institute for International Economics.

Steenbergen, Marco R., and Bradford S. Jones. 2002. Modeling Multilevel Data Structures. *American Journal of Political Science* 46 (1):218–37.

Swank, Duane. 2002a. *Global Capital, Political Institutions, and Policy Change in Developed Welfare States.* Cambridge, UK: Cambridge University Press.

———. 2002b. 21-Nation Pooled Time-Series Data Set, 1950–1999: Political Strength of Political Parties by Ideological Group in Capitalist Democracies. Milwaukee, Wis.: Marquette University. Available at ⟨www.marquette.edu/polisci/Swankpart5099.xls⟩. Accessed January 18, 2005.

Tomz, Michael, Jason Wittenberg, and Gary King. 1999. *Clarify: Software for Interpreting and Presenting Statistical Results.* Version 1.2.1. Cambridge, Mass: Harvard University. Updated version 2.1 (produced 5 January 2003). Available at ⟨http://gking.harvard.edu/stats.html⟩. Accessed January 18, 2005.

[11]

WHY IS TRADE REFORM SO POPULAR IN LATIN AMERICA?

A Consumption-Based Theory of Trade Policy Preferences

By ANDY BAKER*

SCHOLARS, journalists, and politicians alike have been growing more interested in the developing world's reactions to the recently implemented and now nearly ubiquitous free-market reforms. The highly visible, and sometimes violent, protests of antiglobalization activists and angry citizens from Argentina to India have fostered the perception that voters' patience with economic globalization is wearing thin. In Latin America, the region where trade liberalization occurred most rapidly in the 1990s, the concerns of protesters appear to be well founded: free trade has had a detrimental effect on employment opportunities and income equality. Leaders of international financial institutions and promarket heads of state had promised that neoliberal reforms would bear fruit by the end of the 1990s, but the economic roller coaster continued through the turn of the century. However, despite the protests and economic trends, evidence from various surveys indicates that trade liberalization is quite popular throughout Latin America. What explains this popularity? Prevailing explanations of mass attitudes toward free trade cannot solve this puzzle. Trade policy preference theory typically posits that the primary determinants of mass beliefs about foreign trade policy are retrospective economic evaluations and characteristics associated with individuals' earning power. These potential explanations for international trade's popularity, however,

*I am very grateful to Edward Schumacher of *Wall Street Journal Americas* for generously providing the data and to Ethan Scheiner for reading multiple drafts of the paper. Thanks also to Ernesto Calvo, Michael Carter, Raymond Duch, John Fieno, Kenneth Greene, Daniel Nielson, Lila Rosenthal, Mitchell Seligson, Sung Kim Chu, and the anonymous reviewers for providing helpful comments and to Sung Kim Chu for research assistance. The four-city Brazil survey was funded by a Social Science Research Council International Dissertation Fellowship. The title of this paper is an adaptation of the title of Raquel Fernandez and Dani Rodrik, "Why Is Trade Reform So Unpopular?" Discussion Paper no. 391 (London: Centre for Economic Policy Research, 1990).

World Politics 55 (April 2003), 423–55

are clearly incompatible with Latin America's unimpressive economic growth and steadily rising unemployment rates in the postreform era.

This article develops a new theory of trade policy preferences that accounts for this high aggregate support *and* for differences in attitudes across nations and individuals. The theory shifts the explanatory emphasis from determinants of an individual's earning power in a globalized labor market (for example, skills, asset specificity, sector of employment) to more consumption-based characteristics. In developing countries emerging from decades of protectionism, citizens are more likely to assess trade policy based on its highly visible impact on consumer options, not labor markets. Therefore, the impressive degree of support for trade liberalization in Latin America results from the widespread appreciation of its beneficial outcome for the prices, quality, and variety of consumer goods.

To support this argument, I analyze three different cross-national surveys of Latin American public opinion and a more in-depth survey from Brazil. After presenting the evidence of the popularity of international trade in the next section, the subsequent two sections describe the competing theoretical explanations of mass trade preferences and develop the new consumption-based theory. The remaining sections test these propositions with various statistical and qualitative analyses of the survey data.

I. Evidence of Free Trade's Popularity in Latin America

High aggregate support among Latin Americans for free trade and various free-trade agreements is evidenced in numerous surveys and is robust to survey question wording. (Question wordings are in Appendixes 1, 2, and 3.) Tables 1, 2, and 3 show results from four different survey questions in fourteen Latin American nations. Table 1 shows results from the fourteen-nation *Wall Street Journal Americas* survey conducted in January and February 1998. This question measured whether the respondent thought free trade had been good or bad for the country.[1] The vast majority of respondents in every country believed free trade to be "very good" or "somewhat good" for the country.[2]

[1] Translation from Spanish is as follows: "Over the last few years the country has had more and more business and trade with other countries. This tendency is called 'free trade.' Do you think that free trade is good or bad for the country? Very or somewhat?"

[2] All results that are reported may overestimate slightly the degree of aggregate support for free trade because the sampling frame in each country was urban dwellers only. Urban dwellers and free trade proponents tend to be of a higher socioeconomic status, making them, according to results reported below, less protectionist.

TABLE 1
LATIN AMERICANS' BELIEFS ABOUT THE IMPACT OF FREE TRADE ON THEIR COUNTRY[a]

	Very Good	*Somewhat Good*	*Somewhat Bad*	*Very Bad*	*No Response*	*N*
Argentina	28	38	13	6	15	1000
Bolivia	36	46	8	5	5	751
Brazil	45	29	10	7	9	993
Chile	27	52	12	3	7	1000
Colombia	31	49	12	4	4	1000
Costa Rica	45	42	4	3	6	750
Dom. Rep.	39	39	9	5	8	757
Ecuador	52	36	8	2	2	500
Guatemala	55	37	4	2	2	752
Mexico	27	43	12	8	10	1199
Panama	35	39	12	7	7	754
Paraguay	16	43	13	4	24	479
Peru	38	47	6	3	7	1029
Venezuela	48	33	9	6	5	1000

SOURCE: *Wall Street Journal Americas* survey (1998).
[a] Entries are percentage of each national sample.

TABLE 2
THE DISTRIBUTION OF SUPPORT FOR REGIONAL INTEGRATION SCHEMES IN LATIN AMERICA[a]

	Free Trade Agreement of the Americas (1996)					*Latin American Integration (1998)*
	Very Favorable	*Slightly Favorable*	*Slightly Opposed*	*Very Opposed*	*No Response*	*Ratio of "Favorable" to "Against"*
Argentina	23	35	10	10	23	7.2
Bolivia	36	41	9	4	10	4.1
Brazil	46	24	7	8	15	2.8
Chile	29	43	11	5	12	3.1
Colombia	43	36	8	4	9	10.8
Costa Rica	40	36	5	3	17	2.5
Dom. Rep.	35	33	11	9	12	NA
Ecuador	49	32	9	4	7	3.4
Guatemala	46	36	5	6	7	1.6
Mexico	29	39	11	7	15	1.2
Panama	28	29	13	17	14	1.4
Paraguay	19	39	10	6	27	4.1
Peru	34	40	7	5	14	5.6
Venezuela	42	32	9	10	8	2.3

SOURCES: *Wall Street Journal Americas* survey (1998); and Latinbarometer survey (1996).
[a] Entries for FTAA question are percentage of each national sample.

TABLE 3
THE DISTRIBUTION OF SUPPORT FOR FREE TRADE IN BRAZIL[a]

	Strongly Favorable	*Somewhat Favorable*	*Depends*	*Somewhat Opposed*	*Strongly Opposed*	*No Opinion*
Weighted by city population	23	22	3	8	13	30
Unweighted	28	21	3	6	10	32

SOURCE: Four-city Brazil survey (1999).
[a] Entries are percentage of 800-person sample.

In the same survey respondents indicated their degree of support for a potential hemisphere-wide free-trade zone (Free Trade Agreement of the Americas, FTAA). These results, shown in Table 2, also indicate a high level of mass support for the free-market position. The final column of Table 2 also shows the extent of support for greater economic integration with other Latin American countries. These data are from the cross-national Latinbarometer survey administered in 1996. In every country supporters of greater Latin American integration outnumbered opponents, and in most countries they outnumbered them by a ratio of at least two to one. These results are particularly revealing of the region's protrade tendencies because the survey question attempted to induce respondents to consider potential costs of further economic integration: "In general, are you in favor of or against economic integration of the countries in Latin America, even when this might imply some costs or sacrifices for your country?" That a majority of respondents replied positively to this query indicates the robustness of support for trade in Latin America.

A more neutral survey question, administered in four Brazilian cities in 1999, refers neither to potential costs nor to benefits for the country as a whole. Table 3 shows responses to the following survey item: "In the last ten years, Brazil's trade with foreign countries grew. This increase in trade is known as 'trade liberalization' or 'free trade.' Some people favor and others oppose this 'trade liberalization.' Are you in favor of, against, or do you not have an opinion on this policy of trade opening? Are you strongly or slightly favorable/opposed?" Again, a large plurality of respondents in this sample favored free trade.[3] This

[3] Because citizens may not always understand a potentially complex issue such as free trade, a comment on nonresponse levels is merited. High aggregate rates of "don't know" and other "no opinion" responses are typically an indication that citizens, including many who do respond with an opinion, are uncertain or unfamiliar with the policy or issue being queried. See Larry M. Bartels, "Issue Voting under Uncertainty: An Empirical Test," *American Journal of Political Science* 30 (1986). The degree of nonresponse in Tables 1, 2, and 3 varies substantially by question wording but, overall, indicates widespread knowledge and certainty about free trade. Nonresponse rates to a question about the past impact of free trade (Table 1) are very low, in single digits in almost all countries. They are only slightly

result is particularly striking because the survey was administered soon after the major devaluation of Brazil's currency and at the peak of the country's unemployment crisis, events that stemmed in part from its rapid and indiscriminate trade liberalization in the 1990s.

Even recent cross-national data indicate that support for free trade in Latin America remains high. Two-thirds of respondents to the seventeen-nation 2001 Latinbarometer survey believed the FTAA would help the economic development of their country, while over 70 percent favored the economic integration of Latin America.[4] Support for greater Latin American economic integration exceeded 60 percent in every country, and support for FTAA exceeded 60 percent in eight of eleven countries and Central America.[5]

This high aggregate support for free trade contrasts sharply with citizens' attitudes toward privatization, another crucial element of the region's recent economic reform package. In the *Wall Street Journal Americas* survey, free trade is a far more popular policy than privatization, as antiprivatization respondents (39 percent) outnumbered protectionists (18 percent) by a ratio greater than two to one, and the zero-order correlation between attitudes for the two policies was only +.16. Evidence from both the four-city Brazil sample and the 2001 Latinbarometer confirms this pattern. In Brazil free-trade proponents (65 percent) were more numerous than privatization advocates (42 percent). In the seventeen 2001 Latinbarometer countries privatization

higher, although still in the moderately low 7–17 percent range, when respondents were asked about FTAA, a seemingly more complex question about a hypothetical policy that had not yet been enacted (Table 2). (The nonresponse rate in the 1996 Latinbarometer question is 18 percent.) In comparative perspective, these no-opinion rates are about average or even slightly below average, so there is no reason to think that Latin Americans are more uncertain or less knowledgeable about trade than are other democracies' citizens about typical political issues.

At the same time, a potential problem with this assessment of aggregate nonresponse levels is the existence of nonattitudes, or people who do not have real attitudes but offer an opinion nonetheless. See Philip Converse, "The Nature of Belief Systems in Mass Publics," in David Apter, ed., *Ideology and Discontent* (New York: Free Press, 1964). To address this, the four-city Brazil survey (Table 3) offered respondents an "easy out" by including "no opinion" as an explicitly read option. Among those who did offer an attitude, the "realness" or validity of reported opinions could also then be double-checked against open-ended justifications for the response, discussed in more detail in Section IV of this article. Not surprisingly, nonresponse increased (compare Table 1 with Table 3) to 30 percent in Brazil. The remaining 70 percent, therefore, are those with definite attitudes toward free trade, and almost all of their open-ended responses indicated familiarity with the issue. That said, research indicates that offering the "easy out" increases the occurrence of "false negatives," or "no opinion" responses that mask real attitudes. In sum, although nonresponse varies with the issue and question wording, it seems safe to assume that uncertainty or lack of familiarity with free trade varies from about 10 percent to *at most* 25 percent in most of these countries. See Mikael Gilljam and Donald Granberg, "Should We Take Don't Know for an Answer?" *Public Opinion Quarterly* 57 (Autumn 1993).

[4] "An Alarm Call for Latin America's Democrats," *Economist* (July 26, 2001).

[5] The presentation in "An Alarm Call" (fn. 4) aggregates results for six Central American countries (El Salvador, Guatemala, El Salvador, Costa Rica, Honduras, and Nicaragua) into one data point. The eleven countries besides the Central American ones are Argentina, Bolivia, Brazil, Chile, Colombia, Ecuador, Mexico, Paraguay, Peru, Uruguay, and Venezuela.

opponents outnumbered its supporters in all but one nation. Moreover, beliefs about privatization had grown more negative from 1998 to 2001 in every country but one, in contrast to the unchanging support for free trade expressed in both years.[6] In short, aggregate support for free trade is much higher than support for privatization, indicating that positive orientations toward free trade are not simply a vague expression of support for economic liberalization.[7] Instead, many citizens *favorably single out free trade* from the list of Latin America's recent market reforms.

The existence and persistence of support for trade liberalization is all the more impressive in light of the region's recurring economic problems, which are caused in part by trade liberalization itself. Regionwide crises struck in 1995 and 1999. Moreover, no country has sustained economic growth levels over 4 percent, a frequently achieved rate during the import-substitution years. Income inequality has not declined in any country in the postreform era, and in some cases it has worsened.[8] World Bank president James Wolfensohn admitted in 2000 that Latin America was "no better off than . . . in the 1970s." Some of the decline has been linked to free trade itself. The proglobalization Inter-American Development Bank has acknowledged the following: "[Reforms] have slowed the pace of employment growth and may have been one cause of the rise in unemployment rates. . . . Employment rates have declined, and that has happened more forcefully where the structural reforms, and particularly trade and finance reforms, have been deepest."[9] Restructuring due to import competition has increased unemployment and inequality and has shrunk the formal sector.[10] Finally, a recent econometric study demonstrated a negative relationship between trade liberalization and GDP growth.[11]

[6] See "An Alarm Call" (fn. 4).

[7] David E. Hojman, "The Political Economy of Recent Conversions to Market Economies in Latin America," *Journal of Latin American Studies* 26 (February 1994), 210; Kurt Weyland, "Risk Taking in Latin American Economic Restructuring: Lessons from Prospect Theory," *International Studies Quarterly* 40 (June 1996); idem, "Swallowing the Bitter Pill: Sources of Popular Support for Neoliberal Reform in Latin America," *Comparative Political Studies* 31 (October 1998).

[8] Albert Berry, ed., *Poverty, Economic Reform and Income Distribution in Latin America* (Boulder, Colo.: Lynne Rienner, 1998); and John Sheahan, "Effects of Liberalization Programs on Poverty and Inequality: Chile, Mexico and Peru," *Latin American Research Review* 32, no. 3 (1997).

[9] Inter-American Development Bank, *Economic and Social Progress in Latin America: 1997 Report* (Baltimore: Johns Hopkins University Press, 1997), 58. See page 90 for the econometric results backing this assertion. Also concurring are Barbara Stallings and Wilson Peres, *Growth, Employment and Equity: The Impact of the Economic Reforms in Latin America and the Caribbean* (Washington, D.C.: Brookings Institution/ECLAC, 2000).

[10] Stallings and Peres (fn. 9).

[11] David Greenway, Wyn Morgan, and Peter Wright, "Trade Liberalization and Growth in Developing Countries: Some New Evidence," *World Development* 25, no. 11 (1997). See also Francisco Rodriguez and Dani Rodrik, "Trade Policy and Economic Growth: A Skeptic's Guide to the Cross-National Evidence," in Ben Bernanke and Kenneth S. Rogoff, eds., *Macroeconomics Annual 2000* (Cambridge: MIT Press, 2001).

Citizen attitudes reflect this economic malaise. In 2001 citizens in nine of eleven countries (excluding Central America) were more negative about the national economy than they were in 1995.[12] In none of the seventeen Latinbarometer countries did positive assessments of the national economy outnumber negative ones. Similarily, a majority of citizens evaluated the current national economy as "bad" or "very bad" in eight of eleven countries and Central America.

What explains, then, the high degree of support for trade reform, which exists alongside more pessimistic attitudes toward the economy and other neoliberal policies? While this is a question about aggregate public opinion, an accurate theoretical explanation should also account for interpersonal and cross-national differences in trade preferences. The remainder of this paper describes and assesses both aggregate-level and individual-level observable implications of each potential theoretical explanation.

II. Theories Based on Earning Power

Heckscher-Ohlin

The leading economic theory of international trade and its domestic impact, the Heckscher-Ohlin model, provides predictions of interpersonal differences in trade policy preferences and a plausible explanation for Latin America's high aggregate support for free trade.[13] The Heckscher-Ohlin theory states that freely trading countries will tend to export goods that employ their most relatively abundant factor (the four factors being land, capital, unskilled labor, and skilled labor) of production while importing goods whose production relies on their

[12] "An Alarm Call" (fn. 4).

[13] Another leading earning power theory is based on the Ricardo-Viner, or specific factors, model, which claims that individuals who are employed in or who own capital in internationally competitive industries should favor free trade while individuals with assets and employment in uncompetitive industries should favor protection. See Jeffry A. Frieden, *Debt, Development and Democracy: Modern Political Economy and Latin America* (Princeton: Princeton University Press, 1991); and James Alt, Jeffry Frieden, Michael J. Gilligan, Dani Rodrik, and Ronald Rogowski, "The Political Economy of International Trade," *Comparative Political Studies* 29 (January 1996). I disregard Ricardo-Viner because the data to test it rigorously (surveys must record respondents' sector of employment) are not available in any cross-national Latin American survey projects and because it has so far received limited empirical support as a theory of mass trade preferences. See Kenneth F. Scheve and Matthew J. Slaughter, *Globalization and the Perceptions of American Workers* (Washington, D.C.: Institute for International Economics, 2001); and Anne Maria Mayda and Dani Rodrik, "Why Are Some People More Protectionist Than Others?" Working Paper no. 8461 (Cambridge: National Bureau of Economic Research, 2001). The four-city Brazil survey does allow for a test of the Ricardo-Viner model, but it receives no empirical support. (These results are available from the author upon request.) Finally, the Ricardo-Viner model clearly does not provide an answer to this paper's central question about high aggregate support for free trade since only a slim minority of the Latin American population is employed in an internationally competitive sector. In fact, most citizens are not employed in a tradable goods sector at all.

relatively scarcest factor.[14] According to the model, trade restrictions distort these naturally occurring tendencies, thereby favoring scarce factors over abundant ones. As a result, trade liberalization in a protected economy brings income losses to individuals with scarce factor assets (because they face increased competition from imports) and income gains to individuals with abundant factor assets (because foreign demand for their assets increases).

As developing nations, Latin American countries possess a relative abundance of unskilled labor and land over capital and skilled labor, so protectionism during the import-substitution years favored the latter two over the former two. According to the Heckscher-Ohlin model, then, export expansion through trade liberalization should increase the relative wealth of unskilled labor and farmers by decreasing demand for locally produced, capital-intensive goods and by increasing demand for labor-intensive and land-intensive products. Because capital and skilled labor comprise less than 15 percent of most Latin American populations, trade liberalization should reduce wage inequality, thereby producing an enormous protrade coalition of unskilled and rural workers.[15] If this is true, then the relationship between skill level (measured by educational attainment) and support for free trade will be negative in Latin America. At the same time, the strength of this relationship will depend on the relative abundance of skilled labor in each country.[16] Skilled individuals in economies with a moderate supply of skilled labor (like Argentina) will be less protectionist than individuals of the same skill level in countries that are poorly endowed with skilled labor (like Guatemala).

Human Capital

Like Heckscher-Ohlin, the human capital hypothesis claims that trade preferences stem from characteristics that determine an individual's earning power in the labor market.[17] Individuals with a high degree of human capital, namely, formal education, have a relatively large pool of skills from which to draw, thereby increasing their ability to adapt to the shifting configuration of labor demand caused by economic liberalization. Less-educated citizens, by contrast, tend to have skills that are

[14] Eli Heckscher, "The Effect of Foreign Trade on the Distribution of Income," *Readings in the Theory of International Trade*, vol. 4 (Philadelphia: Blakiston, 1949); and Paul Samuelson, "International Trade and the Equalisation of Factor Prices," *Economic Journal* 58 (June 1948).

[15] Ronald Rogowski, *Commerce and Coalitions* (Princeton: Princeton University Press, 1989).

[16] Mayda and Rodrik (fn. 13).

[17] Matthew Gabel, *Interests and Integration: Market Liberalization, Public Opinion, and European Union* (Ann Arbor: University of Michigan Press, 1998).

more specific to a particular sector or type of employment.[18] As a result, contrary to Heckscher-Ohlin's prediction, education should be positively correlated with support for free trade in *all* countries.

The human capital hypothesis also differs from Heckscher-Ohlin in that it predicts a low level of support for free trade in less developed countries because of their undereducated labor forces. Although this seems incompatible with the observed empirical patterns mentioned to this point, I test the relative merits of these two theories nonetheless. To date, scholars have tested these two theories using public opinion data from only the United States and Western Europe, where they both have the same observable implications. Because developed countries have a relative abundance of skilled labor, both theories predict a positive relationship between skill level and support for free trade. Therefore, the relative explanatory power of these theories can be rigorously assessed only with data from the developing world, where the two theories make opposing predictions.

III. A Consumption-Based Theory

The earning-power theories of trade preferences assume that actors' self-interested assessments of trade policy rest largely on the characteristics of their employment or income source and not on the type of goods and services they buy. In other words, while liberalization initially shifts the relative prices of goods and services that foreign and domestic consumers encounter, its most serious impact occurs once the resulting changes in consumer behavior cause a reshuffling of demand for particular types of employable assets. Figure 1 illustrates this logic, with the "x" indicating the empirical link that these theories ignore.

In predicting trade preferences, therefore, these models focus on 3b, the welfare effects of the reshuffling that occurs in 3a. This overlooks the welfare effects in 2b of the shifting prices for consumers in 2a, even though 2a is a more immediate result of the policy change itself than 3a. Most scholars of mass trade preferences have ignored the possibility that individuals may be just as, if not more, likely to form their beliefs about trade liberalization by observing its impact on the prices, quality, and availability of goods and services they buy and consume.[19]

[18] Torben Iversen and David Soskice, "An Asset Theory of Social Policy Preferences," *American Political Science Review* 95 (December 2001).

[19] See Scheve and Slaughter (fn. 13); Mayda and Rodrik (fn. 13); Gabel (fn. 17); Alt et al. (fn. 13); Miguel Basáñez, Ronald Inglehart, and Neil Nevitte, *North American Trajectory* (Ann Arbor: University of Michigan Press, 1996); and Rogowski (fn. 15).

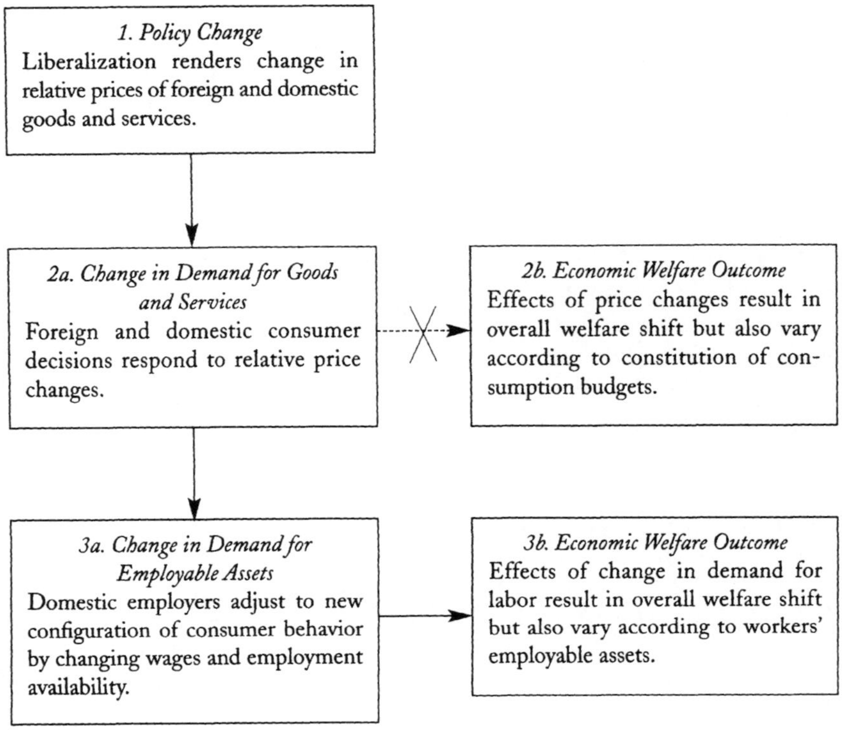

FIGURE 1
THE LOGIC UNDERLYING THE EARNING-POWER THEORIES

The impact of trade and protection on prices and consumer welfare is well established in economic theory, but political scientists have yet to use these principles as a means to generate hypotheses about trade policy preferences. Economic theories of rent seeking claim that a protected industry decreases aggregate national income by artificially increasing prices for its goods.[20] Because citizens would pay less for that industry's good if they had access to world markets, they have less money to devote to other purchases under protectionism. In essence, citizens are charged extra for a protected industry's inefficiencies, so only owners and employees in this industry benefit. As such, ceteris paribus, all consumers (ignoring temporarily the impact of trade on

[20] Gordon Tullock, "The Welfare Costs of Tariffs, Monopolies, and Theft," *Western Economic Journal* 5 (June 1967); and Anne O. Krueger, "The Political Economy of the Rent-Seeking Society," *American Economic Review* 64 (June 1974).

their income) benefit from trade liberalization. Moreover, these benefits vary according to the nature of each person's consumption budget.

Although political scientists have yet to derive and test a consumption-based model of trade preferences, cognitive theories of policy preference suggest that individuals, especially in developing countries, may be more likely to base their free trade attitudes on their own patterns of personal consumption than on their status as producers and income earners.[21] For self-interest to be politicized, the linkage between policy and personal welfare must be evident to an individual, and there is reason to believe that citizens in Latin America have been much more aware of trade's impact on consumer choice than of its impact on employment opportunities. In countries that practiced decades of import substitution, the relaxation of import tariffs had an immediate and obvious impact on consumer choice. During the protectionist decades demand in many product markets was filled by domestic monopolies or oligopolies that sold low-quality goods at well above the world's market price. Consumers had few alternatives and limited purchasing power. With trade liberalization and the influx of imports (combined in many countries with an overvalued exchange rate), consumer options exploded. The quality, variety, and affordability of many goods expanded rapidly and in a process that most consumers perceived.

Why would this process be more visible than job loss and industrial restructuring to Latin American citizens and therefore more likely to shape their trade preferences? First, the cause/effect linkage between unemployment or wage fluctuations and imports may not always be obvious to the affected workers and the unemployed, many of whom are influenced indirectly through a tightened labor market. Second, only a minority of the population works in a tradable goods sector whose employment status and wages would be most visibly touched by trade liberalization. Workers in a given sector are likely to perceive whether they are benefiting from increased exports or losing from greater import competition. However, the remaining majority of the population is either employed in the service sector or not even in the economically active population. Less obvious to these individuals are the effects of foreign trade on their employment (for service sector employees), employment potential (for the unemployed and students), or the employ-

[21] Samuel Popkin, *The Reasoning Voter: Communication and Persuasion in Presidential Campaigns* (Chicago: University of Chicago Press, 1994); William Gamson, *Talking Politics* (Cambridge: Cambridge University Press, 1992); and idem, "Media Discourse as a Framing Resource," in Ann N. Crigler, ed., *The Psychology of Political Communication* (Ann Arbor: University of Michigan Press, 1996).

ment of their main income providers (for homemakers and the retired). Consumer behavior is also more likely to be linked to noticeable trends in aggregate support for trade policy because nearly every citizen is a consumer, while not everyone is a producer. In short, the impact of trade policy on consumer options creates a ready-made information shortcut for citizens to use in developing their preferences.[22]

This asymmetry in perception between the impact of trade on consumption options versus employment opportunities holds the key to understanding high aggregate support for free trade in Latin America. Trade liberalization in heavily protected societies has nothing but positive ramifications for consumer choice. Not only does the influx of foreign goods itself expand and increase the average quality of consumer options, but the increased competition encourages domestic firms (if they survive) to create higher-quality goods at a lower price. If consumers ignore or are unaware of the impact of this beneficial outcome on domestic industry and employment opportunities, then the typical response to free trade will be highly favorable.

Observable Implications of a Consumption-Based Theory

The consumption-based framework posits numerous empirical patterns that are observable at various levels of analysis: multinational, national, and individual. First, the most obvious and important observable implication was demonstrated in the data presented above: in formerly protected countries with small manufacturing sectors, trade liberalization will raise overall consumer welfare and therefore be quite popular. Remaining observable implications are empirically tested in subsequent sections of this article.

Second, due to the visibility of trade's impact, citizens will recognize the positive effects on their consumer options and will tend to justify their support for free trade by referring to these types of gains. Similarly, they will tend to believe that trade has been more beneficial for the availability and price of consumer goods than for wages and employment opportunities. Moreover, justifications of support based on consumer considerations will outnumber justifications of protectionism based on labor-market considerations.

Third, aggregate mass support at the national level will vary inversely with a country's ability to produce its own goods. Under protectionism, individuals living in countries with small, highly concentrated manufacturing sectors have far fewer tradable goods options available for

[22] Popkin (fn. 21); and Paul Sniderman, Richard Brody, and Philip Tetlock, *Reasoning and Choice: Explorations in Political Psychology* (Cambridge: Cambridge University Press, 1991).

purchase than have citizens in countries with large, diversified manufacturing sectors.[23] The beneficial effect of trade liberalization on consumer options is therefore even more pronounced and more visible in a country (like Panama) that historically has not produced a wide variety of manufactured goods than in a country (like Mexico) with a reasonably large and diversified economy. This hypothesis is in sharp contrast to an earning-power approach, which would predict higher support for free trade in countries with large markets. Under protectionism large-market countries can more easily achieve economies of scale, which advantages them in international market competition and creates more jobs.

A fourth and final observable implication pertains to individual-level heterogeneity in trade policy attitudes and merits a lengthier discussion. The relative price changes resulting from free trade will render welfare effects that vary across consumers according to the type of goods and services they tend to buy. Trade liberalization leads to relative declines in the prices of *f*oreign i*m*ports (M_F) and *l*ocally produced goods that compete with i*m*ports (M_L). It also leads to relative increases in the prices of *n*on*t*raded (NT_L) goods and services[24] as well as of locally produced goods in e*x*port-oriented sectors (X_L). Therefore, a theory of trade preferences based on self-interested consumers makes a clear-cut prediction: consumer support for free trade varies according to the individual's consumption budget. Consumers become increasingly disadvantaged by protectionism as the share of M_F and M_L in their consumption budgets increases, so support for trade barriers should vary inversely with this share. In contrast, consumers also become less favored by trade liberalization as the share of NT_L and X_L in their consumption budgets increases, so support for trade barriers should vary directly with this share. In sum, support for trade liberalization should vary directly with the following percentage, which is the share of income that consumer *i* devotes to imports and import-competing goods:

$$\frac{M_{F_i} + M_{L_i}}{M_{F_i} + M_{L_i} + X_{L_i} + NT_{L_i}}, \qquad (1)$$

where each term is the amount of money spent on those types of items.

[23] Peter Katzenstein, *Small States in World Markets: Industrial Policy in Europe* (Ithaca, N.Y.: Cornell University Press, 1985).

[24] This includes financial services such as savings and investment. According to free trade advocates, liberalization increases the demand for, and therefore the prices of, nontraded goods and services because it leads to greater economic growth. For reasons discussed above, I do not make this assumption; however, this does not negate the fact that prices of M_F and M_L will decrease *relative* to those of NT_L.

A precise test of this individual-level element of the theory calls for a data set with detailed information both about citizens' consumption budgets *and* about their trade policy attitudes. Unfortunately, household spending surveys are expensive, time consuming,[25] and therefore rare in Latin America; they are collected by census bureaus just a few times per decade in only a handful of countries. More importantly, the few that do exist are not coupled with attitudinal surveys on political and economic issues. However, existing knowledge and data on household spending do reveal that income can be used as a viable proxy for consumption budgets, especially when proper statistical controls are introduced.

Scholars have used income, like education, to operationalize a vast array of concepts. I introduce a measurement theory of income as consumer interests and argue that it is best conceptualized as a measure of consumer benefits vis-à-vis trade policy. Engel's law, one of the first theorems in modern economics (1857), states that the proportion of income spent on food declines as income rises.[26] A corollary of this original insight is that durable goods and clothing replace food in overall share once the basic need for the latter is fulfilled.[27] At the same time, Keynesian economic theory indicates that upper-class citizens save and invest a greater proportion of their income than does anyone else. The Latin American upper class also spends a larger share of its income on nontradables, namely, on services such as education and health.[28] Therefore, the share of traded, durable goods and clothing in one's consumption budget is at its peak among the middle class. Table 4 shows these patterns with household budget data from various countries.

Latin America has a comparative advantage in products that have relatively little value added and are both land intensive and natural-resource intensive. By contrast, the region has a comparative disadvantage in technology-intensive, high-value-added products. Therefore, clothing and durable goods (which are more processed and higher tech than food and other commodities) constitute a much greater share of

[25] Household budget surveys require family expenditures to be tracked rigorously for at least a week.

[26] H. S. Houthakker, "An International Comparison of Household Expenditure Patterns: Commemorating the Centenary of Engel's Law," *Econometrica* 25 (October 1957); and Debraj Ray, *Development Economics* (Princeton: Princeton University Press, 1998).

[27] Masao Ogaki, "Engel's Law and Cointegration," *Journal of Political Economy* 100 (October 1992); and Masao Ogaki and Carmen M. Reinhart, "Measuring Intertemporal Substitution: The Role of Durable Goods," *Journal of Political Economy* 106 (October 1998).

[28] Inter-American Development Bank, *Economic and Social Progress in Latin America: 1998–1999 Report* (Baltimore: Johns Hopkins University Press, 1998).

TABLE 4
PROPORTION OF INCOME SPENT ON DURABLE GOODS AND CLOTHING BY INCOME PERCENTILE[a]

Poorest									*Richest*
Argentina 1996 and 1997									
0%	10%	20%	30%	40%	50%	60%	70%	80%	90%
.032	.062	.076	.084	.096	.094	.098	.100	.097	.084
Ecuador 1994 and 1995									
0%	12%	43%	78%	88%	93%	95%	97%	98%	99%
.115	.128	.135	.129	.116	.124	.100	.097	.080	.054
Mexico 2000									
0%	10%	20%	30%	40%	50%	60%	70%	80%	90%
.091	.095	.103	.104	.111	.101	.110	.115	.106	.088

SOURCES: Argentina—Instituto Nacional de Estadistica y Censos, *Encuesta Nacional de Gastos de los Hogares 1996/1997*, original data consulted. Ecuador—Instituto Nacional de Estadistica y Censos, *Encuesta Nacional de Ingresos y Gastos de Hogares Urbanos: Resultados Anuales* (Quito, Ecuador: Instituto de Estadistica y Censos, 1995). Mexico—Instituto Nacional de Estadistica, Geografia, e Informatica, *Encuesta Nacional de Ingresos y Gastos de los Hogares* (Aguascalientes, Mexico: Instituto Nacional de Estadistica, Geografia e Informatica, 2000).

[a] Entries in the first row for each country indicate that column group's income level vis-à-vis the rest of the country's population. These percentages should be understood as the percentage of the population with family income smaller than that group. The second row is the mean (median in Argentina) proportion of income that families in that group spent on durable goods and clothing. Census bureaus in these countries each used different classificatory schemes for goods and services, so the categorization of durable goods varies somewhat by country. Details are available from the author upon request.

Latin American imports than exports.[29] According to equation 1, then, middle-class consumers benefit the most from trade liberalization because highly processed goods like consumer durables and clothing, which tend to be imported to Latin America, constitute a greater share of their consumption budgets than of the consumption budgets of any other class. In short, the relationship between income and consumer interests vis-à-vis free trade in the region is nonlinear, so support for trade liberalization should be highest among the middle class and lowest among the poor and the very wealthy. This does not mean that the average prices and quality of items that the lower and upper classes tend to purchase do not improve with free trade. Rather, the average prices and quality of items purchased by middle-class consumers are likely to undergo greater improvements.

Consumer price indices (CPI) from Latin America bear out these

[29] Vivianne Ventura-Dias, Mabel Cabezas, and Jaime Contador, *Trade Reform and Trade Patterns in Latin America* (Santiago, Chile: Economic Commission on Latin America, 1999).

TABLE 5
RELATIVE PRICE CHANGES BY TYPE OF GOOD AND BY CLASS

Country and Starting Year	*Clothing Inflation* / *Food Inflation*	*Durables Inflation* / *Food Inflation*
Argentina 1990	.57	1.15
Bolivia 1981	.69	.86[a]
Brazil 1987	.50	.63
Chile 1974	.29	.73[a]
Colombia 1989	.70	NA
Costa Rica 1986	.55	.93[a]
Dominican Republic 1990	1.02[a]	.94[a]
Guatemala 1986	.57	.78
Mexico 1986	.74	.80
Panama 1991	.40	.91
Paraguay 1986	.67	NA
Peru 1991	.89	.92
Venezuela 1989	.45	.91

Overall Inflation in Mexico by Income, December 1985–December 1997[b]

Lower Class	*Lower-Middle Class*	*Middle Class*
Less than three minimum salaries	Three to six minimum salaries	Six or more minimum salaries
4608	4233	4151

SOURCES: Economic Commission on Latin American and the Caribbean, "America Latina: Índices de Precios al Consumidor" (manuscript); and Instituto Nacional de Estadistica, Geografia y Informatica, *Banco de Información Económica INEGI* (http://www.inegi.gob.mx/estadistica/espanol/economia/feconomia.html, accessed January 2002).

[a] Data are not available for actual year before that in which trade liberalization began. The earliest available data are used in these cases: Bolivia (1988), Chile (1992), Costa Rica (1995), and Dominican Republic (1991).

[b] The "Middle Class" category in the Mexico data includes upper-class citizens, but, because six minimum salaries in Mexico is not much above the poverty level, the vast majority of individuals falling in this category would be middle class.

patterns in relative price changes. Table 5 presents price changes for durable goods[30] and clothing, expressed as ratios to price changes in food. The ratios are based on price changes from the year before trade liberalization began in each country (or the earliest year for which data were available) to 1997.[31] A ratio below one means that prices under

[30] Although the government agencies that record CPIs do not report prices for a "durable goods" category, they do typically report price changes for "home equipment and maintenance." This category consists largely of tradable consumer durables like electronic appliances and furniture.

[31] To determine the first year of trade liberalization, I consulted the commercial policy reform index in Samuel A. Morley, Roberto Machado, and Stefano Pettinato, *Indexes of Structural Reform in Latin America* (Santiago, Chile: ECLAC, 1999).

trade liberalization for goods in that particular category increased at a rate slower than that of food prices. The price of food increased at a faster rate than that of clothing and durables in all but two of twenty-four cases. Table 5 also presents postliberalization price changes for the Mexican lower and middle classes, indicating that inflation was greater for the former.

Summing up this fourth observable implication, then, I use income as a proxy measure in lieu of actual consumption data in attitudinal surveys. From this I generate related hypotheses based on what is known about Latin America's comparative advantage, foreign trade, and inflation patterns, as well as about its citizens' consumption patterns by class. As consumers, the middle class should perceive the most visible benefits from trade liberalization.

IV. Evidence: Addressing the Aggregate Question

This section presents evidence to support the argument that the consumption-based model better accounts for the high aggregate popularity of trade liberalization in Latin America. I demonstrate that Latin Americans (1) recognize and appreciate the benefits of free trade for their consumer options and (2) are more positive overall toward free trade because they recognize these benefits. The subsequent section employs a multivariate model of individual-level survey data to indicate that trade preference heterogeneity among individuals and across countries is also compatible with a consumption-based theory.

Open-Ended Responses in Brazil

Results from open-ended probes about free trade in the four-city Brazil sample strongly indicate that consumer welfare dominates citizen thinking about free trade and is the principal reason for positive reactions toward liberalization. A procedure on the questionnaire prompted interviewers to follow up a close-ended response about free trade (results indicated in Table 3) with the following open-ended query: "And what are your reasons for being favorable/opposed to free trade?" Interviewers then wrote down everything the respondent said and asked "anything else?" until the respondent was finished. A coder read these texts and identified distinct "rationales" that were mentioned by multiple respondents. A single rationale characterized thoughts and phrases of a nearly identical ilk. Because respondents were able to say as much as they wanted about the reforms, many made multiple statements that fell into multiple rationales. After reading all of the open-ended texts

TABLE 6
REASONS FOR SUPPORTING FREE TRADE IN BRAZIL:
OPEN-ENDED RESPONSES[a]

	Raw, Unweighted Frequency	*Weighted Percentage of Sample*	*Weighted Percentage of Supporters*
Free-Trade Supporters	392 of 800	45	100
Consumer Welfare	211	28	60
Lower-priced goods and services	149	21	45
Higher-quality goods and services	62	10	21
Greater variety of goods and services	69	6	14
Employment	120	14	29
Generates jobs	79	9	20
Increases markets for Brazilian goods, exports	47	5	10
Macroeconomic Performance	87	11	24
Spurs economic growth	49	6	12
Enhances technological development	22	4	8
Encourages investment	19	3	6
Relationship with Foreign Countries	25	3	7
Exchange with other countries is good	14	2	3
Economic integration is good for country, world	7	1	2
Tax Revenues: Generates tax revenues to spend on social areas	9	1	2

SOURCE: Four-city Brazil survey (1999).

[a] Sampling weights account for differences in city size. The sums of the *Frame* frequencies and percentages do not sum to the column totals in the top row because many respondents made remarks that fell into multiple frames. Likewise, the sums of the rationale (roman type) frequencies and percentages do not sum to the frame totals because many respondents made remarks that fell into multiple rationales.

and coding them into rationales, the coder grouped each rationale into a limited number of identifiable "frames" that describe the general area of concern, such as employment, prices, or the macroeconomy. The results from this coding are presented in Tables 6 and 7. Frames are underlined and in italics while rationales are in roman type.

The most popular justification for one's attitude toward trade liberalization, either for or against, was a consumer welfare frame. Thirty-three percent of the weighted sample used and 47 percent of all valid responses were justified with a consumer-based rationale.[32] The vast majority of respondents that used this frame, about 90 percent, were

[32] Results were weighted by city size to portray a representative sample of the aggregated four cities.

TABLE 7
REASONS FOR OPPOSING FREE TRADE IN BRAZIL:
OPEN-ENDED RESPONSES[a]

	Raw, Unweighted Frequency	*Weighted Percentage of Sample*	*Weighted Percentage of Supporters*
Free-Trade Opponents	127 of 800	21	100
Employment: Decreases demand for Brazilian goods, businesses fail and jobs disappear	*50*	*11*	*40*
Relationship with Foreign Countries	*59*	*9*	*35*
Need to value and buy more Brazilian goods (free trade "*desvaloriza o produto nacional*")	38	7	32
Brazil must be an independent country	5	0	1
Consumer Welfare	*22*	*5*	*16*
Imports are lower quality	9	3	4
Imports are more expensive	4	1	4
Macroeconomic Performance: Stunts economic growth	*6*	*1*	*1*
Tax Revenues: Imports generate fewer tax revenues than Brazilian goods	*4*	*0*	*1*
Miscellaneous: Brazil has enough to survive on its own	*19*	*5*	*19*
Other Responses			
Depends: Depends on sector or country, or should be more gradual	40	7	—
Nonresponse: Respondent doesn't know or has no opinion	259	30	—

SOURCE: Four-city Brazil survey (1999).
[a] *Frames* are underlined and in italics; rationales are in roman type.

favorable toward free trade, citing the lower prices, higher quality, and/or greater variety of goods brought by the relaxing of trade barriers. In fact, 28 percent of the entire weighted sample and 60 percent of all trade proponents justified their support in this manner.

A labor market or employment frame followed as a close second; it was mentioned by 25 percent of the weighted sample. However, despite the objective evidence about trade's deleterious effects on employment opportunities (especially during the crisis weeks in which the survey was conducted) and the best efforts of leftist politicians to make this an issue during the elections that had occurred five months earlier, a majority of respondents who used a labor-market frame were trade supporters! Almost 60 percent of these respondents believed that free trade in Brazil had helped to generate jobs, mainly by increasing global markets for Brazilian exports. Only 11 percent of the weighted sample (40 percent of free-trade opponents) attributed business failures and unemployment to free trade. In short, many Brazilians exhibited an asymmetry in their perceptions of the impact of trade: realistic understanding of its benefits for their consumer options with unrealistic perceptions of its impact on their employment opportunities. As described above, this is a formula for high aggregate support.

Evaluations of Regional Trade Blocs and Their Impact

In an item on the *Wall Street Journal Americas* survey, respondents were asked if the regional trade bloc of which their country was a member had helped or harmed the following things: (1) the price of consumer goods, (2) employment, and (3) salaries. Responses were coded as follows: (0) harmed a lot, (1) harmed a little, (2) no effect, (3) helped a little, and (4) helped a lot.[33] The results, presented in Table 8, strengthen the argument that Latin American consumers notice and appreciate the impact of free trade on the price of their options as consumers.

Table 8 presents paired difference of mean *t*-tests for whether individuals were more inclined to say that their regional free-trade bloc had helped prices or that it had helped labor markets. A positive and statistically significant difference indicates that respondents did think more highly of their bloc's influence on prices than on either employment or salaries. The results for the aggregated data set of the thirteen countries where these questions were asked are highly statistically significant.[34] In the region as a whole citizens thought that their regional trade bloc had a much more beneficial impact on prices than on employment and salaries.

The country-level results also lend support to this argument. The difference in mean between the assessment of the bloc's impact on prices versus employment is positive and statistically significant in seven of thirteen cases and highly negative in only one case. The latter case, Mexico, is easily explained when one considers that it is the only country to experience some success with export-led job creation. The findings are even more supportive of the consumer-choice argument

[33] Because individuals who had never heard of their country's regional trade bloc were not asked these questions, there was a substantial amount (about 40 percent) of missing data.

[34] These questions were not asked in the Dominican Republic.

TABLE 8
DIFFERENCES BETWEEN ASSESSMENTS OF REGIONAL TRADE BLOC'S EFFECTS ON PRICES AND LABOR MARKETS[a]

	$\bar{x}_{prices} - \bar{x}_{employment}$	$\bar{x}_{prices} - \bar{x}_{salaries}$	*N*
All 13 Countries	.22**	.42**	6021
	(.03)	(.02)	5924
MERCOSUR			
Argentina	.73**	.87**	665
	(.05)	(.05)	650
Brazil	.56**	.70**	394
	(.05)	(.06)	382
Paraguay	–.06	–.02	305
	(.06)	(.05)	301
Chile	.28**	.33**	700
	(.03)	(.03)	695
Andean Pact			
Bolivia	.10*	.20**	321
	(.05)	(.05)	319
Colombia	.10*	.26**	578
	(.04)	(.04)	570
Ecuador	–.03	.08	310
	(.05)	(.06)	310
Peru	.24**	.30**	605
	(.04)	(.04)	592
Venezuela	–.06	.13**	468
	(.05)	(.05)	458
Central American Common Market			
Costa Rica	.09*	.19**	487
	(.04)	(.04)	480
Guatemala	–.09	.11*	352
	(.06)	(.06)	340
Panama	.05	.15**	281
	(.06)	(.06)	275
NAFTA			
Mexico	–.35	.14**	555
	(.05)	(.05)	549

*p < .05; ** p < .01

SOURCE: *Wall Street Journal Americas* survey (1998).

[a] Entries are paired differences in mean evaluations of trade bias impact with standard errors in parentheses. In the variables that are being compared, higher values indicate a more favorable evaluation. All hypothesis tests are one-tailed. Results in the top row are weighted by population. Chile is an associate member of MERCOSUR. Bolivia is an associate member of MERCOSUR and a full member of the Andean Pact, so Bolivians were queried about the latter.

when comparing results from the prices question with those of the salaries question. In all but two countries the results are positive and statistically significant.

V. More Evidence: Cross-National and Individual-Level Patterns

Data and Model Specification

The analyses in the preceding section indicate that the consumption-based framework explains the aggregate question about the popularity of trade in Latin America. However, an accurate theoretical explanation should also be compatible with observed interpersonal and cross-national differences in trade preferences. In this section I describe the specification of two multivariate models that assess the ability of the earning power and consumption-based theories to explain preferences at both the individual and country level. The models are a pair of two-stage least squares procedures with binomial functional forms that pool data from all fourteen nations in the 1998 *Wall Street Journal Americas* data set. The dependent variable in both models is a continuous-variable index of general support for free trade, created from the shared variance between responses to the two *Wall Street Journal Americas* questions in Tables 1 and 2.[35] (See Appendix 1 for more on how the dependent variable was constructed.)

Both models contain the following individual-level variables: education (years of formal education), income (measured in 1997 U.S.$1,000), income squared, knowledge of trade issues, gender, age, town of residence size, presidential approval, and a series of dummy variables measuring occupation. Presidential approval is measured with an instrumental variable created in the two-stage least squares procedure and is explained below. The two models differ only in their treatment of cross-national variation in mean support for free trade. The first model contains three variables that are country specific: supply of skilled labor, GDP of manufacturing sector, and 1997 GDP per capita growth. This

[35] By using a linear combination of these two variables instead of just one of them, I tap an underlying dimension of free trade orientations that is less subject to either item's idiosyncrasies of question wording or measurement error. It is also crucial to note that hypothesized relationships are the same for *both* questions in the dependent variable. Both the Heckscher-Ohlin and consumption-based theories rely on the notions of relative abundance and comparative advantage. Therefore, a comparison of resource endowments between trading partners is necessary to understand economic consequences and to predict individual preferences. Throughout this paper, I have developed predictions based on Latin American countries' comparative advantage as developing countries vis-à-vis the global economy. Both questions are similar in this regard, then, since one refers to unilateral trade liberalization and the other to the FTAA, which would be dominated by the skill-intensive and capital-intensive economy of the U.S.

model also contains a term to capture any potential multiplicative relationship between supply of skilled labor and education. The second model drops these variables and simply includes dummy variables for all but one country. Although atheoretical about cross-national differences, this "fixed effects" model is a robustness check because it allows for a more precise estimation of the regionwide individual-level relationships than the model with the country-level variables. The models employ sampling weights that account for the population of the respondent's country, so the reported results pertain to a sample from the real-world population of these fourteen nations.[36] (See Appendix 1 for more detail.)[37]

Hypotheses

If the Heckscher-Ohlin theory of trade preferences is accurate, such that people possessing scarce factors favor protectionism, then the education coefficient will be negative. Moreover, these coefficients should be more negative in countries with a small supply of skilled labor, so the model includes an interaction term that is the respondent's education level multiplied by the country's supply of skilled labor (measured as the percentage of the population twenty-five and older that has attained some postsecondary education).[38] Heckscher-Ohlin predicts that the coefficient on the interaction term will be positive. If the human capital hypothesis holds, however, then the education coefficient will be positive and the interaction coefficient will be zero. Moreover, if the

[36] The estimation procedure adjusts for the multilevel nature of the data by correcting for nonindependence or clustering within countries. See J. Eltinge and W. Sribney, "Svy4: Linear, Logistic, and Probit Regressions for Survey Data," *Stata Technical Bulletin Reprints* 6 (1997); and Marco R. Steenbergen and Bradford S. Jones, "Modeling Multilevel Data Structures," *American Journal of Political Science* 46 (January 2002).

[37] To avoid a severe loss of cases, the reported estimates are averages of model results from twenty data sets with different imputations for missing values on income (10 percent missing), education (1 percent missing), and the variables used to construct the presidential approval instrument. Gary King, James Honaker, Anne Joseph, and Kenneth Scheve, "Analyzing Incomplete Political Science Data: An Alternative Algorithm for Multiple Imputation," *American Political Science Review* 95 (March 2001). Imputations were made by country using the EMis algorithm in *Amelia, 2.0*; James Honaker, Anne Joseph, Gary King, Kenneth Scheve, and Naunihal Singh, *Amelia: A Program for Missing Data* (Cambridge: Harvard University, 1999) (http://Gking.Harvard.edu, accessed January 2002).

[38] Data are 1999 figures from Robert J. Barro and Jong-Wha Lee, "International Data on Educational Attainment" (http://www.cid.harvard.edu/ciddata/ciddata.html, accessed January 2002). Education is expressed as deviation from the overall weighted sample mean while supply of skilled labor is expressed as deviation from the fourteen countries' mean, and the interaction term is therefore the product of these two variables. Centering these variables in this manner provides a more intuitive and substantive interpretation of the coefficients. The education coefficient is the relationship between education and free trade support in a country with the region's mean supply of skilled labor, while the supply of skilled labor coefficient expresses the relationship between skilled labor and free support for a citizen with the region's mean education level.

human capital argument is useful in solving the puzzle about aggregate preferences, then the first-order measure of supply of skilled labor, which varies by country, will be positive.

If the consumption-based theory holds, then three results will obtain. First, the coefficient on income will be positive. Second, the coefficient on the square of income will be negative. Together, these results would indicate that support for free trade peaks among the middle class, concave with respect to income.[39] Third, the variable measuring GDP of the manufacturing sector will be negative.[40] Consumers in small countries with limited manufacturing sectors stand to benefit more from trade liberalization, so they should be less protectionist on average than are consumers in large, diversified economies.

I test a simple sociotropic policy evaluation model with a measure of GDP per capita growth in 1997,[41] the year before the survey occurred. The sociotropic policy evaluation model states that citizens support an existing policy during periods of economic growth while opposing it during economic slowdowns.[42] If this theory is correct, the coefficient will be positive, since citizens in countries experiencing high economic growth should be less protectionist than are citizens in countries with low or negative economic growth.

The model also controls for several variables whose exclusion would potentially bias the coefficients on the variables of central theoretical import. First, certain occupations, namely, professional and white-collar jobs that tend to be in the nontradable service sector, are more cushioned from international market competition. As such, middle-income individuals may be less protectionist not for consumer-oriented reasons but because their jobs are not as vulnerable to market fluctua-

[39] Income is recalculated as deviations from the sample mean, with income squared equivalent to the square of this value. John Neter, William Wasserman, and Michael H. Kutner, *Applied Linear Regression Models*, 2d ed. (Homewood, Ill.: Irwin, 1989). The decision to measure income in 1997 U.S.$1,000 *without* adjusting for purchasing power parity is crucial. It retains cross-national differences in purchasing power in international markets even though over- or undervalued exchange rates may contribute to these differences.

[40] This variable is not a percentage but a measure of the sheer size of this sector. More specifically, this is the natural log of the country's 1997 manufacturing sector output in US$ at purchasing power parity. Data are from World Bank, *World Development Indicators 2000 CD-Rom* (Washington, D.C.: World Bank, 2000).

[41] World Bank (fn. 40).

[42] Susan Stokes, ed., *Public Support for Market Reforms in New Democracies* (Cambridge: Cambridge University Press, 2001); Kenneth M. Roberts and Moises Arce, "Neoliberalism and Lower-Class Voting in Peru," *Comparative Political Studies* 31 (April 1998); Morris Fiorina, *Retrospective Voting in American National Elections* (New Haven: Yale University Press, 1981); and Donald Kinder and D. Roderick Kiewiet, "Economic Discontent and Political Behavior: The Role of Personal Grievances and Collective Economic Judgements in Congressional Voting," *American Journal of Political Science* 23 (August 1979).

tions. To increase the validity of income as an indicator of consumer interests, then, I control for different occupational types, including white-collar jobs, with a series of dummy variables.

Second, extensive research indicates that many citizens form political attitudes by taking cues from parties and politicians they support.[43] Because presidents, not parties, have been central figures in advocating and implementing Latin America's market reforms, I measure these political orientations with the respondent's approval of the incumbent president.[44] Citizens who support a neoliberal president may be more likely to accept his cues encouraging them to support free trade, while citizens who are opposed to such an incumbent are more prone to reject these promarket messages in favor of protectionist ones. In the rare cases in which statist presidents held office in early 1998 (Colombia and Ecuador), the reverse should obtain, whereby supporters of the incumbent accept more protectionist cues.[45]

While the cue-taking model of attitude formation has extensive empirical support, scholars often test it without accounting for the potential endogeneity involved.[46] A sizable body of evidence, including the widely applied spatial model, indicates that the causal arrow may be reversed: citizens have fixed issue attitudes and evaluate the incumbent based on her or his propensity to support their preferred policy.[47] So that endogeneity does not bias the coefficient estimates, I estimate a two-stage least squares model in which the original presidential approval measure is replaced with an instrumental variable. The instrumental variable is the predicted values from a regression of presidential approval on all the variables used to explain free trade support plus some other exogenous variables, such as ideology and other issue attitudes (listed in Appendix 1), that are correlated with incumbent approval.

Third, a related variable is one's overall degree of exposure to persuasive messages that are positive about trade liberalization. Because the

[43] Robert R. Kaufman and Leo Zuckerman, "Attitudes toward Economic Reform in Mexico: The Role of Political Mediations," *American Political Science Review* 92 (June 1998); and John Zaller, *The Nature and Origins of Mass Opinion* (Cambridge: Cambridge University Press, 1992).

[44] Susan C. Stokes, *Mandates and Democracy: Neoliberalism by Surprise in Latin America* (Cambridge: Cambridge University Press, 2001); and Javier Corrales, "Presidents, Ruling Parties, and Party Rules: A Theory on the Politics of Economic Reform in Latin America," *Comparative Politics* 32 (January 2001).

[45] I categorized each president's economic policy orientation using Stokes's (see fn. 44) classification of the president's government as either "security"-oriented or "efficiency"-oriented (pp. 14–15). For the two security-oriented presidents, I reversed the coding of presidential approval for the respondents in these two countries.

[46] Kaufman and Zuckerman (fn. 43).

[47] Melvin J. Hinich and Michael C. Munger, *Analytical Politics* (Cambridge: Cambridge University Press, 1997).

"Washington consensus" in favor of market orthodoxy has become a near consensus among Latin American political and economic elites as well, Latin American citizens with frequent exposure to elite discourse about trade might be more likely to share these promarket views.[48] Omitting a measure of exposure to elite discourse could bias assessments of the trade theories because this variable is positively correlated with both income and education.[49] Following developments in political psychology, I measure this variable using respondents' score on a "quiz" of objective facts about trade policy, namely, whether they were familiar with their country's regional economic integration scheme and with "fast track" authority.

Finally, because protectionism in Latin America favored urban, industrial sectors at the expense of the agriculture-based rural areas, I hypothesize a negative relationship between town size and support for free trade.[50] Older individuals may be more likely to remember the "glory days" of import-substitution industrialization, when Latin American countries frequently achieved annual GDP growth rates above 5 percent, so I hypothesize a negative relationship between age and the dependent variable. Last, although no research on gender and economic policy preferences in Latin America exists, I hypothesize that women in these fourteen countries, like their counterparts in the developed world, are more economically statist than men.[51]

Multivariate Results

The multivariate results are presented in Table 9. The consumption-based theory passes all tests. In both models, and even more so in the fixed-effects version, income is a positive and statistically significant predictor of support for trade liberalization. At the same time, the relationship is nonlinear since the square of income is negative and statistically significant. Support for free trade is concave with respect to

[48] Sebastian Edwards, *Crisis and Reform in Latin America: From Despair to Hope* (Oxford: Oxford University Press, 1995); and John Williamson, ed., *Latin American Adjustment: How Much Has Happened?* (Washington, D.C.: Institute for International Economics, 1990).

[49] Cue-taking theory dictates an interactive effect between awareness and political orientation, since highly aware citizens are both more exposed to the persuasive messages of their favorite politicians and more likely to reject those of their least preferred politicians. See Zaller (fn. 43). Although I estimated a model with this interaction term, I do not present the results because scholars do not yet know how to calculate the correct standard errors for a model with an interaction term that contains an instrumental variable. Besides this, the inclusion of this variable did not significantly enhance the predictive power of the model nor did it noticeably change any of the other coefficients.

[50] Frieden (fn. 13).

[51] R. Michael Alvarez and Edward J. McCaffery, "Are there Sex Differences in Fiscal Political Preferences?" *Political Research Quarterly* 56 (March 2003)

income: at its peak among the middle class and at its nadir among the lower and upper classes. The inflection point is at about U.S.$1,000 per month, which is approximately the 85th percentile on the region's income ladder. The other main test of the consumer-based theory also turns up the hypothesized result: citizens in countries with large (in absolute size), diversified manufacturing bases are less enthusiastic about trade liberalization, on average, than citizens in countries with a limited manufacturing sector.

Education has a positive and robust relationship with support for free trade, lending substantial credence to the human capital hypothesis.[52] The positive and statistically significant sign on the interaction coefficient in model 1 does support the Heckscher-Ohlin model. However, its magnitude indicates that the relationship between education and support for free trade is positive in all fourteen countries. According to this coefficient, education is positively correlated with free trade support even in Guatemala, the country with the smallest share of individuals with a postsecondary education.[53] This means that skill level in these countries increases one's tendency to support free trade despite their comparatively low-skilled labor forces. In short, the human capital model performs far more impressively than Heckscher-Ohlin in explaining interpersonal heterogeneity in Latin America. However, as mentioned above, this argument cannot explain the high aggregate support for free trade in countries with low levels of human capital. The negative sign on the supply of skilled labor coefficient in model 1 further confirms this suspicion.

The central finding among the control variables is the importance of elite opinion leadership. Citizens who are exposed to media messages about trade are less likely to be protectionist, as evidenced by the statistical significance of the knowledge variable. Moreover, the statistical significance of the presidential approval variable indicates that citizens accept the cues of their incumbent president when they support him and accept countervailing cues when they oppose him. Finally, the results disconfirm the sociotropic policy evaluation model since GDP per capita growth is actually negatively associated with aggregate support for free trade.

[52] This finding on education coincides with the results in Mitchell Seligson, "Popular Support for Regional Economic Integration in Latin America," *Journal of Latin American Studies* 31 (February 1999).

[53] Guatemala's value on the supply of skilled labor variable is −8.8, or almost 9 percentage points below the mean of the fourteen nations. Therefore, the education coefficient for Guatemala would be $-8.8 \times .0011 + .0211 = .011$.

TABLE 9
MASS SUPPORT FOR TRADE LIBERALIZATION IN LATIN AMERICA BY SKILL LEVEL, CONSUMER INTERESTS, AND CONTROL VARIABLES: TWO-STAGE LEAST SQUARES RESULTS[a]

	(1) With Country-Level Variables	*(2) Fixed Effects: With Country Dummy Variables*
Country-Level Variables		
GDP of manufacturing sector	−.0220*	—
	(.0134)	
1997 GDP per capita growth	−.0270	—
	(.0097)	
Supply of skilled labor	−.0077	—
	(.0052)	
Education × supply of skilled labor	.0014*	—
	(.0006)	
Individual-Level Variables		
Income	.0109*	.0182**
	(.0053)	(.0042)
Income^2	-.0006*	−.0010**
	(.0003)	(.0002)
Education	.0237**	.0172**
	(.0046)	(.0044)
Knowledge of trade issues	.0315**	.0312**
	(.0139)	(.0146)
Age	−.0003	−.0003
	(.0008)	(.0009)
Woman	.0056	.0035
	(.0172)	(.0168)
Town size	.0321	.0081
	(.0237)	(.0240)
White-collar workers	0	0
	(0)	(0)
Entrepreneurs (formal and informal sector)	.0317**	.0291**
	(.0127)	(.0107)
Manual laborers	.0438	.0250
	(.0310)	(.0257)
Farmers	.2864**	.2303**
	(.0660)	(.0756)
Unemployed	−.0430	−.0441
	(.0712)	(.0693)
Not in the economically active population	−.0098	−.0075
	(.0151)	(.0167)
Other occupations	−.0274	−.0004
	(.0653)	(.0711)

TABLE 9 *(cont.)*

	(1) With Country-Level Variables	*(2) Fixed Effects: With Country Dummy Variables*
Presidential approval (instrumental variable)	.3799**	.3711**
	(.1135)	(.1064)
Constant	.5304	−.0026
	(.3478)	(.0381)
R^2	.09	.10

*p < .05; **p < .01.

SOURCE: *Wall Street Journal Americas* survey (1998).

[a] N = 11,580. Entries are two-stage least squares coefficients and robust standard errors in parentheses. Standard errors are corrected for clustering within countries. All hypothesis tests, except for those on the education and occupation coefficients, are one-tailed. The results are weighted so that they reflect a sample of the fourteen-nation population. Coefficients on country dummy variables in the second model are not shown.

VI. CONCLUSION: BRINGING THE CONSUMER IN

Latin America's postreform macroeconomic crises and its inability to generate sustained job growth preclude a simple "retrospective evaluations" explanation for the popularity of free trade among the region's citizens. Moreover, the commonly invoked Heckscher-Ohlin trade theory, which appears to explain trade preferences in developed countries, fails to solve this puzzle in Latin America. As a solution, I constructed a theory that shifts the focus from individual earning power to consumption behavior. This explanation succeeded on three empirical fronts. Evidence confirmed that aggregate support for free trade receives a substantial boost because of consumption concerns: citizens are appreciative of how it has improved the quality, price, and variety of goods available to them. In subsequent multivariate analyses, consumption behavior helped explain cross-national and interpersonal differences in mean beliefs about trade policy. The two earning-power theories, by contrast, received more ambiguous empirical support. Neither succeeded in explaining cross-national differences, interpersonal heterogeneity, *and* high aggregate support for free trade, although the human capital hypothesis provided substantial analytical leverage at the individual level.

These results indicate a need to pay greater attention to citizens' interests qua consumers, not simply income earners. Rarely are consumer concerns incorporated into theories of issue attitudes. In particular, most scholarly explanations of economic policy beliefs privilege indicators of earning power despite the fact that citizens, when they are away from work, spend a significant amount of their free time consuming and deciding what to consume. This oversight also colors the conclusions that political economists and politicians make about the sustainability of policy reform. Many political economists once believed that public opposition to market liberalization in developing countries would make these reforms more probable and sustainable in authoritarian regimes, where such outrage could be repressed or ignored. Likewise, politicians in protected, poverty-stricken economies often avoided reform for fear of reprisal from nationalist citizens as well as from angry labor unions and workers. However, trade liberalization in Latin America has actually created a large coalition of supporters who recognize the policy source of the visible change in their consumer options.

This does not, of course, give carte blanche to zealous, promarket politicians in Latin America, especially as they look to negotiate a potential hemisphere-wide trade zone that would include the rather protectionist United States. Evidence does indicate a certain degree of citizen attentiveness to the impact of trade on earning power and employment opportunities. Overly rapid economic integration with the U.S. could alienate undereducated citizens who lack the skills to adjust to global markets, particularly if unemployment rates continue to rise. Moreover, the novelty of being able to buy higher-quality foreign goods may dwindle. Regardless, scholars and politicians alike should not underestimate the ability of citizens to learn about policy consequences in creative and often unexpected ways.

APPENDIX 1: *WALL STREET JOURNAL AMERICAS* SURVEY

The *Wall Street Journal Americas* poll was conducted by RAC & MORI international, headed by Miguel Basáñez, from January 20, 1998, to February 20, 1998. Local polling firms conducted 11,964 face-to-face interviews in fourteen countries (a parallel phone survey in the United States was also administered). The samples are primarily urban, with only 8 percent of respondents residing in cities smaller than fifty thousand people. In each country, a stratified sampling procedure was used in which five homes in two hundred geographic units were each randomly chosen, and respondents within each home were chosen using the "most recent birthday" technique. Regionwide analyses were conducted with population-size probability weights so that results pertain to a sample from the real-world population of these fourteen countries. This shifts only the relative influence of each respondent (based on her or his nationality); it does not artificially change the overall *N*. The weighting factor varies by country and accounts for the country's share of both the Latin American population and the *Wall Street Journal Americas* sample. The weight for a respondent in country *c* is the following:

$$\frac{p_c}{\sum p_c} \times \frac{\sum n_c}{n_c},$$

where p is a country's population and n is the number of respondents from country c in the survey (11,964). This factor was adjusted by city-size sampling weights in the four countries that had them.

The dependent variable was constructed from the free trade evaluation and FTAA support variables listed below. I used the scores from the only extractable factor from a principal components analysis of these two variables (alpha = .50). To avoid a high degree of missing data, individuals with "don't know" responses to one of the two items still received a factor score based on the assumption that they would have scored the same degree of support for free trade on the other item. Respondents were therefore dropped in listwise fashion only when they said "don't know" to both items, resulting in a loss of 384 (3 percent) cases. The index has a mean of –.024 and a standard deviation of .9382, with a minimum of –3.02 and a maximum of 1.14.

—*Free trade evaluation.* "Over the last few years the country has had more and more business and trade with other countries. This tendency is called 'free trade.' Do you think that free trade is good or bad for the country? Very or somewhat?"

—*FTAA support.* "The presidents of North and South America are talking about forming a single free trade zone for the entire continent. Are you in favor of or against this idea? Very or slightly?"

—*Knowledge of trade issues.* Respondents were asked to describe their country's regional trade area (Andean Pact/CACM/MERCOSUL/NAFTA) and "fast-track" authority. Their score on this variable was the number (0 to 2) of which they had an accurate knowledge.

—*Regional trade agreement's impact.* "Do you think that [Andean Pact/CACM/MERCOSUL/NAFTA] helped or harmed (1) the prices of consumer goods, (2) employment, (3) salaries? Greatly or slightly?"

—*Education.* From zero to twelve years, education is coded as the number of years of education. Beyond 12, (13) = undergraduate incomplete, (14) = undergraduate complete, (15) = postgraduate incomplete, (16) = postgraduate complete.

—*Income.* Survey administrators coded income into four categories: lower class (bottom 40 percent of population); middle and lower-middle (next 30 percent); middle-upper class (next 20 percent); upper class (top 10 percent). I converted these figures into income in 1997 U.S.$1,000s using country-level data on GDP per capita and income distribution by decile. Sources for this were Economic Commission on Latin America and the Caribbean, *Statistical Yearbook for Latin America and the Caribbean 2000* (Santiago, Chile: United Nations, 2000); World Bank (fn. 40); and World Bank, *World Development Indicators 2001* (http://www.worldbank.org/data/, accessed January 2002).

—*Town size.* The town size variable is recoded from the manner in which survey administrators recorded it. The code is the middle number of inhabitants for the recorded category divided by 1,000,000: (.0075) rural zone (less than 15,000 inhabitants); (.0325) small city (15,000 to 50,000 inhabitants); (.075) medium city (50,000 to 100,000 inhabitants); (.55) big city (100,000 to 1 million inhabitants), (2) metropolis (over 1 million inhabitants).

Other variables used to construct the presidential approval instrument are:

—*Presidential approval.* "In general, what opinion do you have of President X? Good or Bad? Very or slightly?"

—*Privatization attitude.* "Do you think that the change toward privatization is good or bad for the country?"

—*Foreign direct investment support.* "Which phrase is closer to your way of thinking? Foreign investment is good because it helps the economy grow. Or foreign investment is bad because it gives other countries too much influence over our economy."

—*Neoliberal values.* "With which phrase do you agree more? Government should take care of the well-being of individuals. Or each individual should take care of his own well-being."

—*Left-right self-placement.* "In politics, 'left' and 'right' are often mentioned. On a scale where 0 is left and 10 is right, where would you place yourself?" I created a separate dummy variable to indicate individuals that did not place themselves on this scale.

Appendix 2: Four-City Brazil Survey

The four-city Brazil survey was conducted in late March and April 1999. Respondents were chosen in Belém, Porto Alegre, Recife, and São Paulo with two hundred face-to-face interviews on weekend days in residences in each city. Samples were selected using age, sex, and neighborhood-size quotas (based on census data), with interviewers choosing respondents at their own discretion within neighborhoods. The entire questionnaire lasted an average of thirteen minutes.

—*Free trade support.* "In the last ten years, Brazil's trade with foreign countries grew. This increase in trade is known as 'trade liberalization' or 'free trade.' Some people favor and others oppose this 'trade liberalization.' Are you in favor, against or do not have an opinion on this policy of trade opening? Are you strongly or slightly (favorable, opposed)? And what are your reasons for being favorable/opposed to free trade?"

Appendix 3: Latinbarometer Surveys

The 1996 Latinbarometer was carried out in seventeen Latin American countries with probability samples (about one thousand per country) representative of the urban population of each country. The original data are available for purchase at http://www.latinobarometro.org/.

—*FTAA support (1996).* "In general, are you in favor or against economic integration of the countries in Latin America, even when this might imply some costs or sacrifices for your country?"

Results from Latinbarometer 2001 are those reported in *Economist* (fn. 4). The original data are not yet available to the public domain.

—*FTAA support (2001).* "Generally speaking, are you in favor of or against the economic integration of the countries of Latin America? Would you say that you are very in favor, slightly in favor, slightly against or very against it?" "Do you think the establishment of the Free Trade Area of the Americas will help a lot, somewhat, slightly, or not at all the economic development of your country?"

[12]

Learning to Love Globalization: Education and Individual Attitudes Toward International Trade

Jens Hainmueller and Michael J. Hiscox

Abstract Recent studies of public attitudes toward trade have converged on one central finding: support for trade restrictions is highest among respondents with the lowest levels of education. This has been interpreted as strong support for the Stolper-Samuelson theorem, the classic economic treatment of the income effects of trade that predicts that trade openness benefits those owning factors of production with which their economy is relatively well endowed (those with skills in the advanced economies) while hurting others (low-skilled workers). We reexamine the available survey data, showing that the impact of education on attitudes toward trade is almost identical among respondents in the active labor force and those who are not (even those who are retired). We also find that, while individuals with college-level educations are far more likely to favor trade openness than others, other types of education have no significant effects on attitudes, and some actually reduce the support for trade, even though they clearly contribute to skill acquisition. Combined, these results strongly suggest that the effects of education on individual trade preferences are not primarily a product of distributional concerns linked to job skills. We suggest that exposure to economic ideas and information among college-educated individuals plays a key role in shaping attitudes toward trade and globalization. This is not to say that distributional issues are not important in shaping attitudes toward trade—just that they are not clearly manifest in the simple, broad association between education levels and support for free trade.

A growing body of scholarly research has examined survey data on attitudes toward trade among voters, focusing on individual determinants of protectionist sentiments. These studies have converged on one central finding: fears about the distributional effects of trade openness among less-educated, blue-collar workers lie at the heart of much of the backlash against globalization in the United States and other advanced economies. Support for new trade restrictions is highest among

The authors would like to thank James Alt, Jeffry Frieden, Robert Lawrence, Dani Rodrik, Ron Rogowski, Ken Scheve, Andy Baker, Peter Gourevitch, and Beth Simmons for helpful comments on earlier drafts.

International Organization 60, Spring 2006, pp. 469–498

DOI: 10.1017/S0020818306060140

respondents with the lowest levels of education.[1] These findings are interpreted as strong support for the Stolper-Samuelson theorem, the classic economic treatment of the income effects of trade that predicts that trade openness benefits those owning factors of production with which their economy is relatively well endowed (those with high skill levels in the advanced economies) while hurting others (low-skilled and unskilled workers).

However, the positive relationship between education and support for trade liberalization might also—and perhaps primarily—reflect the facts that more educated respondents tend to be more exposed to economic ideas about the overall efficiency gains for the national economy associated with greater trade openness and tend to be less prone to nationalist and antiforeigner sentiments often linked with protectionism.[2] Studies have shown that measures of economic knowledge are strongly associated with education levels among individuals, and exposure to economics at the college level has especially powerful effects.[3] A large body of research also shows that increased education—and especially college education—tends to socialize students to have more tolerant, cosmopolitan views of the world.[4] It thus seems quite possible that differences of opinion among more and less-educated voters over the trade issue may be shaped less by Stolper-Samuelson–style calculations about the expected distributional effects of trade than by competing ideational and cultural perspectives—that is, education may be important here primarily because it teaches students to think about trade and globalization in different ways and/or to evaluate it according to a different set of values.

Which of these very different interpretations is more correct? The answer to this question is critical to our understanding of the political economy of trade and the nature of the political disagreements over globalization now taking place. Here we reexamine the available survey data on individual attitudes toward trade, conducting a simple test of the effects of education on support for trade that distinguishes clearly between the Stolper-Samuelson interpretation of this relationship and alternative ideational and cultural accounts. We find that the impact of education on attitudes toward trade is almost identical among respondents currently in the active labor force and among those who are not (even those who are retired). That the effects of education on trade policy preferences are not mediated by whether or not individuals are actually being paid for the employment of their skills strongly suggests that it is not primarily a product of distributional concerns. The analysis also reveals clear nonlinearities in the relationship between education and trade preferences: while individuals who have been exposed to college or university education are far more likely to favor trade openness than those who have not, other types of educational attainment have no significant effects on attitudes and some even reduce the likelihood that individuals support trade even

1. See, for example, Scheve and Slaughter 2001a and 2001b; Mayda and Rodrik 2005; and O'Rourke and Sinnott 2002.
2. See Bauer, Pool, and Dexter 1972, 103; and Holsti 1996, 87–88.
3. See Saunders 1980; and Gleason and van Scyoc 1995.
4. See for example, Campbell et al. 1960, 475–81; and Erikson, Luttbeg, and Tedin 1991, 155–56.

though they clearly contribute to skill acquisition. These findings indicate that the particular ideational and/or cultural effects associated with college education, and not the gradual accumulation of skills, are critical in shaping individual attitudes toward trade.

We conclude that the impact of education on how voters' think about trade and globalization has more to do with exposure to economic ideas and information about the aggregate and varied effects of these economic phenomena, than it does with individual calculations about how trade affects personal income or job security. This is not to say that the latter types of calculations are not important in shaping individuals' views of trade—just that they are not being manifest in the simple association between education and support for trade openness. As we discuss in the concluding section, we think it is likely that concerns about the effects of trade on personal income and job security might actually hinge on the particular impact of trade openness in specific industries. One of the key implications of our findings is that future empirical tests of the determinants of individual trade preferences need to be substantially refined to identify the impact of distributional concerns on attitudes toward trade and globalization and distinguish these from the impact of ideational and cultural factors.

Explaining Attitudes Toward International Trade

To date, the analysis of survey data aimed at revealing the determinants of individual attitudes toward trade has focused predominantly on occupational differences among respondents. A principal aim has been to test standard economic models that describe the income effects of trade for different individuals as a function of the types of productive inputs they own. Examining data from recent American National Election Studies (NES) surveys in the United States, Scheve and Slaughter emphasized the importance of respondents' "human capital" or skills (measured principally by years of education), finding that individuals with lower skills were more likely to support restrictions on imports than those with higher skills.[5] Mayda and Rodrik and O'Rourke and Sinnott came to similar conclusions after examining the data from the 1995 ISSP survey: again skill levels, measured either by years of education (Mayda and Rodrik) or occupational categories (O'Rourke and Sinnott), were found to have large effects on attitudes, with lower skilled individuals being the most protectionist in outlook.[6] In terms of economic theory, these findings have been interpreted as providing strong support for the Stolper-Samuelson theorem, which predicts that trade raises real

5. Scheve and Slaughter 2001a and 2001b.

6. See Mayda and Rodrik 2005; and O'Rourke and Sinnott 2002. Similar types of findings are reported by Balistreri 1997; and Beaulieu 2002, who examined data on support for the Canadian-U.S. Free Trade Agreement in Canada; Gabel 1998, who used *Eurobarometer* data on attitudes toward European integration; and Baker 2003, using similar survey data on attitudes toward trade in Latin American nations.

incomes for those who own factors with which the economy is relatively well endowed (that is, labor skills in the developed economies), while disadvantaging owners of other factors (unskilled or low-skilled labor).[7] Scheve and Slaughter highlight as a "key finding" of their study the conclusion that "the preferences about trade and immigration policy align strongly with labor market skills."[8] Mayda and Rodrik report that the results from their analysis of the importance of educational attainment in shaping views about trade are "strikingly supportive of the implications of the factor-endowments model and of the Stolper-Samuelson theorem."[9]

Yet there are other, plausible, ways to interpret the positive relationship between the education levels of surveyed individuals and their support for trade openness. It seems particularly limiting to consider education only as a measure of workers' skill levels, relevant only in the way it affects the expected income effects of trade for each individual. Education may be relevant here for other reasons—other causal mechanisms may be generating the observed association between education levels and protrade attitudes. We think there are two likely candidates: an ideational mechanism that hinges on the role played by economic ideas and knowledge in the formation of economic policy preferences; and a cultural mechanism that relates commitments to key values, such as tolerance and cosmopolitanism, to attitudes toward foreign policy issues.

The ideational argument is fairly straightforward. Highly educated respondents are likely to think about international trade in different ways compared to less-educated counterparts; the highly educated use a more sophisticated set of ideas about cause-and-effect relationships and more information about the effects of trade for themselves and for others.[10] College-educated individuals, in particular, are likely to be far more informed than others about the aggregate efficiency gains associated with expanded trade, especially if they have had any contact at all with economics courses and with the theory of comparative advantage. While there is a firm consensus among economists on the virtues of trade openness, the counterintuitive loveliness of the law of comparative advantage makes it much more difficult to convey the case for trade outside the college classroom.[11] Studies of economic "literacy" among the public have shown that general measures of economic knowledge are strongly associated with education levels among individuals, and college education in particular.[12] Exposure to at least one college-level economics course is an especially powerful predictor of economic knowledge. Crit-

7. Stolper and Samuelson 1941. This theorem has been used extensively in the analysis of trade politics; see Rogowski 1989; and Hiscox 2002.

8. Scheve and Slaughter 2001b, 9.

9. Mayda and Rodrik 2005, 1409.

10. Among scholars who have examined surveys of public attitudes toward trade, the topic is typically regarded as a complex issue about which most survey respondents have low levels of information; see Bauer, Pool, and Dexter 1972, 81–84; Destler 1995, 180; and Pryor 2002.

11. See Krugman 1993.

12. See, for example, Saunders 1980; and Gleason and van Scyoc 1995.

ically, related studies show that higher levels of economic knowledge among surveyed individuals have large positive effects on support for free trade.[13]

This type of ideational argument does have precedents in both the international political economy and broader international relations literatures. Ideas, viewed as beliefs about cause-and-effect relationships, have been assigned key roles in accounts of policymaking in a variety of areas, including international cooperation on environmental issues and arms control.[14] On the trade issue specifically, scholars have linked the removal of mercantilist restrictions on trade in Europe in the nineteenth century to the ideas of Smith and Ricardo and the birth of classical trade theory.[15] The multilateral trade liberalization pursued among Western nations after 1945 has been connected to neoclassical economic theories and the spread of Keynesian ideas in particular.[16] These types of accounts have traditionally focused on the importance of particular ideas among policymakers, and the transmission of ideas to government officials via transnational networks of experts and activists.[17] Examining the distribution of economic ideas among voters, and how this might be connected to policy preferences, might be an interesting and important extension.

Another plausible explanation for the relationship between education and attitudes toward trade focuses on differences in cultural values: highly educated individuals are less prone than others to nationalist and antiforeigner sentiments that are often linked with protectionism in political debates. There is a large scholarly literature showing that education, at least in the United States, tends to socialize students to have more tolerant, pro-outsider views of the world.[18] Education can foster tolerance, not just by increasing students' knowledge of foreign cultures and raising levels of critical thinking, but also by generating more diverse and cosmopolitan social networks, especially at the college level.[19] Indeed, Betts has argued that one aspect of class identity that emerges among the college-educated in Western nations is a commitment to cosmopolitanism and an appreciation for diverse cultures.[20] Studies of survey data also show that various measures of nationalism and national pride are significant predictors of support for trade protection.[21]

13. See Walstad 1997; and Walstad and Rebeck 2002. Walstad and Rebeck 2002 make the larger point that scholarly analysis of public opinion on economic issues makes the erroneous implicit assumption that survey respondents are undifferentiated in terms of their economic knowledge. In fact, individuals differ dramatically in their levels of economic knowledge, as measured by their scores on a set of test questions covering basic economic concepts and facts, and such knowledge scores are significant predictors of attitudes about a range of economic policy issues.

14. For a general discussion, see Goldstein and Keohane 1993; on environmental negotiations, see Haas 1992; on arms control, see Adler 1992; and Price 1998.

15. See Kindleberger 1975; and Bhagwati 1988.

16. See Ruggie 1998; and Goldstein 1988. See also Hall 1989 for essays on the particular impact of Keynesian macroeconomic theory among policymakers in the 1930s and 1940s.

17. For example, Haas 1992; and Keck and Sikkink 1998.

18. For example, Campbell et al. 1960, 475–81; Erikson, Luttbeg, and Tedin 1991, 155–56; and McClosky and Brill 1983.

19. See Case, Greeley, and Fuchs 1989; and Allport 1954.

20. Betts 1988.

21. See Mayda and Rodrik 2005, 1414–16; and O'Rourke and Sinnott 2002, 173. On these points, see also Holsti 1996, 87–88.

This type of argument resonates with a growing body of research in international relations that focuses on the importance of cultural values and conceptions of identity and how they shape the interests pursued by policymakers in international affairs—in areas including military strategy, humanitarian intervention, and support for human rights.[22] It is more difficult to find cultural accounts of trade politics or policymaking, specifically, in the political economy literature, though references to the popular appeal of protectionism when linked with nationalism and xenophobia are common.[23]

How then should we interpret the observed connection between education and support for trade? Besides the standard account, which focuses on Stolper-Samuelson–style distributional concerns, alternative accounts that stress the importance of economic ideas and related values also seem highly plausible. We suggest a simple test to establish whether the education connection is primarily reflecting concerns about the effects of trade on respondents' personal incomes or whether it is a manifestation of broader differences in ideas and/or values among surveyed individuals. We examine the impact of education levels on attitudes toward trade among respondents currently in the active labor force and among those who are not. If the Stolper-Samuelson interpretation of the education effect is accurate, this effect should be contingent on whether or not individuals are actually being paid for the employment of their skills in the labor market.[24]

The Effects of Education on Trade Preferences

Our new empirical tests draw from two key sources of data on individual trade preferences: the NES and the International Social Survey Program (ISSP). These are the same data sets employed by the two most prominent studies of individual attitudes toward trade in recent years: the analyses by Scheve and Slaughter and Mayda and Rodrik.[25] In the following section we briefly describe each dataset and present the results for our split-sample tests.

Tests Using the NES Data

The NES surveys are fielded in the United States around the time of presidential elections and designed to gather data on Americans' social backgrounds, political predispositions, opinions on questions of public policy, and participation in polit-

22. For general discussions, see Wendt 1999; Ruggie 1998; and Finnemore and Sikkink 1998. For studies of strategy, see Katzenstein 1996; on human rights, see Sikkink 1993.

23. For example, Bauer, Pool, and Dexter 1972, 103.

24. Similar split-sample tests have been used in studies of anti-immigrant sentiments to help discern whether greater opposition to immigration among less educated survey respondents (compared with more educated counterparts) reflects different degrees of concern about having to compete with immigrants in the job market: see Scheve and Slaughter 2001c; Mayda 2004; and also Hainmueller and Hiscox 2004.

25. Scheve and Slaughter 2001a and 2001b; and Mayda and Rodrik 2005.

ical life.[26] In 1992, for the first time, the NES included a question that asked respondents about their attitudes toward international trade. The question was the following: *"Some people have suggested placing new limits on foreign imports in order to protect American jobs. Others say that such limits would raise consumer prices and hurt American exports. Do you favor or oppose placing new limits on imports, or haven't you thought much about this?"*

Scheve and Slaughter used responses to this question from the 1992 NES survey as their measure of individual trade policy preferences.[27] We have replicated their approach here to conduct the split-sample test, while also examining data from the 1996 NES survey that included the same trade question.[28] We created the dichotomous dependent variable TRADE OPINION, coded as 1 for responses that favored protection ("new limits on foreign imports") and 0 for those opposed. The "haven't thought much about this" answers are coded as missing, as in the Scheve and Slaughter analysis.

The principal measure of education is SCHOOLING, which simply records the years of full-time education completed by each respondent (a cap is set by the NES at seventeen years). This is the measure employed by Scheve and Slaughter. To allow for nonlinear education effects, we have also constructed a set of dummy variables indicating each respondent's highest level of educational attainment: JUNIOR HIGH (1 = 8 years of schooling; 0 = otherwise); HIGH SCHOOL (1 = high school degree; 0 = otherwise); HIGHER EDUCATION (1 = some years of post–high school education, including junior or community college; 0 = otherwise); COLLEGE (1 = four-year bachelor's degree; 0 = otherwise); and GRADUATE (1 = postgraduate degree; 0 = otherwise).[29] Assuming that education has linear effects on trade preferences seems appropriate if one assumes that each additional year of education (of any type) improves an individual's skills (and changes his or her attitudes) by a roughly constant amount. It is less appropriate if education has other, nonlinear types of effects associated with the ideas and information individuals possess about the way the economy works or the kinds of values and preferences they develop—as noted above, college education appears to play an overwhelming role in terms of its impact on ideas and cultural values among individuals.

For different subsamples of respondents, we estimated binary probit models using TRADE OPINION as the dependent variable, testing for the effects of SCHOOLING or the different education dummy variables while controlling for a variety of other individual characteristics that might plausibly affect trade preferences. We estimated each model with two sets of covariates: a limited set of standard sociode-

26. For details, see Miller et al. 1992; and Rosenstone et al. 1996. For more on NES see ⟨http://www.umich.edu/~nes/⟩. Accessed 10 January 2006.

27. Scheve and Slaughter 2001a.

28. Also examined in Scheve and Slaughter 2001b.

29. Note that there are too few respondents who failed to finish elementary school to allow us to estimate the separate effect of elementary-level education here: the excluded category in our analysis of education effects when using these dummy variables is all those with less than eight years of schooling.

mographic controls (age, in years, gender, and race), which preserved the maximum number of observations across the subsamples; and a more extensive set of controls (the standard controls plus indicators of UNION MEMBERSHIP, PARTY IDENTIFICATION, and IDEOLOGY), which closely matched the more extensive specifications used by Scheve and Slaughter.[30] (See the Appendix for a description of all variables used along with summary statistics).

We expect the measures of education to be negatively associated with support for trade protection (as measured by TRADE OPINION), either because highly skilled individuals expect trade to increase their real wages and poorly skilled respondents expect trade to decrease their real wages (à la Stolper-Samuelson), because more-educated respondents know more about the overall economic benefits associated with trade openness, and/or because the more-educated are less likely to nurture antiforeigner sentiments. If this link between education and individual attitudes toward trade is primarily due to expectations about wages, however, the results from our estimations of trade preferences among respondents not actively engaged in the labor market should differ substantially when compared with those from our estimations of preferences among respondents who are currently employed. To test for this difference, we created subsamples of the full NES survey sample, separating those who were in paid work from those not in paid work.[31] Since those not

30. We have used age in years, because this is the most straightforward approach and is the measure provided in the NES data; Scheve and Slaughter 2001b instead included a range of dummy variables covering separate age brackets. We have reestimated all our results using the respective age dummies and the results are virtually identical. We have also used dummy variables for multiple racial categories here, while Scheve and Slaughter appear to have used a single-race dummy variable. Again, the results are almost identical regardless of how the race variable is entered in the models. The main variables we exclude are the ones constructed by Scheve and Slaughter using non-NES data: SECTOR NET EXPORT SHARE (net exports as a share of output for the industry in which the respondent is employed), and SECTOR TARIFF (customs duties as a share of the total value of imports for the industry in which the respondent is employed). Neither of these variables have significant effects on trade preferences, according to the results reported by Scheve and Slaughter (2001b, 59–60), and their inclusion in the estimations makes no difference at all to the estimated effects of education on trade opinion. We also excluded the other variables Scheve and Slaughter derive from non-NES data—the measure of OCCUPATION WAGE (the national average weekly wage for the respondent's occupation, which they use as an alternative to years of education as an indicator of skill level), and measures of COUNTY EXPOSURE to trade liberalization (the shares of total employment in the respondent's home county accounted for by industries with above average tariffs or net imports). Scheve and Slaughter find that county exposure, when interacted with a dichotomous indicator of home ownership, does have a significant negative impact on support for trade openness, but the inclusion of these added controls in their models has a minuscule and statistically insignificant effect on the estimated impact of education on trade preferences (2001a, 285; 2001b, 64), so we have not attempted to replicate the construction of these added controls here. Note that, because there is very little missing data for variables measured in the NES (the schooling measure has only 6 percent of observations missing in 1992, and 0 percent missing in 1996), and there is less missing data for all the other variables), we do not have to resort to imputation of missing data—Scheve and Slaughter (2001a, 278) report having to impute up to 73.4 percent of the observations for other (non-NES) variables they included in their analysis.

31. The subsamples are determined by answers to a NES question asking respondents about their current employment status. Answer choices included the following: working now, temporarily laid-off, unemployed, retired, student, homemaker, and permanently disabled. Our "currently in paid work" subsample includes those that answered "in work now"; those answering otherwise are classified as "currently not in paid work." Those with missing employment status are coded as missing. We also

currently in paid work include a varied set of individuals, such as those that are unemployed, students, and homemakers (and may be seeking paid work or plan to seek to work soon), we have also isolated one particular group—those individuals who are retired—who are highly unlikely to reenter paid work in the future and be concerned about how their (potential) wages might be affected by trade.[32]

The key results from the estimations are reported in Table 1, which displays the estimated effects of education on individual trade preferences in the full NES sample and in each of the different subsamples. To facilitate comparison across subsamples, rather than showing estimated probit coefficients, we report estimated marginal effects: that is, the change in the probability of favoring protectionism associated with an infinitesimal change in SCHOOLING (for the specific dummy variables for levels of highest educational attainment, the discrete change in the probability is shown).

Comparing the results across the subsamples, we find little difference in the estimated effects of education on attitudes toward trade. In all cases, the estimated effects of SCHOOLING are similar, both in terms of magnitude and level of statistical significance, across all models (none of the coefficients is significantly different from the others across subsamples at conventional levels). This is true for estimations using both the 1992 and the 1996 NES data. For example, in the case of the 1996 survey, using the extensive set of covariates, a change from zero to seventeen years of SCHOOLING (while holding the other covariates at their respective sample means) is associated with an average decrease in the probability of favoring protection of about 0.59 (s.e. 0.05) for the full sample, 0.51 (s.e. 0.09) for those currently in paid work, 0.48 (s.e. 0.11) for those currently not in paid work, and 0.53 (s.e. 0.11) for those who are retired (Models 9 to 12, Panel B).[33] The observed relationship between education and trade preferences becomes even more similar across subsamples once we replace the SCHOOLING measure with the separate education dummies. For example, compared to individuals with less than junior high–level educations, completing a COLLEGE education decreases the probability of being in favor of protection by about 0.28 (s.e. 0.08) for the full

include those few retired/students/disabled/homemakers who also indicated that they are "currently working more than 20 hours per week" in our "currently in paid work" subsample. When the latter are excluded from the "currently in paid work" subsample, the magnitudes of the schooling effect become, if anything, more similar across the in- and out-of-paid-work subsamples than in the results we show here. Full results of these robustness tests are available on request.

32. While pensions for retired workers in some prominent U.S. industries (for example, steel) have been linked to the financial health of their former employers, this is the exception and not the rule. Recent studies of U.S. retirees indicate that less than 17 percent of retirement income in the median household comes from employer-provided pension plans (see Sass 2003, 6; and Social Security Administration 2002). The connection between employer-provided pensions and the financial health of the firm also is attenuated by the standards for funding and fiduciary conduct established by the Employee Retirement Income Security Act in 1974 (see Sass 1997). On this issue, we might also note that we get identical results when we perform the same tests comparing retirees with workers using the ISSP data (see below), drawn from a variety of countries with a variety of pension and retirement income systems.

33. Predicted effects here, and below, are calculated using the "Clarify" software developed by King, Tomz, and Wittenberg 2001. For each such calculation, all other covariates are set at the sample mean values.

TABLE 1. *The effect of education on trade preferences across subsamples—NES data*

Survey	*NES 1992*								*NES 1996*							
Dependent variable	TRADE_OPINION (*1 = favor protectionism; 0 = otherwise*)								TRADE_OPINION (*1 = favor protectionism; 0 = otherwise*)							
Mean of dependent variable	0.67								0.52							
Standard deviation	0.46								0.49							
Subsample	*Full sample*	*Currently in paid work*	*Currently not in paid work*	*Retired*	*Full sample*	*Currently in paid work*	*Currently not in paid work*	*Retired*	*Full sample*	*Currently in paid work*	*Currently not in paid work*	*Retired*	*Full sample*	*Currently in paid work*	*Currently not in paid work*	*Retired*
	Model 1	*Model 2*	*Model 3*	*Model 4*	*Model 5*	*Model 6*	*Model 7*	*Model 8*	*Model 9*	*Model 10*	*Model 11*	*Model 12*	*Model 13*	*Model 14*	*Model 15*	*Model 16*
	Panel A: Limited set of covariates[1]															
SCHOOLING	−0.048***	−0.056***	−0.031***	−0.028**					−0.058***	−0.058***	−0.044***	−0.044**				
	(0.006)	(0.008)	(0.008)	(0.011)					(0.010)	(0.012)	(0.016)	(0.017)				
JUNIOR HIGH					−0.024	0.028	−0.056	−0.029					0.108	0.073	0.118	0.204**
					(0.087)	(0.154)	(0.100)	(0.131)					(0.139)	(0.218)	(0.134)	(0.103)
HIGH SCHOOL					0.028	0.051	0.016	0.070					0.036	0.007	0.065	0.042
					(0.047)	(0.070)	(0.058)	(0.091)					(0.083)	(0.128)	(0.095)	(0.110)
HIGHER EDUCATION					−0.109**	−0.113	−0.079	−0.072					−0.035	−0.022	−0.079	−0.068
					(0.051)	(0.074)	(0.068)	(0.122)					(0.085)	(0.127)	(0.109)	(0.138)
COLLEGE					−0.317***	−0.289***	−0.355***	−0.398***					−0.307***	−0.282**	−0.353***	−0.372**
					(0.053)	(0.073)	(0.098)	(0.132)					(0.078)	(0.112)	(0.119)	(0.149)
GRADUATE					−0.315***	−0.305***	−0.259**	−0.134					−0.348***	−0.315***	−0.365**	−0.297
					(0.061)	(0.081)	(0.113)	(0.149)					(0.075)	(0.102)	(0.163)	(0.197)
Observations	1604	1048	556	227	1563	1021	542	217	843	560	283	167	843	560	283	167
Log likelihood	−962.64	−646.24	−308.66	−128.20	−922.08	−621.46	−293.76	−114.85	−533.13	360.69	−164.87	−89.61	−519.93	−353.56	−158.73	−86.96
Pseudo R^2	0.05	0.06	0.04	0.06	0.07	0.07	0.05	0.11	0.09	0.07	0.09	0.14	0.11	0.09	0.12	0.16

(*continued overleaf*)

(continued)

	Panel B: Extensive set of covariates[2]															
SCHOOLING	−0.049***	−0.057***	−0.032***	−0.025**					−0.057***	−0.054***	−0.047***	−0.056***				
	(0.006)	(0.008)	(0.008)	(0.012)					(0.010)	(0.012)	(0.016)	(0.017)				
JUNIOR HIGH					−0.026	0.010	−0.076	−0.003					0.096	−0.017	0.144	0.196*
					(0.098)	(0.165)	(0.122)	(0.131)					(0.152)	(0.237)	(0.128)	(0.103)
HIGH SCHOOL					0.041	0.072	0.028	0.099					0.046	−0.007	0.083	0.031
					(0.050)	(0.078)	(0.062)	(0.092)					(0.086)	(0.128)	(0.099)	(0.117)
HIGHER EDUCATION					−0.097*	−0.098	−0.057	−0.070					−0.015	−0.033	−0.034	−0.068
					(0.055)	(0.083)	(0.069)	(0.124)					(0.089)	(0.128)	(0.114)	(0.145)
COLLEGE					−0.298***	−0.260***	−0.342***	−0.347**					−0.276***	−0.273**	−0.307**	−0.367**
					(0.058)	(0.083)	(0.103)	(0.142)					(0.083)	(0.113)	(0.131)	(0.161)
GRADUATE					−0.301***	−0.286***	−0.234**	−0.071					−0.329***	−0.316***	−0.303*	−0.261
					(0.065)	(0.090)	(0.115)	(0.146)					(0.080)	(0.103)	(0.182)	(0.214)
Observations	1501	989	512	213	1463	964	499	203	815	537	278	166	815	537	278	166
Log likelihood	−892.72	−604.92	−277.42	−117.09	−856.56	−581.61	−264.24	−104.87	−508.42	−341.85	−158.43	−85.46	−498.29	−335.93	−154.19	−85.23
Pseudo R^2	0.07	0.07	0.06	0.09	0.08	0.09	0.07	0.13	0.10	0.08	0.11	0.17	0.12	0.09	0.13	0.17

Notes: For probit estimations, coefficients are estimated marginal effects ($\partial F/\partial x_k$), that is, the marginal effect on $Pr(y = 1)$, given a unit increase in the value of the relevant (continuous) regressor (x_k), holding all other regressors at their respective sample means. The discrete change in the probability is reported for binary regressors. Robust standard errors in parentheses. Each model includes a full set of controls of the respective covariates set (coefficients not shown here). Cases weighted by the respective NES sample weight (v923008 or v960003).

$*p < 0.10$; $**p < 0.05$; $***p < 0.01$.

1. Limited set of covariates includes age, gender, and race.
2. Extensive set of covariates includes age, gender, race, union membership, party identification, and ideology. For details of variables. See Scheve and Slaughter 2001a and 2001b.

sample, by 0.27 (s.e. 0.11) for those currently in paid work, by 0.31 (s.e. 0.13) for those not in paid work, and by 0.37 (s.e. 0.16) for retirees (see Models 13 to 16, Panel B).[34]

Overall, these results clearly indicate that the link between education and trade preferences reflects a causal mechanism that is not associated with concerns about the labor market and relative wage rates. The findings here are consistent with both types of alternative interpretations, however, suggesting that more-educated individuals favor free trade because they are more likely to understand the economic case for trade openness and/or because they possess more cosmopolitan (or less xenophobic) outlooks—because there is no reason to believe that the effects of education on the economic knowledge or cultural values possessed by different individuals is conditional at all on whether or not they are currently in the workforce.

These alternative interpretations are also supported by the clear nonlinearities that are apparent in the relationship between education and views about trade. Once we relax the linearity restriction imposed by simply counting years of education (the SCHOOLING measure), we can see that the effects of education on trade preferences are described by a nonlinear step function: college education has by far the greatest negative impact on support for protection, about three times larger than HIGHER EDUCATION (which is not itself a robust predictor), and about six times bigger than HIGH SCHOOL education (which is also not itself a robustly significant predictor and seems to have, if anything, a positive effect on support for protection) or completion of JUNIOR HIGH education (which also enters mostly insignificant and with alternate signs); the impact of GRADUATE education is almost identical to the effects of COLLEGE education. For instance, looking again at the estimates in the 1996 NES (full sample), and the limited set of covariates, compared with individuals with less than a JUNIOR HIGH education, completing COLLEGE education reduces the probability of supporting protection by 0.31 (s.e. 0.08), compared to only 0.04 (s.e. 0.09) for HIGHER EDUCATION; finishing HIGH SCHOOL education raises the probability of support for protection by 0.04 (s.e. 0.08) and so does completing JUNIOR HIGH grades by 0.11 (s.e. 0.14), though all three latter effects are not statistically significant. Meanwhile, completing GRADUATE education reduces the probability of protectionist views by 0.35 (s.e. 0.08), an effect not significantly different from that associated with completing an undergraduate college education (see Model 13, Panel A).

There appears to be a clear "plateau" effect here, with exposure to COLLEGE education being the critical contributor to the generally positive relationship between education and support for free trade. This college plateau effect seems out of place with the theory about labor market competition and its effects on trade preferences, especially because it applies to retirees as much as to those individuals currently active in the job market. On the other hand, this pattern fits much better with alternative approaches to explaining attitudes toward trade and foreign affairs

34. Note that since we show marginal effects, the magnitudes of the effects of the dichotomous education variables can be read directly from the table.

that focus on competing ideational and cultural perspectives and the way education—but especially college education—teaches students to think about trade and globalization in different ways or to evaluate it by different standards.

Tests Using the ISSP Data

Our second data set is the 1995 National Identity module of the ISSP, the main data examined by Mayda and Rodrik in their recent study of the determinants of individual trade preferences.[35] The ISSP collects cross-national data by coordinating and combining national surveys on a variety of topics: the 1995 module posed a variety of questions about national identity, patriotism, attachments to local communities, feelings about foreigners, and attitudes toward foreign trade and immigration.[36] It provides information on some 28,500 respondents from twenty-three countries, including the United States, Canada, Japan, many Western and Eastern European countries, and one developing country (the Philippines).[37]

Our treatment of the ISSP data follows precisely the measurement and estimation strategies employed by Mayda and Rodrik. Accordingly, we measure individual trade policy preferences using respondents' answers to the following question:[38]

> *Now we would like to ask a few questions about relations between (respondent's country) and other countries. How much do you agree or disagree with the following statements: (Respondent's country) should limit the import of foreign products in order to protect its national economy.*
>
> *Options:*
>
> - *Agree strongly*
> - *Agree*
> - *Neither agree nor disagree*
> - *Disagree*
> - *Disagree strongly*
> - *Can't choose, don't know*
> - *NA, refused*

Following Mayda and Rodrik, we created two binary variables, labeled PRO-TRADE-DUMMY and AGAINST-TRADE-DUMMY, based on responses to this question. PRO-TRADE-DUMMY is coded 1 for individuals opposing trade protection (that is,

35. Mayda and Rodrik 2005.

36. For details, see ISSP 1998. See also ⟨http://www.issp.org/⟩.

37. The specific countries are West Germany, East Germany, Great Britain, United States, Austria, Hungary, Italy, Ireland, Netherlands, Norway, Sweden, Czech Republic, Slovenia, Poland, Bulgaria, Russia, New Zealand, Canada, Philippines, Japan, Spain, Latvia, and Slovak Republic.

38. See Mayda and Rodrik 2005, 1401, for a discussion of the potential problems associated with the question wording.

for those replying "disagree" or "disagree strongly" to the question), and 0 otherwise. AGAINST-TRADE-DUMMY is coded 1 for individuals favoring trade protection (that is, for those replying "agree" or "agree strongly" to the question), and 0 otherwise. Accordingly, the "Can't choose, don't know" and "NA, refused" responses are coded as zero. Since the results from the estimations of the PRO-TRADE-DUMMY and AGAINST-TRADE-DUMMY are substantively similar, we just emulate Mayda and Rodrik here and present only the results using the analysis of the PRO-TRADE-DUMMY.[39]

Once again the principal measure of education, SCHOOLING is simply a count of the years of full-time education completed by each respondent (we follow Mayda and Rodrik and set a cap at twenty years). In order to test for nonlinearities in the effects of education on attitudes, we again construct a set of highest educational attainment dummy variables that include SECONDARY INCOMPLETE (1 = some secondary education; 0 = otherwise), HIGH SCHOOL (1 = high school degree; 0 = otherwise), and COLLEGE (1 = university education; 0 = otherwise). The reference category here comprises those respondents who have only a primary school education (or less). Unlike the NES data, the ISSP does not allow us to distinguish any finer categories here; no separate coding for graduate education is available, so the college category here includes respondents with advanced or higher university degrees (and those who attended college but did not complete a degree).

Our estimation strategy is identical to the one we applied for the analysis of the NES data. We estimate two series of binary probit models in which the PRO-TRADE-DUMMY is estimated using either SCHOOLING or the set of education dummy variables and other covariates. We estimated all the models for all subsamples using three sets of controls. Our limited set of controls includes just age, gender, and citizenship and a full set of country dummies. This mirrors precisely the baseline specification as presented in the analysis by Mayda and Rodrik.[40] Our extensive set of controls matches those included in their "demographic model" and includes age, gender, citizenship, area of residence (that is, rural, suburban, or urban residence), subjective social class, party affiliation, trade union membership, the log of real income and a full set of country dummies.[41] Our third model mirrors Mayda and Rodrik's "factor endowments model." It includes the covariates AGE, MALE, CITIZEN, and a full set of country dummies, as well as a SCHOOLING*GDP multiplicative term that interacts the schooling measure with the log of gross domestic product (GDP) per capita in the respondent's country alongside the main effect of

39. Mayda and Rodrik note that their results are also unchanged if they treated "Can't choose, don't know" and "NA, refused" as missing data, and the same is true for our findings. In addition, Mayda and Rodrik report that they also used a categorical dependent variable (labeled TRADE_OP) to estimate ordered logit (and OLS regression) models and obtained "very similar" substantive results (2005, 1397).

40. Mayda and Rodrik 2005, 1403, tab. 4, col. 1.

41. Following Mayda and Rodrik 2005, we compute real income using data in local currency from the ISSP dataset and purchasing power parity conversion factors taken from the World Bank's *World Development Indicators* database. See ⟨http://www.worldbank.org/data/wdi2004/⟩. Accessed 10 January 2006.

SCHOOLING.[42] The goal is to capture potential cross-country heterogeneity with respect to the education effect. GDP per capita is used as a simple indicator of relative factor abundance; the assumption is that higher levels of GDP per capita are associated with a greater abundance of skilled labor. According to the Stolper-Samuelson theorem, skilled individuals will gain in terms of real wages and thus should be likely to favor trade openness, in countries that are abundantly endowed with skilled labor, but the size of those gains should be proportional to the degree of skill abundance in each country (and, of course, in countries that are actually poorly endowed with skilled labor relative to potential trading partners, those gains may become losses). In terms of the anticipated results this means that the SCHOOLING*GDP interaction term should be positive. In every model we calculate robust standard errors allowing for potential within-country clustering. (See the Appendix for descriptions of all variables and summary statistics).

Again we created subsamples of the full ISSP survey sample, separating those who were "in paid" work from those "not in paid" work. Since the ISSP variable coding the employment status of respondents also differentiates between those in full- and part-time employment, we define those in (and not in) paid work using both possible combinations (just those in full-time work or all those working).[43] Again, we have estimated the models separately for those individuals who are retired. We estimated all models for the full sample first, and then for each particular subsample. The results are reported in Table 2, which displays just the estimated marginal effects of education on trade preferences.

Overall, the findings from the analysis of the ISSP data are similar to the results from the analysis of the NES data reported above. Here the estimated effects of SCHOOLING on attitudes toward trade are almost identical, both in terms of magnitude and level of statistical significance, across all subsamples, and regardless of whether we examine the baseline (Panel A), the demographic (Panel B), or the factor endowment models (Panel C). None of the schooling effects are significantly different from others across the subsamples at conventional levels. For example, in the baseline model, a shift from zero to twenty years of SCHOOLING (while holding the other covariates at their respective sample means) increases the probability of favoring trade by about 0.34 (s.e. 0.05) in the full sample, by 0.37 (s.e.

42. GDP per capita data is taken from the World Bank's *World Development Indicators* (1995 current international dollars, adjusted for purchasing power parity). Note that the direct effect of country GDP per capita on the attitudes of respondents is captured by the country dummies and is not estimated separately. See Mayda and Rodrik 2005, 1405, for a detailed discussion of the specification.

43. The subsamples are determined by answers to a question asking respondents about their current employment status. Answer choices included the following: full-time employed, part-time employed, less than part-time employed, helping family member, unemployed, student, homemaker, retired, permanently disabled, and other. Our "currently in paid work" subsample includes all those answering "employed (either part-time or full-time)" to this question. Those with missing employment status are coded as missing. We also reestimated all models including those working "less than part-time" in the "currently in paid work" subsamples. The results are substantively identical to those in Table 2 (and are available on request).

TABLE 2. *The effect of education on trade preferences across subsamples–ISSP data*

Survey	ISSP 1995											
Dependent variable	PRO-TRADE-DUMMY (1 = protrade; 0 = otherwise)											
Mean of dependent variable	0.22											
Standard deviation	0.41											
Subsample	Full sample	In work (FT)	Not in work (FT)	In work (FT & PT)	Not in work (FT & PT)	Retired	Full sample	In work (FT)	Not in work (FT)	In work (FT & PT)	Not in work (FT & PT)	Retired
	Model 1	Model 2	Model 3	Model 4	Model 5	Model 6	Model 7	Model 8	Model 9	Model 10	Model 11	Model 12
Panel A: Baseline specification[1]												
SCHOOLING	0.017***	0.019***	0.014***	0.019***	0.013***	0.016***						
	(0.004)	(0.005)	(0.003)	(0.004)	(0.003)	(0.002)						
SECONDARY INCOMPLETE							0.035	−0.003	0.061***	0.008	0.056***	0.073***
							(0.026)	(0.042)	(0.018)	(0.041)	(0.017)	(0.021)
HIGH SCHOOL							0.091**	0.076	0.090***	0.085*	0.082***	0.120***
							(0.036)	(0.051)	(0.028)	(0.049)	(0.028)	(0.021)
COLLEGE							0.186***	0.167***	0.183***	0.181***	0.165***	0.192***
							(0.045)	(0.058)	(0.038)	(0.056)	(0.041)	(0.033)
Observations	26485	12205	13915	14279	11841	4932	28714	12997	15324	15182	13139	5445
Log likelihood	−12632.58	−6366.44	−6087.04	−7396.50	−5070.04	−1882.22	−13617.95	−6730.05	−6691.31	7806.00	5628.82	−1998.99
Pseudo R^2	0.07	0.06	0.07	0.06	0.07	0.09	0.07	0.06	0.08	0.06	0.07	0.10
Panel B: The demographic model[2]												
SCHOOLING	0.015***	0.013***	0.015***	0.013***	0.018***	0.020***						
	(0.003)	(0.004)	(0.003)	(0.003)	(0.003)	(0.005)						
SECONDARY INCOMPLETE							0.019	−0.023	0.070	0.008	0.041	0.018
							(0.036)	(0.040)	(0.044)	(0.052)	(0.029)	(0.041)
HIGH SCHOOL							0.064	0.022	0.101***	0.035	0.115***	0.087***
							(0.039)	(0.048)	(0.034)	(0.055)	(0.026)	(0.031)
COLLEGE							0.137***	0.089*	0.185***	0.108*	0.187***	0.162**
							(0.043)	(0.047)	(0.044)	(0.055)	(0.045)	(0.078)
Observations	5809	3785	1934	4427	1290	503	6547	4138	2313	4834	1615	688
Log likelihood	−2805.44	−1946.62	−815.17	−2241.61	−521.34	−185.57	−3123.02	−2102.24	−968.15	−2421.76	−651.50	−230.39
Pseudo R^2	0.09	0.09	0.11	0.09	0.13	0.16	0.10	0.09	0.11	0.09b	0.13	0.15

(continued overleaf)

(continued)

	Panel C: The factor endowments model[3]											
SCHOOLING	−0.113***	−0.121***	−0.106***	−0.117***	−0.107***	−0.121***						
	(0.021)	(0.019)	(0.025)	(0.019)	(0.025)	(0.025)						
LN(GDP)*SCHOOLING	0.014***	0.015***	0.013***	0.014***	0.013***	0.014***						
	(0.002)	(0.002)	(0.003)	(0.002)	(0.003)	(0.003)						
SECONDARY INCOMPLETE							−0.360***	−0.503***	−0.223***	−0.502***	−0.222***	−0.193**
							(0.049)	(0.041)	(0.079)	(0.046)	(0.071)	(0.081)
LN(GDP)*SEC. INCOMPLETE							0.072***	0.110***	0.040**	0.111***	0.040**	0.040*
							(0.016)	(0.015)	(0.019)	(0.017)	(0.017)	(0.023)
HIGH SCHOOL							−0.497***	−0.624***	−0.393***	−0.623***	−0.383***	−0.275***
							(0.115)	(0.079)	(0.133)	(0.084)	(0.122)	(0.103)
LN(GDP)*HIGH SCHOOL							0.095***	0.116***	0.077**	0.116***	0.077***	0.075**
							(0.027)	(0.021)	(0.031)	(0.022)	(0.029)	(0.033)
COLLEGE							−0.551***	−0.710***	−0.425***	−0.705***	−0.398***	−0.322***
							(0.093)	(0.064)	(0.112)	(0.071)	(0.094)	(0.064)
LN(GDP)*COLLEGE							0.144***	0.164***	0.132***	0.161***	0.137***	0.132***
							(0.029)	(0.022)	(0.040)	(0.023)	(0.038)	(0.028)
Observations	26485	12205	13915	14279	11841	4932	28714	12997	15324	15182	13139	5445
Log likelihood	−12543.62	−6325.67	−6042.16	−7353.64	−5027.18	−1861.63	−13526.51	−6683.06	−6647.11	−7754.93	−5584.56	−1981.49
Pseudo R^2	0.08	0.07	0.08	0.07	0.07	0.10	0.08	0.07	0.08	0.07	0.08	0.11

Notes: For probit estimations, coefficients are estimated marginal effects ($\partial F/\partial x_k$), that is, the marginal effect on Pr(y = 1), given a unit increase in the value of the relevant (continuous) regressor (x_k), holding all other regressors at their respective sample means. The discrete change in the probability is reported for binary regressors. Robust standard errors in parentheses. Each model includes a full set of controls of the respective covariates set (coefficients not shown here). Cases weighted by ISSP sample weight (v342). FT = full-time; PT = part time.

$*p < 0.10$; $**p < 0.05$; $***p < 0.01$.

1. Baseline specification: covariates includes age, gender, citizenship, and country dummies (this set of covariates is equal to Mayda and Rodrik 2005, tab. 4, col. 1).

2. The demographic model specification: covariates includes age, gender, citizenship, subjective social class, log of real income, rural, union membership, partisan orientation, and country dummies (this set of covariates is equal to Mayda and Rodrik 2005, Table 4, Column 2).

0.06) in the in (full-time) work subsample, by 0.31 (s.e. 0.05) for the not-in-full-time-work subsample, and by 0.33 (s.e. 0.05) in the retired subsample (Models 1 to 6, Panel A). These estimated effects of education are very similar regardless of whether those working on a part-time basis are included in the "paid work" subsample or not. The same holds true if we account for potential cross-country heterogeneity with respect to the education effect (Panel C). Both the direct effect of schooling and its interaction with GDP per capita are almost identical across subsamples. The similarity in these effects across the different subsamples of respondents is again clearly at odds with the claim that the SCHOOLING coefficients are primarily indicative of concerns among respondents about the effects of trade openness on labor markets and relative wages.

If we relax the linearity restriction and replace the SCHOOLING measure with the education dummy variables, it is clear that the impact of the education on trade preferences remains very similar across the subsamples. It also becomes apparent again that the effects of education on opinions about trade are nonlinear. Specifically, COLLEGE education has by far the greatest positive effect on individual-level support for free trade, two-to-three times bigger than the impact of HIGH SCHOOL education (which is not a robustly significant predictor of attitudes); meanwhile, INCOMPLETE SECONDARY education appears to have little if any effect on support for free trade (only very few of the coefficients enter significant at conventional levels and some even switch signs). For instance, in the demographic model (Model 7, Panel B), and comparing with individuals with only primary level education, COLLEGE education shifts the probability of being protrade by 0.14 (s.e. 0.04) as compared to only 0.06 (s.e. 0.04) for completing HIGH SCHOOL education; and INCOMPLETE SECONDARY education increases the probability of being pro free trade by a mere 0.02 (s.e. 0.04)—the latter two effects are insignificant at conventional levels. The same nonlinearities are clear when cross-country heterogeneity in the education effect is taken into account. For example, for the full sample in the factor endowments model (Model 7, Panel C), evaluated at the sample mean level of GDP per capita among the ISSP nations ($15,987), a COLLEGE education raises the probability of being protrade by 0.18 (s.e. 0.01) compared to a primary level education; the corresponding effect is only 0.09 (s.e. 0.01) for completing HIGH SCHOOL education, and an INCOMPLETE SECONDARY education increases the probability of being pro free trade by a mere 0.04 (s.e. 0.01). The pattern here strongly resembles the college "plateau" effect found in the analysis of the NES data, and again confirms—this time based on data drawn from surveyed twenty-three nations—that exposure to COLLEGE education among individuals lies at the heart of the observable relationship between education and support for free trade. Regardless of which model we estimate, the college effect is strikingly similar across all subsamples.

One issue we need to address here concerns the cross-country heterogeneity with respect to the education effect that is evident in the results from the estimations of factor endowments model. As reported by Mayda and Rodrik, we find that the SCHOOLING*GDP interaction term is positive—in all of the subsamples. The implication is that the impact of education on individual attitudes toward trade varies by country depending on levels of economic development. For example, examining the full-sample estimates (Model 1, Panel C), a shift from zero to twenty years of SCHOOLING (other covariates at their respective sample means) increases the probability of favoring trade openness by about 0.49 (s.e. 0.03) in a country with GDP per capita of $22,039 (that is, Germany in 1995) but by only 0.27 (s.e. 0.02) in a country with GDP per capita of $11,720 (the Czech Republic in 1995).

This result is consistent with the Stolper-Samuelson theorem, but it also seems consistent with the alternative ideational and cultural accounts of the causal effects of education on attitudes toward trade (accounts that can also explain the similarity in the effects of education across labor-market subsamples in each country). In line with an ideational approach, it seems highly likely that there are important cross-national differences in the content and quality of instruction in economics at the college level that are related to cross-national differences in levels of development across these surveyed countries. Economists and other scholars in less-developed countries may be more concerned than their counterparts in wealthier nations about the adjustment costs associated with trade liberalization, or the fairness of trade negotiations and agreements, and convey these concerns to students. Or, more in line with a cultural account that stresses the link between education and values, it also seems plausible that education systems in richer ISSP nations, which have longer histories of democratic institutions than poorer nations, may place greater emphasis on inculcating tolerance among students, and thus may more effectively discourage antiforeigner (and protectionist) sentiments. The general point here is that there are plausible explanations for the observed differences between richer and poorer ISSP countries in the effects of education on attitudes toward trade that fit with the ideational and cultural accounts; the similarities in the effects of education across subsamples of individuals within each country, and the college plateau effect, are also consistent with these same accounts, but they contradict the Stolper-Samuelson view.[44]

Family Income Effects?

It seems impossible to square the findings we have reported above with a simple Stolper-Samuelson reading of the effects of education on trade policy preferences. One possible counterargument, in defense of the Stolper-Samuelson interpretation, is that individuals who themselves are not employed or seeking employment are nevertheless concerned about the distributional effects of trade because it will have an impact on their total family or household income. Thus individuals who

44. In general we do not place great importance on the finding that the SCHOOLING*GDP interaction term is positive for the ISSP set of countries—in our analysis of the alternative Pew data on individual trade preferences, which includes a much larger and more varied set of countries (see discussion below), we do not find the same, simple positive relationship between GDP per capita and the magnitude of the education effect. The breakdown of this relationship among countries with more varied political and institutional histories suggests that it does not provide firm support for a Stolper-Samuelson interpretation. These results are available at ⟨http://www.people.fas.harvard.edu/~jhainm/Hainmueller Hiscox_IOa.html⟩.

are not employed and describe themselves as "homemakers" may actually be making calculations about the effects of trade on the earnings of their spouse or partner when responding to survey questions. Similarly, retired individuals may be taking into account the effects of trade on the earnings of their children. If these are powerful concerns, and if there is a strong and positive within-family correlation in levels of education, expectations about within-family income transfers might feasibly explain the results we are reporting here in a way that would still be broadly consistent with the spirit of the Stolper-Samuelson theorem. To the best of our knowledge, this family income extension of the theorem has not actually been advanced or tested before—no such claims are made by Scheve and Slaughter or Mayda and Rodrik. On the face of it, we think this potential explanation seems quite implausible, given the clear similarities between the education effects across subsamples, the imperfect correlation between individual education attainment and spouses' or partners' (or children's) education levels, and the uncertainty attached to within-family income transfers. The connection between retirees' incomes and the earnings of their children seems especially tenuous, because most retirees in Western countries rely overwhelmingly on personal savings, retirement accounts, and state-provided pensions for their retirement income.

We tested the alternative explanation using the NES data, which provide the best available data on individual marital status.[45] The NES includes the following question: "Are you married now and living with your (husband/wife)—or are you widowed, divorced, separated, or have you never married?" Following the NES recommendations, we created a dummy variable PARTNER, coded 1 if the respondent indicated he or she is currently living with a spouse or partner and 0 otherwise. To provide an explicit test of spouse and partner effects, we simply repeated all our split-sample analysis using the PARTNER variable to further divide each labor market subsample according to marital status.[46] Dividing the sample in one more dimension results in a limited number of observations within each subsample, of course, so we estimate the model with only the limited set of covariates (including age, gender, and race) here, and we use only the 1992 NES data (the 1996 NES data contains half the total number of observations of the 1992 NES sample, as noted above).[47] Results from these estimations are reported in Table 3. Again we report estimated marginal effects for the education variables so that magnitudes are directly comparable across subsamples.

45. Unfortunately, we cannot conduct a similar analysis for the ISSP survey, because far too much data is missing on the marital status of the respondents. We have repeated these tests using the data from the Pew survey, however, and have found substantively identical results (findings from these additional tests are also available from the authors).

46. We have also rerun our models for each subsample using a multiplicative term (PARTNER* SCHOOLING) alongside the main effect of PARTNER and the results are very similar to the ones reported below. Nonetheless, given the high correlation between the multiplicative and its lower-order terms we prefer the split-sample tests as our identification strategy.

47. Note too, that in the specifications that replace the single SCHOOLING variable with separate educational dummies, we also exclude the JUNIOR HIGH attainment dummy, because there are no observations for this category in some subsamples.

TABLE 3. *The effect of education on trade preferences across labor market and partner subsamples*

Survey	*NES 1992*											
Dependent variable	TRADE_OPINION (*1 = favor protectionism, 0 = otherwise*)											
Mean of dependent variable	0.67											
Standard deviation	0.46											
Subsample 1	*Full sample*			*Currently in paid work*			*Currently not in paid work*			*Retired*		
Subsample 2	*All*	*Partner*	*No partner*	*All*	*Partner*	*No partner*	*All*	*Partner*	*No partner*	*All*	*Partner*	*No partner*
	Model 1	*Model 2*	*Model 3*	*Model 4*	*Model 5*	*Model 6*	*Model 7*	*Model 8*	*Model 9*	*Model 10*	*Model 11*	*Model 12*
Panel A: Limited set of covariates plus schooling												
SCHOOLING	−0.048***	−0.054***	−0.041***	−0.056***	−0.058***	−0.052***	−0.031***	−0.038***	−0.030***	−0.028**	−0.029*	−0.029*
	(0.006)	(0.007)	(0.008)	(0.008)	(0.009)	(0.013)	(0.008)	(0.011)	(0.011)	(0.011)	(0.015)	(0.016)
Observations	1604	981	623	1048	690	358	556	291	265	227	118	109
Log likelihood	−962.64	−575.59	−373.05	−646.24	−425.28	−215.57	−308.66	−149.82	−153.23	−128.20	−61.99	−65.28
Pseudo R^2	0.05	0.08	0.05	0.06	0.07	0.06	0.04	0.07	0.04	0.06	0.09	0.05
Panel B: Limited set of covariates plus educational attainment dummies												
HIGH SCHOOL	0.039	0.099*	−0.104	0.056	0.114	−0.097	0.029	0.083	−0.116	0.067	0.195**	−0.026
	(0.041)	(0.053)	(0.071)	(0.062)	(0.076)	(0.137)	(0.051)	(0.067)	(0.088)	(0.081)	(0.085)	(0.131)
HIGHER EDUCATION	−0.098**	−0.107*	−0.133*	−0.103	−0.089	−0.180	−0.071	−0.107	−0.094	−0.083	−0.022	−0.133
	(0.045)	(0.061)	(0.076)	(0.066)	(0.083)	(0.139)	(0.061)	(0.085)	(0.101)	(0.113)	(0.127)	(0.189)
COLLEGE	−0.303***	−0.301***	−0.339***	−0.284***	−0.266***	−0.328**	−0.317***	−0.393***	−0.443***	−0.412***	−0.282*	−0.658***
	(0.048)	(0.064)	(0.083)	(0.066)	(0.082)	(0.140)	(0.089)	(0.128)	(0.123)	(0.121)	(0.165)	(0.096)
GRADUATE	−0.296***	−0.290***	−0.354***	−0.289***	−0.263***	−0.411***	−0.245**	−0.310**	−0.135	−0.182	−0.150	0.158
	(0.056)	(0.073)	(0.099)	(0.074)	(0.093)	(0.138)	(0.104)	(0.131)	(0.231)	(0.142)	(0.174)	(0.174)
Observations	1672	949	614	1101	666	355	571	280	257	227	112	105
Log likelihood	−981.10	−540.78	−367.22	−666.87	−401.24	−213.79	−308.26	−134.77	−146.58	−120.28	−53.10	−53.81
Pseudo R^2	0.07	0.11	0.05	0.07	0.09	0.06	0.05	0.11	0.06	0.12	0.17	0.18

Notes: For probit estimations, coefficients are estimated marginal effects ($\partial F/\partial x_k$), that is, the marginal effect on $\Pr(y = 1)$, given a unit increase in the value of the relevant (continuous) regressor (x_k), holding all other regressors at their respective sample means. The discrete change in the probability is reported for binary regressors. Robust standard errors in parentheses. Each model includes a full set of controls of the respective covariates set (coefficients not shown here). Cases weighted by the NES sample weight (v923008). Limited set of covariates includes age, gender, and race.
$^*p < 0.10$; $^{**}p < 0.05$; $^{***}p < 0.01$.

The similarities in the effects of education across subsamples appear again here, regardless of whether we limit the analysis to those respondents who have a spouse/partner or to those who do not. In all cases the estimated effects of SCHOOLING are similar, both in terms of magnitude and level of statistical significance. Most importantly, within and across each subsample, we cannot reject the null hypothesis that the education effects are identical (at the 90 percent level). For example, for the full sample estimates, a change from zero to seventeen years of SCHOOLING (while holding the other covariates at their respective sample means) is associated with an average decrease in the probability of favoring protection of about 0.48 (s.e. 0.03) for all respondents, 0.50 (s.e. 0.04) for those respondents that have a partner/spouse, and 0.44 (s.e. 0.06) for those that do not have a partner/spouse. Looking only at those that are currently in paid work, the respective decrease is 0.50 (s.e. 0.04) for all respondents, 0.51 (s.e. 0.05) for those that have a partner/spouse, and 0.47 (s.e. 0.08) for those that do not. For those respondents that are out of the workforce, the respective decrease is 0.35 (s.e. 0.07) for all, 0.38 (s.e. 0.09) for with a partner, and 0.35 (s.e. 0.11) for those without. Finally, for the retired subsample, the respective decrease is again very similar, about 0.32 (s.e. 0.11) for all, 0.33 (s.e. 0.14) for those with and 0.33 (s.e. 0.18) for those without a partner/spouse.

The same results emerge when we rerun the models, replacing the SCHOOLING measure with the EDUCATIONAL ATTAINMENT dummies. Most importantly, the key COLLEGE effect remains strikingly stable across models even if we divide the subsamples using the PARTNER variable. For example for the full sample, completing college education decreases in the probability of favoring protection by about 0.30 (s.e. 0.05) for all respondents, by about 0.30 (s.e. 0.06) for those with partner/spouse, and by 0.34 (s.e. 0.08) for those without (all compared to those that did not complete a high school degree). For those currently in work, the respective decrease is 0.29 (s.e. 0.07) for all respondents, 0.27 (s.e. 0.08) for those with, and 0.33 (s.e. 0.14) for those without a partner/spouse. For those not working, the respective decrease is 0.32 (s.e. 0.09) for all respondents, 0.39 (s.e. 0.13) for those with, and 0.44 (s.e. 0.12) for those without a partner/spouse. The retired subsample reveals the greatest differences in magnitudes of the COLLEGE effect. The decrease in proprotection attitudes associated with completing COLLEGE is 0.41 (s.e. 0.12) for all respondents, 0.28 (s.e. 0.17) for those with, and 0.66 (s.e. 0.10) without a partner. This difference is, if anything, the opposite of what one would expect if one simply assumed that retirees with partners were assessing the effects of trade on the incomes of their (working and similarly educated) partners while retirees without partners were not.

If we just compare the effects of COLLEGE (or SCHOOLING) across subsamples of respondents that do not have partners—a test that presumably excludes the bulk of any family income effects—it is clear that these effects are not significantly different, regardless of whether those respondents are working, not working, or retired. Certainly the effects are not significantly larger for those being paid for the employment of their skills than for others, as implied by a simple Stolper-Samuelson interpretation of the impact of education. Overall, the findings suggest that a broader family or household interpretation of the Stolper-Samuelson theorem cannot account for the results we have found.

Findings and Implications

Previous research has concluded that the simple association that is evident between education and support for trade openness among survey respondents in the United States and other Western nations is proof positive of the Stolper-Samuelson theorem. That is, this relationship is seen as a straightforward confirmation that high-skilled individuals in skill-abundant economies perceive that trade openness raises their real wages while low-skilled individuals calculate that their real wages decrease with trade liberalization. But if these calculations are paramount, the effects of education on individual trade policy preferences should be conditional on whether or not individuals are actually being paid for the employment of their skills in the labor market. Reexamining the available survey data on individual attitudes toward international trade in a variety of nations, we find that this is simply not the case. The impact of education on attitudes toward trade is almost identical among respondents currently in the active labor force and among those who are not—and even among those who are retired from work. In addition, the impact of education on attitudes is overwhelmingly attributable to college education. We have replicated all the tests we report above using two alternative cross-national survey data sets—the third wave of the World Values Survey carried out in 1995–97, and the Global Attitudes Project survey administered by Pew in 2003—and we have found substantively identical results.[48]

Given these results, a fundamental reinterpretation of the survey evidence on attitudes toward trade and globalization appears to be in order. The results reported above indicate that the effects of education levels on trade policy preferences are not primarily a reflection of distributional concerns among survey respondents. We suggest instead that the impact of education on how individuals think about trade and globalization has more to do with ideas and information about the aggregate effects of these economic phenomena. Some part of the effect of education on attitudes toward trade might also reflect the fact that college-educated individuals are less likely than others to harbor antiforeigner sentiments. Which of these two causal mechanisms—ideational or cultural—is more important? Unfortunately, no opinion surveys (of which we are aware) gather all the data that one would need to answer this question definitively. That is, no surveys ask respondents about their views regarding trade, also ask questions designed to measure economic knowledge or exposure to economic ideas, and also ask questions that would gauge individuals' commitments to values such as tolerance and cosmopolitanism. For now we only have some clues provided by studies of partial sets of data—but these clues suggest to us that the smart betting would be on the ideational argument.

48. Full results from all these separate tests are available in a supplement to this paper that can be downloaded at ⟨http://www.people.fas.harvard.edu/~jhainm/HainmuellerHiscox_IOa.html⟩.

One major clue comes from the available data on economic knowledge among the public and its impact upon trade policy preferences. As far as we are aware, the only survey that has actually combined measures of both economic knowledge and attitudes toward trade is the 1992 poll conducted by William Walstad and Max Larsen for the National Center for Research on Economics Education and for Gallup.[49] To gauge "economic literacy"—the main purpose of the study—the survey asked respondents a battery of substantive economic knowledge questions. What is especially interesting, in light of the discussion above, is that once this measure of specialized economic knowledge is included in estimations of individual support for trade openness, the effects of the standard measures of education on attitudes toward trade shrink dramatically in magnitude and none of these effects remains statistically significant.[50] That is, economic literacy appears to account for most of the "raw" impact of education on attitudes about trade.[51] This literacy effect is stable across various subsamples of respondents who are in the active labor force and those who are not.

On the other side of this coin, adding various measures of individuals' commitments to various relevant cultural values (such as tolerance and cosmopolitanism) to estimations of attitudes toward trade appears to have almost no effect at all on the magnitude or significance of the effects of standard measures of education. For instance, using the ISSP survey data that asked a large number of "identity" questions, Mayda and Rodrik introduced an array of controls for (self-expressed) national pride and attachment to local their communities when estimating individual support for trade protection. Many of these cultural variables had significant and sizeable effects on trade preferences, but they had no significant effect at all on the estimated effects of education on such preferences.[52] Using a variety of different measures of racial and cultural tolerance available in the 1992 NES survey, we have found similar results—that is, while the various measures of tolerance among the respondents are themselves significant predictors of views about trade, they account for none of the raw impact of education on trade policy preferences.[53]

Conclusions

Finally, it is important to note that while these results indicate that the impact of education on trade preferences has more to do with ideas and economic literacy than it does with calculations about how trade affects personal income or job security, this is not to say that the latter types of calculations are not important in shaping individuals' views of trade. Our conclusion in this article is just that the

49. See Walstad 1997; and Walstad and Rebeck 2002.

50. See Walstad 1997, 201.

51. Full results from our tests using the Walstad and Larsen data are available at ⟨http://www.people.fas.harvard.edu/~jhainm/HainmuellerHiscox_IOa.html⟩.

52. Mayda and Rodrik 2005, 1414–16.

53. Results from all these separate tests are available from the authors are available at ⟨http://www.people.fas.harvard.edu/~jhainm/HainmuellerHiscox_IOa.html⟩.

simple association between education and support for free trade among surveyed individuals is not a clear manifestation of such distributional concerns. We strongly suspect that concerns about the effects of trade on personal economic well-being do play a large role in shaping trade policy preferences, but they are related much more directly to the impact that trade openness is expected to have in particular industries and firms. "Specific factors" models of the distributional effects of trade that, unlike the Stolper-Samuelson theorem, allow that factors of production are not perfectly mobile between different sectors in the economy, predict that the real incomes of individuals are tied closely to the fortunes of the particular industries in which they are employed or invested.[54]

To date, studies of individual trade preferences have indicated only weak (Mayda and Rodrik) or no (Scheve and Slaughter) support for the prediction that individuals employed in import-competing industries will be much less likely to support trade openness than those employed in exporting industries. But these studies have measured the industry-specific effects of trade in an indirect way, locating respondents by industry using answers to a standard question about the type of business in which they are employed, then controlling for the aggregate trade positions of those industries (for example, their degrees of import penetration) when estimating individual trade preferences.[55] There are at least two major problems with this approach. First, accurately coding respondents by industry of employment using standard industrial classifications is extremely difficult, as respondents typically give vague answers to questions about the type of business in which they work.[56] Second, aggregate industry measures of import penetration and export dependence may offer more information about policy outcomes than policy preferences, and they obscure the obvious variation in positions taken by firms in the subcategories within each broad industry grouping.[57]

One of the implications of our findings is that future survey-based measurements need to be substantially refined to better account for industry-specific effects if we are to accurately gauge the impact of distributional concerns on attitudes toward trade and globalization.[58] Resolving these issues is crucial for improving

54. See Jones 1971; and Mussa 1974. The specific factors approach underpins much of the most recent analysis of the political economy of trade in contemporary advanced economies: see Magee 1980; Grossman and Helpman 1994; and Hiscox 2002.

55. Scheve and Slaughter 2001a and 2001b examine industry effects using this approach and industry coding supplied in the NES. Mayda and Rodrik 2005 were forced to take an extra step: because the ISSP data does not provide coding by industry, they inferred industry of employment from occupational codes assigned to respondents instead.

56. When the staff at the Panel Study of Income Dynamics checked a random sample of surveys, for instance, they found that industry codes differed across coders in 14 percent of cases. See Panel Study of Income Dynamics 1999.

57. The standard concern about using import penetration as a measure of an industry's trade policy preference is that low levels of penetration may reflect the effectiveness of a protectionist lobby (not the absence of concerns about import competition).

58. One recent study, for instance, questioned respondents directly about the likely impact of trade on the security of their particular job, asking them whether they felt that increasing trade made their job more secure, less secure, or had no clear effect (see Hiscox 2004). The estimated probability of support for trade was some 45 percent higher among respondents for whom trade had raised job security compared with those reporting that trade made their job less secure.

our understanding of the determinants of antiglobalization sentiments and the range of policies that might address them.

Appendix: Summary Statistics and Variable Descriptions

TABLE A1. *Summary statistics for NES data*

Variables	Observations	Mean	Standard deviation	Minimum	Maximum
			NES 1992		
TRADE_OPINION	1736	0.674	0.464	0	1
SCHOOLING	2329	12.978	2.733	0	17
GRADUATE	2420	0.076	0.264	0	1
COLLEGE	2420	0.163	0.369	0	1
HIGHER EDUCATION	2420	0.242	0.428	0	1
HIGH SCHOOL	2420	0.343	0.475	0	1
JUNIOR HIGH	2329	0.036	0.187	0	1
AGE	2485	44.271	17.210	17	91
MALE	2485	0.477	0.500	0	1
WHITE	2450	0.845	0.362	0	1
BLACK	2450	0.130	0.336	0	1
INDIAN	2450	0.012	0.110	0	1
ASIAN	2450	0.013	0.114	0	1
TRADE UNION MEMBER	2472	0.108	0.310	0	1
PARTY ID	2445	2.727	2.022	0	6
IDEOLOGY	2277	0.791	0.938	0	2
			NES 1996		
TRADE_OPINION	846	0.524	0.491	0	1
SCHOOLING	1713	13.432	2.581	0	17
GRADUATE	1711	0.099	0.299	0	1
COLLEGE	1711	0.186	0.389	0	1
HIGHER EDUCATION	1711	0.274	0.446	0	1
HIGH SCHOOL	1711	0.315	0.465	0	1
JUNIOR HIGH	1713	0.021	0.143	0	1
AGE	1712	45.529	16.853	18	93
MALE	1714	0.479	0.500	0	1
WHITE	1704	0.852	0.355	0	1
BLACK	1704	0.117	0.322	0	1
INDIAN	1704	0.012	0.108	0	1
ASIAN	1704	0.019	0.136	0	1
TRADE UNION MEMBER	1687	0.120	0.325	0	1
PARTY ID	1695	2.735	2.101	0	6
IDEOLOGY	1651	0.759	0.922	0	2

Note: Cases weighted by respective NES sample weight (v923008 or v960003).

TABLE A2. *Variable descriptions for NES data*

Variables	*Coding*
TRADE_OPINION	Pro–free trade attitudes: "Some people have suggested placing new limits on foreign imports in order to protect American jobs. Others say that such limits would raise consumer prices and hurt American exports. Do you favor or oppose placing new limits on imports, or haven't you thought much about this?" Coded 1 if favored new limits; 0 if opposed. NES variables v923802 and v961327.
SCHOOLING	Years of full-time education completed. NES variables v923905 and v960607
GRADUATE	Highest educational attainment dummy: coded 1 if completed graduate education, and 0 otherwise. NES variables v923908 and v960610.
COLLEGE	Highest educational attainment dummy: coded 1 if completed college education, and 0 otherwise. NES variables v923908 and v960610.
HIGHER EDUCATION	Highest educational attainment dummy: coded 1 if completed some higher education (community or junior college, etc.), and 0 otherwise. NES variables v923908 and v960610.
HIGH SCHOOL	Highest educational attainment dummy: coded 1 if completed high school education, and 0 otherwise. NES variables v923908 and v960610.
JUNIOR HIGH	Highest educational attainment dummy: coded 1 if completed only eight years of schooling, and 0 otherwise. NES variables v923905 and v960607.
AGE	Age in years. NES variables v923903 and v960605.
MALE	Gender: coded 1 if male, and 0 if female. NES variables v924201 and v960066.
WHITE	Respondent's race: coded 1 if White, and 0 otherwise. NES variables v924202 and v960067.
BLACK	Respondent's race: coded 1 if Black, and 0 otherwise. NES variables v924202 and v960067.
INDIAN	Respondent's race: coded 1 if Indian, and 0 otherwise. NES variables v924202 and v960067.
ASIAN	Respondent's race: coded 1 if Asian, and 0 otherwise. NES variables v924202 and v960067.
TRADE UNION MEMBER	Is respondent currently a trade union member: coded 1 if yes, and 0 if no. NES variables v924102/v924101 and v960699/v960698.
PARTY ID	Respondent's party identification: coded from 0 "strong Democrat" to 6 "strong Republican." NES variables v923634 and v960420
IDEOLOGY	Respondent's ideology: coded 0 if conservative, 1 if moderate, and 2 if liberal. NES variables v923513 & v960368.

TABLE A3. *Summary statistics for ISSP data*

Variables	*Observations*	*Mean*	*Standard deviation*	*Minimum*	*Maximum*
PRO-TRADE-DUMMY	30894	0.221	0.408	0	1
AGAINST-TRADE-DUMMY	30894	0.570	0.495	0	1
SCHOOLING	28022	11.375	3.713	0	20
SECONDARY INCOMPLETE	30294	0.218	0.413	0	1
HIGH SCHOOL	30294	0.299	0.458	0	1
COLLEGE	30294	0.230	0.421	0	1
AGE	30666	44.355	16.923	14	98
MALE	30778	0.480	0.500	0	1
CITIZEN	29440	0.973	0.163	0	1
RURAL	24074	1.730	0.894	1	3
PARTY ID	18352	2.905	0.979	1	5
TRADE UNION MEMBER	24662	0.302	0.459	0	1
LN REAL INCOME	21860	9.215	1.700	2.5	13.9
LN GDP PER CAPITA	30894	9.487	0.668	8.1	10.2

Note: Cases weighted by ISSP sample weight.

TABLE A4. *Variable descriptions for ISSP data*

Variables	*Coding*
PRO-TRADE-DUMMY	Pro–free trade attitudes: "How much do you agree or disagree with the following statements: (Respondent's country) should limit the import of foreign products in order to protect its national economy." Coded 1 if answered disagree strongly or disagree, and 0 otherwise. ISSP variable v38.
AGAINST-TRADE-DUMMY	Proprotectionism attitudes: same question as above but coded 1 if answered agree strongly or agree, and 0 otherwise.
SCHOOLING	Years of full-time education schooling (cap at twenty years). Those with no formal schooling are coded as 0. ISSP variable v204.
SECONDARY INCOMPLETE	Highest educational attainment: coded 1 if incomplete secondary education, and 0 otherwise. ISSP variable v205.
HIGH SCHOOL	Highest educational attainment: coded 1 if completed secondary education, and 0 otherwise. ISSP variable v205.
COLLEGE	Highest educational attainment: coded 1 if had college/university education or semi-higher degrees, and 0 otherwise. ISSP variable v205.
AGE	Age in years. ISSP variable v201.
MALE	Gender: coded 1 if male, and 0 if female. ISSP variable v200.
CITIZEN	Citizenship: "Are you a citizen of (country)?" Coded 1 if citizen, and 0 otherwise. ISSP variable v63.
RURAL	Area of residence: coded 1 if urban, 2 if suburban, and 3 if rural. ISSP variable v295.
PARTY ID	Party affiliation: self-placement on a left-right scale. Coded from 1 "far left" to 5 'far right." ISSP variable v269.
TRADE UNION MEMBER	Trade union membership: "Are you a member in a trade union at present?" Coded 1 if answered "Member now," and 0 if answered "Not a member now." ISSP variable v268.
LN REAL INCOME	Log of real income. Data in local currency converted by PPP conversion factors taken from World Bank, *World Development Indicators*. ISSP variable v217.
LN GDP PER CAPITA	Log of GDP per capita 1995, PPP (current international dollars). Taken from World Bank, *World Development Indicators*.

References

Adler, Emanuel. 1992. The Emergence of Cooperation: National Epistemic Communities and the International Evolution of the Idea of Nuclear Arms Control. *International Organization* 46 (1):101–45.

Allport, G. 1954. *The Nature of Prejudice*. Reading, Mass.: Addison & Wesley.

Baker, Andy. 2003. Why Is Trade Reform so Popular in Latin America? *World Politics* 55 (3):423–55.

Balistreri, Edward J. 1997. The Performance of the Heckscher-Ohlin-Vanek Model in Predicting Endogenous Policy Forces at the Individual Level. *Canadian Journal of Economics* 30 (1):1–17.

Bauer, Raymond A., Ithiel de Sola Pool, and Lewis Anthony Dexter. 1972. *American Business and Public Policy: The Politics of Foreign Trade*. 2d ed. Chicago: Aldine-Atherton.

Beaulieu, Eugene. 2002. Factor or Industry Cleavages in Trade Policy? An Empirical Analysis of the Stolper-Samuelson Theorem. *Economics and Politics* 14 (2):99–131.

Betts, Katherine. 1988. *Ideology and Immigration: Australia 1976 to 1987*. Melbourne, Australia: Melbourne University Press.

Bhagwati, Jagdish. 1988. *Protectionism*. Cambridge, Mass.: MIT Press.

Campbell, Angus, Philip E. Converse, Warren E. Miller, and Donald E. Stokes. 1960. *The American Voter: Chicago*. Chicago: University of Chicago Press.

Case, C. E., A. M. Greeley, and S. Fuchs. 1989. Social Determinants of Racial Prejudice. *Sociological Perspectives* 32 (4):469–83.

Destler, I. M. 1995. *American Trade Politics*. 3d ed. Washington, D.C.: Institute for International Economics.

Erikson, Robert S., Norman R. Luttbeg, and Kent L. Tedin. 1991. *American Public Opinion: Its Origins, Content, and Impact*. 4th ed. New York: Macmillan.

Finnemore, Martha, and Kathryn Sikkink. 1998. International Norm Dynamics and Political Change. *International Organization* 52 (4):887–917.

Gabel, Matthew J. 1998. *Interests and Integration: Market Liberalization, Public Opinion, and European Union*. Ann Arbor: University of Michigan Press.

Gleason, J., and L. J. Van Scyoc. 1995. A Report on the Economic Literacy of Adults. *Journal of Economic Education* 26 (3):203–10.

Goldstein, Judith. 1988. Ideas, Institutions, and American Trade Policy. *International Organization* 42 (1):179–217.

Goldstein, Judith, and Robert Keohane, eds. 1993. *Ideas and Foreign Policy: Beliefs, Institutions, and Political Change*. Ithaca, N.Y.: Cornell University Press.

Grossman, Gene, and Elhanan Helpman. 1994. Protection for Sale. *American Economic Review* 84 (4):833–50.

Haas, Peter M., ed. 1992. *Knowledge, Power and International Policy Coordination*. Columbia: University of South Carolina Press.

Hall, Peter A., ed. 1989. *The Political Power of Economic Ideas*. Princeton, N.J.: Princeton University Press.

Hainmueller, Jens, and Michael J. Hiscox. 2004. Educated Preferences: Explaining Individual Attitudes Toward Immigration in Europe. Paper presented at the Annual Meeting of the American Political Science Association, Chicago, September.

Hiscox, Michael J. 2002. *International Trade and Political Conflict*. Princeton, N.J.: Princeton University Press.

———. 2004. Through a Glass and Darkly: Attitudes Towards International Trade and the Curious Effects of Issue Framing. Paper presented at the Annual Meeting of the American Political Science Association, Chicago, September.

Holsti, Ole. R. 1996. *Public Opinion and American Foreign Policy*. Ann Arbor: University of Michigan Press.

International Social Survey Program (ISSP). 1998. International Social Survey Program: National Identity, 1995 [computer file]. ICPSR release. Cologne, Germany: Zentralarchiv für Empirische Sozialforschung/Ann Arbor, Mich.: Inter-University Consortium for Political and Social Research. ⟨www.icpsr.umich.edu⟩.

Jones, Ronald. 1971. A Three-Factor Model in Theory, Trade, and History. In *Trade, Balance of Payments, and Growth*, ed. Jagdish Bhagwati, Ronald Jones, Robert A. Mundell, and Jaroslav Vanek, 3–21. Amsterdam: North-Holland.

Katzenstein, Peter, ed. 1996. *The Culture of National Security: Norms and Identity in World Politics*. New York: Columbia University Press.

Keck, Margaret E., and Kathryn Sikkink. 1998. *Activists Beyond Borders*. Ithaca, N.Y.: Cornell University Press.

Kindleberger, Charles. 1975. The Rise of Free Trade in Western Europe. *Journal of Economic History* 35 (1):20–55.

King, Gary, Michael Tomz, and Jason Wittenberg. 2001. Clarify: Software for Interpreting and Presenting Statistical Results. Version 2.0. Harvard University.

Krugman, Paul A. 1993. What Do Undergrads Need to Know About Trade? *American Economic Review* 83 (2):23–26.

Magee, Stephen. 1980. Three Simple Tests of the Stolper-Samuelson Theorem. In *Issues in International Economics*, edited by P. Oppenheimer, 138–53. London: Oriel Press.

Mayda, Anna Maria. 2004. Who Is Against Immigration? A Cross-Country Investigation of Attitudes Towards Immigrants. IZA Discussion Paper 1115. Bonn, Germany: Institute for the Study of Labor.

Mayda, Anna Maria, and Dani Rodrik. 2005. Why Are Some People (and Countries) More Protectionist than Others? *European Economic Review* 49 (6):1393–430.

McClosky, Herbert, and Alida Brill. 1983. *Dimensions of Tolerance: What Americans Believe About Civil Liberties*. New York: Russell Sage Foundation.

Miller, Warren E., Donald R. Kinder, Steven J. Rosenstone, and the National Election Studies. 1992. American National Election Study, 1992: Pre- and Post-Election Survey [Enhanced with 1990 and

1991 Data] [computer File]. 2d. ICPSR ed. Ann Arbor: University of Michigan, Center for Political Studies, and Inter-University Consortium for Political and Social Research. ⟨www.icpsr.umich.edu⟩.

Mussa, M. 1974. Tariffs and the Distribution of Income. *Journal of Political Economy* 82 (6):1191–203.

O'Rourke, Kevin, and Richard Sinnott. 2002. The Determinants of Individual Trade Policy Preferences. In *Brookings Trade Forum*, edited by Susan M. Collins and Dani Rodrik, 157–96. Washington, D.C.: Brookings Institution.

Panel Study of Income Dynamics. 1999. 1968–1980 Retrospective Occupation-Industry Files Documentation. Ann Arbor: Survey Research Center, University of Michigan.

Price, Richard. 1998. Reversing the Gun Sights: Transnational Civil Society Targets Land Mines. *International Organization* 52 (3):613–44.

Pryor, Frederic. 2002. General Discussion. In *Brookings Trade Forum*, edited by Susan M Collins and Dani Rodrik, 201–3. Washington, D.C.: Brookings Institution.

Rogowski, Ronald. 1989. *Commerce and Coalitions*. Princeton, N.J.: Princeton University Press.

Rosenstone, Steven J., Donald R. Kinder, Warren E. Miller, and the National Election Studies. 1996. American National Election Study, 1996: Pre- and Post-Election Survey [Computer file]. 4th version. Ann Arbor: University of Michigan, Center for Political Studies [producer], 1999. Ann Arbor, MI: Inter-university Consortium for Political and Social Research [distributor], 2000.

Ruggie, John Gerard. 1998. What Makes the World Hang Together? *International Organization* 52 (4):855–85.

Sass, Steven. 1997. *The Promise of Private Pensions*. Cambridge: Harvard University Press.

———. 2003. Reforming the U.S. Retirement Income System: The Growing Role of Work. Issues in Brief 1; Boston College, Mass.: Center for Retirement Research.

Saunders, P. 1980. The Lasting Effects of Introductory Economics Courses. *Journal of Economic Education* 12 (1):1–14.

Scheve, Kenneth F., and Matthew J. Slaughter. 2001a. What Determines Individual Trade-Policy Preferences? *Journal of International Economics* 54 (2):267–92.

———. 2001b. *Globalization and the Perceptions of American Workers*. Washington, D.C.: Institute for International Economics.

———. 2001c. Labor Market Competition and Individual Preferences over Immigration Policy. *Review of Economics and Statistics* 83 (1):133–145.

Sikkink, Kathryn. 1993. Human Rights, Principled Issue-Networks, and Sovereignty in Latin America. *International Organization* 47 (3):411–42.

Social Security Administration. 2002. *2000 Income of the Aged Chartbook*. Washington, D.C.: Government Printing Office.

Stolper, W., and P. Samuelson. 1941. Protection and Real Wages. *Review of Economic Studies* 9 (1):58–73.

Walstad, William B. 1997. The Effect of Economic Knowledge on Public Opinion of Economic Issues. *Journal of Economic Education* 28 (3):195–205.

Walstad, William B., and Ken Rebeck. 2002. Assessing the Economic Knowledge and Economic Opinions of Adults. *Quarterly Review of Economics and Finance* 42 (5):921–35.

Wendt, Alexander. 1999. *Social Theory of International Politics*. Cambridge: Cambridge University Press.

World Bank. Various years. *World Development Indicators*. Washington, D.C.: World Bank.

[13]

Support for Free Trade: Self-Interest, Sociotropic Politics, and Out-Group Anxiety

Edward D. Mansfield and Diana C. Mutz

Abstract Although it is widely acknowledged that an understanding of mass attitudes about trade is crucial to the political economy of foreign commerce, only a handful of studies have addressed this topic. These studies have focused largely on testing two models, both of which emphasize that trade preferences are shaped by how trade affects an individual's income. The factor endowments or Heckscher-Ohlin model posits that these preferences are affected primarily by a person's skills. The specific factors or Ricardo-Viner model posits that trade preferences depend on the industry in which a person works. We find little support for either of these models using two representative national surveys of Americans. The only potential exception involves the effects of education. Initial tests indicate that educational attainment and support for open trade are directly related, which is often interpreted as support for the Heckscher-Ohlin model. However, further analysis reveals that education's effects are less representative of skill than of individuals' anxieties about involvement with out-groups in their own country and beyond. Furthermore, we find strong evidence that trade attitudes are guided less by material self-interest than by perceptions of how the U.S. economy as a whole is affected by trade.

The politics of international trade has been a long-standing puzzle for social scientists. Among economists, there is widespread agreement that free trade is beneficial.[1] Open trade and cross-national market integration help to allocate factors of production efficiently and to promote the welfare of countries and the world as

Earlier versions of this article were presented at the 2006 annual meeting of the American Political Science Association, Philadelphia; seminars at the University of Chicago (Harris School), Emory University, Harvard University, and the University of Virginia; and a conference on Domestic Preferences and Foreign Economic Policy, held at Princeton University. We are grateful to Marc Busch, Jens Hainmueller, So Young Kim, Richard Valelly, the editors of *International Organization*, and two anonymous reviewers for helpful comments; to Rumi Morishima, Matthew Tubin, and Carmela Aquino for research assistance; and to the Christopher H. Browne Center for International Politics and the Institute for the Study of Citizens and Politics for financial assistance.

Note from the editors: Since one of the authors is an associate editor of this journal, the editors handled this article outside of the normal editorial management system and put in place special procedures to ensure rigorous, double-blind peer review.

1. Alston, Kearl, and Vaughan 1992.

International Organization 63, Summer 2009, pp. 425–57

doi:10.1017/S0020818309090158

a whole. Historically, however, open trade has been the exception rather than the rule.

Studies of the political economy of trade often attribute variations in trade preferences to the distributional implications of overseas commerce. Despite the economic benefits that a given country would accrue from open trade, some individuals suffer economic harm as a result. If these individuals form a politically potent constituency, they may be able to pressure policymakers to increase trade barriers even if doing so is economically counterproductive for the country as a whole. If, on the other hand, the individuals who derive welfare gains from trade are particularly influential, then an open trade regime is likely to take hold. Recent research indicates that, in democratic countries, constituency opinion on trade plays a central role in influencing the policy positions of public officials.[2]

There are two principle ways of assessing the distributional consequences of trade. First, the factor endowments approach emphasizes that, in a given country, trade benefits those individuals who own factors of production that are in abundant supply relative to the remainder of the world, and harms owners of factors that are in scarce supply. In countries such as the United States, which has a skilled labor force, free trade benefits highly skilled workers and harms less skilled workers. Second, the specific factors approach predicts that an individual's attitudes toward trade will reflect characteristics of the industry in which he or she works. People employed in industries that depend on overseas markets should be more supportive of open trade than people working in industries that face considerable competition from imports.

A small but growing number of studies have evaluated the strength of these explanations for trade policy preferences. We extend this body of research using two representative national surveys of Americans and more comprehensive measures of industries and occupations than previous studies had available to them. In addition, we link the study of trade preferences to the more extensive body of theory and empirical research on how self-interest enters into the formation of domestic economic policy preferences.

Substantial research in other economic policy domains has demonstrated that self-interest rarely shapes the formation of policy opinions because people have a difficult time understanding the connection between personal economic well-being and government policy. By mounting the most thorough individual-level examination to date of the effects of industry and skill on individual trade preferences, we seek to determine whether trade is, indeed, one of those rare exceptions in which personal experiences are successfully politicized. Alternatively, if attitudes about trade are formed in a manner similar to attitudes about domestic economic domains such as unemployment, then trade policy preferences will be based on how people believe a policy affects the country collectively rather than on narrowly defined self-interest. Importantly, the analysis of aggregate-level data—the

2. See Fordham and McKeown 2003; and Kono 2008.

approach used by most previous studies of trade preferences—cannot differentiate between these two possibilities. Thus, uniquely, this study simultaneously examines both how personal economic self-interest and perceptions of the collective national interest influence trade preferences.

Our findings indicate that accounting for perceptions of how the U.S. economy is affected by trade is important to modeling trade preferences. Consistent with previous research on the impact of self-interest on policy attitudes, our data show little support for either the factor endowments or the specific factors model. By contrast, perceptions of how trade affects the country as a whole—what are often referred to as "sociotropic" perceptions—play a substantial role in shaping attitudes about foreign commerce, a role that is largely independent of self-interest. Indeed, these perceptions are among the most important influences on opinions about trade.

Finally, we further improve our understanding of mass trade preferences by incorporating into our model indicators of domestic ethnocentrism and foreign policy attitudes. There is little support for free trade among people who believe the United States should take an isolationist stance on international affairs more generally or those who feel that members of other ethnic and racial groups are less praiseworthy than their own racial or ethnic group. Although such views have no direct bearing on the economic benefits of trade, they are far more predictive of trade preferences than indicators of economic self-interest.

Taken as a whole, the results of this article cast doubt on the ability of standard political economy models to explain trade preferences. Furthermore, the fact that sociotropic perceptions and out-group anxiety are such powerful predictors of these preferences indicates that research on trade policy would benefit by developing psychologically based models that address how individuals process information about the economy, and how they form attitudes about people and places beyond their borders.

The Origins of Trade Preferences

Much of the existing research on trade preferences has been guided by two models. The factor endowments, or Heckscher-Ohlin, model assumes that all factors of production within a country are mobile across sectors, that markets are perfectly competitive, and that there are constant returns to scale in production. Based on these assumptions, Stolper and Samuelson showed that, in a given country, open trade benefits owners of factors of production that are abundant, relative to the remainder of the world, and harms owners of scarce factors.[3] Consequently, in the United States—a country endowed with an abundance of highly skilled and well-educated labor relative to the rest of the world—free trade benefits highly skilled workers

3. Stolper and Samuelson 1941.

and damages less-skilled individuals.[4] Open trade increases the demand for skilled workers, since the United States has a comparative advantage in the production of goods that use this input intensively. As the demand for such workers rises, so do their wages. Conversely, heightened trade decreases the demand for low-skilled labor in the United States and depresses its wage rate since goods produced using such labor intensively can be produced more efficiently abroad.[5] The factor endowments approach therefore predicts that highly skilled workers in the United States should be protrade, whereas other workers should hold more protectionist views.

Empirical studies of trade policy attitudes have generated a fair amount of support for this theory. In a set of cross-national analyses, O'Rourke and Sinnott and Mayda and Rodrik find that mass opinion about trade corresponds closely to predictions stemming from the factor endowments approach.[6] Scheve and Slaughter provide some additional support for this approach, based on an analysis of public attitudes in the United States; and Balistreri concludes that this model helps to explain Canadian attitudes toward the Canadian–U.S. Free Trade Agreement.[7] Nonetheless, a number of recent studies have raised questions about the fit between trade preferences and the factor endowments model.[8] A key assumption in the Heckscher-Ohlin model is that factors of production can move quickly and easily from one sector to another. In the long run, this assumption is not difficult to justify. In the short run, however, it can be difficult for people (not to mention other factors of production) to change the sector in which they are employed.[9]

The specific factors, or Ricardo-Viner, model is an alternative framework that assumes that, at least in the short run, certain factors of production cannot be shifted across sectors. If workers cannot easily move from one sector to another, then they will base their trade preferences on how changes in trade policy are expected to affect the industry in which they are currently employed. This model suggests that individuals who work in export-oriented sectors of the economy will support open trade because they personally benefit from it, while those in import-competing sectors will be more protectionist. Equally, an individual employed in a nontraded sector of the economy should be more protrade than someone employed in an industry that faces substantial competition from foreign imports.

Few studies have tried to evaluate whether trade preferences correspond to the specific factors model, primarily due to a lack of data on individuals' industry of

4. Leamer 1984.

5. The human capital model makes similar predictions about the attitudes of highly skilled workers in countries with a highly skilled labor force. In this model, however, the reason highly skilled workers should support open trade is that they can more easily shift occupations and industries, and thus adapt successfully to economic change. See Gabel 1998; Baker 2003 and 2005; Kaltenthaler, Gelleny, and Ceccoli 2004; and Kocher and Minushkin 2006.

6. See O'Rourke and Sinnott 2002; and Mayda and Rodrik 2005.

7. See Balistreri 1997; and Scheve and Slaughter 2001.

8. See Baker 2003; and Hainmueller and Hiscox 2006.

9. The model may still prove useful if citizens use a relatively long time frame to evaluate the impact of trade policies. On this point, see Mayda and Rodrik 2005.

employment in most extant surveys. Mayda and Rodrik try to infer respondents' industry from occupational data; but this is an imperfect solution, with many individuals assigned to multiple overlapping sectors because of inadequate information.[10] Nonetheless, Mayda and Rodrik find evidence that is broadly consistent with the specific factors model. In a similarly motivated analysis, Scheve and Slaughter compare the factor endowments and specific factors models, using educational attainment and the average yearly earnings for the respondent's occupation as indicators of skill, and the comparative advantage or disadvantage of the respondent's industry of employment as specific factors indicators.[11] Their study provides evidence for the factor endowments model, but none supportive of the specific factors model.

Notably, the underlying premise in both models described above is that attitudes toward trade are largely a function of who is personally helped or hurt by trade policies. As Mayda and Rodrik note, "to the extent that individuals are motivated by material self-interest, these models provide important hints about an individual's likely attitudes toward trade depending upon his/her factor type or sector of employment."[12] Unfortunately, the explanatory value of these models has been quite limited to date, and even simple demographics often explain more about trade preferences than variables linked to either model.

Beyond these two dominant theoretical frameworks, existing studies have also produced a set of empirical findings that remain in need of a theoretical framework. For example, Mayda and Rodrik find that social status, relative incomes, and values play a more important role than variables highlighted by either economic model.[13] Upper-class people are more likely to be protrade as are those with higher relative incomes. In addition, older people appear to be more protectionist than younger generations.

In the same vein, although educational attainment tends to be highly correlated with support for trade, the appropriate interpretation of this relationship remains unclear.[14] If education is simply serving as a proxy for skill level, then this relationship can be interpreted as support for the factor endowments model. This, in fact, is how these results are typically viewed.

But there are many other plausible explanations for why education might relate to trade preferences. Well-educated people are different from their less-educated counterparts in numerous ways, including levels of tolerance for out-groups (such as foreigners), risk preferences, levels of dogmatism, and preferences for immediate versus delayed gratification. To the extent that trade preferences are driven by

10. Ibid.
11. Scheve and Slaughter 2001.
12. Mayda and Rodrik 2005, 1394.
13. Mayda and Rodrik 2005.
14. For studies that have found such a correlation, see Bauer, Pool, and Dexter 1963, chap. 6; Scheve and Slaughter 2001; O'Rourke and Sinnott 2002; Kaltenthaler, Gelleny, and Ceccoli 2004; and Mayda and Rodrik 2005.

characteristics such as ethnocentricism, out-group hostility, or isolationist foreign policy tendencies, education's influence may have little to do with economic self-interest.

Hainmueller and Hiscox argue that education represents something other than skill level.[15] They find that the effect of education on trade preferences is much the same for Americans who are not currently employed as for those who are working. Equally, there is no distinguishable difference in the effects of education between working individuals and retirees, a subset of nonworking individuals who are unlikely to re-enter the labor force. In their view, the fact that education's impact is not contingent on whether an individual is receiving wages for using his or her skills casts doubt on the factor endowments model. Rather than serving as a proxy for skill, they argue that education represents the effects of exposure to economic ideas among the college-educated. Because mainstream economists generally favor open trade, college-educated individuals will have more exposure to arguments about the economic benefits of foreign commerce than those with less formal education.

This claim is consistent with Hainmueller and Hiscox's findings that college-educated individuals have especially protrade attitudes, but these individuals are distinctive from their less educated counterparts in many other ways as well. As Nie, Junn, and Stehlik-Barry point out, education is a powerful predictor of many civic virtues.[16] Unfortunately, it is poorly understood why education is linked to these outcomes. Empirical research suggests that education affects political preferences in at least two ways: (1) through occupational prominence and position in social networks, and (2) through cognitive proficiency and analytical ability.[17] If education serves as a proxy for skill level, then it falls into the first of these categories. Under these circumstances, education influences trade preferences because of where schooling locates people in socioeconomic strata. But since education also contributes to tolerance of different cultures and countries, as well as a belief on the part of Americans that the United States should be more actively engaged in foreign affairs, it remains to be seen if exposure to arguments about the virtues of international trade is driving Hainmueller and Hiscox's results.[18]

Furthermore, the expected trade attitudes of retirees are far from clear. That education's impact on such attitudes is indistinguishable between workers and retirees could reflect a tendency for trade preferences to persist over the course of a lifetime, rather than changing suddenly at retirement. Thus, based on this analysis alone, it is difficult to determine whether skill level influences the formation of trade preferences.

The common finding that women are more protectionist than men, even after controlling for educational differences, also has been attributed to a college edu-

15. Hainmueller and Hiscox 2006.
16. Nie, Junn, and Stehlik-Barry 1996.
17. Ibid.
18. See Bauer, Pool, and Dexter 1963, chap. 6; Erikson and Tedin 2005; and Fordham 2008.

cation, in this case to differences in the kinds of courses taken by men and women. Burgoon and Hiscox, for example, maintain that college-educated men are more likely than college-educated women to be exposed to mainstream economic arguments about the gains from trade. They argue that the gender gap in trade policy attitudes stems from the fact that protrade ideas reach more men than women through their college coursework.[19]

More generally, Burgoon and Hiscox and Hainmueller and Hiscox make the important point that the kind of information to which citizens are exposed is likely to play a crucial role in shaping trade preferences.[20] To extend their argument beyond the educational environment, it is easy to see how if a person is a union member, they will be exposed to a different kind of information about the impact of free trade policies than a nonunion worker. As new concerns about globalization arise, organizations regularly communicate with their members to encourage certain policy preferences and to inform them about how they think people will be affected by particular policies. Likewise, members of the retiree organization AARP may receive regular information about the perils of financial insecurity in today's global economy, thus cultivating the impression of risk and volatility that could drive perceptions of the need for protectionist policies. Particularly in the current highly specialized media environment, different people receive different information.[21]

Whether this information variability is an outgrowth of the college courses they took, of newsletters, or of the daily newspaper, it helps shape perceptions that may or may not have a basis in the individual's personal economic reality. We refer to this collection of models emphasizing information differences as a source of variance in trade preferences as information-based models.

Intuitively, information of the kind one might be exposed to in college or in a daily newspaper would seem to pale in comparison to the hard reality of economic risk faced by a worker in a given occupation or industry. Surely threats to one's livelihood would seem to be a more potent influence on policy preferences. Surprisingly, the literature on economic policy preferences suggests that self-interest is unlikely to play an influential role in shaping attitudes toward free trade.[22] A large body of research demonstrates that self-interest enters into the formation of policy opinions only under very special and rare circumstances.[23]

Because of the counterintuitive nature of this claim, social scientists have searched extensively for instances in which economic self-interest played a significant role in the formation of policy preferences, but with little success. Evidence suggests that the economic impact of policies on individual families has little, if any, influence on their policy preferences.[24] The lack of self-interested policy pref-

19. Burgoon and Hiscox 2004.
20. See Burgoon and Hiscox 2004; and Hainmueller and Hiscox 2006.
21. Prior 2007.
22. For a review of this literature, see Kiewiet 1983.
23. Sears and Funk 1990.
24. Ibid.

erences occurs not out of a mass tendency toward altruism, but rather because citizens have a difficult time linking their personal economic situations to public policies. Furthermore, this pattern is not restricted to the economic realm. The list of failed attempts to observe the influence of self-interest in the formation of policy preferences is by now quite lengthy.[25] Exceptions to this general rule have received a great deal of attention, if only because of their rarity.[26]

But this is not to say that economic conditions are unrelated to policy preferences. Instead, because people tend to formulate policy preferences on the basis of collective, national-level information (that is, perceptions of how a given policy has affected the nation as a whole), economic conditions can influence these preferences, but through a fundamentally different process than what has been suggested by theories emphasizing self-interest. Even something as personally jarring as losing a job has far less impact on political preferences than the perception that unemployment is worsening as a collective, national problem.[27] Thus, to the extent that trade preferences are similar to attitudes toward other aspects of economic policy, they will stem from people's perceptions of the collective impact that trade policy has on the nation. This pattern has been dubbed sociotropic influence because of the tendency it suggests for relying on collective-level information rather than personal experience.[28]

Sociotropic models are, at root, information-based explanations. They are rooted in people's perceptions (or misperceptions) derived from any number of sources of information, beyond personal life experience. Most interestingly, such perceptions are not mere generalizations from personal experience. The two kinds of information that have been found to influence national-level collective perceptions are: (1) local information, such as information about the local economy, and (2) mass media coverage of economic issues. Citizens tend to process personal-level experiences and concerns in a fashion that compartmentalizes them from the political world.[29] Collective-level information, on the other hand, is more easily linked to government policy. An unemployed person is unlikely to blame the government for his or her personal situation, but people who are aware of rising joblessness in their country or community are likely to hold the government accountable for this development, regardless of their employment status. In the case of trade preferences, if available information convinces a person that many in the United States are being adversely affected by free trade, even if he is not, it

25. For a full review, see ibid.

26. Green and Gerken, for example, found that smoking-related policy preferences were significantly influenced by whether a person was a smoker. The few exceptions are simple policies with straightforward effects on individuals, such as the effects of nonsmoking policies on smokers. As complex, difficult to understand agreements, trade policies would not naturally fall into this category of policies in which one would expect self-interest to affect political preferences. See Green and Gerken 1989.

27. See Sears and Funk 1990; and Mutz 1992.

28. Kinder and Kiewiet 1981.

29. See, for example, Brody and Sniderman 1977; and Mutz 1994.

will be the former, sociotropic perception that shapes his trade policy preferences rather than how trade has influenced his personal economic well-being.

To summarize, research on the role of economic well-being on political preferences would warn against the assumption of self-interest as the driving force behind attitudes toward trade. Studies of mass opinion have repeatedly shown that individuals rarely form political preferences on the basis of economic self-interest. Although early studies of U.S. voting behavior attributed the surge enjoyed by incumbent parties in good economic times, and the anti-incumbent preferences in bad economic times, to so-called "pocketbook" voting, once these studies moved beyond aggregates to the individual level of analysis, it became clear that self-interest was not the mechanism driving economic accountability. The people helped or hurt by the economy were not those rewarding and punishing accordingly; instead, accountability rested on citizens' perceptions of how the nation as a whole was faring—perceptions that might or might not be accurate.

In some ways, this account is quite consistent with the relatively poor performance of the leading political economy models in explaining individuals' trade policy attitudes. Effects have appeared weak to nonexistent in many studies or have been derived from measures such as education, the interpretation of which remains ambiguous. Moreover, because many studies have used aggregate-level measures of preferences and impact, and none have asked about sociotropic perceptions, previous research has not been able to distinguish these various sources of trade preferences.

In this study, we use individual-level data that include multiple measures of attitudes toward trade. To date, few analyses of trade preferences have utilized data gathered at the individual level.[30] In all but a handful of studies, trade attitudes have been inferred from aggregate vote results, patterns of campaign contributions, or the outcomes of the policy debates themselves. Importantly, aggregate-level data can produce evidence of self-interested attitudes toward trade policies that is impossible to distinguish from preferences formed on a sociotropic basis, that is, on the basis of how people think the collective as a whole is influenced.

In addition, previous individual-level studies have generally relied on single-item indicators. Individual questions tend to be unreliable and sensitive to question wording and to the framing of options, problems that are easily avoided if responses across a variety of measures produce a reliable index.[31] We also use these data to expand the potential ways in which self-interest might enter into these policy preferences, beyond skill levels and industry impact.

Interestingly, most research on this topic has not viewed trade as a political issue. Instead, the emphasis in explaining trade attitudes has been on how trade

30. These studies include Bauer, Pool, and Dexter 1963; Balistreri 1997; Scheve and Slaughter 2001; Baker 2003 and 2005; Burgoon and Hiscox 2004; Kaltenthaler, Gelleny, and Ceccoli 2004; Mayda and Rodrik 2005; Hays, Ehrlich, and Peinhardt 2005; Hainmueller and Hiscox 2006; Hiscox 2006; and Kocher and Minushkin 2006.

31. See Bauer, Pool, and Dexter 1963, 84–85; Worldviews 2002; and Hiscox 2006.

positively or negatively affects individuals economically. With these data, we examine not only the dominant political economy models, but also the sociotropic hypothesis, which is the preference formation model most widely documented in public opinion research on economic policy preferences. In so doing, we not only improve our overall understanding of the origins of attitudes toward trade, we also reveal the importance of the kind of political information that reaches citizens in explaining American preferences in this policy domain.

Study Design

Using two representative national surveys, we attempt to move beyond ecological inferences and the limitations of previous individual-level surveys by asking working and temporarily unemployed Americans about their attitudes toward trade and related matters. One was a telephone survey conducted as part of the National Annenberg Election Study (NAES) during the summer of 2004.[32] The other was a survey conducted via Internet or Web TV by Knowledge Networks (KN) in summer 2007.

We focus on the attitudes of Americans for various reasons. First, the United States has been the dominant country in the global trading system for more than half a century. As a result, social scientists have expressed substantial interest in the factors driving U.S. trade policy. The attitudes of Americans toward trade are likely to influence outcomes in this policy arena.[33] Second, a number of key studies of trade attitudes center on the United States.[34] Focusing on the attitudes of Americans should enhance the comparability of our results to these previous analyses.

The Dependent Variables

Two survey questions served to construct the dependent variables in the analyses based on the NAES survey:

1. *As you may know, international trade has increased substantially in recent years. This increase is due to the lowering of trade barriers between countries, that is, tariffs or taxes that make it more difficult or more expensive to buy and sell things across international borders. Do you think government should try to encourage international trade or to discourage international*

32. The conservative AAPOR Response Rate I calculation was 23 percent, which represents a minimum possible response rate.

33. Fordham and McKeown 2003.

34. See, for example, Bauer, Pool, and Dexter 1963; Scheve and Slaughter 2001; Burgoon and Hiscox 2004; and Hainmueller and Hiscox 2006, 474–81, 487–91.

trade? Do you think the government should [encourage/discourage] this a lot or only a little?

2. *I'm going to read you some actions the federal government in Washington can take on a variety of issues. For each one please tell me whether you favor or oppose the federal government doing it.... How about the federal government negotiating more free trade agreements like NAFTA? Do you favor or oppose the federal government doing this? Is that strongly [favor/oppose] or only somewhat [favor/oppose]?*

Each item was scored on a five-point scale, or a four-point scale in the KN survey.[35] The highest (lowest) score was assigned to respondents who believed that the government should encourage (discourage) international trade a lot and who strongly favored (opposed) the government negotiating free trade agreements, respectively.[36]

Our first dependent variable is the mean score for these two items. The second dependent variable is an ordered trichotomous measure that equals 1 if a respondent opposes free trade agreements and believes that international trade should be discouraged, and 3 if he or she favors free trade agreements and believes that international trade should be encouraged. All other respondents were scored as 2. This variable therefore groups individuals based on whether they have a consistent preference for open trade or protectionism, or whether their preferences are inconsistent.[37]

Five survey questions were used to generate the dependent variable for the analysis based on the KN survey. The first two questions were identical to those described earlier, but three additional items were asked as well:

3. *Do you believe that globalization, especially the increasing connections of our economy with others around the world, is good or bad for the United States?*
4. *Should foreign companies be encouraged or discouraged from investing in the United States, for example, by building their factories in this country?*
5. *Do you have a very favorable, somewhat favorable, somewhat unfavorable, or very unfavorable opinion of the WTO, the World Trade Organization?*

Each of these items was scored on a four-point scale. The highest (lowest) score was assigned to respondents who believed that the government should strongly

35. These two items are especially useful because one segment of the literature on trade policy preferences focuses on free trade agreements and another segment addresses more general attitudes toward trade. On this first segment, see, for example, Balistreri 1997; and Baker 2003.

36. For the first item, individuals who expressed no opinion or refused to answer were assigned to a middle category; for the second item, such individuals were grouped with respondents who neither favored nor opposed free trade agreements.

37. Combining these two items has various advantages, chiefly that the dependent variable is a more reliable measure and less prone to problems associated with idiosyncratic wording or measurement error than if we analyzed each item separately. On this issue, see Baker 2003, 444, fn. 35.

encourage (discourage) international trade, who strongly favored (opposed) the government negotiating free trade agreements, who felt that globalization is very good (bad) for the United States, who strongly encouraged (discouraged) foreign investment in the United States, and who had a very favorable (unfavorable) opinion of the WTO. The mean of the responses to these five items is our third dependent variable.

Although these items clearly do not address exactly the same issues, it is noteworthy just how consistent people's preferences were across the questions. Experts on these issues might anticipate that people would have different attitudes on the North American Free Trade Agreement (NAFTA) than on free trade more generally, or toward direct foreign investment than toward the World Trade Organization (WTO). Nonetheless, responses to these five questions indicated a very high degree of internal consistency, with a Cronbach's alpha of greater than 0.80 and a Cramer's V that averages about 0.80 for pairs of the items. In short, people's attitudes are very consistent across these facets of international economic relations, so much so that it would be inaccurate to describe them as anything other than a single underlying protrade or antitrade preference.

The Independent Variables

Our key independent variables fall into three broad categories: (1) indicators of the individual characteristics suggested by the factor endowments and specific factors models, (2) indicators of respondents' perceptions of how trade influences their family's financial conditions as well as the country as a whole, and (3) indicators tapping potential noneconomic influences on trade preferences, including nationalism, ethnocentrism, and attitudes toward intervention in the affairs of other countries.

To analyze self-interest within the first category of models, we include measures of a respondent's skill level and features of his or her industry of employment. Economic studies typically use the average annual wage for an individual's occupation and the extent of an individual's formal education to measure skill, a tack that has been followed in much of the research on trade attitudes.[38] In both surveys, we therefore asked individuals, "In your current (or most recent) job, what kind of work do you do?" Each respondent's occupation was then coded using the U.S. Department of Labor's Standard Occupational Classification (SOC) system. We used data compiled by the Department of Labor's Bureau of Labor Statistics to calculate AVERAGE ANNUAL WAGE in 2003 (for the 2004 survey) and in 2006 (for the 2007 survey) for each occupation in our sample.[39] We also asked

38. See Attewell 1990, 425; Spenner 1990, 407; Balistreri 1997; Scheve and Slaughter 2001; Hays, Ehrlich, and Peinhardt 2005; and Mayda and Rodrik 2005.

39. The data on occupation and wages are taken from U.S. Department of Labor 2008a and 2008b, respectively.

each respondent about his or her formal education and created three dummy variables based on this information. The first, SOME COLLEGE, indicates whether the person graduated from a technical school or a two-year college, or whether the respondent attended but did not graduate from a four-college. The second, COLLEGE GRADUATE, indicates whether he or she graduated from a four-year college; and the third, GRADUATE SCHOOL, indicates whether the person attended graduate school. The reference category is someone who did not receive any formal education beyond high school.

To test the specific factors model using the NAES survey, we asked open-ended questions of each respondent about the industry in which they work, as well as details about their occupations. Because the full range of occupations and industries cannot easily be coded in real time, respondents were probed at length for details. Based on audio recordings of their responses, they were later assigned to one of the U.S. Census Bureau's three-digit North American Industry Codes (NAIC).[40] In the KN survey, we presented respondents with a list of the three-digit NAIC categories and asked them to select the one that best described the industry in which they work or most recently worked. For each industry represented in our sample, i, we constructed one measure of export orientation and another measure of import competition. EXPORT ORIENTATION is defined as the natural logarithm of (X_i/Y_i) and IMPORT COMPETITION is defined as the natural logarithm of (M_i/Y_i), where X_i is sector i's total exports, M_i is the volume of imports in sector i, and Y_i is this sector's total output. These variables are derived using 2003 data for the NAES survey and 2006 data for the KN survey.[41] Various industries in our sample are nontradable and therefore do not export or import goods. Since the natural logarithm of zero is undefined, we arbitrarily add 0.01 to both X_i and M_i. The specific factors model predicts that individuals employed in industries that export a substantial portion of output should support open trade, whereas those working in sectors that face extensive competition from imports should be especially hostile to overseas commerce.

To distinguish evidence of self-interested policy preferences from sociotropic ones, an item in both surveys asked how respondents thought the nation as a whole had been influenced by trade. Respondents answered using a five-point scale ranging from "helped a lot" (5) to "hurt a lot" (1).[42] A parallel item asked about the

40. For a list of the three-digit industry classifications, see U.S. Census Bureau 2008a. Note that our sample is representative of the distribution of workers across industries in the U.S. population as a whole. We compared the distribution of respondents across industries in our sample to the distribution in the U.S. population, using data provided by U.S. Census Bureau 2008b. For each industry, the percentage of respondents in our sample is much the same as the percentage of the U.S. workforce.

41. Data on exports and imports are taken from U.S. International Trade Commission 2008. We used version 2.7.4 of the data when analyzing the NAES survey and version 2.8.4 of the data when analyzing the KN survey. Data on output are taken from U.S. Department of Commerce 2008 (Bureau of Economic Analysis).

42. People who refused to answer this question or who said they did not know the answer were grouped together with people who answered that trade neither hurts nor helps the economy.

perceived effect of trade on the financial situation of the person's family. Although the latter variable might appear to be an indicator of subjectively assessed self-interest, it is included to take into account however much slippage may occur between actual self-interest and what people perceive to be in their economic interests. These perceptions are inevitably a function of personal experience, but they also reflect information that causes people to attribute a particular economic situation to international trade.

As shown in Figure 1, both surveys demonstrate a slight skew toward perceptions that trade has adversely affected the economy. The NAES survey produced a roughly uniform distribution across the five response categories from "helped a lot" to "hurt a lot," whereas the KN results are more bimodal, with most respondents feeling that trade has either helped or hurt the economy "a little."

Importantly, both distributions deviate starkly from the distribution on this same scale for the American public's perceived effects of trade on their family's financial well being. Based on both surveys, there is a striking tendency for respondents to claim that trade has not affected their family's financial situation. Indeed, "no effect" is the modal response when people are asked to assess trade's perceived effects on their personal economic situation, which is consistent with the fact that most Americans are employed in nontradable sectors of the economy.

In the KN survey, we also included three indexes designed to help clarify the role of education in shaping trade preferences. Toward this end, we added items addressing three well-studied orientations that are known to be a function of education and that also are potentially linked to attitudes toward foreign commerce. First, regardless of context, well-educated people tend to favor a more activist role for the United States in foreign policy matters. Such individuals, for example, hold more favorable views of the United Nations, are more willing to normalize relations with Cuba, are more likely to favor signing international treaties, and generally endorse a more active role for the United States in foreign affairs than less-educated individuals.[43] Thus, protrade preferences among the well-educated may be a function of the same underlying tendency to involve one's self in affairs beyond national borders. Second, the poorly educated tend to have a stronger sense of nationalism, which might also account for their hostility to open overseas commerce. Finally, ethnocentrism—that is, the tendency to think less of those who are racially or ethnically different from one's own group—is tied to education and may also promote antitrade preferences. To the extent that the observed effects of education stem from any of these factors, it puts a different cast on what drives attitudes toward trade.

Our first index, ISOLATIONISM, is comprised of five widely used items tapping the extent to which respondents believe the United States should adopt an isolationist or an activist stance on international affairs. Notably, these items do not address economic relations between countries so much as whether the United States should

43. See Bauer, Pool, and Dexter 1963, chap. 6; Erikson and Tedin 2005; and Fordham 2008.

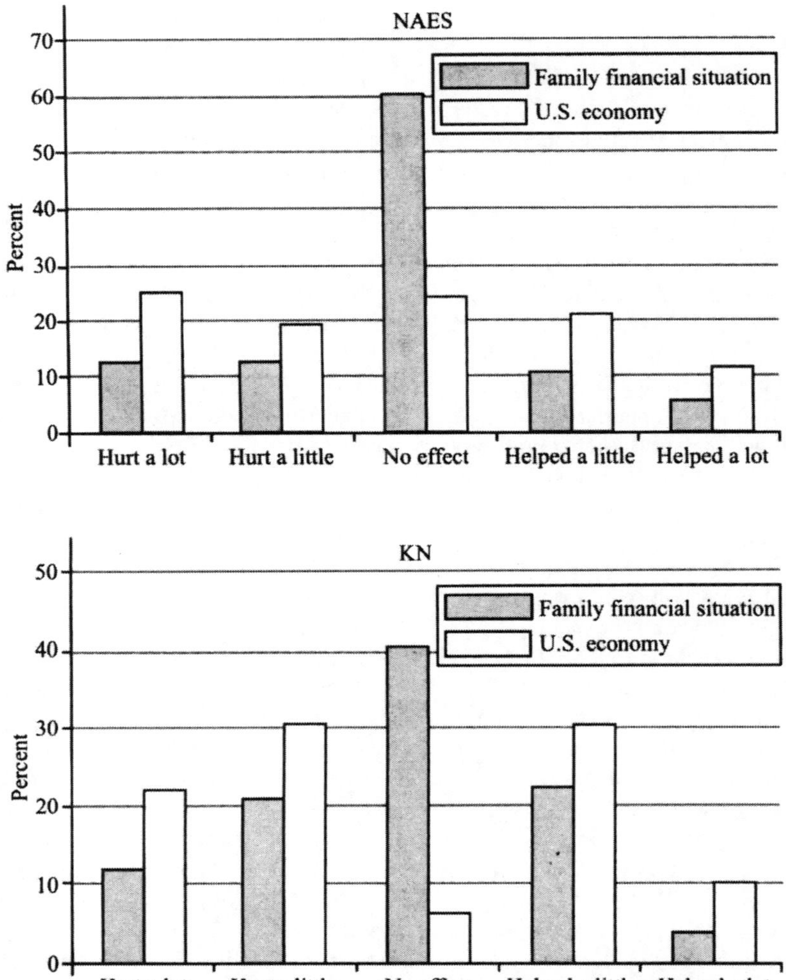

FIGURE 1. *The perceived impact of trade on respondents' families and on the U.S. economy*

intervene to prevent human rights abuses abroad, cooperate with foreign countries to solve global problems, and so forth.[44] The second index, NATIONALISM, draws

44. See Wittkopf and Maggiotto 1983, Maggiotto and Wittkopf 1981; and Herrmann, Tetlock, and Diascro 2001. These five items are as follows. "Please tell us whether you agree or disagree with each of the following statements: [RANDOMIZED ORDER] (1) The U.S. needs to play an active role in

on three previously used questions to assess whether respondents believe that the United States is culturally superior to other countries.[45] The third index, ETHNOCENTRISM, taps "prejudice, broadly conceived."[46] Ethnocentrism scales are designed to measure the "commonplace inclination to divide the world into in-groups and out-groups, the former characterized by virtuosity and talent, the latter by corruption and mediocrity."[47] By asking an individual about some positive and some negative human characteristics with reference to the in-group as well as what are out-groups for that given person, we obtain an indicator of the extent to which the person employs an in-group/out-group mode of thinking.[48] To construct these measures, we use the same racial and ethnic in-groups and out-groups as previous studies (blacks, whites, and Hispanics). Each of these three indexes was highly reliable, with Cronbach's alphas greater than 0.80. All were standardized, with a mean of zero, and coded such that larger positive (negative) values of these variables reflect views that are more (less) isolationist, nationalistic, and ethnocentric, respectively.

In addition, our models include measures of party identification (one variable indicating whether respondents describe themselves as a Democrat and another indicating whether they describe themselves as Republican, with the reference category being someone without a partisan affiliation), whether anyone in the home belonged to a union, whether the respondent was currently unemployed or laid off, age, gender (which equals 1 if the respondent is male and 0 if she is female), and family income.

In the following tests, we use ordinary least squares (OLS) to analyze our nine-point measure of trade policy preferences based on the NAES survey and our measure based on the KN survey, since both of them have a roughly normal distribution. To analyze the ordered trichotomous measure of the consistency of trade policy preferences across the two items, we use an ordered logit specification. All tests

---

solving conflicts around the world; (2) The U.S. government should just try to take care of the well-being of Americans and not get involved with other nations; (3) It is essential for the United States to work with other nations to solve problems, such as overpopulation, hunger, and pollution; (4) It will be best for the future of the country if we stay out of world affairs; (5) The United States has the responsibility to play the role of 'world policeman,' that is, to fight violations of international law and aggression wherever they occur."

45. Rankin 2001. These three items are as follows. "To what extent do you agree or disagree with each of these statements? [RANDOMIZED ORDER]: (1) In the United States, our people are not perfect, but our culture is superior to others; (2) I would rather be a citizen of America than of any other country in the world; (3) The world would be a better place if people from other countries were more like Americans."

46. Levinson 1949, 19.

47. Kam and Kinder 2007, 321. All respondents are asked about their racial ethnic group as well as two out-groups. Ethnocentrism is the difference between the mean for positive-negative characteristics attributed to the in-group and the same characteristics attributed to the out-group. "Next are some questions about various groups in our society. Below are seven-point scales on which you can rate characteristics of people in different groups. Where would you rate physicians in general on this scale? Where would you rate [BLACKS/WHITES/HISPANIC-AMERICANS] in general on these scales?" The scales range from 1 to 7, anchored by Hard Working-Lazy, Efficient-Wasteful, and Trustworthy-Untrustworthy.

48. Levinson 1949.

of statistical significance are based on robust standard errors, which account for any heteroskedasticity in the data and which are clustered by the state in which the respondent resides.

Results

Table 1 shows the results based on the NAES nine-point index of trade opinions, Table 2 reports the results based on the NAES trichotomous index, and Table 3 presents the results based on the mean of the five items on trade opinions from the KN survey. In each table, we start by estimating a model to test the factor endowments and specific factors hypotheses. This model includes occupational wages, education, the industry of employment's exposure to trade, and the control variables. Then we supplement this baseline model with additional variables to evaluate the impact of perceptions of trade's influence on the national economy and to assess the robustness of our results.

Our initial findings offer some apparent support for the factor endowments hypothesis. For each dependent variable, the coefficient estimates of SOME COLLEGE, COLLEGE GRADUATE, and GRADUATE SCHOOL are positive and jointly statistically significant. Furthermore, the results in each table indicate that respondents become increasingly supportive of open trade as they obtain more formal education. The estimated coefficient of SOME COLLEGE is always the smallest among these three variables and the coefficient estimate of GRADUATE SCHOOL is always the largest. Individuals who attended graduate school are much more supportive of open trade than both people with only a high school education and those with some college education. Each coefficient estimate of GRADUATE SCHOOL is statistically significant. Additional analyses of the incremental effect of each additional level of education furnish mixed results.[49] In the KN survey, each additional level of achievement—from high school to some college, and from some college to a four-year college degree—contributes to greater support for trade. Graduate school, on the other hand, does not contribute additional support beyond what one receives by virtue of having completed a four-year college degree. In the NAES study, by contrast, a graduate school education has a statistically significant impact on trade support beyond receiving a four-year degree, whereas prior levels of educational achievement (some college and a college degree) do not contribute significantly.

Whereas education exerts a strong influence on attitudes about trade, the effect of occupational wages is weak. The coefficient estimate of AVERAGE ANNUAL WAGE is positive, which is consistent with the factor endowments approach, but it is

49. The additional analyses to test the incremental effect of each level of educational achievement were conducted by coding education as a set of nested dummy variables. All people with graduate degrees were coded as also having four-year degrees and some college, all who had four-year degrees were coded as also having completed some college, and so forth.

TABLE 1. *The determinants of trade preferences, based on the NAES nine-point index*

Variables	*Model 1*	*Model 2*	*Model 3*	*Model 4*	*Model 5*
SOME COLLEGE	0.068	−0.024	−0.041	−0.025	−0.070
	(0.089)	(0.082)	(0.074)	(0.082)	(0.070)
COLLEGE GRADUATE	0.164	0.111	0.131+	0.110	0.060
	(0.122)	(0.087)	(0.071)	(0.087)	(0.069)
GRADUATE SCHOOL	0.377***	0.304**	0.319***	0.305**	0.248**
	(0.100)	(0.089)	(0.082)	(0.089)	(0.078)
AVERAGE ANNUAL WAGE	0.000	0.000		0.000	
	(0.000)	(0.000)		(0.000)	
EXPORT ORIENTATION	−0.174	−0.033	0.089		0.076
	(0.170)	(0.133)	(0.114)		(0.114)
IMPORT COMPETITION	0.129	0.011	−0.097		−0.090
	(0.163)	(0.126)	(0.108)		(0.109)
TARIFF RATE				−0.025	
				(0.021)	
PERCEIVED EFFECT OF TRADE ON U.S.		0.361***	0.380***	0.363***	0.297***
		(0.024)	(0.020)	(0.024)	(0.020)
PERCEIVED EFFECT OF TRADE ON SELF					0.247***
					(0.033)
UNION MEMBERSHIP	−0.443***	−0.331***	−0.338***	−0.331***	−0.325***
	(0.079)	(0.070)	(0.055)	(0.070)	(0.053)
UNEMPLOYED	−0.168	0.034	0.030	0.033	0.085
	(0.186)	(0.183)	(0.174)	(0.183)	(0.158)
REPUBLICAN	0.014	−0.047	−0.018	−0.047	−0.074
	(0.065)	(0.069)	(0.068)	(0.068)	(0.066)
DEMOCRAT	−0.173+	−0.082	−0.078	−0.080	−0.090
	(0.097)	(0.088)	(0.069)	(0.088)	(0.070)
MALE	0.211*	0.128	0.076	0.123	0.064
	(0.101)	(0.084)	(0.068)	(0.083)	(0.066)
AGE	−0.003	−0.002	−0.002	−0.002	−0.003
	(0.003)	(0.003)	(0.002)	(0.003)	(0.002)
INCOME	0.017	0.000	−0.014	−0.000	−0.014
	(0.026)	(0.024)	(0.019)	(0.024)	(0.017)
Constant	2.992***	2.201***	2.334***	2.184***	1.927***
	(0.212)	(0.204)	(0.166)	(0.220)	(0.155)
R-square	0.077	0.253	0.263	0.252	0.293
Adjusted R-square	0.062	0.240	0.254	0.240	0.284
N	851	851	1084	851	1084

Notes: Entries are ordinary least squares regression estimates with robust standard errors, clustered by the respondent's state of residence, in parentheses. Two-tailed tests of statistical significance are conducted for all coefficient estimates. Statistical significance is indicated as follows: $+ p < .10$; $* p < .05$; $** p < .01$; $*** p < .001$.

small and far from statistically significant. Furthermore, the results offer no support for the specific factors hypothesis since neither EXPORT ORIENTATION nor IMPORT COMPETITION has a statistically significant impact on trade preferences.

There is little evidence that individuals form attitudes about trade based on how trade affects their income. But as shown in the second columns of Tables 1, 2, and 3, there is strong evidence that these attitudes are formed in response to perceptions of how trade affects the U.S. economy. Respondents who feel that trade benefits the economy as a whole are significantly more likely to favor open trade than

TABLE 2. *The determinants of trade preferences, based on the NAES trichotomous index*

Variables	*Model 1*	*Model 2*	*Model 3*	*Model 4*	*Model 5*
SOME COLLEGE	0.111	−0.004	−0.003	−0.006	−0.049
	(0.154)	(0.163)	(0.152)	(0.163)	(0.150)
COLLEGE GRADUATE	0.256	0.216	0.247	0.215	0.130
	(0.220)	(0.179)	(0.151)	(0.180)	(0.151)
GRADUATE SCHOOL	0.598**	0.596**	0.507**	0.597**	0.388*
	(0.187)	(0.190)	(0.166)	(0.191)	(0.163)
AVERAGE ANNUAL WAGE	0.000	0.000		0.000	
	(0.000)	(0.000)		(0.000)	
EXPORT ORIENTATION	−0.280	−0.056	0.172		0.156
	(0.299)	(0.261)	(0.223)		(0.234)
IMPORT COMPETITION	0.209	0.020	−0.181		−0.175
	(0.282)	(0.244)	(0.209)		(0.221)
TARIFF RATE				−0.038	
				(0.044)	
PERCEIVED EFFECT OF TRADE ON U.S.		0.639***	0.669***	0.641***	0.536***
		(0.051)	(0.042)	(0.050)	(0.043)
PERCEIVED EFFECT OF TRADE ON SELF					0.429***
					(0.071)
UNION MEMBERSHIP	−0.626***	−0.493***	−0.487***	−0.493***	−0.474***
	(0.120)	(0.132)	(0.098)	(0.132)	(0.097)
UNEMPLOYED	−0.287	0.020	0.040	0.018	0.132
	(0.340)	(0.402)	(0.379)	(0.402)	(0.369)
REPUBLICAN	0.036	−0.086	−0.047	−0.086	−0.141
	(0.139)	(0.151)	(0.137)	(0.150)	(0.136)
DEMOCRAT	−0.276	−0.159	−0.192	−0.155	−0.219
	(0.185)	(0.195)	(0.161)	(0.194)	(0.161)
MALE	0.393*	0.290+	0.185	0.280+	0.167
	(0.164)	(0.154)	(0.135)	(0.155)	(0.136)
AGE	−0.004	−0.002	−0.005	−0.002	−0.006
	(0.005)	(0.005)	(0.004)	(0.005)	(0.004)
INCOME	0.024	−0.009	−0.031	−0.010	−0.030
	(0.040)	(0.042)	(0.031)	(0.042)	(0.029)
Cut_1	−1.247***	0.003	−0.348	0.020	0.353
	(0.359)	(0.400)	(0.290)	(0.429)	(0.299)
Cut_2	1.125**	2.710***	2.362***	2.725***	3.124***
	(0.378)	(0.409)	(0.295)	(0.439)	(0.313)
Pseudo log likelihood	−829.509	−759.039	−969.012	−759.390	−953.927
Pseudo R-square	0.030	0.113	0.114	0.112	0.128
N	851	851	1084	851	1084

Notes: Entries are ordered logit estimates with robust standard errors, clustered by the respondent's state of residence, in parentheses. Two-tailed tests of statistical significance are conducted for all coefficient estimates. Statistical significance is indicated as follows: + $p < .10$; * $p < .05$; ** $p < .01$; *** $p < .001$.

those who believe that trade is economically harmful, providing considerable support for sociotropic arguments about overseas commerce. Including PERCEIVED EFFECT OF TRADE ON U.S. substantially strengthens the model's explanatory power, increasing the adjusted coefficient of variation (R^2) by about fourfold in Table 1 and by roughly sevenfold in Table 3. In addition, doing so weakens the effects of gender, partisanship, and age.

Our initial results—in the first column of Tables 1, 2, and 3—provide clear evidence of a gender gap, with women holding more protectionist attitudes than men.[50] There is also evidence of a partisan split, although the nature of this split differs across the two surveys. Based on the findings in Table 1, Democrats are more protectionist than either unaffiliated individuals or Republicans. Based on the findings in Table 3, there is no difference between the estimated coefficients of DEMOCRAT and REPUBLICAN, but Republicans are more protectionist than unaffiliated voters. Equally, the results in Table 3 indicate that people become more protectionist as they grow older. All of these relationships except the split between Republicans and unaffiliated voters in Table 3, however, become attenuated once we add the sociotropic variable to the model. Including this variable also reduces the magnitude of education's impact on preferences about overseas commerce, especially when analyzing the KN index.

Consistent with existing research, Tables 1 and 2 further indicate that union membership affects an individual's attitude toward trade.[51] Respondents who either were a union member or had a union member in their family were much less likely to be protrade than those without a union affiliation. However, income seems to have no bearing on trade preferences. In addition, what little evidence there is that unemployment influences these preferences (see the second and third columns of Table 3) becomes much weaker once we account for respondents' perceptions of how trade has influenced their family financial situation (see the fourth column of Table 3).

Taken together, our results indicate that perceptions of how trade affects the U.S. economy, union membership, and education strongly influence mass opinion about trade. To further analyze the impact of these factors, we estimate the effects of a change in each factor on the predicted probability that our trichotomous dependent variable equals 1 (consistent opposition to trade) and 3 (consistent support for trade), respectively. These predicted probabilities are generated using Stata's *prvalue* program, based on the model in the second column of Table 2, and setting the remaining continuous variables to their sample means and the remaining discrete variables to their modal categories.[52]

The results indicate that the perception of trade's effects on the U.S. economy has a sizable impact on trade preferences. A change from not being sure whether trade benefits the U.S. economy (a score of 3) to the view that trade has helped the economy "a little" (a score of 4) yields about a 50 percent increase in the probability that a respondent consistently supports free trade; a change to the belief that trade helps the economy "a lot" (a score of 5) yields roughly a 100 percent increase in this probability.

50. See O'Rourke and Sinnott 2002; Burgoon and Hiscox 2004; Baker 2005; Hays, Ehrlich, and Peinhardt 2005; and Mayda and Rodrik 2005.

51. See Balistreri 1997; and Mayda and Rodrik 2005.

52. On this program, see Long and Freese 2005. Note that these results are virtually identical if we rely on the estimates in the third or fourth columns of Table 2.

TABLE 3. *The determinants of trade preferences, based on the KN index*

Variables	*Model 1*	*Model 2*	*Model 3*	*Model 4*	*Model 5*	*Model 6*
SOME COLLEGE	0.146*	0.072	0.073	0.069	0.050	0.027
	(0.061)	(0.051)	(0.050)	(0.050)	(0.048)	(0.048)
COLLEGE GRADUATE	0.284***	0.155***	0.158***	0.143**	0.107*	0.056
	(0.061)	(0.044)	(0.043)	(0.043)	(0.043)	(0.043)
GRADUATE SCHOOL	0.338***	0.177**	0.181***	0.153**	0.121*	0.031
	(0.063)	(0.051)	(0.051)	(0.054)	(0.057)	(0.050)
AVERAGE ANNUAL WAGE	0.000	−0.000	−0.000	−0.000	−0.000	−0.000
	(0.000)	(0.000)	(0.000)	(0.000)	(0.000)	(0.000)
EXPORT ORIENTATION	0.030	−0.017		−0.043	−0.038	−0.029
	(0.051)	(0.026)		(0.027)	(0.029)	(0.026)
IMPORT COMPETITION	−0.032	0.017		0.040	0.035	0.030
	(0.045)	(0.024)		(0.025)	(0.027)	(0.025)
TARIFF RATE			0.007			
			(0.009)			
PERCEIVED EFFECT OF TRADE ON U.S.		0.300***	0.300***	0.257***	0.254***	0.249***
		(0.010)	(0.010)	(0.011)	(0.011)	(0.012)
PERCEIVED EFFECT OF TRADE ON SELF				0.101***	0.100***	0.075***
				(0.015)	(0.016)	(0.018)
UNION MEMBERSHIP	−0.001	0.045	0.046	0.052	0.054	0.066
	(0.053)	(0.043)	(0.043)	(0.043)	(0.043)	(0.048)
UNEMPLOYED	−0.126	−0.128*	−0.130*	−0.089	−0.089	−0.075
	(0.090)	(0.062)	(0.063)	(0.063)	(0.063)	(0.070)
REPUBLICAN	−0.118*	−0.095*	−0.096*	−0.113**	−0.110*	−0.123*
	(0.052)	(0.041)	(0.041)	(0.042)	(0.042)	(0.047)
DEMOCRAT	−0.081	−0.032	−0.034	−0.034	−0.032	−0.044
	(0.061)	(0.039)	(0.039)	(0.038)	(0.039)	(0.048)
MALE	0.100**	0.035	0.033	0.034	0.024	0.009
	(0.032)	(0.030)	(0.030)	(0.030)	(0.029)	(0.031)
AGE	−0.004*	−0.002	−0.002	−0.002	−0.001	−0.002
	(0.002)	(0.001)	(0.001)	(0.001)	(0.001)	(0.001)
INCOME	0.010	0.010	0.010	0.006	0.003	0.005
	(0.012)	(0.010)	(0.010)	(0.010)	(0.009)	(0.009)
ECONOMICS CLASS					0.044	0.056+
					(0.026)	(0.030)
ECONOMISTS' VIEW OF TRADE					0.062*	0.055+
					(0.026)	(0.027)
ISOLATIONISM						−0.099***
						(0.011)
ETHNOCENTRISM						−0.029**
						(0.010)
NATIONALISM						−0.023
						(0.019)
Constant	2.723***	1.902***	1.936***	1.754***	1.759***	1.886***
	(0.087)	(0.084)	(0.090)	(0.076)	(0.077)	(0.087)
R-square	0.070	0.446	0.446	0.463	0.466	0.480
Adjusted R-square	0.064	0.442	0.442	0.458	0.461	0.474
N	1995	1995	1995	1995	1992	1822

Notes: Entries are ordinary least squares regression estimates with robust standard errors, clustered by the respondent's state of residence, in parentheses. Two-tailed tests of statistical significance are conducted for all coefficient estimates. Statistical significance is indicated as follows: + $p < .10$; * $p < .05$; ** $p < .01$; *** $p < .001$.

Union membership also has a considerable influence on the probability of supporting trade. People with a union member in their household are about 35 percent more likely to oppose trade than other individuals. At first blush, it is tempting to interpret the effect of union membership as an indicator of self-interested preferences. This might be the case if union members work in industries that are adversely affected by trade or are relatively low-skilled workers. However, we have already accounted for the industry of employment and skill level, suggesting that union membership is not simply a feature of self-interest. Instead, unions probably influence attitudes on trade by disseminating information: most major unions oppose trade liberalization and free trade arrangements, and promote such views among their rank and file. Interestingly, most union members in our surveys work in nontradable sectors, such as primary, secondary, and higher education. There is no reason why trade would harm these individuals.

Education also has a marked effect on trade preferences. People with a graduate school education, for example, are about 65 percent more likely to consistently support trade than people with either a high school education or some college education but not a four-year degree. All of these effects are statistically significant.[53]

It is worth considering whether sociotropic perceptions of how trade affects the nation as a whole are potentially rationalized from pre-existing policy opinions. In other words, might people have a priori opinions on trade from some other influence and then rationalize from those issue preferences to an evaluation of how trade affects the nation's economy?

In using sociotropic perceptions of trade's impact as a predictor of trade preferences, we did not assume that such perceptions were completely exogenous. Indeed, previous work suggests that sociotropic perceptions of closely related issues such as unemployment and national economic decline are spawned by media coverage as well as by local economic conditions.[54] Moreover, there is some evidence to suggest that the same pattern of origins is true of trade perceptions.[55] Whereas media coverage may alter sociotropic perceptions, it generally has no direct effect on opinions, thus implying that the ordering we have suggested must be largely correct. Information sources alter collective-level perceptions, and these in turn alter policy preferences.[56]

Importantly, it is obvious from our results that inclusion of the sociotropic variable has no bearing on whether the variables representing self-interest demon-

53. Recall that, based on the results in Table 3, there is also evidence of a split between Republicans and unaffiliated individuals. However, the magnitude of this split is quite modest. A change in party affiliation from unaffiliated to Republican yields less than a 4 percent reduction in the predicted value of the KN index, holding constant the continuous variables in our model at their sample means and the remaining discrete variables at their modal categories.

54. See, for example, Erbring, Goldenberg, and Miller 1980; Conover, Feldman, and Knight 1986; and Mutz 1998.

55. See Busch and Reinhardt 2000; and Mansfield and Mutz 2006.

56. Mutz 1992.

strate influence. Regardless of ordering, we find little evidence that self-interest forms the basis of trade preferences. But if sociotropic perceptions were merely rationalizations of pre-existing issue attachments, one would expect panel data to show null effects from changing sociotropic perceptions over time. However, as in our results, panel analyses show that sociotropic perceptions have a strong and significant influence on political preferences.[57]

The Robustness of the Results

Having generated some initial estimates of our models, we now assess the robustness of our results. First, in coding the data on occupation based on the NAES survey, it was not possible to assign every respondent an SOC code. Consequently, the size of our sample in Tables 1 and 2 is reduced when including AVERAGE ANNUAL WAGE in the model. Since this variable has little impact on trade preferences and to ensure that the effects of the remaining variables remain stable when we analyze the largest possible sample, we estimate the models using the NAES data after dropping AVERAGE ANNUAL WAGE. As shown in the third column of Tables 1 and 2, this change in the model's specification has no bearing on any variable except COLLEGE GRADUATE, which now has a marginally significant effect in Table 1, and MALE, which no longer has a statistically significant effect in Table 2.

Second, our initial findings do not support the specific factors hypothesis. One reason might be the measures we used to test this hypothesis. In addition to measuring the export orientation and import competition of a respondent's industry of employment, a few studies have analyzed whether the tariff rate of this industry affects his or her trade preferences.[58] Hence, we replace the variables tapping export orientation and import competition with a measure of his or her industry's 2003 (for the NAES survey) or 2006 (for the KN survey) tariff rate.[59] Like Scheve and Slaughter, we estimate the effective tariff rate by taking the natural logarithm of the ratio of customs revenue to total imports in each sector, using data compiled by the U.S. International Trade Commission.[60] Nontradable sectors are assigned a tariff rate of zero. Since the natural logarithm of zero is undefined, we arbitrarily add 0.01 to each (unlogged) tariff rate, thereby retaining all of our original observations.

57. See, for example, Kiewiet 1983.

58. See, for example, Scheve and Slaughter 2001.

59. We do not include export orientation, import competition, and the tariff rate in the same model because the first two variables are fairly highly correlated with the latter variable.

60. Scheve and Slaughter 2001. The data are available at U.S. International Trade Commission 2008. We used version 2.7.4 of the data when analyzing the NAES survey and version 2.8.4 of the data when analyzing the KN survey.

Scheve and Slaughter argue that industries marked by extensive protection are likely to be at a comparative disadvantage.[61] As such, the specific-factors model predicts individuals in such industries should be hostile to open trade and should press for protectionism. Our tests, however, continue to provide no support for this approach. As shown in the fourth columns of Tables 1 and 2 and the third column of Table 3, the coefficient estimate of TARIFF RATE is always small and far from statistically significant.

Third, to bolster assessment of self-interest beyond the factor endowments and specific factors measures, respondents in the NAES survey also were asked direct questions about the extent to which their place of work is involved in importing and exporting. They were asked whether their workplace: (1) exports products, (2) imports products, (3) supplies products or services to companies that import or export, or (4) outsources some of its work to other countries. None of these measures of how trade affects their place of employment had a significant bearing on trade preferences. Nor did including these variables have any impact on the remaining results.

To further address whether the effects of trade on an individual's personal life influences or his or her trade preferences, we included in the model respondents' perceptions of how they and their family had been influenced by open trade, as illustrated in Figure 1. Including this variable in our models of trade preferences is particularly important because we want to ensure that the observed effect of people's attitudes about how trade affects the nation is not simply an outgrowth of their attitudes about how trade has influenced them on a personal level. The results in the final column of Tables 1 and 2 and the fourth column of Table 3 show that people who feel that trade has helped them and their family support trade.[62] In all three tables, the coefficient estimate of PERCEIVED EFFECT OF TRADE ON SELF is positive and statistically significant. These estimates are also fairly large. For example, a change from not being sure whether trade benefits a respondent (a score of 3) to holding the opinion that trade helps him or her "a little" (a score of 4) yields about a 40 percent increase in the probability that a respondent consistently supports free trade; a change to the belief that trade helps the person "a lot" (a score of 5) yields roughly a 90 percent increase in this probability. Nonetheless, the effect of this variable is somewhat less than that of the sociotropic variable, whose coefficient is only marginally smaller than in our earlier analysis, and this difference is statistically significant based on the results in Table 3. Even after accounting for subjective perceptions of how trade affects a respondent, perceptions of how trade influences the nation have a strong and sizable impact on whether people support open trade.

Finally, a number of previous studies have included the effects of marital status, race, urban-rural residence, and religiosity in models of trade preferences. To

61. Scheve and Slaughter 2001.

62. We present the results without AVERAGE ANNUAL WAGE to maximize the sample size, but the results do not change when this variable is included.

assess the robustness of our results, we included these variables one at a time and in combination. There is no case in which any of these factors strongly influences trade preferences and including them had no bearing on the remaining results.

Interpreting the Effects of Education

We have found that as Americans obtain more formal education, they become increasingly likely to prefer free trade. Most studies have viewed education as a proxy for skill and therefore interpret findings such as these as supportive of the factor endowments approach. As noted earlier, Hainmueller and Hiscox have challenged this interpretation, maintaining that a college education affects trade opinions, above and beyond increasing human capital and skill, by exposing people to theories about the benefits of trade.[63] This exposure, rather than the occupational skills acquired in the classroom, is why education is positively associated with preferences for open trade in the United States. To test their argument, Hainmueller and Hiscox compared the effects of education (especially a college education) on trade attitudes for people in the workforce and for retirees. If education is a proxy for skill, they reasoned, the factor endowments approach predicts that it should have a much greater influence on the trade policy attitudes of people in the workforce than on retirees. Their results provided no evidence of this sort; nor do ours.

First, we added retirees who were included in the NAES survey to our sample of respondents. We then added four variables to our model: (1) an indicator variable for whether the respondent was retired or in the workforce, and (2) the interaction between this variable and SOME COLLEGE, COLLEGE GRADUATE, and GRADUATE SCHOOL, respectively.[64] (We dropped AVERAGE ANNUAL WAGE, EXPORT ORIENTATION, IMPORT COMPETITION, and UNEMPLOYED since these do not apply to retirees.) Our results indicate that, for any given amount of formal education, the difference in the predicted value of each dependent variable between individuals in and out of the workforce is less than three percent. Clearly, the effects of education do not vary in any meaningful way between these sets of people.

Second, in order to directly test Hainmueller and Hiscox's argument, we included two items on the KN survey. The first asked whether respondents had taken an economics course. The second asked whether economists believe that free trade is good or bad for the economy. We included the latter item to determine whether an understanding of the basic principles of international economics affects trade attitudes, regardless of whether someone has taken an economics course. We then created two dummy variables. ECONOMICS CLASS equals 1 if a respondent has taken such a course, 0 otherwise. ECONOMISTS' VIEW OF TRADE equals 1 if a respondent

63. Hainmueller and Hiscox 2006.
64. Note that retirees make up about 19 percent of the sample in this analysis.

understands that economists believe that free trade is good for the economy, 0 otherwise. If Hainmueller and Hiscox are correct, then the estimated coefficients of these variables should be positive and statistically significant. The coefficients of SOME COLLEGE, COLLEGE GRADUATE, and GRADUATE EDUCATION, however, should not be significant.

The results shown in the fifth column of Table 3 provide some support for Hainmueller and Hiscox's thesis. The estimated coefficients of the two variables tapping exposure to ideas about the benefits of trade are both positive. ECONOMISTS' VIEW OF TRADE has a statistically significant effect, whereas the influence of ECONOMICS CLASS is marginally significant ($p = .105$). Nonetheless, economic knowledge has a small impact on trade attitudes: taking an economics class or understanding that economists argue that free trade is beneficial increases the predicted value of the KN dependent variable by only 2 to 3 percent, holding constant the remaining variables in the model. Equally, the estimated coefficients of SOME COLLEGE, COLLEGE GRADUATE, and GRADUATE SCHOOL, although somewhat smaller than before, remain jointly significant; and the coefficients of the latter two variables remain positive and statistically significant. The impact of education on trade attitudes stems from far more than a knowledge of basic economic principles.

What, then, underlies the influence of education? To gain a better understanding of this issue, we turn to an analysis of noneconomic influences, including ETHNOCENTRISM, NATIONALISM, and ISOLATIONISM, indexes drawn from the KN survey that we described earlier and that are likely to be closely tied to educational attainment. The effects of these variables are reported in the final column of Table 3. The coefficient estimates of all three variables are negative, indicating that there is little support for free trade among people who believe the United States is superior to other countries, hold isolationist views, and exhibit evidence of prejudice toward groups unlike themselves. The effects of isolationist attitudes and ethnocentrism are statistically significant. These effects are also relatively large. A change from the most globally interventionist attitudes registered by respondents to the most isolationist attitudes reduces the predicted value of our measure of trade attitudes by almost 20 percent. A shift from the least ethnocentric views to the most ethnocentric views reduces this predicted value by about 12 percent. Both of these changes are statistically significant.

Not only do ISOLATIONISM and ETHNOCENTRISM have a strong bearing on preferences about trade, they also account for the effects of education. After including ISOLATIONISM, ETHNOCENTRISM, and NATIONALISM in the model, the estimated coefficients of SOME COLLEGE, COLLEGE GRADUATE, and GRADUATE SCHOOL become substantially smaller. Moreover, none of these coefficients are even close to statistically significant and they are no longer jointly significant. The smaller and weaker effects of education stem from the impact of ISOLATIONISM and ETHNOCENTRISM, rather than NATIONALISM. If we exclude ISOLATIONISM and ETHNOCENTRISM but include NATIONALISM, the effects of education grow larger and stronger. In fact, the coefficients of the variables pertaining to education are almost identical to the corresponding coefficients in the fifth column of Table 3, a finding that accords with previous research on the relationship between nationalism and trade attitudes.[65] Consequently, the effects of education reflect differences in attitudes about the extent to which the United States should take an activist stance in international affairs and a general tendency to think less of out-groups relative to in-groups.

At one level, these results might seem curious. Why, for example, does a belief that the United States should play the role of "world policeman" in preventing human rights abuses in other countries have anything to do with trade preferences? Why should how blacks feel about whites and Hispanics (or vice-versa) have anything to do with trade liberalization? Activist foreign policy attitudes, a positive attitude toward out-groups, and a preference for open trade, however, all reflect a sense of cosmopolitanism and inclusion. Isolationism, a negative attitude toward out-groups, and antipathy toward open trade all reflect a sense of insularity and separatism. In short, trade preferences are driven less by economic considerations and more by an individual's psychological worldview.

Conclusion

It is widely acknowledged that any complete model of the political economy of trade must account for the preferences of the mass public.[66] These preferences influence trade policy because government officials need to attend to constituent interests to retain office.[67] Despite the obvious importance of understanding the factors that influence attitudes about trade, however, there have been only a handful of studies on this topic.

Much of the research to date emphasizes that trade preferences are shaped by how overseas commerce affects an individual's income. The factor endowments or Heckscher-Ohlin framework posits that these preferences are affected primarily by a person's skills. In a country such as the United States, highly skilled individuals will benefit economically from open trade and therefore should prefer the expansion of foreign commerce, while less skilled individuals should oppose it. The specific factors or Ricardo-Viner framework posits that people who work in import-competing industries should oppose open trade because foreign competition is likely to degrade their income and threaten their jobs, whereas those who are employed in export-oriented industries should support it.

As with most existing studies of attitudes toward trade, we find limited support for either approach. Occupational wages, a widely used measure of skill, have no

65. See O'Rourke and Sinnott 2002; and Mayda and Rodrik 2005. Note that our measure of nationalism is virtually identical to the measures used in these earlier studies.

66. See Rodrik 1995; Scheve and Slaughter 2001; and O'Rourke and Sinnott 2002.

67. Fordham and McKeown 2003.

effect on attitudes about trade. On the other hand, highly educated Americans are much more likely to support open trade than are less-educated individuals. Some previous studies have interpreted this result as support for the factor endowments approach. However, we have found that that there is reason to be wary of this interpretation. In this study, we conducted the first systematic analysis of the influence of isolationism and ethnocentrism on trade attitudes. Our findings reveal that the observed effects of education reflect negative attitudes toward out-groups, as well as views about whether U.S. foreign policy should be isolationist or interventionist. Isolationism and domestic ethnocentrism are strongly linked to hostility toward free trade. People who have less formal education also hold more negative attitudes toward those different from themselves. Although there are several theories as to how and why education increases tolerance and promotes more cosmopolitan worldviews, there is little doubt that these factors are closely linked. After accounting for the effects of isolationism and ethnocentrism, we find that education has no direct effect on trade attitudes, thus suggesting that its effects represent out-group anxiety rather than economic self-interest.

In addition, we find no support for the specific factors approach. The revealed comparative (dis)advantage of the industry in which an individual is employed does not influence his or her opinions in the way that this approach predicts. Nor does the tariff level of the industry in which he or she works. In short, despite our efforts to gather detailed information on industry of employment and on individual skill levels, the self-interest hypothesis has little explanatory power when it comes to understanding attitudes toward trade.

Besides out-group anxiety, we find that opinions on trade are driven by perceptions of trade's impact on the nation as a whole. While at one level this finding may seem obvious, because existing studies have emphasized that trade preferences are shaped by self-interest, they have largely ignored the influence of the information that drives perceptions of trade's collective-level impact on the nation. We argue that this oversight is a significant shortcoming. Americans' attitudes about trade are guided in powerful ways by whether they believe that trade harms or benefits the national economy, and this perception is not a mere extension of their personal self-interest. If sociotropic perceptions were merely personal interests projected onto the country at large, then we would not expect the impact of perceptions to be consistently strong and influential in shaping trade attitudes in models that simultaneously demonstrate little, if any, impact from indicators of objective self-interest.

The fact that sociotropic perceptions powerfully shape trade attitudes begs the question of where these perceptions originate. Although a thorough analysis of this question is beyond the scope of this study, scholars studying the origins of sociotropic perceptions in other economic policy arenas have identified three likely sources. First, many have found that mass media coverage of the economy plays an important role in forming these perceptions. To the extent that negative economic indicators and downturns are stressed in press coverage, perceptions of the economy also tend to become more negative, regardless of whether people are personally experiencing these downturns.[68] Likewise, when unemployment is emphasized in local and national media, individuals' perceptions of the state of unemployment also become more negative.[69] Any tendency for the press to place greater emphasis on the harmful impact of trade and less emphasis on the beneficial impact might help to account for the negatively skewed sociotropic perceptions shown in Figure 1.

In addition to mass media, local economic conditions that individuals learn about through interpersonal contact and casual conversations also influence their perceptions of the direction of national economic change. Although evidence is less extensive on this point, even those individuals who are not personally affected by trade policies can form impressions of its impact based on acquaintances who have been personally influenced.[70] In the case of trade, formal coursework in economics and related disciplines may also shape perceptions of whether trade is good or bad for the U.S. economy. Finally, perceptions of national-level conditions could be affected by personal experience, although most available evidence suggests that this relationship is fairly weak since people tend to compartmentalize personal-level and collective-level information.[71] Overall, our findings suggest that a better understanding of trade preferences among the mass public requires that we account for the broader information environment in which policy attitudes are formed, as well as the psychological predispositions of individuals.

The strong implication of our study is that standard political economy models are limited in what they can explain about trade preferences. Self-interest accounts for at best only a small portion of the variance in attitudes about trade. Incorporating the effects of sociotropic perceptions, isolationism, and out-group anxiety substantially increases the explanatory power of models of such attitudes. These results conform to what public opinion research has shown about how people form economic policy preferences more generally. Moreover, they point to the need for studies of trade policy to focus more attention on the development of psychologically informed models addressing how people process economic information, and whether political leaders are accurately held accountable for the effects of trade policies.

In one sense our findings were foreshadowed by research almost half a century ago, although this approach did not become dominant in explaining trade preferences. As early as 1963, Bauer, Pool, and Dexter noted that education's importance in shaping attitudes toward foreign trade in the United States exceeded even that of the economic characteristics of a respondent.[72] Unfortunately, they lacked the kind of specific information we have accumulated on individual skill levels

68. See, for example, Adoni and Cohen 1978; Erbring, Goldenberg, and Miller 1980; MacKuen and Coombs 1981; and Behr and Iyengar 1985.

69. Mutz 1992.

70. Conover, Feldman, and Knight 1986.

71. See Tyler 1980 and 1984; and Tyler and Cook 1984.

72. Bauer, Pool, and Dexter 1963.

and industries, and thus they could not differentiate between various explanations as to why education was so influential. These same scholars were also prescient in recognizing the role of communications in shaping perceptions of trade's impact, noting that press coverage in the 1950s was probably what changed public perceptions of whether trade was beneficial for the country. Finally, Bauer, Pool, and Dexter argued, as we have, that attitudes toward trade were driven in part by more general attitudes toward isolationism and internationalism.[73]

The implications of out-group anxiety for trade policy are particularly worrisome because anxiety toward out-groups is such a widespread reaction to what is unfamiliar. Although our findings are limited to a sample of Americans, we suspect that they generalize to other nations as well, precisely because fear of outsiders is so commonplace. Although the structure of economies differs greatly from country to country, human psychology tends to cross national borders easily. The origins of ethnocentric worldviews have been extensively studied, thus enabling some understanding of its origins.

Moreover, our findings may help to explain why previous studies have found that education is positively associated with support for trade liberalization, even in countries in which skilled labor is a scarce factor.[74] To the extent that education promotes cosmopolitanism and reduces out-group anxiety, its effects should be in the same direction in a wide variety of countries. Future approaches to explaining trade preferences will inevitably need to integrate the impact of information about how trade is perceived to affect the economy as well as the symbolic, psychological threat posed by U.S. involvement in foreign markets.

References

Adoni, Hannah, and Akiba A. Cohen. 1978. Television Economic News and the Social Construction of Economic Reality. *Journal of Communication* 28 (4):61–70.

Alston, Richard M., J. R. Kearl, and Michael B. Vaughan. 1992. Is There a Consensus Among Economists in the 1990's? *American Economic Review* 82 (2):203–9.

Attewell, Paul. 1990. What Is Skill? *Work and Occupations* 17 (4):422–48.

Baker, Andy. 2003. Why Is Trade Reform So Popular in Latin America? A Consumption-Based Theory of Trade Policy Preferences. *World Politics* 55 (3):423–55.

———. 2005. Who Wants to Globalize? Consumer Tastes and Labor Markets in a Theory of Trade Policy Beliefs. *American Journal of Political Science* 49 (4):924–38.

Balistreri, Edward J. 1997. The Performance of the Heckscher-Ohlin-Vanek Model in Predicting Endogenous Policy Forces at the Individual Level. *Canadian Journal of Economics* 30 (1):1–17.

Bauer, Raymond A., Ithiel de Sola Pool, and Lewis Anthony Dexter. 1963. *American Business and Public Policy: The Politics of Foreign Trade*. New York: Atherton.

Beaulieu, Eugene, Michael Benarroch, and James Donald Gaisford. 2004. Intra-Industry Trade Liberalization, Wage Inequality and Trade Policy Preferences. Unpublished manuscript, Department of Economics, University of Calgary, Canada.

73. Ibid., 96–99.
74. See Beaulieu, Benarroch, and Gaisford 2004; and Beaulieu, Yatawara, and Wang 2005.

Beaulieu, Eugene, Ravindra A. Yatawara, and Wei Guo Wang. 2005. Who Supports Free Trade in Latin America? *World Economy* 28 (7):941–58.

Behr, Roy L., and Shanto Iyengar. 1985. Television News, Real World Cues, and Changes in the Public Agenda. *Public Opinion Quarterly* 49 (1):38–57.

Brody, Richard A., and Paul M. Sniderman. 1977. From Life Space to Polling Place: The Relevance of Personal Concerns for Voting Behavior. *British Journal of Political Science* 7 (3):337–60.

Burgoon, Brian A., and Michael J. Hiscox. 2004. The Mysterious Case of Female Protectionism: Gender Bias in Attitudes Toward International Trade. Unpublished manuscript, Department of Government, Harvard University, Cambridge, Mass.

Busch, Marc L., and Eric Reinhardt. 2000. Geography, International Trade, and Political Mobilization in U.S. Industries. *American Journal of Political Science* 44 (4):703–19.

Conover, Pamela Johnston, Stanley Feldman, and Kathleen Knight. 1986. Judging Inflation and Unemployment: The Origins of Retrospective Evaluations. *Journal of Politics* 48 (3):565–88.

Erbring, Lutz, Edie N. Goldenberg, and Arthur H. Miller. 1980. Front-Page News and Real-World Cues: A New Look at Agenda-Setting by the Media. *American Journal of Political Science* 24 (1):16–49.

Erikson, Robert S., and Kent L. Tedin. 2005. *American Public Opinion: Its Origin, Content and Impact*. 7th ed. New York: Pearson-Longman.

Fordham, Benjamin O. 2008. Economic Interests and Public Support for American Global Activism. *International Organization* 62 (1):163–82.

Fordham, Benjamin O., and Timothy J. McKeown. 2003. Selection and Influence: Interest Groups and Congressional Voting on Trade Policy. *International Organization* 57 (3):519–49.

Gabel, Matthew J. 1998. *Interests and Information: Market Liberalization, Public Opinion, and European Union*. Ann Arbor: University of Michigan Press.

Green, Donald P., and Ann E. Gerken. 1989. Self-Interest and Public Opinion toward Smoking Restrictions and Cigarette Taxes. *Public Opinion Quarterly* 53 (1):1–16.

Hainmueller, Jens, and Michael J. Hiscox. 2006. Learning to Love Globalization: Education and Individual Attitudes Toward International Trade. *International Organization* 60 (2):469–98.

Hays, Jude C., Sean D. Ehrlich, and Clint Peinhardt. 2005. Government Spending and Public Support for Trade in the OECD: Am Empirical Test of the Embedded Liberalism Thesis. *International Organization* 59 (2):473–94.

Herrmann, Richard K., Philip E. Tetlock, and Matthew N. Diascro. 2001. How Americans Think About Trade: Reconciling Conflicts Among Money, Power, and Principles. *International Studies Quarterly* 45 (2):191–218.

Hiscox, Michael J. 2006. Through a Glass and Darkly: Attitudes Toward International Trade and the Curious Effects of Issue Framing. *International Organization* 60 (3):755–80.

Kaltenthaler, Karl C., Ronald D. Gelleny, and Stephen J. Ceccoli. 2004. Explaining Citizen Support for Trade Liberalization. *International Studies Quarterly* 48 (4):829–52.

Kam, Cindy, and Donald R. Kinder. 2007. Terror and Ethnocentrism: Foundations of American Support for the War on Terrorism. *Journal of Politics* 69 (2):320–38.

Kiewiet, D. Roderick. 1983. *Macroeconomics and Micropolitics: The Electoral Effects of Economic Issues*. Chicago: University of Chicago Press.

Kinder, Donald R., and D. Roderick Kiewiet. 1981. Sociotropic Politics: The American Case. *British Journal of Political Science* 11 (2):129–61.

Kocher, Matthew A., and Susan Minushkin. 2006. Trade and Investment Policy Preferences and Public Opinion in Mexico. Paper presented at the 47th Annual Convention of the International Studies Association, March, San Diego, Calif.

Kono, Daniel Y. 2008. Does Public Opinion Affect Trade Policy? *Business and Politics* 10 (2): Article 2. Available at ⟨http://www.bepress.com/bap/vol10/iss2/art2⟩. Accessed 31 March 2009.

Leamer, Edward E. 1984. *Sources of International Comparative Advantage*. Cambridge, Mass.: MIT Press.

Levinson, Daniel J. 1949. An Approach to the Theory and Measurement of Ethnocentric Ideology. *Journal of Psychology* 28 (1):19–39.

Long, J. Scott, and Jeremy Freese. 2005. *Regression Models for Categorical Outcomes Using Stata*. 2d ed. College Station, Tex: Stata Press.

MacKuen, Michael Bruce, and Stephen Lane Coombs. 1981. *More Than News: Media Power in Public Affairs*. Beverly Hills, Calif.: Sage Publications.

Maggiotto, Michael A., and Eugene R. Wittkopf. 1981. American Public Attitudes toward Foreign Policy. *International Studies Quarterly* 25 (4):601–31.

Mansfield, Edward D., and Diana C. Mutz. 2006. What Determines Perceptions of Trade's Influence on the US Economy? Paper presented at the 102d Annual Meeting of the American Political Science Association, August-September, Philadelphia.

Mayda, Anna-Maria, and Dani Rodrik. 2005. Why Are Some People (and Countries) More Protectionist Than Others? *European Economic Review* 49 (6):1393–430.

Mutz, Diana C. 1992. Mass Media and the Depoliticization of Personal Experience. *American Journal of Political Science* 36 (2):483–508.

———. 1994. Contextualizing Personal Experience: The Role of Mass Media. *Journal of Politics* 56 (4):689–714.

———. 1998. *Impersonal Influence: How Perceptions of Mass Collectives Affect Political Attitudes*. New York: Cambridge University Press.

Nie, Norman H., Jane Junn, and Kenneth Stehlik-Barry. 1996. *Education and Democratic Citizenship in America*. Chicago: University of Chicago Press.

O'Rourke, Kevin H., and Richard Sinnott. 2002. The Determinants of Individual Trade Policy Preferences: International Survey Evidence. In *Brookings Trade Forum, 2002*, edited by Susan M. Collins and Dani Rodrik, 157–206. Washington, D.C.: Brookings Institution.

Prior, Markus. 2007. *Post-Broadcast Democracy: How Media Choice Increases Inequality in Political Involvement and Polarizes Elections*. New York: Cambridge University Press.

Rankin, David M. 2001. Identities, Interests, and Imports. *Political Behavior* 23 (4):351–76.

Rodrik, Dani. 1995. Political Economy of Trade Policy. In *Handbook of International Economics*. Vol. 3, edited by Gene M. Grossman and Kenneth Rogoff, 1457–94. Amsterdam: Elsevier.

Scheve, Kenneth F., and Matthew J. Slaughter. 2001. What Determines Individual Trade-Policy Preferences? *Journal of International Economics* 54 (2):267–92.

Sears, David O., and Carolyn L. Funk. 1990. Self-Interest in Americans' Political Opinions. In *Beyond Self-Interest*, edited by Jane J. Mansbridge, 147–70. Chicago: University of Chicago Press.

Spenner, Kenneth I. 1990. Skill: Meanings, Methods, and Measures. *Work and Occupations* 17 (4): 399–421.

Stolper, Wolfgang Friedrich, and Paul A. Samuelson. 1941. Protection and Real Wages. *Review of Economic Studies* 9:58–73.

Tyler, Tom R. 1980. Impact of Directly and Indirectly Experienced Events: The Origins of Crime-Related Judgments and Behaviors. *Journal of Personality and Social Psychology* 39 (1):13–28.

———. 1984. Assessing the Risk of Crime Victimization: The Integration of Personal Victimization Experience and Socially Transmitted Information. *Journal of Social Issues* 40 (1):27–38.

Tyler, Tom R., and Fay L. Cook. 1984. The Mass Media and Judgments of Risk: Distinguishing Impact on Personal and Societal Level Judgments. *Journal of Personality and Social Psychology* 47 (4): 693–708.

U.S. Census Bureau. 2008a. North American Industry Classification System (NAICS). Available at ⟨http://www.census.gov/epcd/www/naics.html⟩. Accessed 31 March 2009.

———. 2008b. DP-3, Profile of Selected Economic Characteristics: 2000. Available at ⟨http://factfinder.census.gov/servlet/QTTable?_bm=y&-geo_id=01000US&-qr_name=DEC_2000_SF3_U_DP3&-ds_name=DEC_2000_SF3_U&-_lang=en&-_caller=geoselect&-state=qt&-format=⟩. Accessed 30 April 2009.

U.S. Department of Commerce. 2008. Industry Economic Accounts. Bureau of Economic Analysis. Available at ⟨http://www.bea.gov/industry/gdpbyind_data.htm⟩. Accessed 30 April 2009.

U.S. Department of Labor. 2008a. Standard Occupational Classification. Bureau of Labor Statistics. Available at ⟨http://www.bls.gov/soc/⟩. Accessed 30 April 2009.

———. 2008b. Occupational Employment Statistics. Bureau of Labor Statistics. Available at ⟨http://www.bls.gov/oes/oes_dl.htm⟩. Accessed 30 April 2009.

U.S. International Trade Commission. 2008. USITC Interactive Tariff and Trade DataWeb. Available at ⟨http://dataweb.usitc.gov/scripts/user_set.asp⟩. Accessed 30 April 2009.

Wittkopf, Eugene R., and Michael A. Maggiotto. 1983. Elites and Masses: A Comparative Analysis of Attitudes Toward America's World Role. *Journal of Politics* 45 (2):303–34.

Worldviews. 2002. American Public Opinion and Foreign Policy. Chicago Council on Foreign Relations. Available at ⟨http://www.worldviews.org/detailreports/usreport.pdf⟩. Accessed 30 April 2009.

[14]

International Studies Quarterly

International Studies Quarterly (2012) **56**, 484–500

Lost in Globalization: International Economic Integration and the Sources of Popular Discontent[1]

Yotam Margalit

Columbia University

What are the sources of popular opposition to economic globalization? A common answer in the literature is the adverse impact of trade liberalization on some people's labor market standing and earning prospects. Recent studies also note a correlation between nationalist and ethnocentric sentiments and support for trade protectionism, yet do not test whether these non-economic sentiments are actually a cause of the opposition to freer trade. I argue that many individuals fear not only the oft-cited material consequences of trade openness, but also what they perceive to be its social and cultural consequences. I use cross-national survey data and a survey experiment to test this causal claim. The argument also helps explain why less-educated individuals are consistently more apprehensive about international economic integration than more educated individuals, even in the countries in which economic theory predicts otherwise. The findings have implications for the debate over the policy tools for compensating globalization's losers and sustaining popular support for further economic integration.

The liberalization of national economies and their opening up to international trade in recent decades have produced substantial gains for many, but have also generated deep discontent among many others (Rodrik 1997; Stiglitz 2002). Politicians in various countries have taken note of this discontentment and routinely attempt to seize upon it to shore up political support: condemnations of job losses due to offshoring, attacks on the unfair practices of foreign trading partners, and calls for protectionist trade policies can all be seen in this light. Notably, this phenomenon is not limited to a specific country or region. Anti-openness appeals are often embraced by a wide array of political parties and candidates, ranging from the recent wave of leftist populists in Latin America, through postcommunist parties in Eastern Europe, to the far right in Western Europe.[2] Yet despite the fact that disaffection with economic globalization is a politically salient issue, not much is known about the constituencies that feel harmed by economic openness.[3] What characterizes the individuals that view themselves as losing out from their country's integration into the global economy? What specific aspects of economic openness cause them to view it as harmful?

Popular opposition to economic globalization has commonly been attributed to its impact on people's earning capacity. Much of the scholarly focus has thus been on exploring the association between individuals' labor market standing, measured either by their sector of employment or by the factor of production they own (for example, skill level), and their attitudes on trade liberalization. Yet while arguments based on changes in the labor market offer some important insights into people's attitudes toward economic openness, the explanatory power of these arguments has been shown to be quite limited. First, analyses of survey data find only a weak association between the exposure of people's employment sector to foreign competition and their attitudes on trade policy (for example, Scheve and Slaughter 2001). Furthermore, survey data consistently reveals a pattern that is at odds also with the second factor-based explanation. Whereas the classic Stolper–Samuelson theorem suggests that lower-skilled individuals should be more (less) opposed to trade openness than skilled individuals in advanced (developing) economies, cross-national data show that less-educated (and presumably lower-skilled) individuals are consistently more opposed to trade openness than their higher-educated counterparts, regardless of their country's relative factor endowment and position in the glo-

[1] For helpful comments and suggestions, the author would like to thank Alberto Cayeros-Diaz, Josh Cohen, Jim Fearon, Judy Goldstein, Alex Kuo, David Laitin, Doug Rivers, Natan Sachs, Ken Scheve, Mike Tomz, Jeremy Weinstein, and participants at the International Relations workshop at Stanford University. Earlier versions of the paper were presented at the 2007 Annual Meeting of the Political Science Association and at The Society for Comparative Research, Yale University. The article was written when the author was a graduate student in the Political Science Department of Stanford University. Data, additional appendices, and replication information can be found on the author's website at www.columbia.edu/~ym2297.

[2] On the Western European case, see Swank and Betz (2003); Kriesi, Grande, Lachat, Dolezal, Bornschier, and Frey (2006). On the effects of globalization on Eastern European politics and the appeal of postcommunist parties, see the edited volume of Bozóki and Ishiyama 2002, particularly chapter 17. See the *Economist*, "The Return of Populism," 12 April 2006, for a discussion of the sources of populist success in Latin America.

[3] Throughout the article, I use the terms "economic globalization," "economic integration," and "economic openness" interchangeably.

Margalit, Yotam. (2012) Lost in Globalization: International Economic Integration and the Sources of Popular Discontent. *International Studies Quarterly*, doi: 10.1111/j.1468-2478.2012.00747.x

bal economy (for example, Baker 2003; Beaulieu, Bennaroch, and Gaisford 2004). This "education puzzle" suggests that an explanation based on a factor-based model is insufficient by itself for explaining variation in mass attitudes on trade openness.[4]

In examining similar survey data on individual attitudes, various scholars also point to the correlation between opposition to trade openness and nationalist–chauvinist attitudes (O'Rourke and Sinnott 2001; Mayda and Rodrik 2005) or ethnocentrism (Mansfield and Mutz 2009). These studies advance the debate by suggesting that attitudes on trade openness may be influenced also by non-economic concerns. However, these observational studies do not deal with the crucial question of whether there is a causal link between non-economic sentiments and attitudes on trade openness, nor do those studies attempt to explore the direction in which causality runs. It could be, for example, that the adverse material effects of openness to international trade underlie *both* the opposition to trade liberalization and the emergence of chauvinist–nationalist views, rather than the latter causing the former. Yet if non-economic sentiments are not a cause of support for trade protectionism, then the correlation these scholars find is irrelevant for explaining the sources of popular opposition to trade openness. Without a theoretical account to explain this empirical association between non-economic sentiments and views on trade openness, as well as a research design that can test for a causal relationship, the nature of this association remains an unresolved question.

This paper builds on and extends the literature by putting forward and testing an argument about the sources of people's perception that international economic integration is harmful. I contend that many individuals fear not only the oft-cited material consequences of trade liberalization, but also what they perceive to be its social and cultural consequences. They view the material effects of trade liberalization as part of a broader "package" of openness, which also includes processes such as growing exposure to foreign influences, westernization, and shifting moral codes. Anxiety about this broader set of changes that people intuitively perceive as byproducts of economic openness underlies some of the opposition to trade liberalization. Furthermore, I argue that anxiety about the perceived social and cultural consequences of economic integration helps explain why less-educated individuals are consistently more opposed to economic integration than those more educated, even in countries where a factor-based model would predict otherwise.

I use data from two cross-national surveys and an experiment to test this "openness package" argument. The cross-national data reveal a strong empirical relationship between people's views about social–cultural aspects of openness and their views about the impact of international trade. The survey experiment, designed to illuminate the causal nature of this relationship, demonstrates that a heightening of cultural concerns intensifies people's view of trade liberalization as harmful. Importantly, this effect is found to be strong only among less-educated individuals, a finding that helps account for the "education puzzle" noted above. I also test other mechanisms for explaining people's perceptions of being harmed by economic integration, such as labor market effects and concerns about *relative* economic change. The analysis shows that even when accounting for the effect of these alternative mechanisms, social–cultural factors have major explanatory power.

In sum, this article makes three contributions. First, it develops an argument and presents data about the important role of the perceived social–cultural consequences of openness as a source of popular discontentment with international economic integration. The empirical analysis compares the explanatory strength of the argument to a broad set of alternative explanations, including some that have not been explored before. Second, the article presents experimental results that offer the first evidence of a causal link between cultural concerns and opposition to trade liberalization. Finally, the article goes some way toward resolving a key empirical puzzle in the literature, namely the finding that less-educated individuals are more trade protectionist than highly educated members of their country, regardless of their country's relative position in the global economy.

The rest of the paper proceeds as follows. Next, I review the main insights in the literature regarding the winners and losers from trade openness. I then discuss the limitations of existing approaches and lay out the paper's argument. The subsequent sections present the results of the analysis of observational cross-national data, followed by experimental evidence from the U.S. The final section outlines the argument's broader implications and concludes.

Sources of Opposition to Economic Globalization

Interest in understanding of the underpinnings of mass attitudes toward economic globalization has spawned a substantial literature on the determinants of individual preferences on trade policy. The literature has focused primarily on the distributive consequences of trade as the source of those preferences. According to the classic Heckscher–Ohlin (H–O) model and the Stolper–Samuelson theorem built on it, trade brings a country to export goods whose production is intensive in its abundant factor while importing goods that are intensive in their relatively scarce factor. This logic implies that the losers from trade openness are the unskilled laborers in skill-abundant countries and the skilled laborers in skill-scarce countries.[5] Indeed, several studies have found evidence that among more skilled individuals (typically measured by their level of education), support for free trade is lower in economies that are relatively skill-scarce than in economies that are skill-abundant (for example, Beaulieu et al. 2004; Baker 2005). However, as noted earlier, these studies also find that even in the skill-scarce countries, less-educated individuals are substan-

[4] While economic globalization also includes other aspects such as foreign direct investment and capital flows, the empirical section of this paper focuses on people's views on trade openness.

[5] In an interesting theoretical elaboration, Baker (2005) argues that the distributive consequences of trade openness on individuals as consumers, not just as laborers, is also consistent with the H–O logic.

tially more opposed to trade openness than the higher educated individuals.[6] For example, in a study of 15 skill-scarce Latin American economies, Beaulieu et al. (2004) find that educated individuals are more supportive of trade than the less educated in *all* 15 countries.[7] This finding poses a challenge to the central prediction of the H–O model and has led scholars to suggest that education, perhaps through the content of the curricula, has an independent effect on the way people assess the benefits of open markets (Hainmueller and Hiscox 2006).

Others have posited that due to the immobility of certain factors of production, the key cleavage along which support and opposition to trade lies in the short run is the industry in which individuals are employed. This specific factors approach, often referred to as the Ricardo–Viner (R–V) model, suggests that the losers from trade openness are first and foremost those working in import-sensitive industries (Magee 1978; Irwin 1996). While certainly a plausible explanation, empirical analyses find that industry affiliation is an inconsistent or weak predictor of individual attitudes on trade (for example, Scheve and Slaughter 2001; Hays, Ehrlich, and Peinhardt 2005; Mansfield and Mutz 2009).

Material-based discontentment with economic openness could also be the result of subjective notions about one's *relative* economic standing in society, a mechanism explored in the "economics of happiness" literature (for example, Blanchflower and Oswald 1999; Easterlin 2001). Indeed, individuals living in recently liberalized developing economies often perceive their personal situation to be worse off than in the pre-liberalization period, despite experiencing real income gains following the transition (Graham and Pettinato 2002). The key explanation the authors offer for this apparent dissonance is that those dissatisfied individuals are comparing themselves to others in society who have fared better than they have, leading to what the authors describe as the "frustrated achievers" phenomenon. In the context of this paper, the argument suggests that opposition to trade openness may be driven by discontentment about changes in one's relative standing in society, rather than by losses in absolute terms.

Other analyses of trade attitudes also incorporate controls that proxy for non-economic sentiments (O'Rourke and Sinnott 2001; Mayda and Rodrik 2005; Mansfield and Mutz 2009). These studies find a strong association between individuals' views on trade openness and nationalist–chauvinist or ethnocentric inclinations.[8] These associations hold even when controlling for a range of other individual-level characteristics. Yet as noted, the nature of the correlation between ideological factors and people's preferences on trade policy is ambiguous for a number of reasons. First, it could be that the correlation is spurious and does not represent any causal link in people's minds. Second, it could also be that the adverse economic effects of international trade underlie both people's nationalist views and their opposition to trade openness, rather than the former causing the latter. Given that trade openness tends to be beneficial for countries at the aggregate (that is, national) level, it is not a priori obvious why holders of nationalist sentiments should oppose trade openness.[9] In other words, to make the claim that non-economic concerns are shaping attitudes on trade openness (in this case, nationalism–chauvinism causing protectionist sentiments), both a clearer theoretical elaboration of this association is needed and an empirical strategy to test it. This is the task to which I now turn.

The Openness "Package"

International economic integration is a unique economic phenomenon in that it has not only material effects but also wide-reaching cultural and social consequences. Increases in trade (particularly of cultural goods and services), migration of labor, foreign direct investment, and the growing presence of foreign multinationals are all changes that have unambiguous social and cultural aspects. Indeed, much of the voluminous literature on globalization is dedicated to analyzing these non-economic aspects, emphasizing a range of processes that globalization brings about. These include the growing exposure to foreign influences and changing domestic value orientations (for example, Giddens 2000; Inglehart 2000), a shift from a collectivist toward a more individualistic society (Beck 1992; Triandis 1995), and growing Western and American economic and cultural dominance (Ritzer 2000; Beck 2006).

Yet despite the recognition that global integration is a multidimensional phenomenon with significant social and cultural consequences, the debate over the determinants of popular support for openness to trade has predominantly centered on the economic dimension, focusing on the impact of trade liberalization on people's labor market standing and consumption opportunities. The key question is whether this view is justified: In forming attitudes about the impact of trade openness on their well-being, do individuals disentangle the broad and complex effects of "openness" and separately assess the material effects of trade?

I argue that many individuals do not. Instead, they perceive international trade as having the oft-cited economic impacts, but also associate it with substantial social and cultural consequences. People view the

[6] The one exception is Mayda and Rodrik's finding that in Thailand, a developing economy, less-educated individuals were more pro-trade than educated.

[7] The difference between the mean attitudes of the skilled and unskilled was statistically significant in eight of the cases.

[8] Sinnott and O'Rourke divide nationalist sentiments into two separate categories: patriotic and chauvinistic sentiments. They define their measure of patriotism as capturing a "preference and sense of superiority of one's own country" and chauvinism as an exclusive sense of nationality of the "my country right or wrong" variety. Both measures are found to be strongly correlated with preferences for trade protectionism. Mayda and Rodrik (2005) use the same survey data and categorize similar survey items under one label as capturing nationalist sentiments.

[9] See Krugman and Obstfeld (1994) for a review of the basic theoretical argument why trade openness is welfare enhancing at the aggregate level. See Sachs and Warner (1995) and Wacziarg and Welch (2008) for empirical evidence on the positive relationship between trade liberalization and growth (but also see Rodriguez and Rodrik (2000) for a more skeptical view of the evidence).

material effects of trade as only one component of a broader "package" of openness that includes processes such as those discussed in the literature mentioned above, be it the increasing exposure to foreign influences, a shift towards a less traditionalist society, or growing American cultural dominance. I conjecture that people's deep apprehension about these social–cultural processes translates also into a negative view of the broader openness "package," accounting for some of the discontentment with trade liberalization and economic integration more broadly.[10]

An Illustrative Example

It is probably safe to say that individuals do not perceive *all* economic phenomena to have significant social and cultural implications. To illustrate why economic integration is different in this respect, let us briefly consider the case of trade in cultural goods and services, which nicely illustrates some of the characteristics of the social–cultural dimension on which my argument rests.[11]

Since 1980, the size of the cultural and creative industries has grown almost threefold and in 2002 accounted for more than 7% of the world's GDP.[12] Between the years 1994–2002, the period covered by the latest UNESCO report, absolute *levels* of exports and imports in cultural goods were highest in the advanced economies, but *growth* in the imports of cultural goods was fastest in the low-income and lower-middle-income economies, increasing at an astounding average annual rate of 26.7% and 12.4%, respectively.[13]

Overall, the United States has been the largest exporter of cultural goods and services combined,[14] dominating the export markets for core cultural goods both to developing and to advanced economies.[15] For example, a country like Brazil imports approximately 30% of its cultural goods from the United States while it imports only 14% from all other Latin American countries combined.[16] Similarly, in 2003, South Africa imported only a fraction of its core cultural goods from other African countries, while the United States and the United Kingdom alone accounted for half its imports.

Importantly, American dominance can be seen also in its trading relations with other *advanced* economies. Exports of American films, for example, have grown from representing 35% of box office revenue in continental Europe in the mid-1960s to above 80% by 2000.[17] And in the broadcasting content domain, the EU countries sustained a trade deficit with the United States that was almost 15 times the value of their exports to North America.[18] Notably, these imbalances have taken place despite European legislation explicitly designed to protect local cultural production.

This example of trade in cultural goods and services suggests that individuals may associate trade liberalization with more than "just" its distributive consequences.[19] This expectation indeed finds grounding in a growing body of public opinion research which shows that people's attitudes on a range of phenomena associated with international integration fuse both economic and social–cultural concerns. For example, various studies offer evidence that attitudes toward immigrants and immigration policy are largely driven by individuals' cultural values and beliefs, not just by fears about the fiscal or labor market consequences of immigration (Citrin, Green, Muste, and Wong 1997; Sniderman, Hagendoorn, and Prior 2004; Hainmueller and Hiscox 2007, 2010). Similarly, in examining support and opposition to EU integration, several studies find that people's stances are better accounted for by measures of cultural anxieties than by demographic or occupational characteristics (De Master and Le Roy 2000; McLaren 2002). These studies support the notion that non-economic concerns are important factors in shaping people's view of economic integration as harmful.

Empirical Implications

People's views on the impact of their country opening up economically represent considerations on a number of dimensions, be it the impact of economic openness on the availability and the variety of products on the shelves, the quality of available jobs, or the changing price levels of goods. The social–cultural consequences that my argument emphasizes are also important outcomes that people associate with international economic integration but certainly not the only ones. It is thus likely that attitudes on economic integration vary temporally as a function of how salient each of these different dimensions of openness is in people's minds at a given point of time: In periods when the negative social–cultural aspects of openness are made more salient (for example, due to controversies in the news or public statements by politicians),

[10] The argument does not imply that all individuals threatened by the social–cultural aspects of openness necessarily view economic integration as harmful, but suggests that there is a substantial group of individuals for which this is the case. In line with Prospect Theory's notion that losses loom larger than gains (Kahneman and Tversky 1979), it is likely that individuals whom openness has made better off in one dimension (economic or cultural) and worse off in the other will tend to focus on the adverse effect of the openness process. In other words, only a few individuals harmed by economic integration will support it because they approve of its cultural consequences.

[11] To be clear, trade in cultural goods does not comprise the sole source of change underlying the perception that globalization has a social-cultural dimension. Nonetheless, this case is a useful illustration of the logic underlying the argument that people perceive economic integration as part of a broader openness "package."

[12] UNESCO Institute for Statistics 2005, p. 9.

[13] Ibid, p.69, Table III-3.

[14] The US exports $7 billion in cultural good and services; the second largest exporter is the U.K. ($1.5 billion).

[15] Core cultural goods are defined as goods with an explicit cultural content.

[16] The figures are based on the UN COMtrade DESA/UNSD data, 2004, and reported in UNESCO Institute for Statistics 2005, p. 34.

[17] See Puttnam (1998,p. 266). See Cowen (2002) for an analysis of this trend (pp. 74–83).

[18] Data are based on the ETS/European Audiovisual Observatory, 2002, and reported in UNESCO Institute for Statistics (2005, p. 48).

[19] Importantly, the relevant empirical question here is not whether individuals are correct in attributing these social-cultural consequences to economic integration, but whether or not this is how people perceive the consequences of economic integration.

apprehension about economic integration is likely to increase.[20]

Yet the degree to which concerns along the various dimensions shape the public's views on economic integration is likely to vary not only as a function of the relative *salience* of each dimension at a given moment in time, but also as a function of the prevalence of each set of concerns across different segments of society. One key source of variation in people's degree of concern with the cultural dimension of openness is likely to be their level of education, since multiple studies find a strong negative association between educational attainment and measures of out-group bias and intolerance of other cultures (for example, Bobo and Licari 1989; Coenders and Scheepers 2003). Less-educated individuals are also found to exhibit stronger feelings of in-group superiority along lines of ethnicity, race, or nation (Wagner and Zick 1995). Scholars attribute such findings not only to cognitive and personal development, but also to the role of education in exposing individuals to foreign cultures and by creating more cosmopolitan social networks (Vogt 1997; Chandler and Tsai 2001). These findings thus suggest that the argument advanced here could also, at least partially, account for the "education puzzle" described earlier: If one were to find that cultural concerns about openness are not only more prevalent among individuals with a lower level of education, but are also causally related to a negative view of international economic openness; this would help explain the consistent empirical association observed between lower education and greater opposition to trade liberalization.

In sum, the argument developed here has three key observable implications, which can be specified as distinct hypotheses:

Hypothesis 1: *Individuals apprehensive about social and cultural openness are more likely to view trade liberalization as harmful, controlling for other socioeconomic characteristics.*

If this relationship between social–cultural anxieties and attitudes on trade openness is causally interlinked (and not merely a correlation), opposition to trade liberalization should be greater when the social–cultural threat is more salient. This implies that:

Hypothesis 2: *An increase in the salience of negative social–cultural issues associated with openness should lead to greater hostility toward free trade.*

And finally, as noted earlier, if social–cultural concerns about openness are more prevalent among less-educated individuals, the implication would be that:

Hypothesis 3: *An increase in the salience of social–cultural processes associated with openness should have, on average, a greater negative effect on the way less-educated individuals perceive the impact of trade liberalization than on the views of highly educated individuals.*

In the empirical sections that follow, I present tests for each of the three propositions.

Data and Empirical Approach

The data discussed in this section and used in the subsequent analysis are based on the *Pew Global Attitudes Project*, a data set comprised of 40 national surveys carried out in five continents in 2002 (Pew 2003).[21] In the online appendix, I present the results of an additional analysis that relies on a different cross-national data set, the *International Social Survey Program* (ISSP) from 2003. By testing the implications of the theory on two different data sets, one can draw greater confidence that the findings are not driven by artifacts in the design of a specific survey such as ordering effects or question framing.[22]

The Pew survey is well suited for this research since it includes questions on both economic and cultural aspects of globalization. Having both sets of questions is crucial for testing the paper's argument. The dependent variable used in the analysis is based on respondents' answers to the following question (henceforth referred to as the "main question"):

> Now thinking about you and your family—do you think the growing trade and business ties between our country and other countries are very good, somewhat good, somewhat bad, or very bad for you and your family?

I categorize the self-perceived *Losers* as those respondents who answered the main question as either "somewhat bad" or "very bad"; conversely, *Gainers* are those who answered "somewhat good" or "very good."

To test the argument that people's sense of personal harm from economic integration is driven in part by apprehension about the social–cultural changes they associate with openness, I use factor analysis to construct a measure of cultural threat based on responses

[20] For example, during the debate over the GATT agreement, French Minister of Culture Jacques Toubon described his opposition as a fight for the "survival of [French] culture" and for the French "way of life." ("GATT et culture: Laisser respirer nos âmes!", *Le Monde*, 1 October 1993). Similarly, then-president Francois Mitterrand stated: "What is at issue is the cultural identity of nations, the right of each people to its own culture, the freedom to create and choose one's images. … A society that relinquishes to others its means of representation, is an enslaved society" (McMahon 1995).

[21] The original data set includes 44 countries. However, in several countries, a set of important questions necessary for the analysis were not asked. The analyses thus exclude Egypt, Vietnam, China, and Uzbekistan. Approximately 91% of the respondents answered the question on the effects of trade openness on themselves and their family. To avoid losing additional observations, missing observations were imputed for several independent variables, most notably education (6.4% of the observations). Substantive results were unchanged when conducting the analyses with and without the imputed observations. See appendix 1 for a complete list of the countries included in the study.

[22] To reduce clutter and avoid confusion regarding the measurement of the variables used in the two analyses, I defer the results from the analysis of the ISSP survey to the online appendix.

to a set of seven survey items listed in Table 1. These items deal with some of the most common non-economic issues mentioned in the context of international integration: exposure to foreign influences, the spread of American ideas, changes to the traditional way of life, and the import of cultural goods ("foreign TV and movies"). A principle factor analysis shows the seven survey items load on a single dimension.[23] I then construct the *cultural threat* variable as a weighted sum of the responses to the seven items and standardize it with a mean of zero and a standard deviation of one.[24] Table 1 reports the scoring coefficient weights of each item used in constructing the *cultural threat* measure.

The survey items capture a somewhat narrow aspect of the range of issues associated with globalization and ignore other relevant issues, in particular people's attitudes on immigration. While the issue of immigration is an important and ubiquitous aspect in the globalization debate, I intentionally exclude direct questions about immigration since the responses to these questions may be interpreted as representing economic concerns about labor market threat rather than individuals' views on social and cultural issues (Mayda 2006; Malhotra, Margalit, and Mo 2010). By limiting the constructed factor to these seven items that focus more directly on cultural aspects of openness, the analysis provides a clearer and more exacting test of the paper's argument.[25]

To test the hypothesis derived from the Heckscher–Ohlin model (henceforth H–O), I use educational attainment as a proxy for respondents' skill level.[26] The factor endowment argument holds that an individual that completed their high school education in a skill-scarce country, such as Bolivia, has a very different standing in the local labor market than a high school graduate in a skill-abundant country, such as Germany. To account for the differential effect of skill on people's attitudes as a function of their standing in the labor market, I again follow the standard approach in the literature and include an interaction term of individual skill and the country's skill endowment. Measurement of a country's skill endowment is problematic due to lack of comparable cross-national data. I therefore use the natural log of a country's per capita GDP as a proxy for a country's skill abundance. The interaction term of skill and skill abundance is represented with the *Education* × GDP per capita variable.[27] In addition, as another set of controls, I include in the model a set of dummy variables for respondents' employment status. The categories include full-time employees, part-time employees, self-employed, pensioners, and individuals not in the labor market (for example, homemakers).

TABLE 1. Factor Analysis of Items Dealing With Cultural and Social Change

Survey Item	*Weight*
Our Traditional Way of Life is Getting Lost (/remains strong)	0.072
Our Way of Life Needs to be Protected Against Foreign Influence	0.044
Having the Opportunity to Watch Movies and TV and Listen to Music from Different Parts of the World is a Good (/bad) Thing	0.159
I Like (/I Do Not Like) The Pace Of Modern Life	0.111
Consumerism and Commercialism are a Threat (/not a threat) to Our Culture	0.095
It's good (/bad) that American Ideas and Customs are Spreading here	0.214
I like (/dislike) American Music, Movies, and Television	0.307

Source: Author's calculations using data from PEW Global Attitudes Survey (2003).

As an additional measure for testing the role of labor market concerns as the source of attitudes on economic integration, I also generate a variable based on people's *subjective view* of change in the labor market over the past 5 years, and whether they attribute the change to globalization or not. The variable is constructed from two questions: First, the survey asked whether the "availability of good paying jobs" has changed over the past 5 years for better, worse, or not at all. The follow-up question asked whether they attribute this change "largely to the world becoming more connected" or "mostly to other reasons." I use the responses to the two questions to generate a variable that ranges from one (job situation improved, largely because of globalization) to seven (job situation worsened, largely because of globalization).[28]

To assess the empirical strength of the hypothesis that people's *relative* position in society affects their subjective perceptions of gain and loss, one would ideally need a good panel data set that tracks changes in people's economic well-being as well as their attitudes on economic globalization over time. Since such measures are not available, I examine the explanatory power of two different indicators that proxy for relative position. The first is centered on earnings, com-

[23] The first (and only) retained dimension has an eigen value of 1.43. The next dimension has an eigen value of 0.37.

[24] The weights of each item in constructing the index are obtained using a varimax-rotated matrix and are provided on the right column of the table. For a test of robustness, I re-ran all the analyses reported in the subsequent sections using a factor analysis after dropping any one of items from the seven-item list. The results are substantively similar indicating that no single survey item is responsible for the obtained results. I also re-estimated the models after dropping the questions pertaining to US influence, since these may be construed as measuring anti-Americanism rather than a social-cultural concern. Once again, the substantive results all hold, and both the magnitude and the statistical significance of the *cultural threat* variable remain high.

[25] The Pew survey also includes two items about immigration: One asking about the perceived influence of immigrants on the "way things are going in [survey country]" (q15) and the other asking respondents to rate the degree to which they view immigration as "a problem" (q35). Inclusion of respondents' answers to these two questions in the factor analysis shows them to load on the same dimension as the other seven items and further strengthens the results reported in Table 2. Both the marginal effect associated with this alternative cultural threat measure and the overall fit of the model increase. However, to minimize the possible "contamination" of the cultural threat measure by questions that may be construed as capturing an economic concern, I err on the side of caution and exclude these two questions from the reported analysis.

[26] This is a highly imperfect measure, albeit a commonly used one in the literature on trade preferences (for example, Scheve and Slaughter 2001; Mayda and Rodrik 2005).

[27] I do not include a separate control for GDP per capita due to the inclusion of country fixed effects.

[28] See appendix 1 for more detail on the coding of the variable.

paring whether an absolute measure of real income or a measure of relative income is a stronger predictor of perceived loss from economic openness. Since a $30,000 annual household income places an individual in the third income quintile in a country like Germany, but in the top income quintile in a country like India, the question of interest is whether, when pooling observations from all countries together, attitudes on trade openness are better predicted by one's absolute income or measures of relative income.

The variable *Income* denotes the absolute household earning of each respondent. To control for differences across countries in the cost of living, I convert the reported incomes from the local currency into US dollars at the date of the survey, standardize the incomes as annual earnings, and adjust for purchasing power parity. The income figure is then logged. I also calculate the *Relative Income* variable as the income quintile into which the respondent falls within their own country.

A second test of the logic of relative change is based on a measure of respondents' self-reported level of well-being. Respondents were asked to rate both their current situation and their situation 5 years ago on a 10-step "ladder of life" ranging from 1 to 10 (from the worst to the best "possible life for you"). I use these two measures to generate two different variables: *Current State* denotes the answer to the question about the respondent's current standing; the variable *5-year Change* is calculated by subtracting the current well-being from the (retrospective) well-being reported for 5 years ago. These two measures enable us to test whether (i) the self-perceived losers from economic globalization are simply "gripers," that is, individuals who are unhappy about life in general and (ii) whether a sense of relative change in well-being is associated with perceived harm from trade openness.

In addition to the variables described above, I control for gender, since women are consistently found to be more apprehensive about free trade, possibly due to child-rearing considerations that affect their prospects in the labor market (Burgoon and Hiscox 2003). Finally, I also control for respondents' age, since older people may find it more difficult to adjust to new skill requirements in the labor market and thus view economic integration as more detrimental.

Results

In order to examine the sources of people's perception of being harmed by economic globalization, it is useful to begin by examining the variation in such perceptions across countries with different levels of economic openness and development. Figure 1 provides a rough indication of the variation in the size of the group of self-perceived losers in a range of countries. The size of the group varies significantly across the different countries, as less than six percent of the respondents in the United Kingdom, but close to 20% in Bolivia, believe that economic openness is harmful to their families.[29]

An intuitive explanation for this variation might be the varying types of shocks that different economies have undergone as a result of integration into world markets: Countries more exposed to trade and capital flows may have experienced deeper changes and therefore may have a larger constituency of self-perceived losers. The data, however, do not support this conjecture. The correlation between trade openness and perceptions of the effect of economic integration is low ($r = .07$).[30] Similarly, the correlation between a country's GDP and respondents' attitudes is also low ($r = .1$). There seems to be a limited empirical relationship between macroeconomic indicators of development or trade openness and the extent of perceived gains or losses from economic integration. This leaves the open question of what *does* account for the observed variation in people's perceptions, and what are the characteristics of the self-perceived losers.

To address these questions, I proceed by examining the relationship between cultural concerns and the sense of being harmed by international economic integration. The lower panel in Figure 2 compares the mean levels of the *cultural threat* measure among groups that differ with respect to how they perceive the impact of economic integration on their families. As the figure demonstrates, cultural threat is much greater among those that view economic integration as harmful than among those that view it as beneficial. Moreover, since the measure of cultural threat is standardized, one can see that the rate of cultural threat is below average among those who feel that they are gaining from economic integration, but above average among the self-perceived losers. In fact, among those who feel most harmed by economic integration, the average rate of cultural threat is within the top quartile of the distribution on the *cultural threat* variable. The differences between each of the four groups are highly significant in statistical terms ($p < .01$).

The upper panel of Figure 2 examines the mean rates of cultural threat among groups with different education levels. Again, a clear pattern emerges whereby cultural anxieties are much greater among less-educated individuals. As noted, this pattern is consistent with a large literature that documents the relationship between education level and cultural attitudes.

Next, we introduce additional controls into the analysis. Table 2 presents the results of the multivariate regression estimates in which the dependent variable is a binary measure based on the Main Question that takes the value "1" if the respondent perceives their family to be harmed by economic integration and zero otherwise. For ease of interpretation, the reported

[29] For clarity of presentation, the graph includes only a sample of the countries in the survey.

[30] Attitudes on trade at the national level are calculated as the mean score of the respondents to the Main Question (higher values mean greater apprehension about the effects of trade). Trade openness is calculated as the sum of a country's exports and imports as percentage of its GDP. When excluding Kenya and Jordan, two outliers with over 45% of respondents saying trade openness is harmful to them, the correlation between trade openness and attitudes on trade is somewhat higher ($r = .17$).

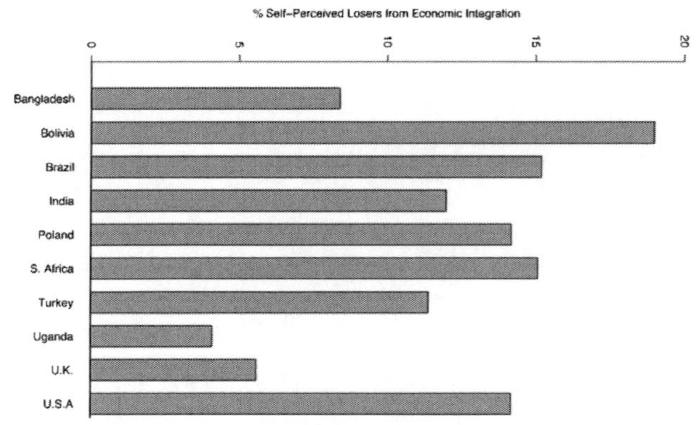

FIG 1. Self-Perceived Losers from International Economic Integration, by Country
Note: Self-perceived ''losers'' are defined as those that described the effect of growing trade and business ties with other countries as ''somewhat bad'' or '''very bad'' for their families.
(*Source*: PEW Global Attitudes Project, 2003).

results are the estimated marginal effects.[31] Column (1) shows that self-perceived loss is associated with lower levels of education, lower income, older age, unemployment, not participating in the labor market, or being employed in a part-time job. Women are also more likely to view themselves as worse off from trade openness, though the effect is not well specified.

The results also indicate that *cultural threat* is strongly associated with self-perceived loss: The magnitude of the effect is large and statistically significant under all the different specifications. As columns (3–5) demonstrate, individuals that are more anxious about social–cultural changes are much more likely to believe that economic integration is making them worse off. Also notable is the fact that inclusion of the *cultural threat* measure in the model consistently decreases the magnitude of the *education* variable, reduces the significance of the *pensioner* variable, and reverses the sign associated with *age*. These changes suggest that at least some of the negative attitudes among less-educated and older individuals toward trade openness can be accounted for by concerns regarding social and cultural change.

Holding all variables in column (4) at their means, a change from a respondent being culturally ''secure'' (associated with responses in the bottom 10th percentile on the *cultural threat* variable) to one that is culturally threatened (at the 90th percentile level) increases the likelihood of the respondent perceiving herself as worse off from economic integration almost fivefold (from 4.3% to 20.4%). Holding all other variables at their means, a positive change of one standard deviation in the *cultural threat* measure increases the likelihood of the respondent perceiving trade as having an adverse effect by six percentage points. In comparison, a downward change of one standard deviation in the income variable increases the same probability by slightly less than a single percentage point. In other words, the association between cultural threat and views on international trade is substantial both in an absolute and a relative sense.[32]

How well does the cultural threat argument perform compared to the other explanations? Hypotheses centered on the labor market as the source of attitudes on trade policy receive mixed results. On the one hand, and as noted above, some of the variables pertaining to people's labor market standing are indeed associated with people's attitudes (in particular, part-time employment and not being in the labor market). Moreover, *Job Situation,* the subjective measure of people's perceptions of globalization's impact on the labor market, is significant in all specifications. An individual who thinks that globalization has had a detrimental effect on the overall availability of well-paying jobs is substantially more likely to hold negative views about the impact of economic integration on their own well-being than someone who thinks that globalization has improved the offerings in the labor market (11.8% versus 7.1%).

Furthermore, the findings are consistent with the expectation of the H–O logic, as the sign on the coefficient for the interaction term *Education* × GDP per capita is negative and statistically significant (column 4). This relationship implies that for a given level of skill (as measured by educational attainment), a respondent in a skill-abundant country is less likely to view herself as worse off from trade openness than someone with an equivalent skill in a skill-scarce

[31] In substantive terms, this measure denotes the marginal effect on the probability of a respondent viewing herself as harmed by economic globalization given a one-unit increase in the value of the predictor variable, while holding all other variables at their sample means. I also estimated a set of ordered probit models using a dependent variable measured along a four-point scale instead of a dichotomous measure. The results remain substantively and statistically very similar.

[32] As noted, I also estimated the same specifications using an alternative measure of cultural threat that includes also attitudes on immigration. Re-estimating the benchmark specification in column (4), the marginal effect associated with this alternative measure of *cultural threat* increases to 6.0%, and the overall fit of the model increases from 0.175 to 0.181.

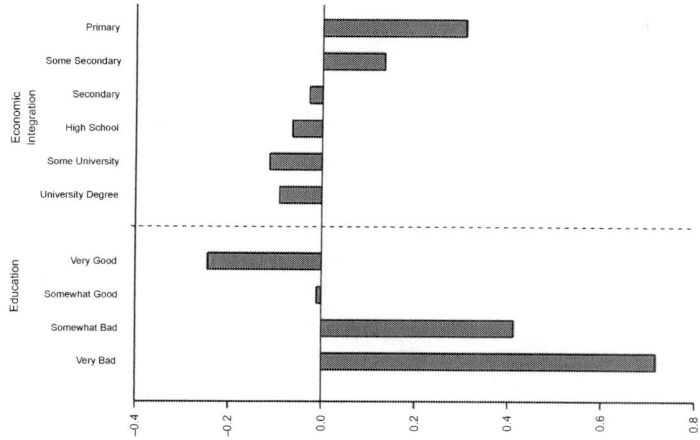

FIG 2. Cultural Threat Perceptions, by Education and Views on Economic Integration
Note: In both charts, the mean level of cultural threat is measured along the *X*-axis. The groupings in the bottom panel of the chart (that is, below the dotted line) are based on respondents' perception of how economic openness integrate their family. Respondents in the upper panel are grouped by level of education.

TABLE 2. Predictors of Perceived Loss from International Economic Integration

	(1)	*(2)*	*(3)*	*(4)*	*(5)*
Education	−0.013 (0.002)**	−0.013 (0.002)**	−0.010 (0.002)**	0.035 (0.016)*	0.037 (0.016)*
Cultural Threat			0.058 (0.003)**	0.057 (0.003)**	0.057 (0.003)**
Real Income (USD, ppp)	−0.013 (0.003)**	−0.012 (0.003)**	−0.009 (0.003)**	−0.007 (0.003)**	
Age	0.0007 (0.0002)**	0.0006 (0.0002)**	−0.0002 (0.0002)	−0.0003 (0.0002)	−0.0003 (0.0002)
Female	0.003 (0.005)	0.003 (0.005)	0 (0.005)	0.002 (0.005)	0.002 (0.005)
Part-time Employee	0.020 (0.011)+	0.022 (0.011)*	0.020 (0.01)+	0.020 (0.01)+	0.019 (0.01)+
Pensioner	0.024 (0.012)*	0.025 (0.012)*	0.014 (0.011)	0.012 (0.011)	0.012 (0.011)
Self-employed	−0.008 (0.008)	−0.008 (0.008)	−0.009 (0.007)	−0.008 (0.007)	−0.009 (0.007)
Unemployed	0.014 (0.011)	0.012 (0.011)	0.011 (0.01)	0.007 (0.01)	0.008 (0.01)
Not in Labor Force	0.015 (0.007)*	0.017 (0.007)*	0.015 (0.007)*	0.015 (0.007)*	0.015 (0.007)*
Job Situation		0.011 (0.001)**	0.008 (0.001)**	0.008 (0.001)**	0.008 (0.001)**
Edu × GDPpc(logged)				−0.005 (0.002)**	−0.005 (0.002)**
Current State				−0.005 (0.001)**	−0.005 (0.001)**
Five-year. Change				0.0003 (0.001)	0.0005 (0.001)
Relative Income					−0.007 (0.002)**
Pseudo Log-likelihood	−7993.13	−7911.56	−7568.47	−7548.5	−7543.03
Pseudo R^2	.13	.136	.173	.175	.176
N	23,797	23,705	23,705	23,705	23,705

(*Notes*: The coefficients of the probit analysis are estimated marginal effects (∂F/∂xk), that is, the marginal effect on Pr(y = 1) given a unit increase in the value of the relevant (continuous) regressor (xk), holding all other regressors at their respective sample means. Each model includes a full set of country dummies (coefficients not reported). +Significant at 10%; *Significant at 5%; **Significant at 1%.)

country. Conversely, unskilled laborers are less likely to view economic integration favorably in economies that are more skill abundant.[33]

However, even when accounting for this cross-national pattern, individuals with lower levels of education are more disposed to feel harmed by economic integration than their highly educated counterparts irrespective of the country's position in the global economy. This is the case when restricting the analysis to the more advanced economies (those with per capita GDP over $15,000) or to the least developed ones (those with per capita GDP below $2,000): In both settings, the coefficient associated with education is negative. These findings mirror the results of previous studies that have documented this education effect and point to the limits of using the H-O model to explain people's views on trade openness.[34] Notably, the results hold in a range of robustness tests, including estimations that use un-weighted data,

[33] I also estimated a logistic mixed-effect hierarchical model that accounts for the inclusion of a country-level variable in the model (GDP per capita). The substantive results are almost unchanged: The interaction of education and country income remains negative ($\beta_{Educ \times GDP} = -0.052$, $p = .004$), and the *cultural threat* variable remains positive and highly significant ($\beta_{cultural\ threat} = 0.62$, $p < .001$).

[34] For example, Hainmueller and Hiscox 2006; Beaulieu et al. 2004.

exclude imputed observations, or use an altogether different data set.[35]

Next, I test the hypothesis that people's relative standing in the labor market is a key factor in explaining attitudes on trade openness. Table 2 compares the explanatory strength of measures of respondents' absolute and relative income. Column (4) uses the log of respondents' absolute income in US dollars (adjusted for purchasing power parity), and column (5) replaces this measure with the income quintile of the respondent. As the table shows, the overall fit of the models using either of the measures is almost identical, suggesting that neither of the measures has substantially stronger explanatory power. In substantive terms, holding all other variables at their means, a change from being located at the top income quintile to the bottom income quintile is associated with a three–percentage point increase in the likelihood of a respondent perceiving economic globalization as harmful to their family's well-being.

A second measure of relative change is constructed by differencing respondents' reported subjective well-being at the present time with the same assessment of their well-being 5 years earlier. Although the results show a negative correlation between people's sense of well-being and their propensity to view economic integration as harmful, there does not seem to be a significant relationship between the perceived *change* in people's standing (from 5 years ago) and self-perceived loss from economic integration. The estimated effect of *5-year change* is miniscule, and the standard error is large. In sum, the two tests of the importance of relative standing, both across subjects (in terms of income) and within subjects (in terms of changes in an individual's well-being over time) do not indicate that concerns about relative standing are a major factor explaining negative views of economic integration.

Notably, the set of findings presented in Table 2 and discussed above are not driven by a specific country or geographical region. Table 3 presents results from two separate estimations for different geographic regions, one estimation with and the other without the *cultural threat* variable. The estimation of both models includes the same control variables used in column (1) of Table 2 (coefficients for the controls are not reported). The results make two points evident: First, the effect of the *cultural threat* variable is positive, statistically significant, and substantively large in all geographic regions. Furthermore, in all regions, the model that includes the *cultural threat* predictor is shown to have substantially greater explanatory power than the model without the predictor. In some regions (for example, Western Democracies, Asia), a model that controls for respondents' views on cultural openness explains almost three times more of the variation than the nested model without the *cultural threat* control. Second, the size of the effect associated with education consistently decreases, in some cases quite substantially, once respondents' level of cultural threat is included in the estimation. This suggests that while education has an independent effect on perceptions about the impact of economic globalization—perhaps as a proxy for skill attainment, perhaps by education increasing sophistication about the gains from trade—this effect is smaller once we account for individuals' cultural concerns. In the next section, I present an experiment that further explores this relationship between cultural concerns, education level, and views on economic openness.[36]

Survey Experiment

The analysis of the cross-national data reveals a strong empirical association between people's views on cultural openness and their perceptions of how economic integration affects them. Yet such analysis cannot ascertain whether a causal relationship exists, nor reveal the direction of causality. Establishing whether cultural concerns generate opposition to international trade is meaningful since if the correlation is spurious, or if the causal process operates only in the reverse direction, then cultural concerns are irrelevant for explaining the opposition to trade openness.

To address this issue, I carried out a randomized survey experiment on a national sample of US respondents. As before, the hypothesis underlying the experiment holds that people's view on the impact of international trade is influenced by their concerns about social and cultural changes that they associate with growing economic openness. If the two are unrelated in people's minds, then a prime that increases the prominence of such social–cultural concerns is expected to have no effect on people's assessments of the impact of international trade. Yet if the cultural prime is found to exert a discernable impact on people's views on trade liberalization, this would suggest that the cultural issues that individuals associate with openness do indeed influence their assessments of international trade.[37]

Such a priming experiment, it should be noted, assumes that people's views on the merits of international trade vary over time as a function of the extent to which they think of, and worry about, the social–cultural aspects of openness in a given period. Otherwise, exposure to primes that make the social–cultural aspects more prominent would have no impact on people's assessment of trade.

[35] See the online appendix for full results of a second set of tests with different cross-national data.

[36] Interestingly, the magnitude of the *cultural threat* variable varies across regions and is, for example, almost three times larger in the Middle East and North Africa than in Asia. One of course should *not* interpret this finding as if cultural threat is itself three times larger in the Middle East and North Africa than in Asia but rather that the association between cultural threat and negative attitudes on the impact of economic openness is substantially larger in the former region than in the latter. Explaining this variation as well as identifying the exact sources of people's sense of cultural threat are challenges beyond the scope of this paper, but certainly merit further study.

[37] To make the logic underlying this contention clearer, let us consider the hypothesis that one of the factors shaping opposition to immigration is people's perception that immigration leads to higher rates of crime. If people do not associate immigration with crime, then priming individuals with information that makes the issue of crime more salient in people's minds should not affect their attitudes on immigration (assuming that there is no other pathway by which individuals make the connection between crime and immigration). Yet if immigrants are associated in people's minds with crime, then the prime is likely to strengthen respondents' anti-immigrant sentiment.

TABLE 3. Education, Cultural Threat, and Perceived Loss from International Economic Integration, by Region

	Western Democracies		*Eastern Europe*		*Asia*		*Middle East & North Africa*		*Sub-Saharan Africa*		*Latin America*	
	(1)	*(2)*	*(1)*	*(2)*	*(1)*	*(2)*	*(1)*	*(2)*	*(1)*	*(2)*	*(1)*	*(2)*
Education	−0.019	−0.017	−0.022	−0.018	−0.010	−0.009	−0.023	−0.021	−0.007	−0.004	−0.013	−0.010
	(0.005)**	(0.004)**	(0.007)**	(0.006)**	(0.005)*	(0.005)*	(0.008)**	(0.008)**	(0.004)+	(0.004)	(0.004)**	(0.004)*
Cultural Threat		0.050		0.072		0.049		0.119		0.042		0.067
		(0.006)**		(0.006)**		(0.007)**		(0.012)**		(0.004)**		(0.006)**
Pseudo R^2	.037	.089	.076	.152	.03	.074	.117	.156	.246	.272	.073	.113
N	2,893	2,893	2,580	2,580	5,466	5,466	2,369	2,369	5,932	5,932	4,836	4,836

(*Notes*. The coefficients of the probit analysis are estimated marginal effects ($\partial F/\partial xk$), that is, the marginal effect on Pr(y=1) given a unit increase in the value of the relevant (continuous) regressor (xk), holding all other regressors at their respective sample means. All regressions include country's fixed effects and controls for income, age, gender, part-time employee, pensioner, self-employed, unemployed, and not in labor force (coefficients not reported).

+Significant at 10%; *Significant at 5%; **Significant at 1%.)

By collecting demographic data on the respondents, this experimental design also enables us to examine whether there are systematic differences in the way educated and less-educated individuals respond to the priming of cultural issues. The expectation is that if more of the less-educated individuals are anxious about the social–cultural aspects of openness, then exposure to the cultural prime would have a greater negative impact on their support for trade liberalization than on the highly educated. If such a systematic difference exists, it could provide at least a partial explanation for the "education puzzle" reported earlier.

Finally, to provide another yardstick for assessing the impact of cultural issues on people's thinking about economic integration, I test the effect of another priming treatment that triggers an altogether different set of associations. Since it could be that people view free trade positively (or negatively) because they generally support minimal government intervention, I prompt one treatment group with a "libertarian" prime. In the next section, I describe the design of the experiment, followed by a presentation of the results.

Experimental Design

The survey experiment fielded by the online polling firm YouGov/Polimetrix, Inc., in August 2006 included 1,455 American respondents and was carried out as follows: Respondents were randomly assigned into either a control or one of two treatment groups. The first treatment group was exposed to a "cultural" prime and the other treatment group to a "libertarian" prime. Participants in each of the groups were asked a set of four initial questions that differed in their content. The cultural prime treatment consisted of a set of questions about social and cultural issues such as their perceptions of changes in Americans' traditional way of life or whether the US anthem should be allowed to be sung in schools in a language other than English. The libertarian treatment consisted of questions relating to respondents' views on the optimal role of government. Finally, respondents in the control group were prompted with a set of "filler" questions about their preferences on outdoor activities.[38] Following this set of initial questions, *all three* groups were asked the exact same question about their view on the impact of economic integration: "Do you think that growing trade and business ties of the United States with other countries have made the average American better or worse off?"[39]

[38] See appendix 2 for the complete question protocol.

[39] The five-point scale ranged from (1) "A lot better off" to (5) "A lot worse off." The cross-national survey and the experimental study do not use the exact same question wording: While the Pew survey asked respondents about trade's impact on them personally, the experimental question gauges respondents' views on trade's impact on the average American. Other research, however, suggests that the results would be similar if the two dependent variable questions were the same. For example, Sears and Funk (1990) find that people typically rely on collective-level information rather than personal experiences in formulating policy views. More pertinently, Mansfield and Mutz (2009) find that people's assessments of trade openness represent socio-tropic considerations, that is, trade views are closely tied to how individuals perceive trade openness to affect the broader population.

Conducting the experiment with American subjects poses a hard test for the argument, since concerns in other countries about foreign cultural influences are often considered to be at least partially due to apprehension about "Americanization" and a consequent concern about the loss of local traditions. In the United States, a key exporter of culture rather than an importer, concerns regarding cultural exposure are therefore likely to be of smaller magnitude than in most other countries. Results found in the United States may thus be regarded as measuring a lower bound of the phenomenon discussed here.

Experiment Results

The results of the experiment are reported in Figure 3. The figure shows that respondents exposed to the cultural prime offered more negative assessments of the impact of economic integration than individuals exposed to the libertarian prime or those in the control group. However, the cultural prime is shown to have had a significant effect only on the attitudes of less-educated respondents (measured here as those with no college education). Following exposure to the cultural prime, less-educated respondents held more negative views on the effect of economic integration than those in the control group. The mean response rate was 3.37 versus 3.0, respectively, a difference of 14% along the five-point rating scale (the difference is significant at the $p < .03$ level).[40] To interpret this difference in more substantive terms, consider the following: While 44% of respondents in the control group described economic integration as harmful, the corresponding figure among those exposed to the cultural prime rose to 54%.[41] Notably, there was no treatment effect among respondents exposed to the libertarian questions; their views were not different from those in the control group. And again, the treatments had no effect on the attitudes of highly educated individuals.

To test whether the results were driven by any other confounding variables for which the random assignment of respondents did not account, I examine the results also in a multivariate regression. Table 4 below reports the results of the analysis. As before, the dependent variable is respondents' views on the impact of economic integration measured on a five-point scale. Results reported in column (1) confirm that the cultural prime did not have a statistically significant effect on the population at large. However, column (2) shows that exposure to the cultural prime did cause less-educated individuals to assess the impact of economic integration more negatively. The interaction term of education and the cultural prime is negative and highly significant in statistical terms ($p < .05$), in line with *H3*. Furthermore, as column (3) confirms, these results hold also when controlling for other possible confounding factors.

One interpretation of this finding is that the views on trade liberalization of less-educated individuals were more negatively affected by the cultural prime than the views of the highly educated because apprehension about cultural openness is more prevalent among the less educated. Indeed, this contention is supported by the data, which shows that 51.6% of the less-educated held culturally "protectionist" views on all the questions used to construct the cultural prime, while among highly educated individuals the corresponding figure was only 41.8% (difference significant at $p < .05$). Yet an alternative explanation may be that the effect of the prime on individuals with lower education was stronger not because of their cultural sensitivities but simply because they are more susceptible to priming. This experiment cannot definitively rule this explanation out; however, it should be noted that the literature on priming offers no evidence to suggest that less-educated individuals are systematically more susceptible to primes (in fact, a number of experimental studies find the opposite relationship).[42] Furthermore, the experiment shows that the less educated were unaffected by the libertarian prime, a finding that indicates that the specific content of the prime (and not simply education level) determines whether or not individuals' responses are affected by the prime.

In sum, the results offer further evidence in support of the hypothesis that concerns about cultural and social change that individuals associate with openness influence their views on international economic integration. Importantly, this link between the economic and cultural aspects of openness is shown to be pronounced among less educated individuals. This result is in line with the finding that educated individuals are on average more positively disposed toward economic integration than less-educated individuals, regardless of the skill abundance of the country in which they live. Hainmueller and Hiscox (2006) documented this pattern and hypothesized that the education effect on support for trade may have to do with greater exposure to economic curricula. The experimental findings presented here suggest that lower-educated individuals may, at least in part, be more apprehensive about economic integration for a different reason, namely that they are more likely to associate economic integration with a set of social and cultural consequences that they view as harmful.[43]

Conclusion

This article argues that people's assessments of the impact of international economic integration are

[40] See Table A2 for full results and *t*-statistics.

[41] As before, respondents are coded as viewing economic integration as harmful if they describe it as "somewhat bad" or "very bad."

[42] For example, see Petty and Wegener 1991; Petty 2001; Schwarz, Bless, and Bohner 1991; Kuo and Margalit forthcoming.

[43] Hainmueller and Hiscox (2006) report that including predictors associated with nationalist attachments in an analysis of ISSP data from 1995 had no substantial effect on decreasing the magnitude of the education measure as a predictor of trade attitudes. The actual size of the effect is not reported. The Online Appendix reports a similar test using the ISSP data from a latter wave (2003). Once a measure of cultural threat is included in the regression, the magnitude associated with the education variable decreases by almost 30%. Note that this change is comparable in size to the effect found when using the Pew Data (columns (2) and (3) in Table 2).

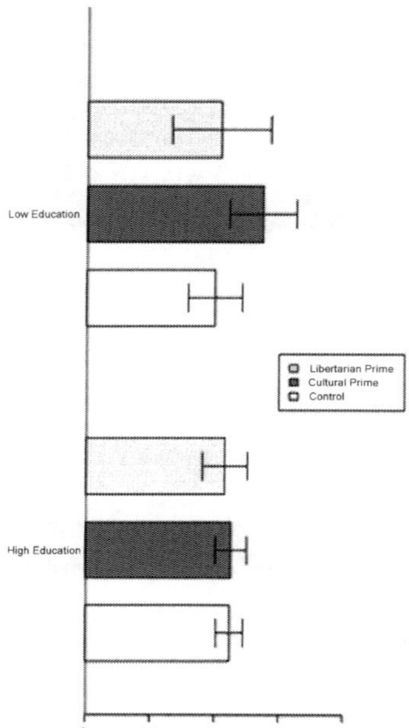

FIG 3. Experimental Treatment, Education Level, and Perception of Economic Integration as Harmful

Note: The *X*-axis denotes the mean response to the question about the perceived impact of economic integration on the average American. Possible answers: (1) "very good"; (2) "somewhat good"; (3) "neither good nor bad"; (4) "somewhat bad"; (5) "very bad". Each bar represents the mean response of a different treatment group. The difference of means among less-educated individuals between the cultural prime and the control group is highly significant ($p < .003$); differences between other experimental groups are not statistically significant.

TABLE 4. Experimental Treatment, Education, and Attitudes on Economic Integration

	(1)	*(2)*	*(3)*
Cultural Prime	0.071 (0.062)	0.666 (0.296)**	0.704 (0.296)**
Libertarian Prime	−0.016 (0.077)	0.128 (0.364)	0.106 (0.365)
Education		0.123 (0.1)	0.13 (0.101)
Cultural Prime × Education		−0.328 (0.159)**	−0.351 (0.16)**
Libertarian Prime × Education		−0.08 (0.197)	−0.069 (0.197)
Female			0.225 (0.056)***
Age			0.001 (0.002)
Psuedo R^2	.000	.006	.011
N	1,455	1,455	1,455

(*Notes.* Dependent variable is respondents' attitude on the impact of economic integration, ranging from (1) very good to (5) very bad. Standard errors in parentheses. Reported entries obtained from estimating in an ordered probit model.
*Significant at 10%; **Significant at 5%; ***Significant at 1%.)

partly shaped by the social and cultural changes that they associate with growing economic openness. Individuals apprehensive about these social–cultural consequences are more disposed to view economic integration as harmful. The analysis demonstrates that the empirical association between social–cultural views and attitudes on economic integration holds across geographical regions, countries that differ in terms of their level of economic development, and different sets of cross-national survey data. Furthermore, the study offers the first test of a causal relationship between attitudes on cultural change and opposition to economic openness, providing further evidence in support of the article's argument. While other explanations proposed in the literature, such as those centered on employment effects (Scheve and Slaughter 2001; Mayda and Rodrik 2005) or on people's concerns about relative economic standing (Graham and Pettinato 2002) are also shown to have explanatory power, the size of the variation accounted for by the measure of social–cultural threat indicates that this is a major factor explaining popular apprehension about international economic integration.

These findings suggest that in thinking about the political manifestations of discontentment with globalization, the anti-openness political "camp" should be seen as encompassing individuals with highly divergent concerns and beliefs. Some oppose economic integration because it exposes them to the risks of lower income, job insecurity, and unemployment. Others, however, oppose economic integration because it is seen as part of a broader process of change that affects some of the things they care most deeply about, be it the values and ideas that their children are exposed to, the traditions respected in their society, or their national and cultural identity. Studying the opposition to trade liberalization and economic globalization more broadly as driven merely by its distributive consequences is therefore a framework that is too narrow and which leaves out much of what is politically significant about the phenomenon in question.

The evidence put forward here contributes to the growing literature on the impact of economic globalization on domestic political competition (for example, Mughan and Lacy 2002; Meunier 2004; Kriesi et al. 2006; Walter 2010; Margalit 2011). It suggests that in studying the electoral repercussions of globalization, future research should examine how political parties use anti-openness messages to appeal to voters' discontentment with international integration. The findings also offer insight as to why political parties with diverse agendas such as the People's Party (SVP) in Switzerland, "Self-defense" in Poland, or Rafael Correa's Alianza PAIS in Ecuador do not only aim their anti-openness message at the labor market effects of economic integration. Instead, they also incorporate traditionalist, nationalist, or even religious appeals that offer a sense of protection on the social–cultural dimensions of economic integration. A promising avenue for future research would be to explore whether this phenomenon is a result of political entrepreneurs exploiting the connection voters are making intuitively between the economic and the social–cultural aspects of openness, or whether the politicians themselves are those making this connection salient to voters.

Finally, the findings presented here also speak to the ongoing debate regarding the policies needed to sustain popular support for open markets. Scholars often note that although international trade can have sharp distributive consequences with clear winners and losers, the *aggregate* gains from trade imply that the surplus can be used to compensate the losers and assuage their opposition to trade liberalization. This is the rationale underlying calls for expanding public funding for active labor market programs that provide wage insurance and retraining services for workers hurt by trade, such as the TAA program in the United States and similar programs in Western Europe (Marcal 2001; Davidson, Matusz, and Nelson 2007). Others cast doubt on the ability of such programs to effectively assuage the losers' discontentment and call instead for a substantial redistribution of income (Scheve and Slaughter 2007). The evidence presented here suggests that while such measures could help alleviate some of the opposition toward economic globalization, they are likely to have only a limited effect; substantial opposition among the constituencies that feel socially and culturally discomfitted by growing openness is likely to remain strong.

References

BAKER, ANDY. (2003) Why Is Trade Reform So Popular in Latin America? A Consumption-Based Theory of Trade Policy Preferences. *World Politics* 55 (3): 423–455.

BAKER, ANDY. (2005) Who Wants to Globalize? Consumer Tastes and Labor Markets in a Theory of Trade Policy Beliefs. *American Journal of Political Science* 49 (4): 924–938.

BEAULIEU, EUGENE, MICHAEL BENNAROCH, AND JIM GAISFORD. (2004) *Intra-Industry Trade Liberalization, Wage Inequality and Trade Policy Preferences.* Mimeograph: University of Calgary.

BECK, ULRICH. (1992) *Risk Society: Towards a New Modernity.* London: Sage Publications.

BECK, ULRICH. (2006) *The Cosmopolitan Vision.* Cambridge, UK: Polity.

BLANCHFLOWER, DAVID G., AND ANDREW J. OSWALD. (1999) *Well-Being, Insecurity and the Decline of American Job Satisfaction.* Working paper, Hanover, NH: Dartmouth College.

BOBO, LAWRENCE, AND FREDERICK C. LICARI. (1989) Education and Political Tolerance: Testing the Effects of Cognitive Sophistication and Target Group Affect. *Public Opinion Quarterly* 53: 285–308.

BOZÓKI, ANDRES, AND JOHN T. ISHIYAMA. Eds. (2002) *The Communist Successor Parties of Central and Eastern Europe.* Armonk, NY: M. E. Sharpe.

BURGOON, BRIAN, AND MICHAEL HISCOX. (2003) The Mysterious Case of Female Protectionism: Gender Bias in the Attitudes and Politics of International Trade. Paper Presented at the Annual Meeting of the American Political Science Association, Chicago.

CHANDLER, CHARLES R., AND YUNG-MEI TSAI. (2001) Social Factors Influencing Immigration Attitudes: An Analysis of Data from the General Social Survey. *Social Science Journal* 38 (2): 177–188.

CITRIN, JACK, DONALD P. GREEN, CHRISTOPHER MUSTE, AND CARA WONG. (1997) Public Opinion toward Immigration Reform: The Role of Economic Motivations. *Journal of Politics* 59 (3): 858–881.

COENDERS, MARCEL, AND PEER SCHEEPERS. (2003) The Effect of Education on Nationalism and Ethnic Exclusionism: An International Comparison. *Political Psychology* 24: 313–341.

COWEN, TYLER. (2002) *Creative Destruction.* Princeton, NJ: Princeton University Press.

DAVIDSON, CARL, STEVEN J. MATUSZ, AND DOUGLAS R. NELSON. (2007) Can Compensation Save Free Trade? *Journal of International Economics* 71 (8): 167–186.

DE MASTER, SARA, AND MICHAEL K. LE ROY. (2000) Xenophobia and the European Union. *Comparative Politics* 32 (4): 419–436.

EASTERLIN, RICHARD A. (2001) Income and Happiness: Towards a Unified Theory. *The Economic Journal* 111: 465–484.

GIDDENS, ANTHONY. (2000) *Runaway World: How Globalization Is Reshaping Our Lives.* New York: Routledge.

GRAHAM, CAROL, AND STEFANO PETTINATO. (2002) Frustrated Achievers: Winners, Losers and Subjective Well-Being in New Market Economies. *The Journal of Development Studies* 38 (4): 100–140.

HAINMUELLER, JENS, AND MICHAEL HISCOX. (2006) Learning to Love Globalization: The Effects of Education on Individual Attitudes toward International Trade. *International Organization* 60 (2): 469–498.

HAINMUELLER, JENS, AND MICHAEL HISCOX. (2007) Educated Preferences: Explaining Individual Attitudes toward Immigration in Europe. *International Organization* 61 (2): 399–442.

HAINMUELLER, JENS, AND MICHAEL HISCOX. (2010) Attitude Towards Highly Skilled and Low Skilled Immigration: Evidence from a Survey Experiment. *American Political Science Review* 104 (1): 61–84.

HAYS, JUDE C., SEAN D. EHRLICH, AND CLINT PEINHARDT. (2005) Government Spending and Public Support for Trade in the OECD: An Empirical Test of the Embedded Liberalism Thesis. *International Organization* 59: 473–494.

INGLEHART, ROLAND. (2000) Globalization and Postmodern Values. *Washington Quarterly* 23 (1): 215–228.

IRWIN, DOUGLASS A. (1996) Industry or Class Cleavages Over Trade Policy? Evidence from the British General Election of 1923. In *The Political Economy of Trade Policy: Papers in Honor of Jagdish Bhagwati*, edited by R. C. Feenstra, G. M. Grossman, and D. A. Irwin. Cambridge, MA: MIT Press.

KAHNEMAN, DANIEL, AND AMOS TVERSKY. (1979) Prospect Theory—Analysis of Decision Under Risk. *Econometrica* 47 (2): 263–291.

KRIESI, HANSPETER, EDGAR GRANDE, ROMAN LACHAT, MARTIN DOLEZAL, SIMON BORNSCHIER, AND TIMOTHEOS FREY. (2006) Globalization and the Transformation of the National Political Space: Six European Countries Compared. *European Journal of Political Research* 45 (6): 921–956.

KRUGMAN, PAUL R., AND MAURICE OBSTFELD. (1994) *International Economics*, 3rd edition. New York: Harper-Collins.

KUO, ALEX, AND YOTAM MARGALIT. Measuring Individual Identity: An Experimental Approach. *Comparative Politics.* Forthcoming.

MAGEE, STEPHEN P. Ed. (1978). *Three Simple Tests of the Stolper-Samuelson Theorem. Issues in International Economics.* London: Oriel.

MALHOTRA, NEIL, YOTAM MARGALIT, AND CECILIA H. MO. (2010) Economic Explanations for Opposition to Immigration: Distinguishing Between Prevalence and Magnitude. Paper presented at the Annual Meeting of the American Political Science Association Meeting, Washington, DC, August.

MANSFIELD, EDWARD, AND DIANA MUTZ. (2009) Support for Free Trade: Self-Interest, Sociotropic Politics, and Out Group Anxiety. *International Organization* 63 (2): 423–457.

MARCAL, LEAH E. (2001) Does Trade Adjustment Assistance Help Trade-Displaced Workers? *Contemporary Economic Policy* 19 (1): 59–72.

MARGALIT, YOTAM. (2011) Costly Jobs: Trade-Related Layoffs, Government Compensation and Voting in U.S. Presidential Elections. *American Political Science Review* 105 (1): 166–188.

MAYDA, ANNA M. (2006) Who Is Against Immigration? A Cross-Country Investigation of Attitudes Towards Immigrants. *Review of Economics and Statistics* 88 (3): 510–530.

MAYDA, ANNA M., AND DANI RODRIK. (2005) Why Are Some People (and Countries) More Protectionist Than Others? *European Economic Review* 49 (6): 1393–1430.

MCLAREN, LAUREN M. (2002) Public Support for the European Union: Cost/Benefit Analysis or Perceived Cultural Threat. *Journal of Politics* 64 (2): 551–566.

MCMAHON, DARRIN. (1995) *Echoes of a Recent Past: Contemporary French Anti-Americanism in Historical and Cultural Perspective.* International Security Studies at Yale University.

MEUNIER, SOPHIE. (2004) Globalization and Europeanization: A Challenge to French Politics. *French Politics* 2: 125–150.

MUGHAN, ANTHONY, AND DEAN LACY. (2002) Economic Performance, Job Insecurity and Electoral Choice. *British Journal of Political Science* 32: 513–533.

O'ROURKE, KEVIN H., AND RICHARD SINNOTT. (2001) What Determines Attitudes Towards Protection? Some Cross-Country Evidence. Paper read at the Brookings Trade Forum.

PETTY, RICHARD E. (2001) Subtle Influences on Judgment and Behavior: Who Is Most Susceptible? In *Social Influence: Direct and Indirect Processes,* edited by J. Forgas, and K. Williams. Philadelphia, PA: Psychology Press.

PETTY, RICHARD E., AND DUANE T. WEGENER. (1991) Thought Systems, Argument Quality, and Persuasion. In *The Content, Structure, and Operation of Thought Systems,* edited by Robert S. Wyer Jr. and Thomas Srull. Hillsdale, NJ: Lawrence Erlbaum Associates, Inc. Publishers.

PEW RESEARCH CENTER. (2003) The Pew Global Attitudes Project. Available at http://people-press.org/pgap/.

PUTTNAM, DAVID, WITH NEIL WATSON. (1998) *Movies and Money.* New York: Alfred A. Knopf.

RITZER, GEORGE. (2000) *The McDonaldization of Society.* Thousand Oaks, CA: Pine Forge Press.

RODRÍGUEZ, FRANCISCO, AND DANI RODRIK. (2000) Trade Policy and Economic Growth: A Skeptic's Guide to the Cross-National Evidence. In *NBER Macroeconomics Annual 2000,* edited by Bernanke Ben, and Rogoff Kenneth. Cambridge, MA: MIT Press.

RODRIK, DANI. (1997) *Has Globalization Gone Too Far?.* Washington, DC: Institute for International Economics.

SACHS, JEFFREY D., AND ANDREW WARNER. (1995) Economic Reform and the Process of Global Integration. *Brookings Papers on Economic Activity* 1: 1–118.

SCHEVE, KENNETH F., AND MATTHEW J. SLAUGHTER. (2001) What Determines Individual Trade-Policy Preferences? *Journal of International Economics* 54 (2): 267–292.

SCHEVE, KENNETH F., AND MATTHEW J. SLAUGHTER. (2007) A New Deal for Globalization. *Foreign Affairs* 86 (4): 34–47.

SCHWARZ, NORBERT, HERBERT BLESS, AND GERD BOHNER. (1991) Mood and Persuasion: Affective States Influence the Processing of Persuasive Communications. In *Advances in Experimental Social Psychology,* edited by M. P. Zanna. San Diego, CA: Academic Press.

SEARS, DAVID O., AND CAROLYN L. FUNK. (1990) Self-Interest in Americans' Political Opinions. In *Beyond Self-Interest,* edited by Jane J. Mansbridge. Chicago: University of Chicago Press.

SNIDERMAN, PAUL M., LOUK HAGENDOORN, AND MARKUS PRIOR. (2004) Predispositional Factors and Situational Triggers: Exclusionary Reactions to Immigrant Minorities. *American Political Science Review* 98: 35–50.

STIGLITZ, JOSEPH E. (2002) *Globalization and its Discontents,* 1st edition. New York: Norton.

SWANK, DUANE, AND HANS-GEORG BETZ. (2003) Globalization, the Welfare State and Right-Wing Populism in Western Europe. *Socio-Economic Review* 1: 215–245.

TRIANDIS, HARRY C. (1995) Individualism & Collectivism. *New Directions in Social Psychology.* Boulder: Westview Press.

UNESCO INSTITUTE FOR STATISTICS. (2005) International Flows of Selected Goods and Services, 1994–2003: Defining and Capturing the Flows of Global Cultural Trade. Available at http://unesdoc.unesco.org/images/0014/001428/142812e.pdf.

VOGT, W. PAUL. (1997) *Tolerance & Education: Learning to Live with Diversity and Difference.* London: Sage.

WACZIARG, ROMAIN, AND KAREN HORN WELCH. (2008) Trade Liberalization and Growth: New Evidence. *World Bank Economic Review* 22: 187–131.

WAGNER, ULRICH, AND ANDREAS ZICK. (1995) The Relation of Formal Education to Ethnic Prejudice: Its Reliability, Validity and Explanation. *European Journal of Social Psychology* 25: 41–56.

WALTER, STEFANIE. (2010) Globalization and the Welfare State: Testing the Microfoundations of the Compensation Hypothesis. *International Studies Quarterly* 54 (2): 403–426.

Appendix 1: Measurement of Control Variables

Education

Variable is coded based on the highest level of education attained by the respondent. The categories are 1. No formal education; 2. Completed primary education; 3. Some secondary education; 4. Completed high school; 5. Some university or college education; and 6. Completed university or college degree.

Income

The variable is coded based on responses to the question: "Here is a list of incomes. Which of these does your household fall into counting all wages, salaries, pensions, and other incomes that come in? Just give the letter of the group your household falls into, before taxes and other deductions." In each country, the responses were a set of ranges. To generate a specific dollar figure, I assigned each of the respondents the middle point within that range (that is, if a respondent earns in the range of $2,500–$3,000 US dollars, the respondent's income was calculated as $2,750). The income of respondents in the bottom income category (between $0 and $X) was calculated as 80% of the upper bound (that is, as 0.8 * $X). The income of the top category, which was often "above X dollars," was calculated as 25% above the category's lower bound (that is, 1.25 * $X).

Job Situation

The variable is coded based on responses to two questions: (i) Has each of the following gotten better or worse over the last 5 years in our country: The availability of good-paying jobs?" (1. Better; 2. Worse; 3. Has not changed; 4. Don't know and (ii) Do you think this change in the availability of good-paying jobs is largely because of the way the world has become more connected or mostly for other reasons? 1. Largely because world more connected; 2. Mostly other reasons; 3. DK. The *Job Situation* variable is coded as follows (the first number in the parentheses corresponds to respondents' answer to the first question; the second number to the second question): 1. (1,1); 2. (1,3); 3. (1,2); 4. (3 or 4 in Q1); 5.(3,2); 6.(3,3); 7.(3,1).

Current State

The variable is coded on a 1–10 scale, based on the response to the following question: Here is a ladder representing the "ladder of life." Let's suppose the top of the ladder represents the best possible life for you, and the bottom the worst possible life for you. On which step of the ladder do you feel you personally stand at the present time?

Five-year change

Deducting *current state* from the response to the follow-up question: On which step would you say you stood 5 years ago?

Countries included in the PEW Global Attitudes survey and covered in the analysis: Angola, Argentina, Bangladesh, Bolivia, Brazil, Bulgaria, Canada, Czech Republic, France, Germany, Ghana, Great Britain, Guatemala, Honduras, India, Indonesia, Italy, Ivory Coast, Japan, Jordan, Kenya, Lebanon, Mali, Mexico, Nigeria, Pakistan, Peru, Philippines, Poland, Russia, Senegal, Slovak Republic, South Africa, South Korea, Tanzania, Turkey, Uganda, Ukraine, Venezuela, and the USA.

Appendix 2: Experimental Treatments

Listed below are the questions used as the opening questions in each experimental treatments. These questions were followed by the dependent variable on the effects of trade and economic openness.

Questions to the Control Group

In a typical week, how often do you do physical exercise (for example, jogging, hiking)?

1. Five times or more; 2. 3–4 times; 3. 1–2 times; 4. Hardly ever.

Do you like doing outdoor activities (such as hiking, biking, climbing)?

1. Very much like; 2. Somewhat like; 3. Somewhat dislike; 4. Strongly dislike.

Of the following sporting activities, which do you like best?

1. Jogging; 2. Playing team sports; 3. Hiking; 4. Working out in the gym; 5. None of the above.

Over the last 2 years, how often have you visited any of the national parks?

1. Five times or more; 2. 1–4 times; 3. Did not visit any national parks.

Cultural Prime Questions

There has recently been a debate about whether the US National anthem, the Star Spangled Banner, should be sung in some schools in Spanish and not in English. Some people think that singing the National anthem in another language hurts our culture. What do you think?

"The Star Spangled Banner should be sung only in English (or in any language)".

In some countries, homosexual (gay) couples are legally allowed to marry and are recognized by the law in exactly the same way as a married heterosexual (straight) couple. There is now a growing debate within the United States about whether similar legislation should be enacted. Do you favor or oppose allowing gay marriages in the United States? (1. Strongly favor—5. Strongly oppose).

Do you agree or disagree with the following statement: "Our traditional way of life is getting lost".

(1. Strongly agree—5. Strongly disagree).

Do you agree or disagree with the following statement: "These days American culture is increasingly threatened". (1. Strongly agree—5. Strongly disagree).

Libertarian Prime Questions

We would now like to ask you a few questions about issues discussed in the news. For each of the following statements, please select the answer that best describes your view:

"The current level of taxation in the United States is too low" (1. Strongly agree—5. Strongly disagree).

"Governments tend to be wasteful" (1. Strongly agree—5. Strongly disagree).

"To accommodate the growing numbers of convicted felons, the federal government should build more prisons" (1. Strongly agree—5. Strongly disagree).

"Freedom is having a government that doesn't interfere in my life" (1. Strongly agree—5. Strongly disagree).

TABLE A1. Descriptive Statistics Pew Global Attitudes Data

Variable	*Mean*	*SD*	*Min*	*Max*
Age	37.904	14.882	18	97
Cultural Threat	−0.024	0.984	−2.038	2.244
Current State	5.552	2.165	0	10
Edu × GDPpc(log)	30.191	13.682	6.326	61.594
Education	3.564	1.491	1	6
Female	0.478	0.500	0	1
Five-year Change	0.035	2.532	−10	10
Income (quintile)	2.617	1.475	1	5
Job Situation	4.528	1.984	1	7
Loss from Econ. Integration	0.126	0.332	0	1
Not in Labor Force	0.307	0.461	0	1
Part-time Employee	0.078	0.268	0	1
Pensioner	0.091	0.287	0	1
Real Income (log)	8.699	1.439	0	11.736
Self-employed	0.156	0.363	0	1
Unemployed	0.071	0.256	0	1

N = 23,705

TABLE A2. Perception of Economic Integration as Harmful, by Exposure to Treatment and Education Level

	Education: Low			Education: High		
Treatment	Mean	*t*-stat	*N*	Mean	*t*-stat	*N*
Control	3.0		137	3.12		561
Cultural prime	3.37	2.2**	89	3.13	0.15	413
Libertarian prime	3.04	0.2	48	3.08	0.34	207

(*Note.* Mean score denotes the average view of respondents on the effect of economic openness rated on a 1 (very good) to 5 (very bad) scale. The *t* statistic is obtained from a *t*-test comparing the treatment and control group.)

TABLE A3. Descriptive Statistics: Survey Experiment

	Cultural Prime		*Libertarian Prime*		*Control*		*Full Sample*			
	Mean	*SD*	*Mean*	*SD*	*Mean*	*SD*	*Mean*	*SD*	*Min*	*Max*
Econ. integration	3.17	1.25	3.07	1.28	3.09	1.27	3.09	1.27	1	5
Education	1.82	0.38	1.81	0.39	1.80	0.40	1.80	0.40	1	2
Female	1.54	1.50	1.53	1.50	1.51	1.50	1.51	1.50	1	2
Age	49.60	15.12	49.35	15.43	51.15	15.23	51.15	15.23	18	90
N	502		255			698		1,455		

Part III
The Great Recession and International Trade

[15]

NOTE

IS PROTECTIONISM ON THE RISE? ASSESSING NATIONAL TRADE POLICIES DURING THE CRISIS OF 2008

Hiau Looi Kee, Cristina Neagu, and Alessandro Nicita*

Abstract—This paper quantifies trade policy changes and the associated trade impacts for about 100 countries between 2008 and 2009. Results show that there has been no widespread increase in protectionism. Only a few countries, including Russia, Argentina, Turkey, and China, have increased tariffs on major imported products. The United States and the EU, by contrast, rely mainly on antidumping duties to shield domestic industries. Overall, while the rise in tariffs and antidumping duties may have jointly caused global trade to drop by US$43 billion, it explains less than 2% of the collapse in world trade during the crisis period.

I. Introduction

WITH the dramatic collapse of world trade in the wake of the biggest global recession in recent history, many have feared that governments may respond by increasing tariffs and other trade policy barriers to protect their domestic economies, which may indirectly prolong the recession and lead to domestic unrest. In fact, in December 2008, the first of the crisis-related demonstrations erupted in several cities in Russia over the increase in car tariffs (Levy, 2008).

Has protectionism been rising since fall 2008? To answer this question, we compare the overall trade restrictiveness Indices (OTRI) of a wide range of countries in 2008 and 2009. The OTRI summarizes the trade policy stance of a country by calculating the uniform tariff that will keep its overall imports at the current level when the country in fact has different tariffs for different goods. Unlike trade-weighted average tariffs, the OTRI takes into account the importance of each good in total imports, as well as the responsiveness of the import of each good with respect to its tariff. Thus, not only are the weights proportionate to the import value of the goods, but goods that have a larger fall in imports when tariffs are imposed (those goods that are highly elastic in demand) are also given larger weights. The empirical methodology of the OTRI was first developed by Kee, Nicita, and Olarreaga (2008, 2009), based on the theoretical underpinning of Anderson and Neary (1994, 1996, 2003). Irwin (2010) also uses a similar methodology to study the historic protection level of the United States from 1867 to 1961. A major benefit of looking at the changes in the OTRI over the crisis period is that it allows us not only to measure the changes in trade policy but also to quantify the drop in trade due to those changes. This is the point of departure of our paper from the previous literature, which tends to focus on only average tariff increases or the percentage of tariff lines that have increased during the crisis period.

Received for publication May 25, 2010. Revision accepted for publication June 8, 2011.

* Kee and Neagu: World Bank; Nicita: U.N. Conference on Trade and Development.

We are grateful to the International Trade Center in Geneva for kindly sharing the data with us and to Richard Newfarmer and Elisa Gamberoni for facilitating the request. We are indebted to Chad Bown for sharing his data on antidumping duties and all the stimulating discussions and comments. We also thank Ann Harrison for feedback on a previous draft. Feedback from Daniel Lederman, Caglar Ozden, and participants of the World Bank DECRG Crisis Workshop in January 2010 is acknowledged. The findings, interpretations, and conclusions expressed in this paper are entirely our own and should not be attributed to the World Bank or the United Nations Conference on Trade and Development.

A supplemental appendix is available online at http://www.mitpressjournals.org/doi/suppl/10.1162/REST_a_00241.

Many recent papers have studied the trade impact of the global crisis in 2008 (see Baldwin & Evenett, 2009, and Baldwin, 2009). While consensus has yet to emerge among researchers, the two leading explanations for the large and synchronized drop in trade are the role of international supply chains (Yi, 2009) and the lack of trade credits and finance during the crisis period (Amiti & Weinstein, 2009; Chor & Manova, 2009). In a unified framework, Eaton et al. (2010) merges an input-output framework with a gravity trade model of the world and shows that changes in demand play the most significant role in explaining the large drop in trade-to-GDP ratio during the crisis, while trade frictions, which include trade policies and trade credits, explain at most about 15% of the collapse in trade. Thus, trade policy as a protectionist device has not been seen to play a substantial role in the global collapse of trade—neither as a cause nor a consequence. Nevertheless, anecdotal evidence suggests that some countries are actively tinkering with their trade policies. For example, during the crisis period, Bolivia, Ecuador, and Turkey have altered their tariffs on a large share of their imported products, and India increased its use of antidumping (AD) duties. How important are those changes in explaining or prolonging the collapse in world trade? The objective of this paper is to carefully compare the trade policies of a wide range of countries over the crisis period and assess the extent of the fall in trade due to the increase in tariffs and AD duties of these countries. For the purpose of this paper, we narrowly define trade policies to include only tariffs and AD duties. Due to data limitations, we do not look at other policies that may affect trade, such as government bailouts and buy-national requirements, which could play a much larger role than tariffs and AD in affecting trade during the crisis period.

To achieve our objective, we obtained the most favored nations (MFN) applied tariff schedules and the bilateral tariff schedules for a wide range of countries in 2008 and 2009.[1] The MFN-applied tariffs tend to overestimate the level of protection because they do not account for the existence of bilateral or regional tariff preferences. Hence, it is important for us to construct the OTRI based on the bilateral tariff schedules. This significantly complicates the calculation of the OTRI because each country may have up to 200 trading partners and each bilateral tariff schedule consists of nearly 5,000 Harmonized System (HS) 6 digit products. To capture the effect of antidumping, we also merge the bilateral tariff schedules with the World Bank Global Antidumping Database. Thus, changes in the OTRI reflect trade policy changes related to both the changes in applied tariffs and antidumping duties during the crisis period.

In addition, we need bilateral import demand elasticities and bilateral trade flow data to properly weigh these bilateral tariffs. We modify the multilateral import demand elasticity estimates in Kee et al. (2008) to obtain bilateral import demand elasticities. Bilateral trade flow data are from Comtrade. Finally, to make sure that changes in the OTRI period purely capture changes in trade policies, we use the 2008 bilateral trade flows and elasticities as fixed weights. As such, changes in trade or elasticity due to demand shocks will not affect our OTRI measures.

[1] As a robustness check, we also compare the tariffs of 2007 to those of 2009. The results are very similar and available on request.

Going through the schedules of all countries in our data set, we found that overall, there has been no widespread increase in tariffs. Although many countries have increased tariffs on imported products, the trade impact has generally been minimal. However, for a handful of countries, tariff increases on important items in agriculture and manufacturing pushed up their OTRI and significantly affected trade. Russia, Malawi, and Argentina all increased tariffs on manufacturing products that caused their OTRI to increase by 0.9 to 1.2 percentage points and their trade flows to drop by US$4.8 billion, US$29 million, and US$914 million, respectively. Turkey increased tariffs on a wide range of agricultural products, which raised its OTRI by 0.8 percentage points and caused its trade flow to decrease by US$2.2 billion. With the removal of a temporary tariff reduction on palm oil and the introduction of some antidumping duties, India had a large increase in the level of protectionism on agriculture products (8.3 percentage points), even though this was offset by tariff liberalization in the manufacturing sector such that India's OTRI increased only by 0.1 percentage points. Other countries that had large drops in trade due to increases in tariffs include China (US$5 billion), Canada (US$1.8 billion), and Brazil (US$991 million). Finally, for the United States and the EU, although the tariff schedules remained roughly the same throughout our period of analysis, spikes in antidumping duties caused their OTRI to increase by 0.5 percentage points, and 0.1 percentage points, respectively. Jointly, if we add up all the decreases in trade for all countries during the crisis period due to changes in tariffs and antidumping duties, in the worst-case scenario, the total decrease in imports is about US$43 billion, which is less than half a percent of the world's imports in 2008. According to the latest estimate of the World Trade Organization (2010), the world's imports decreased by 24% from its precrisis level. Thus, trade policies can explain at most 2% of the sharp drop in world trade. This suggests that protectionism was not the main culprit behind the collapse of world trade and the collapse of world trade did not cause protectionism to increase.

Countries have been restrained in terms of raising their tariffs and AD for several reasons. First, most countries are part of bilateral, regional, or multilateral trade agreements, which may have significantly restricted their ability to adjust tariffs during the crisis period. The limitations in policy space due to multilateral obligations are more relevant for developed countries, such as the EU and the United States, where the difference between bound and applied rates is generally small. This is not the case for most developing countries. Those are generally more constrained by obligations within regional and preferential trade agreements. Second, countries may recognize the adverse long-run impact of those protectionist policies in the context of an increasingly globalized economy. This is particularly the case if the exports of the countries depend heavily on imported materials: higher tariffs will severely affect exports, thus further hindering economic recovery. Similarly, global production chains and foreign direct investment (FDI) that span national borders have made it harder to distinguish domestic from foreign. Thus, many multinational firms find that traditional forms of protectionism are contrary to their interests. This could explain why most countries continued to liberalize their tariff policies during the crisis rather than raising tariffs. In this regard, carefully targeted AD may well be the more suitable policy choice. However, the modest increase in AD cases during the crisis suggests that firms may also have found this instrument inadequate to protect their interests.

This paper is organized as follows. We first briefly discuss the methodology behind the OTRI calculation in section II. Section III presents the data coverage. Section IV discusses the results, and section V concludes.

II. Change in the Overall Trade Restrictiveness Index

The OTRI summarizes the impact of each country's trade policies on its aggregate imports. The OTRI's conceptual framework was first proposed in Anderson and Neary (1994, 1996, 2003), it was simplified in Feenstra (1995), and it was empirically estimated in Kee, Nicita, and Olarreaga (2008, 2009). The OTRI answers the following question: What is the uniform tariff that, if imposed on home imports, would leave the aggregate imports at their current level? In a partial equilibrium, when we ignore the substitution between products and the potential income effect due to tariff revenue redistribution, the OTRI is just a more sophisticated way to calculate the weighted average tariff of a country, with the weight of a good set equal to the product of the good's import demand elasticity and its share in total import. Irwin (2010) also applies the same approach to study the historic level of protection of the United States.

We refer readers to Kee, Nicita, and Olarreaga (2008, 2009) for the formal derivation of the OTRI of a country. In this paper, we adopt a fixed-weight method to compare the OTRI of a country across two years, where the bilateral trade flow data and elasticity estimates of the base year, 2008, are used as weights:[2]

$$OTRI_c^{2009} - OTRI_c^{2008} = \frac{\sum_n \sum_p m_{ncp}^{2008} \varepsilon_{ncp}^{2008} \left(t_{ncp}^{2009} - t_{ncp}^{2008}\right)}{\sum_n \sum_p m_{ncp}^{2008} \varepsilon_{ncp}^{2008}}, \tag{1}$$

where m_{ncp} is the bilateral import value of country c for good n from partner country p, t_{ncp} is the ad valorem tariff of country c on good n from country p, and ε_{ncp} is the import demand elasticity of country c for good n from country p. Superscripts indicate the year of the variables. In this way, the difference in the OTRI of a country between 2008 and 2009 captures only trade policy changes and does not reflect the collapse of trade during the crisis period.

While the trade policy of a country could also consist of other nontariff measures, here, due to data limitations, we focus mainly on tariffs. However, unlike the earlier papers, we use the bilateral tariffs between country pairs at the HS 6 digit good level in our calculation of the OTRI. Moreover, we also employ the bilateral import demand elasticity at the same level of aggregation as the tariffs. Finally, when possible, we include any antidumping duties that were imposed during the crisis period.

Once the change in the OTRI of a country is calculated, some back-of-the-envelope calculations can be made to figure out the impact on trade-flows. One way is to use the change in the OTRI multiplied by the trade-weighted import demand elasticities of the country. Then,

$$\text{Change in trade using the OTRI} = \left(OTRI_c^{2009} - OTRI_c^{2008}\right) \sum_n \sum_p m_{ncp}^{2008} \varepsilon_{ncp}^{2008}. \tag{2}$$

Note that there is no bound for the calculation of change in trade in this formula, and thus it is possible for the change in trade to be higher than the existing level of trade. An alternative approach would be to calculate the change in tariff at the tariff line level for each product from each partner country, multiply that by the bilateral import demand elasticity

[2] For the purposes of this paper, we also calculated bilateral import demand elasticities, which vary across countries, products, and partners. For each product n imported by country c from partner country p, we rely on the following formula and on estimates of the GDP function parameter, a_{nn}, from Kee et al. (2008) to construct bilateral import demand elasticities, where s_{nc} is the share of trade in product n in the GDP of country c in 2008 and s_{ncp} is the share of trade in product n from partner country p in the GDP of country c in 2008 (refer to Kee et al., 2010, for a proof):

$$\varepsilon_{ncp} = \frac{a_{nn}}{s_{nc}} + s_{ncp} - 1.$$

FIGURE 1.—COMPARING AVERAGE BILATERAL TARIFFS, 2008 VERSUS 2009

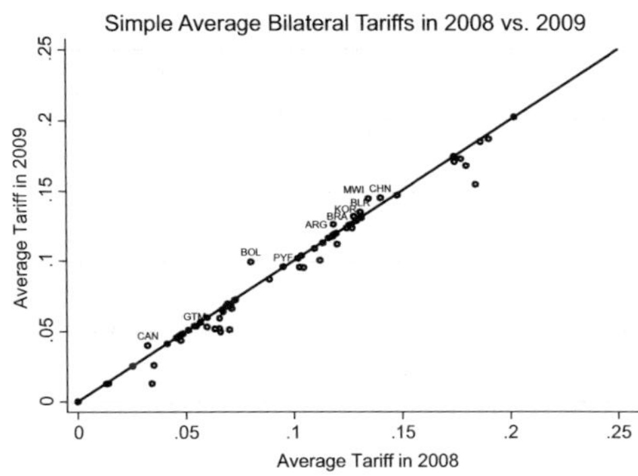

TABLE 1.—ANTIDUMPING DUTIES AFFECTED IMPORTS IN 2008–2009

Country	Value (US$000)	Share in Total Import (%)	Share of AD Import with AD Data (%)
Argentina	336,499	0.59	32.33
Australia	50,931	0.03	100.00
Brazil	657,543	0.38	76.14
Canada	578,787	0.14	100.00
Chile	350	0.00	100.00
China	990,444	0.10	100.00
Colombia	21,919	0.06	100.00
European Union	8,560,695	0.38	100.00
India	1,405,095	0.44	23.35
Japan	27,417	0.004	1.00
Mexico	3,171	0.00	100.00
Turkey	361,681	0.18	2.03
United States	3,538,908	0.16	100.00

Data retrieved from the Global Anti-Dumping Database of the World Bank. For India, the actual AD-affected trade is US $2.2 billion; however, only $1.4 billion is matched to tariff reclassifications.

to obtain the change in trade at tariff line level, and then constrain the fall in trade to be no more than the level of imports in 2008. Summing all changes in trade at the tariff line level across all partners gives the total change in trade:

$$\text{Change in trade using tariffs} = \sum_n \sum_p \max\left[m^{2008}_{ncp}\,\varepsilon^{2008}_{ncp}\left(t^{2009}_{ncp} - t^{2008}_{ncp}\right), -m^{2008}_{ncp}\right]. \qquad (3)$$

III. Data

We obtained tariff data for 135 countries from the International Trade Center (ITC) in Geneva. For India, Japan, and South Korea we supplemented the ITC data with MFN schedules from other sources.[3] Figure 1 summarizes the raw data by plotting the average bilateral tariff of 2008 against that of 2009, along with a 45 degree line. Only ten countries have higher average tariffs in 2009 than those of 2008. These countries are labeled in the figure and include Korea, Brazil, Argentina, China, and Canada. For Canada, the average bilateral tariff was 3.2% in 2008 and 4.0% in 2009.[4]

Data for antidumping duties are retrieved from the publicly available Global Antidumping Database of the World Bank, which is maintained by Chad Bown (2009a). The data set provides detailed information on antidumping cases. While data can be traced back as far as the early 1990s, given that our focus is the changes during the 2008–2009 period, we use only those cases that are initiated between June 2008 and September 2009, net of antidumping duties that were removed during the same period. By doing so, we capture only the change in antidumping duties during the two-year period and not the level of antidumping for each of the two years. This is an important point, because many antidumping duties in 2008 and 2009 are due to cases filed before the crisis. As long as these duties were not removed from the second quarter of 2008 onward, they do not affect the change in the level of protectionism. Only the new cases and the removal of old duties are factored into the calculations.

Table 1 presents some summary statistics on the countries that have added antidumping duties since the second quarter of 2008.[5] For the most part, changes in antidumping duties affect less than 1% of imports, ranging from US$8.5 billion in the EU to US$350,000 in Chile. Nevertheless, given that some countries cannot unilaterally increase their tariffs without violating WTO agreements, AD may well be one of those few legitimate channels to increase trade protection during the crisis period. In addition, given that AD duties are imposed at the tariff line level, which for many countries is represented by eight- or ten-digit HS codes, we first need to identify the share of these goods in the bilateral trade of the corresponding HS 6 categories, and impose AD duties only on the goods affected. In doing so, we avoid imposing AD duties on all tariff-line goods within an HS 6 category, even though we are still making the assumption that AD duties affect all bilateral trade within HS 8 goods and are not distinguishable among different firms that export. For some countries, such as Turkey and India, only a portion of AD cases have information on the actual AD duties imposed (see table I, last column). For the missing AD duties, we use the inverse of our bilateral import demand elasticity estimates to infer the minimum prohibitive AD duties.

IV. Results

Figure 2 plots the level of OTRI constructed using bilateral tariffs in 2008 against the level of OTRI constructed using bilateral tariffs in 2009 and AD imposed during the 2008–2009 period.[5] Most are located below

[3] India's 2008 and 2009 MFN schedule as well as Japan's 2008 MFN schedule come from TRAINS. Japan's 2009 MFN schedule was obtained from http://www.customs.go.jp/english/tariff/2010/index.htm. South Korea's 2009 MFN schedule comes from http://english.customs.go.kr/kcsweb/user.tdf?a=user.customtariff.CustomTariffApp&c=1001&mc=ENGLISH_INFORMATION_KOREA For these three countries, we lacked ad valorem equivalents of 2009 specific tariffs; hence, we used the 2008 values.

[4] A detailed data summary table is available on request, and it is also included in the working paper version of this paper (Kee, Neagu, & Nicita, 2010).

[5] In addition to the thirteen countries listed in table 1, the global antidumping database also has information for five more countries of the 135 in our data set. Pakistan is not included because we have no data on its 2009 tariff schedules; and we also have no trade flow data for South Korea and South Africa at the tariff line level; and we fail to match the AD data with trade data for Indonesia and Peru due to tariff reclassification.

[6] In the working paper version of this paper, we also compare the OTRI constructed using MFN tariffs with the OTRI constructed using bilateral tariffs. We found that MFN tariffs tend to overestimate the level of protection of a country by 75%. On the other hand, allowing for bilateral import demand elasticities marginally increases the overall level of protection, as bilateral elasticities tend to be larger than multilateral elasticities that are common across all trading partners within an imported product. At the sample mean, the OTRI constructed using bilateral elasticities is 2% larger than the OTRI constructed using multilateral elasticities. Finally, our results are robust to the exclusion of AD from the calculation.

the 45 degree line, indicating that most have further liberalized during the crisis. However, there are quite a few exceptions, notably Malawi, Russia, Turkey, China, Argentina, Canada, and Brazil. Malawi's OTRI for 2008 is 7.1%, and for 2009 it is 8.3%, which implies an increase of 1.2 percentage points. Russia increases its OTRI from 9.6% to 10.8%. For Turkey, the increase in tariffs of agricultural products pushes up its OTRI from 2% to 2.7%. The OTRI of China, Argentina, and Canada each increases by 0.3 percentage points. Although small, such increases in the overall level of tariff protection could significantly disrupt trade if imports are very elastic.[7]

For most countries, adding AD does not change their OTRI in any significant way, with the exception of the United States, the EU, and India. Incorporating AD duties increases the OTRI of the United States by half a percentage point. This seemingly small number in fact prompted trade to decrease by US$24 billion, if we allow AD to affect more than the existing level of preAD trade (see equation [2]), or by US$3 billion if we assume the maximum effect of AD and other tariff increases cannot exceed the existing trade in 2008 (see equation [3]). Likewise, for the EU, incorporating AD duties causes its OTRI to increase by 0.1 percentage point. As a result, imports of the EU drop by US$2 billion. This exercise shows that while antidumping may not increase the overall level of protection by much, it has been in fact the main instrument used by the United States and EU. Another heavy user of AD is India. Without AD duties, the OTRI of India decreases by 0.2 percentage points from 2008 to 2009.[8] Once AD duties are included, the change becomes positive 0.1 percentage points, indicating that AD duties have made the overall level of trade restrictiveness of India worse. The net trade effect of the changes in tariff and AD duties for India is about US$306 million.[9] Nevertheless, on a global scale, such duties hardly explain the huge collapse in trade, which further suggests that this global collapse in trade is probably not because countries are becoming more protectionist but instead relates to factors such as demand shocks.

Detailed analysis further shows that for most countries, most of the changes in the OTRI are driven by increased protection in the agricultural sector. For example, in India, the removal of a temporary tariff reduction on palm oil and the introduction of some antidumping duties on agriculture products in 2009 resulted in an increase in protectionism in the agricultural sectors by about 8.3 percentage points. Likewise, Turkey increased tariffs on a wide range of agricultural products, which pushed its OTRI for agricultural goods from 21.2% to 31.4%. Canada and Malawi also have large increases in their OTRI on agricultural products. On the other hand, the overall increases in the OTRI of Russia,

FIGURE 2.—COMPARING THE OTRI IN 2008 AND 2009

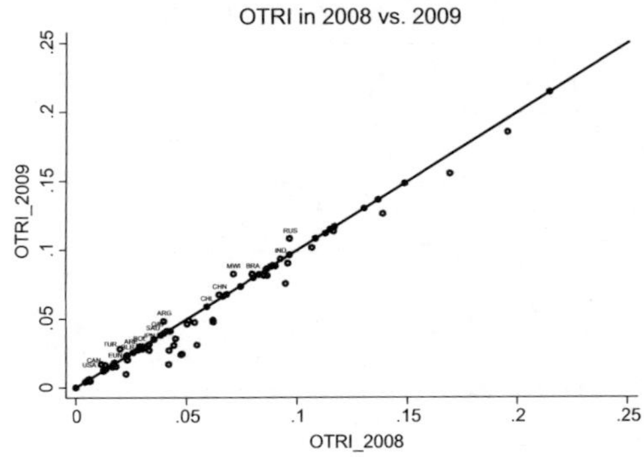

Argentina, and China are mainly driven by increases in tariffs in the manufacturing sector (the rise in the car tariffs of Russia and textile tariffs of Argentina).[10]

Overall, if we sum up all the negative trade impacts due to increased tariffs and AD duties, total world's imports may have decreased by US$43 billion. In 2008, the value of world imports was about $11 trillion, which implies that the changes in trade policy may have decreased the world's imports by 0.4%. According to the latest estimate of the WTO (2010), the world's imports contracted by 24% in 2009. Thus, our results show that the trade policy changes we have discussed can explain less than 2% of the collapse in the world's imports.

V. Conclusion

The fear that countries may raise tariffs to protect their domestic markets in the wake of the largest global recession since the Great Depression has not materialized. Comparing the published 2008 and 2009 tariff schedules of a wide range of countries shows that only a handful of countries have raised their tariffs significantly. These countries include Russia, Malawi, Argentina, Turkey, and China. The increase in motor vehicle tariffs in Russia not only restricted imports; it also caused one of the first reported crisis-related demonstrations. For some other countries, such as the United State and the EU most of the policy actions during the crisis are not about tariffs but antidumping duties. Nevertheless, even after taking antidumping duties into account, evidence provided in this paper suggests that the trade impact due to trade policy changes can explain no more than 2% of the collapse in the world trade.

[7] Detailed OTRI estimates for each of the countries are available on request and are also available in the working paper version of this paper (Kee et al., 2010).

[8] For Chile, India, and Japan, we use their MFN tariffs and AD to calculate their OTRI, since 2009 bilateral tariff schedules are not available.

[9] Our estimated changes in trade are not directly compatible to Bown (2009b). For example, for the worst-case scenarios, Bown's estimates of the AD impact in the United States, EU, and India are US$7 billion, US$8 billion, and US$4 billion, respectively. The differences can be attributed to the following. First, our estimates are based on tariff line (HS 8 digit) data rather than HS 6 digit data. In other words, within an HS 6 digit category, only the HS 8 digit goods that are affected by AD are included in the calculation, whereas Bown's estimates use HS 6 digit trade flows. Second, we use 2008 trade value in our calculation, whereas Bown's estimates are based on 2007 trade value. Third, our AD coverage is from June 2008 to September 2009, and Bown's estimates are from the first quarter of 2008 to the first quarter of 2009. Fourth, we take into account the bilateral import demand elasticities in the calculation of trade impact due to AD. Finally, we include tariffs and AD in our calculation of trade changes, while Bown's estimates focus on only AD. For the EU and India, the negative impacts on trade flows due to AD are partially offset by their overall tariff reduction during the two-year period.

[10] The detailed analysis can be found in the working paper version of this paper (Kee et al., 2010) or are available on request.

REFERENCES

Amiti, Mary, and David Weinstein, "Exports and Financial Shocks," NBER working paper 15556 (2009).

Anderson, James E., and J. Peter Neary, "Measuring the Restrictiveness of Trade Policy," *World Bank Economic Review* 8 (1994), 151–169.

——— "A New Approach to Evaluating Trade Policy," *Review of Economic Studies* 63 (1996), 107–125.

——— "The Mercantilist Index of Trade Policy," *International Economic Review* 44 (2003), 627–649.

Baldwin, Richard, *The Great Trade Collapse: Causes, Consequences and Prospects* (London: Centre for Economic and Policy Research, 2009).

Baldwin, Richard, and Simon Evenett, *The Collapse of Global Trade, Murky Protectionism, and the Crisis: Recommendations for the G20* (London: Center for Economic and Policy Research, 2009).

Bown, Chad P., "Global Anti-dumping Database" [Version 5.1] World Bank (2009a).

——— "The Global Resort to Anti-Dumping, Safeguards, and Other Trade Remedies amidst the Economic Crisis" (pp. 91–118), in Simon J. Evenett, Bernard M. Hoekman, and Olivier Cattaneo (eds.), *Effective Crisis Response and Openness: Implications for the Trading System* (London: CEPR and World Bank, 2009b).

Chor, Davin, and Kalina Manova, "Off the Cliff and Back? Credit Conditions and International Trade during the Global Financial Crisis," unpublished manuscript (2009).

Eaton, Jonathan, Samuel Kortum, Brent Neiman, and John Romalis, "Trade and the Global Recession," unpublished manuscript (2010).

Feenstra, Robert, "Estimating the Effects of Trade Policy" (vol. 3, pp. 1553–1595), in Gene Grossman and Kenneth Rogoff (eds.), *Handbook of International Economics* (Amsterdam: Elsevier, 1995).

Irwin, Douglas, "Trade Restrictiveness and Deadweight Losses from U.S. Tariffs." *American Economic Journal: Economic Policy* 2 (2010), 111–133.

Kee, Hiau Looi, Cristina Neagu, and Alessandro Nicita, "Is Protectionism on the Rise? Assessing National Trade Policies during the Crisis of 2008," World Bank Policy Research working paper 5274 (2010).

Kee, Hiau Looi, Alessandro Nicita, and Marcelo Olarreaga, "Import Demand Elasticities and Trade Distortions," this REVIEW 90 (2008), 666–682.

——— "Estimating Trade Restrictiveness Indices," *Economic Journal* 119 (2009), 172–199.

Levy, Clifford J., "Protests Erupt in Rusia over Raising of Car Tariffs," *New York Times*, December 21, 2008.

World Trade Organization, "Consultation with Ecuador," Background Document by the Secretariat, WT/BOP/S/15/Rev.1 (2009).

——— "World Trade 2009, Prospects for 2010," press/598 (2010).

Yi, Kei-Mu, "The Collapse of Global Trade: The Role of Vertical Specialization," in Richard Baldwin, and Simon Evenett (eds.), *The Collapse of Global Trade, Murky Protectionism, and the Crisis: Recommendations for the G20* (London: Centre for Economic Policy Research, 2009).

[16]

Journal of International Economics 90 (2013) 50–64

Contents lists available at SciVerse ScienceDirect

Journal of International Economics

journal homepage: www.elsevier.com/locate/jie

Import protection, business cycles, and exchange rates: Evidence from the Great Recession☆

Chad P. Bown [a,*], Meredith A. Crowley [b,1]

[a] Development Research Group, Trade and International Integration (DECTI), The World Bank, 1818 H Street, NW, MSN MC3-303, Washington, DC 20433, USA
[b] Federal Reserve Bank of Chicago, Economic Research, 11th floor, 230 South LaSalle, Chicago, IL 60604, USA

ARTICLE INFO

Article history:
Received 11 April 2012
Received in revised form 8 December 2012
Accepted 10 December 2012
Available online 22 December 2012

JEL classification:
F13

Keywords:
Antidumping
Safeguards
Temporary trade barriers
US
EU
Macroeconomic fluctuations

ABSTRACT

This paper estimates the impact of macroeconomic fluctuations on import protection policies over 1988:Q1–2010:Q4 for five industrialized economies — the United States, European Union, Australia, Canada and South Korea. We find evidence of a strong countercyclical trade policy response in the pre-Great Recession period of 1988:Q1–2008:Q3 during which increases in domestic unemployment rates, real appreciations in bilateral exchange rates, and declines in the GDP growth rates of bilateral trading partners led to substantial increases in new temporary trade barriers. We then apply this pre-Great Recession empirical model to realized macroeconomic data from 2008:Q4 to 2010:Q4 and find that it predicts a surge of new import protection during the Great Recession — e.g., for the US and EU, the model predicts that new trade barriers would cover an additional 15 percentage points of nonoil imports, well above the baseline level of 2–3% of import coverage immediately preceding the crisis. Finally, we examine why the realized trade policy response differed from model predictions. While exchange rate movements played an important role in limiting new import protection during the Great Recession, we provide evidence of one particularly important change in trade policy responsiveness; i.e., in this period, governments refrained from imposing new temporary trade barriers against foreign trading partners experiencing their own weak or negative economic growth.

We underscore the critical importance of rejecting protectionism and not turning inward in times of financial uncertainty. In this regard, within the next 12 months, we will refrain from raising new barriers to investment or to trade in goods and services, imposing new export restrictions, or implementing World Trade Organization (WTO) inconsistent measures to stimulate exports.
– G20 Declaration, November 15, 2008

1. Introduction

The imposition of the Smoot–Hawley tariffs during the early days of the Great Depression has since established a widespread presumption that import tariffs and other forms of trade protection rise during periods of macroeconomic weakness. During the Great Recession, the fear of new import restrictions led to pre-emptive statements like the G20 Declaration of November 2008.

This paper uses quarterly data for the United States, European Union, Australia, Canada, and South Korea to estimate the impact of macroeconomic shocks on import protection policies over 1988–2010. We find evidence of a robust countercyclical trade policy response in the pre-Great Recession period of 1988:Q1–2008:Q3. For example, a one standard deviation increase in the change in the domestic unemployment rate is associated with a 52% increase in the number of imported products over which an economy initiates new temporary trade barrier investigations in the following quarter. Other macroeconomic factors also have important effects on trade policy; a one standard deviation appreciation in the bilateral real exchange rate leads to a 33% increase in import protection while a one standard deviation *decrease* in the growth rate of real GDP in a foreign trading partner results in a 60% increase. Finally, when we extend our analysis through 2010:Q4 so as to

☆ Thanks to seminar participants at the Chicago Fed, World Bank/WTO/IMF Trade Workshop, Graduate Institute, ETSG, and Econometric Society NASM, and Vanderbilt for their helpful comments, as well as two anonymous referees, and Hiau Looi Kee, Aart Kraay, Jay Shambaugh, Tom Prusa, Marcelo Olarreaga, Michele Ruta, Robert Staiger, Doug Irwin, and Nuno Limão for useful discussions. Aksel Erbahar, Chrissy Ostrowski, and Jake Fabina provided outstanding research assistance. Any opinions expressed in this paper are the authors' and should not be attributed to the World Bank or the Federal Reserve Bank of Chicago. All remaining errors are our own.

* Corresponding author. Tel.: +1 202 473 9588; fax: +1 202 522 1159.
E-mail addresses: cbown@worldbank.org (C.P. Bown), crowley.meredith@gmail.com (M.A. Crowley).
URL: http://econ.worldbank.org/staff/cbown (C.P. Bown).
[1] Tel.: +1 312 322 5856.

0022-1996/$ – see front matter © 2012 Elsevier B.V. All rights reserved.
http://dx.doi.org/10.1016/j.jinteco.2012.12.001

analyze the Great Recession, one noteworthy change is to the relationship between import protection and a *trading partner's* economic growth. During the Great Recession, governments refrained from imposing new temporary trade barriers against trading partners experiencing their own weak or negative economic growth.

Our evidence paints a complex picture of the role that macroeconomic shocks play in determining trade policy for countries bound by the WTO. In particular, our results indicate that the empirical relationships between macroeconomic shocks and trade policy are changing over time and across trading partners in ways that ultimately impact the worldwide distribution of import protection beyond that which takes place through tariff liberalization negotiations and trade agreements. To document this phenomenon, our approach is to analyze determinants of *temporary trade barriers* (TTBs) — the relatively substitutable import restrictions under antidumping, countervailing duty, global safeguards, and the China-specific safeguard policies — because these are the predominant means through which industrialized countries have implemented *new* protection under the GATT and WTO since the 1980s.[2] Quantitatively, these restrictions have been economically important; e.g., the European Union and United States subjected 4–6% of their imported products at the 6-digit Harmonized System level to these policies at various points during our sample period (Bown, 2011a; Prusa, 2011). We focus on five economies – the United States, European Union, Australia, Canada and South Korea – for three reasons. First, they are economically important — together they constituted more than 40% of world imports and more than half of world GDP in 2010. Second, we can accurately track and consistently measure trade policy changes over time and at high frequency (i.e., quarterly) due to the similarity of their trade policy institutions and international commitments. Third, these economies have high quality macroeconomic data at the quarterly frequency over a relatively long time series which facilitates an examination of business cycles.

Given the severity of macroeconomic shocks that took place during the Great Recession, an open research question is why was the trade policy response so mild relative to expectations? Our formal analysis tackles this question by proceeding in three steps. Our first step is to estimate a model of macroeconomic determinants of import protection for these five policy-imposing economies over the pre-crisis period of 1988:Q1–2008:Q3. For each economy, Fig. 1 shows the time series of real exchange rate fluctuations, changes to domestic unemployment rates, and counts of imported products subject to new TTB policies in the quarterly data over 1988–2010.

Our second step is to use the model estimates from 1988:Q1 to 2008:Q3 to generate out-of-sample predictions for trade policy responses during 2008:Q4–2010:Q4, given the macroeconomic shocks that arose during the Great Recession. The model predicts a surge in import protection for the United States and European Union in particular in 2009:Q3. In terms of trade values, back of the envelope calculations put the forecasted *new* TTB import protection during 2008:Q4–2010:Q4 as covering up to an additional 15% and 14% of non-oil imports in the US and EU, respectively. This projected new coverage would have added roughly five to seven times as much import protection as the entire US and EU stock of imports cumulatively covered by TTBs immediately prior to the crisis (Bown, 2011a).

Finally, in order to understand why the predicted surge of import protection did not materialize, our third step is to re-estimate the empirical model on data that includes 2008:Q4–2010:Q4. This enables us to compare how the responsiveness of import protection policies to macroeconomic shocks changed during the crisis, relative to the earlier period. First, we find robust evidence that policy-imposing economies refrained from imposing new import restrictions against those trading partners with weak GDP growth. This contrasts strongly with TTB determination before 2008, and it is an important force for dampening the overall incidence of import protection during the Great Recession given that so many trading partners were undergoing periods of macroeconomic contraction. Second, our estimates indicate that bilateral real appreciations are typically associated with more TTBs. Thus, for the United States and European Union, sharp real currency depreciations, especially in late 2009 through early 2010, likely contributed to a dampening of the trade policy response throughout 2010.

This paper contributes to the empirical literature on the determinants of import tariffs and other trade restrictions. Trefler (1993), Goldberg and Maggi (1999), and Gawande and Bandyopadhyay (2000) pioneered empirical investigations into political-economic theories of endogenous trade policy formation (Hillman, 1982; Grossman and Helpman, 1994). While the evidence indicated that lobbying for protection impacts trade policy; the quantitative effect of such political-economic determinants was perhaps smaller than had been expected. More recent empirical research explores classical economic theories regarding the role of the terms of trade in tariff determination (Bagwell and Staiger, 1990, 1999). For example, Broda et al. (2008) directly test the optimal tariff theory in a cross-section of hundreds of imported products for a set of countries that faced no internationally-binding external constraints in setting trade policy. Their evidence supports the theory that governments set higher tariffs when export supply is more inelastic. In a different setting, Bagwell and Staiger (2011) find broad empirical support for terms-of-trade models of international agreements through a cross-sectional examination of negotiated tariff reductions for countries acceding to the WTO. Finally, Bown and Crowley (forthcoming) analyze a panel of time-varying US trade policy decisions and find that tariff increases are more likely in sectors with larger potential terms-of-trade gains, a theoretical prediction arising from dynamic models of self-enforcing trade agreements.

The current paper further informs our understanding of import tariffs by providing a detailed investigation into the macroeconomic determinants of time-varying trade policy. While there is an empirical presumption that import protection rises during recessions, with the exception of papers like Bagwell and Staiger (2003) and Crowley (2010), there is surprisingly little economic theory articulating the channels through which the countercyclical relationship between new import restrictions and macroeconomic shocks arises.[3] Thus, one purpose of this paper is to provide, in as much detail as possible, evidence on the explicit linkages between macroeconomic shocks and import protection.

[2] A reasonable question is the extent to which our singular focus on TTB policies fully captures the new import protection activity during 2008–2010 by the five economies in our sample. According to data from the Global Trade Alert, TTBs are by far the predominant trade policy instruments through which these economies directly erected new import-restricting trade barriers in 2008–2010. Appendix Table 1 lists the *only other* examples from these economies that the Global Trade Alert characterizes as "red" – i.e., the measure has been implemented and almost certainly discriminates against foreign commercial interests – and is directed at imports. From this list, it appears that only a South Korean increase in tariffs on 16 different products in January 2009 would be characterized as a substantial protectionist import restriction that is not captured by our focus on TTBs.

[3] In their theoretical paper, Bagwell and Staiger (2003, pp. 1–2) best articulate the failure of "political" or "distributional" theories for trade policy to explain the countercyclical relationship between business cycles and import protection policies with "... a common argument is that tariffs are higher in recessions, because the political pressure from import-competing firms is then most pronounced. This explanation, however, is incomplete, since it ignores the political influence of other production sectors that might press for *less* protection in recessions ... In light of these competing political influences, the common argument for countercyclical tariffs fails to be convincing, as it does not explain why the political pressures from import-competing sectors dominate in recessions but not in booms." Bagwell and Staiger (2003) also contains extensive reference to a number of empirical papers from earlier periods documenting the countercyclical relationship between business cycles and import protection.

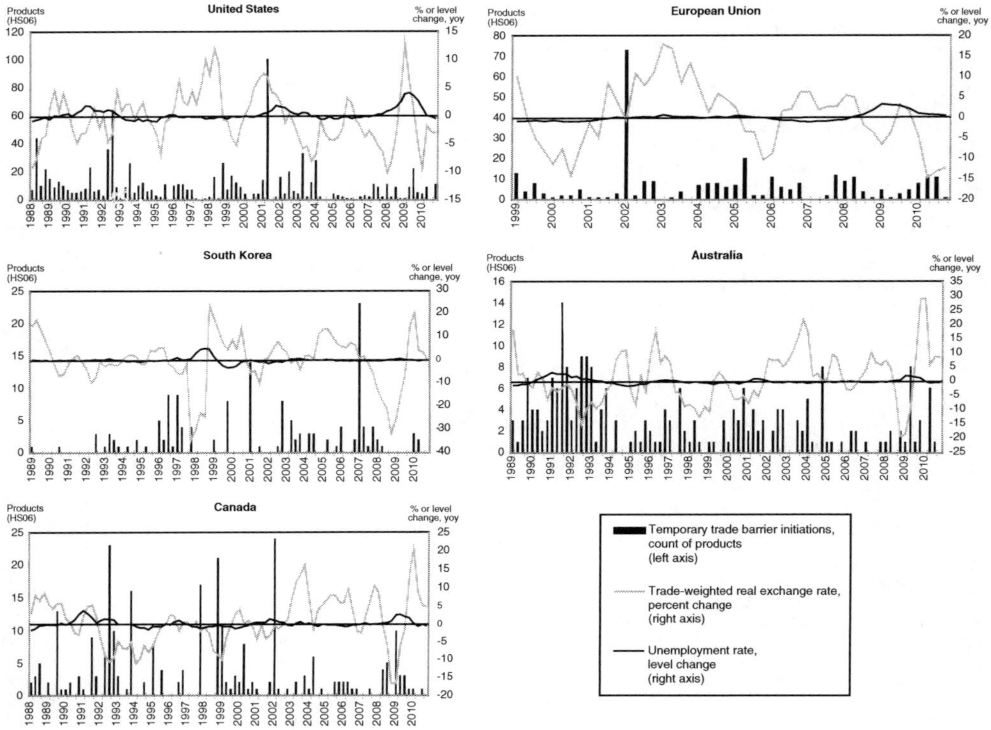

Source: constructed by the authors from quarterly data from OECD, USDA, and IMF and Bown (2011b). Increases in the real exchange rate series reflect appreciations of the domestic currency. EU data for 1999:Q1-2010:Q4 only.

Fig. 1. Import protection, real exchange rates, and unemployment, 1988:Q1–2010:Q4. Notes: Increases in the real exchange rate series reflect appreciations of the domestic currency. EU data are for 1999:Q1–2010:Q4 only.
Source: constructed by the authors from quarterly data from OECD, USDA, and IMF and Bown (2011b).

Our paper is most closely related to the literature on the macroeconomic determinants of antidumping protection that includes Feinberg (1989), Knetter and Prusa (2003), and Crowley (2011).[4] Relative to that work, our approach makes a number of advances, extensions and refinements by taking advantage of newly available and detailed data at the product-level from the World Bank's *Temporary Trade Barriers Database* (Bown, 2011b). First, we examine not just the antidumping policy, but we also consider use of other, relatively substitutable forms of import protection that have taken on particular importance in the first decade of the 2000s, such as global safeguards, China-specific safeguards, and countervailing duties. Second, we focus our analysis on precise, bilateral measures of import protection — i.e., between a policy-imposing economy and a particular trading partner. This bilateral emphasis is important given the discriminatory (i.e., trading partner-specific) nature of import protection.[5] Third, we construct our trade barrier measures at the quarterly frequency and use quarterly macroeconomic data. This allows us to better address the relationship between business cycles, exchange rates, and import restrictions and capture the precise timing of any trade policy changes taking place during the Great Recession.[6]

The rest of the paper proceeds as follows. Section 2 presents the predictions of the theoretical literature on temporary trade barrier policies such as antidumping, safeguards, and countervailing duties, the empirical model, and the panel data set that is used to estimate the model. Section 3 presents our basic results regarding the relationship

[4] Feinberg (1989) focused on the 1982–1987 period for the United States and found evidence that more antidumping cases were associated with dollar depreciations. Knetter and Prusa (2003) examine annual data for the US, Canada, Australia and the EU over 1980–1998 and find strong evidence of a relationship between antidumping cases and local currency appreciations over this longer time series of data. Crowley (2011) uses a cross-country, cross-industry panel from 1980–2001 and finds that the US imposed antidumping against foreign trading partners with weakness in manufacturing sectors.

[5] Antidumping is explicitly a bilateral policy. Although it was often imposed simultaneously on multiple foreign trading partners in the 1980s and 1990s (see Hansen and Prusa, 1996), there is less evidence of this more recently (e.g., Bown, 2010).

[6] Other papers on trade policy during the Great Recession include Kee et al.'s (forthcoming) study of Overall Trade Restrictiveness Indices, Gawande et al.'s (2011) examination of applied MFN tariffs for emerging economies, Bown's (2011a) work on TTB measurement and trade policy churning, and economy-specific case studies by Prusa (2011), Vandenbussche and Viegelahn (2011), Ludema and Mayda (2011) and Kang and Park (2011).

between trade restrictions and macroeconomic fluctuations based on historical data leading up to the Great Recession. Section 4 analyzes the import protection response after the onset of the worldwide financial crisis. Section 5 concludes.

2. Theory, empirical model and data

2.1. Theoretical models of temporary trade barriers and macroeconomic shocks

A large theoretical literature examines the role of temporary trade barriers in international agreements such as the GATT and WTO. Nevertheless, despite substantial research documenting the countercyclical nature of business cycles and import protection dating back to at least the Great Depression (Irwin, 2011a,b), there is not one universal theory linking the imposition of new import restrictions to macroeconomic shocks. Bagwell and Staiger (2003), Crowley (2010) and Knetter and Prusa (2003) are the theoretical contributions that inform our basic empirical approach.

Bagwell and Staiger (2003) model dynamic, self-enforcing trade agreements that are characterized by trade policy that fluctuates in response to macroeconomic conditions.[7] They relate business cycles to tariff increases in a model with serially correlated shocks to growth. In this rich model, two large symmetric countries play a trade policy game in which each period's one-shot game for every traded product is characterized by a terms-of-trade-driven prisoner's dilemma. An international business cycle is modeled as fluctuations in the rate of growth of new product entry, and the international economy moves between periods of high growth and low growth according to two Markov-switching processes. Because of the possibility of terms-of-trade gains, the static welfare gain of a tariff hike increases with trade volume, and this would otherwise result in tariff increases being pro-cyclical. However, in the presence of the kind of positive, serially correlated growth shocks that give rise to recessions, cooperation to maintain low tariffs is more difficult in periods in which the expected rate of future trade growth is low. Thus, unilateral tariff increases are less costly in welfare terms during recessions with persistently underperforming growth because it is precisely then that the cost of a trade war is relatively low. This basic intuition generates the key empirical prediction of the model: import restrictions increase during recessions.

We turn to two partial equilibrium models (Crowley, 2010; Knetter and Prusa, 2003) for guidance regarding two macroeconomic variables that exhibit considerable bilateral variation — real foreign GDP growth and real bilateral exchange rates. Crowley (2010) builds from the seminal, reciprocal dumping model of Brander and Krugman (1983) to show that import restrictions increase in response to macroeconomic weakness abroad. This theory focuses on the international rules regarding antidumping, one of the policies of particular emphasis for our empirical analysis. In a model of imperfect competition in which domestic and foreign firms have capacity constraints, the foreign firm increases its exports to the domestic market at a "dumped" price when the foreign country's own demand for the product falls. In this environment, it is welfare-improving for the importing country to impose import restrictions against the foreign country that is trying to export its way out of a recession. The cross-sectional empirical prediction of this model is that an importer will impose trade restrictions against those trading partners that are experiencing negative demand shocks in their own markets.[8]

Finally, Knetter and Prusa (2003) develop a stylized model of pricing behavior in a market with imperfect competition. Their focus is on understanding how international rules regarding dumping, i.e. pricing below average cost, are impacted by exchange rate fluctuations. In their model of a foreign firm that prices to market, an appreciation of the domestic currency leads to a decline in the foreign firm's marginal cost in terms of the importing country's domestic currency. At the same time, pricing to market under imperfect competition implies a relatively smaller decline in the domestic currency price of the foreign good. Thus, the foreign firm will simultaneously increase its sales in the domestic market (increasing the likelihood of injury to the domestic import-competing industry) and be less likely to be guilty of dumping. Because an exchange rate movement has opposite effects on the two criteria for dumping, the model gives ambiguous empirical predictions regarding the relationship between an exchange rate appreciation and new antidumping import restrictions.[9]

In summary, the literature on macroeconomic fluctuations suggests that temporary trade barriers increase when domestic macroeconomic conditions are weak (Bagwell and Staiger, 2003) and foreign macroeconomic conditions are weak (Bagwell and Staiger, 2003; Crowley, 2010). An appreciation of the domestic currency relative to a trading partner's currency implies more import restrictions if a national authority's antidumping investigation places more weight on the criterion of injury to the domestic industry than it places on the criterion of dumping (Knetter and Prusa, 2003).

2.2. Empirical model

This section presents an empirical model of the determinants of the number of imported products from a particular trading partner that a policy-imposing economy subjects to new temporary trade barrier investigations. The model relates the number of products under an antidumping, global safeguard, China safeguard, or countervailing duty investigation in a given quarter to the first lag (quarter $t-1$) of the percent change in the bilateral real exchange rate, the change in the domestic unemployment rate, and foreign real GDP growth.

The dependent variable is the number of products that economy j (United States, European Union, South Korea, Australia, Canada) imported from trading partner i in quarter t that is subjected to a new TTB investigation. Empirically, the dependent variable is a non-negative count which exhibits over-dispersion in that the variance of the number of investigations per time period exceeds the mean (see Table 1).

We formally model temporary trade barrier formation as generated by a negative binomial distribution (Hausman et al., 1984). In this model, the number of imported products under TTB investigations, y_{ijt}, follows a Poisson process after conditioning on the explanatory variables, x_{ijt}, and unobserved heterogeneity, $u_{ijt}>0$. Specifically,

$$y_{ijt}|x_{ijt}, u_{ijt} \sim \text{Poisson}\left(u_{ijt} m\left(x_{ijt}, \beta\right)\right), \text{ where } u_{ijt} \sim \text{gamma}(1, \alpha).$$

Thus, the distribution of counts of products subject to temporary trade barriers, y_{ijt}, given x_{ijt} follows a negative binomial with conditional mean and variance

$$E\left(y_{ijt}|x_{ijt}\right) = m\left(x_{ijt}, \beta\right) = \exp\left(x_{ijt}\beta\right) \text{ and } \text{Var}\left(y_{ijt}|x_{ijt}\right) = \exp\left(x_{ijt}\beta\right) + \left(\alpha \exp\left(x_{ijt}\beta\right)\right)^2.$$

We estimate the model using maximum likelihood with pair-wise fixed effects for importing country-foreign trading partner combinations. The model is identified off both inter-temporal and cross-

[7] Bagwell and Staiger (2003) build from an earlier model (Bagwell and Staiger, 1990) of self-enforcing trade agreements that links changes in trade policy to *iid* trade volume shocks. Bown and Crowley (forthcoming) use a sample of annual US data from 1997 to 2006 to provide evidence from much more disaggregated, industry-level relationships in support of the Bagwell and Staiger (1990) theory.

[8] Crowley (2011) examines US antidumping data for industries over 1980–2001 and finds evidence in support of this theory at the relatively disaggregated level.

[9] While Knetter and Prusa (2003) acknowledge the ambiguous theoretical predictions of their model, they find strong empirical evidence at the annual frequency for 1980–1998 linking exchange rate appreciations to aggregated counts of antidumping filings for a sample that includes data from the US, EU, Australia and Canada.

54 C.P. Bown, M.A. Crowley / Journal of International Economics 90 (2013) 50–64

sectional variation in domestic unemployment rates, bilateral real exchange rates, and foreign trading partner GDP growth rates.

2.3. Data and variable construction

There are a number of innovations in our data and modeling approach relative to the previous literature (e.g., see Knetter and Prusa, 2003).

Our first innovation concerns how to measure time-varying import protection. We construct quarterly series of bilateral trade policy actions at the universally-defined, 6-digit Harmonized System (HS-06) product level from 1988:Q1 to 2010:Q4.[10] Specifically, our dependent variable is the count of HS-06 imported products on which the government of economy j conducts a *new* temporary trade barrier investigation against trading partner i in quarter t and against which there is not already an existing TTB in place.[11] Inclusion of all forms of temporary import restrictions is important because more recent episodes of import protection – including the 2001–3 global safeguard on steel products imposed by the US, EU, and a number of other countries, and the 2009 China-specific safeguard the US imposed on imports of tires – took place under these alternative temporary trade barrier policies and would not be captured by an analysis restricted to antidumping.[12] In robustness checks, we also construct the count of products investigated under antidumping policy alone and we re-estimate the model using this dependent variable to illustrate the implications.

A second innovation in our approach is to examine data at the quarterly frequency; this is potentially important because macroeconomic shocks may cross calendar years. The key macroeconomic determinants of import protection in our model are bilateral real exchange rates, domestic unemployment rates, and the foreign trading partner's real GDP growth, with each of the variables reflecting year-over-year changes at the quarterly frequency.[13] We define the exchange rate variable as the percent change in the real bilateral exchange rate between the foreign and local currencies, so that an increase indicates an *appreciation* of the local (policy-imposing economy's) currency.[14] The domestic unemployment variable is defined as the level change in the domestic unemployment rate. Our focus on unemployment follows Irwin (2005); in robustness checks we use domestic real GDP growth in lieu of unemployment and find that temporary trade barriers are typically more responsive to domestic unemployment changes than to real GDP growth.

The third innovation that we stress in our panel data approach is to focus on bilateral relationships between policy-imposing economies j and their key trading partners i.[15] This is potentially important for two reasons. First, industrialized economies frequently impose import restrictions through temporary trade barriers bilaterally.[16] Furthermore, we wish to examine whether import protection is applied against trading partners that are experiencing negative economic shocks at home. Thus a modeling approach that considered only the use of import protection aggregated over trading partners may not accurately capture the importance of bilateral shocks.

Table 1 presents the summary statistics for the quarterly data used in the empirical analysis. Appendix A provides more information on the underlying sources of the data.

3. Baseline estimates from the pre-crisis period

Table 2 presents our first set of results for the "pre-crisis" period 1988:Q1–2008:Q3. We utilize a panel data set comprised of five economies j – the United States, the European Union, South Korea, Australia and Canada – and fifteen of each economy's top trading partners i. The dependent variable is defined as the count of HS-06 imported products against which the government of economy j has newly initiated a temporary trade barrier investigation against trading partner i in quarter t.

As is common practice for negative binomial regression models, the tables report estimates for incidence rate ratios (IRRs) for the explanatory variables. That is, we report the ratio of counts predicted by the model when the first lag of an explanatory variable of interest is one unit above its mean value (and all other variables are at their means) to the counts predicted when all variables are at their means. An estimated IRR with a value that is statistically greater than 1 is evidence of a positive effect of the determinant of interest; i.e., the explanatory variable is associated with an increase in the number of imported products from trading partner i in quarter t that economy j subjects to a new TTB investigation. Conversely, an estimated IRR that is statistically less than 1 is evidence that an increase in the explanatory variable is associated with a reduction in the count of imported

[10] These series are derived from data in the World Bank's *Temporary Trade Barriers Database* (Bown, 2011b). Because the Harmonized System has been in place and utilized across countries only since 1988, the time series dimension of our data begins in 1988:Q1.

[11] We focus on products subject to new investigations, given research from Staiger and Wolak (1994) which has shown that even an investigation can have trade-destroying effects. Nevertheless, in unreported results available from the authors, we confirm that the evidence below extends to a redefinition of the dependent variable to counts of products under investigations that only conclude with formal trade barriers being imposed.

[12] This measure is carefully constructed for each policy-imposing economy by trading partner and by quarter in a conservative way that does not allow for redundancy. At any point in time in the sample period under the Harmonized System, there are roughly 5000 HS-06 imported products that could be imported from any particular trading partner. In terms of policy, governments impose these import restrictions at the 8- or 10-digit product level; unfortunately the HS-06 level is the most finely disaggregated level of data that is comparable across countries. First, so as to avoid double counting in cases in which new import protection at the 8-digit level falls into the same HS-06 category as a previously imposed barrier, we do not include such products. Second, for our baseline import protection measure that expansively covers all four TTB policies, we also do not include products that were subject to a simultaneous or previously imposed barrier under a different policy. This phenomenon is particularly relevant for countervailing duties as most have been imposed simultaneously with antidumping duties on the same products against the same trading partners. For a discussion, see Bown (2011a).

[13] We are forced to use year-over-year changes in these variables as opposed to quarter-to-quarter changes due to how quarterly real GDP for China, one of the key trading partners in the analysis, is defined and available in the underlying data. Thus each of the key macroeconomic determinants is defined as a year-over-year change; i.e., quarter 1 of year t over quarter 1 of year $t-1$, quarter 2 of year t over quarter 2 of year $t-1$, etc.

[14] To coincide with the introduction of the euro in 1999, the estimates for the EU are based on a panel of data beginning only in 1999:Q1. Furthermore, there are a number of other issues associated with variable construction for the EU over this time period that merit discussion. The EU underwent a sizeable membership expansion during the period 1999–2010 — from 15 countries at the beginning of the period to 27 by the end of the sample. Once a country becomes a member of the EU it can no longer be targeted by EU antidumping, safeguard, or countervailing duty policies — as such, 12 countries that were significant EU trading partners (and hence potential antidumping targets) in 1999 cannot be included in the sample because they were part of the EU by 2007. Furthermore, the expanding membership means that the definition of the economies comprising domestic unemployment and being subject to a common EU exchange rate is changing over time, which creates potential additional issues of measurement error.

[15] Appendix A provides a list of the fifteen trading partners included for each of the five policy-imposing economies' bilateral relationships. These trading partners cumulatively account for the source of 75% (EU) to 94% (Canada) of each policy-imposing economy's non-oil imports during the sample periods. We condition on trading partners targeted by TTBs because non-targeted trading partners would be dropped from the estimation given the nature of the included country fixed effects.

[16] Even in the case of the application of global safeguards – which are supposed to be applied on a nondiscriminatory basis against all import sources of a product – economies typically apply them in a discriminatory fashion to exclude PTA partners or some developing countries. For a discussion, see Bown and McCulloch (2003). The construction of the policy variables in our bilateral panel data set only counts global safeguards against trading partners that were included in the policy.

Table 1
Summary statistics, 1988:Q1–2010:Q4.

Variables	Policy-imposing economy … Full sample	US only	EU[a] only	Australia, Canada, Korea only
Dependent variables				
All temporary trade barrier initiations *ijt* (products per quarter per trading partner), 1988:Q1–2008:Q3	1.25	2.76	1.98	0.51
	(6.41)	(10.28)	(9.13)	(2.41)
All temporary trade barrier initiations *ijt* (products per quarter per trading partner), 2008:Q4–2010:Q4	0.37	0.70	0.62	0.16
	(1.65)	(2.87)	(1.56)	(0.81)
Antidumping initiations only *ijt* (products per quarter per trading partner), 1988:Q1–2008:Q3	0.76	1.81	0.53	0.40
	(3.46)	(5.93)	(1.73)	(2.09)
Explanatory variables				
Percent change in bilateral real exchange rate *ijt*, 1988:Q1–2008:Q3	0.85	0.24	1.47	0.96
	(14.70)	(15.87)	(12.38)	(14.69)
Percent change in bilateral real exchange rate *ijt*, 2008:Q4–2010:Q4	−1.35	−0.28	−5.87	−0.06
	(14.37)	(15.69)	(13.19)	(13.97)
Domestic unemployment rate change *jt*, 1988:Q1–2008:Q3	−0.13	−0.02	−0.35	−0.13
	(0.86)	(0.66)	(0.51)	(0.97)
Domestic unemployment rate change *jt*, 2008:Q4–2010:Q4	1.06	1.82	1.75	0.51
	(1.35)	(1.73)	(1.04)	(0.99)
Domestic real GDP growth *jt*, 1988:Q1–2008:Q3	3.41	2.92	2.45	3.80
	(2.30)	(1.41)	(1.02)	(2.65)
Real GDP growth of trading partner *it*, 1988:Q1–2008:Q3	4.08	4.06	4.11	4.09
	(3.50)	(3.56)	(3.10)	(3.56)
Real GDP growth of trading partner *it*, 2008:Q4–2010:Q4	2.18	2.19	2.19	2.17
	(5.42)	(5.40)	(5.37)	(5.45)
Import growth from trading partner *ijt*, 1988:Q1–2008:Q3	11.50	8.46	11.80	12.60
	(23.03)	(11.69)	(14.21)	(27.32)
Import growth from trading partner *ijt*, 2008:Q4–2010:Q4	0.96	0.14	−7.09	4.29
	(29.87)	(25.74)	(20.59)	(33.50)
Observations	5036	1195	719	3122

Notes: sample means are reported with standard deviations reported below in parentheses.
[a] EU is defined throughout as EU-27, its data are for 1999:Q1–2010:Q4 only.

products subject to new import protection. The table also reports *t*-statistics (in parentheses) for whether the estimated IRR is statistically different from 1.

The three macroeconomic determinants of interest are the percent change in the bilateral real exchange rate, the change in the domestic unemployment rate, and the foreign trading partner's real GDP growth. The baseline model also includes a time trend as well as importer and exporter combined (pair-wise) fixed effects to control for time-invariant, bilateral relationship-specific heterogeneity in policy treatment. For example, China's designation as a non-market economy under antidumping provisions could affect the way that the United States treats China's exporters relative to another economy's exporters or relative to how Australia treats China's exporters.

3.1. Pre-crisis estimates for the full sample of policy-imposing economies

The baseline results in column (1) of Table 2 indicate a countercyclical trade policy response over 1988:Q1–2008:Q3. Increases in the domestic unemployment rate and declines in foreign GDP growth are associated with more trade barriers and the IRR estimates are statistically significant at the 1% level.

The IRR of 1.62 on the change in domestic unemployment rate in the second row of column (1) is greater than 1 and indicates that import protection increases when the domestic economy is weakening through rising unemployment. The IRR of 0.88 on foreign real GDP growth is evidence that additional import protection is used against trading partners that are going through their own periods of weak economic growth. Furthermore, an estimated IRR of 1.02 indicates that a real appreciation of the domestic currency is associated with increased import protection through TTBs. This evidence is consistent with related results from a 1980–1998 sample of data on antidumping policy use reported by Knetter and Prusa (2003). Finally, the time trend estimate of 0.99 indicates that, on average, import protection through these policies has been declining over the sample period.

Specification (2) provides our first sensitivity analysis by replacing the variable capturing the domestic macroeconomic shock – the change in the domestic unemployment rate – with a variable defined as the growth rate of domestic real GDP in $t-1$. Theory predicts an IRR that is less than 1; i.e., weak domestic growth is associated with a higher incidence of TTBs. The estimated IRR is 0.93 and statistically significant. The IRR estimates for the other determinants of interest are qualitatively unaffected by this alternative indicator of the health of the domestic macroeconomy.

Before proceeding with additional robustness checks, consider next the economic magnitude of the estimated IRRs; Fig. 2 provides a graphical interpretation. We present the percent increase in the count of imported products per trading partner per quarter subject to new TTBs that is associated with a one standard deviation change in each macroeconomic determinant. Specifically, we compute the median of the model's predicted estimates of import protection evaluated using the sample data; and we then introduce (one at a time) a one standard deviation shock to each of the macroeconomic determinants of interest, holding everything else constant, and regenerate the model's predictions of import protection.

The gray bars of Fig. 2 present estimates based on specification (1) of Table 2, whereas the black bars illustrate impacts based on specification (2). First note from Table 1 that a one standard deviation increase in the percent change of the bilateral real exchange rate is roughly a 15% appreciation. Fig. 2 indicates that this 15 percent appreciation is associated with a 33% (34%) increase in imported products subject to TTB protection per trading partner per quarter according to specification (1) (alternatively, specification (2)). Next, the figure illustrates a sizeable estimated impact of domestic macroeconomic shocks. A one standard deviation increase to the change in the domestic unemployment rate – i.e., 0.86 or nearly one full percentage point (see again Table 1) – is associated with, per trading partner, a 52% increase in import protection. In specification (2), when we use a one standard deviation decline in domestic real GDP

Table 2
Negative binomial model estimates of macroeconomic determinants of import protection, 1988:Q1–2008:Q3.

	Dependent variable: bilateral (*ij*) count of products initiated under all temporary trade barrier policies in quarter *t*							
Explanatory variables	Baseline (1)	Substitute real GDP for un-employment (2)	Modify country fixed effects (3)	Substitute second lag for macro variables (4)	AD only (5)	Interaction of domestic and foreign shocks (6)	Add tariffs and TTB stock (7)	Same restricted subsample (8)
Percent change in bilateral real exchange rate *ijt* − 1	1.02[a]	1.02[a]	1.02[a]	1.02[a]	1.00	1.02[a]	1.02[a]	1.02[a]
	(3.97)	(3.98)	(4.54)	(4.92)	(0.29)	(4.01)	(3.60)	(4.08)
Domestic unemployment rate change *jt* − 1	1.62[a]	–	1.62[a]	1.18[b]	1.36[a]	1.54[a]	1.81[a]	1.78[a]
	(6.61)		(6.57)	(2.05)	(4.30)	(3.71)	(5.14)	(5.05)
Domestic real GDP growth *jt* − 1	–	0.93[b]	–	–	–	–	–	–
		(2.28)						
Real GDP growth of trading partner *it* − 1	0.88[a]	0.86[a]	0.97[c]	0.90[a]	0.93[a]	0.88[a]	0.90[a]	0.89[a]
	(6.13)	(6.70)	(1.96)	(4.58)	(3.82)	(5.95)	(3.91)	(4.07)
Time trend	0.99[a]	0.99[a]	0.99[c]	0.99[a]	0.99[a]	0.99[a]	0.96[a]	0.96[a]
	(2.99)	(3.84)	(1.80)	(2.95)	(3.24)	(2.99)	(7.01)	(7.20)
Domestic unemployment rate change *jt* − 1 × real GDP growth of trading partner *it* − 1	–	–	–	–	–	1.01	–	–
						(0.59)		
Change in the share of imported products under WTO discipline in *jt* − 1	–	–	–	–	–	–	1.04	–
							(1.58)	
Stock of TTBs against trading partner *ijt* − 1	–	–	–	–	–	–	0.99[b]	–
							(2.47)	
Importer and exporter combined fixed effects	Yes	Yes	No	Yes	Yes	Yes	Yes	Yes
Importer and exporter separate fixed effects	No	No	Yes	No	No	No	No	No
Observations	4406	4406	4406	4380	4406	4406	3218	3218

Notes: Policy-imposing economies *j* (Australia, Canada, EU, South Korea, US) vis-à-vis one of the 15 trading partners *i* (listed in Appendix A) over 1988:Q1–2008:Q3. Data for the EU as policy imposer are restricted to 1999:Q1–2008:Q3 throughout. In (7) and (8), data for the other four policy-imposing economies are restricted to 1995:Q1–2008:Q3. Incidence rate ratios (IRRs) are reported in lieu of coefficient estimates, with t-statistics in parentheses. Model includes a constant term whose estimate is suppressed. Superscripts a, b, and c indicate statistical significance at the 1, 5, and 10 percent levels, respectively. AD = antidumping.

growth – i.e., 2.3 percentage points – there is a significant, albeit smaller, 18% increase in import protection.[17] Finally, Fig. 2 illustrates the importance of economic growth in foreign trading partner *i*. A one standard deviation reduction to a trading partner's real GDP growth – i.e., 3.5 percentage points – is associated with a 60% increase in import protection against that partner based on specification (1) and a 70% increase based on specification (2).

The remaining columns of Table 2 examine the robustness of our results to alternative specifications of the underlying model.

Column (3) of Table 2 reports a specification with alternative fixed effects. Instead of importer *j* and exporter *i* pair-wise fixed effects, we introduce *separate* importer *j* and exporter *i* fixed effects. The qualitative pattern to the results is unchanged; the only distinction is a reduction to the estimated size differential (away from 1) of the IRRs on foreign real GDP growth and the statistical significance of the IRRs for foreign real GDP growth and the time trend being reduced to the ten percent level.

In column (4), we modify the baseline model by substituting the second lag of each of the macroeconomic variables for the first lag. The qualitative pattern to the results is unchanged; however, estimated magnitudes of the impact of the domestic unemployment rate change and the foreign trading partner's real GDP growth are slightly smaller. We return to this issue of the timing of shocks in more detail in our economy-specific estimates discussed below.

Next we redefine the dependent variable in column (5) so that it includes only antidumping (AD) import protection. The estimated IRR on the impact of an appreciating domestic currency is no longer statistically different from 1. Furthermore, while the qualitative nature of the IRRs is similar to column (1), there is again a slight reduction to the size differential (away from 1) of the estimated IRRs for the domestic unemployment rate change and the foreign trading partner's real GDP growth. This result stands in contrast to research covering earlier periods of data whereby an exclusive focus on TTBs through AD policy alone may have been sufficient to capture the relationship between macroeconomic shocks and import protection (e.g., Knetter and Prusa, 2003). One important implication of our results is that a sole focus on antidumping underestimates the relationship between macroeconomic shocks and time-varying import protection for these economies.

In specification (6), we introduce a new covariate to the baseline model — the *interaction* of the domestic unemployment rate change *jt* − 1 with real GDP growth of trading partner *it* − 1. We include this interaction term in addition to each variable entering independently. The interaction term examines the possibility that economy *j* may be

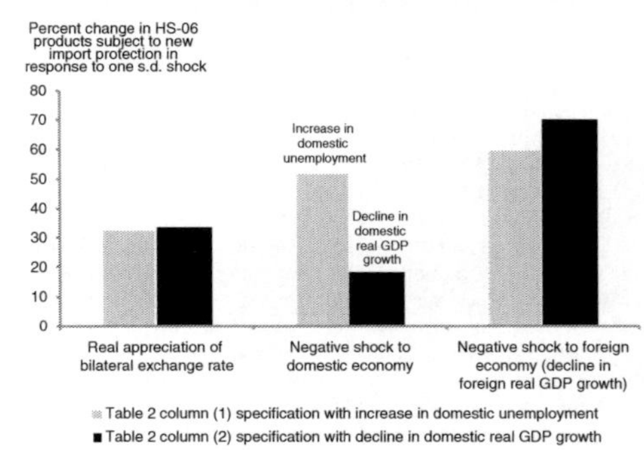

Fig. 2. Trade policy responsiveness to macroeconomic shocks, pre-crisis.
Notes: Percent increase in HS-06 products subject to new import protection per quarter per trading partner. Based on Table 2 model estimates and a one standard deviation change in each explanatory variable away from the sample mean, holding all other variables constant.

[17] This is consistent with earlier results for the United States alone based on annual data (e.g., Irwin, 2005).

less likely to impose new import protection against trading partner *i* – despite *j*'s own domestic economic contraction – if there is a simultaneous negative economic shock abroad. If this were the case, since a negative shock to the domestic economy is captured as an increase in the domestic unemployment rate, we would expect an estimated IRR that is less than 1 for the interaction term and a potentially insignificant IRR estimate for the domestic unemployment change variable. However, we find no evidence of these relationships for this time period and this sample of policy-imposing economies.[18]

Finally, in specifications (7) and (8), we address the issue that the five economies might face different choice sets of import restrictions. First, the extent to which WTO commitments restrict an economy's freedom to raise its applied most-favored-nation (MFN) tariff rates might vary across economies.[19] In specification (7), we control for this by introducing a new variable defined as the annual change in the share of economy *j*'s HS-06 products subject to strict WTO discipline, i.e., the share of products for which its applied MFN tariff is equal to (or above) its WTO legal maximum tariff binding.[20] We expect the IRR on this variable to be larger than 1 so that as more imported products fall under WTO discipline, the restricted policy choice set induces more substitution of import protection toward TTB policies. The estimated IRR of 1.04 on this variable in specification (7) is larger than 1 as expected, though it is not statistically significant. Second, we also introduce a TTB "stock" variable defined as the count of HS-06 products over which the policy-imposing economy *j* already had a TTB in effect against trading partner *i* in $t-1$. We expect an IRR that is less than 1 for this variable; i.e., the more imported products already subject to a TTB, the less scope for the economy to impose new TTBs. The estimated IRR is 0.99 and statistically significant.[21]

The downside to including these two variables is that it restricts our sample to the post-1995 period, further limiting the business cycle variation in the data.[22] Therefore, to understand how our results are affected by omitting these controls for the available policy choice set, specification (8) re-estimates the baseline model on the smaller sample of data used in specification (7). A comparison of specification (7) to (8) reveals very little change to the IRRs for the key macroeconomic determinants. We conclude that omitting controls for the trade policy choice set does not appear to affect the results for these policy-imposing economies over this time period.

To summarize Table 2, we present evidence from 1988:Q1–2008:Q3 that macroeconomic shocks impact import protection through temporary trade barriers.[23] First, there is strong evidence of a countercyclical relationship between negative shocks to domestic employment (and to a lesser extent, domestic real GDP growth) and new import protection. Second, our comprehensive temporary trade barrier (TTB) measure exhibits greater measured co-movement with macroeconomic variables than the antidumping measure used in the prior literature. Estimates on antidumping alone fail to capture the true impact of these shocks on import protection, especially with respect to movements in bilateral real exchange rates. The third point worth highlighting is that the estimated IRR for foreign real GDP growth is less than 1 in all specifications of Table 2. This is evidence that, on average, these economies tended to impose new import protection on trading partners that were themselves undergoing a period of weak economic growth or an economic contraction. This result is particularly important for understanding the *differential* government policy responses during the Great Recession, as we discuss in Section 4.

3.2. Pre-crisis estimates for subsamples of the US, EU and smaller economies

Table 3 presents estimation results from the 1988:Q1–2008:Q3 period restricted to subsamples of data based on policy-imposing economies. We consider three subsamples in particular: estimates for the United States, European Union, and a combined sample of data jointly covering Australia, Canada, and South Korea. For each subsample of data, we present results from three different specifications. Columns (1), (4) and (7) of Table 3 present the same baseline model specification as Table 2, specification (1). We then consider robustness checks in columns (2), (5) and (8) in which we substitute the explanatory variables at the second lag ($t-2$) for the first lag. Finally, in columns (3), (6) and (9), we consider the impact of these determinants on the antidumping policy alone, as opposed to the more comprehensive dependent variable that covers all TTBs.

The results for the United States in Table 3 are consistent with the overall results reported in Table 2. Import protection through TTBs is associated with a real appreciation of the US dollar, an increase in the US unemployment rate, and a decline in trading partner real GDP growth. Furthermore, while importer *j* and exporter *i* combined fixed effects were also included as part of the model estimates in Table 2, we did not report them to conserve space. We report one fixed effect estimate in Table 3 in order to highlight the policy-imposing economy's relationship with

[18] During the revision process, we became aware of a paper by Davis and Pelc (2012) that examines related questions on product-level data at the annual frequency for a heterogeneous sample of industrialized and developing economies for 1997–2009. Over this sample period, the authors present evidence consistent with the idea that countries may be less likely to impose protection against partners undergoing a *simultaneous* contraction. While we present evidence of a similar result for the period covering the Great Recession in Section 4.2 below, here we examine whether such a relationship existed in the pre-Great Recession period. As column (6) indicates, we fail to find evidence of this relationship in data from *prior to* the Great Recession; i.e., countries were no more or less likely to impose new bilateral import restrictions during a domestic downturn if that was synchronized with the trading partner's downturn.

[19] We anticipate that this issue does not matter much across these particular industrialized economies as they each have applied MFN tariff rates relatively close to their WTO tariff bindings. By design, this institutional similarity influenced the focus of this paper to these five policy-imposing economies. Put differently, one contributing explanation as to why we deliberately chose not to include a number of emerging economies in the empirical analysis is because there is substantial variation across those countries, products, and time as to the extent to which WTO commitments discipline their trade policies. We speculate that a much more serious treatment of the choice set of available trade policy instruments is required to analyze the impact of macroeconomic shocks on the import protection for such policy-imposing countries; thus we leave it to future research.

[20] The variable is constructed from HS-06 data on WTO maximum tariff bindings and applied MFN tariffs derived from WITS; the data are available from 1995 to 2010 only. Note that we define this variable as equal to *or above* (as opposed to simply equal to) because the early WTO period involved many of these economies phasing in reductions to their applied tariffs to levels that were only eventually at or below their bindings. We have also considered other modifications to the definition of this variable – e.g., defining it more flexibly as a product's applied tariff being within a 1, 5 or 10 percentage point cutoff of the binding – and we obtain similar results. One key drawback to this variable worth noting is that data availability is limited to the *annual* frequency. This lack of inter-temporal variation, relative to all of the other variables included in the estimation which are defined at the *quarterly* frequency, in addition to the lack of trading-partner variation, is likely a contributing explanation to the statistically insignificant IRR estimate described in the text.

[21] In unreported results available from the authors, we have also estimated versions of the model in which we introduce each of these two variables separately, and the broad pattern of results does not change.

[22] First, the required data on WTO tariff bindings is only relevant and available for the post-1995 period. Second, the TTB stock variable is only constructed for TTBs imposed since the HS system has been in effect beginning in 1988. The implication is that earlier in our sample, the stock measure based on available HS data would severely underestimate the actual TTBs in effect as it is not able to consider all of the TTBs imposed prior to 1988 that were still in effect in the early 1990s. This is important for the historical users of TTBs such as Australia, Canada, European Union, and the United States. Thus the TTB stock measure constructed from HS-06 data becomes more accurate over our sample period as (unaccounted for) TTBs that governments imposed prior to 1988 are increasingly removed.

[23] A related research question is whether government decisions on TTB *removals* are symmetrically affected by macroeconomic conditions. For example, when a government examines its previously-imposed antidumping import restrictions under the WTO's guidelines for Sunset Reviews, is it less likely to remove such a measure if the domestic economy is undergoing a period of weak growth or a high rate of unemployment? This is an important and unaddressed question that we leave for future research, as it is beyond the scope of the current analysis for data limitation reasons.

58 C.P. Bown, M.A. Crowley / Journal of International Economics 90 (2013) 50–64

Table 3
Economy-Specific estimates of macroeconomic determinants of import protection, 1988:Q1–2008:Q3.

	Dependent variable: bilateral (ij) count of products initiated under all temporary trade barrier policies or antidumping (AD) in quarter t by country(ies) listed below								
	United States			European Union‡			Australia, Canada, & South Korea		
Explanatory variables	Baseline (1)	Second lag (macro variables) (2)	AD only (3)	Baseline (4)	Second lag (macro variables) (5)	AD only (6)	Baseline (7)	Second lag (macro variables) (8)	AD only (9)
Percent change in bilateral real exchange rate $ijt-1$	1.03[a] (3.53)	1.04[a] (5.26)	1.00 (0.15)	1.03[b] (2.28)	1.05[a] (3.91)	1.02 (1.61)	1.00 (0.64)	1.00 (0.04)	1.00 (0.54)
Domestic unemployment rate change $jt-1$	2.16[a] (4.62)	1.69[a] (2.72)	2.00[a] (4.70)	10.80[a] (6.33)	1.61 (1.17)	0.95 (0.16)	1.43[a] (4.36)	1.12 (1.29)	1.27[a] (2.61)
Real GDP growth of trading partner $it-1$	0.86[a] (4.69)	0.94[b] (2.03)	0.88[a] (4.01)	0.90[c] (1.65)	0.81[a] (2.65)	1.01 (0.29)	0.94[b] (1.97)	0.94[b] (2.13)	0.96 (1.16)
Time trend	0.98[a] (3.74)	0.98[a] (3.61)	0.98[a] (4.42)	0.93[a] (4.96)	0.95[a] (3.33)	0.98[c] (1.78)	1.00 (0.26)	1.00 (0.05)	1.00 (0.81)
China as trading partner	22.66[a] (6.01)	10.58[a] (4.52)	32.18[a] (6.78)	65.66[a] (5.02)	66.58[a] (4.54)	72.85[a] (4.78)	62.25[a] (3.46)	66.15[a] (3.48)	39.37[a] (3.05)
Import and exporter combined fixed effects	Yes	Yes	Yes	Yes	Yes	Yes	Yes	Yes	Yes
Observations	1060	1053	1060	584	583	584	2762	2744	2762

Notes: The trading partners i of each importer j are listed in Appendix A. ‡Data for the EU as policy imposer j in specifications (4), (5) and (6) are restricted to 1999:Q1–2008:Q3. Incidence rate ratios (IRRs) are reported in lieu of coefficient estimates, with t-statistics in parentheses. Model includes a constant term whose estimate is suppressed. Superscripts a, b, and c indicate statistical significance at the 1, 5, and 10 percent levels, respectively. Each explanatory variable is lagged two quarters (at $t-2$) in lieu of one quarter ($t-1$) in specifications (2), (5), and (8). AD = antidumping.

China. In specification (1), the IRR of 22.66 is evidence that China was substantially more likely than the omitted trading partner (in this case, Australia) to face US import protection.[24] As has been well documented (e.g., Bown, 2010), this China phenomenon is pervasive across policy-imposing economies. Next, in specification (2), when we substitute the macroeconomic determinants at the second lag (quarter $t-2$) for the first lag, there is a reduction to the estimated size differential (away from 1) of the IRRs on the US unemployment rate change and the foreign trading partner's real GDP growth compared to the baseline. Finally, specification (3) confirms for the US a finding in the full sample of data (Table 2, column 5). Limiting the dependent variable to antidumping yields an insignificant estimate of the relationship between real bilateral US dollar fluctuations and new import protection.

Consider next the Table 3 results for the European Union, which we have noted are estimated on a shorter time series of data (1999: Q1–2008:Q3) to coincide with the introduction of the euro in 1999. Estimates of the baseline EU model in column (4) are also in line with the theory. When we substitute the second lag for the first lag of the macroeconomic determinants in specification (5), the estimated IRR for the change in the EU unemployment rate drops considerably, and it is no longer statistically significant. There is no qualitative change to the other key determinants. Finally, when the dependent variable is defined as antidumping *alone* in specification (6), there is no statistically significant evidence of a relationship between macroeconomic shocks and import protection. This specification notably omits an extensive set of import restrictions on steel products through the EU's global safeguard policy in 2002.

Fig. 3 provides information on the magnitudes of the estimated IRRs for the US and EU samples of data. The US panel is based on specifications (1) and (2), and the EU panel is based on specifications (4) and (5). The figure follows the approach of Fig. 2 by presenting the percent increase in the count of imported products per trading partner per quarter subject to new TTBs that are associated with a one standard deviation change in each macroeconomic determinant. For the United States, a one standard deviation appreciation of the dollar is 16% (see Table 1) and is associated with a 21% (99%) increase in imported products being subject to TTBs per trading partner per quarter, relative to the model's estimates in specification (1) (specification (2), respectively) at the means of the data. For the EU, a one standard deviation appreciation of the euro is 13% and it leads to 49% (85%) more protection according to specification (4) (specification (5), respectively). A one standard deviation increase in the domestic unemployment rate leads to 41% (65%) more protection for the United States, and 26% (221%) more protection for the EU. Finally, a

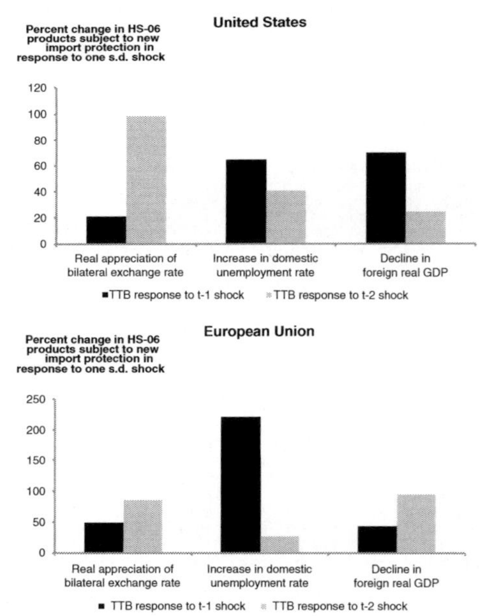

Fig. 3. US and EU trade policy responsiveness to macroeconomic shocks, pre-crisis. Notes: Percent increase in HS-06 products subject to new import protection per quarter per trading partner. Based on Table 3 model estimates and a one standard deviation change in each explanatory variable away from the sample mean, holding all other variables constant.

[24] The IRRs for the other trading partners are not reported in the table but are available from the authors upon request. In terms of scale, the estimated IRR for China in the US models, for example, is typically twice as large as that for the second-highest trading partner.

one standard deviation decline in trading partner real GDP growth is associated with 25% (70%) more US import protection and 43% (95%) more EU import protection.

Returning to Table 3, the remaining columns apply the modeling approach and robustness checks to the subsample of the relatively smaller economies of Australia, Canada, and South Korea. On average for these three countries, the estimated IRRs are in line with the theory; however, the IRRs are not consistently statistically significant across different specifications. Thus the estimated trade policy response through these TTBs to macroeconomic shocks appears to be somewhat weaker for smaller industrialized countries than for the United States and European Union.[25] One likely contributing explanation is that these economies are less frequent users of TTBs, on average, than the US and EU (see again Table 1).[26]

4. Import protection during the Great Recession

4.1. Protectionist expectations

During the early period of the Great Recession, a widespread fear of "protectionism" among policymakers led to the coordinated, G20 Declaration of November 2008 cited above. Furthermore, policymakers asked major multilateral institutions to establish new trade policy surveillance initiatives in order to monitor and report on national changes in policies that could impact international trade.[27]

Fig. 4 provides one explanation for the increased concern over "protectionism" and the associated response. The left panels of Fig. 4 take the US and EU model estimates from Table 3 – i.e., based on pre-crisis data – and generate the *predicted* import protection response over 2008:Q4–2010:Q4 given the realized macroeconomic data from this period. The historical models for the US and EU predict a sharp increase in import protection beginning in 2009:Q2 and lasting through 2010:Q1, peaking in 2009:Q3. To provide some context, the median number of products subject to new US TTBs against these 15 trading partners per quarter between 1988:Q1 and 2008:Q3 was 12. The model's US prediction for 2008:Q4–2010:Q4 peaks at *647 products* being subject to new TTBs in 2009:Q3. The median number of products subject to new EU TTBs against these 15 trading partners per quarter between 1999:Q1 and 2008:Q3 was 9. The model's EU prediction for new TTBs peaks at *264 products* in 2009:Q3.

To provide additional context, our back-of-the-envelope calculations suggest that the historical models forecast an upper bound of roughly 15% of US and EU nonoil imports becoming subject to *new* import protection during the Great Recession. In particular, the US model predicted that cumulatively 1558 new imported product-trading partner combinations would become subject to new TTB investigations during the period of 2008:Q4 through 2010:Q4. If we multiply the value of imports for a relevant target in 2007 by the predicted number of TTBs, we arrive at an upper estimate that 15.4% of US non-oil imports could expect to face new US TTBs.[28] Similarly for the EU, the cumulative effect of its predicted 623 imported product-trading partner TTBs (see again Fig. 4) translate into 14.0% of EU non-oil imports.[29] Estimates from Bown (2011a) put the trade-weighted share of US and EU imports subject to the existing stock of TTBs at only 2–3% immediately preceding the crisis in 2007. The implication is that TTB coverage of imports was predicted to increase 5–7 times above pre-crisis levels.

The reasons for the predicted run-up in new import protection illustrated in Fig. 4 are clear given the results of Table 3 for the US and EU and the magnitude of the worldwide recession — i.e., new import protection was historically associated with rising domestic unemployment and economic contraction abroad. The unemployment rate rose significantly in both economies. The simultaneity of the recession *across the world* implied that virtually every US and EU trading partner was also undergoing a sharp decline in real GDP growth during this period. These factors combined to create a perfect storm of conditions for a large increase in new import protection, given the way policymakers in the US and EU had historically responded, as documented in Table 3.

Nevertheless, as the solid line of the right panel of Fig. 4 illustrates, the realization of new import protection for the US and EU was different from the model predictions. While the timing of the predicted US peak in 2009:Q3 corresponds with the realized peak of TTBs, the *magnitude* of the realized increase was much smaller. Cumulatively across the 15 trading partners under study, the US responded with 16 times fewer TTBs than the pre-crisis model estimates predicted. Similarly, the EU responded with nearly 8 times fewer new TTBs than the model predicted. US TTBs affected 0.9% of nonoil imports, far less than the forecasted upper limit of 15.4%. EU TTBs affected 1.9% of nonoil imports, also far less than its forecasted upper limit of 14.0%. Furthermore, for the EU, the difference between the left panel and the solid line of the right panel also illustrates that the *timing* of new import protection was delayed by three quarters (from 2009:Q3 to 2010:Q2) relative to the pre-crisis model's predictions.

4.2. Why did so little import protection arise?

Given the severity of macroeconomic shocks that took place during the Great Recession, a fundamental question is what explains the import protection that did and did not arise? To address this question systematically, we re-estimate our preferred specifications from Tables 2 and 3 on a time series of data that extends through the crisis period of 2010:Q4. We introduce pre-crisis (1988:Q1–2008:Q3) and crisis (2008:Q4–2010:Q4) dummy variables to interact with the three key macroeconomic determinants so that we can test for whether import protection responded to macroeconomic shocks

[25] An interesting empirical question is whether the South Korean experience during the Asian Financial crisis of 1997–1998 foreshadowed what would happen in the US and EU during the Great Recession. Like the US and EU during 2008–2010 that we detail below, South Korea did not turn to heavy TTB use during 1997–1998. However, in other regards the two crises appear more different than similar. While South Korea did experience a sharp increase in its unemployment rate, the behavior of its real exchange rate and of the GDP growth of foreign trading partners was markedly different from the analogous variables facing the US and EU during the Great Recession. In contrast to the real US dollar, which appreciated sharply at the start of the more recent global financial crisis, the real Korean won depreciated sharply in 1997. Further, the Asian Financial Crisis did not lead to a slowdown in GDP growth around the world. Thus, the applicability of the South Korean experience to later financial crises in industrialized economies is limited.

[26] In unreported results, we have also investigated whether including the WTO discipline variable – introduced in Section 3.1 and included in Table 2, specification (7) – improves upon the estimates for this subsample of countries. It does not, which suggests that the main impact captured by the WTO discipline variable in Table 2, specification (7) is due to variation across the five policy-imposing economies – e.g., the US and EU have relatively more products bound by WTO disciplines than do Australia, Canada and South Korea – and not from inter-temporal variation within one of these policy-imposing economies.

[27] Bown (2011c) provides a discussion of the World Bank's initiatives, as well as efforts by the World Trade Organization Secretariat and the establishment of the high-profile Global Trade Alert.

[28] To clarify the thought experiment, the import data used to construct these shares are all taken from 2007, to remove any potential contamination associated with the 2008–9 trade collapse. Nevertheless, the products in focus would not become subject to TTB policies until 2008:Q4–2010:Q4. The mean value of annual imports in 2007 for one of the 94 product-trading partner combinations that were actually confronted with new US TTBs between 2008:Q4 and 2010:Q4 was $133.4 million. The estimate of 15.4% is derived by taking this $133.4 million, multiplying it by 1558 product-trading partner combinations, and dividing by $1.34 trillion — i.e., the total US non-oil imports from these 15 trading partners in 2007. The estimate is an upper limit given that product-trading partner combinations affected by US TTBs in the data ($133.4 million) are much higher than the mean product-trading partner combination in the entire sample ($30.2 million) which includes non-TTB affected products.

[29] Even though the EU had a much lower predicted count of TTBs (623 versus 1558), the mean value of EU annual imports in 2007 for the 84 relevant product-trading partner combinations was $247.3 million. Finally, EU non-oil imports from its sample of 15 trading partners in 2007 were $1.1 trillion.

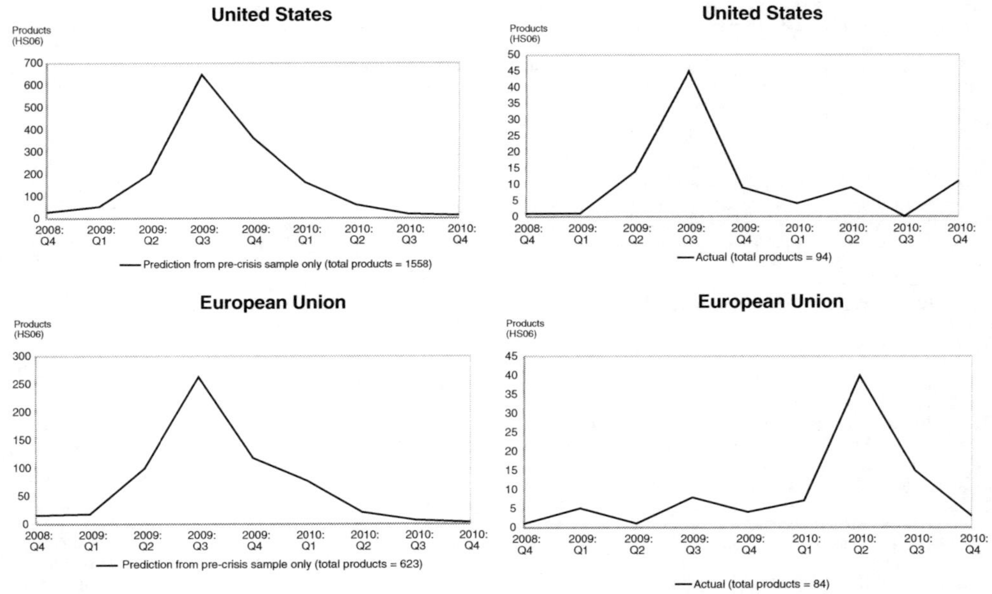

Fig. 4. United States and European Union: Predicted versus realized trade policy response to macroeconomic shocks during 2008:Q4–2010:Q4.
Notes: Prediction of the number of imported products from 15 trading partners per quarter subject to new TTBs from the pre-crisis sample based on estimates from Table 3 specification (2) for the US and specification (5) for the EU. For context, the median number of products subject to new US TTBs against these 15 trading partners per quarter between 1988:Q1 and 2008:Q3 was 12, and for the EU between 1999:Q1 and 2008:Q3 the median was 9.

differentially across the two sub-periods.[30] We consider three different samples of data; the full sample of all five policy-imposing economies, and then two subsamples in which the United States or the European Union is the policy-imposing economy. Table 1 again provides summary statistics that highlight the differences in means and standard deviations of the underlying data series across the two sub-periods.

Table 4 presents our results under this approach. First consider the estimates on the full sample of data. For the 1988:Q1–2008:Q3 period, the estimated IRRs for each of the three macroeconomic determinants are close to the size of the corresponding estimates in Table 2 that we discussed in Section 3.1.[31]

How did the trade policy responsiveness to macroeconomic fluctuations *change* during 2008:Q4–2010:Q4? According to the baseline specification (1), in which the macroeconomic determinants are each defined at one lag ($t-1$), the Chi-squared test statistics with one degree of freedom (reported in square brackets) indicate that there is a statistically significant change in each of the estimated IRRs between the pre-crisis and post-2008:Q3 period. The IRR estimate of 1.00 on the bilateral real exchange rate is statistically different from the pre-crisis IRR estimate of 1.02, the IRR estimate of 1.06 on the domestic unemployment change is statistically different from the pre-crisis IRR estimate of 1.63, and the IRR estimate of 1.03 on foreign GDP growth is statistically different from the pre-crisis IRR estimate of 0.88. However, not all of these changes are robust to slight modifications to the baseline model. In specification (2), for example, if we redefine the determinants to each be at the second lag ($t-2$) instead of the first lag, then the statistically significant differential for the domestic unemployment rate change is eliminated. Specification (3) introduces one additional explanatory variable, defined as the growth rate in bilateral imports.[32] This variable is included to address the concern that import protection through TTBs is typically associated with substantial import growth; thus the muted import protection response during 2008:Q4–2010:Q4 could be due to the global collapse in trade flows that took place in 2008-2009 (Baldwin and Evenett, 2009).[33] The estimated IRR on this variable for the pre-crisis period is not statistically different from 1; more importantly, controlling for imports does not affect either the qualitative or the quantitative nature of our results for the pre-crisis estimates of the other macroeconomic determinants of interest. However, inclusion of this variable in specification (3) does eliminate the statistically significant *differential* (across sub-periods) for the variable defined as the percent change in the bilateral real exchange rate. On balance, the model estimates are not sufficiently robust across specifications to allow us to conclude that there was a change in the relationship

[30] The qualitative pattern to our results does not change if we move the definition of the beginning of the crisis period by 1 or 2 quarters.

[31] The estimates for the 1988:Q1–2008:Q3 period in Table 4 are not identical to the corresponding Table 2 or Table 3 estimates because the empirical models embed an assumption that the importer *i* and exporter *j* combined fixed effects are the same across both the 1988:Q1–2008:Q3 and 2008:Q4–2010:Q4 sub-periods.

[32] Due to a lack of quarterly data on trading-partner specific import price indices, these data are in nominal terms. However, because this variable is also constructed from year-over-year data, we are not concerned with potential seasonality issues.

[33] In principle, a necessary legal condition under WTO rules for applying each of the TTB policies is that the domestic industry should be injured *because of* imports – whether they be dumped (antidumping), subsidized (countervailing duties) or surging (safeguards). In theory, evidence that imports had recently been in decline could make it more difficult for government authorities to impose TTBs.

C.P. Bown, M.A. Crowley / Journal of International Economics 90 (2013) 50–64 61

Table 4
Differential impacts on policy response during the Great Recession.

	Dependent variable: bilateral *(ij)* count of products initiated under all temporary trade barrier policies in quarter *t* by country(ies) listed below						
	All countries			United States		European Union‡	
Explanatory Variables	First lag (1)	Second lag (2)	Second lag (3)	First lag (4)	Second lag (5)	First lag (6)	Second lag (7)
Percent change in bilateral real exchange rate	1.02^a	1.02^a	1.02^a	1.03^a	1.04^a	1.03^a	1.05^a
$ijt-1$, 1988:Q1–2008:Q3	(4.23)	(5.00)	(5.03)	(3.58)	(5.31)	(2.60)	(4.45)
Percent change in bilateral real exchange rate	1.00	1.00	1.01	1.06	1.06^c	0.93^b	0.94^b
$ijt-1$, 2008:Q4–2010:Q4	(0.26)	(0.34)	(0.90)	(1.59)	(1.94)	(2.46)	(2.53)
[Test statistic]	$[4.23]^b$	$[3.17]^c$	[1.38]	[0.63]	[0.15]	$[10.65]^a$	$[16.84]^a$
Domestic unemployment rate change $jt-1$,	1.63^a	1.17^b	1.16^c	2.16^a	1.67^a	10.00^a	1.58
1988:Q1–2008:Q3	(6.72)	(2.01)	(1.87)	(4.55)	(2.58)	(6.60)	(1.19)
Domestic unemployment rate change $jt-1$,	1.06	1.16	0.96	1.87^b	1.77^b	0.59	2.31^c
2008:Q4–2010:Q4	(0.46)	(1.05)	(0.24)	(2.56)	(2.20)	(1.29)	(1.94)
[Test statistic]	$[8.34]^a$	[0.00]	[1.01]	[0.22]	[0.03]	$[26.84]^a$	[0.44]
Real GDP growth of trading partner $it-1$,	0.88^a	0.90^a	0.90^a	0.84^a	0.92^a	0.91^c	0.85^b
1988:Q1–2008:Q3	(6.41)	(4.90)	(4.64)	(5.31)	(2.62)	(1.66)	(2.46)
Real GDP growth of trading partner $it-1$,	1.03	1.01	1.04	1.09	1.08	1.08	1.09
2008:Q4–2010:Q4	(0.90)	(0.37)	(1.14)	(1.24)	(1.30)	(1.01)	(1.07)
[Test statistic]	$[19.56]^a$	$[10.70]^a$	$[13.02]^a$	$[12.17]^a$	$[6.15]^b$	$[4.34]^b$	$[8.30]^b$
Import growth from trading partner $it-1$,	–	–	1.00	–	–	–	–
1988:Q1–2008:Q3			(0.48)				
Import growth from trading partner $it-1$,	–	–	0.98^c	–	–	–	–
2008:Q4–2010:Q4			(1.82)				
[Test statistic]	–	–	[2.65]	–	–	–	–
Time trend included	Yes	Yes	Yes	Yes	Yes	Yes	Yes
Import and exporter combined fixed effects	Yes	Yes	Yes	Yes	Yes	Yes	Yes
Observations	5036	5010	5007	1195	1188	719	718

Notes: "All countries" include the five economies *j* (Australia, Canada, EU, South Korea, US) vis-à-vis one of the 15 trading partners *i* (listed in Appendix A) over 1988:Q1–2010:Q4. ‡Data for the EU as policy imposer are restricted to 1999:Q1–2010:Q4 throughout. Incidence rate ratios (IRRs) are reported in lieu of coefficient estimates, with t-statistics in parentheses. Chi-squared test statistics with one degree of freedom are reported in square brackets. Model includes a constant term whose estimate is suppressed. Superscripts a, b, and c indicate statistical significance at the 1, 5, and 10 percent levels, respectively. Each explanatory variable is lagged one quarter (at $t-1$) in specifications (1), (4), and (6) and two quarters (at $t-2$) in specifications (2), (3), (5), and (7).

between trade policy and the exchange rate or between trade policy and domestic unemployment during the Great Recession.[34]

Nevertheless, the one variable for which there is an important estimated change is foreign real GDP growth. For example, the pre-crisis IRR estimate of 0.88 in specification (1) indicates that policy-imposing economies had used import protection against trading partners with weak economic growth. In contrast, the estimated IRR on foreign real GDP growth is 1.03 during 2008:Q4–2010:Q4. While this second IRR was not statistically greater than 1, the pre-crisis and crisis IRRs are statistically different *from one another*, thus signaling a change in behavior. Therefore, these economies switched toward implementation of new TTB import protection against those trading partners that were experiencing relatively stronger economic growth during the Great Recession. This is a particularly important contributor to the low levels of import protection that arose during this period.

Columns (4) through (7) confirm this result for the United States and the European Union. In fact, the only statistically significant estimated IRR change that is robust across these two sub-periods for both the United States in specifications (4) and (5) and the European Union in specifications (6) and (7) is the differential on foreign real GDP growth. As in the full sample of data, there is evidence that the US and EU switched away from imposing import protection on trading partners that were experiencing macroeconomic weakness, as had been the historical pattern, and toward those that were growing. With so many US and EU trading partners undergoing economic contraction during 2008:Q4–2010:Q4, the implication of this effect was to reduce new US and EU import protection overall relative to pre-crisis predictions.

Consider next the two other macroeconomic determinants of interest for each of the subsamples of data in Table 4. For the United States, the estimated IRRs for these two determinants did not change during the crisis in statistically meaningful ways away from the 1988:Q1–2008:Q3 estimates. For example, in specification (4), the IRR estimate of 1.06 on the bilateral real exchange rate is not statistically different from the pre-crisis IRR estimate of 1.03, and the IRR estimate of 1.87 on the domestic unemployment change is not statistically different from the pre-crisis IRR estimate of 2.16. The same pattern holds when we redefine the macroeconomic determinants at $t-2$ in specification (5). Furthermore, results from the European Union sample are like the United States in that the IRR estimate on the domestic unemployment rate change during 2008:Q4–2010:Q4 is not consistently different from the IRR estimate from prior to the crisis. While specification (6) presents evidence of a differential, this is not robust to redefining the macroeconomic determinants at two lags. As described earlier, the estimated IRR for the unemployment rate change appears particularly sensitive to the relatively shorter time series of available data for the EU sample.

[34] During the revision process, we became aware of a paper by Rose (2012) that challenges the idea that import protection is countercyclical. Rose analyzes a number of trade policy indicators at the annual frequency – including a coarse measure of antidumping cases rather than a count of affected HS-06 products – for thirty economies through 2009. In results available upon request, we estimate our baseline model on annual data and find that trade policy is countercyclical prior to the Great Recession (over 1988–2007) regardless of whether trade policy is measured as products subject to all TTBs or antidumping alone and for domestic business cycle measures including both lagged changes in unemployment (our preferred measure) and real GDP growth (Rose's measure). In our model, when using the change in the unemployment rate at the annual frequency for data extended through 2009, the point estimate for the IRR continues to show evidence of a countercyclical relationship, although the IRR is less precisely estimated. When using real GDP growth at the annual frequency in data extended through 2009, the point estimate for the IRR is no longer precisely estimated.

However, there is one other robust differential between estimated IRRs from the European Union sample. The estimated IRRs for the EU's bilateral real exchange rate for 2008:Q4–2010:Q4 are less than 1 and they are statistically less than the EU's IRR estimate for the earlier period. Thus there is some evidence of a change in that the EU imposed fewer TTBs in response to the euro appreciation early in the crisis period (see again Fig. 1), given the EU's 1999:Q1–2008:Q3 IRR estimate which indicated that an appreciation of the euro currency historically led to more TTBs.

Nevertheless, a final contributing explanation for the lack of a major import protection response by the United States or the European Union during 2008:Q4–2010:Q4 is related to the movements in each economy's bilateral real exchange rates over the period. The historical evidence for the EU and US is that real currency appreciations led to more import protection through TTBs. As the gray line in Fig. 1 again illustrates for the EU, for much of the 2008–2010 period the euro is depreciating. Furthermore, shortly after the sharp appreciation of the US dollar in 2009:Q1, the dollar *depreciated* by a nearly identical amount, and then continued a period of weakening throughout 2009–2010. These real depreciations suggest another dampening effect on new EU and US import protection.

4.3. Model predictions for import protection during other recessions

In light of the evidence from the last section that IRR estimates changed for the Great Recession relative to 1988:Q1–2008:Q3, one last question we investigate is the ability of the model to predict new TTB import protection during *earlier* cyclical downturns. Here we consider the question in the context of the United States. Our approach is to estimate the US model with data from 1988:Q1 to 2000:Q4 and to then use the estimated IRRs to predict out-of-sample TTBs for 2001:Q1–2007:Q4, given the realizations of aggregate variables during that period.[35] We continue to implement a basic model that also allows for trading partner-specific channels of aggregate fluctuations to bilateral real exchange rates and foreign real GDP growth to affect the formation of new TTBs. Nevertheless, the exercise can also be viewed as examining whether identification of the model's parameters for a period that includes only one major US recession – i.e., the 1990–1991 downturn – can be used to predict trade policy activity alongside the subsequent domestic recession of 2001.

The estimated IRRs for the model for 1988:Q1–2000:Q4 are qualitatively similar to the IRR estimates from the full sample for the period of 1988:Q1–2008:Q3 in Table 3. They continue to align with theoretical expectations although the IRR for the real exchange rate is smaller in magnitude and it is not precisely estimated in the limited sample.[36]

Fig. 5 illustrates the predicted amount of new TTBs over 2001:Q1–2007:Q4 using the US model estimates based on the 1988:Q1–2000:Q4 data and the realized macroeconomic data for this later period. We illustrate predictions in comparison to the actual US TTBs taking place during that period.

As Fig. 5 illustrates, the model does a reasonable job at predicting the quantity of protection over several quarters. First, the model predicts a general increase in TTBs for the period of 2001:Q1–2003:Q2. Over that time period, the model predicts that 989 total new TTBs would arise; the US initiated 1209 in practice. The increase in TTBs taking place during this period is related to the sharp appreciation of the US dollar and the rising unemployment rate. However, as Fig. 1 again illustrates, note that the largest quarterly increase in the real exchange rate was in 2001:Q1, whereas the peak quarterly increase in the unemployment rate was considerably later in 2001:Q4. Second, the model also predicts *low* levels of TTBs over the period 2004:Q2 through 2007:Q4; this compares well with the realized data on new TTBs.

On the other hand, the model cannot match the magnitude of the spike in realized US TTBs in 2001:Q2. These were almost entirely associated with one single policy decision, i.e., the US steel safeguard initiation in June 2001. However, the US steel safeguard had a number of unique properties, from the perspective of this modeling exercise. First, it was a single action covering hundreds of products. Furthermore, and despite the exclusions and exemptions which pierced the full nondiscriminatory nature of the policy (Bown, 2004), the import restriction still covered many trading partners, a number of which may not have been substantial suppliers of US steel import products. Finally, in the quarterly data, the singular timing of this policy action also ends up being recorded as quite different from a set of similar (in the aggregate) antidumping actions in 1991-1992, for example. Because those many separate antidumping actions fell over a couple of different quarters (e.g., 1992:Q2, 1992:Q3) there was not as large a spike in any one quarter as was recorded during the 2001 recession.

5. Conclusion

This paper uses quarterly data for the United States, European Union, and three other industrialized economies to estimate the impact of macroeconomic shocks on import protection over 1988:Q1–2010:Q4. Estimates from a data sample taken before the Great Recession exhibit evidence of three key relationships. First, there is strong evidence of a countercyclical relationship between domestic macroeconomic shocks – increases in domestic unemployment rates or reductions in domestic real GDP growth – and governments initiating new temporary trade barrier investigations over significantly more imported products per trading partner per quarter. Second, we find that these economies used such bilateral import restrictions against trading partners that were going through their own periods of weak economic growth. Third, a real appreciation of the bilateral exchange rate defined in terms of the domestic currency is associated with increases to these forms of import protection. Overall, we find that this evidence is especially strong for import protection by the United States and European Union, and the evidence is weaker for smaller economies such as Australia, Canada, and South Korea.

In a second exercise, we use estimates from the pre-Great Recession model to then show the expected trade policy response during 2008:Q4–2010:Q4 given the realized macroeconomic shocks. The historical models for the US and EU in particular predicted a sharp increase in import protection taking place beginning in 2009:Q2 and lasting through 2010:Q1, peaking in 2009:Q3. While the increase in import protection during the Great Recession was not as large as the potential additional 15 percentage point coverage of imports that some historical models predicted, arguably the fear of this realization contributed to the pre-emptive "anti-protectionism" G20 Declaration of November 2008 and a number of initiatives to actively monitor trade policy (by the WTO, World Bank, and Global Trade Alert) beginning in early 2009.

Third, we re-estimate the models on data from the Great Recession period in order to explain deviations to the realized protectionist response away from historical behavior. We do not find robust evidence of a change to the countercyclical relationship between *domestic* unemployment and new import protection. However, we do provide evidence that these policy-imposing economies "switched" from their historical behavior; during the Great Recession they shifted new import protection away from those trading partners that were contracting and toward those experiencing relatively stronger economic growth. This evidence, in addition to the sharp and

[35] We estimate the same specification as that presented in Fig. 4, i.e., Table 3, specification (2), in which the determinants are each defined at two lags.

[36] We do not present the estimates in a table so as to conserve space. Nevertheless the estimated IRRs (and t-statistics) for the key determinants for the 1988:Q1–2000:Q4 period are: 1.01 (1.06) for the real exchange rate, 2.01 (3.42) for the change in unemployment, and 0.90 (2.91) for the foreign trading partner real GDP growth rate.

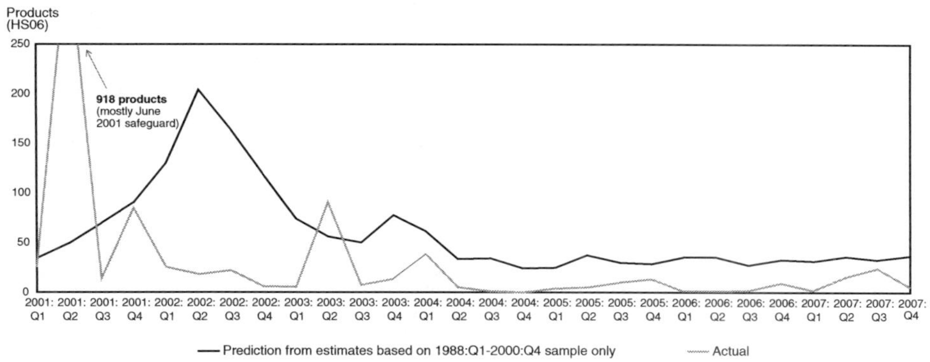

Fig. 5. Out-of-sample model predictions for United States TTBs, 2001:Q1–2007:Q4.
Notes: Prediction of number of imported products from 15 trading partners per quarter subject to new TTBs from IRRs estimated on the 1988:Q1–2000:Q4 data sample and macroeconomic data from 2001:Q1-2007:Q4 based on the same model specification as Table 3, column (2). The estimated IRRs are reported in footnote 36.

persistent real depreciations of the US dollar and euro after their initial run-up in 2009, was a particularly important contributor to the relatively low levels of import protection that arose given that so many trading partners were themselves experiencing periods of severe economic contraction during 2008–2010.

Finally, our results contribute to a substantial literature that has evolved to explain the role of trade agreements and the use of temporary trade barriers under the WTO. Our paper identifies the importance of bilateral channels through which new trade barriers arise, and how these channels differed in 2008–2010 relative to periods before the Great Recession. Nevertheless, even this research is just one additional step in understanding the role of trade agreements, including the potential limits to what trade agreements can accomplish in maintaining trade policy cooperation across countries. Indeed, economies like the United States and European Union are no longer the "biggest" users of temporary trade barrier policies. Whether the major new emerging economy users of these policies – India, China, Brazil, Argentina, and Turkey, for example – respond similarly to macroeconomic shocks remains an open question.

Appendix A. Data description

Temporary trade barrier data under antidumping, countervailing duty, global safeguards, and the China-specific safeguard policies at the Harmonized System 6-digit level by trading partner for 1988–2010 is compiled by the authors from the World Bank's *Temporary Trade Barriers Database* (Bown, 2011b) which is publicly available at http://econ.worldbank.org/ttbd/.

Bilateral real exchange rate series come from the USDA's Agricultural Exchange Rate Data Set. For each quarterly observation we use the value as of the last month of the quarter.

Domestic unemployment rate change is calculated at the quarterly frequency as the year-over-year changes with data from the International Labor Organization.

Real GDP growth is calculated as the year-over-year changes. There are a total of 18 economies from which we require data on real GDP growth. Unless otherwise noted, each economy had data available for 1988:Q1–2010:Q4 in the form of a seasonally adjusted, quarterly real GDP series taken from OECD. The EU (EU27) and Israel's series began in 1995:Q1. Turkey's series began in 1998:Q1. Furthermore, series for Brazil (beginning in 1996:Q1), Japan, Indonesia (beginning in 1990:Q1), and India (beginning in 1996:Q2) are from Haver OECD MEI. Mexico and South Africa's series are from IFS. China's quarterly year-on-year real GDP growth series are from official government statistics and began in 1992:Q1. Taiwan's series are from official government statistics.

The variable defined as the change in the share of imported products under WTO discipline is calculated at the annual frequency for 1995–2010 based on HS-06 applied MFN tariffs and WTO binding data available from UNCTAD (TRAINS) and the WTO's Integrated Database through WITS.

Trading partners: For each of the five policy-imposing economies *j*, with the exception of South Korea, the bilateral relationship is with one of its 15 trading partners *i*. The 15 partners are determined as the most frequent targets against which each economy used such import protection over the sample period, conditional on the availability of that trading partner's macroeconomic data at the quarterly frequency. The trading partners for each are:

- United States (15): Australia, Brazil, Canada, China, European Union, India, Indonesia, Japan, Mexico, New Zealand, South Africa, South Korea, Switzerland, Taiwan, China; and Turkey. These economies were the source of 85% of non-oil imports during this period.
- European Union (15): Australia, Brazil, China, India, Indonesia, Japan, Mexico, New Zealand, Norway, South Africa, South Korea, Switzerland, Taiwan, China; Turkey, and United States. These economies were the source of 75% of non-oil imports during this period.
- South Korea (10): Canada, China, European Union, India, Indonesia, Japan, New Zealand, Switzerland, Taiwan, China, and United States. These economies were the source of 79% of non-oil imports during this period.
- Australia (15): Brazil, Canada, China, European Union, India, Indonesia, Israel, Japan, Mexico, Norway, South Africa, South Korea, Taiwan, China; Turkey, and United States. These economies were the source of 81% of non-oil imports during this period.
- Canada (15): Australia, Brazil, China, European Union, India, Indonesia, Japan, Mexico, New Zealand, South Africa, South Korea, Switzerland, Taiwan, China; Turkey, and United States. These economies were the source of 94% of non-oil imports during this period.

Appendix Table 1. The only other (non-TTB) import restricting policies for these five economies, 2008–2010

Country, non-TTB import-restricting policy	Date of inception
Australia	
Increase of excise rates on imports of tobacco	April 30, 2010
Customer price index adjustment for alcohol and tobacco products	August 2, 2010
Canada	
Temporary tariff-rate quota on milk protein substitutes	March 1, 2009
Lower threshold for delisting wines in provincial liquor stores	July 20, 2009
South Korea	
Increased tariffs for 16 selected products	January 1, 2009
Restoration of tariff on imports of crude oil to 3%	March 1, 2009
United States	
Reclassification subjecting certain solar panels to a 2.5% tariff	January 9, 2009
Ban on poultry imports from China	March 11, 2009
Adoption of a ban against imports of Mexican shrimp	April 20, 2010
Ban on the importation of Asian carp	December 14, 2010

Source: compiled by the authors from Global Trade Alert at www.globaltradealert.org, last accessed 29 February 2012. See discussion in footnote 1.

References

Bagwell, Kyle, Staiger, Robert W., 1990. A theory of managed trade. American Economic Review 80 (4), 779–795.

Bagwell, Kyle, Staiger, Robert W., 1999. An economic theory of GATT. American Economic Review 89 (1), 215–248.

Bagwell, Kyle, Staiger, Robert W., 2003. Protection and the business cycle. Advances in Economic Analysis & Policy 3 (1), 1–43.

Bagwell, Kyle, Staiger, Robert W., 2011. What do trade negotiators negotiate about? Empirical evidence from the World Trade Organization. American Economic Review 101 (4), 1238–1273.

Baldwin, Richard, Evenett, Simon J. (Eds.), 2009. The Collapse of Global Trade, Murky Protectionism, and the Crisis: Recommendations for the G20. CEPR and VoxEU.org, London UK (March).

Bown, Chad P., 2004. How Different are Safeguards from Antidumping? Evidence from U.S. Trade Policies Toward Steel. Brandeis University manuscript . (July).

Bown, Chad P., 2010. China's WTO entry: antidumping, safeguards, and dispute settlement. In: Feenstra, Robert C., Wei, Shang-Jin (Eds.), China's Growing Role in World Trade. University of Chicago Press for the NBER, pp. 281–337.

Bown, Chad P., 2011a. Taking stock of antidumping, safeguards and countervailing duties, 1990–2009. The World Economy 34 (12), 1955–1998.

Bown, Chad P., 2011b. Temporary Trade Barriers Database. The World Bank . (July. Available on line at http://econ.worldbank.org/ttbd/).

Bown, Chad P., 2011c. Introduction. In: Bown, Chad P. (Ed.), The Great Recession and Import Protection: the Role of Temporary Trade Barriers. CEPR and World Bank, London, UK, pp. 1–51.

Bown, Chad P., Crowley, Meredith A., forthcoming. Self-enforcing trade agreements: evidence from time-varying trade policy. American Economic Review.

Bown, Chad P., McCulloch, Rachel, 2003. Nondiscrimination and the WTO agreement on safeguards. World Trade Review 2 (3), 327–348.

Brander, James, Krugman, Paul, 1983. A 'reciprocal dumping' model of international trade. Journal of International Economics 15 (3–4), 313–321.

Broda, Christian, Limão, Nuno, Weinstein, David E., 2008. Optimal tariffs and market power: the evidence. American Economic Review 98 (5), 2032–2065.

Crowley, Meredith A., 2010. Split decisions in antidumping cases. B.E. Journal of Economic Analysis and Policy 10 (1) (Article 68).

Crowley, Meredith A., 2011. Cyclical dumping and US antidumping protection: 1980–2001. Federal Reserve Bank of Chicago Working Paper (WP-2007-21).

Davis, Christina, Pelc, Krzysztof, 2012. Cooperation in Hard Times: Self-Restraint of Trade Protection. Princeton University manuscript . (June. Available on line at http://www.princeton.edu/~cldavis/files/DavisPelc_selfrestraint.pdf).

Feinberg, Robert M., 1989. Exchange rates and unfair trade. The Review of Economics and Statistics 71 (4), 704–707.

Gawande, Kishore, Bandyopadhyay, Usree, 2000. Is protection for sale? Evidence on the Grossman–Helpman theory of endogenous protection. The Review of Economics and Statistics 82 (1), 139–152.

Gawande, Kishore, Hoekman, Bernard, Cui, Yue, 2011. Determinants of trade policy responses to the 2008 financial crisis. World Bank Policy Research Working Paper Series No. 5862 (October).

Goldberg, Pinelopi Koujianou, Maggi, Giovanni, 1999. Protection for sale: an empirical investigation. American Economic Review 89 (5), 1135–1155.

Grossman, Gene M., Helpman, Elhanan, 1994. Protection for sale. American Economic Review 84 (4), 833–850.

Hansen, Wendy, Prusa, Thomas J., 1996. Cumulation and ITC decision-making: the sum of the parts is greater than the whole. Economic Inquiry 34, 746–769.

Hausman, Jerry, Hall, Bronwyn H., Griliches, Zvi, 1984. Econometric models for count data with an application to the patents–R&D relationship. Econometrica 52 (4), 909–938.

Hillman, Arye L., 1982. Declining industries and political-support protectionist motives. American Economic Review 72 (5), 1180–1187.

Irwin, Douglas A., 2005. The rise of U.S. antidumping activity in historical perspective. The World Economy 28 (5), 651–668.

Irwin, Douglas A., 2011a. Peddling Protectionism: Smoot–Hawley and the Great Depression. Princeton University Press, Princeton, NJ.

Irwin, Douglas A., 2011b. Trade Policy Disaster: Lessons from the 1930s. The MIT Press, Cambridge, MA.

Kang, Moonsung, Park, Soonchan, 2011. South Korea: temporary trade barriers before and during the crisis. In: Bown, Chad P. (Ed.), The Great Recession and Import Protection: the Role of Temporary Trade Barriers. CEPR and World Bank, London, UK, pp. 163–197.

Kee, Hiau Looi, Neagu, Cristina, Nicita, Alessandro, forthcoming. Is protectionism on the rise? Assessing national trade policies during the crisis of 2008. The Review of Economics and Statistics.

Knetter, Michael M., Prusa, Thomas J., 2003. Macroeconomic factors and antidumping filings: evidence from four countries. Journal of International Economics 61 (1), 1–17.

Ludema, Rodney D., Mayda, Anna Maria, 2011. Canada: no place like home for antidumping. In: Bown, Chad P. (Ed.), The Great Recession and Import Protection: the Role of Temporary Trade Barriers. CEPR and World Bank, London, UK, pp. 131–161.

Prusa, Thomas J., 2011. United States: evolving trends in temporary trade barriers. In: Bown, Chad P. (Ed.), The Great Recession and Import Protection: the Role of Temporary Trade Barriers. CEPR and World Bank, London, UK, pp. 53–83.

Rose, Andrew K., 2012. Protectionism isn't counter-cyclic (anymore). NBER Working Paper No. 18062 (May).

Staiger, Robert W., Wolak, Frank A., 1994. Measuring industry-specific protection: antidumping in the United States. Brookings Papers on Economic Activity: Microeconomics, pp. 51–118.

Trefler, Daniel, 1993. Trade liberalization and the theory of endogenous protection: an econometric study of U.S. import policy. Journal of Political Economy 101 (1), 138–160.

Vandenbussche, Hylke, Viegelahn, Christian, 2011. European Union: no protectionist surprises. In: Bown, Chad P. (Ed.), The Great Recession and Import Protection: the Role of Temporary Trade Barriers. CEPR and World Bank, London, UK, pp. 85–129.

[17]

Global Supply Chains and Trade Policy Responses to the 2008 Crisis

Kishore Gawande, Bernard Hoekman, and Yue Cui *

The collapse in trade and the contraction of output that occurred during 2008–9 was comparable to, and in many countries more severe than, the Great Depression of the 1930s. However, it did not give rise to the rampant protectionism that followed the Great Crash. The idea that the rise in the fragmentation of production across global value chains – vertical specialization – may be a deterrent against protectionism is underappreciated in the literature. Institutions also played a role in limiting the extent of protectionist responses. World Trade Organization discipline raises the cost of using trade policies for member countries and has proved to be a stable foundation for the open multilateral trading system that has been built over the past 50 years. Using trade and protection data for seven large emerging market countries that have a history of active use of trade policy, the influence of these and other factors on trade policy responses to the 2008 crisis are empirically examined. An instrumental variables strategy is used to identify their impact. Participation in global value chains is found to be a powerful economic factor determining trade policy responses. JEL codes: F13, F5, L52

The contraction in output and collapse in trade that followed the 2008 financial crisis was comparable to what occurred in the early years of the Great Depression of 1930. Eichengreen and O'Rourke (2012, Figure 2) depict, in parallel, how far and how fast trade collapsed following the Great Depression and the

* Kishore Gawande (corresponding author) is the Helen and Roy Ryu Professor of Economics and Government, Bush School of Government and Public Service, Texas A&M University. His email address is kgawande@tamu.edu. Bernard Hoekman is the Director of the Global Economics Program, Robert Schuman Centre for Advanced Studies at the European University Institute. His email address is bernard.hoekman@eui.eu. Yue Cui is a Senior Transfer Pricing Analyst at Ernst & Young LLP. Her email is yue.cui@ey.com. She was a graduate student at the Bush School while co-authoring the paper. This paper is a contribution to the UK-supported Global Trade and Financial Architecture project. We thank Guillaume Daudin for very generously sharing data as well as seminar participants at CERDI, the European University Institute, the Peterson Institute for International Economics, Seoul National University, and the Bush School, Texas A&M University for helpful suggestions. The revised paper has benefitted greatly from comments made by reviewers and the editor. Responsibility for any errors is ours. A supplemental appendix to this article is available at http://wber.oxfordjournals.org/.

THE WORLD BANK ECONOMIC REVIEW, VOL. 29, NO. 1, pp. 102–128 doi:10.1093/wber/lht040
Advance Access Publication January 23, 2014

2008 crisis. In the two years following the 2008 crisis, trade fell faster than during the first two years of the Great Depression.[1] The trade collapse during the Great Depression coincided with walls of tariffs rising around the world as countries closed their economies to protect producers and to keep employment from falling even further. In contrast, the 2008 crisis and its recessionary aftermath did not fuel rampant protectionism.

Most developing and emerging market countries had substantial policy latitude to raise tariffs and still remain compliant with their WTO commitments. Table 1 presents the pre- and post-crisis averages of bilateral tariffs imposed by seven large emerging market nations on their imports. Of relevance are the simple and import-weighted averages of the actual applied rates (t).[2] Clearly, the Depression-era scenario did not materialize and has not as of this writing. Argentina, Brazil, and Turkey show a slight increase in weighted tariff averages, whereas both measures actually *dropped* after the crisis for the other four countries. Even where protectionism by means other than tariffs was perceived after the 2008 crisis, the share of trade affected was limited. Calculations of the Anderson-Neary trade restrictiveness index (Anderson and Neary 1994; Kee, Nicita, and Olarreaga 2009) by Kee, Neagu, and Nicita (2013) suggest that less than 2% of the trade collapse may be attributed to protectionism.

The primary objective of this paper is to unpack the reasons why the deep post-2008 recession was unaccompanied by widespread protectionism. One contrast with the Depression era is that the high tariffs of that time were due to the rigid adherence of countries to the gold standard and the associated unwillingness to allow their currencies to depreciate (Irwin 2012). This predominantly macroeconomic explanation for the rise in protectionism is consistent with the inexperience that countries had with Keynesian policies, which became known much later.[3] However, the scope for governments to undertake large-scale fiscal easing is limited by high debt and mounting deficits. When macroeconomic policy is thus constrained, will protectionism surge?

Trade theory suggests good reasons why this may not be the case. One-way trade flows that involve the exchange of final consumption goods in one sector for final consumption goods in another have gradually been replaced by two-way

1. There is an emerging consensus that a decrease in demand for investment goods and consumer durables was a major cause of the 2008 trade collapse and that this may have been compounded by trade finance liquidity constraints. See Eaton et al. (2011) and Levchenko, Lewis, and Tesar (2010) on the former and Chor and Manova (2012) and Ahn, Amiti, and Weinstein (2011) on the latter. A number of initial analyses of the great trade collapse are collected in Baldwin (2009).

2. For a country such as India, these are averages taken across the country's bilateral tariffs t_{ip}, which may vary across partners p and commodities i. The simple average is taken only over non-zero imports. Weighted averages weight t_{ip} with imports m_{ip}. Because tariffs lower imports, weighted averages understate tariffs, and because simple averages disregard commodity import volumes, they overstate tariffs.

3. In the 1930s, fixed exchange rates of countries remaining on the gold standard led to real exchange rate appreciation and reduced the competitiveness of their products. Today, few of the large trading countries maintain fixed exchange rates and are able to exercise monetary policy.

TABLE 1. Simple and Weighted Average, 6-Digit HS Bilateral Tariffs

		Simple Mean			Import-Weighted Mean		
		Applied tariff (t)	Bound tariff (t_{BND})	MFN tariff (t_{MFN})	Applied tariff (t)	Bound tariff (t_{BND})	MFN tariff (t_{MFN})
ARG	2006–8	10.37	31.69	12.12	5.46	31.94	11.89
	2009	9.85	31.23	11.50	5.96	31.98	12.90
BRA	2006–8	12.51	30.67	13.76	7.16	30.23	9.35
	2009	13.31	30.69	14.75	7.83	30.49	10.61
CHN	2006–8	8.84	9.47	9.30	4.80	5.22	4.97
	2009	8.04	9.58	9.23	4.22	5.02	4.59
IND	pre-2009	13.13	38.08	13.37	9.38	30.22	9.54
	2009	9.31	37.99	9.53	8.69	32.99	8.85
MEX	pre-2009	7.23	34.97	14.07	2.66	35.61	12.54
	2009	4.78	34.97	11.11	1.81	35.41	8.36
TUR	pre-2009	2.43	19.67	4.66	1.97	20.62	4.79
	2009	2.89	20.06	5.17	3.04	22.11	5.60
ZAF	2006–8	7.84	20.52	9.72	6.29	21.86	7.33
	2009	7.40	20.10	9.78	6.21	21.25	7.65

Notes: 1. The three pre-2009 years for the following countries are India: 2005, 2008; Mexico 2005–6, 2008; Turkey 2005–6, 2008.

2. The import-weighted applied rates are significantly lower for countries' trade agreements (ARG, BRA, MEX).

Source: Authors' analysis based on tariff data in WITS database (described in the text).

intermediate input trade within the same sector. Trade in intermediates intrinsically discourages protectionism because it penalizes downstream domestic firms that rely on these imports. This process has accelerated in the past two decades as specialization has increased because of the reduction in trade costs following trade reforms and technological advances. A second trend is in evidence over the past decade as rapidly declining transport and communication costs have allowed the stages of production for a good to be separated across different borders, creating international supply chains. The classic case of Mexican maquiladoras performing the labor-intensive stages of production of auto parts to be shipped back to the US for further processing is no longer exceptional. The iPhone's supply chain, which traverses more than ten countries for eventual assembly in China, is the new "new". Because a multinational firm and its network of affiliates and arms-length suppliers drive the supply chain on both sides of the border, it has every incentive to reduce protection to zero to implement activities along the chain at the least cost.[4]

4. Supply chains may also be more resilient to trade collapses. Altomonte and Ottaviano (2009) hypothesize that the sunk cost of setting up supply chains makes firms adjust the entire chain along the intensive margin (value per trader) rather than the extensive margin (number of traders), and they find evidence that supports this hypothesis. Large multinational corporations at the center of supply chains alleviate the liquidity constraints of suppliers, protecting their chains from finance shortages.

Although the growth in integrated supply chains may restrain protectionism, the role of GATT/WTO rules and discipline in containing protectionism may be as important. These institutions have proved to be stable foundations for building multilateral trading relations over the last 50 years. Indeed, the proliferation of global supply chains is due to that stability. High-income OECD countries have all made binding commitments to keep most of their tariffs at low levels, often approximately 5% or less. During the crisis, there were no instances in which OECD countries raised tariff levels; insofar as these countries used trade policy, it was through instruments of contingent protection such as antidumping and safeguards (Bown 2011a).

In contrast, developing countries have greater scope to raise tariffs because their WTO bindings are less complete and often involve ceilings that are far higher than applied tariffs. As Table 1 indicates, the bound rates (t_{BND}) substantially exceed the actual applied MFN rates (t_{MFN}) for most developing countries. This "water" in the tariff allows countries to raise levels of protection without fear of retaliation by OECD trading partners. Because OECD countries do not have this policy space for increasing their MFN tariffs, the focus of this paper is on the behavior of the seven large emerging markets listed in Table 1: Argentina, Brazil, China, India, Mexico, South Africa, and Turkey. We use pre- and post-crisis trade and protection data to investigate the different explanations for observed trade policy responses and find an important role for international specialization – participation in global value chains – in preventing protectionism.

The plan of the paper is as follows. Section 2 presents statistics suggesting trends in protection in the seven countries that are the subject of the paper. Section 3 briefly describes forces based on both economic interest and institutions that may encourage or discourage protectionism and how they are measured in the econometric model. Section 4 reports the empirical results. An identification strategy allows causal inferences about the impact of these forces and how their impact after the crisis differed from that in period preceding the crisis. Section 5 concludes.

I. Trends in Tariffs and Related Policies

As noted, trade protection data for Argentina, Brazil, China, India, Mexico, South Africa, and Turkey are analyzed in the paper. In addition to the fact that all of these countries are trade dependent, they were chosen because (i) their WTO bound rates exceed their actual applied MFN rates, allowing them trade policy space[5] and (ii) they are users of WTO-permitted instruments of contingent protection, such as antidumping and safeguard actions. These are disparate countries, which allow for a robust research design. Some are members of

5. The exception here is China, which bound its tariffs at applied rates upon joining the WTO in 2001. As noted, developed countries such as Canada, the EU, Japan, and the US are unable to raise tariffs because their applied tariffs have been bound.

customs unions, whereas others participate in shallower preferential trade agreements (PTAs); some keep their applied tariffs close to bound rates, whereas others apply tariffs far below their bound rates; some are large, open countries and are able to dictate terms of trade in specific goods, whereas others are small and have little market power; some are proximate to large markets, whereas others are geographically distant. All have a long history of trade policy activism driven by industrial policy, economic development, and non-economic objectives. Consistent inferences about protectionism across these heterogeneous countries would therefore suggest that such findings may be generalized.

The primary measure of protection used in the analysis, taken from the WITS database [http://wits.worldbank.org/wits/ (last accessed September, 2012)], is bilateral tariffs at the 6-digit level of the Harmonized System (HS). The disaggregate level is necessary because protection is determined at the product, not the sector, level. The MFN tariff $t_{i,\ \mathrm{MFN}}$ is the rate that a country decides to impose on imports of commodity i regardless of which WTO member is the source. An exception to this non-discrimination occurs when a country enters a PTA with other countries and imposes a lower preferential tariff $t_{i,\ \mathrm{PRF}}$ ($\leq t_{i,\ \mathrm{MFN}}$) on imports from PTA partners. A country's actual applied tariff on imports of commodity i, t_i, is therefore equal to $t_{i,\ \mathrm{PRF}}$ or $t_{i,\ \mathrm{MFN}}$, depending on the source (possibly higher if the source is a non-WTO country). Appendix Table S.1 (in the supplemental appendix available at http://wber.oxfordjournals.org/) shows the average applied tariff t that the seven countries impose on imports from their top 15 partners. For example, US exports to Argentina face a (trade-weighted) average tariff of 7.40%, whereas exports from Brazil are free. The average difference in post-crisis and pre-crisis applied tariffs (Δt) indicates little change except in these atypical cases: the weighted average of Argentina's applied tariffs on French imports rose by 3.04 percentage points (from 5.27% to 8.31% after the crisis); Brazil's applied tariffs on Korean imports rose by 4.12%; India's applied tariffs on imports from Hong Kong rose by 4.22%; Mexico's applied tariffs on Brazilian imports rose by 3.69%; and Turkey's applied tariffs on Russian and Uzbek imports rose by 2.89% and 3.89%, respectively (most likely as a revenue-raising device because these are primary commodity imports, mainly oil and gas). The Δt column indicates these are clearly exceptions; increases in the average tariff were barely perceptible across partners, and in many cases, the average tariff was actually lower post-crisis.

Bound tariff rates ($t_{i,\ \mathrm{BND}}$) are what WTO members negotiate for each commodity i during multilateral trade rounds. The bound rate is the maximum MFN tariff a country may levy on commodity i. WTO members can and do keep their applied MFN tariffs below bound levels. Those that do so have the flexibility to increase their applied tariffs while abiding by WTO rules. The commitment made by countries to these bound rates means that the bound rates are ceilings for actual applied rates. As shown in Table 1, the average bound tariffs in most emerging countries are three times the average applied rates, implying the existence of significant water in the tariff. The last column in Table S.1 (online appendix) shows the average of the difference in difference $\Delta(t - t_{BND}) = \Delta t - \Delta t_{BND}$ between the actual and bound rates for important partners.[6] The $\Delta(t - t_{BND})$ column indicates that, except for the few cases noted, the available policy latitude remained unused. Avenues other than tariffs – antidumping duties (AD), countervailing duties, safeguards, and other nontariff barriers (NTBs) – were not overly used, even though the seven countries have an active track record as users of such measures.[7] Bown (2011a) indicates no significant upsurge in contingent protection (temporary trade barriers such as AD) in these countries. Finally, according to the Global Trade Alert (GTA) database, which tracks the flow of non-tariff measures other than transparently documented NTBs such as AD and countervailing duties (CVD), the overall increase in protectionism has remained limited.[8] The following sections address the main question of why the trade shock did not translate into significant increases in tariffs.

II. Econometric Model of Trade Policy and Identification

Model

The empirical analysis is framed as a clash between two classes of explanations, interest-based and institutions-based. Both are clearly relevant, and the model attempts to quantify their influence. The following econometric model posits that a country's bilateral tariffs are formed as

$$t_{ip} = \mathrm{S}_{ip}\Delta + \mathrm{R}_{ip}\mathrm{B} + \mu_p + e_{ip}, \tag{1}$$

where t_{ip} is the country's applied tariff on commodity i sourced from partner p, S_{ip} is a vector of variables that measures institutions, and R_{ip} is a vector of variables that measures interest. The vector of coefficients Δ and B measure their respective marginal impact on protection. Because the institution and interest

6. Because $(t - t_{BND}) \leq 0$, if $\Delta(t - t_{BND}) > 0$, it is implied that the applied tariffs approached their bounds from below; that is, the applied rates were closer to the bound rates in 2009 than in the years immediately before the crisis.

7. The Global Trade Alert (GTA) database (http://www.globaltradealert.org/) documents new non-tariff barriers (NTBs) after November 2008. Table S.2 in the (online) appendix indicates an assortment of measures designed to protect domestic producers (Evenett 2010). As of March 2011, there were 1,385 actions discriminating against foreign producers ("red" measures), including industry-specific guarantees, subsidies, tax relief, export credit insurance, and loans. Because the GTA starts in November 2008, it is not possible to assess whether measures increased in 2009. It appears that the number of new NTBs imposed in the period following the crisis was relatively stable, with little yearly variation.

8. See also Bown (2011b, Figure 2), who suggests that the trend toward greater NTB use started before the recession in 2007. In the same article, Table 2 indicates that only China showed any noticeable increase in the amount of imports on which temporary trade barriers were imposed after the crisis.

measures are sector specific (below), μ_p captures partner-fixed effects. The model's error term e_{ip} is likely to be correlated with some regressors and may have within-commodity correlations. An effective instrumental variables (IV) strategy accounts for such endogeneity and a correction for clustering for such correlations. The model is extended to detect whether and how structural change in the post-crisis period affected tariffs in the seven countries.

INTEREST. This paper suggests a new interest-based explanation: vertical specialization. Among the major transformations that separate today from the Depression era are exponentially lower transport and communication costs. Not only has trade expanded substantially, but lower costs have also allowed stages of production to be separated without concern for geography in search of the production locations with the lowest cost. Global supply chains now enable multiple countries to contribute intermediate inputs to different stages before the final good is delivered to its destination.

Combining input-output data with bilateral trade data, Johnson and Noguera (2012) quantify the current extent of multi-country production sharing by computing the ratio of the domestic content of exports or *value added exports* to gross exports – the "VAX ratio". Without trade in intermediates, the VAX ratio equals one, whereas production sharing across borders lowers it.[9] The bilateral VAX ratio for the US varies between 0.57 with Canada (a large amount of production sharing) and 0.96 with Japan (little production sharing). The same ratio for imports varies between 0.62 (Canada) and 1.07 (Japan). In general, the US VAX ratio with EU partners France, UK, and Germany is around one; with geographically close partners such as Canada and Mexico and Asian partners such as Malaysia, Taiwan, China, and Korea, it drops to approximately 0.6. The same ratio for imports is of similar magnitude with these partners.

These findings have implications for the demand for protection. If output is falling, protectionism cannot shelter a domestic market. Protecting a stage of production is different from protecting the market for a good with no production sharing. Protecting a stage of production raises the cost of vertically specialized intermediates produced in that stage to the next user downstream, which may be

9. This also implies that gross bilateral exports incorrectly state the amount of *value added* by a country that is incorporated in its exports to a destination. A correct measure of domestic content embodied in a country's exports must take account of the production sharing across borders before these stages of production deliver a final good to a destination. If semi-processed Japanese goods enter Singapore, where a small amount of value is added before the good is shipped for consumption to India, then gross Singapore-India exports overstate the true domestic content (value added) of Singapore that is embodied in Singapore-to-India exports, and gross Japan-India exports understate Japan's true domestic content that is embodied in Japan-to-India exports. The VAX ratio is therefore much lower than one for Singapore's exports to India and greater than one for Japan's exports to India.

located in a partner country, lowering demand for the output from the protected stage. With cross-border production sharing, where stages alternate across borders (US-Canada trade in auto parts), there is even less incentive to demand protection because it raises the costs of intermediates to downstream producers within the protected country itself. With large vertically integrated enterprises, the same firm performs different stages of production. It makes little sense for a firm to take an action that ultimately raises its own costs. This situation suggests a simple maxim: the greater production-sharing (participation in international supply chains) is, the lower incentives are for local producers to demand import protection.[10]

To see whether the maxim is empirically true, two measures of vertical specialization are used. These measures, based on Hummels, Ishii, and Yi (2001) and Yi (2003),[11] have recently been constructed by Daudin, Rifflart, and Schweisguth (2011). The first measure, *VS*, is the share of imports in a sector that is used directly and indirectly—that is, embedded as intermediate inputs in the country's own exports. The second measure, *VS*1, is the proportion of a sector's exports that is used as intermediates by exporters in *other* countries. This measure captures the intensity of two sources of anti-protectionist pressure. High tariffs on imports in a sector undermine the competitiveness of the sector's exports that intensively use those imports. Input-output tables indicate that the same sector is the largest user of imports by that sector. Exporters of that sector are therefore a source of anti-protectionism because they will lobby against tariffs that raise their input costs, making them uncompetitive. The second source of anti-protectionism is foreign lobbying (e.g., Gawande, Krishna, and Robbins 2006) by exporters in countries that are dependent on the source country to supply them with the intermediate inputs. Low or zero tariffs in the source country are desirable for keeping their input costs down. In industries that are less linked, *VS* and *VS*1 are low, and incentives to restrict trade remain.

More generally, any interest-based source for trade policy should account for the fact that trade in intermediates comprises two-thirds of world trade. The explosion in intermediate trade appears to verify the large gains from trade demonstrated in Ethier (1982), affirming Ethier's idea that trade expands production possibilities by widening the range of intermediates that can be used. This is potentially a source of strong anti-protectionist pressure. Downstream users of intermediate goods are natural lobbyists against border tariffs on such goods because tariffs only increase their input costs. Car producers, for example, want low or no tariffs on steel. Gawande, Krishna, and Olarreaga (2012) show how lobbying by downstream industries may counter the demand for protection by

10. The collapse in trade, triggered by the collapse of output during the US financial crisis, was amplified by the linkage effects of international supply chains (Bems, Johnson and Yi 2009). The reverse implication is that as output picks up, trade should rapidly increase, as has occurred after 2011.

11. Guillaume Daudin generously provided the disaggregated measures, for which we are very grateful. Vertical specialization measures are constructed at the GTAP level of aggregation of 57 sectors, which are mapped to the HS6 level according to a concordance provided by GTAP.

upstream producers that compete with imports. In their model, all else held constant, tariffs should vary inversely with the intermediate use-to-gross output ratio across commodities.[12] Intermediate use-to-gross output ratio is used to capture the intensity of counter-lobbying by downstream users against protection to upstream industries. This variable (*%IntermediateUse*) is constructed by aggregating the proportions across sectors (columns) in input-output use matrices from the OECD.[13]

A different logic was advanced in the "new" trade theory originating in the 1980s to explain two-way intra-industry trade. For such trade in finished goods, Krugman's (1981) model with different countries specializing in different *varieties* of similar products demonstrated large gains from trade. However, models featuring domestic and foreign duopolies indicated that – unlike models assuming zero-profit monopolistic or perfect competition – intra-industry trade does not necessarily mean freer trade because these market structures allow rents to be shifted from foreign to home firms through strategic tariff policy. Although the optimal action for both countries is to reduce tariffs, the unilateral incentive is for governments to use tariffs to play zero-sum games. If tariffs are strategic, a positive correlation between intra-industry trade and rents imply that tariffs should be positively associated with intra-industry trade.[14]

Intra-industry trade in goods is proxied using the Grubel-Lloyd (1971) measure, defined at the HS 6 digit level as $IIT = 1 - |\text{Imports-Exports}|/(\text{Imports} + \text{Exports})$. *IIT* lies between 0 (no intra-industry trade) and 1 (two-way trade in equal amounts). Measuring *IIT* at a higher level of aggregation (say the 4-digit ISIC level, as is current practice) captures both horizontal and vertical *IIT* because higher levels of aggregation involves trade in intermediates as well as more processed goods that constitute a specific 4-digit sector. Disaggregating at the 6-digit HS allows *IIT* to better capture two-way trade in differentiated products. To the extent that *IIT* is correlated with *VS* measures and *%IntermediatesUse*,

12. Gawande, Krishna, and Olarreaga (2012) extend Grossman and Helpman (1994) to generate the following counter-lobbying model: $\frac{t_i}{1+t_i} = \frac{1}{a}\left[\frac{z_i}{e_i} - \frac{z_i}{e_i}\sum_{j=1}^{\infty}\frac{a_{ij}\cdot y_i}{y_i}\right]$, where z_i is sector i's inverse import-to-gross output ratio, e_i is the absolute import demand elasticity in sector i, a is the political economy parameter indicating the relative weight government puts on a dollar of welfare relative to a dollar of contributions from industry lobbies, and $\sum_{j=1}^{\infty}\frac{a_{ij}\cdot y_i}{y_i}$ is the intermediate use for good i, where a_{ij} units of good i are used to produce one unit of good j and y_j is the gross output of good j. When there is no intermediate use ($a_{ij} = 0$), the model reverts to that of Grossman and Helpman (1994).

13. *%IntermediateUse* for good i is defined as $\sum_{j=1}^{\infty}\frac{a_{ij}\cdot y_i}{y_i}$; see the previous footnote. It is calculated using OECD input-output (I-O) tables, available at http://www.oecd.org/sti/inputoutput/. The tables are constructed for 48 sectors (OECD's STAN system), which are first mapped into ISIC rev. 3 according to the concordance in De Backer and Yamano (2008, Table 2) and then mapped into HS6. The I-O tables are chosen, based upon availability, from the years closest to 2005. For the seven countries, the I-O matrices are for the following years: ARG 1997; BRA 2005; CHN 2005; IND 2003-04; MEX 2003; TUR 2002; and ZAF 2005.

14. Jorgensen and Schroder (2006) show that an optimal tariff exists below which welfare is reduced because there are too few domestic varieties and beyond which there are too many inefficiently produced, costly domestic varieties.

conditioning on these should separate incentives for and against protection in each measure.

INSTITUTIONS. Institutions such as the WTO and PTAs constrain the scope for tariffs to be increased when producers are faced with shocks that shrink their export markets and intensify competition at home. Mechanisms by which these institutions overcome negative externalities, described below, are a dominant theme in explaining their emergence and endurance.

The ability of the GATT/WTO to solve the terms of trade (TOT) externality, without which countries would impose optimal tariffs against each other, is a prevailing explanation for these institutions (Bagwell and Staiger 1999; Johnson 1954). Ossa (2011) advances the idea that, in addition to TOT externalities, the WTO allows governments to internalize production-location externalities.[15] This argument is in line with the role of the WTO in quelling protectionism because of countries' desires to use policy to shift production to domestic locations – a major reason why tariffs exploded in the 1930s – rather than for optimal tariff (i.e., TOT) reasons. The WTO principles of reciprocity and nondiscrimination enable governments to internalize this externality by allowing them to negotiate rules that restrict their ability to engage in production-relocation efforts.

Membership in the WTO provides a mechanism for governments to deflect protectionist pressures from domestic special interests. The need to abide by WTO commitments and rules can be invoked by a government as a valid reason for telling lobbies that adherence to those rules as a signatory to the WTO limits its policy latitude. The same is true for PTAs (Ethier 1998). This role of trade agreements as a commitment device is a core element of the policy literature (Hoekman and Kostecki 2009) and has been theoretically examined by Staiger and Tabellini (1999), Maggi (1999), and, in the context of regional trade agreements, Maggi and Rodriguez-Clare (1998). Empirical support for this idea has been presented in Bown (2004).

Whether WTO rules and PTAs eliminate some type of externality or provide a commitment device to governments seeking to escape the influence of powerful lobbies, they may prevent trade wars. This is another potential reason why the large trade and output collapses following the 2008 crisis were not accompanied by an outbreak of protectionism.

To measure the influence of these institutions on tariffs, this paper takes a grassroots approach. A strategic reason for a country to negotiate high bound rates in multilateral negotiations is to give it the policy space to raise tariffs in the

15. By making a foreign product more expensive in the domestic market, a tariff shifts consumer expenditure toward domestic output. The greater profitability for domestic producers induces entry into the home market and exit out of the foreign market. Because of trade costs due to geography, this relocation of production increases domestic welfare and reduces foreign welfare. The share of goods consumed by domestic consumers that is subject to trade costs is reduced, whereas the share of goods consumed by foreign consumers that is subject to trade costs increases.

future. Therefore, the measure of the influence of institutions is based on $t_{i,\mathrm{BND}}$ (as amended below). A political economy basis for this measure is that bound rates are largely determined by a tariff-cutting formula referenced to a previous unilaterally determined structure. Because the structure of bound rates reflects the historical structure and the political economy embedded in that structure, it may be expected that applied rates are scaled down similarly so that the political status quo is maintained in the new structure of applied tariffs. In the extreme case that the applied rate structure is simply the result of a linear formula applied to the bound rates, the regression (1) should indicate the formula for each country, with nothing left for other variables to explain.

Deviations from the bound (and MFN) rate obviously occur.[16] The primary example of this is preferential tariffs and reciprocal concessions by trading partners in PTAs. Foletti et al. (2011) note that PTAs are a primary reason why the level of the tariff binding exaggerates the amount of policy latitude. Preferential tariffs among PTA partners lower the level of "water" in the tariff by constraining the scope to increase tariffs on PTA partners.[17] The influence of institutions is represented by the variable $t_{ip,\mathrm{BNDPRF}}$, equal to a country's WTO bound on commodity i ($t_{i,\mathrm{BND}}$), but it is replaced by the PTA tariff ($t_{ip,\mathrm{PRF}}$) whenever it applies.[18]

For each of the seven countries, the 6-digit HS level data are pooled across partner countries. Table 2 reports descriptive statistics for the variables used in the analysis.

Identification

An instrumental variables (IV) strategy is used to address the endogeneity of the three variables *VS, VS1,* and *%IntermediatesUse*. The endogeneity is because shocks to tariffs in sector i make imports in sector i costlier. Input-output tables use data at the ISIC 4-digit level and indicate that the largest using sector is usually the *same* sector. An increase in tariffs reduces the competitiveness of the sector's output by raising its cost to using sectors and enhances the competitiveness of global suppliers of the same product. Because manufacturing sectors are their own largest users, as the output of a sector shrinks, so does the demand for the output from users in the same sector. Therefore, *%IntermediatesUse* is affected by tariff shocks. Further, the loss of competitiveness means that demand from

16. By placing an upper bound on the cost of accessing a market, tariff bindings reduce uncertainty facing exporters. Because this uncertainty deters investments to produce in or for a market, reductions in policy uncertainty will increase the risk-adjusted rate of return and spur greater entry, raising welfare (Francois and Martin 2004; Handley and Limão 2012).

17. Another reason that Foletti et al. offer is that if the bound rate is too high, it exceeds the prohibitive tariff at which imports fall to zero. Then, the prohibitive tariff defines the effective bound. Nevertheless, they conclude that most countries still have substantial leeway to increase their applied tariffs; the policy space remains, on average, at more than 60% of the "water" (i.e., the difference between applied and bound rate).

18. More precisely, for imports from WTO member countries, $t_{ip,\mathrm{BNDPRF}} = t_{i,\mathrm{BND}}$ for non-PTA partners and $t_{ip,\mathrm{BNDPRF}} = t_{ip,\mathrm{PRF}}$ for PTA partner p. Note that $t_{i,\mathrm{BND}}$ is the same across WTO members (hence the absence of subscript p), but it may be different for non-member country partners.

TABLE 2. Descriptive Statistics

	ARG		BRA		CHN		IND		MEX		TUR		ZAF	
	mean	sd	mean	sd	mean	sd	mean	sd	mean	sd	mean	sd	mean	sd
t	10.185	7.253	12.734	7.471	8.786	6.069	11.889	12.085	7.114	9.721	2.660	11.266	12.605	12.639
t_{BND}	31.601	6.228	30.631	6.865	9.665	6.130	38.052	26.123	35.023	3.514	20.212	20.069	27.652	24.119
t_{BNDPRF}	26.990	12.324	27.706	10.831	8.964	6.136	36.594	26.312	16.475	17.002	8.372	18.610	21.887	24.342
IIT	0.075	0.196	0.104	0.223	0.197	0.276	0.181	0.274	0.079	0.198	0.132	0.243	0.085	0.206
%IntermediatesUse	0.774	0.263	0.638	0.268	0.771	0.278	0.604	0.282	0.777	0.294	0.757	0.317	0.684	0.311
VS	0.290	0.085	0.166	0.054	0.266	0.059	0.257	0.075	0.266	0.138	0.291	0.077	0.192	0.049
*VS*1	0.206	0.090	0.210	0.097	0.226	0.097	0.236	0.082	0.125	0.076	0.220	0.068	0.206	0.111

Notes: 1. The sample is organized bilaterally for each country. Only large partners are included (imports from partner >$750 Mn. in 2009).

2. Data for all countries pooled across 2006–9, except India: 2005, 2008, 2009; Mexico 2005–6, 2008, 2009; Turkey 2005–6, 2008, 2009. Sample size: ARG: 145642; BRA: 199533; CHN: 275344; IND: 75930; MEX: 232019; TUR: 91401; ZAF: 119400.

3. Agriculture, Mining, Manufacturing sectors included in analysis.

Variable

t Applied Tariff at HS-6 digits. Percentage points. *Source:* WITS database.

t_{BND} Bound Tariff Rate at HS-6 digits. Percentage points. *Source:* WITS.

t_{BNDPRF} Bound Tariff Rate, replaced by Preferential rate at HS-6 digits. $t_{BNDPRF} = t_{BND}$, but replaced by t_{PRF} where applicable. *Source:* WITS.

IIT Bilateral intra-industry trade: IIT $= 1 - |\text{Imports-Exports}|/(\text{Imports} + \text{Exports})$. HS 6 digits. *Source:* WITS database.

%IntermediatesUse Fraction of output used as intermediates inputs by all other sectors. (See eq. (1)) *Source:* UNCTAD Input-output data (aggregated at 48 sectors).

VS Vertical Specialization Measure 1: % of output used as intermediates by exporters in the same country (*Source:* VS in Daudin et al. 2011). Contructed at GTAP aggregation of 55 input-output sectors, then mapped into HS 6 digits.

*VS*1 Vertical Specialization Measure 2: % of output used as intermediates by exporters in all countries (*Source:* VS1 in Daudin et al. 2011). Contructed at GTAP aggregation of 55 input-output sectors, then mapped into HS 6 digits.

users outside the sector drops. Because the drop in demand includes using sectors located in other countries, *VS* and *VS1* are also affected. Not accounting for this endogeneity induces downward bias in the coefficients of the three variables.

The IV strategy is simple: variables for the US are used to instrument for the corresponding variables for the sample countries. Thus, the *VS, VS1,* and *%IntermediatesUse* measures for the United States are used to instrument India's *VS, VS1,* and *%IntermediatesUse* measures. Using India as an example clarifies why this IV strategy is effective. Shocks to India's tariffs in sector *i* affect Indian users of the output of that sector as intermediate inputs much more than American users of (sector *i*'s) Indian output. Even if American users were dependent on imports from India, they could search the world for the next lowest cost producer of good *i*. In general, input-output tables indicate that using sectors are more dependent on domestic producers than imports, reflecting trade costs due to geography and other factors. Thus, *%IntermediatesUse* in sector *i* in the US is more immune to an Indian tariff increase in sector *i* than is India's *%IntermediatesUse* in the sector.

Similarly, *VS* for sector *i* in the US is immune to an Indian tariff increase in sector *i* because the tariff increase lowers the Indian competitiveness of that sector's output in the world export market more than it lowers the American competitiveness of that sector's output (unless the sector is heavily dependent on imports of *i* from India). The same argument applies for *VS1*. The US is relatively inward looking in the sense that American users source a greater proportion of their goods and services domestically compared with most other open countries. Its large size creates a home bias, as gravity models have affirmed. In that sense, the US variables are more immune to tariff shocks in other countries, making them appropriate instruments. The empirical relevance of the instruments comes from matching cross-sectional variation in the US variables with those of the corresponding variables in the countries in the sample. Because the structure of production in terms of intermediate use is not dissimilar across countries, the US variables are not expected to suffer from the weak instruments problem.

The exogeneity of t_{BNDPRF} is maintained. Bound rates are set via a multilateral bargaining process that determines actual tariffs but is not determined by them. In a dynamic sense, actual tariffs and the water in the tariffs may allow bound rates to decrease during the subsequent bargaining process, but these changes are infrequent and determined by a process that is exogenous in the short run, certainly over the duration of the data used here. For similar reasons, preferential rates are taken to be determined exogenously. Intra-industry trade is also considered exogenous in the analysis, although it is possible that shocks to tariffs may inhibit *IIT*. The coefficient on *IIT* is therefore biased downwards. Empirically, *IIT* correlates poorly with the other variables, so any bias in the coefficient on *IIT* does not affect other coefficients.

III. Results

Baseline IV Model

A baseline set of results from (1) is first presented in Table 3. These results are intended to demonstrate that the cross-sectional pattern of bilateral tariffs at the HS6-digit level accords with the "interest and institutions" specification in the seven countries. Although the interest variables *VS, VS1,* and *%IntermediatesUse* distinguish the use of a sector's output by different users, they remain correlated.[19] For India and South Africa, for example, collinearity requires that the variables be included one at a time. In Table 3, the results from three models are presented with different combinations of interest variables. Partner fixed effects are included. Standard errors are corrected for clustering on HS6 products; otherwise, the standard errors are underestimated.

There are four main results:[20]

(i) The coefficients on the bound rates are sharply estimated. However, with the exception of China, they are not close to unity, indicating the availability of substantial policy space. In other countries, t_{BNDPRF} is not the sole, or even the most important, determinant of the applied tariff structure. Although Argentina and Brazil belong to the Mercosur agreement, the coefficient on t_{BNDPRF} is far below 1, and interest plays a large role in determining which sectors may or may not receive protection.[21] The same is true for India, Mexico, South Africa, and Turkey.

(ii) Intermediate use of a country's output by *foreign* exporters (*VS1*) is a powerful force against protectionism in *all* country samples. The negative coefficients on *VS1* suggest that home governments are keen to advance the interests of their exporters by reducing tariffs on the inputs used by (upstream) home exporters to enhance their competitive position with foreign users. That these supply chains crisscross the home country a number of times is an added reason to keep tariffs down. The negative coefficients on *VS1* may also be taken as evidence for the idea that exporters in *foreign* countries may politically influence home tariffs because their competitiveness depends on the supply of cheap inputs from home producers. One mechanism to achieve this is to press their own governments

19. The data sets are appropriately constructed at HS6 because the tariff policy (the dependent variable) is formulated at that level of disaggregation. The variables *VS, VS1,* and *%IntermediatesUse* are constructed a higher level of aggregation and are replicated at the HS6 level. This is one reason for the strong correlations among them. See also the robustness-for-clustering discussion at the end of Section 4.

20. OLS estimates from the same model with partner fixed effects are reported in the online appendix (Table S.3). The models fit the data well. Although many OLS inferences hold up in the IV models, differences remain. Our working paper, Gawande et al. (2011), provides details.

21. If the GATT/WTO rules kept applied tariffs in check, then the small coefficient on t_{BNDPRF} should not necessarily be a feature of belonging to PTAs (Argentina and Brazil). The row of coefficients on t_{BNDPRF} indicates that this is indeed the case: the small coefficient on t_{BNDPRF} is the rule, not the exception, even for countries that trade actively outside regional blocs.

TABLE 3. Baseline Models of Applied Bilateral Tariffs Instrumental Variables with Partner Fixed-Effects and Errors Clustered on HS6-digit Products

	ARG				BRA		CHN			IND		
t_{BNDPRF} (+)	0.143***	0.225***	0.152***	0.277***	0.315***	0.275***	0.965***	0.968***	0.962***	0.212***	0.260***	0.253***
Bound or Preferential Rate	[0.015]	[0.015]	[0.016]	[0.015]	[0.014]	[0.014]	[0.006]	[0.005]	[0.006]	[0.038]	[0.025]	[0.024]
IIT (−)	1.757***	1.869***	1.207***	1.128***	1.573***	1.137***	−0.067***	−0.0486**	−0.069**	−0.228	−1.072***	−1.073***
Intra-industry Trade	[0.203]	[0.206]	[0.243]	[0.164]	[0.166]	[0.163]	[0.024]	[0.0236]	[0.028]	[0.293]	[0.238]	[0.234]
VS (−)	17.99***			28.18***			1.961***			−40.09**		
% used by domestic X	[2.621]			[5.467]			[0.560]			[16.59]		
VS1 (−)	−8.583***		−34.40***	−28.34***		−25.68***	−0.883***		−4.323***	–		−27.55***
% used by dom + foreign X	[1.472]		[4.111]	[1.933]		[2.260]	[0.198]		[1.074]	–		[3.775]
%IntermediateUse (−)		4.469***	13.57***		−3.185***	3.699***		0.303**	2.012***		−5.928***	–
% used by all domestic users		[0.695]	[1.668]		[0.464]	[0.934]		[0.151]	[0.565]		[1.278]	–
N	145228	144033	144033	199776	197671	197671	285365	271125	271125	75424	75259	75259
partner FE	Yes	Yes	Yes	Yes	Yes	Yes	Yes	Yes	Yes	Yes	Yes	Yes
#Instruments	2	1	2	2	1	2	2	1	2	1	1	1
# clusters	3823	3768	3768	4033	3980	3980	4122	3877	3877	2596	2593	2596
Kleibergen-Paap WI stat.	1231	106526	6814	5192	165149	21191	7769	48239	2336	844.8	17198	368418
Anderson-Rubin (*F*)	16.74	43.33	51.94	165.9	47.96	140	12.71	4.069	12.76	6.681	21.71	53.96
Anderson-Rubin (*p*-val)	0.000	0.000	0.000	0.000	0	0.000	0.000	0.043	0.000	0.010	0.000	0.000

(*continued overleaf*)

Table 3. Continued.

	MEX				TUR			ZAF	
t_{BNDPRF} (+)	0.227***	0.237***	0.236***	0.398***	0.400***	0.392***	0.268***	0.135**	0.201***
Bound Rate (= Preferential if applicable)	[0.014]	[0.015]	[0.015]	[0.051]	[0.050]	[0.0474]	[0.071]	[0.060]	[0.062]
IIT (−)	0.14	−0.478***	−1.166***	−1.086***	−1.155***	−1.071***	0.682*	0.674	0.216
Intra-industry Trade	[0.304]	[0.141]	[0.154]	[0.318]	[0.334]	[0.333]	[0.376]	[0.413]	[0.307]
VS (−)	−37.72***			5.114			104.6***		
% used by domestic X	[7.904]			[4.018]			[13.87]		
VS1 (−)	−59.11***		−37.83***	−24.16***		−34.08***	–		−25.64***
% used by dom + foreign X	[7.799]		[2.583]	[3.713]		[12.18]	–		[3.242]
%IntermediateUse (−)		−0.984***	4.988***		−3.708***	2.288		−13.55***	–
% used by all domestic users		[0.337]	[0.654]		[1.031]	[2.868]		[1.962]	–
N	261343	228664	228664	94983	90294	90294	239796	117107	239796
partner FE	Yes	Yes	Yes	Yes	Yes	Yes	Yes	Yes	Yes
#Instruments	2	1	2	2	1	2	1	1	1
# clusters	4181	3712	3712	1990	1868	1868	3880	1921	3880
Kleibergen-Paap WI stat.	1319	153039	24090	7916	51662	3123	7899	43987	383549
Anderson-Rubin (*F*)	184.8	8.526	164.8	26.55	12.69	26.56	65.11	48.47	24.73
Anderson-Rubin (*p*-val)	0.000	0.00352	0.000	0.000	0.000376	0.000	0.000	0	0.000

Notes: 1. Standard errors in brackets; ***$p < 0.01$, **$p < 0.05$, *$p < 0.10$

2. Corresponding US variables used as instruments.

Source: Authors' analysis based on data described in the text.

to bargain with the home government to reduce their tariffs; another mechanism involves directly lobbying the home government. Because *VS1* is closely related to multinational activity with their affiliates and the foreign direct investment (FDI) undertaken by these multinational enterprises (MNEs) (Hummels, Ishii, and Yi. 2001; Alfaro and Charlton 2009), it may well proxy those influences. The quantitative impact of *VS1* is striking. For example, as the share of output of Brazilian exporters that is used by exporting firms in partner countries increases from 0 to the country mean of 0.21, Brazil's tariffs are lowered by 5.95 percentage points (model 1). Across the board, countries in the sample have similarly large estimates on *VS*1. It may be surmised that China's would be similar if its tariff bindings were less constraining.

(iii) Intermediate use of a sector's output by domestic users (*%IntermediatesUse*) is a deterrent force against tariff increases only in models where the effect of *VS1* is not conditioned out. After accounting for *VS*1, it does not appear that intermediate use by domestic sectors is a source of anti-protectionism. A possible reason in this sample of emerging countries may be that taxing *%IntermediateUse* in sectors whose output is not heavily used by foreign processors (which is conditioned out by *VS1*) is an effective revenue raiser.

(iv) In all countries except Argentina and Brazil, intra-industry trade (*IIT*) has a negative coefficient, in line with the Krugman (1981) gains from variety in differentiated final goods. The gains from trade in these countries appear to overwhelm the incentives to use tariffs for other motives. The positive coefficients on *IIT* for Argentina and Brazil indicate that intra-industry trade is associated with an increase in their tariffs. This may reflect profit-shifting motives, industrial policy, or simply the use of tariffs to raise revenue.

Finally, diagnostics reported at the bottom of the table indicate no weak instruments problem. The Kleibergen-Paap weak instrument (WI) statistics are uniformly large, indicating that the small sample bias in the coefficients on the endogenous variables is very small compared to the ordinary least squares (OLS) bias. The large WI statistics are a consequence of the large sample size. They mainly indicate that the bias in the 2SLS instrumented coefficient is less than 5% of the bias in the OLS estimate of the coefficient. The Anderson-Rubin (weak-instrument robust) statistic rejects the hypothesis that the coefficients on the endogenous variables are all zero. Because the number of instruments is equal to the number of endogenous variables, the coefficients on the endogenous variables are exactly identified. The main results of the paper are presented next.

Pre- and Post-Crisis

Table 4 considers models in which each variable is interacted with a post-crisis dummy. This approach allows us to ascertain whether the relationships observed

TABLE 4. Difference-in-differences: Before and After 2009. Instrumental Variables with Partner Fixed-Effects and Errors Clustered on HS6-digit Products

	ARG	ARG	BRA	BRA	CHN	CHN	IND	IND
t_{BNDPRF}	0.142***	0.154***	0.266***	0.264***	0.973***	0.970***	0.233***	0.271***
Bound Rate (= Preferential if applicable)	[0.015]	[0.016]	[0.016]	[0.014]	[0.005]	[0.005]	[0.038]	[0.025]
$t_{BNDPRF} \times I_{2009}$	0.006***	−0.008**	0.045***	0.044***	−0.032***	−0.032***	−0.0831***	−0.037***
	[0.002]	[0.003]	[0.003]	[0.003]	[0.006]	[0.006]	[0.027]	[0.012]
IIT	1.770***	1.164***	1.201***	1.223***	−0.088***	−0.085***	−0.540*	−1.290***
Intra − industry Trade	[0.205]	[0.248]	[0.158]	[0.157]	[0.022]	[0.025]	[0.303]	[0.243]
IIT × I_{2009}	0.037	0.338*	−0.179	−0.262*	0.069***	0.052*	1.402***	0.984***
	[0.167]	[0.191]	[0.130]	[0.134]	[0.027]	[0.032]	[0.266]	[0.209]
VS	19.61***		22.19***		1.887***		−31.81*	
% used by domestic exporters	[2.573]		[5.049]		[0.511]		[16.33]	
VS × I_{2009}	−10.23***		24.19***		0.307		−35.18**	
	[1.500]		[2.637]		[0.490]		[15.44]	
VS1	−10.08***	−36.46***	−24.27***	−23.14***	−0.808***	−3.237***	–	–
% used by domestic + foreign exporters	[1.418]	[4.153]	[1.791]	[2.169]	[0.180]	[0.898]	–	–
VS1 × I_{2009}	9.409***	12.32***	−16.25***	−10.27***	−0.373*	−4.753***	–	–
	[0.864]	[1.473]	[1.063]	[1.112]	[0.194]	[1.254]	–	–
%IntermediateUse		13.64***		3.381***		1.450***		−5.365***
% used by all domestic users		[1.672]		[0.899]		[0.467]		[1.274]
%IntermediateUse × I_{2009}		−0.847		1.378***		2.417***		−2.127***
		[0.527]		[0.423]		[0.667]		[0.652]
I_{2009}	0.453	−2.498***	−0.971***	0.956***	0.0494	−0.757***	8.630*	−1.025**
	[0.314]	[0.248]	[0.300]	[0.150]	[0.125]	[0.248]	[4.842]	[0.403]
N	145228	144033	199776	197671	285365	271125	75424	75259
partner FE	Yes	Yes	Yes	Yes	Yes	Yes	Yes	Yes
#Instruments	4	4	4	4	4	4	2	2
# clusters	3823	3768	4033	3980	4122	3877	2596	2593
K-P (Weak Instr.)	503.2	3002	669.2	3106	1055	262	400.1	5719

(Continued)

A-R (*F*)	69.84	73.94	104.4	87.93	7.299	8.359	8.135	15.55
A-R (*p*-val)	0.00	0.00	0.00	0.00	0.00	0.00	0.00	0.00

	MEX	MEX	TUR	TUR	ZAF	ZAF
t_{BNDPRF}	0.238***	0.244***	0.381***	0.376***	0.197***	0.119**
Bound Rate (= Preferential if applicable)	[0.014]	[0.015]	[0.052]	[0.048]	[0.063]	[0.056]
$t_{BNDPRF} \times I_{2009}$	−0.070***	−0.068***	0.049***	0.047***	0.153**	0.184***
	[0.003]	[0.003]	[0.015]	[0.014]	[0.065]	[0.056]
IIT	0.307	−1.028***	−1.043***	−1.041***	−0.371	0.493
Intra-industry Trade	[0.321]	[0.162]	[0.323]	[0.337]	[0.446]	[0.431]
IIT × I_{2009}	−0.400**	−0.176	−0.112	−0.0685	0.231	0.833**
	[0.165]	[0.132]	[0.174]	[0.179]	[0.325]	[0.407]
VS	−38.47***		4.45		123.7***	
% used by domestic exporters	[8.035]		[3.929]		[16.90]	
VS × I_{2009}	4.638*		2.082		−20.43***	
	[2.711]		[1.625]		[7.886]	
VS1	−59.35***	−39.47***	−22.92***	−31.96***	−47.20***	–
% used by domestic + foreign exporters	[7.849]	[2.632]	[3.615]	[11.49]	[5.074]	–
VS1 × I_{2009}	2.623	8.199***	−3.905***	−6.412	7.755*	–
	[2.659]	[1.270]	[1.420]	[4.265]	[4.154]	–
%IntermediateUse		5.655***		2.001		−13.55***
% used by all domestic users		[0.667]		[2.700]		[1.965]
%IntermediateUse × I_{2009}		−3.167***		0.852		2.391
		[0.397]		[1.082]		[1.459]
I_{2009}	−2.326**	0.473**	0.221	0.701***	−0.487	−5.646***
	[1.041]	[0.196]	[0.371]	[0.271]	[0.901]	[2.130]
N	261343	228664	94983	90294	239796	117107
partner FE	Yes	Yes	Yes	Yes	Yes	Yes
#Instruments	4	4	4	4	4	2
# clusters	4181	3712	1990	1868	3880	6136
K-P (Weak Instr.)	203.9	4661	3498	479	3383	141.3
A-R (*F*)	95.95	91.86	13.81	13.32	37.1	30.89
A-R (*p*-val)	0.00	0.00	0.00	0.00	0.00	0.00

Notes: 1. Standard errors in brackets; *** $p < 0.01$, ** $p < 0.05$, * $p < 0.10$

2. $I_{2009} = 1$ if year = 2009, and zero if year ≤ 2008.

Source: Authors' Analysis Based on Data Described in the Text.

in Table 3 remained unaltered through the crisis or were fundamentally changed by it. These difference-in-differences indicate the *source* of the change (if any) in protectionism following the crisis.[22] Inference about *%IntermediateUse* is made conditionally on *VS1*. Where collinearity does not allow the full set of variables (India, South Africa), *VS1* is dropped.

Consider the coefficient on the interaction term $t_{BNDPRF} \times I_{2009}$. The negative and statistically significant coefficients for China, India, and Mexico indicate that although tariff water allowed policy discretion, those countries instead *lowered* their tariffs on average in 2009. Conversely, Brazil, South Africa, and Turkey responded to pressures to raise tariffs where t_{BNDPRF} allowed them the latitude. In the case of South Africa, for example, the coefficient on t_{BNDPRF} increased by 0.184 (second model) in 2009 over a pre-crisis coefficient of 0.12, signaling a readiness to increase tariffs up to bound levels.

The coefficient on $\%IntermediateUse \times I_{2009}$ is positive and significant for Brazil and China and negative and significant for India and Mexico. There is no change in the influence of this variable in South Africa and Turkey. The estimates for Brazil and China indicate that post-crisis, other forces, such as revenue objectives, trump the incentives to provide domestic downstream sectors with cheaper intermediate inputs. Heavy downstream users of intermediate inputs whose final output primarily supplies the domestic market (e.g., utilities, construction) do not deter governments from taxing upstream sectors producing these intermediates. Because these sectors are captive and may even be regulated, they may not have the bargaining or lobbying power of other downstream users that compete in the export markets.

In contrast, users who are part of global supply chains face greater competition, and the quantity of use is far more price sensitive. This is evident from the vertical specialization difference-in-differences $VS \times I_{2009}$ and $VS1 \times I_{2009}$: either one or the other shows a tariff-reducing effect. $VS1 \times I_{2009}$ has a large negative coefficient for Brazil, indicating that in the post-crisis period, exporting sectors in Brazil's partner countries appear to have had a strong influence on lowering Brazilian tariffs specifically on products they import from Brazil for their own intermediate use. Keeping the cost of those inputs down makes them more competitive, in turn increasing their purchases from Brazilian suppliers and expanding Brazil's exports. This source of anti-protectionism is also evident for China and Turkey. In the case of Argentina, India, and South Africa, *VS* is the main source of anti-protectionism after the crisis; domestic exporters are the prime movers in demanding lower protection on the imported goods that they use intensively. In India's case, there is no discernible change in the influence of *VS* and *VS1* on tariffs in 2009.

A country-by-country summary highlights the heterogeneity in the sources of economic and political pressure on trade policy in 2009. Although Argentina

22. The results corresponding to the second model in Table 3 are not reported for brevity but are available from the authors.

and Brazil are Mercosur partners, Argentina further liberalized intermediate use by domestic exporters (*VS*), whereas Brazil responded only to intermediate use by *foreign* exporters. In fact, Brazil stepped up the taxation of domestic users and domestic exporters after the crisis: $I_{2009} \times IntermediateUse$ and $I_{2009} \times VS$ both have positive statistically significant coefficients. China raised import taxes on domestic users of intermediates (*IntermediateUse*), whereas Mexico did the same on intermediate use by domestic exporters (*VS*). Although China's WTO commitments kept tariffs at already low levels, the liberalizing influence of foreign exporters that use Chinese output (via *VS*1) is in evidence after the crisis. The liberalizing influence of *VS1* and *IIT* is evident in Turkey, where proximity to the EU markets provides opportunities for producers to participate in European supply chains. South Africa appears to have become more responsive to its domestic exporters after the crisis.

In sum, three new findings from tariffs at the HS commodity level are in evidence. First, conditional on institutionally determined upper bounds on tariffs and despite the fact that most countries had significant policy space to raise tariffs, only a small subset revealed a desire to use the policy space after the crisis. Second, the difference-in-differences indicates that vertical specialization can strongly deter tariffs. In Argentina, India, and South Africa, the post-crisis period saw further liberalization in sectors whose output was used as intermediate inputs by domestic exporters. In Brazil, China, and Turkey, the post-crisis period saw liberalization in sectors whose output was used as intermediate inputs by domestic *and* foreign exporters.

Less auspiciously, evidence also indicates that revenue needs or industrial policy motivations may undermine incentives to liberalize. Countries appear to choose to raise tax revenue though tariffs in sectors where intermediate use by domestic users is heavy. In 2009, Brazil, China, and Mexico stepped up tariffs in sectors whose output was heavily used by domestic users.

Robustness: Incidence of Antidumping Investigations

In the first of three robustness checks, the model is estimated using a non-tariff measure. Countries use instruments of contingent protection as a complement or alternative to increasing statutory tariffs. For countries such as China, whose tariffs are bound at applied rates, these non-tariff instruments may be used to protect domestic firms and industries. Here, the WITS data are combined with Chad Bown's temporary trade restrictions database at the 6-digit HS level to examine whether contingent protection instruments, such as antidumping (AD) investigations, increased after the crisis in the sample of countries.[23] The dependent variable is the incidence of antidumping investigations that were initiated, regardless of whether these led to a favorable judgment, were dropped, or were overturned.

23. Available at http://econ.worldbank.org/ttbd/.

Table 5 uses linear probability models to show whether the incidence of AD investigations changed in 2009 in the five countries – Argentina, Brazil, China, India, and Turkey – for which data are available. Here, HS6-digit commodities for which investigations occurred are compared with the (overwhelming) number of cases in which there were no such investigations. The main characteristic of the data on contingent protection is that they are sparse, which is one reason why empirical investigations of AD actions in the literature restrict their samples to cases where investigations were conducted.[24] In the country samples, the model coefficients are small in magnitude because of the overwhelming number of zeros.

The positive coefficients on the applied tariff interactions $t \times I_{2009}$ in Table 5 indicate that after the crisis, the incidence of AD investigations was increased (in all countries except Brazil) for commodities for which applied tariffs are high. Thus, a country's AD investigations complemented its tariffs. In China's case, the results indicate that the restricted tariff policy space was expanded through the use of AD. The magnitudes indicate that although the estimated probability of increasing AD investigations was positive in four countries, it was still low.

Vertical specialization failed to deter AD investigations in 2009, but the low estimated probabilities indicate that in the absence of their anti-protectionist influence, more AD investigations might have been undertaken than actually occurred. In India, the coefficient on $VS1 \times I_{2009}$ is 0.114, the highest among the five countries. That is, a one standard deviation increase in *VS1* of 0.08 raised the estimated probability of an AD investigation by 0.114×0.08, or less than 1%, over the pre-crisis period. The fact that the coefficient on *VS1* was not statistically significantly different from zero before the crisis period but became positive in 2009 is cause for concern. Looking at just the number of new AD investigations would overstate the amount of protectionism, but these results indicate that the (unconditional) propensity to protect remains small.[25]

Robustness: Additional Instruments

As an IV robustness check, the set of US instruments is augmented with the same variables from Germany, France, the Japan, and UK. Each endogenous variable can therefore instrumented using five IVs. The results are qualitatively similar to those reported in Tables 3 and 4. The validity of instruments is also confirmed

24. Linear probability is more easily estimable than nonlinear logit models due to the sparseness in the data. Instrumenting adds to the problem with estimating nonlinear models.

25. Conditioning the sample to only imported goods, or to only specific partners, will probably increase these probability estimates, but there is no good reason to exclude some partners and keep others in the context of this study. Parallel results, in which the set of observations with no within variation for a specific partner is dropped, are available from the authors. The logic for dropping those observations is that they provide no discriminating information. These results may be missing a sample selection model of characteristics of commodities that make them prone to AD investigations. This is a topic for further research. The results from this abridged sample (reported in Table S.4 in the online Appendix) qualitatively affirm the inferences from the full sample in Table 5. Quantitatively, the results are not very different.

TABLE 5: Difference-in-differences: Incidence of Antidumping Investigations Before and After 2009 Instrumental Variables with Partner Fixed Effects and Errors Clustered on HS6-digit Products

	ARG	ARG	BRA	BRA	CHN	CHN	IND	IND	TUR	TUR
t	2.8e − 05**	2.4e − 05*	6.3e − 05***	7.0e − 05***	−1.5e − 05***	−1.0e − 05**	−0.028	−1.3e − 05*	2.55E-06	−5.3e − 06*
Applied tariff	[1.4e − 05]	[1.4e − 05]	[1.6e − 05]	[1.7e − 05]	[5.9e − 06]	[5.2e − 06]	[2.4e − 05]	[7.6e − 06]	[3.8e − 06]	[2.8e − 06]
$t \times I_{2009}$	0.0001***	0.0001***	−5.5e − 05***	−5.7e − 05***	5.4e − 05***	5.07e − 05**	4.87E-05	1.94e − 05*	1.85e − 05*	1.9e − 05***
	[4.6e − 05]	[4.7e − 05]	[1.4e − 05]	[1.5e − 05]	[2.0e − 05]	[2.0e − 05]	[3.0e − 05]	[1.1e − 05]	[1.0e − 05]	[7.1e − 06]
IIT	9.95E-05	9.58E-05	−0.0001	−0.00005	−0.0003*	−0.0002	−0.0004	−0.0001	0.0003**	0.0003***
Intra-industry trade	[0.0004]	[0.0004]	[0.0003]	[0.0003]	[0.00016]	[0.0002]	[0.0004]	[0.0005]	[0.0001]	[0.0001]
IIT × I_{2009}	0.0001	9.50E-05	4.21E-04	4.42E-04	−0.0002	−0.00008	2.23E-04	−0.0003	0.0005	0.0004
	[0.001]	[0.001]	[0.0004]	[0.0004]	[0.0003]	[0.0003]	[0.0006]	[0.0007]	[0.0005]	[0.0004]
VS	−0.003***		0.0045***		0.001		−0.007		−0.0006	
% used by dom. exporters	[0.001]		[0.0014]		[0.001]		[0.011]		[0.001]	
VS × I_{2009}	0.0076**		−0.005***		0.005**		0.020		0.0035**	
	[0.0038]		[0.0016]		[0.002]		[0.012]		[0.0018]	
VS1		−0.003		0.003***		0.006***		−0.066		−0.009**
% used by domestic + foreign exporters		[0.003]		[0.001]		[0.002]		[0.041]		[0.004]
VS1 × I_{2009}		0.00896		−0.00127		0.00953*		0.114**		0.009*
		[0.00552]		[0.00209]		[0.00568]		[0.0487]		[0.005]
%IntermediateUse	0.0005	0.0015	−0.0001	−0.0008*	−0.0000	−0.002***	0.007**	0.027*	0.002***	0.004**
% used by all domestic users	[0.0005]	[0.001]	[0.0003]	[0.0004]	[0.0002]	[0.0009]	[0.003]	[0.016]	[0.0006]	[0.001]
%IntermediateUse × I_{2009}	−0.003*	−0.005*	0.0005	0.0005	0.0002	−0.004	−0.007***	−0.043**	−0.002***	−0.004**
	[0.001]	[0.0028]	[0.0003]	[0.0006]	[0.0003]	[0.0025]	[0.0027]	[0.018]	[0.0008]	[0.0018]
I_{2009}	−0.0009	0.001	0.0009**	0.0002	−0.002***	0.0006	−0.002	−0.0016*	0.0006	0.0009***
	[0.001]	[0.001]	[0.0003]	[0.0002]	[0.0006]	[0.0007]	[0.002]	[0.001]	[0.0006]	[0.0003]
N	144033	144033	197671	197671	271125	271125	106423	106423	185864	185864
#Instruments	4	4	4	4	4	4	4	4	4	4
# clusters	3768	3768	3980	3980	3877	3877	3432	3432	3742	3742
K-P (Weak Instr.)	663.8	1677	20170	1993	4905	264.6	74.82	76.55	5260	493
A-R (*F*)	2.417	1.181	3.636	2.938	2.968	3.455	5.68	5.627	3.261	2.871
A-R (*p*-val)	0.05	0.32	0.01	0.02	0.02	0.01	0.00	0.00	0.01	0.02

Note: Standard errors in brackets; ***$p < 0.01$, **$p < 0.05$, *$p < 0.10$

Source: Authors' analysis based on AD data from Bown's database at http://econ.worldbank.org/ttbd

from weak-instrument diagnostics. The logic that the variables from these countries are uncorrelated with shocks to the endogenous variables (the same variable in India, for example) is most likely weaker in the case of these countries than it is for the US. These countries are all more trade dependent than is the US and have less of a home bias. Perhaps for that reason, the Hansen test does not always validate the exclusion restrictions presumed in the use of the five instruments. These results are available from the authors.

Robustness: Clustering of Data

In the results reported, statistical significance is based on error clustering at the HS6-digit level on the logic that adherence to MFN will cause within-commodity clustering across partners. Indeed, the *t*-values reported are lower than without the clustering correction by a magnitude of three or four. Another source of clustering may be due to the aggregate measurement of the three interest variables at the ISIC or I-O levels. Mapping them into the finer HS6-digit level replicates their values. The recent literature suggests error cluster correction at the highest level of the aggregation (Cameron and Miller 2011). Doing this at the ISIC level reduces the statistical significance of the interest variables and overly penalizes the use of IVs at the more aggregate level. A truer test of the economic and statistical significance of these interest variables requires their measurement at the finer commodity level. It is hoped that the results of this paper will encourage work in this direction.[26]

IV. Conclusion

WTO and PTA commitments constrain the policy space of member governments to varying degrees depending on the depth of the commitments. With the exception of China (and other countries that acceded to the WTO after 1995), most developing countries and emerging markets have substantial freedom to raise tariffs. In practice, however, most countries did not resort to this policy space following the 2008 financial crisis. This paper's analysis suggests a new explanation for countries' limited use of the significant headroom available, one that involves the changing structure of global trade and production. The regressions indicate that the position of domestic and foreign exporters in the global supply chain exerted offsetting forces in many countries. The demand for cheap inputs by downstream users, both domestic suppliers and exporters, and the demand for a country's exports by vertically specialized producers in partner countries exerted countervailing pressure against protectionist pressure from domestic lobbies. Thus, the economic interest of users and vertically specialized firms that has been a factor driving unilateral liberalization in recent decades (Baldwin 2010) helped keep protectionism in check globally during the crisis. The tariff structures of the

26. An example is the study by Jensen, Quinn, and Weymouth (2013), of which we have recently become aware. It uses firm- and transaction-level micro-data to assess the determinants of trade disputes.

seven large emerging countries examined in the paper are influenced by the demands of vertically specialized foreign exporters that depend on home exporters for their inputs. In Argentina, India, and South Africa, the demand of vertically specialized domestic exporters restrained protectionism after 2008. In Brazil, China, and Turkey, the demand of vertically specialized foreign exporters is the more important factor supporting tariff reductions and market openness.

Different countries behave differently in their trade policies. Although this heterogeneity is an important finding, the main message of the paper's results is that the nature of trade today produces powerful incentives against protectionism. Certainly, institutions such as the WTO and PTAs have contributed to the prevalence of open markets. However, negotiated reciprocal agreements to internalize terms of trade externalities and address the economy forces that generate pressure for trade barriers are just one factor undermining protectionism. The results presented in the paper suggest that a more powerful force is the increase in specialization brought about by both the large reductions in trade costs and the integration of populous countries that has multiplied the scale of global trade. The greatest benefit of the WTO may well be that by reducing trade policy uncertainty and supporting a decades-long process of multilateral liberalization of trade, it has facilitated the greater specialization manifested in global supply chains and the associated profusion of FDI that is now a potent force for maintaining open markets.

Based on the heterogeneity of policy responses across countries, the results of this paper provide a longer-term view of the forces at work and depict more than just a snapshot; the immediate post-crisis change in the coefficients contains important information about future trends. Whether this new constellation of trade interests will be able to withstand a sluggish world economy and high unemployment in addition to inflation and currency appreciation, which only increase pressure on governments to promote domestic economic activity, will most likely be the ultimate test of these new results.

References

Ahn, J.B., M. Amiti, and D. Weinstein. 2011. "Trade Finance and the Great Trade Collapse." *American Economic Review: Papers & Proceedings* 101 (3): 298–302.

Alfaro, L., and A. Charlton. 2009. "Intra-industry Foreign Direct Investment." *American Economic Review* 99 (5): 2096–119.

Altomonte, C., and G. Ottaviano. 2009. "Resilient to the Crisis? Global Supply Chains and Trade Flows." In R. Baldwin, ed., *The Great Trade Collapse: Causes, Consequences and Prospects*, 95–100. London: CEPR.

Anderson, J. E., and J. P. Neary. 1994. "Measuring the Restrictiveness of Trade Policy." *World Bank Economic Review* 8 (2): 151–69.

Bagwell, K., and R. W. Staiger. 1999. "An Economic Theory of GATT." *American Economic Review* 89 (1): 215–48.

Baldwin, R., ed. 2009. *The Great Trade Collapse: Causes, Consequences and Prospects*, London: CEPR.

———. 2010. "Unilateral Tariff Liberalization." *The International Economy* 14: 10–43.

Bems, R., R. C. Johnston, and K.-M. Yi. 2009. "The Collapse of Global Trade: Update on the Role of Vertical Links." In R. Baldwin, ed., *The Great Trade Collapse: Causes, Consequences and Prospects*, 79–86. London: CEPR.

Bown, C. 2004. "On the Economic Success of GATT/WTO Dispute Settlement." *Review of Economics and Statistics* 86: 811–23.

———. ed. 2011a. *The Great Recession and Import Protection: The Role of Temporary Trade Barriers.* Washington DC: CEPR and World Bank.

———. 2011b. "Import protection and the Great Recession." (12/2012) http://www.voxeu.org/article/import-protection-and-great-recession.

Cameron, A. C., and D. L. Miller. 2011. "Robust Inference with Clustered Data." In A. Ullah, and D. E. Giles, eds., *Handbook of Empirical Economics and Finance*, 1–28. Boca Raton: CRC Press.

Chor, D., and K. Manova. 2012. "Off the Cliff and Back: Credit Conditions and International Trade during the Global Financial Crisis." *Journal of International Economics* 87 (1): 117–33.

Daudin, G., C. Rifflart, and D. Schweisguth. 2011. "Who Produces for Whom in the World Economy?" *Canadian Journal of Economics* 44 (4): 1403–37.

De Backer, K., and N. Yamano. 2008. "The Measurement of Globalization using International Input-Output Tables." STI, OECD Working Paper 2007/8.

Eaton, J., S. Kortum, B. Neiman, and J. Romalis. 2011. "Trade and the Global Recession." NBER Working Paper No. 16666, January 2011.

Eichengreen, B., and K. O'Rourke 2012. "A Tale of Two Depressions Redux." (12/2012) at http://www.voxeu.org/article/tale-two-depressions-redux.

Ethier, W. J. 1982. "National and International Returns to Scale in the Modern Theory of International Trade." *American Economic Review* 72 (3), 389–405.

———. 1998. "Regionalism in a Multilateral World." *Journal of Political Economy* 106 (6): 1214–45.

Evenett, S. J., ed. 2010. *Tensions Contained. . . For Now: The 8th GTA Report.* London: Centre for Economic Policy Research.

Foletti, L., M. Fugazza, A. Nicita, and M. Olarreaga. 2011. "Smoke in the (Tariff) Water." *The World Economy* 34 (2): 248–64.

Francois, J., and W. Martin. 2004. "Commercial Policy, Bindings and Market Access." *European Economic Review* 48: 665–79.

Gawande, K., B. Hoekman, and Y. Cui. 2011. "Global Supply Chains and Trade Policy Responses to the 2008 Crisis." World Bank Policy Research Working Paper *No. 5862.*

Gawande, K., P. Krishna, and M. Olarreaga. 2012. "Lobbying Competition and US Trade Policy." *International Economic Review* 53: 115–32.

Gawande, K., P. Krishna, and M.J. Robbins. 2006. "Foreign Lobbying and U.S. Trade Policy." *Review of Economics and Statistics* 88 (3): 563–71.

Grossman, G., and E. Helpman. 1994. "Protection for Sale." *American Economic Review* 84 (4): 833–50.

Grubel, H., and P. Lloyd. 1971. "The Empirical Measurement of Intra-Industry Trade." *Economic Record* 47 (4): 494–517.

Handley, K., and N. Limão. 2012. "Trade and Investment under Policy Uncertainty: Theory and Firm Evidence." NBER Working Paper 17790.

Hoekman, B., and M. Kostecki. 2009. *The Political Economy of the World Trading System.* Oxford: Oxford University Press.

Hummels, D., J. Ishii, and K.-M. Yi. 2001. "The Nature and Growth of Vertical Specialization in World Trade." *Journal of International Economics* 54 (1): 75–96.

Irwin, D. 2012. *Trade Policy Disaster: Lessons from the 1930s.* Cambridge: MIT Press.

Jensen, J. B., D. Quinn, and S. Weymouth. 2013. "Why Currency Undervaluation Provokes Trade Disputes in Some Settings But Not Others." Manuscript.

Johnson, H. 1953–4. "Optimum Tariffs and Retaliation." *Review of Economic Studies* 21 (2): 142–53.

Johnson, R. C., and G. Noguera. 2012. "Accounting for Intermediates: Production Sharing and Trade in Value-Added." *Journal of International Economics* 86: 224–36.

Jorgensen, J., and P. Schroder. 2006. "Tariffs and Firm-Level Heterogeneous Fixed Export Costs." *Contributions to Economic Analysis & Policy* 5 (1): Article 18.

Kee, H. L., A. Nicita, and M. Olarreaga. 2009. "Estimating Trade Restrictiveness Indices." *Economic Journal* 119 (534): 172–99.

Kee, H. L., C. Neagu, and A. Nicita. 2013. "Is Protectionism on the Rise? Assessing National Trade Policies during the Crisis of 2008." *Review of Economics and Statistics* 95 (1): 342–6.

Krugman, P. R. 1981. "Intra-industry Specialization and the Gains from Trade." *Journal of Political Economy* 89 (5): 959–73.

Levchenko, A., L. Lewis, and L. Tesar. 2010. "The Collapse of International Trade during the 2008-2009 Crisis: In Search of the Smoking Gun." *IMF Economic Review* 58 (2): 214–53.

Maggi, G. 1999. "The Role of Multilateral Institutions in International Trade Cooperation." *American Economic Review* 89 (1): 190–214.

Maggi, G., and A. Rodriguez-Clare. 1998. "The Value of Trade Agreements in the Presence of Political Pressures." *Journal of Political Economy* 106 (3): 574–601.

Ossa, R. 2011. "A 'New Trade' Theory of GATT/WTO Negotiations." *Journal of Political Economy* 119 (1): 122–52.

Staiger, R. W., and G. Tabellini. 1999. "Do GATT Rules Help Governments Make Domestic Commitments?" *Economics and Politics* 11 (2): 109–44.

Yi, K.-M. 2003. "Can Vertical Specialization Explain the Growth of World Trade?" *Journal of Political Economy* 111 (1): 52–102.

[18]

THE SYSTEM WORKED
Global Economic Governance during the Great Recession

By DANIEL W. DREZNER*

I. INTRODUCTION

THE 2008 financial crisis posed the biggest challenge to the global economy since the Great Depression. During the first ten months of the "Great Recession," global stock market capitalization plummeted lower as a percentage of its precrisis level than during the first ten months of the 1930s depression.[1] Housing prices in the United States declined more than twice as much as they did during the Great Depression.[2] Banks and other financial institutions lost more than $4 trillion in the value of their holdings as a result of the crisis.[3] The global decline in asset values in 2008 was conservatively estimated to be $27 trillion, or roughly 50 percent of global economic output.[4] Five years after the start of the subprime mortgage crisis, concerns about systemic risk were still elevated.

The demand for global economic governance structures to perform effectively is at its greatest during crises. I define *global economic governance* as a set of formal and informal rules that regulate the global economy and the collection of authority relationships that promulgate, coordinate, monitor, or enforce said rules. As Menzie Chinn and Jeffry Frieden note: "The 1929 recession became a depression largely

*Previous versions of this article were presented at the University of Toronto, Nuffield College, The Ohio State University, and the Council on Foreign Relations. I am grateful to Steven Bernstein, Brad Glosserman, Peter Gourevitch, Todd Hall, James Lindsay, John Mueller, Carla Norrlof, Rebecca Perlman, Stewart Patrick, Randall Schweller, Duncan Snidal, Alexander Thompson, Martin Weiss, Pan Rui, Trish Dorff, and Amare Bekele for their feedback and assistance. I am grateful to both the Council on Foreign Relations International Institutions and Global Governance program and the Michael and Andrea Leven Family Foundation for their generous financial support during the drafting of this paper.

[1] Eichengreen and O'Rourke 2010.

[2] Reinhart and Rogoff 2009, 226.

[3] IMF 2009.

[4] Roxburgh, Lund, and Piotrowski 2011.

World Politics 66, no. 1 (January 2014), 123–64

doi: 10.1017/S0043887113000348

because of the collapse of international cooperation; the current crisis may head in that direction if international collaboration fails."[5] One of the primary purposes of global economic governance is to provide public goods—most importantly, keeping barriers to cross-border exchange low. An open global economy lessens the stagnation that comes from a financial crisis, preventing a downturn from metastasizing into a depression.[6]

Since the Great Recession began, there has been no shortage of scorn for the state of global economic governance in public perception, policy analysis, and scholarly assessment. Nevertheless, a closer look at the global response to the financial crisis reveals a different picture. Despite initial shocks that were more severe than the 1929 financial crisis, global economic governance responded quickly and robustly. Whether one looks at economic outcomes, policy outputs, or institutional resilience, these governance structures either reinforced or improved upon the status quo after the collapse of the subprime mortgage bubble. These regimes performed particularly well during the acute phase of the crisis in the fall of 2008, ensuring the continuation of an open global economy. To be sure, there remain areas where global governance either faltered or failed. Even if the policy outcomes have been suboptimal, they have not been subpar. International institutions and frameworks performed contrary to expectations. Simply put, the system worked—the open global economy survived because of "good enough" global governance.

If global economic governance has worked, why has there been such a widespread consensus that it has not? Misperceptions about global economic governance persist because the Great Recession has disproportionately affected the core economies, a fact that is also the center of gravity for commentary about the global political economy. Commentators based in the advanced industrialized states have conflated national governance with global governance. They have also overestimated the effectiveness of prior periods of global economic governance. *Why* the system has worked better than expected remains a more open question. We can tentatively conclude that both the power of the United States and the resilience of neoliberal economic ideas were underestimated during the depths of the Great Recession.

The rest of this article is divided into eight sections. Section II discusses the widespread perception that post-2008 global economic governance has been a failure. Section III discusses the methodologi-

[5] Chinn and Frieden 2011, xvi. See also James 2001.

[6] Claessens, Kose, and Terrones, 18.

cal challenges to assessing the effectiveness of global economic governance. Sections IV, V, and VI consider the performance of global economic governance in terms of economic outcomes, policy outputs, and governance processes. Section VII considers why there is so much misperception on this issue. Section VIII proffers some preliminary explanations for why the system worked. Section IX concludes.

II. The Perceived Crisis in Global Economic Governance

Even if states are the principal actors in world politics, they rely on global governance structures to coordinate action on the global scale. These structures can range from hard law treaty-based organizations with autonomous secretariats and operational authority to soft law groupings and arrangements that act merely as focal points for national governments.[7] For some issues, such as taxation or investment, the "regime complex" that governs these issues includes a network of bilateral arrangements as well.[8]

International relations scholars have posted a welter of causal mechanisms through which global economic governance facilitates economic growth and international cooperation. Even skeptics about international institutions acknowledge that they can serve as useful focal points to coordinate the global rules of the game.[9] International relations theorists have posited a number of additional roles for these regimes. These include reassuring participating actors about the future course of action; monitoring and enforcing the actors' compliance with the rules of the game; providing expertise and advice on policy issues; offering a means for leaders to blunt domestic pressures to act unilaterally; securing legitimacy, accountability, and representation for global public policy; and fostering shared understandings between policy principals.[10] When global economic governance functions well, it reduces the transaction costs of policy coordination. When it functions poorly, a lack of trust and a surfeit of uncertainty stymie responsible authorities from cooperating in situations where a bargaining core exists.

Prior to the 2008 financial crisis, there was mounting concern about the ability of these governance structures to handle severe challenges.

[7] Snidal and Abbott 2000.

[8] Raustiala and Victor 2004. On BITs, see the symposium in this issue: *World Politics* 66, no. 1 (January 2014).

[9] Goldsmith and Posner 2005.

[10] On reassurance, see Martin 1992. On monitoring/enforcement, see Axelrod and Keohane 1985. On expertise, see Haas 1992. On blunting domestic pressures, see Goldstein 1996. On legitimacy and socialization arguments, see Johnston 2001.

Public confidence in multilateral institutions was trending downward before the subprime mortgage bubble popped.[11] Policy elites were also sounding warning alarms about a looming crisis in global economic governance.[12] There appeared to be a growing mismatch between the global distribution of power and the institutional prerogatives within global governance structures. If those mismatches were allowed to fester, many feared a breakdown of the open economic order in favor of a more balkanized, mercantilist set of arrangements.

Some modest steps were taken to address these issues prior to the crisis, but pre-2008 global economic governance seemed to confirm the worst expectations of dysfunction. Despite rising macroeconomic imbalances, China vetoed any serious discussion of exchange rate issues at the IMF. Fund discussions of financial mismanagement in the eurozone area were suppressed prior to the crisis.[13] By the spring of 2008, the IMF leadership opted to sell off some gold reserves to shrink its operating deficit.[14] The Basel Committee on Banking Supervision's core banking standards not only failed to prevent banking crises across Europe—but, arguably, the "Basel II" standard exacerbated the banking crises.[15] The Doha Round of world trade talks was stalemated. G8 efforts to reach out and include the BRIC economies in their summitry bordered on the insulting.

The Great Recession provided a severe stress test for global economic governance—and there has been no shortage of scorn for the state of global economic governance since 2008. Public opinion polls reveal frustration with the status quo and a desire for more robust global governance structures. In early 2009 an overwhelming majority of global respondents supported "major reforms" of the international economic system. In July 2009 majorities in seventeen of nineteen countries polled wanted a more powerful global financial regulator.[16] Four years after the collapse of Lehman Brothers, public pessimism about the global economy had not dissipated.[17]

Global public policy elites have been just as disdainful as the mass public. In early 2011 Richard Samans, Klaus Schwab, and Mark Malloch-Brown noted that "nearly every major initiative to solve the new century's most pressing problems has ground to a standstill amid

[11] PIPA 2006.

[12] Abdelal and Segal 2007; Drezner 2007.

[13] On China, see Beattie and Oliver 2010. On Europe, see Doyle 2012.

[14] Dunphy 2008.

[15] Levinson 2010; Bair 2012; Zaring 2009–10, 483.

[16] PIPA 2009.

[17] Pew Research Center 2012.

political gridlock, summit pageantry, and perfunctory news conferences."[18] The World Economic Forum similarly concluded: "As the financial crisis unfolded in 2008 and 2009, the world lacked an appropriate and effective crisis response mechanism."[19] Ian Bremmer and Nouriel Roubini characterized the G20 as toothless, proclaiming instead that we live in a "G-Zero" world: "[T]he divergence of economic interests in the wake of the financial crisis has undermined global economic cooperation, throwing a monkey wrench into the gears of globalization." By January 2012, Bremmer had concluded that "the effectiveness of many global institutions is under severe strain, as they remain largely unchanged from their postwar forms."[20] Alan Beattie concurred, noting that "the collective response of the world's big economies since 2007 has been slow, disorganized, usually politically weak and frequently ideologically wrong-headed."[21]

The current skepticism about global economic governance extends beyond publics and pundits to include a broad array of social scientists. Tom Hale, David Held, and Kevin Young note that "in recent years the problem of addressing global policy challenges seems to have grown worse," attributing the problem to "gridlock" in global governance. In a joint report, Jeffry Frieden, Michael Pettis, Dani Rodrik, and Ernesto Zedillo conclude that with the exception of monetary policy, "on virtually every other important global economic issue, international cooperation is stalled, flawed, or non-existent." Historian Mark Mazower notes: "With the WTO's Doha Round paralyzed and the World Bank chastened, the IMF incapable of helping to rectify the global imbalances that threaten the world economy . . . the institutions of international governance stand in urgent need of renovation." David Zaring posits that international financial institutions "have been ineffective or, at best, marginally useful" since the start of the crisis. Naazneen Barma, Ely Ratner, and Steven Weber conclude: "It's not particularly controversial to observe that global governance has gone missing."[22]

Scholars provide two reasons for why global economic governance has failed. The first is that the current era echoes the interwar period all too ominously.[23] As Charles Kindleberger famously explained in *The World in Depression*: "In 1929 the British couldn't and the United States

[18] Samans, Schwab, and Malloch-Brown 2011, 80.

[19] World Economic Forum 2012.

[20] Bremmer and Roubini 2011, 4; Bremmer 2012.

[21] Beattie 2012a, 18.

[22] Hale, Held, and Young 2013, 2; Frieden et al. 2012, 2; Mazower 2012, 424; Zaring 2009–10, 475; Barma, Ratner, and Weber 2013, 56.

[23] See, for example, Mastanduno 2009; Cohen and DeLong 2009; and Chinn and Frieden 2011.

wouldn't [stabilize the world economic system]. When every country turned to protect its national private interest, the world public interest went down the drain, and with it the private interests of all."[24] Now it is the developed world that is willing but unable and the developing world that is able but unwilling. Charles Kupchan warns that "emerging powers will want to revise, not consolidate, the international order erected during the West's watch." Christopher Layne concludes that "in the Great Recession's aftermath . . . a financially strapped United States increasingly will be unable to be a big time provider of public goods to the international order."[25] China's rise has led to claims that it is articulating a "Beijing Consensus" as an alternative to the discredited Washington Consensus. Because this consensus rests on principles of mercantilism and state capitalism, it is antithetical to the liberal economic order.[26] China therefore acts like a spoiler rather than a supporter state.

The other proffered reason is that power itself is diffusing so rapidly that no actor or concert of actors can successfully wield authority anymore. Moises Naim argues: "Today's panoply of international threats and crises . . . come as the hierarchy of nations is in flux and the very exercise of state power is no longer what it used to be." Bruce Jentleson believes we are now in a "Copernican world" characterized by "power diffused and diluted more than realists portray, post–World War II norms and institutions more contested than liberal internationalists acknowledge, and the nation state still more central than most theories of global governance convey." Randall Schweller goes even further, concluding that we are now living in "age of entropy" in which "world politics is being subsumed by the forces of randomness and enervation, wearing away its order, variety, and dynamism."[27] In such a world of disorder, efforts at global governance would seem particularly foolhardy.

III. How Can We Tell If Global Economic Governance Works?

In theory, global governance structures can provide a welter of services to facilitate economic growth and international cooperation. In practice, however, empirical assessments about whether global governance

[24] Kindleberger 1971, 292.
[25] Kupchan 2012, 7; Layne 2012, 211.
[26] Halper 2010; Bremmer 2009.
[27] Naim 2013, 158; Jentleson 2012, 140–41; Schweller 2011, 287.

"works" or is "effective" do not suffer from an abundance of analytical clarity.[28] Part of the problem is conceptual and part of the problem is empirical. Conceptually, any definition of global economic governance that shows it to be "working" is freighted with peril, because the counterfactual is often so difficult to determine. For example, did the joint G20 statements in late 2008 and early 2009 advocating fiscal and monetary expansion provide vital reassurance and policy coordination to the great powers, or are they simply epiphenomenal to a harmony of preferences? Even the best counterfactual analysis cannot completely eliminate this uncertainty.

Empirically, critics of the current system of global governance tend to rely upon a few stylized facts that are meant to imply general dysfunction. Almost any list includes the collapse of the Doha Round; the spike in protectionist actions contravening G20 pledges in the six months after the first G20 summit; the accusations of "currency wars" among the great powers; the failure of the 2009 Copenhagen climate change summit; and the ongoing sclerosis of the eurozone economies.

These facts, though true, are not the whole truth. To ascertain the effectiveness of global economic governance after the 2008 financial crisis, I follow Tamar Gutner and Alexander Thompson's framework of examining three different levels of analysis to assess the performance of global economic governance.[29] First, what do the *policy outcomes* look like? How have global output, trade, and capital flows responded since the start of the Great Recession compared with their responses to similar crises in the past? Second, what do the *policy outputs* look like? Have key international institutions provided policies that a consensus of experts would consider significant and useful in response to a global financial crisis? Would the policies have been implemented in the absence of these global governance structures? Finally, have these governance structures demonstrated *improved policy processes*? A common complaint prior to 2008 was that these institutions had not adapted to shifts in the distribution of power. Have these structures maintained their relevance and authority? Have they ensured that rising actors continue to view participation and compliance with existing arrangements as incentive compatible?

The advantage of looking at all three levels of performance is that it permits a check against standard counterarguments that global economic governance is either irrelevant or ineffective. It is frequently

[28] Gutner and Thompson 2010.
[29] Gutner and Thompson 2010, 234–37.

posited that global governance structures are merely the "low-hanging fruit" of international political economy, in which a harmony of preferences makes governance easy to achieve.[30] This would render global economic governance epiphenomenal. For this case, however, examining the process level in particular helps to refute this claim. The post-2008 goal at the process level was to reallocate influence among states within these structures. Traditionally, such governance reforms are intrinsically difficult to execute, because such steps go against the interests of those actors whose power is diluted. If process reforms nevertheless went through, we can infer that there was genuine policy coordination rather than a simple harmony of preferences.

IV. Policy Outcomes

How well has the global economy recovered from the 2008 crisis? The burgeoning literature on economic downturns suggests two factors that impose significant barriers to a strong recovery from the Great Recession: it was triggered by a financial crisis and it was global in scope. Whether measuring output, per capita income, or employment, financial crashes trigger downturns that last longer and have far weaker recoveries than standard business cycle downturns.[31] Furthermore, the global nature of the crisis makes it extremely difficult for individual states to simply "export their way" out of the problem. Countries that have experienced severe national financial crises since World War II have usually done so when the rest of the global economy was unaffected.[32] That was not the case for the Great Recession, which affected wide swaths of the global economy. The proper baseline for comparison is therefore the last severe global financial crisis—the Great Depression.

By any metric, the global economy post-2008 rebounded much more robustly than did the global economy of the Great Depression. Economists Barry Eichengreen and Kevin O'Rourke have compiled data to compare global economic performance from the start of the crises (see Figures 1 and 2).[33] Two facts stand out in their comparisons. First, the percentage drop in global industrial output and world trade levels at the start of the 2008 financial crisis was more precipitous than the falloffs following the October 1929 stock market crash. The drop

[30] Keohane 1984.

[31] Reinhart and Rogoff 2009, 223–39; Claessens, Kose, and Terrones 2011; Reinhart and Reinhart 2010; Eichengreen 2011; Jorda, Schularick, and Taylor 2012.

[32] One example would be the Scandinavian countries that experienced severe banking crises in the early 1990s.

[33] Eichengreen and O'Rourke 2010; Eichengreen and O'Rourke 2012.

in industrial output was greater one year into the 2008 financial crisis than it was eighty years earlier after the same time period. The drop in trade flows was more than twice as large. Second, the post-2008 rebound has been far more robust. Four years after the onset of the Great Recession, global industrial output is 10 percent higher than when the recession began. In contrast, four years after the 1929 stock market crash, industrial output was only two-thirds of its precrisis levels.

A similar story can be told with aggregate economic growth. According to calculations from Angus Maddison's historical database, global economic output shrank by approximately 3 percent in 1930 and then contracted at annual rates of approximately 4 percent for the next two years. In contrast, global economic output shrank by 0.59 percent in 2009, followed up by growth in 2010 of 5.22 percent and 3.95 percent in 2011. Indeed, the average growth in global output between 2010 and 2012 was on par with the average growth rate in the decade that preceded the financial crisis.[34] More intriguingly, the growth continued to be poverty reducing. Despite the 2008 financial crisis, extreme poverty continued to decline across all the major regions of the globe. In the teeth of the Great Recession, the World Bank reported that the developing world achieved its first Millennium Development goal of halving 1990 levels of extreme poverty.[35] The United Nations Development Programme noted that despite the crisis, the data showed a more rapid improvement in human development in recent years than during the 1990s—in no small part because poorer countries were able to access global markets.[36]

An important reason for the quick return to positive economic growth is that cross-border flows did not dry up after the 2008 crisis. Compared with the Great Depression, post-2008 trade flows rebounded extremely well. As Eichengreen and O'Rourke observe, four years after the 1929 stock market crash, trade flows were off by 25 percent compared with their precrisis levels. Four years after the start of the Great Recession, trade flows are more than 5 percent higher. Even compared with other postwar recessions, the current period has seen robust cross-border exchange. Indeed, the growth in world trade since 2008 has been more robust than growth was in all other postwar recoveries.[37]

[34] IMF 2013.

[35] Lowery 2012.

[36] United Nations Development Programme 2013, 75–77.

[37] At http://www.cfr.org/geoeconomics/quarterly-update-economic-recovery-historical-context/p25774, accessed July 2012.

FIGURE 1
WORLD INDUSTRIAL PRODUCTION:
GREAT DEPRESSION VS. GREAT RECESSION

SOURCE: Eichengreen and O'Rourke 2010, data provided by authors.

Other cross-border flows have also rebounded from Great Recession lows. Total cross-border capital flows are still below 2007 highs, but even financial analysts acknowledge that those precrisis flows were due to several unsustainable trends, including excessive leverage and the carry trade.[38] The more resilient components of cross-border capital flows have rebounded well. Global foreign direct investment (FDI) returned to robust levels. The precrisis average of FDI inflows between 2005 and 2007 was $1.49 trillion. The postcrisis three-year FDI inflow average, between 2010 and 2012, was $1.47 trillion—a negligible

[38] Lund et al. 2013, 17.

FIGURE 2
WORLD TRADE VOLUMES:
GREAT DEPRESSION VS. GREAT RECESSION

SOURCE: Eichengreen and O'Rourke 2010, data provided by authors.

difference.[39] Furthermore, as with economic growth more generally, an increasing proportion of FDI was targeted at the developing world. Multiple private sector analyses conclude that global foreign investment assets have fully recovered from the financial crisis and are now valued at 10–15 percent higher than at their precrisis highs. Remittances from migrant workers have also become an increasingly important revenue stream to the developing world—and the 2008 financial crisis barely dented that income stream. Cross-border remittances to developing countries quickly rebounded to precrisis levels and then

[39] United Nations Commission on Trade and Development 2013, xvi.

rose to an estimated all-time high of $389 billion in 2012. Total cross-border remittances were more than $519 billion in 2012 and are estimated to exceed $700 billion by 2016.[40] Excluding intra-European bank lending, other cross-border capital flows now approximate precrisis levels. At the same time, the McKinsey Global Institute estimates that current account imbalances have shrunk by 30 percent since the start of the 2008 financial crisis.[41] With FDI and remittances now occupying a greater share of cross-border capital flows, they are far more resilient to financial shocks than precrisis capital markets.

The final significant outcome addresses a dog that hasn't barked: the effect of the Great Recession on cross-border conflict and violence. During the initial stages of the crisis, multiple analysts asserted that the financial crisis would lead states to increase their use of force as a tool for staying in power.[42] They voiced genuine concern that the global economic downturn would lead to an increase in conflict—whether through greater internal repression, diversionary wars, arms races, or a ratcheting up of great power conflict. Violence in the Middle East, border disputes in the South China Sea, and even the disruptions of the Occupy movement fueled impressions of a surge in global public disorder.

The aggregate data suggest otherwise, however. The Institute for Economics and Peace has concluded that "the average level of peacefulness in 2012 is approximately the same as it was in 2007."[43] Interstate violence in particular has declined since the start of the financial crisis, as have military expenditures in most sampled countries. Other studies confirm that the Great Recession has not triggered any increase in violent conflict, as Lotta Themnér and Peter Wallensteen conclude: "[T]he pattern is one of relative stability when we consider the trend for the past five years."[44] The secular decline in violence that started with the end of the Cold War has not been reversed. Rogers Brubaker observes that "the crisis has not to date generated the surge in protectionist nationalism or ethnic exclusion that might have been expected."[45]

[40] For FDI data, see OECD/UNCTAD 2012; OECD/UNCTAD 2013. For foreign investment assets, see Lund et al. 2013. For remittance flows, see World Bank 2012.

[41] Lund et al. 2013, 6.

[42] See, for example, Rogers 2008, Kurlantzick 2009; and Brubaker 2011, 93.

[43] Institute for Economics and Peace 2012, 37.

[44] Themnér and Wallensteen 2012, 566. See also Human Security Report Project 2010.

[45] Brubaker 2011, 94.

V. Policy Outputs

It could be that the global economy has experienced a moderate bounceback in spite of, rather than because of, the global policy response. At the beginning of the twentieth century, for example, cross-border flows grew dramatically despite efforts by states to raise barriers to exchange.[46] In assessing *policy outputs*, Charles Kindleberger provided the classic definition of what should be done to stabilize the global economy during a severe financial crisis: "maintaining a relatively open market for distress goods" and providing liquidity to the global financial system through "countercyclical long-term lending" and "discounting."[47] Serious concerns were voiced in late 2008 and early 2009 about the inability of anyone to provide these kinds of public goods, threatening a repeat of the beggar-thy-neighbor policies of the 1930s.[48]

By Kindleberger's criteria, however, public goods provision has been quite robust since 2008. On the surface, the open market for distressed goods seemed under threat. The stalemate of the Doha Round, the rise of G20 protectionism after the fall 2008 summit, and the explosion of antidumping cases that occurred at the onset of the financial crisis suggested that markets were drifting toward closure. According to WTO figures, antidumping initiations surged by 30 percent in 2008 alone. In a June 2013 assessment, the free trade group Global Trade Alert warned of a massive spike in protectionist measures leading to "a quiet, wide-ranging assault on the commercial level playing field."[49]

A closer look, however, reveals that warnings about an increase in protectionism have been vastly overstated. The surge in nontariff barriers following the 2008 financial crisis quickly receded; indeed, as Figure 3 shows, the surge never came close to peak levels of these cases. By 2011, antidumping initiations had declined to their lowest levels since the founding of the WTO in 1995. Both countervailing duty complaints and safeguards initiations have also fallen to precrisis levels.

Some post-2008 measures are not captured in these traditional metrics of nontariff barriers, but similar results hold. Most temporary trade barriers were concentrated in countries such as Russia and Argentina that had already erected higher barriers to global economic integration.[50] Even including these additional measures, the combined effect of protectionist actions for the first year after the peak of the financial crisis

[46] O'Rourke and Williamson 1999, chaps. 6, 10.
[47] Kindleberger 1971, 292.
[48] *Economist* 2009; Kurlantzick 2009; Abdelal and Segal 2009.
[49] Evenett 2013.
[50] Bown 2012.

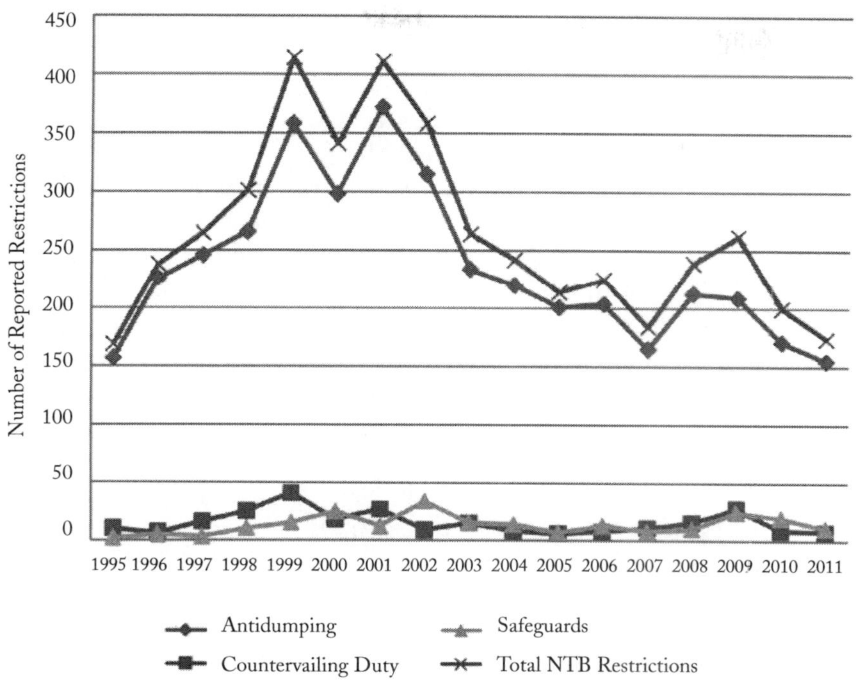

FIGURE 3
TRADE RESTRICTIONS, 2006–11

SOURCE: WTO.

affected less than 0.8 percent of global trade.[51] Furthermore, the use of these protectionist measures declined further in 2010 to cover only 0.2 percent of global trade. Five years after the start of the Great Recession, the effect of these measures remains modest, affecting less than 4 percent of global trade flows. The WTO's June 2013 estimate is that the combined effect of all postcrisis protectionist measures by the G20 had reduced trade flows by a total of 0.2 percent.[52] The WTO estimate jibes with academic estimates of post-2008 trade protectionism playing a minimal role in affecting cross-border exchange. The overwhelming consensus is that "the Great Recession of 2009 does not coincide with any obvious increase in protectionism."[53] The quick turnaround

[51] Dadush, Ali, and Odell 2011.
[52] WTO 2013.
[53] Rose 2012, 4. See also Kee, Neagu, and Nicita 2013; Kim 2013, 7.

and growth in trade levels further show that these measures have not seriously impeded market access.[54]

The multilateral trade system played a significant role in this outcome. The WTO's dispute-settlement mechanism helped to contain the spread of protectionist measures that the Great Recession triggered; there is no evidence that compliance with these rulings waned after 2008.[55] This is consistent with research that shows membership in the WTO and related organizations acted as a significant brake on increases in tariffs and nontariff barriers.[56] The major trading jurisdictions—the United States, the European Union, and China—adhered most closely to their WTO obligations. As Alan Beattie acknowledged: "The 'Doha Round' of trade talks may be dead, but the WTO's dispute settlement arm is still playing a valuable role."[57] The WTO's Government Procurement Agreement (GPA) helped to blunt the most blatant parts of the "Buy American" provisions of the 2009 fiscal stimulus, thereby preventing a cascade of "fiscal protectionism."

Policy advocates of trade liberalization embrace the "bicycle theory" —the belief that unless multilateral trade liberalization moves forward, the entire global trade regime will collapse because of a lack of forward momentum.[58] The last four years suggest that there are limits to that rule of thumb. The *Financial Times*/Economist Intelligence Unit surveys of global business leaders reveal that concerns about protectionism have stayed at a low level. Figure 4 shows that compared with popular concerns about economic and political uncertainty, corporate executives were far less concerned about either protectionism or currency volatility. Reviewing the state of world trade, Uri Dadush and his colleagues conclude: "The limited resort to protectionism was a remarkable aspect of the Great Recession."[59] Former US trade representative Susan Schwab concurs, noting, "Although countries took protectionist measures in the wake of the crisis, the international community avoided a quick deterioration into a spiral of beggar-thy-neighbor actions to block imports."[60] At a minimum, the bicycle of world trade is still coasting forward.

From the earliest stages of the financial crisis, there was also concerted and coordinated action among central banks to ensure both dis-

[54] Dadush, Ali, and Odell 2011. See also Bussière et al. 2011.
[55] On pre-2008 compliance, see Wilson 2007.
[56] Gawande, Hoekman, and Cui 2011; Baccini and Kim 2012; Kee, Neagu, and Nicita 2011.
[57] Beattie 2012b.
[58] Bhagwati 1988, 4,1 was the great popularizer of the term.
[59] Dadush, Ali, and Odell 2011, 3.
[60] Schwab, 2011, 112.

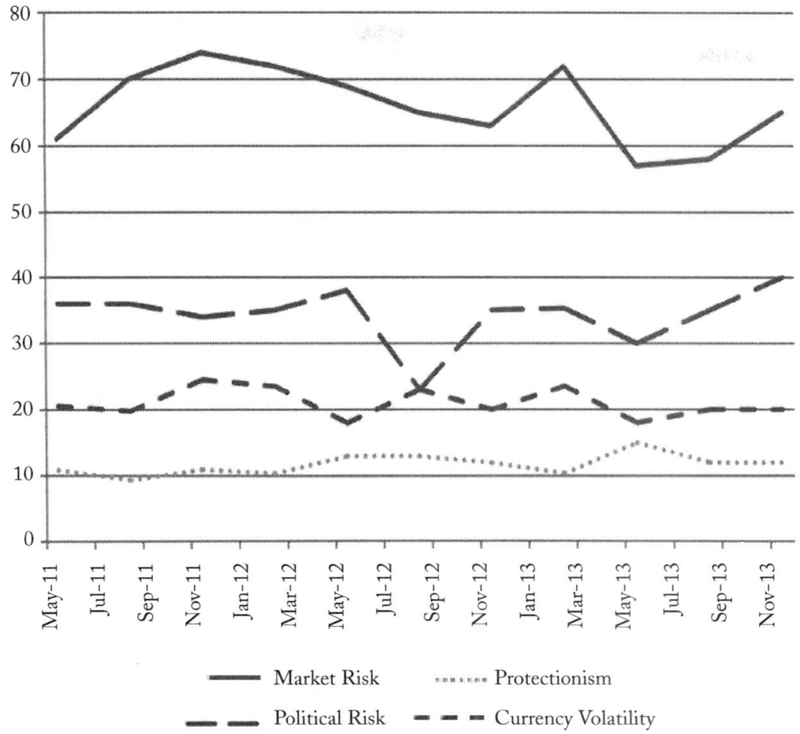

FIGURE 4
PRIVATE SECTOR PERCEPTIONS OF THREATS AND RISKS TO THE GLOBAL ECONOMY

SOURCE: *Financial Times*/Economist Intelligence Unit.

counting and countercyclical lending. Indeed, even global governance skeptics acknowledge the success of global economic governance on this point.[61] As the extent of the subprime mortgage crisis became clear, central banks of the major economies slowly cut interest rates in the fall of 2007. A few months later, the central banks of the United States, Canada, the United Kingdom, Switzerland, and the eurozone announced currency swaps to ensure liquidity.[62] By the fall of 2008 they were cutting rates ruthlessly and in a coordinated fashion—"the first globally coordinated monetary easing in history," as one assessment put it.[63] Global real interest rates fell from an average of 3 percent

[61] See, for example, Beattie 2012a, 10–11; Frieden et al. 2012, 2.
[62] Irwin 2013, 127–32.
[63] Irwin 2013, 161.

prior to the crisis to zero in 2012—in the advanced industrialized economies, the real interest rate was effectively negative.[64] Not content with lowering interest rates, most of the major central banks also expanded emergency credit facilities and engaged in more creative forms of quantitative easing. Between 2007 and 2012, the balance sheets of the central banks in the advanced industrialized economies more than doubled. The Bank for International Settlements acknowledged in its 2012 annual report that "decisive action by central banks during the global financial crisis was probably crucial in preventing a repeat of the experiences of the Great Depression."[65]

Central banks and finance ministries also took coordinated action during the fall of 2008 to try to ensure that cross-border lending would continue, so as to avert currency and solvency crises. In October of that year, the G7 economies plus Switzerland agreed to unlimited currency swaps in order to ensure that liquidity would be maintained in the system. The United States then extended its currency-swap facility to Brazil, Singapore, Mexico, and South Korea. The European Central Bank expanded its swap arrangements for euros with Hungary, Denmark, and Poland. China, Japan, South Korea, and the ASEAN economies broadened the Chang Mai Initiative into an $80 billion swap arrangement to ensure liquidity. The International Monetary Fund also negotiated emergency financing for Hungary, Pakistan, Iceland, and Ukraine. In the ten months after September 2008, the IMF executed more than $140 billion in stand-by arrangements to seventeen countries.[66]

Over the longer term, the great powers bulked up the resources of the international financial institutions to provide for further countercyclical lending. In 2009 the G20 agreed to triple the IMF's reserves to $750 billion. In 2012, in response to the worsening European sovereign debt crisis, G20 countries combined to pledge more than $430 billion in additional resources. The Fund created multiple new credit facilities for its least developed members and established a flexible credit line that enabled members to sign up for precautionary arrangements without triggering market panic. Multiple outside reviews of the IMF's performance concluded that the IMF response to the Great Recession "was larger in magnitude, was more rapid, and carried fewer conditions" than in prior crises.[67] The World Bank's International

[64] Bank of International Settlements 2012, 39.
[65] Bank of International Settlements 2012, 41.
[66] Joyce 2013, 170.
[67] Joyce 2013, 168.

Development Association (IDA), which offers up the most concessionary form of lending, also increased its resources. The sixteenth IDA replenishment in December 2010 was a record $49.3 billion, an 18 percent increase of IDA resources from three years earlier. Using Kindleberger's criteria, global economic governance worked rather well in response to the 2008 financial crisis.

To be sure, there are global public goods that go beyond Kindleberger's initial criteria, as Kindleberger and successive IPE scholars have observed. Macroeconomic policy coordination would be an additional area of possible cooperation, as would coordinating and clarifying cross-border financial regulations. Again, however, the international system acted in these areas after 2008. Between late 2007 and the June 2010 G20 Toronto summit, the major economies agreed on the need for aggressive and expansionary fiscal and monetary policies in the wake of the financial crisis. Even reluctant contributors like Germany—whose finance minister blasted the "crass Keynesianism" of these policies in December 2008—eventually bowed to pressure from economists and G20 peers. Indeed, in 2009 Germany enacted the third largest fiscal stimulus in the world.[68] Germany's actions, which contravened its *ordoliberal* preferences, are an example of global economic governance leading to greater policy coordination.[69]

Progress was also made on regulatory coordination in finance and investment rules. There were developments in two particular areas: investor protectionism and banking regulation. The rise of sovereign wealth funds prior to 2008 had precipitated a ratcheting up of restrictions to cross-border investment by state-owned enterprises and funds. The OECD articulated its own guidelines for recipient countries but warned that unless these funds demonstrated greater transparency, barriers to investment would likely rise even further.[70] In September 2008 an IMF-brokered process approved a set of "Generally Accepted Principles and Practices" for sovereign wealth funds. These voluntary guidelines—also called the Santiago Principles—consisted of twenty-four guidelines addressing the legal and institutional frameworks, governance issues, and risk management of these funds. Contemporaneous press reports characterized the new rules as "a rare triumph for IMF financial diplomacy."[71] The expert consensus among financial analysts, regulators, and academics was that these principles—if fully implemented—address most

[68] Prasad and Sorkin 2009.
[69] Farrell and Quiggin 2011.
[70] OECD 2008, 6.
[71] Davis 2008.

recipient country concerns.[72] Since the IMF approved the Santiago Principles, furthermore, investor protectionism has declined.[73]

With respect to banking, international regulators have significantly revised the Basel core banking principles. At the November 2010 Seoul summit, the G20 approved the Basel III banking standards. Basel III took only two years to negotiate in the Basel Committee on Banking Supervision—an extraordinarily brief period given that the Basel II standards took more than six years to hammer out. The new rules, scheduled to be phased in over the rest of this decade, take a number of steps to improve bank stability. The primary "microprudential" step was to triple the amount of "Tier 1" reserve capital that qualifying banks needed to keep on hand. Basel III further created a leverage ratio—the ratio of Tier 1 capital to a bank's total exposure—of more than 3 percent by 2018. For the first time, Basel III also instituted "macroprudential" measures designed to ensure that banks could function even when asset markets seized up. By 2019 banks are expected to have a "liquidity coverage ratio" —the proportion of "high-quality liquid assets" to the estimated net liquidity outflows over a thirty-day period of "market stress"—of 100 percent. A net stable funding ratio proposed a similar 100 percent ratio of a bank's available stable funding over a calendar year to required funding over the same year. Finally, systemically important banks would be required to amass additional countercyclical capital buffers to prevent financial institutions from engaging in procyclical lending.

Financial sector analysts and scholars have debated whether Basel III is a sufficient upgrade in regulatory stringency and whether it will be implemented too slowly, or not at all.[74] There is consensus, however, on three points. First, if implemented, Basel III clearly represents an upgrade over the Basel II standards for preventing bank failures.[75] Second, the dampening effects of the new standards on economic growth are negligible; indeed, the preliminary evidence shows that banks have significantly augmented their capital reserves while still increasing their lending.[76] Third, the Basel Committee did not substantively alter its draft set of standards despite fierce resistance from the global banking industry.[77]

[72] Deloitte Touche Tohmatsu 2008; Cohen and DeLong 2009, 89.
[73] OECD/UNCTAD 2012; OECD/UNCTAD 2013.
[74] See, for example, Bair 2012; Lall 2012; Baker 2013.
[75] Chinn and Frieden 2011, 214; Véron 2012.
[76] Cohen 2013.
[77] Interviews with BCBS officials; see also Wilf 2013. It should be noted that the BCBS has altered its macroprudential standards somewhat from its original draft, but bank lobbying is not the primary reason for these changes.

VI. Governance Processes

The degree of institutional resiliency and flexibility at the global level has been remarkable. Once the acute phase of the 2008 financial crisis began, the G20 quickly supplanted the G7/G8 as the focal point for global economic governance. At the September 2009 G20 summit in Pittsburgh, the member countries explicitly designated the G20 to be the "premier forum" for international economic cooperation. This move addressed the problem of the G8's waning power and relevancy. The G20 grouping comprises 85 percent of global economic output, 80 percent of global trade, and 66 percent of global population, making it a far more legitimate and representative body than the G8. As Geoffrey Garrett puts it: "[T]he G20 is globally representative yet small enough to make consensual decision-making feasible."[78] As a club of great powers, consensus within the G20 would lead to effective policy coordination across a wide range of issues.

The perception is that G20's political momentum stalled out years ago after countries disagreed on macroeconomic imbalances and the virtues of austerity. By 2010, various G20 finance ministers were accusing each other of "currency wars." The reality is a bit more complex. On the currency question, actual currency volatility did not appear to faze business executives too much, as Figure 4 demonstrates. This is likely in part because, despite media reports about currency wars, the data indicate a downward secular trend in exchange rate volatility to levels below the precrisis average.[79] It is certainly true that consensus on macroeconomic policy broke down, but the rest of the G20's Framework for Strong, Sustainable and Balanced Growth agenda went forward. According to the University of Toronto's G20 Information Centre, compliance with G20 commitments actually increased over time. They measured G20 adherence to "chosen priority commitments." Measured on a per country average, G20 members have steadily improved since the 61.5 percent compliance rate for the April 2009 London Summit commitments, rising all the way to 77 percent for the June 2012 Los Cabos Summit.[80]

The obvious rejoinder is that this kind of assessment inflates compliance because the pledges made at these summits are increasingly modest.[81] Indeed, the G20 has likely scaled back its ambitions—even in

[78] Garrett 2010, 29.
[79] Hood 2012, chart 3.
[80] G20 Information Centre 2013.
[81] Downs, Rocke, and Barsoom 1996; Gutner and Thompson 2010.

its "priority commitments"—making compliance easier. There are examples, however, of great powers using the G20 as a means of blunting domestic pressures for greater protectionism—at precisely the moment when the group was thought to be losing its momentum. For example, the G20 has served as a useful mechanism for defusing rising domestic tensions concerning China's undervalued currency. In response to congressional pressure for more robust action, in April 2010 Treasury Secretary Timothy Geithner cited the G20 meetings as "the best avenue for advancing U.S. interests" on China's manipulation of its exchange rate.[82] This successfully deflected momentum in Congress to take unilateral action against China.

In June 2010, President Obama sent a letter to his G20 colleagues stressing the importance of "market-determined exchange rates." Three days after Obama's letter was sent, the People's Bank of China announced that it would "enhance the RMB exchange rate flexibility." For the next two years, the renminbi nominally appreciated at a rate of 5 percent a year—and more so if one factors in the differences in national inflation rates. Significant appreciations in the renminbi occurred in advance of G20 meetings.[83] By late 2012, as the renminbi hit record highs against the dollar, there was mounting evidence that China had dramatically curtailed its intervention into exchange rate markets.[84] In the three years after China's pledge, the renminbi has appreciated by 15 percent against China's major trading partners. This has contributed to a shrinking of global current account imbalances of more than 30 percent since the start of the crisis.[85]

Other key financial bodies also strengthened their membership and authority as a response to the 2008 crisis. In March 2009 the Basel Committee on Banking Supervision expanded its membership from thirteen advanced industrialized states to twenty-seven members by adding the developing country members of the G20. The Financial Stability Forum was renamed the Financial Stability Board in April 2009 and given greater responsibilities for regulatory coordination; it also expanded its membership to include the developing country members of the G20. During this period the Committee of the Global Financial System also grew in size from thirteen countries to twenty-two, adding Brazil, China, and India, among others. The Financial Action Task Force on Money Laundering has added China, India, and

[82] Geithner 2010.
[83] Rickards 2011, 113.
[84] Bradsher 2012; Rabinovitch 2012.
[85] Lund et al. 2013, 6.

South Korea to its grouping since 2007. Prior to 2008, the G7 countries dominated most of these financial standard-setting agencies. That is no longer the case in terms of membership. In the future, this expansion might impair the efficacy of these groups, but their legitimacy has been enhanced since 2008. Indeed, the G20 assessment process has enhanced the monitoring powers of many of these institutions. In requesting reports from the FSB, as well as organizations ranging from the WTO to UNCTAD, the G20 has implicitly burnished the expertise and legitimacy of these governance structures.

The International Monetary Fund and World Bank also changed after the financial crisis, though on the surface that might not appear to be the case. The implicit compact in which a European is given the IMF managing director slot and an American is appointed to the World Bank presidency has continued. Despite the scandals that engulfed Dominique Strauss-Kahn in 2011 and Paul Wolfowitz five years earlier, former French finance minister Christine Lagarde replaced Strauss-Kahn in 2011 and an American, Jim Yong Kim, replaced Robert Zoellick as the new World Bank president in 2012.

Beneath the surface, however, the Bank and the Fund have witnessed significant evolution. Power within the IMF is based on quota size, calculated using a complex formula of economic variables. Prior to 2007 the allotment of quotas in the IMF bore little resemblance to the distribution of economic power. This has changed. A significant step has been two rounds of quota reform in the IMF that were implemented in 2011. An additional proposed quota reform was proposed in 2010 and is pending, awaiting US congressional approval and implementation. The explicit goal of these reforms has been to expand the voting power of advanced developing economies to better reflect the distribution of economic power. Once the latest round of quota reform is completed, China will possess the third largest voting share in the Fund, and all four of the BRIC economies will be among the ten largest shareholders in the IMF. There will also be a planned shift to an all-elected executive board for the IMF that is designed to allow a further reduction in the number of European representatives to the board.

The World Bank Group underwent a parallel set of reforms. Between 2008 and 2010, the voting power of developing and transition economies within the main World Bank institution (the International Bank for Reconstruction and Development) had been increased by 4.59 percentage points, and China became the third largest voting member. The International Finance Corporation (IFC) approved an even larger shift of 6.09 percentage points. More importantly, the Bank's

Development Committee agreed that Bank and IFC shareholding would be reviewed every five years beginning in 2015, thereby routinizing the process.[86]

While the appointments of Lagarde and Kim might appear retrograde, their appointments represent political bargaining that reflected the greater influence of the advanced developing countries. In both cases, the nominee had to woo developing countries to secure political support in advance of voting. China, for example, was an early supporter of both Lagarde and Kim despite the possibility of emerging market candidates.[87] The appointment of Chinese national Min Zhu to be a deputy managing director of the IMF at the same time that Lagarde took over might have been one reason for this preference. This highlights a shift in the distribution of senior-level appointments toward the advanced developing economies.

The content of Bank and Fund policies has also shifted to better reflect developing country concerns. In the wake of the 2008 financial crisis, the IMF began to change its attitude about the wisdom of capital controls. In February 2010 an IMF staff paper concluded that under some circumstances, capital controls could be a legitimate and useful policy tool.[88] Dani Rodrik characterized the change in the IMF's tune as a "stunning reversal" of its previous orthodoxy.[89] By November 2012 the staff note had translated into the IMF's official position. The Fund allowed that capital controls could be "useful" in some circumstances and that "[t]here is . . . no presumption that full [capital account] liberalization is an appropriate goal for all countries at all times."[90] As for the Bank, Kim's appointment to the presidency in 2012 highlights the shift in priorities. Trained as a doctor and an anthropologist, Kim's entire career had focused on health policy. This suggests that the Bank will use a more capacious notion of development going forward, consistent with a shift toward developing country preferences.

The trade and investment regimes have displayed somewhat less vigor than global financial governance, but these regimes have not withered on the vine either. The multilateral trade regime would appear to have suffered the most from the Great Recession. The failure to complete an ambitious Doha Round was a blow to the World

[86] World Bank 2010.

[87] Subramanian 2013, 4.

[88] Ostry et al. 2010.

[89] Rodrik 2010.

[90] International Monetary Fund 2012, 1. It should be noted that the change in the IMF's position on capital controls did not lead to a wholesale rejection of capital account liberalization. Rather, restrictions on capital flows were temporary and market based.

Trade Organization. Nevertheless, the institution has endured, as the December 2013 trade facilitation deal in Bali demonstrates. Indeed, it has expanded its reach in several ways. Geographically, the WTO finally secured the accession of the Russian Federation, the last G20 non-member, after a slow-motion fifteen-year negotiation process. Since the start of 2007 the WTO has added seven additional members, including Ukraine and Vietnam.

The WTO also adapted to play a crucial role in constraining the rise in protectionism. The WTO's impact was felt through both enhanced monitoring and acting as a focal point for plurilateral liberalizaton. Beginning in late 2008, the WTO's secretariat used the Trade Policy Review Mechanism (TPRM) to report on a regular basis to the G20 on increases in protectionism. After initial reluctance, WTO members accepted the move as a useful increase in monitoring and transparency.[91] A comparison of the WTO's monitoring with that of Global Trade Alert further shows that the monitoring of the latter is based on less reliable metrics and exaggerates the increase in protectionism.[92] WTO members also shifted their approach to pushing for greater trade liberalization by switching to expanding or starting plurilateral agreements. China is now negotiating to join the Government Procurement Agreement. The United States, the European Union, and eighteen other countries have accelerated talks on a services liberalization agreement that would encompass most of the OECD economies as well as advanced developing countries.

Enthusiasm for greater trade liberalization has also found an additional outlet: the "open regionalism" of regional and bilateral free trade agreements (FTAs). The traditional expectation that an economic downturn would dampen enthusiasm for greater openness has not been borne out by the data on FTAs. In the four years prior to the collapse of Lehman Brothers, fifty-one FTAs were reported to the World Trade Organization. In the four years since, fifty-eight free trade agreements were registered.[93] The United States and eleven other countries are currently negotiating a Trans-Pacific Partnership. The United States and the European Union are negotiating a Transatlantic Trade and Investment Partnership as well.

To be sure, not all of these FTAs were created equal. Some of them have greater coverage of goods and services than others. Some of them might promote more trade diversion than trade creation. Neverthe-

[91] Wolfe 2012, 787–79; Kim 2013.
[92] Wolfe 2012.
[93] World Trade Organization 2012.

less, the patterned growth of these FTAs mirrors how they spread in the late nineteenth century.[94] Even if these FTAs do not possess the most-favored-nation provision that accelerated trade liberalization in the nineteenth century, the political economy of trade diversion still generates competitive incentives for a growth in FTAs, thereby leading to a similar outcome.[95] Through their own shared understandings and dispute-settlement mechanisms, they act as an additional brake on protectionist policies.[96]

There is no multilateral investment regime to display resiliency. Instead, investment is governed by a network of bilateral investment treaties (BITs). Compared with the data on free trade agreements, it would appear that the pace of BITs has slowed since 2008. According to UNCTAD data, an annual average of seventy-eight BITs were completed in the three years prior to 2008; an average of only sixty-one per annum were negotiated in the three years after 2008. That indicates a slowdown. A look at the longer time series, however, reveals that the Great Recession is not the cause of this slowdown. As Figure 5 shows, the peak of BIT negotiations took place in the decade after the end of the Cold War. From 1992 to 2001, an annual average of 160 BITs were negotiated. After 2001, however, the number of negotiated BITs declined, following a standard diffusion pattern. Based on that kind of pattern of diffusion, the last three years have seen expected levels of BIT growth. Furthermore, in 2012 the United States introduced a new "model BIT" and started negotiations with China, India, and other countries on bilateral investment treaties, suggesting that there will be more significant liberalization going forward.[97]

VII. Why the Misperception?

There is considerable evidence that global economic governance functioned comparatively well in response to the 2008 financial crisis and the Great Recession. Even through the initial drop in output and trade levels was more acute in 2008 than in 1929, by any measure the global economy has rebounded more robustly in the past five years than during the era of the Great Depression. The great powers and global governance structures successfully coordinated policy outputs that alleviated the worst effects of the financial crisis. Key multilateral insti-

[94] Lazer 1999; Drezner 2006.

[95] Indeed, the US endorsement of the Trans-Pacific Partnership has already caused China to accelerate its own strategy of signing regional free trade agreements. See Song and Yuan 2012.

[96] Dadush, Ali, and Odell, 8–9.

[97] Politi 2012.

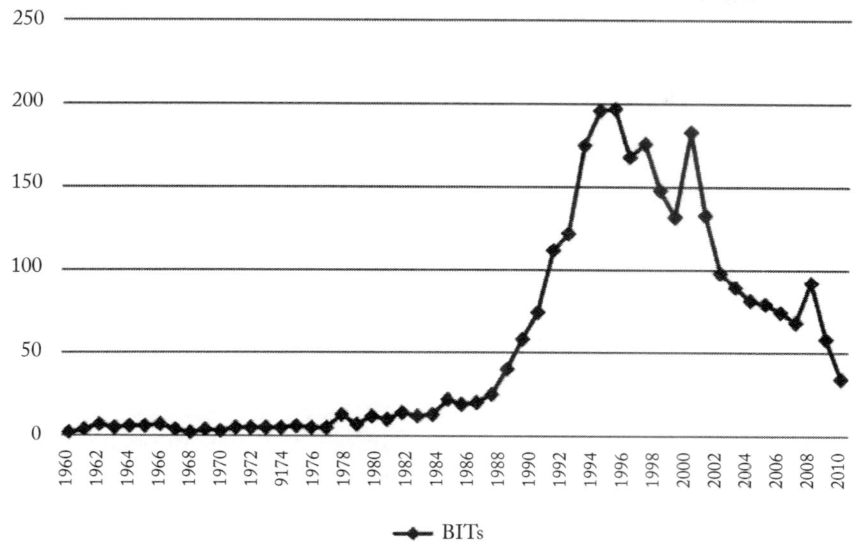

FIGURE 5
ANNUAL COUNT OF BILATERAL INVESTMENT TREATIES, 1960–2011

SOURCE: UNCTAD.

tutions, particularly in the financial realm, expanded their policy competencies and adjusted their governance structures to better reflect the distribution of power in the world. Contrary to precrisis expectations, global economic governance performed the necessary tasks to prevent the 2008 financial crisis from metastasizing into a prolonged depression.

Why is there such a profound gap between perceptions and reality in evaluating the performance of multilateral economic institutions?[98] The simplest explanation is that the core economies—the advanced industrialized democracies—have not rebounded as vigorously as expected. Two trends have marked most postwar global business cycles: economies rebound as vigorously as they drop, and the advanced industrialized states suffer less than the economic periphery. Neither of these trends has held during the Great Recession. As previously noted, the recovery from a financial crisis tends to be longer and slower than standard business-cycle recessions. After the 2008 financial crisis, the recovery has been particularly weak in the advanced industrialized

[98] See Kahler 2013 for a notable exception.

economies. According to the Economist Intelligence Unit, the OECD economies averaged GDP growth of 0.5 percent between 2008 and 2012. The non-OECD economies averaged 5.2 percent during the same period. A weak economy feeds perceptions of institutional breakdown. The 2012 Edelman Trust Barometer reflects this phenomenon. It shows that trust of elite institutions is significantly higher among developing countries than in the developed world.[99] This is a reversal of traditional findings that show lower levels of trust in emerging markets. Since the study of global economic governance has been anchored in the developed world, it is not surprising that this literature suffers from a pessimism bias.

Pessimism about current economic conditions in the developed world might also be causing analysts to conflate poor domestic and regional governance with poor global governance. The primary causes for domestic economic weakness in the United States, Europe, and Japan are not global in origin—and neither are policies at the global level necessarily the best possible response.[100] Japan's economic woes have been a function of two decades of slack economic growth combined with the aftereffects of the Fukushima disaster. US economic misfortunes have had little to do with either the global economy or global economic governance. Indeed, the United States benefited from the postcrisis state of international affairs through lower borrowing costs and higher exports. Domestic policy stalemates and political uncertainty, by contrast, tamped down the US recovery.

Europe's situation is more complex because of the sui generis nature of the eurozone. To be sure, the Great Recession was the trigger for the eurozone's sovereign debt crisis. The international response to the crisis has been that of a modest supporting role. The IMF has proffered both its technical expertise and its financial support in excess of $100 billion to Greece, Portugal, and Ireland. The United States and other major economies have offered to reopen swap lines with the European Central Bank to ensure liquidity. European and national policy responses to the crisis, however, have badly exacerbated the economic situation. Greece's reckless precrisis levels of government spending and borrowing made that economy a target ripe for market pessimism. The initial European bailout package for Greece was inadequate, allowing the crisis to fester. The austerity policies advocated in some quarters have not panned out as expected. The European Central Bank's decision to raise

[99] The Edelman Trust Barometer data can be accessed at http://trust.edelman.com/trust-download/global-results/.

[100] Frieden et al. 2012.

interest rates prematurely in early 2010 helped to stall out the nascent recovery on the Continent. On the fiscal side of the equation, austerity-related policies led to a double-dip recession in Great Britain and the eurozone, higher borrowing costs in Spain and Italy, and continued uncertainty about the euro's future. Europe's fiscal and monetary policies have been less expansionary than in the United States. This, in turn, has prevented any appreciable private sector deleveraging in Europe, thereby guaranteeing a longer downturn before any sustained recovery is possible.[101]

The IMF has come under criticism for failing to exert more influence over the eurozone crisis. One high-ranking staffer resigned in June 2012, blasting the Fund for its "European bias" and the consensus culture that keeps the Fund from criticizing countries in the middle of lending programs.[102] There are two counterpoints to this argument. First, the IMF *has* been critical at various moments during the eurozone crisis. Fund staff issued warnings about the health of the European banks in August 2011, and IMF managing director Lagarde called explicitly for debt sharing among the eurozone countries in June 2012.[103] The first criticism received significant pushback from the European Central Bank and eurozone governments, and Germany ignored the second criticism. This leads to the second point: it is highly unlikely that national governments would feel compelled to respond to IMF criticism in the absence of a market response. The Fund must walk a tightrope between transparent criticism and setting off market panic. This is hardly an ideal vantage point for strong-arming governments with sizable IMF quotas.

A final reason for misperception about global economic governance is exaggerated nostalgia for prior eras of global economic governance. The presumption in much of the commentary on the current global political economy is that both governance structures and hegemonic leadership were better and stronger in the past. Much of this commentary evokes the era of the 1940s, when the creation of the Bretton Woods institutions, backstopped by the United States, ushered in a new era of global governance. The contrast between US leadership then and now seems stark.

This comparison elides some inconvenient facts, however. The late 1940s were indeed the acme of American hegemonic leadership. Even during that peak, however, the United States failed to ratify the Havana

[101] Reinhart and Rogoff 2009; Roxburgh et al. 2012.
[102] Doyle 2012.
[103] Beattie and Giles 2011; Kanter 2012.

Charter that would have created an International Trade Organization with wider scope than the current WTO. With the Marshall Plan, the US decided to act outside the purview of Bretton Woods institutions, weakening their influence. After the late 1940s American leadership and global financial governance experienced as many misses as hits. The logic of the Bretton Woods system rested on an economic contradiction that became known as the Triffin dilemma. Extravagant macroeconomic policies in the United States, combined with a growing reluctance to accommodate the US position, eroded that global financial order. As the logical contradictions of the Bretton Woods regime became more evident, existing policy coordination mechanisms failed to correct the problem. Despite initial efforts to have the IMF exercise leverage over surplus countries as well as deficit countries, the Fund found itself incapable of pressuring countries running surpluses.[104] By 1971, when the United States unilaterally decided to close the gold window, all of the major economies had chosen to ameliorate domestic interests rather than coordinate action at the global level.[105] In ending Bretton Woods, the United States also undercut the IMF's original raison d'être.

Post–Bretton Woods global economic governance was equally haphazard. An increase in antidumping, countervailing duties, and nontariff barriers weakened the rules of the global trading system over the next two decades. Neither the United States nor any global governance structure was able to prevent OPEC from raising energy prices from 1973 to 1986.[106] Exchange rates and macroeconomic policy coordination devolved from the IMF to the G7. A predictable cycle emerged: other G7 countries would pressure the United States to scale back its fiscal deficits. In turn, the United States would pressure Japan and West Germany to expand their domestic consumption in order to act as locomotives of growth. Not surprisingly, the most common outcome on the macroeconomic front was a stalemate.[107]

Even perceived successes in macroeconomic policy coordination have had mixed results. While the 1985 Plaza Accord helped to depreciate the value of the dollar while allowing the yen to rise in value, it was also the beginning of an unsustainable asset bubble in Japan. In Europe the creation of the euro would seem to count as an example of successful coordination. The Growth and Stability Pact that was attached

[104] Barnett and Finnemore 2004, chap. 3.
[105] Gowa 1984.
[106] Keohane 1980.
[107] Putnam and Bayne 1987.

to the creation of the common European currency, however, was less successful. Within a year of the euro's birth, five of the eleven member countries were not in compliance; by 2005, the three largest countries in the eurozone were ignoring the pact.[108] Regardless of the distribution of power or the robustness of international institutions, the history of macroeconomic policy coordination is not a distinguished one.[109] In comparison with this historical standard, three years of successful macroeconomic policy coordination is quite remarkable.

None of this is to deny that global economic governance was useful and stabilizing at various points after 1945. Rather, it is to observe that even during the heyday of American hegemony, the ability of global economic governance to solve ongoing global economic problems was limited. The original point of Kindleberger's analysis of the Great Depression was to discuss what needed to be done during a global economic crisis. By that standard, the post-2008 performance of key institutions has been far better than extant commentary suggests. The obvious defects of recent global economic governance remain clear: the 2008 collapse of the Doha Round, the 2009 breakdown in climate change negotiations, the 2010 breakdown of macroeconomic policy coordination, and the complete absence of any international regime to tackle cybercrime. Expecting more than an effective crisis response might be unrealistic, however. Global economic governance has not been optimal, but it has been good enough.

VIII. Why Has the System Worked?

Global economic governance did what was necessary during the Great Recession—but *why* did the system work? The precrisis observations about sclerotic international institutions and a looming power transition did not seem too far off the mark. How did these actors manage to produce the necessary policy outputs and reforms to stave off systemic collapse? It is impossible to provide a definitive answer in the space provided, but a preliminary evaluation is warranted.

The most commonly provided answer is that the shared sense of crisis spurred the major economies into joint action—and when the immediate crisis subsided, so did the degree of policy coordination. This is not a compelling argument, however. The same crisis mentality did not lead to sustained cooperation during the Great Depression.

[108] Dominguez 2006.
[109] Willett 1999.

Significant postwar economic crises—such as the end of the Bretton Woods regime, the oil shocks of the 1970s, and the breakdown of the European exchange rate mechanism in the early 1990s—also failed to spur meaningful great power cooperation. What caused powerful actors to think of the 2008 crisis as a "shared" one?

A more sophisticated version of this argument stems from open economy politics.[110] It argues that globalization has locked in powerful interests that give strong preference to an open global economy. These interests then pressured governments into taking necessary actions at the national and global levels so as not to interfere with the global supply chain. The problem with this explanation is that there are too many instances in which powerful interests either lost or compromised their positions. Neither Germany's government nor German business interests were predisposed toward Keynesian macroeconomic policies in late 2008. Neither China's government nor its exporting interests preferred allowing the renminbi to appreciate in 2010. Large financial firms were firmly opposed to the Basel III banking accord. European governments resisted the dilution of their influence in the World Bank and International Monetary Fund. There are too many instances of policy coordination—rather than a harmony of preferences—for a strictly interest-based approach to explain post-2008 outcomes.

A fuller answer requires additional research, but some tentative answers can be proffered here. The distribution of power and the role of economic ideas are among the primary conceptual building blocks of international political economy—and both of these factors offer a partial explanation for the performance of global economic governance.[111] Comparing the current situation with the analogous moment during the Great Depression along both of these dimensions, we can discern why events have unfolded differently this time around. Looking at the distribution of power, for example, the interwar period was truly a moment of great power transition. At the start of the Great Depression, the United Kingdom's lack of financial muscle badly hampered its leadership efforts. Even as it was trying to maintain the gold standard, Great Britain possessed only 4 percent of the world's gold reserves.[112]

By contrast, American power and leadership during the recent crisis turned out to be more robust than many experts perceived.[113] This was particularly true in the financial realm. Despite occasional grumblings

[110] For a review, see Lake 2009.
[111] Drezner and McNamara 2013.
[112] Frieden 2006, chap. 8.
[113] Norrlof 2010; Ikenberry 2011; Beckley 2011–12.

among the BRICS, the US dollar's hegemony as the world's reserve currency remained unchallenged, giving the United States the financial power that the United Kingdom lacked eight decades earlier.[114] Nor was the dollar's status as a reserve currency the sole basis for American financial power. The IMF estimated that the United States housed 25 percent of global capital markets in 2010; private sector analysts estimate that American capital was responsible for more than a third of global asset markets. While domestic politics might have prevented a more robust US policy response, partisan gridlock did not prevent the United States from pursuing emergency rescue packages (via the 2008 Troubled Assets Relief Program), expansionary fiscal policy (via the 2009 American Recovery and Reinvestment Act and the 2010 payroll tax cut), stress tests of large financial institutions, expansionary monetary policy (via interest rate cuts, three rounds of quantitative easing, and Operation Twist), and financial regulatory reform (via Dodd-Frank). These acts of US leadership helped to secure multilateral cooperation on macroeconomic policy coordination for two years, as well as Basel III.

Another way to demonstrate the significance of US economic power is to compare and contrast the finance and trade dimensions. As just noted, US market power in the financial realm remained significant even after the crisis; American policy outputs were significant enough to display leadership on these issues. The picture looks very different on trade. US relative power on this issue had faded: according to WTO figures, US imports as a share of total world imports declined from 18.1 percent of total imports in 2001 to 12.3 percent a decade later. US policy on this issue was more inert. The executive branch's trade-promotion authority expired, and legislative demands for protectionism spiked. Not surprisingly, the global policy response on trade has been somewhat more muted than on finance. Intriguingly, as the US economy has recovered more quickly than other advanced industrialized states, even previous skeptics of US power have acknowledged that the death of its hegemony may have been exaggerated.[115]

The other difference between the interwar era and the current day is the state of economic ideas. As the Great Depression worsened during the decade of the 1930s, there was no expert consensus about the best way to resuscitate the global economy.[116] Prominent economists like John Maynard Keynes, who had been staunch advocates of free trade a

[114] Cohen and Benney 2012; Stokes 2013.
[115] See, for example, Subramanian 2013, 4.
[116] James 2001.

decade earlier, reversed themselves as the depression worsened. There was no agreement on the proper macroeconomic policy response to the downturn; nor was there any agreement about whether and how to fix the broken gold standard.

To be sure, there has also been a rethinking of causal beliefs after the 2008 financial crisis—but this rethink has been much less radical. Former Federal Reserve chairman Alan Greenspan made headlines when he admitted that his faith in the intellectual edifice of self-correcting markets had "collapsed." As previously noted, the IMF has reversed course on the utility of temporary capital controls. While the Washington Consensus might be fraying, however, it has not been dissolved or replaced by a "Beijing Consensus." Indeed, such a policy consensus does not even exist within China.[117] If anything, the fifth generation of Chinese leadership has shifted away from the state-led capitalist model. The *China 2030* project, endorsed by China's top leaders, emphasized a transition away from the state-owned enterprises. In a major speech outlining his plan for further economic reform, Prime Minister Li Keqiang stressed the need to "further develop the market's fundamental role in allocating resources." In not articulating an alternative to the current open economic order, China has acted like a responsible stakeholder—not a spoiler.[118]

Mass public attitudes about the global economy suggest the relative robustness of market-friendly economic ideas about the global economy. A general assumption in public opinion research is that during a downturn, demand for greater economic closure should spike, as individuals scapegoat foreigners for domestic woes. The global nature of the 2008 crisis, combined with anxiety about the shifting distribution of power, should have triggered a fall in support for an open global economy. The reverse is true, however. Beginning in 2002 Pew's Global Attitudes Project has been surveying a wide spectrum of countries about globalization.[119] The results show resilient support for expanding trade and business ties with other countries. Twenty-four countries were surveyed in both 2007 and at least one year after 2008, including a majority of the G20 economies. By 2011, twenty of twenty-four countries showed greater or equal support for trade compared with 2007. Indeed, between 2007 and 2012, the unweighted average support for more trade in these countries *increased* from 78.5 percent to 83.6 percent.

[117] Ferchen 2013; Kennedy 2010.
[118] See Johnston 2013, 32–33.
[119] Pew 2012.

After more than a half-century of laying the intellectual groundwork for an open global economy and more laissez-faire domestic economic policies, it would appear that the ideas animating the Washington Consensus are more resilient than expected.[120] As one recent history of free-market thought concluded: "the hold of market advocacy on the popular imagination has remained far stronger than in the early 1930s. . . . Capitalism may be in crisis, but the horizon of alternatives has narrowed."[121] Postcrisis surveys of leading economists suggest that a powerful consensus persists on several key international policy dimensions. The University of Chicago has run an economic experts panel for the past few years since the crisis started. The survey results show a strong consensus on the virtues of freer trade and a rejection of returning to the gold standard to regulate international exchange rates. There is, however, much less consensus on macroeconomic policy, including about the relative merits of quantitative easing and fiscal austerity.[122] This absence of agreement reflects a much greater policy debate on this area. This helps to explain why macroeconomic policy coordination has been less robust.

IX. Conclusion

When the subprime mortgage crisis began, there were rampant fears that global economic governance was too dysfunctional and unprepared to cope with a severe crisis. The Great Recession then exacerbated those fears. A review of policy outcomes, outputs, and processes shows a different picture. Global trade and investment levels have recovered from the plunge that occurred in late 2008. A mélange of international coordination mechanisms facilitated the provision of key policy outputs from 2008 onward. Existing global governance structures, particularly in finance, have been revamped to accommodate shifts in the distribution of power. The evidence suggests that multilateral institutions adapted and responded to the 2008 financial crisis in a robust fashion. They passed the stress test—global economic governance has been good enough. The picture presented here is at odds with prevailing conventional wisdom on this subject.

This does not guarantee that global economic governance will continue to function effectively going forward. It is worth remembering

[120] Yergin and Stanislaw 1997; Burgin 2012.

[121] Burgin 2012, 216.

[122] Gordon and Dahl 2013. For further evidence of the absence of consensus on macroeconomic policy, see Weisenthal 2012; and Blyth 2013.

that there were genuine efforts to provide global public goods in 1929 as well, but they eventually fizzled. The failure of the major economies to assist the Austrian government after the CreditAnstalt bank failed in 1931 led to a cascade of bank failures across Europe and the United States. The collapse of the 1933 London conference guaranteed an ongoing absence of policy coordination for the next several years. The start of the Great Depression was bad, but international policy coordination failures made it worse. Such a scenario could play out again.

It is equally possible, however, that the postcrisis system has increased in resiliency. The 2013 Cyprus crisis failed to trigger the same financial contagion as prior eurozone episodes, for example. Furthermore, a renewed crisis could trigger a renewed surge in policy coordination. As John Ikenberry has observed: "The last decade has brought remarkable upheavals in the global system—the emergence of new powers, financial crises, a global recession, and bitter disputes among allies. . . . Despite these upheavals, liberal international order as an organizational logic of world politics has proven resilient. It is still in demand."[123] Despite uncertain times, the open global economic order that has been in operation since 1945 does not appear to be closing anytime soon.

References

Abdelal, Rawi, and Adam Segal. 2007. "Has Globalization Passed Its Peak?" *Foreign Affairs* 86, no. 1: 103–14.

———. "Yes, Globalization Has Passed Its Peak." Foreignaffairs.com, March 17. At http://www.foreignaffairs.com/articles/64856/rawi-abdelal-and-adam-segal/yes-globalization-passed-its-peak, accessed November 29, 2012.

Axelrod, Robert, and Robert Keohane. 1985. "Achieving Cooperation under Anarchy: Strategies and Institutions." *World Politics* 38, no. 1 (October): 226–54.

Baccini, Leonardo, and Soo Yeon Kim. 2012. "Preventing Protectionism: International Institutions and Trade Policy." *Review of International Organizations* 7, no. 4: 369–98.

Bair, Sheila. 2012. *Bull by the Horns*. New York, N.Y.: Free Press.

Baker, Andrew. 2013. "The New Political Economy of the Macroprudential Ideational Shift." *New Political Economy* 18, no. 1: 112–39.

Bank of International Settlements. 2012. *82nd Annual Report*. June 24. At http://www.bis.org/publ/arpdf/ar2012e.htm, accessed July 3, 2012.

Barma, Naazneen, Ely Ratner, and Steven Weber. 2013. "The Mythical Liberal Order." *National Interest*, no. 124: 56–68.

Barnett, Michael, and Martha Finnemore. 2004. *Rules for the World*. Ithaca, N.Y.: Cornell University Press.

[123] Ikenberry 2011, 6.

Beattie, Alan. 2012a. *Who's in Charge Here?* New York, N.Y.: Penguin.
———. 2012b. "Decommission the Weapons of Trade Warfare." *Financial Times*. August 8.
Beattie, Alan, and Chris Giles. 2011. "IMF and Eurozone Clash over Estimates." *Financial Times*. August 31.
Beattie, Alan, and Christian Oliver. 2010. "Accord on IMF Board Masks Lack of Progress." *Financial Times*. October 25.
Beckley, Michael. 2011/12. "China's Century? Why America's Edge Will Endure." *International Security* 36, no. 1: 41–78.
Bhagwati, Jagdish. 1988. *Protectionism*. Cambridge, Mass.: MIT Press.
Blyth, Mark. 2013. *Austerity: The History of a Dangerous Idea*. New York, N.Y.: Oxford University Press.
Bown, Chad. 2012. "Import Protection Update: Antidumping, Safeguards, and Temporary Trade Barriers through 2011." VoxEU.org, August 18. At http://voxeu.org/article/import-protection-update-antidumping-safeguards-and-temporary-trade-barriers-through-2011, accessed August 10, 2012.
Bradsher, Keith. 2012. "On China Currency, Hot Topic in Debate, Truth Is Nuanced." *New York Times*. October 17.
Bremmer, Ian. 2009. *The End of the Free Market*. New York, N.Y.: Portfolio.
———. 2012. "Decline of Global Institutions Means We Must Embrace Regionalism." *Financial Times*. January 27. At http://blogs.ft.com/the-a-list/2012/01/27/decline-of-global-institutions-means-we-best-embrace-regionalism/, accessed July 13, 2012.
Bremmer, Ian, and Nouriel Roubini. 2011. "A G-Zero World." *Foreign Affairs* 90, no. 2: 2–7.
Brubaker, Rogers. 2011. "Economic Crisis, Nationalism, and Politicized Ethnicity." In Craig Calhoun and Georgi Derlugian, eds., *The Deepening Crisis: Governance Challenges after Neoliberalism*. New York, N.Y.: New York University Press.
Burgin, Angus. 2012. *The Great Persuasion: Reinventing Free Markets since the Great Depression*. Cambridge, Mass.: Harvard University Press.
Bussière, Matthieu, Emilia Pérez-Barreiro, Roland Straub, and Daria Taglioni. 2011. "Protectionist Responses to the Crisis: Global Trends and Implications." *World Economy* 34, no. 5: 826–52.
Chinn, Menzie, and Jeffry Frieden. 2011. *Lost Decades: The Making of America's Debt Crisis and the Long Recovery*. New York, N.Y.: W. W. Norton.
Claessens, Stijn, M. Ayhan Kose, and Marco Terrones. 2011. "Financial Cycles: What? How? When?" IMF Working Paper WP/11/76.
Cohen, Benjamin J. 2013. "How Have Banks Adjusted to Higher Capital Requirements?" *BIS Quarterly Review* 17, no. 3: 25–41.
Cohen, Benjamin J., and Tabitha Benney. "What Does the International Currency System Really Look Like?" Manuscript, University of California at Santa Barbara.
Cohen, Stephen, and J. Bradford DeLong. 2009. *The End of Influence*. New York, N.Y.: Basic Books.
Dadush, Uri, Shimelse Ali, and Rachel Esplin Odell. 2011. "Is Protectionism Dying?" Carnegie Papers in International Economics. May. At http://carnegieendowment.org/files/is_protectionism_dying.pdf, accessed June 20, 2012.

Davis, Bob. 2008. "Foreign Funds Agree to Set of Guiding Principles." *Wall Street Journal*. September 3.

Deloitte Touche Tohmatsu. 2008. *Minding the GAPP: Sovereign Wealth, Transparency, and the "Santiago Principles."* October.

Dominguez, Kathryn. "The European Central Bank, the Euro, and Global Financial Markets." *Journal of Economic Perspectives* 20, no. 4: 67–88.

Downs, George, David Rocke, and Peter Barsoom. 1996. "Is the Good News about Compliance Good News about Cooperation?" *International Organization* 50, no. 3: 379–406.

Doyle, Peter. 2012. Resignation letter to the IMF executive board. At http://cnnibusiness.files.wordpress.com/2012/07/doyle.pdf, accessed July 12, 2012.

Drezner, Daniel W. 2006. *U.S. Trade Strategy: Free versus Fair*. New York, N.Y.: Council on Foreign Relations Press.

———. 2007. "The New New World Order." *Foreign Affairs* 86, no. 2: 34–46.

Drezner, Daniel W., and Kathleen R. McNamara. 2013. "International Political Economy, Global Financial Orders and the 2008 Financial Crisis." *Perspectives on Politics* 11, no. 1: 155–66.

Dunphy, Harry. 2008. "IMF Approves Eventual Gold Sale." Associated Press. July 7.

Economist. 2009. "The Return of Economic Nationalism." February 5.

Eichengreen, Barry. 2011. "Crisis and Growth in the Advanced Economies: What We Know, What We Don't Know, and What We Can Learn from the 1930s." *Comparative Economic Studies* 53, no. 3: 383–406.

Eichengreen, Barry, and Kevin O'Rourke. 2010. "A Tale of Two Depressions." VoxEU.org. March 8. At http://www.voxeu.org/index.php?q=node/3421, accessed July 3, 2012.

———. 2012. "A Tale of Two Depressions Redux." VoxEU.org. March 6. At http://www.voxeu.org/article/tale-two-depressions-redux, accessed August 2, 2012.

Evenett, Simon. 2013. "Protectionism's Quiet Return: The GTA's Pre-G8 Summit Report." VoxEU.org. June 13. At http://www.voxeu.org/article/protectionism-s-quiet-return-gta-s-pre-g8-summit-report, accessed June 15, 2013.

Farrell, Henry, and John Quiggin. 2011. "Consensus, Dissensus and Economic Ideas: The Rise and Fall of Keynesianism during the Economic Crisis." Manuscript, George Washington University.

Ferchen, Matt. 2013. "Whose China Model Is It Anyway? The Contentious Search for Consensus." *Review of International Political Economy* 20, no. 2: 390–420.

Frieden, Jeffry. 2006. *Global Capitalism*. New York, N.Y.: W. W. Norton.

Frieden, Jeffry, Michael Pettis, Dani Rodrik, and Ernesto Zedillo. 2012. *After the Fall: The Future of Global Cooperation*. Geneva, Switzerland: International Center for Monetary and Banking Studies.

G20 Information Centre. 2013. *2012 Los Cabos G20 Summit Final Compliance Report*. September 4. At http://www.g20.utoronto.ca/compliance/2012/loscabos-final/index.html, accessed October 3, 2013.

Garrett, Geoffrey. 2010. "G2 in G20: China, the United States, and the World after the Global Financial Crisis." *Global Policy* 1, no. 1: 29–39.

Gawande, Kishore, Bernard Hoekman, and Yue Cui. 2011. "Determinants of

Trade Policy Responses to the 2008 Financial Crisis." World Bank Policy Research Working Paper no. 5862. October.

Geithner, Timothy. 2010. "Statement on the Report to Congress on International Economic and Exchange Rate Policies." April 3. At http://www.ustreas.gov/press/releases/tg627.htm./, accessed July 12, 2012.

Goldsmith, Jack, and Eric Posner. 2005. *The Limits of International Law*. New York, N.Y.: Oxford University Press.

Goldstein, Judith. 1996. "International Law and Domestic Institutions." *International Organization* 50, no. 4: 541–64.

Gordon, Roger, and Gordon Dahl. 2013. "Views among Economists: Professional Consensus or Point-Counterpoint?" *American Economic Review* 103, no. 3: 629–35.

Gowa, Joanne. 1984. *Closing the Gold Window: Domestic Politics and the End of Bretton Woods*. Ithaca, N.Y.: Cornell University Press.

Gutner, Tamar, and Alexander Thompson. 2010. "The Politics of IO Performance: A Framework." *Review of International Organizations* 5, no. 3: 227–48.

Haas, Peter. 1992. "Introduction: Epistemic Communities and International Policy Coordination." *International Organization* 46, no. 2: 1–35.

Hale, Thomas, David Held, and Kevin Young. 2013. *Gridlock: Why Global Cooperation Is Failing When We Need It Most*. London, UK: Polity.

Halper, Stefan. 2010. *The Beijing Consensus*. New York, N.Y.: Basic Books.

Human Security Report Project. 2010. *Human Security Report 2009/2010: The Causes of Peace and the Shrinking Costs of War*. New York, N.Y.: Oxford University Press.

IGM Forum. 2012a. "Gold Standard." January 12. At http://www.igmchicago.org/igm-economic-experts-panel/poll-results?SurveyID=SV_cw1nNUYOXSAKwrq, accessed July 3, 2012.

———. 2012b. "Free Trade." At http://www.igmchicago.org/igm-economic-experts-panel/poll-results?SurveyID=SV_0dfr9yjnDcLh17m, accessed July 3, 2012.

Ikenberry, G. John. 2011. *Liberal Leviathan*. Princeton, N.J.: Princeton University Press.

Institute for Economics and Peace. 2012. *Global Peace Index 2012*. June.

International Monetary Fund. 2009. *Global Financial Stability Report: Responding to the Financial Crisis and Measuring Systemic Risks*. Washington, D.C.: International Monetary Fund.

——— 2012. "The Liberalization and Management of Capital Flows: An Institutional View." November 14. At http://www.imf.org/external/np/pp/eng/2012/111412.pdf, accessed June 10, 2013.

———. 2013. *World Economic Outlook: Hopes, Realities and Risks*. Washington, D.C.: International Monetary Fund.

Irwin, Neil. 2013. *The Alchemists: Three Central Bankers and a World on Fire*. New York, N.Y.: Penguin Press.

James, Harold. 2001. *The End of Globalization: Lessons from the Great Depression*. Cambridge, Mass.: Harvard University Press.

Jentleson, Bruce. 2012. "Global Governance in a Copernican World." *Global Governance* 18, no. 2: 133–48.

Johnston, A. Iain. 2001. "Treating International Institutions as Social Environments." *International Studies Quarterly* 45, no. 4: 487–515.

———. 2013. "How New and Assertive Is China's New Assertiveness?" *International Security* 37, no. 4: 7–48.

Jorda, Oscar, Moritz Schularick, and Alan Taylor. 2012. "When Credit Bites Back: Leverage, Business Cycles, and Crises." NBER Working Paper no. 17621. October.

Joyce, Joseph. 2013. *The IMF and Global Financial Crises*. New York, N.Y.: Cambridge University Press.

Kahler, Miles. 2013. "Economic Crisis and Global Governance: The Stability of a Globalized World." In Miles Kahler and David Lake, eds., *Politics in the New Hard Times: The Great Recession in Comparative Perspective*. Ithaca, NY: Cornell University Press.

Kanter, James. 2012. "IMF Urges Europe's Strongest to Shoulder Burdens of Currency Bloc." *New York Times*. June 21.

Kee, Hiau Looi, Cristina Neagu, and Alessandro Nicita. 2013. "Is Protectionism on the Rise? Assessing National Trade Policies during the Crisis of 2008." *Review of Economics and Statistics* 95, no. 1: 342–56.

Kennedy, Scott. 2010. "The Myth of the Beijing Consensus." *Journal of Contemporary China* 19, no. 65: 461–77.

Keohane, Robert. 1980. "Theory of Hegemonic Stability and Changes in International Economic Regimes, 1967–1977." In Ole Holsti, Randolph Siverson, and Alexander George, eds., *Change in the International System*. Boulder, Colo.: Westview Press.

———. 1984. *After Hegemony*. Princeton, N.J.: Princeton University Press.

Kim, Soo Yeon. 2013. "Protectionism during Recessions: Is This Time Different?" *Political Economist* 9, no. 2: 6–8.

Kindleberger, Charles. 1971. *The World in Depression, 1929–1939*. Berkeley, Calif.: University of California Press.

Kupchan, Charles. 2012. *No One's World*. New York, N.Y.: Oxford University Press.

Kurlantzick, Joshua. 2009. "The World Is Bumpy." *New Republic*. July 15. At http://www.newrepublic.com/article/the-world-bumpy, accessed June 10, 2013.

Lake, David A. 2009. "Open Economy Politics: A Critical Review." *Review of International Organizations* 4, no. 3: 219–44.

Lall, Ranjit. 2012. "From Failure to Failure: The Politics of International Banking Regulation." *Review of International Political Economy* 19, no. 4: 609–38.

Layne, Christopher. 2012. "This Time It's Real: The End of Unipolarity and the *Pax Americana*." *International Studies Quarterly* 56, no. 1: 203–13.

Lazer, David. 1999. "The Free Trade Epidemic of the 1860s and Other Outbreaks of Economic Discrimination." *World Politics* 51, no. 4 (July): 447–83.

Levinson, Marc. 2010. "Faulty Basel." *Foreign Affairs* 89, no. 3: 76–88.

Lowrey, Annie. 2012. "Dire Poverty Falls Despite Global Slump, Report Finds." *New York Times*. March 6.

Lund, Susan, Toos Daruvala, Richard Dobbs, Philipp Härle, Ju-Hon Kwek, and Ricardo Falcón. 2013. *Financial Globalization: Retreat or Reset*? Washington, D.C.: McKinsey Global Institute.

Martin, Lisa L. 1992. "Interests, Power, and Multilateralism." *International Organization* 46, no. 4: 765–92.

Mastanduno, Michael. 2009. "System Maker and Privilege Taker: U.S. Power and the International Political Economy." *World Politics* 61, no. 1 (January): 121–54.

Mazower, Mark. 2012. *Governing the World: The History of an Idea.* New York, N.Y.: Penguin.

Hood, Michael. 2012. "The Volatility Conundrum." JPMorgan Institutional Market View. September 30.

Naim, Moises. 2013. *The End of Power.* New York, N.Y.: Basic Books.

Norrlof, Carla. 2010. *America's Global Advantage: U.S. Hegemony and International Cooperaion.* Cambridge, UK: Cambridge University Press.

OECD. 2008. *Sovereign Wealth Funds and Recipient Country Policies.* Paris, France: Organization for Economic Cooperation and Development.

OECD and UNCTAD 2012. "7th Report on G20 Investment Measures." May 31. At http://www.wto.org/english/news_e/news12_e/igo_31may12_e.htm, accessed July 10, 2012.

———. 2013. "9th report on G20 investment measures." June 17. At http://www.wto.org/english/news_e/news13_e/igo_17jun13_e.htm, accessed June 24, 2013.

O'Rourke, Kevin H., and Jeffrey G. Williamson. 1999. *Globalization and History.* Cambridge, Mass.: MIT Press.

Ostry, Jonathan, Atish R. Ghosh, Karl Habermeier, Marcos Chamon, Mahvash S. Qureshi, and Dennis B. S. Reinhardt. 2010. "Capital Inflows: The Role of Controls." IMF Staff Position Note SPN/10/04. February 19.

Pew Research Center. 2012a. "Key Indicators Database: Views on Trade." June 17. At http://www.pewglobal.org/database/?indicator=16&survey=13&response=Good%20thing&mode=table, accessed July 13, 2012.

———. 2012b. "Pervasive Gloom about the World Economy." July 12. At http://www.pewglobal.org/2012/07/12/pervasive-gloom-about-the-world-economy/, accessed July 13, 2012.

PIPA. 2006. "U.N. Continues to Get Positive, though Lower, Ratings with World Public." Program on International Policy Attitudes. January 24. At http://www.worldpublicopinion.org/pipa/articles/btunitednationsra/163.php, accessed December 8, 2012.

———. 2009. "Publics Want More Aggressive Government Action on Economic Crisis." July 21. At http://www.worldpublicopinion.org/pipa/articles/btglobalizationtradera/626.php, accessed December 8, 2012.

Politi, James. 2012. "US Revises Investment Treaty Approach." *Financial Times.* April 20.

Prasad, Eswar, and Isaac Sorkin. 2009. "Assessing the G-20 Stimulus Plans: A Deeper Look." Brookings Institution. March.

Putnam, Robert, and Nicholas Bayne. 1987. *Hanging Together: Cooperation and Conflict in the Seven-Power Summits.* Cambridge, Mass.: Harvard University Press.

Rabinovitch, Simon. 2012. "Renminbi Hits 19-Year High against Dollar." *Financial Times.* October 12.

Raustiala, Kal, and David Victor. 2004. "The Regime Complex for Plant Genetic Resources." *International Organization* 58, no. 2: 277–309.

Reinhart, Carmen, and Vincent Reinhart. 2010. "After the Fall." NBER Working Paper no. 16334. September.

Reinhart, Carmen, and Kenneth Rogoff. 2009. *This Time Is Different: Eight Centuries of Financial Folly*. Princeton, N.J.: Princeton University Press.

Rickards, James. 2011. *Currency Wars: The Making of the Next Global Crisis*. New York, N.Y.: Portfolio.

Rodrik, Dani. 2010. "The End of an Era in Finance." Project Syndicate. March 10. At http://www.project-syndicate.org/commentary/the-end-of-an-era-in-finance#dkuJB92AvW6Fckoy.99, accessed July 3, 2012.

Rogers, Paul. 2008. "The Tipping Point?" Oxford Research Group. November. At http://www.oxfordresearchgroup.org.uk/sites/default/files/thetippingpoint_0.pdf, accessed July 3, 2012.

Rose, Andrew K. 2012. "Protectionism Isn't Counter-Cyclic (Anymore)." NBER Working Paper no. 18062.

Roxburgh, Charles, Susan Lund, and John Piotrowski. 2011. *Mapping Global Capital Markets 2011*. Washington, D.C.: McKinsey Global Institute.

Roxburgh, Charles, Susan Lund, Toos Daruvala, James Manyika, Richard Dobbs, Ramon Forn, and Karen Croxson. 2012. *Debt and Deleveraging: Uneven Progress on the Path to Growth*. Washington, D.C.: McKinsey Global Institute.

Samans, Richard, Klaus Schwab, and Mark Malloch-Brown. 2011. "Running the World, after the Crash." *Foreign Policy*, no. 184: 80–83.

Schwab, Susan. 2011. "After Doha." *Foreign Affairs* 90, no. 3: 104–17.

Schweller, Randall. 2011. "Emerging Powers in an Age of Disorder." *Global Governance* 17, no. 3: 285–97.

Snidal, Duncan, and Kenneth Abbott. 2000. "Hard and Soft Law in International Governance." *International Organization* 54, no. 3: 421–56.

Song, Guoyou, and Wei Jin Yuan. 2012. "China's Free Trade Ageeement Strategies." *Washington Quarterly* 35, no. 3: 107–19.

Stokes, Doug. 2013. "Achilles' Deal: Dollar Decline and US Grand Strategy after the Crisis." *Review of International Political Economy*. DOI: 10.1080/09692290.2013.779592.

Subramanian, Arvind. 2013. "Preserving the Open Global Economic System: A Strategic Blueprint for China and the United States." Peterson Institute for International Economics PB13-16. June.

Themnér, Lotta, and Peter Wallensteen. 2012. "Armed Conflicts, 1946–2011." *Journal of Peace Research* 49, no. 4: 565–75.

United Nations Commission on Trade and Development. 2013. *World Investment Report 2013*. New York, N.Y.: UNCTAD.

United Nations Development Programme. 2013. *2013 Human Development Report*. New York, N.Y.: UNDP.

Véron, Nicolas. 2012. "Financial Reform after the Crisis: An Early Assessment." Peterson Institute for International Economics Working Paper 12-2. January.

Weisenthal, Joe. 2012. "The Biggest Tragedy in Economics." *Business Insider*. September 7. At http://www.businessinsider.com/the-biggest-tragedy-in-economics-2012-9, accessed June 13, 2013.

Wilf, Meredith. 2013. "A Stake in the International: US Banks and Basel III Regulatory Announcements." Manuscript, Princeton University.

Willett, Thomas. 1999. "Developments in the Political Economy of Policy Coordination." *Open Economies Review* 10, no. 2: 221–53.

Wolfe, Robert. 2012. "Protectionism and Multilateral Accountability during the Great Recession: Inferences from Dogs Not Barking." *Journal of World Trade* 46, no. 4: 777–813.

World Bank. 2010. "World Bank Group Reform: An Update." September 30. At http://siteresources.worldbank.org/DEVCOMMINT/Documentation/22723851/DC2010-0014(E)Reform.pdf, accessed June 12, 2013.

———. 2013. *Migration and Development Brief 21*. October 2. At http://siteresources.worldbank.org/INTPROSPECTS/Resources/334934-1288990760745/MigrationandDevelopmentBrief21.pdf, accessed October 15, 2013.

World Economic Forum. 2012. "Global Agenda Council on Geopolitical Risk." Davos-Klosters, Switzerland. January 29.

World Trade Organization. 2012. "Regional Trade Agreements Information System." At http://rtais.wto.org/UI/PublicMaintainRTAHome.aspx, accessed July 3, 2012.

———. 2013. "WTO Report on G-20 Trade Measures." June 17. At http://www.wto.org/english/news_e/news13_e/igo_17jun13_e.htm, accessed June 20, 2013.

Yergin, Daniel, and Joseph Stanislaw. 1997. *The Commanding Heights*. New York, N.Y.: Simon and Schuster.

Zaring, David. 2009/10. "International Institutional Performance in Crisis." *Chicago Journal of International Law* 10, no. 2: 475–504.